LOCKHEED BLACKBIRD

BEYOND THE SECRET MISSIONS

Paul F Crickmore

LOCKHEED
BLACKBIRD
BEYOND THE SECRET MISSIONS

Paul F Crickmore

First published in Great Britain in 1993 by Osprey Publishing, Elms Court, Chapel Way, Botley, Oxford OX2 9LP, United Kingdom.
Email: info@ospreypublishing.com

Revised edition published 2004

A CIP catalogue record for this book is available from the British Library

ISBN 1 84176 694 1

Paul F. Crickmore has asserted his right under the Copyright, Designs and Patents Act, 1988, to be identified as the Author of this Work

Editor: Paul E. Eden
Design: Ken Vail Graphic Design, Cambridge, UK
Index by Alan Thatcher
Maps by The Map Studio Limited
Originated by The Electronic Page Company, Cwmbran, UK
Printed in Hong Kong through Bookbuilders

04 05 06 07 08   10 9 8 7 6 5 4 3 2 1

For a catalogue of all books published by Osprey Military and Aviation please contact:

Osprey Direct UK, P.O. Box 140,
Wellingborough, Northants, NN8 2FA, UK
E-mail: info@ospreydirect.co.uk

Osprey Direct USA, c/o MBI Publishing,
P.O. Box 1, 729 Prospect Ave,
Osceola, WI 54020, USA
E-mail: info@ospreydirectusa.com

www.ospreypublishing.com

CONTENTS

ACKNOWLEDGEMENTS

This book is dedicated to my wife Ali, for her tireless support and unconditional love.

The material from this book came from two basic sources: open literature including books, newspapers, professional journals and various declassified reports, and first-hand accounts from pilots, RSOs and other people associated with the various programmes.

Much of the information contained within these pages was pieced together during the course of numerous interviews (many of which were taped, others being conducted over the internet), with those intimately connected with Oxcart, Kedlock, Tagboard and the Senior Crown programme. Several contributed information with the proviso that their anonymity be respected.

My deepest appreciation therefore goes to Cols Don Walbrecht, Frank Murray, Larry Brown, Tom Allison, Rich Graham and Barry MacKean. Also Denny Lombard, Heinz Berger, Rolf Jonsson and Dr Jeff Richelson.

My grateful thanks also go to Dave Adrian, Bob Gilliland, Jim Eastham, Jay Miller, TD Barnes, Cols 'Slip' Slater, Buddy Brown, Don Emmons, Ed Payne, Tom Pugh, BC Thomas, Jerry Glasser, Frank Stampf, 'Buzz' Carpenter, Curt Osterheld, Rod Dyckman, Per-Olof, and Lt-Cols Blair Bozek and Tom Veltri. Also, Bob Murphy, Jeannette Remak, Valery Romanenko, James Bebhardt, Ilva Grinberg, Maj. Mikhail Myagkiv, Lutz Freund, Gen. Al Joersz and Tim Brown.

I also wish to thank Maj-Gens Doug Nelson, Pat Halloran and Mel Vojvodich; Brig-Gens Dennis Sullivan and Buck Adams; Cols Tony Bevacqua, Pat Bledsoe, Larry Boggess, George Bull, Gary Coleman, Ken Collins, Dave Dempster, Bruce Douglass, Carl Estes, Tom Estes, Ty Judkin, Joe Kinego, John Kraus, Jack Layton, Jay Murphy, Dewain Vick, Jim Watkins, Rich Young and Jack Maddison; Lt-Cols Ben Bowles, Nevin Cunningham, Bill Flanagan, Jim Greenwood, Dan House, Tom Henichek, Bruce Leibman, 'GT' Morgan, Bob Powell, Maury Rosenberg, Tom Tilden, Ed Yielding, Reg Blackwell and 'Stormy' Boudreaux; Majs Brian Shul, Doug Soifer and Terry Pappas and also Keith Beswick, Kent Burns, Russ Daniell, Kevin Gothard, Graham Luxton, Lindsay Peacock, Marta Bohn-Meyer, Colin Grice, MBE, Dave Wilton, Betty Sprigg, Rich Stadler, Jane Skliar, Berni Mearns, Mike Hirst, Ellen Bendell, Steve Davies, Jim Goodall, James Hepburn, Peter Merlin, Chris Pocock, Bill Park, Lou Schalk and Bill Weaver.

Finally, thanks goes to my editor, Paul E. Eden, and for their endless support and encouragement my eternal gratitude goes to my Dad, Neil, Pauline, Alberto, Karen, Nicola, Matthew and Gilly. This book also welcomes Benjamin William John into the world.

Jock Heron's recollections of his 29 June 1965 visit to Area 51 are reproduced by courtesy of the Rolls Royce Heritage Trust (Bristol)

Paul F. Crickmore

PREFACE

I'd shot half a dozen films during the course of this air-refuelling (AR) sortie in a KC-135, replenishing F-15 Eagle receivers from Bitburg Air Base, West Germany. Recovering back at RAF Mildenhall, we taxied slowly back to our allotted stand on the apron and I spotted the unmistakable, seductively sleek lines of a Lockheed SR-71. The type had begun operating sporadically out of the English base a few years earlier, but its movements were shrouded in secrecy. This was after all, at the height of the Cold War, and its strategic reconnaissance mission was a vital one.

As I jumped from the final rung of the tanker's nose ladder, I was immediately met by my escort officer and friend, Major Jim Morrow. He enquired as to how the sortie had gone, and did I think I'd got some good shots. 'Great', I replied, 'but what are the chances of getting involved in an AR sortie with the "Blackbird"?' – my mother always maintained that I had a long neck! Jim replied that that would be an altogether different affair and the matter wasn't discussed any further.

Some five weeks later, the telephone at home rang. At once I identified the 'gravel' voice on the other end as that belonging to Jim Morrow. 'Paul', he said, 'That airplane that you were talking about when we last met'. My heart leapt, 'Yes', I replied, knowing precisely what he was talking about and also remembering that we were conversing on an unsecure phone line. 'Can you be outside the Mildenhall main gate at 6:30 tomorrow morning', he continued. As chance would have it, it was my day off. 'Yes … can I bring my camera' – that neck again! – 'Yes', was the reply, then the line went dead.

So began an association with an aircraft programme and a remarkable set of people that transcended the wildest dreams of the most optimistic dreamer. My KC-135Q flight, on 6 October 1981, was commanded by one Captain Marc Blacketter, and to this day I've never met anyone who could handle a big jet like him. Our AR mission was classified secret and the navigation charts were liberally stamped 'Top Secret' but today, long after the tumultuous events of late 20th century world geopolitics, I can now say that we flew in formation with KC-135Q serial 58-117 to the Viking North air- refuelling anchor point off Bødo, northern Norway. Our receiver SR-71A, serial 64-17964, crewed by Capt Rich Judson and Maj

Frank Kelly, took on a split fuel load from the two tankers, having already completed its reconnaissance 'take' of the Soviet Northern Fleet, stationed in the ice-free ports of the Kola peninsular. With fuel tanks once again full, the crew completed their mission with an anticlockwise loop around the Baltic, before recovering back into RAF Mildenhall. In the refuelling track my luck had held despite the northern latitude and time of year. The clear skies and light conditions were perfect for air-to-air photography and my trusted Canon A-1 camera performed flawlessly.

Back on watch at London Air Traffic Control Centre at RAF West Drayton, my dear friend Kevin Gothard – an outstanding controller – badgered me mercilessly about getting the shots published. I eventually plucked-up the courage and approached *Air Enthusiast* magazine, which published several shots. The editor then asked if I was prepared to write an article. I pointed out that this was something I had never done before, but agreed anyway.

Before sending the article off for publication I passed it by the SR-71 Detachment Commander of the time, Lt-Col Barry McKean, for review. I already had a fair idea what was sensitive, so when Barry returned the work only a couple of sentences had been removed.

Shortly after the second part of the article had been published, Dennis Baldry, Osprey's larger-than-life editor at that time, called. He explained that he'd enjoyed my article and had obtained my phone number from Air Enthusiast. He then proceeded to ask if I would write a book about the SR-71! In my supreme naivety (or stupidity) I agreed; however, it's true to say that Dennis really earned his editorial salary knocking that book into shape, producing in the process a highly successful sales generator.

In 1990, the SR-71 Senior Crown programme was on the brink of cancellation and Tony Holmes, who had become Osprey's Aerospace Editor, contacted me and asked if I would undertake a full-scale update of the earlier work. During the intervening period, friends in the SR-71, or Senior Crown, programme had provided me with unprecedented access to the 'Blackbird' or Habu; so I talked over Tony's proposal with several of them. They agreed that it was probably time to reveal some of the programme's hitherto classified accomplishments – not least because this might provide wider support for the mortally-wounded programme. My good friend and ex-SR-71 pilot Col Don Walbrecht, was central in obtaining further support for my efforts as well as an objective editorial edge to my work prior, to submitting it to Osprey. Fortunately, *Lockheed SR-71 The Secret Missions Exposed*, was also a great sales success and was further updated in the spring of 1993, when the programme was finally shut down.

In August 2002, Jane Penrose, Osprey's Editorial Director, asked if I would again update the book on the basis that the Cold War was now over and even more previously classified material was now available. What you now have before you is therefore the culmination of recent and previous research efforts on the subject. As ever, my aim was to write as detailed, accurate and balanced an account as possible; an account that is worthy of being associated with such an amazing programme and some very special life-long friends.

Paul F. Crickmore

FOREWORD

During the course of modern history, there have been remarkable leaps in technology that have captured the imagination of mankind and inspired increasingly ambitious human endeavours. The steam engine took the realm of transportation from the horse and buggy to the age of the railroad. The railroad, in turn, broke industry and commerce out of their local and regional boundaries and allowed expansion to transcontinental scope. The publication of this book comes at a time when the world celebrates its first century of powered flight, which in itself has expanded the transcontinental boundaries of human interaction to its current global scale. And beyond global reach, we now stand at the threshold of interplanetary travel, should we choose to pursue that next 'leap' in technology. However, of all the marvels of technology we have seen through the past century or more, only one has so completely intertwined the inspiration of the 'machine' with the hearts and souls of the men and women who designed, built, supported, and flew it. The SR-71 'Blackbird' – the Habu.

Anyone with enough interest in aviation to have read or heard stories about the incredible SR-71 'Blackbird' will be familiar with the term 'Habu'. Operating in heavy secrecy during its initial operational deployments to Okinawa during the early to mid-1960s, the Okinawans caught only a few brief glimpses of the 'Blackbird's' long, sleek forebody as it taxied out of its guarded hanger and roared off the runway to disappear rapidly into the skies over the South China Sea. As the airplane returned hours later, touching down gracefully in its characteristic nose-high attitude, the combination of its slender black fuselage and the wide, flatly-curved chines of its nose undoubtedly gave it the look of the hooded, poisonous viper indigenous to the island, called 'Habu' by the locals. And so the unofficial name was born. Habu came to refer not only to the airplane itself, but to those few crewmembers fortunate enough to have flown it operationally during its more than a quarter-century of service. It was only after a year of intensive training, then deployment overseas and finally their first operational mission, that a new 'Blackbird' crew could wear the coveted Habu shoulder patch on their flight suits.

It is a safe bet to say that few, if any, of those aviators who were privileged to become 'Habus' had any idea initially of how deeply the experience and all it entailed would imbed itself in their lives. I had never even seen the airplane when, in 1975, as a junior captain backseater flying RF-4Cs in Cold War Europe, I decided that I wanted to apply for what was referred to as 'The Program'. I still joke about not knowing why it was referred to as 'The Program', and to this day I'm not certain what drew me to that decision. But four years later, having finally logged the minimum number of flying hours to apply, I did just that. Somewhat to my surprise, I was accepted and, in 1979, began one of the most fascinating and enduring chapters of my life, both professionally and personally.

Right from the beginning, the challenges, mysteries, and often flat-out frustrations of going through the SR-71 training programme as a 'new guy' brought not only appreciation of the airplane's incredible capabilities, but a true sense of humility in one's own ability to absorb it all. Fortunately for me, this was a two-man airplane, and the pilot I was lucky enough to be crewed with – Captain Gil Bertelson – possessed the flying skills, patience, and possibly most important, the sense of humour to see us through to operational Habu status. Of the relatively small number of Habus I have come to know over the past 20 years, some flew the first intensely exciting and eminently more dangerous initial sorties over hostile territory in the early 1960s, and retired from active duty before I even started. Others shared the same segment of the airplane's history during the Cold War as I, and still others came after me. When, where, or with whom a Habu crewmember flew the mission is irrelevant. The bonding among Habus and their commitment to the integrity and honour of 'The Program' is the same. I have no doubt it always will be.

Like so many other fascinating systems, there was more than met the eye to what made the SR-71 so successful over more than 25 years in service. Much more went on behind the scenes than was visible to an outside observer. Crewmembers got much of the glory, but it took hard work, dedication and sacrifice on the part of so many others to get the 'crew dogs' off the ground in this

Captain Frank Stampf (at right), poses with his pilot, Captain Gil Bertelson. As a crew they were involved in the important missions which monitored the tense situation in Poland during the late winter of 1981. Such was the nature of SR-71A operations that the majority of sorties was flown 'in anger', with the professionalism of the aircraft's crews reflecting the importance placed by senior military and intelligence personnel on their missions. (via Frank Stampf)

magnificent machine; the absolute brilliance of 'Kelly' Johnson and his hand-picked crew of engineers who designed it; the maintenance troops and civilian contractors who maintained it and kept it safe; the planners who translated complex, detailed intelligence requirements into a flyable operational language so that the aircrews could execute the mission; the KC-135Q tanker crews who gave the Habu its 'legs' (and many times saved the SR crewmembers' butts!); and in an even less visible sense, the air traffic controllers on the ground who most often never even got to see the airplane, but from their darkened radar operations centres guided us and kept other aircraft away from our sometimes not so flexible flight paths so that we could make it all

look so easy. Paul Crickmore was based at the London Air Traffic Control Centre during the time Gil and I flew SR-71 missions out of Mildenhall. Fortunately for us, he and his contemporaries carried out their mission-critical function flawlessly, usually in complete radio silence, using complex, pre-arranged classified procedures known only by the Habu crews and the controllers.

Having come to know Paul Crickmore over 20 years ago while flying out of our detachment at RAF Mildenhall in the early 1980s, I can attest that his thorough knowledge and exhaustive research about the SR-71 are matched only by his intense enthusiasm for the airplane, 'The Program', and its history. In addition to incredibly detailed accounts of specific 'Blackbird' missions, beginning before the days of the Vietnam War, throughout that conflict, and well into the Cold War, Paul expertly conveys the 'heart' of 'The Program' to the reader. He does that by giving one the sense of being there when the engines are cranked, the canopies are closed encapsulating the crewmembers, and as the aircraft leaps off the runway to reach for the fringes of the atmosphere …

I thought I had read just about everything written about this phenomenal machine, and have even written a bit about it myself. But I can say with complete confidence that this work introduced me to 'pieces' of its history that I had never seen before, including accounts of interviews with the Soviet MiG-25 and MiG-31 pilots who had flown attempted intercepts against us over the Barents Sea, the Baltic Sea, and east of Vladivostok … Clearly, their perception of our vulnerability to their air-to-air weapons was quite a bit different from ours. These accounts simply confirm what most aviators already know – it's no secret that fighter pilots the world over tell their 'war stories' the way they want them to be heard! Having said that, I have also heard first hand how much the Soviet fighter pilots respected (and hated) the SR-71's capabilities, and what those capabilities meant in terms of American technological superiority.

As a member of the Habu fraternity, I commend Paul on what he refers to as his 'Labour of Love'. This work is a tribute to what arguably became the past century's greatest integration of technology and human spirit into a single entity … Perhaps that's why it was referred to as 'The Program'.

Frank Stampf

INTRODUCTION
Chapter 1

The name of an 11th century Holy Roman Emperor, Frederick Barbarossa, King of Germany, occupies an indelible place in contemporary history. At dawn on 22 June 1941, Nazi Germany launched Operation Barbarossa, its invasion of the Soviet Union. As its Panzer Divisions rolled east, smashing everything in their path, Soviet industry sought protection deep within the motherland. When, after World War II, 'An iron curtain … descended across the Continent' and relations between the victorious eastern and western powers chilled into the Cold War, it was soon discovered that the accuracy of maps and target intelligence held by Britain and the United States pertaining to their new common adversary was woefully inadequate. With limited human intelligence (Humint) being provided by agents in the field, large gaps remained in the knowledge of Soviet industrial and military capability. Stand-off aerial reconnaissance of peripheral targets provided a partial solution to the problem, but the vastness of the Soviet Union left only one option given the level of technology available at that time – overflight. So began the so-called PAROP (Peacetime Aerial Reconnaissance Operations) programme.

For several years, sorties were conducted using converted bombers manned by extremely courageous aircrews, as well as specialised variants of existing designs. For example, de Havilland Mosquito PR.Mk 34s flying with No. 540 Sqn, Royal Air Force (RAF), based at RAF Benson in Oxfordshire, conducted reconnaissance flights from altitudes in excess of 43,000 ft (13106 m) over such places as Murmansk and Archangel. Operations from such altitudes proved to provide a haven from interception by Soviet fighters and No. 540 Sqn continued such sorties until at least 1949.

In June 1948, the Soviet Union enforced a food blockade upon the Western zones of Berlin; the Allies responded by mounting a round-the-clock airlift; the United States highlighted the seriousness of the situation by redeploying bombers back to Britain. As Allied reconnaissance operations continued, it was only a question of time before such actions provoked the ultimate response. It occurred on 11 April 1950, when a US Navy Consolidated PB4Y Privateer, Bureau of Aeronautics Number 59645, nicknamed *Turbulent*

Turtle and operated by VP-26, with a crew of ten, was shot down and crashed into the Baltic, off Soviet occupied Latvia – there were no survivors.

World destabilisation continued when at dawn on 25 June 1950, communist North Korea invaded its southern neighbour, sparking off the Korean War. Back in Europe, surveillance operations against the USSR continued; the 5th Strategic Reconnaissance Group (SRG), from Travis AFB, California, operated Boeing RB-29 Superfortresses from RAF Sculthorpe and Burtonwood in the UK. Like the RAF's Mosquitos, their high-altitude performance and long range made them ideal photographic and electronic intelligence (Photint and Elint), gathering platforms. In February 1951, North American RB-45 Tornados from the 322nd, 323rd and 324th Strategic Reconnaissance Squadrons (SRSs), 91st Strategic Reconnaissance Wing (SRW), United States Air Force (USAF), based at Lockbourne AFB, Ohio, began rotating through RAF Sculthorpe on three-month temporary duty (TDY) assignments. They flew along the periphery of the Soviet Union and occasionally over Soviet satellite countries. Later, four of these Tornados were 'loaned' to Great Britain and painted in RAF markings. On the night of 21 March 1952, one of these aircraft, flown by an RAF crew, ventured into East Germany to gauge how the Soviets would react to such an incursion. Suitably encouraged, the Allied planners put together an audacious mission that was implemented on the night of 17 April 1952. Three RB-45Cs, in RAF colours and similarly crewed departed Sculthorpe, each heading for a separate air refuelling track. One was located over the North Sea, another over Denmark and a third south of Frankfurt. Having completed tanking from US Air Force KB-29s, they climbed to 35,000 ft (10668 m) and proceeded in total radio silence on routes that took them deep into the Soviet Union. The route flown by each was designed to overfly the maximum number of targets possible. One aircraft covered targets in Estonia, Latvia, Lithuania, Poland and in the former German province of East Prussia; another flew across Belorussia as far as Orel and the third, piloted by Sqn Ldr John Crampton, flew the longest and most southerly route, crossing the Ukraine and penetrating 'denied airspace' as far as

Rostov, on the Black Sea, before returning safely back to Sculthorpe after a flight lasting ten hours and 20 minutes. The operation was judged to be a success and another similar mission was flown, again by three 'RAF' RB-45s on 28 April 1954, after which the RAF exited its brief and highly classified relationship with the type (a similar three-ship mission was flown by the 19th Tactical Reconnaissance Squadron after Strategic Air Command (SAC) had retired the aircraft from its inventory sometime later).

Perhaps not surprisingly, the Soviet Union was becoming increasingly sensitive to Western incursions into its airspace and retaliated by pressing home a series of attacks on any aircraft suspected of violating its sovereignty. In April 1952, an Air France Douglas DC-4 was attacked and damaged in the Berlin corridor and less than two months later a Swedish air force Douglas C-47 was downed into the Baltic Sea, east of Gotland. Even a search and rescue Consolidated PBY Catalina was attacked while looking for survivors. The Russians certainly meant business, as witnessed at 17:33 local time on 13 June 1952, when RB-29 serial 44-61810, assigned to the 91st SRS and operating out of Yokota Air Base (AB), Japan, was shot down by two Soviet Mikoyan-Gurevich MiG-15 'Faggots' of the 165th Air Division of the Naval air force, stationed at Unashi airfield. The entire 12-man crew aboard the reconnaissance aircraft was lost.

Virtually a repeat performance followed at 14:30 local, on 7 October 1952, when RB-29 44-61815, named *Sunbonnet King* and also from the 91st SRS, was destroyed by two Soviet Lavochkin La-11 'Fang' fighters from the 368th Air Defence Fighter Aviation Regiment, during the process of conducting a reconnaissance mission northeast of the Island of Hokkaido, Japan. Yet again all eight crewmembers were killed.

The lumbering World War II vintage converted bombers, crewed by highly skilled and courageous flyers, were proving to be no match for Soviet fighters, which were exacting a terrible price on the Photint and Elint gatherers. But technology and the jet age at last caught up with the strategic reconnaissance business in the form of Boeing's sleek, new RB-47B Stratojets. Powered by six General Electric J47-GE-25 turbojets, each developing 6,000 lb (26.68 kN) of static thrust, the aircraft cruised at a useful 495 mph (797 km/h) and at altitudes of up to 40,000 ft (12192 m). But the RB-47Bs were only around for a couple of years and were replaced between March 1953 and August 1955, by no less than 240 RB-47Es. These were completed by Boeing-Wichita and also replaced the ageing piston-engined RB-29s and Boeing RB-50. Later models of the jet also included specialist Elint gathering versions, designated RB-47H and ERB-47H.

But the shoot-downs continued throughout 1953, the first on 10 March, when a USAF Republic F-84 Thunderjet was shot down over Bavaria by Czech MiG-15s. Two days later, an RAF Avro Lincoln (serial RF531) of the Central Gunnery School was shot down in the Berlin Corridor, again by MiG-15s; seven crew lost their lives. Yet another incident followed on 15 March, when an RB-50 of the 38th SRS, 55th SRW, flown by Lt-Col Robert Rich was intercepted by Soviet MiG-15s. The gunner, T/Sgt Jesse Prim, returned fire and the MiGs withdrew. However, on 29 July another RB-50 from the same wing was not so lucky. Attacked by MiG-15s southeast of Vladivostok during an electronic 'ferret' flight, aircraft serial 47-145 crashed into the Sea of Japan near Askol'd Island. The co-pilot, Capt John E. Roche was the only survivor from a crew of 17.

As the cost in aircrew lives continued to mount, it became apparent that a new approach to gathering such vital intelligence was needed. With high altitude having already been established as the 'safest' operational environment for such missions, it was a US Air Force Major who articulated the way forward. Having spent some time as an aeronautical engineer with Chance Vought, John Seaburg had been recalled to active duty following the outbreak of the Korean War. It was while serving as Assistant Chief in the New Developments Office, Bombardment Branch, at Wright Field, near Dayton, Ohio, that he articulated high-altitude strategic reconnaissance philosophy, by proposing to mate an aircraft with an extremely efficient high-aspect-ratio wing to the new generation of turbojet engines. Such a union, he believed, should enable a platform to cruise at altitudes far in excess of any other aircraft then in service.

Spurred on by his new boss, William Lamar, Seaburg had, by March 1953, created a formal specification, requiring the aircraft to cruise at an altitude of 70,000 ft (21336 m) and possess a range of 1,500 nm (1,727 miles; 2780 km), while carrying a camera payload weight of up to 700 lb (318 kg). In addition, it was stipulated that this new aircraft should be in service by 1956. These initial proposals were subsequently released to just three of the smaller aircraft manufacturing companies; the rationale being that since large-scale production was not envisioned, the project would receive a higher priority than if placed with the big players.

Both Bell and Fairchild were requested to submit proposals for the design and construction of a totally new aircraft; Martin was asked to apply improvements to the Martin B-57 Canberra (a design built under licence by the company, but actually designed and developed by the British

English Electric Company). In July 1953, six-month study contracts had been agreed with each company and the project, now identified as MX-2147, was given the classified code name of Bald Eagle.

Developments in camera and film technology, required to gather surveillance data from high altitude, had been proceeding in parallel with advances made by the aerospace industry. Having established the Photographic Laboratory at Wright Field before World War II, Brig-Gen George Goddard recruited two individuals, Col Richard Philbrick and Amrom Katz, who continued working after the war. With the organisation renamed as the Aerial Reconnaissance Laboratory, Goddard also helped establish a group of optical research specialists that formed the Boston University Optical Research Center; these included its director, Dr Duncan MacDonald. In addition, there were notable industrialists and academics serving on various presidential panels that also played a key role in the development of procuring high altitude reconnaissance imagery; people such as Harvard astronomer Dr James Baker, Edwin Land − inventor of the Polaroid camera − Allen Donovan and Col Richard Leghorn, an airborne reconnaissance expert from Eastman Kodak. But it was Jim Baker who had, by the end of World War II, produced the first 100-in (2540-mm) focal length precision lens for an aerial camera, and his work was continued at Boston by Dunc MacDonald and his team in the early post-war years, work that culminated in the production of a massive 240-in (6100-mm) focal length lens, which at 14 ft (4.27 m) long, could only fit into a giant Convair RB-36 Peacemaker!

Concerns in the US concerning a possible surprise Soviet Intercontinental Ballistic Missile (ICBM) attack had caused the Air Force to set up a Boston-based study group to look into the aerial reconnaissance problem. Code-named Beacon Hill, it was chaired by Carl Overhage and first assembled in May 1951, for the first time bringing together Baker, Land and Donovan. In mid-1952, the group submitted its report to the Air Force, basically confirming that aircraft involved in such work should be built to fly higher and faster. Later, part of this team became members of the so-called Killian Committee (set up by President Eisenhower in 1954, it served under the chair of Dr James R. Killian).

By January 1954, Bell, Fairchild and Martin had completed their studies and submitted them to Wright Field for evaluation. Apart from all three companies nominating the new Pratt & Whitney J57 axial flow turbojet engine (with high altitude modifications, the full designation would become J57-P-37), the design submissions varied considerably. As requested, Martin's proposed Model 294 was a 'big wing' version of the B-57; Bell's Model 67 was a frail-looking, twin-engined craft, while the single-engined Fairchild M-195 featured an over-the-fuselage intake and a stub-boom mounting for its vertical and horizontal tail surfaces.

On 1 February 1954, Richard Bissell Jr, (a brilliant economist who lectured at both Yale and MIT) was named Director for Planning and Coordination by the Director of Central Intelligence (DCI), Allen Dulles. Later that year, in response to Congressional criticism of the CIA, the Hoover Commission established a Special Study Group, chaired by Gen James Doolittle, to investigate the Agency's covert activities. When it reported back on 30 September, it expressed the belief that every known technique should be used, and new ones developed, to increase US intelligence by high altitude photographic reconnaissance and other means.

By March, engineers at Wright Field had nominated Martin's B-57D as the interim design, while the Bell proposal was felt to be the more suitable, longer-term design option. In April, Seaburg briefed all three designs to the Air Research and Development Command (ARDC) and SAC. This was followed a month later by yet another briefing, this time to Air Force Headquarters in Washington DC. Shortly afterwards Seaburg received approval to proceed with the B-57D; consequently a list of B-57 modifications was sent to ARDC headquarters, to enable urgent Air Force intelligence requirements in Europe to be met. Tentative approval was also obtained for the Bell Model 67 design; however, on 18 May an unsolicited proposal originating from Lockheed hit Seaburg's desk.

It was perhaps inevitable that someone in the Pentagon would leak details of the classified high-altitude reconnaissance proposal to Lockheed's Advanced Development Projects (ADPs) boss, aircraft design genius, Clarence L. 'Kelly' Johnson. However, after a short but detailed review, Seaburg and his staff rejected the Lockheed design, designated CL-282, and in June 1954 Kelly received a letter officially rejecting his proposal. Undaunted, Kelly decided to pursue funding for his high-altitude reconnaissance solution from alternative sources. Shortly afterwards he therefore presented a refined design submission to a CIA study committee.

On 9 October 1954, a Technological Capabilities Panel (TCP) of the Office of Defense Mobilisation's Surprise Attack Committee was established under Dr James Killian, with Dr Edwin Land as its Chairman. In a letter from the panel to the DCI dated 5 November, it recommended that the CIA establish a programme of photo-reconnaissance

flights over the USSR, with the assistance of the Air Force. In a subsequent meeting, held on 19 November in the office of the Secretary of the Air Force, Harold Talbott, the CIA and USAF agreed to pursue the TCP's proposal on a joint basis. This was followed up four days later by a memorandum signed by members of the Intelligence Advisory Committee (IAC), in support of the photo-reconnaissance programme.

With the Killian Committee having been briefed earlier on all four Bald Eagle contenders, Kelly met with the Government Advisory Board on 19 November 1954. During the course of that meeting he was told that he: 'was essentially being drafted for the project'.

The Killian Committee's decision to back the refined CL-282 proposal was communicated to Secretary of Defense Charles Wilson and DCI Allen Dulles. On 24 November, a meeting was held at the White House with President Eisenhower to present and seek authorisation for the CL-282 proposal, and funds to produce twenty aircraft, at a total cost of $35 million. This was duly sanctioned.

That same day, Kelly received a phone call giving him the go-ahead for the project that was accorded the classified cryptonym Aquatone (during the Agency's association with the U-2, which was developed from the CL-282 and which finally ended on 30 July 1967, the cryptonym changed on two occasions in order to preserve security when this was believed to have been compromised; it therefore became Chalice on 1 April 1958, and Idealist after Francis Gary Powers was shot down on 15 May 1960). Within

Lockheed's U-2 relied on its high-altitude capabilities for survival over denied territory. Cruising at altitudes in excess of 70,000 ft (21336 m), the glider-like spyplane's period of immunity was relatively short, however, its own early success in overflights of the Soviet Union helping spur on that country to develop the weapons system that would prove to be the U-2's nemesis – the SA-2 'Guideline' surface-to -air missile. (Lockheed)

days Lockheed's ADP office, better known as the 'Skunk Works', had by default become a full-scale, advanced design, engineering and production facility. The requirement for absolute secrecy meant that in the years ahead, the Skunk Works team was assured a high degree of autonomy from the rest of the Lockheed Corporation; additionally, the high level of specialised support required to run the programme, coupled with the lack of CIA expertise in this field, ensured Lockheed's participation in the programme for the life of the aircraft; in one step, a series of precedents had been set for future aircraft programmes.

A WINNING FORMULA
The Skunk Works had come into being back in 1943, following Lockheed's successful bid to build the United States' first jet fighter. Kelly recruited the finest engineers from the company's Burbank facility and put them to work in an area isolated and secure from the rest of the plant – building the XP-80 in just 143 days! The high level of secrecy surrounding the facility's activities, together with its location adjacent to the unit's awful smelling plastics manufacturing plant, caused Ervin Culver, a talented engineer on Kelly's

team (who later invented the rigid rotor system for helicopters), to constantly answer the telephone using the name 'Skunk Works', after a location in a popular wartime comic strip, written by Al Capp – the name stuck.

The team Kelly recruited to design and build the new reconnaissance aircraft included Dick Boehme (project engineer), Art Viereck (head of manufacturing), Ed Baldwin and some 50 other key engineers. Kelly nominated Tony LeVier (chief test pilot on the XF-104), to be the project's chief test pilot, but his first task was to find a secret site from which to conduct flight tests. Edwards and Palmdale were initially considered as possible sites, but both were soon discounted by the US government, which deemed them to be too visually accessible to the public.

In response, LeVier and Dorsey Kammerer – a Skunk Works logistics specialist – borrowed the company Beech Bonanza and conducted a two-week aerial survey of remote desert areas in southern California and Nevada. They then submitted a short list of possible options. However, none appealed to Bissell or Col Ozzie Ritland – the USAF's liaison officer to the CL-282's Development Project Staff (DPS). To settle the issue, in mid-April 1955, LeVier flew Johnson, Bissell and Ritland up to some likely sites near the Nevada nuclear test range. Ritland, a pilot who was once assigned to the B-29 test squadron which had dropped nuclear weapons at the range, directed LeVier towards an old World War II airfield which he remembered just to the north of the test range and adjacent to Groom Dry Lake. They landed on the lake-bed and according to Ritland: 'within 30 seconds we knew it was the place'.

In early May 1955, contracts were issued by the DPS, worth $800,000 for construction work at the secret site. It was to consist of a 5,000-ft (1524-m) long runway, a control tower, a mess hall and three hangers. Johnson, with generous amounts of irony, referred to this parched desert location as Paradise Ranch and this was inevitably soon shortened to 'The Ranch'.

On 7 May 1956, an elaborate cover story, devised to mask the true purpose of the U-2 programme, was issued to the press in the name of Dr Hugh Dryden, director of the National Advisory Committee for Aeronautics (NACA) – the predecessor of the National Aeronautics and Space Administration (NASA) – wherein it announced that the first U-2 aircraft were participating in an upper atmosphere research programme and 'flying from Watertown Strip in Southern Nevada'. Watertown was in fact now the 'official' name for the Ranch, the CIA naming the site after a town in upstate New York that was the birthplace of its DCI, Allen Dulles. The Nevada test site was vast and divided into many areas. Part of it had been a World War II gunnery range and a walk across the lakebed would reveal countless spent 50-calibre rounds, shell cases and links. The site fell within the boundaries of the main Atomic Energy Commission (AEC) nuclear test site. Therefore the area had to be cleared and fenced off and a restricted airspace zone established. Within three months, under the auspices of Richard Bissell, a large team of AEC construction crews worked round the clock to transform the site into a basic test facility.

To ensure that 'Kelly's Angel' (as the high-altitude design was being referred to by some in the Skunk Works) maintained a competitive edge over its rival, the Bell 67 (now officially designated X-16 by the Air Force as a cover), Kelly promised that his design would be airborne in no less than eight months after the first metal was cut. The initial batch of 20 aircraft was built at the Burbank plant; thereafter further production was moved to Oildale, near Bakersfield, California. By 15 March 1955, wind tunnel testing of the design had been successfully completed and on 21 May the fuselage of 'Article 341', the prototype, was removed from its jig. On 20 July, the completed aircraft was handed over to inspection for final checks. The next day it was disassembled and loaded into loading carts. At day break on 24 July, Article 341 was loaded into an Air Force Douglas C-124 Globemaster II and flown to Groom Lake. There it was reassembled in the semi-completed hangers and three days later static engine runs were initiated. With taxi tests completed – the third of which culminated in the aircraft inadvertently getting airborne, to an altitude of 35 ft – the schedule first flight took place at 15:55 on 4 August 1955. Witnessed by several key Skunk Works and 'Agency' people, Tony LeVier, (using the call sign ANGEL 1), was chased by a Lockheed operated C-47, flown by company test pilot Bob Matye accompanied by Kelly Johnson (Matye would be the second pilot to fly Article 341).

It was during phase one of the flight test programme that the aircraft was officially designated U-2, the 'U' for Utility, again designed to hide the machine's true mission. Bell's X-16 had also been progressing well, with construction getting underway in September 1954 and its first flight scheduled for early 1956. However, with the Agency, not the Air Force, now responsible for high-altitude reconnaissance, the X-16's raison d'etre had disappeared. Consequently, two months after the U-2 took to the air, a decision was made to terminate the X-16 contract – it was a bitter blow for Bell and one that was to have serious financial implications for the company for several years.

The first of six RB-57s was delivered to SAC, under Project Black Knight, in March 1956.

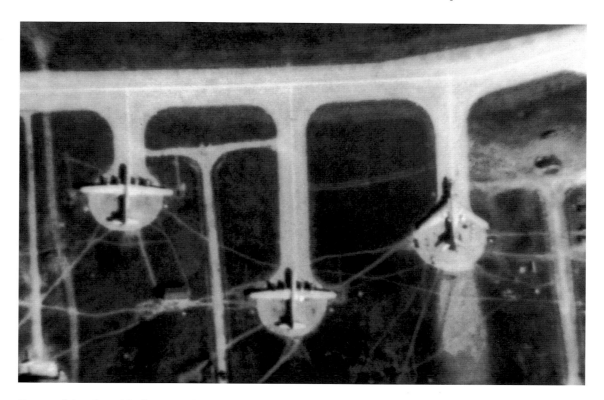

Operated by the 4025th Strategic Reconnaissance Squadron (SRS), 4080th Strategic Reconnaissance Wing (SRW), located at Turner AFB, Georgia, the aircraft were operationally deployed for the first time, under Operation Sea Lion, just four months after their activation. Most of these early operations were Elint/Sigint missions, flown from Operating Locations (OLs), at Yokota AB, Japan, and briefly Eielson Air Force Base (AFB), Alaska.

Highly classified, these so-called ferret sorties utilised specialist equipment designated Model 320 or SAFE (Semi-Automatic Ferret Equipment), which had been tested during 1956 and 1957, under the Blue Tail Fly project. Thereafter, it was declared operational and deployed onboard the RB-57s. In addition, the unit conducted high-altitude sampling, during which particles were collected from the upper atmosphere, following nuclear tests undertaken by China and the Soviet Union. This enabled scientists to ascertain the weapon's characteristics, yield, efficiency, etc.

In February 1957, the 4025th relocated from Turner to Laughlin AFB, Texas, and one month later it received the last of 20 RB-57Ds ordered by the Air Force. For six months further air sampling flights were conducted, this time from Eniwetok Proving Grounds, on the Marshall Islands. Then, in early 1959, under Operation Bordertown, the unit deployed to Europe, where it continued to conduct air sampling and Elint/Sigint missions, before

This typical piece of U-2 imagery shows a pair of Tupolev Tu-4 'Bull' bombers and a single Tupolev Tu-16 'Badger' bomber on dispersal at a Soviet air base. The quality of image obtained by the mid-1950s' optics of the U-2 is clearly impressive. The Tu-4 was reverse engineered by the USSR from Boeing B-29 Superfortress aircraft force landed in the Soviet far east during the closing stages of World War II. More significantly in this image, the Tu-16 was a modern, swept-wing, jet-powered bomber, the gathering of intelligence on technology such as this driving the U-2 programme. (CIA)

returning to Laughlin and deactivating in mid-1959.

By 1 September 1955, Tony LeVier had completed a total of 20 flights in the U-2 and he left Project Aquatone, having been promoted to Director of Flying back at Burbank. Future test flight planning now became the responsibility of Ernie Joiner and test flying was undertaken by Bob Matye and Ray Goadey.

CAMERAS AND CREWS

Early model U-2s had their mission payload located in a cavernous, pressurised area behind the cockpit, known as the Q-bay. The acquisition of Photint was to be the aircraft's primary mission and Dr Jim Baker proved to be pivotal in the conceptualisation of the camera system deployed on the U-2. Three camera systems were worked up: the Type A was primarily refurbished Air Force stock and a stop-gap; the Type C, with its 180-in (4572-mm) focal length lens, would be overtaken by events; and the Hycon Type B camera would prove to be Project Aquatone's workhorse. Optimised with a 36-in (914-mm) focal length lens with an f/10 aperture, the camera's large-format film was loaded onto two contra-winding 9½-in by 18-in (24 × 46 cm) rolls either 4,000 or 6,500 ft (1219 or 1981 m) long. The system was programmed to produce parallel images with an overlap of 50 or 70 per cent. When the two 4,000-ft reels were loaded, the combined film and camera weight was 484 lb (220 kg) which increased to a hefty 577 lb (262 kg) when the two 6,500-ft reels were carried. Also located in the Q-bay was a 35-mm tracker camera. This scanned from horizon to horizon throughout the flight, thereby providing the photographic interpreters with an accurate ground track of the aircrafts flight path.

Pilots recruited by the Agency into Project Aquatone came straight from the Air Force, on a 'suspended contract', their 'grey suit' time during the period of 'secondment' counting as time served in the military. Having passed various interviews, conducted by mysterious civilians at insalubrious hotels, they then spent a week undergoing one of the most rigorous medicals ever devised, at the Lovelace Clinic, Albuquerque, New Mexico. In all, about 25 pilots, in three intakes, were recruited into the Agency programme.

During the Geneva Summit, on 21 July 1955, President Eisenhower had proposed that an 'Open Skies' plan should be considered between the United States, the Soviet Union and other participating countries, wherein a limited number of annual reconnaissance overflights would be made in order to verify claims of declared force strengths. Surprised by the proposal, the Soviet delegation reacted favourably and agreed to confer with their Party Secretary, Nikita Khrushchev. However, his deep mistrust of the West, and his paranoia, conspired to ensure that he neither signed up to nor rejected the proposal. Such prevarication ensured that 'Open Skies' failed one month later, when a vote was taken in the United Nations.

By June 1956, the initial flight test and training objectives of the U-2 programme had been completed, and six pilots, together with ten U-2s, were readied for operational deployment. History was about to prove that the death of Eisenhower's 'Open Skies' proposal would have a profound impact, both within the intelligence fraternity and on the stage of international power politics, when in response the US President sanctioned an initial ten day period for the execution of Operation Overflight.

In anticipation, two U-2s had been air freighted to RAF Lakenheath, England, on 30 April 1956, where the first of three Agency detachments was formed, under the entirely fictious designation of 1st Weather Reconnaissance Squadron, Provisional (WRSP-1). Within the 'inner circle', however, this was known as 'Detachment A' and consisted of Agency and Air Force personnel, and contracted civilians. However, on 16 May, Prime Minister Anthony Eden wrote to President Eisenhower requesting a postponement of Det A's operations from the UK, following an embarrassing incident with the Soviet Union over an attempt by Royal Navy frogman to covertly survey the cruiser *Ordzhonikdze* while it was in Portsmouth harbour and carrying Nikita Khrushchev. Consequently no operational sorties were flown from the UK and the unit redeployed to Wiesbaden, West Germany on 15 June. This new location was situated close to Camp King, the Agency's main West German intelligence gathering facility, from within which intelligence reports from defectors were collected and then used, in part as a basis for generating U-2 overflight requests.

The first operational U-2 sortie was flown just four days after Det A's arrival at Wiesbaden. Piloted by Carl Overstreet, the platform overflew Warsaw, Berlin and Potsdam, before recovering back into Wiesbaden without incident. Image quality from the Type B camera was breathtaking, surpassing anything previously seen, and the stage was set for Overflight to begin operations against the Soviet Union. This historic event was achieved by Hervey Stockman, flying Article 347, on US Independence Day, 4 July 1956. He flew over East Berlin then across northern Poland via Poznan, and onward to Minsk and Leningrad, before exiting via the Baltic states of Estonia, Latvia and Lithuania, landing again without incident back at Wiesbaden after a flight lasting eight hours 45 minutes.

The very next day the same aircraft was again airborne, this time with Carmen Vito at the controls on an overflight that encompassed the Soviet capital, Moscow. Again image quality was exceptional, but on this occasion Soviet fighters tried, unsuccessfully, to intercept the flight. Yet another mission was successfully completed the following Monday, by which time the Soviet 'diplomatic cage' had been well and truly rattled. On 10 July the Soviet Ambassador in Washington DC delivered a formal, public protest against the flights. Eisenhower was very concerned at the level of provocation that these flight inevitably caused and insisted that henceforth, ten day blanket clearances were rescinded, and instead replaced by a policy of one clearance, one flight.

The imagery secured by these first sorties was developed and duplicated at Wiesbaden, before one set was despatched by special courier aircraft to Washington (the other set was retained at Wiesbaden in the event that the first was lost or

Clarence Leonard 'Kelly' Johnson was the genius behind both the U-2 and A-12/F-12/SR-71 programmes – here he is accompanied by the third and final YF-12A. Universally known as 'Kelly', Johnson joined the Lockheed company as a designer in 1933 at the age of 23. His first projects included the Orion and Electra airliners, before he moved onto a series of legendary types including the P-38 Lightning, P-80 Shooting Star, F-104 Starfighter, U-2 and A-12/F-12/SR-71. 'Kelly' Johnson left the company in 1975 and died in 1990, in time to see the revolutionary F-117 Nighthawk fly. (Lockheed)

damaged in transit). Once in Washington, the images ended up in a run down neighbourhood where Art Lundahl, of the Agency's Photographic Intelligence Division, had set up a secret process and interpretation centre aptly code-named Auto Mat, on the upper floors of an auto repair shop.

The vast amount of quality imagery collected by Overflight soon put the Agency at odds with gloomy Air Force predictions about the strength of the Soviet bomber fleet, which forced a downward reappraisal of the National Intelligence Estimate (NIE). One disturbing aspect revealed by the flights, however, was the ease with which Soviet defences were able to track them with early warning and height finding radars. This led the Skunk Works to undertake a series of evaluations using various techniques to reduce the U-2's radar cross section (RCS). The first of these, code-named Project Dirty Bird, utilised Article 341 at Watertown Strip, and saw the aircraft's planform framed by wires of different dipole lengths running from tail to wing. Another evaluation used radar absorbent material (RAM), in the form of a metallic grid, known as a Salisbury Screen, attached to '341's lower surfaces this was then covered in 'Echosorb', a microwave-absorbent coating based on black rubber foam, but neither technique proved effective.

In August 1956, the second cadre of Agency pilots had completed their training at Groom Lake and was shipped to Incirlik AB, Turkey, to form 'Detachment B', which consisted of seven pilots

and five aircraft. A third U-2 operating location – 'Detachment C' ('Det C'), was established at Atsugi airfield near Tokyo in 1957, and in February that same year the last Agency pilots graduated and were dispersed to the three Dets. By now Det A had again moved, this time to Giebelstadt, just south of Wurzburg, and shortly afterwards it was merged with Det B.

The U-2 programme's accomplishments were approaching legendary status; in addition to revealing the truth about the Soviet bomber fleet, it had, while operating out of Lahore and Peshawar, Pakistan, discovered the location of a new ICBM test site at Tyuratam, which turned out to be the primary test facility for the new R-7 ICBM (later known to NATO as the SS-6 'Sapwood').

But the U-2 flights had also provided a further spur to Soviet surface-to-air missile (SAM) development, that culminated in the production and deployment of the SA-2 'Guideline'. With the weapon touting a kill pattern of about 400 ft (122 m), U-2 mission planners gave known SA-2 sites a berth of up to 30 miles (48 km). Further precautions also saw the development and introduction of a rudimentary electronic countermeasures (ECM) suite designated System 9. This simple range-gate pull-off (RGPO) device was located in a small aft-facing compartment at the root of the vertical fin. Switched on by the pilot upon entering denied territory, it had the capability of breaking lock if illuminated by an airborne intercept radar. Additional comfort came from the first major U-2 upgrade which had just been initiated. Five aircraft were reworked into U-2C models, powered by an up-rated Pratt & Whitney J75 engine, which enabled the aircraft to climb an additional 5,000 ft (1524 m).

On the diplomatic stage, a visit by Khrushchev to the United States prompted a reciprocal invitation for Eisenhower to visit the Soviet Union during 1960. In the meantime, it was agreed a summit would be held in Paris, to which both the British and French would be invited. A thaw in the frosty relationship between the two superpowers seemed in prospect. However, all this was about to slide over the precipice.

MAYDAY

By the spring of 1960, the U-2 had successfully completed about 30 overflights of the Soviet Union and considerably more peripheral missions. On 1 May 1960, at 06:26 local time, operation Grand Slam, mission 4154, was launched from Peshawar, Pakistan. The ambitious sortie planned to transit the entire Soviet mainland from south to north, a distance of some 3,800 miles (6115 km), by overflying Afghanistan and then targets located at Tyuratam, Aralsk, Sverdlovsk, Kirov, Plesetsk, Archangelsk and Murmansk, before recovering into Bødo, Norway.

To help draw attention away from the deep penetration mission, a diversionary peripheral flight left from Incirlik. However, three hours and 27 minutes into the flight, the pilot of U-2C Article Number 360, Francis Gary Powers, was stunned to feel and hear what seemed to be a dull explosion below and behind his aircraft. Almost immediately afterwards the sky turned bright orange and seconds later '360's right wing dropped. Turning the control yoke left, Powers managed to correct the roll, but then the nose pitched downward – due to damage sustained by the horizontal tail. As the U-2 pitched violently forward both wings were ripped from the fuselage. Power's faceplate frosted over, his partial pressure suite inflated and what was left of the aircraft entered an inverted flat spin. Centrifugal forces pinned the hapless pilot to the instrument panel precluding use of the ejection seat. Glancing at the unwinding altimeter, Powers noted he was descending through 34,000 ft (10363 m). Reaching up he pushed the canopy open, unlatched his seat harness and was thrown forward. Now half out of the cockpit, he realised he hadn't disconnected his oxygen hose. He attempted to re-enter the cockpit. When this failed, he began frantically pulling on the hose in an effort to break it; finally he broke-free from the doomed aircraft and almost immediately his parachute deployed – triggered by a barometric sensor set to activate at 15,000 ft (4572 m). Powers was captured after landing in a field and four days later the political impact of the shoot down reverberated across the front pages of newspapers all around the world. Operation Overflight, the United States' most clandestine reconnaissance operation, had literally been blown apart at the seams. An immediate cessation of all CIA U-2 overflights followed and this was later backed-up by the retraction of all 'Agency' U-2 operations around the world. But with 90 per cent of all photographic reconnaissance data on Soviet military developments originating from the U-2 platform, the question to be addressed was, with what would it be replaced?

OXCART

Chapter 2

Air Force analysts at Wright Field deduced that the U-2's ability to safely execute deep penetration missions, particularly over the Soviet Union, would inevitably be time-limited as a result of expected advances in anti-aircraft technology. Consequently, even before the aircraft's first flight they embarked upon a series of studies into replacement options capable of wresting back from the CIA the strategic reconnaissance overflight mission.

SUNTAN

Despite various post-war studies in the United States proving that liquid hydrogen was a viable, albeit volatile, fuel for both rockets and aircraft,

nothing in the way of concept flight testing got under way until the mid-1950s.

On 24 March 1954, a British engineer named Randolph Rae personally delivered to the Air Force's new development offices at Wright Field, a proposal outlining the development of a unique, liquid hydrogen-fuelled aircraft. Propeller driven, the machine was optimised to cruise at an altitude

The CL-400 design emerged under the Suntan programme aimed at the development of a platform for use in deep-penetration strategic reconnaissance missions and with greater survivability than the U-2. Designed to employ liquid hydrogen as its fuel, the CL-400 design never reached hardware stage, although components and prototype engines were constructed and tested. (Lockheed)

CL-400 GENERAL ARRANGEMENT

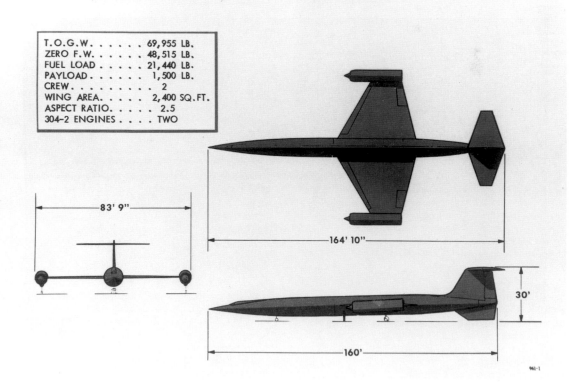

T.O.G.W.	69,955 LB.
ZERO F.W.	48,515 LB.
FUEL LOAD	21,440 LB.
PAYLOAD	1,500 LB.
CREW	2
WING AREA	2,400 SQ. FT.
ASPECT RATIO	2.5
304-2 ENGINES	TWO

83' 9"

164' 10"

30'

160'

961-1

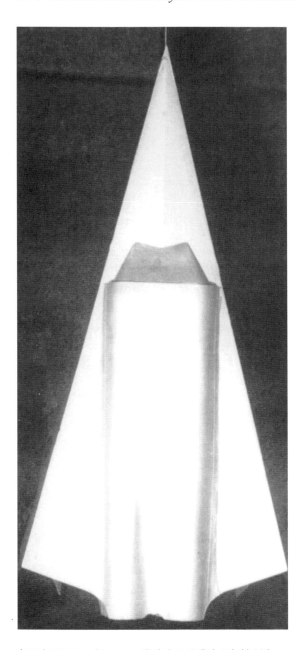

Arrow I was among the many exotic designs studied, and ultimately abandoned, during the search for an aircraft to replace the U-2. Interestingly, the delta planform, which would ultimately be a feature of the A-12, was incorporated into many of the concepts. (Lockheed Martin Skunk Works)

in excess of 75,000 ft (22860 m) and at a speed of about 500 mph (805 km/h). Although these performance figures were in themselves outstanding, it was the Rex I engine that attracted most interest from the Air Force engineers.

Randolph Rae was formally associated with the Summers Gyroscope Company. However, during the subsequent review process of his drawings and calculations at Wright Field, the company had been quietly acquired by the Garrett Corporation, specifically to gain access to the engine's patent. Unfortunately the ensuing, protracted litigation continued to follow the Rex I throughout its life.

The Skunk Works became involved in the project in mid-1954 when, under the original proposal, it was agreed that it would be provided with $50,000 to conduct an airframe analysis. However, ongoing legal problems over the patent issue delayed contract ratification between Rae and the Garrett Corporation until October 1955. All seemed on track until the Air Force issued a work statement a few weeks later, calling for a high-altitude, supersonic design, the range of which was of secondary importance.

Not wishing to forgo the Air Force funding allocated for the Rex engine – one of the three designs now available was for a supersonic-cruise aircraft – Garrett decided to pursue an airframe study that had earlier been given to Rae, and since the Skunk Works had been involved in the initial airframe negotiations back in mid-1954, it was invited to provide airframe input under a Skunk Works contract. However, after reviewing Garrett's data, the Skunk Works engineering team concluded that the proposed engines would be incapable of producing the required levels of thrust to meet the Air Force performance specification. Further calculations indicated that the engines would need to be 50 per cent larger if a cruise speed of Mach 2.25 was to be achieved. This in turn forced the Air Force to re-evaluate Garrett's ability to build such an engine – certainly to date the company had only built auxiliary power unit type turbines.

On 15 February 1956, two Skunk Works design proposals, designated CL-325-1 and CL-325-2 and powered by the supersonic Rex III liquid hydrogen engine, were presented to the Air Force at Wright Field. However, after extensive studies the Air Force became convinced that Garrett was incapable of building an engine as complex as that proposed. Consequently, on 18 October 1956, it issued a directive demanding that all work on both projects be stopped, except for the completion of a final summary report.

Impressed by the notion of a hydrogen-fuelled aircraft and encouraged by the Air Force to develop a U-2 follow-on, Kelly Johnson and his Skunk Works team had begun their own studies into the concept a year before cancellation of the Rex III design submissions. During a Pentagon meeting with Lt-Gen Donald Putt, head of ARDC, in early January 1956, Kelly offered to build two prototype hydrogen-fuelled aircraft powered by more conventional engines and have them delivered within 18 months of contract signing.

Based upon the CL-325, they would be capable of cruising at an altitude of over 99,000 ft (30175 m) at a speed of Mach 2.5 and have a range of 2,500 miles (4023 km).

A second meeting was held at the Pentagon on 18 January, during which it was decided to fund Air Force studies to verify Kelly's proposal and to select a qualified manufacturer to design and build a hydrogen-fuelled engine. By the end of February, proposals from Pratt & Whitney and General Electric had been reviewed and on 1 May 1956 a six-month study contract was signed with Pratt & Whitney for the engine, and with the Skunk Works to evaluate airframe configuration and material options. Air Force programme management was headed by Lt-Col John Seaburg, who was assisted by Maj Alfred Gardner (engine development) and Capt Jay Brill (logistics). As the aircraft's mission would be the penetration of 'denied territory', just 25 people were cleared into this special access-required programme, code-named Suntan.

In 1956, the Skunk Works signed a contract to produce four production aircraft for the Air Force, in addition to the two prototypes and a single static test specimen. The design was now designated CL-400.

Having joined the Skunk Works in 1954 as an entry-level engineer specialising in thermodynamics, Ben Rich became a key member of the Suntan project and became involved in the feasibility studies that would prove liquid hydrogen was safe and practical to produce in large batches. To produce the highly volatile fuel,

a production facility was established in a remote corner of the Lockheed complex at Burbank airport that had served in World War II as a communal air raid shelter for workers from a nearby Boeing B-17 Flying Fortress factory. As Ben later noted: 'It had 8-ft (2.44-m) thick walls and underground bunkers and was located about as far away from the rest of the Skunk Works as it could be, in case something went wrong and we blew up!' Dave Robertson joined Ben, together with 12 Skunk Works shop workers and mechanics, and in less than three months they were producing more than 200 US gal (757 litres) of liquid hydrogen a day, within the walled compound that had become known as Fort Robertson. Despite the temperamental nature of the fuel, not a single accident occurred and visitors cleared into the project and touring the site were often given Martini icicles: the gin and vermouth mixture was poured into a Dixie cup, a lollypop stick inserted and the complete ensemble then immersed in liquid hydrogen. The result was a frozen Martini on a stick!

On 18 August 1957, Pratt & Whitney had completed its first Model 304 engine. It was then transported from the company's facility at East Hartford, Connecticut, to its new plant at West Palm Beach, Florida. On 11 September, static tests

This Archangel I model dates to October 1957 and perhaps represents one of the less radical concepts in the process that resulted in the A-12. With the U-2 having become 'Kelly's Angel', some of the new designs acquired the name Archangel. (Lockheed Martin Skunk Works)

Archangel II was a mixed-powerplant design, featuring a pair of turbojets mounted at mid-span and a ramjet at each wing tip. The turbojets were to have been J58s and the aircraft could have flown a 4,000-mile (4437-km) mission with an operational ceiling in the region of 100,000 ft (30480 m). (Lockheed Martin Skunk Works)

were initiated, using nitrogen to check the engine's rotating elements and fuel system. During October the first runs took place, followed by a second series in December after engine inspection. A second engine began tests on 16 January 1958, with an improved engine, Model 304-2, being delivered and tested for the first time on 24 June. The tests went extremely well, with both Pratt & Whitney and the Air Force gaining considerable confidence in the hydrogen-fuelled engines.

All seemed to be running according to schedule: the Air Force had allocated $95 million to Suntan, Kelly had ordered no less than $2\frac{1}{2}$ miles (4 km) of aluminium extrusion for airframe production, the 304 engine continued to perform as planned, Air Products was constructing a large hydrogen liquefaction plant in Florida and the Massachusetts Institute of Technology was working on an inertial guidance system.

But over the next six months something continued to bother Kelly. Despite his having successfully sold the aircraft to the Air Force, it was becoming increasingly apparent to him that the CL-400's severe range limitations could not be designed out of the aircraft. The design fell short of its estimated original lift-over-drag ratio by 16 per cent. Stretching the fuselage to increase fuel capacity would result in only a 3 per cent increase in range. Pratt & Whitney estimated that no better than a 5–6 per cent improvement in specific fuel consumption (SFC) could be achieved with its Model 304 engine over a five-year period of operation. Such low growth potential, coupled with the logistical problems associated with pre-positioning liquid hydrogen to forward operating locations, convinced Kelly that 'the aircraft was a dog'. In March 1957, during a meeting with James Douglas Jr, then Secretary of the Air Force, and Lt-Gen Clarence Irvine, deputy Chief of Staff for material, Kelly bluntly informed them of his misgivings and by the middle of that year others were voicing similar concerns. In February 1959, and at Kelly's insistence, Suntan was cancelled. The Skunk Works returned almost $90 million and yet again another proposed strategic overflight programme slipped from the Air Force's grasp.

GUSTO AND OXCART

Concerns about the U-2's possible vulnerability were not solely the preserve of the Air Force; shortly after its first flight, Richard Bissell – DCI Allen Dulles' Special Assistant for Planning and Coordination – called for research studies that would ultimately lead to its successor.

The Scientific Engineering Institute (SEI), a Boston based CIA proprietary that had been conducting work aimed at reducing the U-2's vulnerability, had also been investigating the possibility of designing an aircraft with a small radar cross section (RCS). These so-called 'radar camouflage studies', code named Rainbow, soon indicated that if such a design also incorporated the use of radar absorbent materials (RAM) and was capable of flying at both supersonic speeds and extreme altitude, the chances of detection by radar were greatly reduced. In August 1957, these findings were presented to Bissell and shortly thereafter they became enshrined in a CIA general operation requirement, specifically designed to produce a U-2 replacement. The project was given the secret code name Gusto and John Parangosky was nominated as the CIA's project manager. It was from Parangosky's office that both Kelly Johnson and Robert Whidmer of the Convair Division of General Dynamics were informed of the SEI's findings; but due to security constraints, both were asked to submit designs without a formal contract or government funding. They agreed to this, on the basis that funding would be forthcoming at 'the appropriate time' and over the following

18 months, configurations were developed and refined, all at no expense to the CIA.

It was immediately apparent to Bissell that Gusto would be both hi-tech and high risk for the two participating aircraft companies, neither of whom were in a position to guarantee success. It therefore followed that the US government would have to assume practically all of the liability, which in turn meant that a number of high-ranking officials would need to be cleared for access in order to secure the necessary funding. Consequently, on 19 November 1957 Bissell reported the project to Deputy Secretary of Defense Quarles, who agreed that it should also be reported to the President's Board of Consultants on Foreign Intelligence Activities. To ensure that those who held the purse strings had the most definitive information available as programme advances occurred, Bissell also established an evaluation panel and again called upon Edwin

Gusto 2 was designed with invisibility to radar as its primary defence, the type's projected performance being subsonic. It had been discovered that Soviet radar systems were able to acquire the U-2 and, as such, the ability to avoid this detection – 'stealth' – was a keen motivation in the continuing design process. (Lockheed)

While Lockheed was working on proposals including Archangel II, Convair, and latterly General Dynamics, were working on the unlikely-named Fish. In this wind-tunnel model the Fish aircraft is mounted below its B-58 Hustler launch aircraft. A later development, Kingfish, did away with the need for the B-58. (Jay Miller Collection)

Land to serve as chairman of the advisory group. Other members of the so-called Land Panel included Edward Purcell, who had earlier served on the Technological Capabilities Panel (TIP), Allen F. Donovan, of the Cornell Aeronautical Laboratory and Eugene P. Kiefer, Bissell's assistant.

Perhaps not surprisingly, Kelly Johnson and his team of Skunk Works engineers had already been looking at various designs that would replace the U-2. Ben Rich recalled that some were referring to the design in-house as the 'U-3'. These same engineers often referred to the U-2 as 'Kelly's Angel', cognisant that the proposed capabilities

inherent in this new advanced aircraft represented an enormous leap forward, Kelly noted on 21 April 1958, in what was to become his A-12 log/diary: 'I drew up the first Archangel proposal for a Mach-3.0 cruise airplane having a 4,000-nm [4,606-mile; 7412-km] range at 90,000 to 95,000 ft [27432 to 28956 m]'. To power the ADP design, two engine types were examined, the Pratt & Whitney J58 and the General Electric J93. By June, studies concluded that the former of the two would provide superior performance.

On 23 July 1958, Kelly presented his Gusto Model G2A to the Programme Office and noted later in his diary that it was well received. During a meeting with the Land Panel on 14 August, Kelly was asked to comment on a US Navy/Boeing proposal for a 190-ft (58-m) long ramjet-powered, inflatable aircraft capable of cruising at an altitude of 150,000 ft (45720 m) and carried aloft by a balloon. After a few rapid notes and calculations, Kelly informed the board that the carrying balloon would need to be over a mile in diameter!

Some of the designs worked on by the Skunk Works at this time were also inflatable and required the use of ramjet propulsion. However, following a presentation to the board in September, Kelly noted: 'The inflatable airplane concept appears to have been dropped for our particular mission'. He went on to mention that he had presented Gusto 2A and a revised version of the Archangel design that developed a higher altitude performance and that Convair had proposed a Super Hustler design, powered by a ramjet, capable of Mach 4.0 and launched from a B-58. In fact, the Land Panel approved the subsonic Gusto design, but only as a back-up to the high-speed project.

During the 12-month study period, while Kelly concentrated on refinements to his Archangel II proposal, the General Dynamics team (Convair had by now become part of General Dynamics) headed by Bob Widmer and Vincent 'Vinko' Dolson, continued to evolve its Super Hustler. The name of this design similarly underwent a metamorphosis,

being latterly referred to as Fish, then, following a major redesign, the enlarged version became known as Kingfish. Fish, it was proposed, would be powered by a mixture of ramjets and two retractable General Electric J85 turbojets that provided propulsion for final approach and landing, but Kingfish was to be powered by two J58s. It would cruise at Mach 3.25 (as opposed to Fish, at Mach 4.25); however, the major advantage of this design was that it did not require the use of a specially modified, stretched B-58 to get airborne. It was also thought to be far more operationally practicable.

On 25 November 1958, the Land Panel conducted a review of studies provided to it by the two competing design teams and decided that each company would be granted a year to refine its initial proposal and generate a definitive aircraft design. This decision was relayed to

These two views show a Kingfish mock-up and give an idea of how the aircraft might have looked. Note that the machine would have featured canted engine air intakes and that provision was made on the edges of its lifting surfaces for the incorporation of wedges of radar absorbent material. (both Jay Miller Collection)

President Eisenhower and he, together with the Killian Comittee, reviewed both the Gusto programme and the other design options. On conclusion of that meeting, the President agreed that funding would – as with the U-2 – be made available from the CIA's special Contingency Reserve Fund and would be allocated for the development of either the Lockheed or General Dynamics Mach-3.0 reconnaissance platform. Gusto became ever less relevant as the high speed designs progressed and it eventually succumbed. On 18 February 1959, following an internal CIA restructure, an office, hitherto known as the Development Project Staff, was re-designated the Development Projects Division (DPD). One of the components of this organisation was the 1007th Air Intelligence Service Group (AISG), which served as a cover unit for DPD Air Force assignees, but, on 17 June, this too was re-designated and became the 1149th Special Activities Squadron – it was this unit that would operate the new high-flier.

For some 12 months, Kelly and the Lockheed Programme Manager, Dick Boehme, went into overdrive and studied no less than ten major design models designated A-3 to A-12. Each of these was further subdivided into a number of variations on the 'parent' design. On 18 May 1959, at the request of Gen Thomas White, Air Force Chief of Staff, a CIA/Air Force working level technical panel was formed, to further provide expert advice in respect of the looming design selection process. On 20 August, the final design submissions from Lockheed (A-12) and General Dynamics were delivered to the joint Department of Defense/Air Force/CIA selection panel. Interestingly, despite the strikingly different external appearances of the two designs, their performance was very similar:

	A-12	Kingfish
Speed	Mach 3.2	Mach 3.2
Range (total)	4,120 nm	4,000 nm
Range (at altitude)	3,800 nm	3,400 nm
Cruise Altitudes Start Mid-range End	84,500 ft 91,000 ft 97,600 ft	85,000 ft 88,000 ft 94,000 ft
Dimensions Length Wing span	102 ft 57 ft	79 ft 6 in 56 ft
Gross weight	110,000 lb	101,700 lb
Fuel Weight	64,600 lb	62,000 lb
Time to first flight	22 months	22 months

On 29 August 1959, Lockheed received official notification that it had won the competition with

its A-12 design submission. On 4 September it received $4.5 million by way of an advanced feasibility contract, covering the period 1 September to 1 January 1960. Concurrently, the top secret project received its equally classified cryptonym: Oxcart.

Viewed in the context of the best front-line fighters of the day – the early Century Series jets, like the North American F-100 Super Sabre and the McDonnell F-101 Voodoo – the A-12 would be a giant leap into the technically unknown, almost doubling and trebling the altitude and speed envelopes, respectively, of these fighters. This single-seat hot rod would cruise in afterburner at Mach 3.2, possess an unrefuelled range of 4,000 miles (6437 km) and have an end of cruise climb ceiling of between 84,500 and 97,600 ft (25756 and 29748 m). Above 80,000 ft (24390 m) the ambient air temperature is −69°F (−56°C) and atmospheric air pressure is just 0.4 psi (2.7 kPa). However, cruising at a speed of 1 mile (1.6 km) every two seconds, the A-12's airframe temperatures would vary from 473 to 1,030°F (245 to 565°C). The two Pratt & Whitney J58 turbojet engines each produced 29,500 lb (131.12kN) of thrust and required 100,000 cu ft (2832 m³) of air per second. Such an awesome performance envelope ensured that virtually everything on the aircraft had to be invented and built from scratch. Accordingly, 85 per cent of the aircraft's structural weight was of titanium metal to cope with the extreme temperature environment that the airframe would experience (advanced composites were not then available).

At Mach 3.2, the turbine inlet temperature (TIT) reached over 2,102°F (1100°C), which necessitated the development of a unique fuel. Developed jointly by Pratt & Whitney, Ashland Shell and Monsanto, it was known originally as PF-1and later as JP-7. With this fuel enjoying a much higher ignition temperature than standard JP-4 fuel, the next problem was that standard ignition systems were incapable of producing the required heat for combustion, so a chemical ignition system (CIS) was developed, using a highly volatile pyrophoric fluid known as triethyl borane (TEB). TEB is extremely flash sensitive when oxidised, and a small TEB tank was carried on the aircraft to allow afterburner start up, both on the ground and aloft. After a 'shot' of TEB had been used, the tank was pressurised using gaseous nitrogen to ensure the system remained inert. Liquid nitrogen was carried in three dewar flasks to provide a positive head of gaseous nitrogen in the fuel tanks. This prevented the depleted tanks from crushing as the aircraft descended into denser air to land or refuel; additionally, it reduced the risk of inadvertent vapour ignition.

MISSION SENSORS
Viewscope
The Baird-Atomic 6642-1 periscope system enabled the pilot to see the ground below. It had two settings, wide-angle, that provided a view forward of about 85° forward of nadir – a point on the earth's surface, directly below the aircraft – and a narrow field of view which provided a coverage of about 47° forward of nadir.

Cameras
Although three different cameras were developed for the A-12, or Oxcart programme, recently declassified documents indicate that only the Perkin-Elmer Type I camera was used during operational missions. Equipped with an f/4, 18-in (457-mm) lens and 6⅔-in (16.76-cm) wide, 5,000-ft (1524-m) supply of film, the system enjoyed a ground resolution of 1 ft (0.30 m) at nadir, and 3 ft (0.91-m), depending upon 'squint' angle and haze degradation. Film transport utilised a concentric supply and take-up system in order to ensure that

An aircraft as complex as the A-12 and as revolutionary in its performance was always going to require a drawn-out development process. This document shows the evolution from Arrow I to A-12. The chined delta made an appearance with the A-10, while the 'A-10 WITH TREATMENT' has been modified for anechoic testing. (Lockheed)

the film weight remained centralised, thereby minimising potential changes in the aircraft's centre-of-gravity (cg) as the film advanced. A rotating cube mirror was used as a scanner head and at cruise altitude obtained a ground swathe of about 70 miles (113 km) wide, with a 30 per cent stereo overlap. Since in-flight temperatures could vary from between -40 and 554°F (-40 and 290°C), an isothermal window was provided as a protective barrier between such severe temperature gradients and the camera's film. This was sealed to the Type I camera and a pump was then used to create a vacuum between the camera base and the glass. The entire assembly was located in a compartment behind the pilot, known as the Q-bay and the camera lens sought out its targets through a high quality quartz window that measured 22 × 23 in (55.88 × 58.42 cm). Problems encountered when bonding the window to its metal frame were eventually overcome during a three-year, $2-million programme, which developed a unique fusing process using high frequency sound waves.

Birdwatcher
Birdwatcher was a monitoring system unique to the A-12. It utilised a multiplexed high frequency/single sideband (HF/SSB) radio system

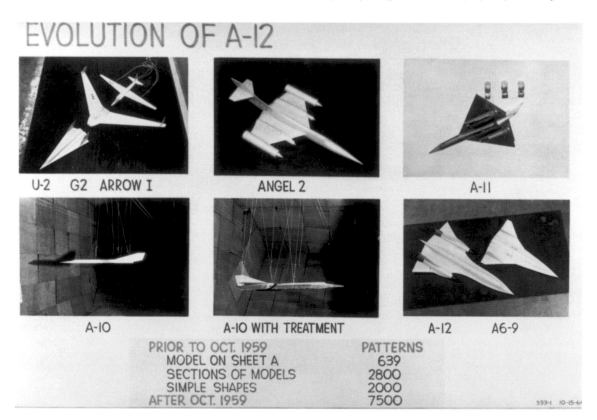

EVOLUTION OF A-12

U-2   G2   ARROW I

ANGEL 2

A-11

A-10

A-10 WITH TREATMENT

A-12   A6-9

PRIOR TO OCT. 1959
MODEL ON SHEET A
SECTIONS OF MODELS
SIMPLE SHAPES
AFTER OCT. 1959

PATTERNS
639
2800
2000
7500

533-1   10-15-6

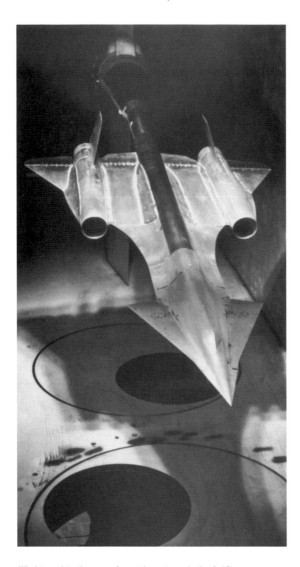

Wind-tunnel testing was of great importance in the A-12 programme, particularly in these pre-computer simulation days. Canards were tested in an attempt to bestow greater pitch stability on the A-12, but without success. (Lockheed)

the ground plane furnished by the airframe and made a fairly efficient antenna. Of its 40 channels, 32 were used to monitor individual aircraft systems: channel 54, for example, covered the starboard engine's exhaust gas temperature (EGT); channel 7 covered the starboard engine's fuel flow; and channel 3 covered the aircraft's altitude. If any preset parameters of the systems being monitored were breached, Birdwatcher keyed and modulated the HF transmitter with a coded signal. This consisted of three consecutive half-second bursts, each separated by a five-second period of silence. During each of the half-second bursts, the aircraft's identity and the condition of each of the systems being monitored was transmitted. These three bursts could be heard through the pilot's headphones as three chirps – hence the name Birdwatcher. The A-12 pilot had only limited control over the system. In the cockpit there were two switches, labelled 'A' and 'B'. The 'A' code was usually used by the pilot to signify to the ground station that the aircraft had reached a pre-designated point in the mission and that it was in a 'go' condition, such as at the end of a successful air refuelling (AR), or upon reaching a predetermined distance to go (DTG) point, or turn point. The pilot activated the 'B' code usually to indicate that the aircraft had experienced some sort of abort condition. The two buttons could be used sequentially to indicate that something unusual had occurred. For example, 'B' followed by 'A' might be interpreted to mean that the Article (each of the A-12s was known to Lockheed as an Article, each with its own number) had an abort condition, but was not in an emergency situation. Involuntary Birdwatcher codes were transmitted automatically by the system when any one of a number of sensors tripped the encoder. The system also transmitted a code when the Oxcart's electronic countermeasures (ECM) equipment was tested with the built-in-test (BIT) switch. All radio emitters on the A-12 could be inhibited by the pilot by activating a 'mute' switch – except the Birdwatcher. The mute system was installed on the aircraft to prevent accidental transmissions by a device such as the TACAN (Tactical Air Navigation), UHF radio, etc. The pilot was usually instructed to operate the 'mute' switch by the mission film strip, prior to entering denied territory.

Birdwatcher could also be interrogated by appropriately equipped ground stations. A command post could, if required, cause Birdwatcher to transmit a short burst of information that would only include the coded identification of the Oxcart – if no other sensors had already tripped. To the dismay of a couple of pilots, some of those monitoring the aircraft's progress from the ground station at Kadena

and was designed to telemeter signals concerning the operation/ non-operation of various aircraft systems down to a specially equipped ground station. The frequencies selected for any particular mission were briefed and noted by the pilot on hand cards; they were also annotated on the mission film strip, which was displayed to the pilot in the cockpit. The system consisted of two main elements, an air element and a ground element. The air element was a subset of the aircraft's HF/SSB radio, the antenna consisting of a tube structure within the A-12's pitot/static system located at the front of the aircraft. The relatively short antenna was closely matched to

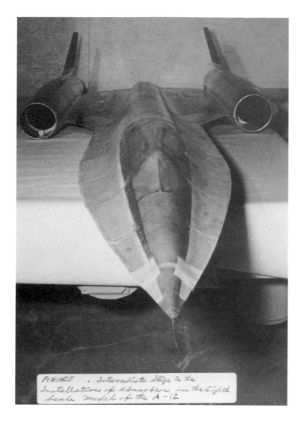

FIGURE . Intermediate Stage in the Installation of absorbers on the eighth scale model of the A-12

In the quest to make the A-12 as invisible to radar as possible, panels of RAM were added to and tested on scale models. Here an intermediate stage in this process is illustrated. (Lockheed)

occasionally interrogated the aircraft when it was over enemy territory.

The ground station for Birdwatcher at Area 51 was located just outside the entrance to the Command Post, in the Secure Communications Room – an area that no one was allowed access to without good reason. From here an operator monitored the Birdwatcher decoder using an oscillograph paper recorder upon which was recorded the Birdwatcher's 'chirping'. Lights were then used to develop the oscillograph paper to a point where it was possible that the technician could place the paper on a read-out cursor and see which sensor had tripped. He then activated a switch that illuminated an appropriate light on a light board located in the CP, thereby alerting other officers as to the aircraft's status.

Elint

The A-12 was also equipped with an Elint capability, via equipment known as System 6. This wide-band collection system comprised a miniaturising wide-frequency receiver which monitored C, L, X and P bands. These were then split and recorded by two three-channel recorders

working at $2\frac{1}{2}$ in per second; C- and X-band information, together with capture time and left or right of track directional information, was channelled to one recorder, while the same data for L and P bands was stored by the other unit.

ECM

Very little changed on Oxcart's ECM suite from the first installations. All were activated by a single, three-position power switch that was mounted on the console control panel and labelled 'OFF', 'Standby' and 'ON'. Also mounted on this panel was a BIT switch. This activated a logic test to ensure that each element worked correctly. The first element to be checked in the BIT sequence was the direction finding (DF) element; this was followed by the launch indication (LI) sub-system and finally the active element of the ECM suite, or 'Jam Green'. These checks were undertaken by the pilot prior to entering denied territory. Satisfactory completion of the checks caused Birdwatcher to chirp, confirming to the ground station that the aircraft was about to penetrate hostile airspace. If the BIT check failed, it was mandatory for the pilot to abort the mission.

The only elements of the system that were visible to the pilot were a series of five lights positioned above the viewscope and enclosed in the cockpit glare shield. The outboard lights were marked 'DF', the set inboard of these was marked LI and the larger centre light was known as the 'Jam Green' or 'Jam Red' light. The DF lights illuminated when the ECM system detected that a SAM system was tracking the Oxcart. If only one of these two lights was on, it indicated the general direction of the tracking radar; if both were on, it meant that the SAM system was either ahead or on both sides of the flight path. The LI lights illuminated when the SAM site's radar had gone into a high PRF (pulse repetition frequency) mode and usually indicated that the site had actually launched one or more missiles. Oxcart pilot Frank Murray recalls the usual sequence of events: 'When a SAM site was on you, the DF light or lights would come on and this started the Birdwatcher chirping. Then the LI light(s) would come on, indicating a missile launch. Then came the moment of truth! Sometime into the missile flight time, the active parts of the ECM suite would activate and the "Jam Green" light would illuminate. This indicated to the pilot that the ECM system was working to counter the missile's guidance system. If, however, the "Jam Red" light illuminated, this indicated that the active elements of the system weren't working correctly, in which case the pilot then had to depress and hold down a button marked "JAM O'RIDE", located on the top-right portion of the flight control stick. This activated the noise jammer part

A-12 construction was complicated by the use in quantity of titanium and the scope of generally new techniques involved. Building 309/310 of plant B-6 housed A-12 production, with Article Number 133 shown above in an advanced stage of construction, while a rather more complete machine is shown at right. (Lockheed Martin Skunk Works)

of the ECM suite. I have to say though, that I'm not aware of anyone in the program having to use the "JO" switch.'

The various elements of the ECM suite were given cryptic names. The system known as Pin Peg was the SAM detection system. Blue Dog was a large deceptive radar countermeasure system, weighing in at 480 lb (218 kg) and requiring 1,100 Watts of electrical power for liquid cooling and a further 1,600 Watts for air cooling. The noise-jammer was known as Big Blast; however, a deceptive radar countermeasures system known as Mad Moth was added with the intention of replacing Big Blast. Mad Moth used range-gate pull-off techniques to confuse the SA-2 'Guideline' SAM's command guidance system.

AREA 51
Development

It was almost inevitable that Oxcart flight testing would be conducted from Groom Lake, or Watertown strip as it had been known to the U-2 community. When the U-2 programme moved out, the base remained more or less unoccupied. All that was about to change, but before any of the new aircraft arrived an enormous amount of work was required to bring the base up to standard, since virtually all its facilities were inadequate to support such a significant flight-test programme.

A small army of contractors would be required to carry out this work. Nevada law required that all contractor personnel staying in the state for more than 48 hours report to state authorities, but such an undertaking by so many individuals would inevitably attract unwanted attention and breach the project security. The CIA's general council, however, came up with the answer when it was discovered that government employees were exempt from this requirement. Consequently, all site contractor personnel received appointments as government consultants.

One of the first tasks undertaken was to drill a new water well. New recreational facilities were also provided for the workers who were billeted in trailer houses. In September 1960 work began in earnest and thereafter continued in double-shift schedules until mid-1964. In addition to building a new runway, 18 miles (29 km) of off-base highway was resurfaced to allow 500,000 US gal (1892700 litres) of specially developed PF-1 fuel to be trucked in every month.

The runway

The runway was made of reinforced concrete, 12,000 ft (3658 m) of which was actually laid on the lakebed, with approximately 8,000 ft (2438 m) more covering native soil. In addition, each end was provided with a 1,000-ft (305-m) graded overrun. The 8,000-ft section extended out to the southeast and included a taxiway located at the lakebed edge. A returning A-12 could usually land and halt within this section and use the taxiway to exit the runway. Difficulties, however,

Article 123's forward fuselage appears to display a tandem cockpit arrangement, but actually displays the cockpit with the Q-bay aft. The sign pronouncing 'SERIAL 123' is misleading. This aircraft carried Lockheed's article number 123, but was actually serial 60-6926. Having become only the second A-12 to fly, it was lost on 24 May 1963, as a result of inaccurate flight data being displayed to pilot Ken Collins in the cockpit. (Lockheed via Buddy Brown)

arose if the aircraft overshot the taxiway entrance, since the runway was not wide enough to turn an A-12 around on without it having to venture onto the lakebed, so a turnaround pad was added to the lakebed section in 1965. A fire truck pad was positioned near the intersection of the runway and lakebed and when A-12s were flying one of the trucks stood alert on the pad. Take-offs and landings were made to the northwest, enabling use to be made of the extended runway and, if necessary, the lakebed.

In fact the lakebed proved to be extremely useful, especially during a high-speed abort at, or beyond, refusal speed – especially if the emergency condition was further complicated by a drag chute failure. To aid the stopping process in this condition, an Archimedes curve was painted onto the lakebed and tightened as it extended off to the east of the runway; this increased deceleration drag and to aid pilot acquisition a few dead trees were positioned along the length of the curve.

One early test called for an A-12 to demonstrate a maximum gross weight take-off, but unfortunately the mainwheel tyres burst on rotation. The pilot elected to continue with the take-off, then, once airborne, he dumped fuel before landing safely on the lakebed on what was left of the wheels.

The lakebed could also be used if the main runway crosswind was excessive. However, there were times when it was off limits due to standing water, since its surface is not very load-bearing when wet.

NAVIGATION AIDS
ILS
Prior to the A-12's operational deployment to Kadena AB, Okinawa, some aircraft were retrofitted with an instrument landing system (ILS) receiver. In order to test this equipment, a temporary ILS was constructed at the eastern end of the lakebed, with test approaches being made to the west.

TACAN
Area 51 is situated about 3 miles (5 km) south-southwest of Bald Mountain, which rises to a height of 9,300 ft (2835 m) above mean sea level. Another area of high ground, known as Papoose Ridge, is located less than a mile to the west-southwest of the runway. Ideally a TACAN beacon would have been placed on the airfield, as close as possible to the runway that it was to serve, but in the case of Area 51, this was not possible. Instead the TACAN was situated on the top of Bald Mountain – or Baldy as it was referred to by the

Left: As well as giving a fine impression of the of the A-12 'production line', this image also gives an excellent view of the RAM wedges along the aircraft's trailing edges. Two part-built Articles are visible, surrounded by the gantries and ladders typical of the hand-building process that produced the A-12s. (Lockheed via Buddy Brown)

On 26 February 1962, the first A-12, Article 121, made the journey from Burbank to Groom Lake in specially built containers. The width of the trailers restricted the convoy's speed and the co-operation of highway patrols from two states was required to enable the operation to go off smoothly. (Lockheed)

pilots. Such elevation gave the equipment an outstanding range capability; however, instrument approaches into the Area were complicated by the mountainous terrain. Consequently, all instrument approaches were made to align the aircraft inbound to runway 32. The TACAN approach was a basic teardrop let down, with a left hand procedure turn back to the beacon on a radial that would allow the pilot to locate the runway at a specified TACAN distance and altitude. On most occasions it was used to position the aircraft to a point where the ground controlled approach (GCA) precision radar could acquire it.

After reassembly at Groom Lake, Article 121 underwent engine and fuel flow tests. Problems with leaking fuel tanks were eventually overcome, prior to the start of taxi tests. The large areas with removed panels on the inboard upper sections of the wings show the locations of the main wing fuel tanks. (Lockheed)

GCA: AN/FPN-16

The base's GCA radar trailers were located almost directly in front of the control tower, to the west of the main runway and in between it and the main taxiway. The facility comprised two trailers, an Operations Trailer and a Maintenance Trailer. Both were mounted on a platform that could be rotated to align the precision approach radars using the metal radar reflectors that were located at the approach end of the runway. The radar itself was powered by the base's main power grid, backed-up by a generator housed in the Maintenance Trailer. Also located in this trailer were air conditioning units and the surveillance radar. The Operations Trailer housed the precision approach radar (PAR) and the scopes were located in both the trailer and a building situated near the tower.

A total of 25 men was assigned air-traffic control (ATC) duties, which included working in the

Ignominiously mounted inverted on 'the Pole', Article 122, the second A-12, was used for extensive radar scatter tests. With testing complete, the aircraft completed its first flight, before going on to fly some 177 hours 54 minutes in the course of 161 flights. (Lockheed)

control tower, and at Approach Control at the nearby Nevada Test Site (NTS). Eight of the enlisted controllers were dual rated for GCA duties.

FACILITIES

In 1963, most of the housing at Area 51 consisted of old, wood frame, Babbitt duplex family accommodation that had been acquired from the ammunition depot at Hawthorne, Nevada. More than eighty of the units were dismantled, transported through the wilderness of Nevada and, once at the new site, erected and arranged in a quadrangle in the middle of the base and reconfigured to sleep four to six people. Each house featured two bathrooms and two living rooms and they were also equipped with evaporation cooling systems and propane fired furnaces – most incumbents agree that they were quite comfortable. One of the buildings was fitted out as the Oxcart pilots' dining room. Here special low residue meals were prepared for when extended missions were to be flown. Another building, referred to as 'House 6' served as an informal gathering place and do-it-yourself bar.

In the early years of the programme, the mess hall consisted of a couple of old adjoined buildings situated next to the Operations facility.

After the evening meals had been served it doubled as a film theatre, managed by Jim Casteel. Later a new mess hall was constructed, where food was served 24 hours a day. Throughout the entire programme everyone agrees that the food, served by Reynolds Electric Company (Reeco), was outstanding.

For recreation there was a gym, squash and tennis courts, and a small pitch-and-putt golf course. Several of the pilots and support staff also got into building and flying radio-controlled model aircraft from the dry lakebed during the evenings. Later the base was also supplied with its own swimming pool. This doubled up as a training facility for Oxcart pilots learning water survival techniques while wearing the full pressure suit. During their training, Oxcart pilots also used a parasail in order to get up to altitude before being lowered into Lake Mead, again for water survival training. A Coast Guard power launch provided the tug to launch the pilots into the air. One pilot recalls that it was not the safest thing he had ever been told to do: trying to run to lift-off in a complete pressure suit and survival kit without falling on the lake beach was, he said, decidedly 'dicey'.

The Base Headquarters building housed the 1129th Special Activities Squadron's commander together with his administrative staff, the CIA station chief and his staff, the Base Security Section and the Medical Facility from where the flight surgeons worked.

As with all operational bases, The Mission Operations Building was the hub for all flying operations and included regular base ops functions, a main mission briefing room, a flight planning section and a personal equipment section where the pilots' flight suits and pressure suits were kept and maintained. It also housed the Standardisation and Evaluation (Stan/Eval) section. The Stan/Eval pilots were responsible for training and maintaining flying standards. There were also offices for the Project pilots. Within the inner sanctum of the building was located the Command Post or CP. On one large wall was a map of the United States, upon which were detailed all the usual A-12 flight routes. Its backing was sheet steel and small magnetic A-12 silhouettes, on which individual serial numbers were engraved, were positioned along the routes being flown, enabling CP personnel to keep a check on proceedings. Adjacent to the CP was the Secure Communications Room. Radios were used to monitor most missions within the US, and included single sideband HF and the tailor-made Birdwatcher systems. Finally, at the rear of the building, the Meteorological/Weather section and a small Link Trainer room were located. A separate building located near the main taxiway served the security needs for classified document control. This facility was fenced and patrolled by security guards. It was opened for access by the 'crew bus' which carried Project pilots to the 'Agency' hangers and contractor test pilots to the Lockheed hangers and their dedicated test aircraft.

HANGARS

A-12 hangars and the main parking-ramp were located on the southern perimeter of the base and connected to the main runway by a taxiway. Three large ex-Navy hangers were moved to the test site and used to house the A-12s while they were being re-assembled. They also provided hangarage for two Lockheed F-104 Starfighter chase aircraft, and the A-12 test Articles 121, 122 and 129 also spent some time in this accommodation while undertaking flight test duties before being returned to the 'Agency' as mission aircraft. There remained on site several old hangers from the U-2 days and these were utilised as engine and machine shops; other smaller buildings housed

the avionics facility and another the inertial navigation system (INS) repair station. An extremely large metal-clad warehouse was home to the Logistics Supply Center; while a large fuel dump, located away from most other structures, stored the various fuels required by aircraft and base vehicles.

Custom-built hangars housed the Project aircraft and these were provided with doors at either end to facilitate drive-in, drive-out operations and in-hangar engine starting. A large central bay, flanked each side by five or so hangars, provided offices for the maintenance staff and several specialisation shops. Opposite these hangars was located the 'peak building', where the camera systems were installed. This building was designed to cover the nose section of the A-12 while the highly classified camera was being installed. The Oxcart was towed, nose first, into the building and sliding doors at either side were closed to encapsulate the forward section of the aircraft. In addition to providing additional security, it also kept wind-blown sand and other debris away from sensitive optics.

Another single-bay hanger was used for the maintenance of support aircraft and housed several F-101 chase aircraft.

RATSCAT RANGE

A radar target scatter, or RatScat, range was built north of the main Lockheed hangars. It comprised threat simulators, precision radars and some optical systems. The latter could be used to track A-12s from the ground as they flew local test sorties. The RatScat equipment was used to assess the radar cross section (RCS) of both sub-scale and full-scale aircraft during the early development days of the A-12. The aircraft was mounted atop a hydraulic lift, located some distance from the radar head on the dry lakebed, and then positioned at various aspects; the hydraulic lift device was then masked with Echosorb and readings taken of the aircraft's RCS. A-12 Article 122 spent several months on 'the Pole'.

FALLOUT AND SELECTION

As mentioned earlier, the sheer quality and quantity of imagery secured by the U-2 overflight programme had became highly addictive to the US intelligence community and, despite misgivings, President Eisenhower had agreed to sanction further penetrations of the Soviet Union – albeit on a more regulated, one clearance one flight basis – from late November 1956. The shooting down of Frank Powers and 'his' U-2 would prove to have a profound impact on the Oxcart programme, as detailed in a top secret memo for the record, dated 2 June 1960, and written by Brig-Gen Andrew Goodpaster, military aide to President

This early Groom Lake photograph shows to good effect the wedges of radar absorbing material that completely skirted the aircraft's outer edges. Their individual shape was intended to trap any incident radar beam, causing it to reflect from one side of the wedge to the other. As it did so, its energy was gradually absorbed into the RAM, causing the A-12's radar signature to be much smaller than that of a similarly sized conventional aircraft. (CIA)

Eisenhower: 'I spoke to the President early this week about the question of whether work should go forward on the successor to the U-2. After considering the matter, he said he was inclined to think that it should go forward, on low priority, as a high performance reconnaissance plane for the Air Force in time of war. I suggested it might be useful for Mr Allen Dulles [DCI], Mr Gates [Thomas Gates – Defense Chief] and Mr Stans [Maurice Stans – Budget Bureau Chief] to get together to consider the matter, and he agreed. He said he did not think the project should now be pushed at top priority. In fact, they might come to the conclusion that it would be best to get out of it if we could. Alternatively, they may feel that we have so much invested in it that we should capitalise on this through carrying it forward.'

The future of Oxcart was far from certain in those early months immediately following the Frank Powers shoot-down. Nonetheless, flight crew selection evolved by the Pentagon's Special Activities Office representative (Col Houser Wilson) and the Agency's USAF liaison officer (Brig-Gen Jack Ledford – later succeeded by Brig-Gen Paul Bacalis) – got underway in 1961. Ken Collins, one of the first pilots to be recruited into Oxcart, now recalls the process: 'The primary professional selection criteria was that a pilot should have more than 1,000 hours in 'Century' aircraft and a total of 2,000 flight hours. At the

time, I was an experienced instructor pilot in the RF-101, having over 50 air-air refuelling training sorties and about ten transatlantic deployments, each with multiple air-air refuellings. This was the easy part of the Pentagon selection process. Either you had it or you didn't. All of your flight, professional and medical records were meticulously scrutinised at all levels before your name was released for further evaluation.

'On the personal side of things, they were adamant that you were married, preferably with children – this was because they'd experienced problems with the previous U-2 programme. Their rationale being that the family unit was more socially established, dedicated and dependable. Later during the process our wives were interviewed and evaluated separately; expanded background investigations were also run on them. My wife Jane was told that she wasn't to talk to anyone about the interviews, neither was she told what I'd be doing. She could if asked say that I had decided to resign from the Air Force and to work for Hughes Aircraft.

'At this stage in the proceedings (April 1961), we didn't know what we were being evaluated for, each of us were separately tasked for these various events, for example, I was unaware that another pilot from Shaw AFB – Capt Walter Ray – was also undergoing these interviews and evaluations. We started running into each other about a year later, when the field of consideration was narrowed by elimination. From day one you were given the option of withdrawing from the selection process at any time, without prejudice – an option that remained throughout the programme.

'Our medical records were acceptable for the initial evaluation, because we were all on flying status, however, they weren't extensive enough as the selection process continued and we were all about to find out what that really meant. I was scheduled for my "astronaut" physical examination at the Lovelace Clinic, in Albuquerque, New Mexico. This is the same facility in which the original astronauts and the early U-2 pilots received their medical evaluations. The clinic was founded by Dr Lovelace, one of the pioneers of aviation medicine and his work was continued by his son, Dr Randy Lovelace, until he, his wife and their pilot were killed in a flying accident.

'My government contact at the clinic was an Air Force flight surgeon, he established my schedules and appointments and observed the tests, we also had dinner together, but this was more as part of the evaluation than being social. I arrived on a Sunday and departed the following Saturday; during those five days they checked-out every bodily orifice, X-rayed me from head to toe, flushed me out and took samples and measurements of everything — I even had to carry a large brown bottle around for 48 hours, to collect every drop of urine. They also conducted extensive ECGs and EEGs. I was hydrostatically weighed in a large water tank, ran the bicycle pulmonary functions and passed other physical stress exercises. They then flew me to Los Alamos Laboratory to be inserted into the "body counter", this mapped fat versus muscle tissue in the body and when correlated with the data from the hydrostatic weighing, it theoretically enabled them to determine total body capacity, regardless of size. After that I was ready for the hospital.

'I was also subjected to many different types of personal and professional evaluations. In Philadelphia, I was put into a soundproof black box, where I had to remain in total darkness and without sleep for 12 hours. Then there was a polygraph and numerous dinners and lunches with a variety of people with "professional", medical, intelligence and senior manager backgrounds, all there to get an opinion. After all the sorting was nearly complete, I learned that eight people would be selected for the initial programme. This sounded reasonable, since that was the average group size for the astronaut programme.

'Finally I received orders assigning me to Headquarters USAF, at the Pentagon, where I was to report on 28 October 1962. The packers had completed their task, but the night before Jane and I were due to leave Shaw AFB I received a phone call from Lt-Col Clyde East, my squadron commander over at the 20th TRS, instructing me to report on base immediately, because the unit's RF-101s were on alert for immediate deployment to Mac Dill AFB, Florida, as what came to be the Cuban missile crisis had just erupted. I would have liked to deploy with my squadron, but

Before joining the Oxcart programme, Dennis Sullivan flew Convair F-106 Delta Darts with the 318th Fighter Interceptor Squadron, based at McChord AFB, Washington. His Cygnus call sign was DUTCH 23. (USAF)

clearly, and unknown to them, other things were happening in my flying career.

'Having been informed earlier that my new assignment wasn't into the astronaut programme, but a project to fly and test an exotic new airplane for the CIA, I was again offered the option to withdraw. There were still no pictures of the aircraft or any other details, but I declined to opt-out. On arrival in Washington I met other successful candidates that were soon to become close colleagues, Bill Skliar, Lon Walter and Walt Ray — who I already knew from Shaw. I signed on the dotted line and was told that I was to be in LA by November and that further contact and instructions would follow when I got there, so the next day Jane and I, together with our four kids, headed west.'

In addition to Ken Collins, the other project pilots that successfully completed the arduous selection process were Jack Layton, Francis Murray, Dennis Sullivan, Mele Vojvodich, Jack Weeks, William Skliar, Walter Ray, Alonzo Walter, David Young and Russ Scott (although only the first six were destined to fly the Oxcart on operational missions).

Frank Murray joined the programme via a more circuitous route, graduating from the USAF Aviation Cadet Programme as a pilot at Laredo AFB, Texas, in Class 53C (which means that he completed the course in May 1953), and undergoing gunnery training in the Lockheed T-33 and Republic F-84B and C Thunderjet. He then went to France, completing his first operational tour with the 48th Fighter Wing, flying the F-84G and North American F-86F Sabre, before returning to the United States to fly F-84Fs with SAC. In early 1957 he was reassigned to another SAC wing, flying F-101As and Cs, at Bergstrom AFB, Texas. However, in 1958, the wing disbanded and its aircraft were sent to the 81st Fighter Wing at RAF Bentwaters/Woodbridge, England. Having just recently returned from a tour of duty with United States Air Forces Europe (USAFE), Frank was instead posted to the 60th Fighter Squadron, an Aerospace Defence Command unit based at Cape Cod, MA, that was about to be re-equipped with the new F-101B interceptor. This was to be Frank and his wife Stella's home for the next five years, at the end of which time he volunteered to become a support pilot for NASA. Little did he know at the time, but this was a cover, used by the CIA to entice USAF fighter pilots to put their names forward, from which list they could select pilots and support staff for the Oxcart programme. Like all those selected, Frank had an outstanding military record, with over 1,500 hours flying the F-101 in his log-book. He arrived at Area 51 in July 1963 as an instructor and chase pilot in the F-101, checking-out other pilots on the aircraft and conducting chase duties and routine Proficiency and Instrument Flight Checks. By 1965 some of the earlier Oxcart project pilots elected, for various reasons, to opt out of the programme. Frank was approached and asked if he was interested in becoming an A-12 driver – he leapt at the chance and became, as he puts it, the 'junior wienie'.

SUPPORT

On 15 November 1961, Col Robert Holbury was appointed base commander of Area 51. Other members of his staff included Col Doug Nelson, his Director of Operations (DO); Lt-Col Anderson, Assistant DO; Lt-Col Barrett, Chief of Base Operations; Chief of Standardisation and Evaluation (Stan/Eval) Lt-Col Ray Hampt and Maj Burgeson. During the spring of 1962, eight F-101B/F Voodoos arrived, to be used mainly as chase aircraft and flown by the project pilots. Two F-104s were also assigned as high-speed chase. These were mainly flown by Lockheed flight test pilots before being re-assigned to Edwards AFB when the three YF-12s were relocated. In addition, two T-33As were provided for mission support and proficiency flying for the many military staff pilots. Light air transport was provided by a Cessna U-3B 'Blue Canoe', flown by some of the staff and a civilian-registered Cessna 180 – later replaced by a Cessna 210 – was used for medical evacuation (medevac). Base rescue, fire

suppression and local security were covered by a Kaman HH-43 Huskie before it too was replaced, by a Bell UH-1 'Huey'. Logistics support, particularly for ferrying the J58 engines in and out of the base, was conducted by a Lockheed C-130 Hercules. The weekly commute of staff into Area 51 from Las Vegas, as well as the airlift of special devices used for local technical studies, was initially achieved with a Douglas C-47 Skytrain (this was later replaced by a Fairchild F-27, although both aircraft were operated under contract from CARCO Inc). The majority of contractors, Lockheed workers and project pilots alike, made the Monday/Friday trip into and out of Area 51 in Lockheed Constellations operating into Burbank. Another visitor to the desert base was Lockheed's prototype, twin-engined, JetStar. This was used by the likes of Kelly Johnson and his senior team.

That the physical location of Area 51 was an ideal, secure site from which to conduct the Oxcart test programme is beyond dispute. However, there were additional, special needs that had to be met to ensure that the aircraft and its associated chase planes could operate safely. In response, an agreement was reached between the Federal Aviation Administration (FAA), the Air Force and the Agency that set aside a vast area of airspace. This joined the northern borders of Restricted Areas 4806, 4807, 4808 and 4809 and ran north in a box that was bordered by the navigation aids (navaids) at Wilson Creek and Coaldale. The area extended north, to 42° North and was bordered to the east by 115° West and to the west by 118° West. This enormous area (the size of England), designated as the Yuletide Special Operations Area (SOA), stretched vertically from 24,000 ft (7315 m) to 60,000 ft (18288 m) above mean sea level (amsl). Flight above this altitude was not subject to FAA positive control; however, for additional safety, when A-12s began operating routinely above this altitude, their pilots used a simple code to hide their actual height from eavesdroppers, by reporting that they were at an altitude of Base plus a number. For additional security, the base altitude would change daily, so if for example it was briefed as 50,000 ft, and the Oxcart was cruising at 85,000 ft (25908 m), the pilot would report to the centre that he was at Base plus 35. In this way ATC could keep a watchful eye out for other high flying traffic and later, when SR-71s and U-2s were flying in those upper reaches, controllers would sometimes report 'Company Traffic' at an azimuth relative to the Oxcart's flight path. To accommodate an airway that ran between the Wilson Creek VORTAC (VHF omni-range TACAN) and that at Coaldale, a 'tunnel' 10 nm (11.5 miles; 18.5 km) wide and from between 24,000 ft (7315 m) and 40,000 ft (12192 m) was established. Area 51 traffic had to either fly below or

This near perfect underside planform shot of Article 123, taken on 22 December 1962, serves to illustrate the A-12's futuristic design. The aircraft was unpainted, allowing the various panels of its skin to show up clearly. (Lockheed)

above this air route, or obtain prior clearance from Salt Lake Air Traffic Control Center, if it was intended that flight was to penetrate the corridor. When the A-12 began test operations out of Area 51, most pilots elected to fly beneath the corridor northbound after take-off, en route to the tanker, and fly over the top when southbound, especially if the A-12 was on the descent into the SOA. When the SOA was not required to support A-12 operations, the airspace reverted to Salt Lake Center, for use by airline and general aviation traffic.

THE PROTOTYPE ARRIVES

Final checks were carried out on aircraft number one (Article Number 121, Air Force serial number 60-6924) at ADP during January and February 1962. The airframe was dismantled for transportation to 'the Area' and loaded onto a custom-built trailer costing $100,000. On 26 February 1962, with help from the California and Nevada Highway Patrols, the slow-moving, wide-bodied trailer and its convoy left Burbank at three o'clock in the morning and arrived late the next evening at its Groom Lake destination. Another delay occurred after the aircraft was reassembled. While preparing for the first flight it was discovered that the special sealing compounds had failed to adhere to the surfaces between the fuel tanks and the metal skin of the aircraft, causing the filled tanks to leak profusely. The defective tank sealant was removed and the area relined with new materials that temporarily solved the problem.

By 24 April 1962, engine test runs were completed and low and medium-speed taxi tests had been successfully carried out. Now it was time for Chief test pilot Lou Schalk to take the aircraft on a high-speed taxi run that would culminate in a momentary lift-off and landing roll-out onto the salty lakebed. For this first 'hop' the Stability Augmentation System (SAS) was left uncoupled; it would be properly tested in flight. As 121 accelerated down the runway, Lou Schalk recalled: 'It all went like a dream until I lifted off. Immediately after lift-off, I really didn't think I was going to be able to put the aircraft back on the ground safely because of lateral, directional and longitudinal oscillations. The aircraft was very difficult to handle but I finally caught up with everything that was happening, got control back enough to set it back down, and to chop engine power. Touchdown was on the lake bed instead of the runway, creating a tremendous cloud of dust into which I disappeared entirely. The tower controllers were calling me to find out what was happening and I was answering, but the UHF antenna was located on the underside of the aircraft (for best transmission in flight) and no one could hear me. Finally, when I slowed down and started my turn on the lake bed and re-emerged from the cloud of dust, everyone breathed a sigh of relief'. That night Kelly asked Lou if the aircraft ought to fly again the next day. Lou (as chief test pilot) thought it should fly but added, 'I also think we ought to turn the SAS dampers on'.

The first real test flight was made two days later, on 26 April 1962. This trouble-free sortie lasted 35 minutes, the aircraft's landing gear remaining extended throughout the flight to avoid 'historic first-flight gear retraction problems'. The SAS performed admirably, the aircraft failing to repeat the 'bucking bronco ride' of two days earlier even after each of the three SAS stability dampers (one for each axis) was switched off individually in proper test-flight sequencing. With all three dampers of the SAS re-engaged, Schalk terminated the first true A-12 flight with an 'absolutely uneventful' landing. He flew 121 on its second test flight four days later. The jet (at 72,000 lb/ 32659 kg gross weight) lifted off at 170 kt (196 mph; 315 km/h) and easily climbed to 30,000 ft (9144 m) where it attained a top speed of 340 kt (392 mph; 631 km/h). That smooth flight lasted 59 minutes and attained all second-flight test objectives. Four days later Lou broke Mach 1.

When word of these initial successes was passed to Washington DC, John McCone, the new director of the CIA, telegrammed congratulations to Kelly; but the programme was a year behind schedule and much work still remained to prepare the new aircraft for its operational debut.

A-12 BUILD-UP

Over the next few months 121 was joined by more of its stablemates. Article 122 arrived on 26 June, but was destined to spend three months conducting ground radar tests before taking to the air. Aircraft number three (Article 123) arrived in August and flew in October. In November the two-seat pilot trainer was delivered, which helped smooth transition training. The aircraft was to have been powered by J58 engines, but Pratt & Whitney was still having production problems. Since the Agency needed to get on with pilot training, it was decided to equip the two-seater with J75 engines and let the checked out pilots go on to high-Mach flight on their own. Once this decision was seen through, aircraft number four (the 'Titanium Goose') undertook its first maiden flight in January 1963 fitted with the less powerful engines. Aircraft number five (Article 125) was delivered to the site on 19 December 1962.

Lou Schalk had been contracted to perform the first 12 experimental test flights in the A-12 and to thoroughly check out all important stability characteristics. An element of superstition also led him to fly the 13th sortie on the aircraft. The burden of added test flying was shared with two other experienced test pilots, Bill Park and Jim Eastman, who began to build up flight time on the aircraft. Early trials proved the soundness of the overall design, and specific in-flight tests were performed on the cameras and sensors, the inertial navigation system and some of the more sensitive stability controls.

When pilots destined to eventually fly the aircraft operationally first saw an A-12 they were eager to confer a nickname upon Kelly's new Skunk Works masterpiece. Being aware of Lockheed's penchant for christening its aircraft designs with names of celestial bodies, Jack Weeks came up with Cygnus (the Swan), which was the name of a constellation in the Northern Celestial Hemisphere, lying between Pegasus and Draco in the Milky Way. The name was particularly apt for the secretive A-12 programme because research astronomers believe that Cygnus may contain one of the most mysterious of nature's invisible bodies – a black hole.

As time went by there was still no sign of the much-vaunted J58 engines. The CIA became increasingly impatient to see some progress in return for the government's multimillion dollar investment in advanced propulsion. Senior Agency officials decided that the A-12 should be capable of Mach 2.0 with its J75 powerplant. Since the J75s powered the USAF's Convair F-106 Delta Dart interceptor to Mach 2.0, then the A-12, they reasoned, should also be able to match that speed. They did not seem to understand that the A-12 had been designed to house a pair of J58s and that the J75s were mismatched with the inlet systems. This caused an inlet airflow vibration or 'duct-shudder' as Mach 2.0 was approached. However, in order to placate the directors who controlled the Agency's purse strings, Bill Park dived an A-12 to Mach 2.0, relieving at least some of the high-level pressure on the design team.

World events were soon to provide the Oxcart project with a 'necessity' boost. Following Maj Steve Heyser's historic U-2 overflight of Cuba on 14 October 1962, undeniable photographic evidence was obtained of the presence of Soviet SS-N-4 Medium Range Ballistic Missiles (MRBMs) and SS-N-5 Intermediate Range Ballistic Missiles (IRBMs) on the island. Consequently, U-2 overflight activities were increased to a peak level of five flights per day. On Saturday 27 October 1962, Maj Rudolph Anderson was shot down by an SA-2, while flying a U-2 over Cuba. As with the Gary Powers incident two and a half years earlier, the U-2's vulnerability had been demonstrated in a most spectacular fashion. Regrettably, Maj Anderson was killed in the Cuba overflight shoot down, but from that moment, the Oxcart programme assumed greater significance than ever and the achievement of 'operational status' became one of the highest national priorities.

One question being voiced in some quarters concerned the Oxcart's ability to avoid detection by Soviet radars. As part of an ongoing effort to measure the range and power of various Soviet defence radar systems, the CIA implemented the Quality Elint programme. A highly classified element of that programme was code-named Palladium. Its objective was to determine the sensitivity of various Soviet radars. To achieve this, a special electronic transmitter, capable of projecting a 'ghost signal' onto a P-12 'Spoon Rest' surveillance and missile acquisition radar was developed. The knowledge gained from the Quality Elint power and coverage measurements enabled technicians to simulate an aircraft of any RCS and 'fly-it' along any particular path at a pre-determined speed and altitude. By electronically varying the size of the radar returns and enlisting the cooperation of the National Security Agency (NSA), which intercepted and decrypted the relevant communications channels, it was possible to determine a radar's sensitivity based upon which signals were being tracked.

During the Cuban Missile Crisis, the US intelligence community had monitored the construction of no less than 19 SA-2 SAM sites on the island and these provided the CIA, together with the Oxcart planners, with an ideal opportunity for determining the sensitivity of the

Inflight refuelling was a vital element in A-12 and, later, SR-71 missions. As such, the procedure was an important element in any A-12 pilot's initial course on the AT-12 two-seater. Even though it was J57 powered, this aircraft behaved much like the J58-engined single-seater during refuelling operations. (Lockheed)

A bare titanium Cygnus comes home to roost at Groom Lake. All A-12 operations were carried out from the desert base until a detachment was established on Okinawa in 1967, for missions over Vietnam. (CIA)

weapon's radar receiver. One night, a US Navy destroyer equipped with one of the Palladium transmitters positioned itself beyond the detection range of a Soviet P-14 'Tall King' A-band early warning radar situated near the capital Havana, and with its antenna protruding just above the horizon the destroyer produced signal returns that appeared to be emanating from a US fighter out of Key West and making a high speed dash towards the capital. At a predetermined time a US Navy submarine surfaced near Havana Bay, just long enough to time-release a series of balloons carrying radar reflectors of varying sizes. The idea was that having detected the 'aircraft', the Soviets would switch on the SA-2's target-tracking radar, in preparation for engaging the target. Release of the balloons, ahead of the original target, would produce a number of other returns. The smallest reported would therefore represent the highest level of radar sensitivity. The operation worked like clockwork, Cuban interceptors were scrambled to hunt down the 'intruder' and when one of the pilots told his ground controlled intercept (GCI), controller that he had acquired the 'target' on his radar, the technician on the destroyer flicked a switch and the 'US fighter' disappeared!

After analysing all the intelligence data collected from this sortie and by other means, the CIA's Office of Scientific Intelligence (OSI), was able to conclude that Soviet radar capability would indeed be able to track and 'lock on' to an Oxcart, despite the aircraft's radar-attenuating design features, but despite these discouraging findings flight testing continued.

J58 ENGINES

In July 1962 the J58 finally completed its Pre-Flight Rating Test. An engine was taken to Area 51 and at last installed in Article 121, which, until confidence levels in the new engine grew, would fly with a proven, but far less powerful J75 in the other nacelle. Even this arrangement had its usual crop of problems. One early hiccup concerned ignition – the engine would not start no matter what procedure was tried by the Pratt & Whitney engineers! The small-inlet wind tunnel model did not reveal that the engine's appetite for air was so great that instead of air flowing out of the compressor's fourth stage bleed ducts, flow reversal occurred and air was drawn into the compressor from the back end. As a temporary fix, Lockheed removed an inlet access panel to facilitate ground starts. It subsequently cut holes into the rear section of the nacelle and installed two sets of suck-in doors, while Pratt & Whitney added an engine bleed to the nacelle to improve airflow through the powerplant during ground starts.

On 15 January 1963, the first test flight of the A-12 powered by two new J58s occurred. By the end of the month ten engines were available. Again, the Pratt & Whitney engineers and the Lockheed test pilots were faced with a multitude of problems that needed to be solved in order to attain Kelly's design goal for sustained high altitude flight at full Mach. As the envelope extension programme slowly began to edge up the aircraft's top speed, other problems were highlighted. Initial flight results with the aircraft in this new configuration were not at all encouraging for Lou Shalk, and he confided in Bill Park, who had chased him in an F-104: 'Look Bill, you're going to fly this airplane pretty soon, but don't say too much about how bad it accelerates, we're never gonna make Mach 3. But let's not get this programme cancelled till someone figures out how to make this thing run right'. After Park flew Article 121 equipped with the two J58s he said: 'Lou, you're right, but let's keep it under our hats'. Perhaps the two test pilots were joking, but there certainly remained cause for concern.

Heavy wear and cracks on the long drive shafts between the engine and its remote gearbox became a problem, together with twisting and heavy spline wear. This was caused by a 4-in (10-cm) displacement of the gearbox relative to the engine during high Mach transients. A double universal joint on a new shaft between the two components solved that problem. It was also discovered that the aircraft's fuel system ahead of the engine showed signs of fatigue and distortion. Measurements from a fast recorder showed that pressure levels at the engine fuel inlet were going off the scale. This over-pressuring was caused by feed back from the engine hydraulic system. The phenomenon had failed to materialise in rig tests and during engine ground tests because large fluid volumes were not involved.

Resourceful as ever, the Skunk Works invented a 'high temperature sponge' – promptly named the football – that was installed ahead of the engines and reduced pressures to more tolerable levels. Yet another problem turned up during certain manoeuvres that crushed engine plumbing. This was found to be as a result of the outer half of the nacelle rotating into the engine. Pratt & Whitney solved this by redesigning the rear engine mounting and incorporating a tangential link between the underside of the engine and the outboard side of the nacelle. A finite distance was thereby always maintained between engine and nacelle.

Transonic flight induced unacceptably high fuel consumption. Test instrumentation recorded in-flight thrust measurements, Mach number, and ejector operation. This showed that the ejector went supersonic long before the aircraft. This problem rectified itself when one of the test pilots went transonic at lower altitude and raised the equivalent airspeed datum from 350 to 400 kt (403/649 to 461 mph/742 km/h).

As greater speeds and altitudes were attained, cockpit cooling became an issue. Bill Park recalled that the control stick got so hot that he had to change hands regularly to keep hold of it – even though he was wearing his pressure-suit gloves. In fact, temperatures got so high in the upper areas of the cockpit that they blackened the 130° templates fixed on the pilots helmets. By redirecting the incoming flow from the AiResearch air conditioning unit and employing a special bootstrap-cooling unit, the Skunk Works eventually provided a tolerable cockpit environment.

AIR INDUCTION SYSTEM
However, the biggest hurdle remaining was to perfect airflow in the air induction system, which was designed to vastly augment engine thrust. To achieve this the inlet spike's aft-movement schedule had to be programmed very accurately as speed increased and the same equally applied to the position of various bypass doors. When this fine-tuned control over the high-speed inlet drag equation was finally achieved, the jet's thirst for fuel was notably reduced.

On 20 July 1963, Article 121 was the first A-12 to reach Mach 3.0. Kelly later noted in his diary: 'On the second flight, we blew an engine at design speed. It was very difficult to slow down and it rattled Lou Schalk around for three minutes. The aircraft stability augmentation system did precisely as I asked it to do three years ago and no high structural loads were obtained'. In all, it took 66 flights to push the speed envelope out from a marginal Mach 2.0 to the full design-speed of Mach 3.2.

These envelope expansion flights from Area 51 trod a well-worn path across the emptiness of Nevada, northward over Wendover, Utah, high across southern Idaho and then turned east or west along a smooth 180° arc just short of the Canadian border, before heading back south toward Arizona or California and finally back down into the 'roost', north of Las Vegas. Sonic booms were heard all over the western United States and complaints were conveniently shifted toward the Arizona Air National Guard Fighters at Phoenix, then onward to the naval aviators at Fallon, Nevada, and then onward still, toward any flying outfit capable of booming! This convenient shifting of blame was ignored by the Oxcarters

In spite of its radical external appearance and awesome capabilities, in the cockpit the A-12 was generally conventional, as this 8 November 1965 shot taken by Lockheed technicians illustrates. (Lockheed)

and FAA controllers who knew the truth. During the return leg to Las Vegas, the A-12 would reach its test-point objectives above 72,000 ft (21946 m), an altitude that would also allow the pilot to make a steep but safe recovery back to the 'Ranch' in the event of an in-flight emergency.

The cockpit workload for one person during A-12 test flying was extremely high since the turbine inlet temperature (TIT) tended to wander. This variation needed close monitoring if engine damage was to be avoided. At 7,300 rpm, unstable temperatures caused thrust variations, so two toggle switches were introduced to allow the pilot to 'trim' the fuel flow in small increments, without having to adjust the throttle positions, to keep turbine temperatures within operable limits. Two rotating wafer switches controlled the inlet spike position (forward and aft), while a third set varied the bypass door positions (open to closed). The task of flying the aircraft, while manually operating those six control switches and determining the optimum inlet schedule of door and spike positions, created a situation where the pilot was saturated with switch movement activity during acceleration to high Mach. It was soon realised that it would be nearly impossible to

fly the aircraft during unstable situations without the SAS operating. This gyro-stabilised system, coupled into the autopilot, made life in the cockpit more tolerable, despite the disheartening effect of using more than a third of the total fuel load accelerating to full speed due to poor inlet scheduling. The slow initial progression 'to full speed' was the result of a 'trial and error' positioning of door and spike inlet schedules.

During these early tests, the speed was gently increased by one tenth of a Mach number before the next spike progression increment was selected. If all worked well, that day's work was analysed in the laboratories and incorporated into the schedule. More often, however, the spike position would not match the inlet duct requirements and a hard 'unstart' (the violent and sudden expulsion of the normal shockwave from the internal throat of the inlet to the outside of the inlet) would cause a harsh yaw movement which swung the nose sharply to the direction of the unstarted inlet, snapping the pilots head quickly to one side in the process. To break a sustained unstart and to recapture the disturbed inlet shock wave, the pilot would have to open the bypass doors on the unstarted side and move the spike fully forward, before slowly returning them to the smooth-flowing, but less efficient, position that they occupied prior to the disturbance. Incessant problems in the air induction system caused Lockheed's propulsion engineers to change the inlet geometry and trim schedules. In addition, the manual trim schedule was speeded-up to allow the aircraft to be accelerated more quickly, and to save fuel during the climb to high altitude.

During that first year of development testing, the inlet control system was changed often, and on many flights the two inlets never seemed to work together. Project pilot Walt Ray (wearing a Beatles' wig at a time when all the pilots had short hair), after returning from a night training sortie filled with many unstarts, joked to the debriefing team at Area 51: 'Man, that was a hairy flight!'. Unstarts came to be expected on nearly all of the early A-12 flights. Ultimately the optimum pattern of door and spike sequencing was perfected and the inlet system was programmed to operate automatically with the assistance of inlet computers.

Thermodynamic considerations had minimised the number of electrical systems in the aircraft. Pneumatic pressure gauges were installed on the inlet systems to sense pressure variations of as little as 0.25 psi (1.72 kPa). Translating the position of the inlet spike was based on a schedule derived from pneumatic pressure readings. After a multitude of inlet malfunctions and unstarts, it became apparent that these pneumatic instruments were not sensitive enough for the job of accurately scheduling the spikes. Aircraft were

coming off the production line with the pneumatic system installed, but Kelly decided that it should be replaced by an electronically controlled system. Although the Garrett Corporation's new system initially required far more maintenance per flight hour than the pneumatic system, its in-flight performance was far superior to the old equipment.

Despite the added cost, the electrical system was retrofitted to all aircraft already delivered and was incorporated in the remaining A-12s being produced at Burbank from aircraft number nine onwards.

Before the new spike control system was flight tested, many electromagnetic induction (EMI) tests were carried out on the ground to ensure non-interfering operations. It was thought that all was well with the EMI tests until a radio check made the inlet spikes retract! Thus, it was back to the drawing boards and more tests. When Bill Park briefed the other pilots about the new system he added that unstarts would soon be almost a thing of the past. None believed him, but the new system immediately began to prove its worth and the number of unstarts decreased dramatically. Fuel consumption also decreased significantly, due to the tighter inlet spike and door scheduling. By the end of 1963, the Agency's fleet of A-12s based at Area 51 numbered nine and during 573 flights they had chalked-up 765 flying hours. In November, the aircraft finally reached its design speed, Mach 3.2, and attained an altitude of 78,000 ft (23774 m). By the end of 1964, the fleet

This view of the right console panel illustrates some of the equipment unique to the A-12 and its successors. The 'STAB AUG' panel controlled the Stability Augmentation System, while other switches aft of this controlled navigation functions. (Lockheed)

numbered 11, but only six hours and 23 minutes total flying time was at or above Mach 3.0 – just 33 minutes of this was at Mach 3.2.

PROJECT PILOT TRAINING

Ken Collins now recalls his flight training for Oxcart: 'I began flying training by rechecking out in the F-101. Since I had already accumulated over 1,000 hours in the RF-101A, C and B (trainer) as a combat-qualified crew member and a flight instructor less than three months before, this was achieved in short order. All flying was accomplished in accordance with current Air Force Standardization and Evaluation regulations.

'The project pilots studied existing A-12 procedures documents, and reviewed the systems with aircraft systems engineers and the Lockheed test pilots, they also got all the cockpit familiarisation time possible. It's important to point out that during these early days there was little in the way of established test data and procedures. Kelly Johnson repeatedly said that this was a truly experimental test programme. The systems were new and untried, changes evolved and were being made daily with the completion of each test flight; procedures were developed in flight and during the debriefings, every flight was critically reviewed by the project pilots, the system engineering staff and the Lockheed test pilots.

'A-12 flight training began with three or four flights in the AT-12 two-seat trainer which was equipped with J57 engines and afterburners. The cockpit and flight systems were basically the same as on other A-12s, but the trainer would only get out to Mach 2+. There was no flight simulator, so the trainer was the best available and it was good. My first A-12 trainer flight was on 6 February 1963, Bill Skilar was the first project pilot to fly the aircraft and he checked out two days earlier. Walt Ray followed me on 10 February and Lon Walter some time after that – Lon opted out of the programme shortly after he started flying the J58 A-12. Take-offs and landings were very similar to the operational A-12, as was air refuelling. I wanted to ensure that I got all the trainer flight time possible in preparation for my first flight in the single-seater, equipped with J58 engines.

'The most critical event that the trainer could not prepare you for was the inlet unstarts, because it didn't have a variable geometry inlet and could not get to Mach 3. Other important points at this juncture were that the A-12 did not have aft bypass doors, or spike and door position indicators, it only had spike/door restart switches, its fuel controls were unreliable and the inlet controls were unreliable.

'As soon as possible after the AT-12 trainer checkout, we were put on the A-12 schedule. Once there, every flight was different with the exception that every flight had multiple inlet unstarts. When you began the climb and acceleration out to 80,000 ft [24384 m] and Mach 3, you were certain that there would be a "popped shock" and an unstart between 2.5 Mach and 2.9 Mach. You never knew the extent of these, true to say, however, that all unstarts were severe and serious in the beginning. The problem was, since we only had a toggle switch for each inlet (no inlet position indicators until much later) you were reacting, usually too late, to an unstart that was already in progress. An inlet unstart "popped" the shock out of the throat of the inlet, immediately stopping the air flow through that inlet and causing an engine compressor stall and afterburner blow-out, both of which were essential to your acceleration and retaining altitude. At this phase of the test programme you were only guessing which system unstarted, left or right. For any hope of restarting the inlet and continued acceleration, you hit both inlet toggle switches immediately. By making a quick guess you reactivated that inlet toggle hoping that you could catch it before the unstart compressor stalled the engine and blew-out the afterburner. Even after guessing right, you were usually too late, because it all happened in a nanosecond. After the unsuccessful attempt to get an immediate restart, you were in for head knocking, rapid deceleration and a shuttering dive toward the ground. At this point, you weren't concerned about the inlets, your primary efforts were directed toward getting the engine restarted, because the severity of the initial inlet unstart placed the aircraft in a hard yaw, which then caused the other inlet to unstart, which in turn caused that engine to compressor stall and the other afterburner to flame out, leaving you with an even more serious problem and very few options. You had to get at least one engine re-started. Reflecting back to those days, we always got at least one turning and burning again. The most serious problem occurred when the TEB probes started "cooking", this caused a chemical residue to build-up on the engine/afterburner starting TEB probe, restricting the flow of TEB, which was required to re-ignite the engine and/or the afterburner. We had a lot of other mechanical and electronic system problems throughout the program, but none as big as the inlet unstarts.'

Virtually all of these training sorties required a fuel top-off shortly after take-off and the tracks, or anchors, were located within the Yuletide SOA, about 20 miles (32 km) further north of the 'tunnel', as described earlier. For missions planned to the north, the refuelling track was orientated on a north-south axis, for flights to the east or west, there was an east-west orientated track. If the weather within the SOA was not conducive to air refuelling operations, the 'Oxcarters' would use SAC anchors – a track located to the north of Lake Tahoe, in western Nevada, was used on several occasions for weather avoidance. The A-12 was refuelled at an altitude of 30,000 ft (9144 m) (some 4,000–6,000 ft/1219–1829 m higher than the SR-71, because it was lighter and carried less fuel). On completion of the air refuelling task, the A-12 would turn onto its outbound course and carry out a climb/dive manoeuvre, referred to by Oxcart pilots as a 'Whifferdill' and designed to accelerate the aircraft rapidly through Mach 1 in order to reduce transonic drag and associated increased fuel consumption. This 'Whifferdill' manoeuvre would remain a standard part of A-12 operations and remained crucial to SR-71 operations, albeit under the revised name 'Dipsy Doodle'. The most often used track was that to the north – the AT-12 flew within the SOA since its less powerful J57s could not power it above the positive control areas. It flew practically every Monday night to keep the pilots current in both night flying and night air refuelling. The main test hop, however, was known as the Wells Route. After air refuelling and completing the 'Whifferdill', the Oxcart headed directly for the small town of Wells, in northern Nevada. Climbing through 60,000 ft (18288 m), the pilot checked in with Salt Lake Center and informed them that he was above the SOA. Shortly after level-off at 75,000 ft (22860 m) and when the aircraft was starting its cruise-climb, the autopilot coupled to the INS would roll it into a left turn over the old mining village at Midas (about 50 miles (80 km) north of Battle Mountain, Nevada), and consequently both Wells and Battle Mountain received regular 'boomings'. After passing over Area 51, the A-12 would then complete a descending left turn, to arrive back in the SOA for a let down into base. A variation of this route extended flight beyond Area 51 before completing a wider left, teardrop turn, followed by a deceleration into the SOA. This track enabled the aircraft to burn off more fuel and thereby achieve a much higher altitude. Both routes ultimately terminated in the SOA, from which point the aircraft proceeded either under, over, or through the tunnel, before landing back at 'home plate'. To provide project pilots with the opportunity to experience an extended fight with multiple 'hot legs' for 'graduation' or final flight training, a route was established to the west. After completing the first air refuelling and hot leg, the pilot descended for another top off near Hawaii, before completing a second and final hot leg back to the SOA. For the 'graduation' flight, the Stan/Eval section often planned the tanker in the Hawaiian anchor to be out of position, in order to give the new pilot a chance to

exercise the lost tanker drill. During his first attempt at this route, Frank Murray recalls having 'great fun', experiencing a severe 'unstart' at about Mach 2.4 at 60,000 ft (18288 m) on the climb out. He recalls: 'It was so severe that it broke the sunshade visor on my helmet and managed to break-off one of the canopy-mounted, over-the-shoulder cameras. Needless to say, I didn't graduate that day and returned to base a very weary and sobered young aviator.'

There were also routes to the east, one involving a single top off followed by an easterly hot leg of about 800 miles (1287 km), before turning back home for a run over the base. Another easterly route was named Super Continental. This included a second air refuelling near the east coast, before turning back and recovering into Area 51. Some of these training routes included the use of the aircraft's camera and electronic warfare (EW) systems. Area 51 was equipped with a variety of different threat simulators that could trigger a response from various pieces of onboard equipment for the purpose of testing both the equipment and pilot.

F-101 CHASE DUTIES

All A-12 flights out of 'the Area', were assigned an F-101 chase. During the early years many of these sorties were documented by a camera operator (frequently a Lockheed employee, sitting in the back seat of the '101, using a movie camera). However, once the number of sorties increased, photo chase flights declined. Typically, the chase pilot attended the A-12 pre-flight briefing and was ready to roll shortly after the Oxcart's brake release. After reaching a few thousand feet and 350 kt (403 mph; 649 km/h), the A-12 usually came out of afterburner and the '101 would join-up in close formation and look over the Article for signs of any leaks, loose panels, etc. Chase then flew a loose route formation while the A-12 proceeded to the refuelling track designated for that mission. Typically during this period the flight remained below 24,000 ft until north of the Wilson Creek–Coaldale airway. Once clear, the Oxcart climbed to the pre-contact refuelling altitude and following a final 'nod of the boom', by the tanker boom operator, the A-12 closed and boom contact completed the radio silent rendezvous. Throughout, the entire operation was carefully monitored by the chase pilot and once the Oxcart had topped-off, cleared the tanker and accelerated away, the chase aircraft could ease into position and top off its tanks. The A-12's fuel burned without a problem in the '101's engines, but was not reliably re-ignited by the aircraft's spark plug ignition system if an engine re-light sequence became necessary – as chase pilot Dick Roussell discovered one day while demonstrating an air start to a passenger. As a rule, chase stayed with the tanker until it departed. Occasionally, A-12 test sorties called for a second AR, in which event chase would again be in position to monitor the situation. All of the project pilots and several of the military staff officers at Area 51 were qualified as chase pilots. In addition, as mentioned earlier, during the early years two F-104s provided by Lockheed were also used on high-speed chase duties to document A-12 flight tests.

Denny Sullivan recalls undertaking an early morning F-101 chase flight: 'I chased Bill Park on a 6 am routine non-refuelled test flight early on. As he accelerated, I got the '101 supersonic and stayed with him out to about Mach 1.3 or so. He then climbed and pulled away. But on this particular flight, while out at about 1.5 and climbing, he suddenly came out of burner and turned back towards the Area. As I caught up with him, I asked, "What's the problem?" He answered, "Aft bypass". This was quite confusing, as the aft bypass doors on the engine didn't come into play at that speed. I later met him on the ground to talk over the flight. Turns out he aborted due to the need of a quick trip to the "out-house". It was either a case of abort the flight, or "do it" in the pressure suit – it was probably one of the most expensive trips to a toilet on record.'

Heavy maintenance on the F-101s was conducted at Hill AFB, Utah. Both staff and Oxcart project pilots were rostered to position the chase aircraft to Hill and collect and return them back to Area 51 as dictated by the maintenance cycle. To prevent identification of individual Oxcart crewmembers and prevent awkward questions being asked, they were issued with blue NASA flying suits and jackets. All, of course, carried Department of Defense (DoD) identification and official orders, which authorised the bearer to undertake such flights in the event that they were challenged, but the pilots' names were not displayed on any of their flight gear. Instead a four digit identity number was stencilled onto white tape that was then sown inside their collars – these same numbers were stamped onto their pressure suits and helmets and were replicated across the top shelf of each pilot's cubicle in the personal equipment room back at Area 51. The base ops staff at Hill AFB were soon used to seeing flight plans filed by blue-suited pilots declaring their destination to be one of the many airfields within the Nellis area – which was more or less correct.

Since there were no weather reporting stations within the special rules area, a weather scout provided this much needed service. During the summer it launched from Area 51 at about 06:00 hours or at first light during other seasons. The weather scout, flying one of the F-101s, usually flew a couple of hundred miles to the north, paying particular attention to cloud conditions in the refuelling areas and reporting conditions to Area 51's Weather Station on UHF radio. Having completed these duties the scout was free to return to home plate via any route desired – usually returning before any other aircraft had taken off. One or two of the more mischievous pilots used the opportunity to check out the Security Guard post on the dirt road leading to the east of Bald Mountain – it seems that many a guard was startled back into reality by an extremely fast and very low returning weather scout! Upon landing the '101 pilot reported to both the Weather Station and Command Post and related his report in more detail if required.

Another duty performed by both staff and project pilots before the start of a day's flying was a security check of the area's 'perimeter'. This was flown in the Cessna 210 as well as the HH-43/UH-1 Huey.

A flight in the AT-12 was set up for Kelly Johnson to enable the aircraft's designer to get a feel for the platform's early performance. Lou Schalk was the 'instructor pilot' in the Titanium Goose and recalls: 'I took off, cleaned it up then "gave it" to Kelly. He climbed the airplane, levelled off with the afterburners in and accelerated out to Mach 1.4. That was the first time he had ever been supersonic and he was delighted. The airplane behaved beautifully as we proceeded to take an INS trip to one of our checkpoints on the course. I rolled the airplane into a steep bank and there was the checkpoint – a city down in Utah – right on the money. I then contacted the tanker for a refuelling rendezvous – which at times could be a bit hit and miss. He answered my call immediately and was right where he said he was. I picked him out, slid into position and the boom operator, who was red hot that day, plugged me off and we'd taken on 5,000 lb [2268 kg] of fuel and were gone again before we hardly knew what had happened. Maybe it wasn't a good idea to have such a good flight with the Boss, to whom you were supposed to impress with all the problems that you were having, but it was a beautiful flight and I'm sure glad he was there'.

During a chase sortie on 26 September 1967, F-101B 56-0286 was returning to home plate and in company with the Titanium Goose. It was already quite dark, and while the AT-12 was nearing the approach to runway 32 and at about 8,500 ft (2591 m), it appears that the chase pilot, James S. Simon Jr, lost visual contact with his charge. The Oxcart pilot told Simon that he was okay and had no further need for the chase aircraft; the A-12 then turned onto final. When asked where he was, chase replied: 'in trail and moving over to the right side'. Shortly thereafter a fireball was seen to streak across the desert and the AT-12 pilot initiated a go-around at 500 ft (152 m) and 190 kt (219 mph; 352 km/h). The wreckage of '0286 was subsequently found 4,000 ft (1219 m) short of runway 32 and 2,000 ft (610 m) to the right of its extended centreline. It was determined that James Simon had made no attempt to eject and the CIA accident report concluded that he had inadvertently flown into the ground.

THE FIRST LOSS

As with most flight-test programmes, success was not obtained without loss. The first A-12 loss occurred on 24 May 1963. At the time, the A-12 was experiencing problems with its engine fuel controls during acceleration and cruise. Ken Collins was scheduled to fly aircraft 60-6926, Article Number 123, to conduct a series of subsonic engine test runs. He now takes up the story: 'Jack Weeks was scheduled as my F-101 chase pilot. Take-off and initial cruise was routine. I made the planned right turn to 180° and climbed to 27,000 ft [8230 m] to stay out of the building cloud formations. During these missions the chase plane was to stay close enough to observe the engine nacelles and the afterburner areas, but far enough away to maintain safe flight.

'The F-101 had a historical pitch-up problem, if it got too slow in flight. As we continued south in the Windover Danger Area (northwest of the Great Salt Lake) I entered an area of heavy cumulus cloud formations. My chase moved in to keep visual contact. Minutes later, Jack signalled that we were getting too slow for the F-101. The A-12 instruments (airspeed and altitude) were giving normal indications. Jack signalled that he could not stay with me. I waved him off, he cleared to my right and disappeared into the clouds.

'I dedicated all my efforts to determining what the real problems were. I engaged the autopilot and reviewed all of the instruments and systems. There were no observable failures or abnormal indications. I then disengaged the autopilot, maintaining my planned airspeed and 30,000 ft [9144 m] altitude. In a matter of seconds all hell broke out. Without any noticeable change of aircraft attitude or speed the altimeter was rapidly 'unwinding', indicating a rapid loss of altitude and the airspeed indicator was also 'unwinding', displaying a rapid loss of airspeed. In the heavy clouds, with no visual references and with what felt like a solid platform under me, I advanced the throttles attempting to stop the indicated loss of airspeed, but with no obvious results. At this

point I could not assume that any of my flight or engine instruments were providing correct data and I was right. Without any warning the A-12 pitched up and went into a flat inverted spin.

'Realising that I had no effective controls and that the aircraft was unrecoverable from this flat inverted spin and that I had no true indication of my actual altitude, it was time to eject. I could have been much lower and over higher mountains, which would put me dangerously close to the ground or hill-tops. I closed my helmet visor, grabbed the ejection 'D' ring between my legs, firmly pushed my head against the ejection seat headrest and pulled. The aircraft canopy instantly flew off, the boot stirrups snapped back into the seat retainers locking my feet securely for the ejection and the rocket jet charge fired shooting me down and away from the aircraft. The man/seat separator worked great. Shortly after separating from the seat my chute opened. I looked up to confirm that I did indeed have a good chute (this was my first ejection), then looked down at the ground to get a general idea of the terrain where I would land. At that moment the chute broke away, separating from my parachute harness. I knew that my luck had just run out! There was momentarily a quieting sensation; a pause in my life. Just as suddenly, this beautiful 35-ft [10.67-m] canopy blossomed quickly, slowing my descent (the A-12 parachute system consisted of two elements, the first, a smaller drogue chute, deployed shortly after ejection and seat separation, its primary purpose being to slowly decelerate the pilot when ejecting at high speed and altitude. The main chute was of greater diameter than usual to compensate for the extra weight of the pressure suit. If the main deployed at high altitude and excessive speed, the pilot would be killed by the deceleration forces). When I ejected, I did not know what my altitude was. After ejection I was just happy that I had a parachute and was out of the clouds. I had separated safely from the aircraft. When descending through 15,000 ft [4572 m], the drogue chute is programmed to separate and the main chute is scheduled to deploy. At that moment I truly thought that my parachute was gone.

'During my descent, I saw the A-12 spiralling toward the ground and then a large black column of smoke and flames billowed from behind a hill. I had time to 'look around'. I saw a road miles to the right and a lot of rough terrain covered with rocks and sage. As I got closer to the ground, I assumed the parachute landing position, with feet together and knees bent. I hit the ground and rolled on my right side into a standing position. I immediately released the riser safety clips and collapsed the chute. You keep the parachute canopy for survival. I was in the middle of a hilly desert, with little prospect of being rescued soon. My chase plane (Jack Weeks) did not know where I was and because of the programme classification, we did not maintain radio contact with base operations. I began collecting all my flight checklist pages, which broke loose during the ejection, together with any other aircraft items lying around. Much to my amazement, I saw a pickup truck bouncing across the rocks coming toward me with three men in the cab. When they stopped, I saw that they had my aircraft cockpit canopy in the truck bed. They asked me if I wanted a ride. They said that they would take me over to my airplane. I told them it was an F-105 fighter with a nuclear weapon onboard. They got very nervous and said that if you're going with us get in quick, because they weren't staying around. There were four of us in the truck cab. I asked them to drop me off at the nearest Highway Patrol Office, which was in Windover, Utah. I thanked them and that was the last I saw of them. I made my 'secret' phone call. The base sent a Lockheed Constellation loaded with security people and aircraft engineers in less than two hours. Kelly Johnson's jet arrived behind the 'Connie' to pick me up. Our flight surgeon and I flew directly to Albuquerque, New Mexico, to the Lovelace Clinic for my physical check-up.

'An intense accident investigation was conducted. I submitted to sodium pentothol to confirm all my statements relating to the flight and the accident. The person who solved the true technical causes of the accident (inadequate pitot tube provision caused the air data computer to fail) was Norm Nelson, a dedicated government engineer and a fine, caring man, who later became Vice President of the Skunk Works. As always, the initial belief is that there was pilot error, fortunately the real cause of the accident was discovered and corrected. Ten years after the accident, I received a package in the mail. Unwrapping it, I found a shadow-box frame with the 'D' ring mounted inside with the inscription: to Ken Collins 'A Friend In Need'. It was my ejection 'D' ring from the A-12 and was sent to me by Keith Beswick, a Lockheed engineer on the Oxcart programme.' The wreckage of Article 123 was recovered in two days and persons at the scene were identified and requested to sign secrecy agreements. Interestingly, the press cover story describing the accident as having occurred to an F-105 still remains listed this way on official records, the fact that the Oxcart was on a "low altitude" sortie and that Ken was therefore not wearing his moon suit gave further credence to the story.

In an ironic twist of fate, some time after the loss of Article 123, a Republic F-105 Thunderchief from Nellis was lost and members of Oxcart were involved in the search for the crash site, Frank Murray now recalls: 'Earlier in the day, four of the big Republic aircraft had taken off for a sortie in the Pahrump Valley area, west of Spring Mountains, near Las Vegas. After some in-trail formation aerobatics, the flight was minus number four. The CP at Area 51 ordered both the base helicopter and Cessna 210 to help in the search. One of the Flight Surgeons, Roger Anderson and I, got airborne in the Cessna and set up a search pattern in the southern half of the valley 1,000 ft [305 m] agl on an east-west track. We soon located the crash site near a small lake adjoining the property of one of the brothels in the area known as Ash Meadows Ranch. From the air, it appeared that the '105 had impacted the ground, wings level in a slight dive. Marks on the ground were consistent with where first the drop tanks and then the tail pipe contacted before the aircraft broke up.

'The brothel provided a small dirt runway, graded out, to allow its customers the option of air travel into the facility. Our party, attired in Air Force flight gear, landed and taxied to the main building where we were greeted by a gent. We explained that we were part of a search party and that we'd located a crash site and requested transport to check for possible survivors. Happy to oblige, we were driven the few miles in the Ranch van and upon reaching the site the flight surgeon confirmed that the pilot had perished in the accident. At about this time a chopper from Indian Springs arrived at the site and I provided the crew with a brief written report and returned to Ash Meadows. By now it was lunchtime and the Madam had got the cook to rustle up lunch. During the course of a rather guarded but polite conversation with the madam, my aviation curiosity got the better of me and I asked her what was the largest aircraft ever to use the landing strip. She replied that light twins were regular visitors, but the largest was an Army C-7A Caribou packed full with GIs from an Army base in California. "Mind you …" she added mischievously, "they weren't looking for downed airplanes!" After lunch the three of us said our goodbyes and departed for a life back at our own "Ranch".'

As a final footnote to Ash Meadows Ranch; one of the 'lovelies' discovered that a resident, who never actually 'indulged' himself, seemed to have a rather questionable background, further suspicions prompted the madam to notify the FBI. 'Slip' Slater recalls being subsequently briefed by Nick Zubon, the Area 51 resident Agency Chief of Security and it turned out that the individual in question turned out to be a ships radio operator from an Eastern Bloc country. Following a raid on his room, an array of hi-tech communications equipment was discovered. It spelled the end of his days in espionage, but to date, no one actually seems to know who he was or what subsequently happened to him.

DUTCH 30, Mel Vojvodich, deployed A-12 serial 60-6937 to Kadena on 22 May 1967; he flew the same aircraft on Black Shield's first operational mission nine days later. (CIA)

MORE FLIGHTS, MORE LOSSES

Lou Schalk experienced what was perhaps the most 'thrilling' flight of his distinguished test flight career while flying '924 on an inlet-schedule flight in 1963 with the electrically-controlled spike actuator installed. 'I was approaching Wendover, Utah, from the south and the aircraft was accelerating like it had never done before. It was apparent that I would be at Mach 3 before I left Utah (well before reaching the turn point short of the Canadian border), so I throttled back and started my turn early. Emerging from the turn, I pushed the throttles to full burner and continued to climb. I got so far behind the aircraft that I didn't notice that the fuel flow fell off slightly which led to a loss in rpm on one engine. The next thing I knew, I had an unstart, where upon I attempted to open the bypass doors to break the unstart but that action didn't seem to help. Then the other inlet unstarted and so it went on with terrific oscillations continuing, one after another. I made a single radio transmission saying that I was in real trouble. I thought I ought to bail out, but stayed with the aircraft because it still seemed to be in one piece and still flying, although these violent oscillations continued all the way down to Mach 1.4. I then realised that I'd left the right engine in burner and that the left engine had flamed out. I was holding tremendous rudder pressure with one leg in an attempt to fly straight

without even trimming out some of that pressure with the rudder trim switch. When I finally came out of afterburner it was much easier to handle, so I restarted the flamed-out engine and headed back to base.

'At the debriefing I learned that the engineers had decided at their Monday morning maintenance planning briefing that the slow acceleration and high fuel consumption could be due to the bypass doors leaking air after they had closed. They therefore decided to 'bolt' them closed, but no one had told me about this decision and that's why the aircraft had taken off on me like 'a scorched dog'. It then also became clear why I couldn't break the unstart and why, when I tried to switch the bypass doors open, nothing happened to change the inlet airflow. After the lesson in the lack of communication between the engineers and pilots, I attended all the Monday morning maintenance planning briefings!'

All seemed to be progressing well until 9 July 1964, when Bill Park experienced a complete lock-up of his flight controls in Article 133 as he descended for landing following a high-Mach flight. Despite trying to save the aircraft from rolling under while turning on to final approach, Park could not stop the bank angle from increasing. Realising he was 'going in' he yanked the D-ring between his legs, which fired the rocket beneath his ejection seat, and succeeded in 'punching-out' at about 200 kt (230 mph; 370 km/h) in a 45° bank, not more than 200 ft (61 m) above the ground as the brand new Article 133 exploded in a spectacular fire ball ahead of him. After just one quick swing under the quickly deployed canopy of his parachute, his feet were on the overrun to runway 32! The 'Road Runners' were all certain that they had just witnessed their first fatality in the programme. To the great surprise and relief of those hurrying to the scene, Bill was picked up walking toward the wreckage uninjured.

It is not uncommon for developmental flight-testing to be punctuated by varying periods of stand down to evaluate mistakes, or to make changes in hardware or procedures. One day, when Mele Vojvodich came to the the site's main hanger, Article 126 (which he was to fly the following day) was lying about in bits and pieces across the hanger floor. He joked that this aircraft 'was never going to fly again', not knowing how prophetic his words would prove to be. On 28 December 1964, Mele taxied 126 out for a training flight and lit the burners for what he thought would be another run to altitude. As he reached rotate speed, he gently applied back-pressure to the stick for rotation to lift-off attitude. Instead of 126's nose rising smoothly, it yawed viciously to one side, whereupon Mele stood on the rudder pedals to correct the yaw. Instead of rectifying the yaw, the rudder input made 126 pitch-up. The rash of instinctive responses that followed resulted in a series of counter movements opposite to those that an experienced pilot would expect to occur. It was indeed a pilot's nightmare. When the aircraft became airborne, it pulled itself toward the ground and back stick pressure caused another hard yaw movement that could not be corrected by counter rudder pressure without an increasingly sharp pitch movement. In the midst of this wild pitching and yawing, Mele pulled the D-ring between his legs and at an altitude of not more than a 100 ft (30 m), he blasted free of his unmanageable aircraft and rode his parachute to the only safe landing possible. Narrowly missing the flaming pyre that billowed up from yet another lost A-12, Mele landed safely after just six seconds of flight in a brand new aircraft – almost a new world record for the shortest ever test flight!

The subsequent accident board established that the SAS had been cross-wired, and that 'Murphy's Law' had claimed yet another jet. The pitch SAS had been connected to the yaw SAS actuators and vice-versa. Inside the cockpit there were no warning lights available to warn the pilot of his predicament, and with no SAS effect felt until rotation, Mele had no possible opportunity to identify the potential problem until the gyro-sensed SAS reacted to rotation as if it were a yaw input at the most critical moment of flight – lift-off. Through a series of tests in the new SR-71 simulator then being installed at Beale AFB, it was determined that none of the trained A-12 pilots who repeatedly tried to fly out of such a situation could have saved 126. Indeed, it was considered 'miraculous' for Mele to have been able to escape with his life. From that experience, the SAS connectors were made 'Murphy proof'.

UNINVITED VISITORS

Mindful of the wilder imaginings of some elements of the media, several members of the Oxcart programme have confirmed that there were definitely no aliens at Area 51, adding – tongue in cheek – at least not during their stay at the isolated base! However, uninvited visitors did 'drop in' from time to time. Denny Sullivan recalls that on one night a young lady and her rather drunk pilot boyfriend arrived at the base: 'It seems that he convinced her that it was a good idea to fly from Reno down to Las Vegas in this light plane to continue the party. He evidently lost his way and was getting low on fuel when he saw this nice big runway and landed. He was met by the security folks and as I understand it, during the session with security, the gal got into seriously

berating the guy for his stupidity and whacked him one with her purse!'

On another occasion Frank Murray missed the last Friday night 'Connie' flight back to Burbank due to the late completion of a Functional Check Flight (FCF). He was in his base house on the Saturday morning when he heard the sound of a light aircraft flying over the base, so he ventured out to see what was going on, as he now recollects: 'At about this time one of the security guys drove up and told me that someone was landing on the taxiway. I jumped in the truck and went to see. As we caught-up with our "guest" he was shutting down on the apron in front of the big hangers. The guy then stepped out and said "God, am I glad to be down, I've been flying around his huge desert, lost." It turned out that he was a student pilot, ex-USAF navigator, flying one of his solo cross-countries out of Apple Valley, California. Security checked out his story and decided to let him go with the usual signing away of his life about the Area. We filled-up his little airplane with Mogas and told him to taxi out to the main runway and head off southeast and don't turn. He flew off to the cut in the ridges southeast of the Area and I never saw him again. I then went back to the house to continue work on building my radio-controlled model aircraft'.

Although similar incursions occasionally punctuated life at the test area, it is believed that there is only one case of a 'guest' actually seeing an Oxcart. Late on the morning of 29 June 1965, RAF exchange officer Flt Lt Jock Heron got airborne from Nellis AFB in F-105D 59-1772 of the 4526th Combat Crew Training Squadron (CCTS), 4520th Combat Crew Training Wing (CCTW), on a simulated nuclear weapons delivery sortie to one of the Nellis ranges.

Jock now recalls that sortie: 'Having released a practice bomb I pulled off the target and suddenly the cockpit filled with smoke. Despite following the usual emergency procedures the problem remained so with thoughts that an internal fire had developed, I declared an emergency and had little alternative but to seek authority to land immediately at the "Ranch", which lay on the edge of a dry lake bed some 15 miles [24 km] to the south east inside the prohibited area of the test site. Permission was duly gained and my credentials were passed to the control tower using the emergency frequency. The airfield looked deserted as I passed through the overhead before setting up for my approach and landing. The "Thud" was well over maximum landing weight and I flew a wide circuit before making my final approach at a higher than normal speed to allow for the extra 8,000 lb [3629 kg] of fuel. Touchdown was straightforward and gentle, the braking parachute deployed normally and the aircraft slowed gradually to normal taxiing speed before I turned it off the long runway. I then shut down the engine and electrical power because of the continuing risk of an internal fire from the source of the smoke, which did not disperse until the canopy was opened.

Two vehicles met me, one of which was an engineering truck and crew, the other contained two men in civilian clothes. Having dismounted from the aircraft and ascertained that there were no external signs of fire I left the aircraft in the hands of the ground crew and was invited to board the second vehicle which took me to one of the hangers adjacent to the aircraft parking area. Conversation was limited to the events surrounding the aircraft's emergency and I was escorted to a room without windows where I was given a welcome cold drink. The ensuing debriefing was courteous but prolonged and I was reminded of the classified nature of the airfield. After about an hour, one of the ground crew appeared and confirmed the cause of the smoke in the cockpit. Apparently the cold air turbine for the cabin air refrigeration system had seized and the overheated lubricant had ignited within the system. Although there was no real danger to the aircraft, the effects in the cockpit were consistent with the system failure. In the light of the evidence of a genuine malfunction, the two men adopted a more relaxed manner and we exchanged flying banter for a time. It was agreed that I could return to base without the cold air system which, because of the failure, would be isolated by the engineers.

'One of the hosts looked at his watch and invited me to follow him outside. We stood in the baking mid-day sun at the edge of a large dispersal pan where there were two aircraft parked, an F-104D Starfighter and an F-101B Voodoo, both of which were two-seaters. There was an audible deep engine noise that wasn't generated by either the J79 of the F-104 or the two J57s of the F-101, but there was no sign of any other aircraft. A few minutes later the F-101 started its engines and my host then said: "You'll be interested in this". The doors of the hangarette opposite opened to reveal the source of the earlier unidentified engine noise. It was an aircraft pointed straight at our position, which I was to identify later as the forerunner of the SR-71. This sleek black shape then emerged from its cover, passed us while taxing to the end of the runway and took off with the Voodoo in pursuit. Naturally as a young Flight Lieutenant I was awestruck to have been so close to this spectacular product of the Lockheed Skunk Works.

'After a quick snack lunch I was returned to reality because my aircraft was pronounced ready to fly and it was time to leave the remote test site

and fly back to Nellis. After a final word from my host of the need for complete discretion I boarded my "Thud", started the engine, taxied to the end of the runway and took off for the short flight back to Nellis. Because of the lack of air conditioning, I climbed to a relatively cool 10,000 ft [305 m] and turned my back on the "Ranch", conscious that I was privileged to have been there. The following day I was flying another "Thud" on the same bombing range with a student flying on my wing when he suffered a fuel transfer emergency and again the procedure for such a failure was to land as soon as possible. When asked by the air traffic control tower at the test site to pass my flight details on the emergency frequency, I said merely "Same as yesterday". I was told that I could return to Nellis after monitoring my student's landing. Perhaps the authorities had seen enough of the visiting Scot at the "Ranch" and two days running was too much!'

OPERATIONS

On 1 January 1964, unique equipment used to support the A-12 and stored at Mira Loma Depot was moved to a location at San Bernardino Air Material Area, Norton AFB, California; concurrently, Air Logistics Command at Wright-Patterson AFB assumed full manpower and logistics control at the new depot for Oxcart, the D-21 drone project (Tagboard) and the up-coming Air Force SR-71 programme. A year later, on 27 January 1965, the first in a series of long-range, high-speed, high-altitude proving flights, code-named Silver Javelin, occurred. Article 129 completed the 2,580 nm (2,971 mile; 4781 km) flight in just one hour 40 minutes, one hour 15 minutes of which was spent at speeds above Mach 3.1 and cruising altitudes of between 75,600 and 80,000 ft (23043 and 24384 m) were achieved. Later that year, on 18 March 1965, the heads of both the CIA and DoD agreed to take preparatory steps towards operating the A-12 over Communist China and by year's end, all the Agency's project pilots were Mach-3 qualified. However, despite this near state of readiness, political sensitivities surrounding the overflight conundrum ensured that the A-12 would never conduct sorties over the Soviet Union or China. Where, then, was this multi-million dollar national security asset to earn its keep? One possible short-term answer appeared to be in a classified project, code-named Upwind.

In 1964, KH-4 Corona satellite imagery obtained what some analysts believed was an anti-ballistic missile site, located at Tallinn in Estonia. Photographic interpreters contended that 12–18-in resolution imagery was needed to determine the size of the missile, the antenna pattern and configuration of the engagement radars associated with the so-called Tallinn system. However, the resolution of satellite, or 'overhead' imagery available at that time was not capable of producing the required level of detail necessary to resolve the ensuing debate. To settle the issue, the Office of Special Activities (OSA) proposed that a composite mission should be flown consisting of an Oxcart equipped with a high-resolution camera, and a U-2 configured for gathering Elint. The highly classified proposal had the unclassified code name Project Scope Logic and a classified cryptonym, Project Upwind. The A-12 would fly from the United States into the Baltic Sea, where it would rendezvous with the U-2. Thereafter, the former would proceed north of Norway, and then south, along the Soviet/Finnish border. Just prior to reaching Leningrad, the A-12 would head west-southwest, down the Baltic Sea, skirting the coasts of Estonia, Latvia, Lithuania, Poland and East Germany before heading back west, to the United States. The 11,000-mile (17702 km) flight would take eight hours 40 minutes to complete and require four air refuellings. Although not violating Soviet airspace, it was hoped that the high speed, high altitude target would provoke Soviet radar operators into activating the Tallinn system. The A-12, with its Type 1 camera, would secure high resolution imagery of the Tallinn site and the more vulnerable U-2 would be standing-off, beyond SA-2 range, recording the radar's signal characteristics. Both Agency and Defense Department officials supported the proposal; however, Secretary of State Dean Rusk was strongly opposed and the influential 303 Committee never forwarded the proposal to President Johnson for his approval.

Another possible area of operations for Oxcart was Cuba. By early 1964, Project Headquarters had already begun planning for possible 'contingency overflights' under a programme code-named Skylark. Four of the 13 A-12s now at Area 51 were initially designated as primary Skylark aircraft, namely Articles 125, 127, 128 and 132. They were later joined by aircraft 129 and 131 following the installation of further modifications.

A luncheon meeting held on 15 September in Secretary of State Dean Rusk's dining room and attended by McNamara, McGeorge Bundy and McCone, discussed the limitations of satellite coverage of Cuba in the context of monitoring assurances made by the Soviet Union not to re-deploy nuclear missiles on the island following the 1962 crisis. The discussion also covered vulnerability of the U-2 to undertake such missions in the light of a very real SAM threat. It was pointed out that Oxcart overflights would be 'far less vulnerable than the U-2, but not entirely invulnerable; however it would be known because

of the sonic boom in addition to radar detection'. McNamara took a slightly opposing view, believing that vulnerability of the A-12 would only increase 'if we engaged in frequent flight over a pre-determined pattern when the Cubans might put some of their SAMs in a state of alert which would very possibly catch an Oxcart'. However, he thought that one flight every 30 days would provide enough coverage of the island to fulfil the United States Intelligence Board (USIB) requirements. Others in attendance disagreed, particularly on the number of sorties required, given a study of the history of weather over Cuba, especially if substantial coverage of the island was to be achieved. It was agreed that the subject should receive further study and that this should include Oxcart vulnerability under the Skylark programme and a substantive judgement as to the number of flights required from November 1964 to November 1965 in order to accomplish acceptable coverage of the island with usable photography.

To bring the A-12s up to the necessary standard required to participate in the envisaged missions, a two-point plan was developed, both Phase I and II were to begin simultaneously on 1 March 1965. Phase I focused on increasing the aircraft's speed envelope out from Mach 2.9 to Mach 3.05. While Phase II concentrated on providing Oxcart with the capability to undertake three air refuellings during the course of a mission, an element, code named Supermarket, related to improvements in the A-12's ECM system. The latter seemed to be taking a disproportionate amount of time to resolve, causing the CIA to try a different approach – Project Kempster. This project proposed the development of electron guns that would be located at the front of the Oxcart and fire an ion cloud ahead of the aircraft to hide its presence. Innovative Kempster certainly was, but it proved to be a non-starter and ultimately the other modifications proposed for Skylark provided the A-12s with the required capability. In the interim, on 5 August 1965, the Director of the National Security Agency, Gen Marshall S. Carter, directed that Skylark was to achieve emergency operational readiness by 5 November. Should security considerations dictate, any contingency sorties would have to be executed below the optimum capability of the A-12 (nearer to Mach 2.8). In order to meet this tight time frame, the Oxcarts would have to deploy without their full ECM suite, but despite all the difficulties, a limited Skylark capability was ready on the date prescribed by Gen Carter. In the event, these Cuban contingencies were never implemented (on 15 September 1966, the 303 Committee voted not to commit Oxcart to Cuban reconnaissance missions, on the basis that it could disturb the prevailing political calm). Instead, a

THE ROAD RUNNIN'EST

The unofficial emblem of the 1129th Special Activities Squadron was, rather appropriately, a 'hotted-up' Cygnus. The 1129th SAS ultimately received an Air Force Outstanding Unit Award in honour of its Lockheed A-12 operations. (via Frank Murray)

more critical situation had developed in Southeast Asia and this took priority.

BLACK SHIELD

On 22 March 1965, Brig-Gen Jack Ledford briefed Deputy Secretary of Defense Cyrus Vance on project Black Shield – the planned deployment of Oxcart to Okinawa – in response to the increased SA-2 threat that was facing U-2 and Ryan Firebee drone reconnaissance vehicles used over Communist China. Overflights of China would obviously have to be approved by the President himself, but Secretary Vance was willing to make $3.7 million available to provide support facilities at Kadena AB, which were to be ready by the fall of 1965. On 3 June 1965, Secretary McNamara consulted with the Under Secretary of the Air Force on the build-up of SA-2 missile sites around Hanoi and the possibility of substituting A-12s for the vulnerable U-2s on recce flights over the North Vietnamese capital. He was informed that Black Shield could operate over Vietnam as soon as adequate aircraft performance was validated.

On 20 November 1965 the final stage of the Silver Javelin validation process was completed when a maximum-endurance flight of six hours and 20 minutes was achieved, during which time the A-12 demonstrated sustained speeds above Mach 3.2 at altitudes approaching 90,000 ft (27432 m). Four A-12s were selected for Black Shield operations, Kelly Johnson taking personal responsibility for ensuring that the aircraft were completely 'squawk free'. On 2 December 1965, the highly secretive 303 Committee received a

formal proposal to deploy Oxcart operations to the Far East. The proposal was quickly rejected, but the Committee agreed that all steps should be taken to develop a quick-reaction capability for deploying the A-12 reconnaissance system within a 21-day period anytime after 1 January 1966.

SCOTCH MIST

The likelihood of deployment abroad spurred other preparations, one of which was code-named Scotch Mist. In the spring of 1966 it was decided to flight-test a windshield rain-clearing system, developed to enable the pilot to maintain forward visual contact with the ground during descent in heavy rain. In addition, Scotch Mist would also examine the flight characteristics of an Oxcart when operating at sea level. The A-12 had only ever been flown routinely out of Area 51, which was well above sea level. It was decided that the tests would be conducted from McCoy AFB, near Orlando, Florida, as meteorological (met.) conditions were similar to those expected at Kadena. The deployment consisted of one A-12, with support provided by one F-101 and the C-130. The pilot selected for the project was Walt Ray.

McCoy is a joint-use Air Force/civil airport and, at the time, few directly outside the programme had ever seen the likes of such an aircraft, as 'Slip' Slater relates: 'When the bird rolled out for take-off, no one had ever seen a "Blackbird" and you could actually see the airliners tip as all the passengers rushed to the side windows to get a peek. Another interesting event occurred on the first few attempts to get the bloody machine airborne. Walt would get to the end of the runway for take-off and when he came back on the PLA (throttle), the engine would quit! Well, that brought a rash of P&W, Lockheed and United Aircraft (fuel control) guys out from Connecticut, to identify and rectify the problem. They discovered that the T-2 sensor in the engine nacelle had to be repositioned – that cured the problem'.

The rain clearance system was tested by flying the aircraft through local showers, a switch activated in the cockpit causing a chemical water-wetting agent to be sprayed from nozzles located along the 'Barracuda' blade (situated at the apex of the cockpit windshield) to dissipate rain drops. To date, records commenting on the effectiveness or otherwise of the system remain elusive. However, Frank Murray recalls using the system once 'in anger' having returned to Kadena after completing a Black Shield mission. 'It was "raining like a dog", Denny Sullivan was out at the Mobile [acting as the Mobile Crew, checking for runway debris, etc prior to Murray's landing] and I recall thinking, here's a great chance to try the vaunted rain clear system. I told Denny, but when I activated the switch, the stuff came out as white as milk and I couldn't see a thing through the windshield. Denny helped me by saying, "Okay, get the chute, get the chute!" He was saying for me to "deploy the drag-chute." I could only see the sides of the runway – so much for the rain clear system. Turns out that the fluid had to be changed regularly and not kept indefinitely since it coagulated from the heat accumulated during cruise.'

Throughout 1966, numerous requests were made to the 303 Committee to implement the Black Shield Operations Order, but all requests were turned down. A difference of opinion had arisen between two important governmental factions that advised the Committee: the CIA, the Joint Services Committee (JSC) and the President's Foreign Intelligence Advisory Board favoured the deployment, but Alexis Johnson of the State Department and Robert McNamara and Cyrus Vance of the Defense Department opposed it.

Meanwhile, throughout 1966 training and testing continued, while mission plans and tactics were prepared to ready the operational 'package' for deployment should the Black Shield plan be executed. Deployment timing was further cut from 21 to 11 days and the Okinawa-based maintenance facility was stocked with support equipment. To further underwrite the A-12's capability to carry out long-range reconnaissance missions, Bill Park completed a non-stop 10,200-mile (16415 km) flight in just over six hours on 21 December 1966.

Fifteen days after Park's proof-of-range flight, tragedy struck the programme with the crash of yet another jet, but this time the incident claimed the life of its pilot. Walt Ray had logged 358 hours in the A-12 when he got airborne from Area 51 at 11:50 am (local) on 5 January 1967, using his personal call sign DUTCH 45. The flight was scheduled as a routine training and test sortie and shortly after take-off he successfully completed his first AR, taking onboard 36,000 lb (16330 kg) of fuel. Completing the first high-speed, high-altitude leg of the sortie, he descended for a second AR. This time his fuel off-load from the tanker was 61,000 lb (27670 kg). This was some 4,000–5,000 lb (1814–2268 kg) less than planned, since the tanker reported that it was running low on gas. To make up for the fuel shortfall, Walt planned to execute a fuel-saving, reduced-power climb during the next leg. His fuel management skills seemed to have paid off when, having completed his final turn back to 'home-plate' he was a manageable 800–1,000 lb (363–454 kg) off schedule. However, nearing Framington, New Mexico, the aircraft should have had about 13,000 lb (5897 kg) onboard, but at 3:22 pm Walt reported that he was down to 7,500 lb (3402 kg) and commented on the R/T: 'I don't know where it's gone'. Thirty minutes later during the descent near Hanksville, Utah, he reported that he was low on fuel and just one minute later, he declared an emergency. At 3:56:27 pm, Walt radioed that he was 130 miles (209 km) out, had just 4,000 lb (1814 kg) of fuel left and that he was losing this at an excessive rate. Five minutes later he reported that the fuel low-pressure lights had illuminated, then, after 30 seconds, he reported that the engines were starting to flame out. At 4:03 pm Walt made his final radio call, stating that both engines had flamed out and that he was ejecting. Article 125 (60-6928) had run out of fuel some 70 miles (113 km) short of Area 51. After 'gliding' to a lower altitude and executing what appeared to be a controlled bailout, Walt couldn't separate his parachute from the ejection seat and was killed when he hit the ground.

The circumstances leading up to the loss of this outstanding pilot and extremely popular member of the programme were particularly ironic. Almost a year earlier, on 25 January 1966, SR-71A test vehicle 64-17952 was lost by Lockheed flight test crew Bill Weaver and Jim Zwayer, during a range-extension test in which Zwayer was killed. Post-accident investigations revealed that the back-seater had died from a broken neck, sustained as the aircraft disintegrated following a Mach 3 pitch-up. The violent 'whiplash', that had resulted from the high-speed break-up of the aircraft and the subsequent g forces that slung Zwayer and Weaver about as they were forcibly torn from their non-ejected seats, slammed Zwayer's head back against the seat's headrest. It was further determined that, because of Zwayer's short stature, that his headrest was further back due to the thickness of the parachute's back-pack.

Subsequent to that accident, Lockheed undertook flight-safety modifications to the seat's headrest cushion, tailoring it more closely to the contours of individual crew members to provide support and protection from future 'whiplash' injuries. Regrettably, Walt's extended headrest had caused his parachute to become trapped between the seat well and the headrest, to the degree that the 'butt-snapper' straps (which had attempted to work as advertised) could not push him free from his seat. The accident was a bitter blow to the deployment timing of Oxcart. The *Los Angeles Times* reported the accident and identified the aircraft as an 'SR-71 Experimental Reconnaissance jet' and Walt Ray as a 'Lockheed test pilot'.

In May 1967, the National Security Council was briefed that North Vietnam was about to receive surface-to-surface ballistic missiles. Such a serious escalation of the conflict would certainly require hard evidence to substantiate the claim. Consequently, President Johnson was briefed on the threat. Richard Helms of the CIA again proposed that the 303 Committee authorise the deployment of Oxcart, since it was ideally equipped to carry out such a surveillance task, having both superior speed and altitude capabilities to the U-2s and pilotless drones, as well as a better camera. President Johnson approved the plan and in mid May an airlift was begun to establish Black Shield at Kadena AB.

At 08:00 hours on 22 May 1967, Mele Vojvodich departed Area 51 in Article 131 (60-6937) and headed west across California for his first refuelling. Having topped off, he accelerated to high Mach toward the next air-refuelling control point (ARCP) near Hawaii. A third rendezvous took place near Wake Island to ensure that he had enough reserve fuel to divert from an intended landing at Kadena to either Kunsan AB, South Korea, or Clark AFB in the Philippines, (some 1,200 miles/1931 km beyond Kadena) should weather over Okinawa deteriorate. When Mele arrived, however, the weather was fine and he let down for landing after an uneventful flight of just over six hours in duration. Had it not been for the deployment's secrecy, the flight could have been recognised as a new transpacific speed record.

Two days later Jack Layton set out to repeat Mele's flight, but aircraft 127 (60-6930) experienced an air data computer failure shortly after take-off. As a result, Jack lost important instrument readings on his Triple Display Indicator (TDI), which showed KEAS, Mach number and altitude read-outs. Loss of the TDI instrument was an abort item on his 'Go-No-Go' checklist, but Jack (like all the Oxcart team), was acutely aware of the pressure on the programme to succeed. He therefore chose to continue the flight toward Okinawa by calculating bypass door and inlet spike position schedule changes using temperature gauge indications. That careful action proved successful and Jack landed the second aircraft at Kadena in under six hours. Jack was met after engine shut-down by his old flying instructor and now A-12 Detachment (Det) commander, Col 'Slip' Slater, who asked him if there were any maintenance write-ups, to which Jack replied, 'Only the TDI'. 'When did you lose that?' 'Slip' pressed. 'Away back', answered the A-12 driver. 'How far away back?' continued the Colonel. 'Well, just after take-off actually', Jack admitted. 'You crazy SOB', 'Slip' laughed and never again mentioned the incident.

Jack Weeks left Area 51 on 26 May, but due to INS and radio problems, he was forced to divert into Wake Island. An Oxcart maintenance team arrived in a KC-135 from Okinawa the following day to prepare 129 (60-6932) for the final 'hop' to Kadena. After completing the journey, Jack's aircraft was soon declared fit for operational service along with 127 and 131. As a result, the Detachment was declared ready for operations on 29 May and following a weather reconnaissance flight the day after, it was determined that conditions over North Vietnam were ideal for an A-12 photo run.

Project Headquarters in Washington then placed Black Shield on alert for its first ever operational mission. Avionics specialists checked various systems and sensors and, at 16:00 hours, Mele Vojvodich and back-up pilot Jack Layton attended a mission alert briefing that included such details as the projected take-off and landing times, routes to and from the target area and a full intelligence briefing of the area to be overflown. At 22:00 hours (12 hours before planned take-of time) a review of the weather confirmed the mission was still on, so the pilots went to bed to ensure they got a full eight hours of 'crew rest'.

They awoke on the morning of the 31st to torrential rain – a new phenomenon for the 'desert dwelling' A-12s. The two pilots ate breakfast, dressed and proceeded to prepare for the mission, despite local rain. Since met. conditions over the 'collection area' were good, at 08:00 hours Kadena received a final clearance from Washington that Black Shield flight X001 was definitely on. The rain, however, continued without letup, casting serious doubts over the launch of the aircraft. The pilot had the final say in the matter since conditions were within Air Force take-off limits. Mele – well aware of the pressure on the programme to deliver – elected to launch. After brief medical checks, Mele and Jack both donned their S-901 full pressure suits and began breathing 100 per cent pure oxygen to purge their bodies of potentially harmful nitrogen. By taxi time, the rain was falling so heavily that a staff car had to lead Mele from the hanger to the end of the main

During his meritorious overflight mission against North Korea on 26 January 1968, Frank Murray captured some outstanding imagery. Among it was the shot (above) of the area around Wonsan where the USS *Pueblo* was thought to be held. He also photographed the hapless vessel itself (right). (National Archive via Tim Brown)

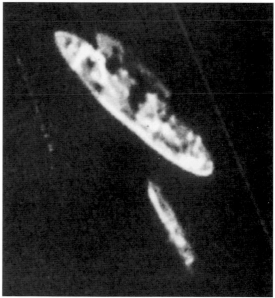

runway. After lining up for what would be the first instrument-guided take-off, on cue Mele engaged both afterburners and accelerated 131 rapidly down the runway to disappear completely into the rain and then upward through the drenching clouds.

A few minutes later he burst through cloud and flew 60-6937 up to 25,000 ft (7620 m) to top off the tanks from his waiting KC-135 tanker. Disengaged from the KC-135's boom, he accelerated and climbed to operational speed and altitude having informed Kadena ('home-plate') that aircraft systems were running as per the book and the back-up services of Jack Layton would not be required. He penetrated hostile airspace at Mach 3.2 and 80,000 ft (24384 m) during a so-called 'front door' entry over Haiphong, then continuing over Hanoi before exiting North Vietnam near Dien Bien Phu. A second air refuelling took place over Thailand, followed by another climb to speed and altitude, and a second penetration of North Vietnamese airspace made near the Demilitarised Zone (DMZ), after which he recovered the aircraft, after three instrument approaches in driving rain, back at Kadena. In all, the flight had lasted three hours and 40 minutes. Several SA-2s were fired at the aircraft but all detonated above and well behind their target. The 'photo take' was downloaded and sent by a special courier aircraft to the Eastman Kodak plant in Rochester, New York for processing. In all 60-6937's camera successfully photographed ten priority target categories, including 70 of the 190 known SAM sites.

A roster was set up for the six operational Black Shield pilots, on the basis that at least two were required to be on station at Kadena at any one time. Frank Murray recalls: 'We flew out to the OL [Operating Location] on US flag airlines, in Business Class, one guy at a time. Some allowance was made if a guy went on holiday and the like and when it was time for one pilot to be replaced the new guy would fly in, a week or two before the other left. We were all housed in an old Quonset Hut housing area, called "Morgan Manor". The Agency had them overhauled and they were deluxe by anyone's standards, a fresh coat of paint on the outside, but really well fitted out inside. A couple of good-sized portable buildings were joined to make the Mess Hall and offices and it was all located at the adjunct of a major intersection called Kadena Circle, near the base gates. The briefing room was situated on-base, within a small fenced compound close to our hanger area. Also inside the compound the Agency had a very large Log Periodic antenna tower, used for their radio traffic and to monitor our Birdwatcher equipment – unfortunately a typhoon blew the first one down before the footings were cured!

'The usual build-up for a Black Shield mission at the OL started with a pre-notice. With only two pilots and three aircraft to support the mission, both pilots were alerted to be ready for a "Go". Most of our missions were over North Vietnam, so we'd usually receive the alert about mid morning the day before the planned sortie. We then usually

Among the targets photographed by Frank Murray during his time over denied North Korean territory, was this airfield, Sanan Up. The search for *Pueblo* allowed previously arranged plans for overflights of the country to be instigated. (National Archive via Tim Brown)

conducted a pre-brief consisting of a weather forecast in the general area of interest; the intel [intelligence] guys would go over the expected areas of interest and the expected defences we were likely to face if we were detected and acted upon. Our ground crews would be busy readying the aircraft, the selected camera system and other recording devices. We always readied two aircraft for Southeast Asia missions. Both Oxcart pilots attended the briefings, one would be designated primary, the other standby, in case primary had to abort. The Agency was completely focused in ensuring the flight was "on time" no matter what. From memory, I think that the back-up aircraft was ready to launch should primary abort anytime up to completion of the first tanker top off.

'The day of the sortie, we'd attend the Mission Briefing, also there was the Det CO [Commanding Officer] and his assistant, the weather guy, an intel Officer and the Nav [navigation] section guys, who briefed the route of flight and where our tanker support would be. We were then told a special little bit about where we could expect help if we were downed – I don't think any of us had too much faith in this part of the briefing. This entire final briefing took no more than an hour to complete, then we were off to the suit room and have a little physical examination so that the flight surgeons could verify that we were still alive! I was never told if at this point they detected a slight increase in our blood pressure. Then the crew bus delivered us to the hanger, we'd get in and get on with it.'

During the first three months of Black Shield operations nine missions were successfully completed. One of those 'alerted' but subsequently aborted was to be Jack Layton's first operational flight. All had gone well until Jack plugged into the KC-135 just southwest of Okinawa. The boom operator's first remark to Jack as the A-12's fuel tanks began to fill was, 'You don't want to go supersonic with this aircraft, Sir'. The puzzled A-12 pilot enquired why, since there were no cockpit indications that supported such a remark and the aircraft seemed to be handling well. 'I don't think you'll want to go fast, Sir', the Boomer insisted, 'because the left side of your aircraft is missing'. After further consultation with him and other tanker crewmembers who went aft to view the unusual sight, Jack decided that prudence should dictate that he abort his first important mission, however reluctantly. As he turned back to Kadena, an F-102 interceptor was

This enlarged image from Murray's camera, caught these MiG-17 'Fresco' fighters in the open at Hwangju airfield. Such aircraft posed no threat to the A-12 whatsoever. (National Archive via Tim Brown)

scrambled from Naha AB, Okinawa, to serve as escort in the event of controllability problems. As the Delta Dagger drew alongside the crippled Cygnus, the '102 pilot reported that the A-12 had lost practically all of its left chine panels from nose to tail. In addition, large panels on the top of the wing (which also covered the top side of the wheel well) had also disappeared, allowing the chase pilot to see right through part of the aircraft's left wing. As some of these panels had broken loose, at least one had impacted the top of the left rudder, causing even more damage.

As the two aircraft descended below 20,000 ft (6096 m), they dipped into clouds and the A-12's cockpit fogged-up so badly that Jack was unable to see his hand in front of his face, let alone read his flight instruments. He quickly called for the F-102 pilot to report the A-12's attitude, since he was becoming very concerned that it might depart its flight envelope by stalling or diving. Relieved that he had remained within normal flight parameters, Jack managed to climb back out of the clouds. By turning the cockpit temperature control to full-hot, he managed to eliminate the humidity that had caused the fogging, but the hotter-than-normal cockpit soon became extremely uncomfortable. Nevertheless, he was able to safely recover back at Kadena without further incident.

By mid July, A-12 overflights had determined with a high degree of confidence that there were no surface-to-surface missiles in North Vietnam. However, such recce flights soon became invaluable, since they provided timely information to mission planners as to what SA-2 sites were occupied, as well as high quality bomb damage assessment (BDA) imagery.

From September to the end of December 1967, the three Black Shield-operated A-12s completed 13 operational missions, the highest period of activity being reached in October, when seven sorties were flown. One of Frank Murray's early sorties was a so-called 'double-looper'. Frank commenced his first photo run at an altitude above 80,000 ft (24384 m) on a track deep into North Vietnam with all systems functioning well. But as he was about to turn off his cameras before heading south toward his air refuelling rendezvous, his left engine started vibrating. This was shortly followed by a left inlet unstart. Frank recalled: 'I had my hands full for a while. In fact, I ended up having to shut the engine down. I

A more plausible threat to A-12 operations was posed by the SA-2 'Guideline' SAM. Frank Murray was able to photograph 12 of the 14 known North Korean SAM sites on his 26 January 1968 mission, including this SA-2 site. (National Archive via Tim Brown)

increased power on the good engine and flew it at maximum temperature for about an hour before I hooked up with the tanker. Because of the shut-down engine, I decided to divert into Takhli and the tanker crew relayed messages back to Kadena that I was diverting. Because I kept my radio calls to a minimum for security reasons, I didn't identify myself to the Takhli air traffic controllers until I was on final approach for landing. I landed without incident, but inadvertently screwed up a complete F-105 strike mission launch when I jettisoned the big brake chute on the main runway. I turned off the runway and sat there with the engine running and asked that the base commander come out to the aircraft as there were certain things I had to tell him. My presence was causing a pandemonium of curiosity; there was this most unusual black aircraft with no markings, the like of which nobody on that base had ever seen before, that had dropped in completely unannounced, disrupting a major operation and its pilot insisting on the base commander coming out to see him! While this was going on guys on base with cameras were clicking away like mad. Eventually they sent out the Thai base commander which was no good because I wanted the US base commander. He eventually arrived and (despite all

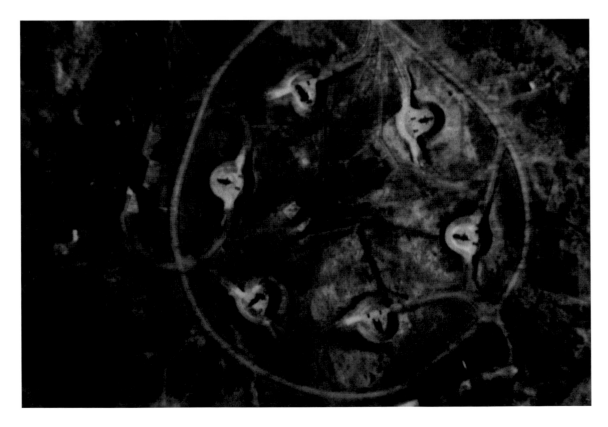

my disruptions to his war operations) was extremely helpful.'

After Frank's aircraft had been safely tucked away in an Agency U-2 facility on the base, the Air Force security Police had a field day confiscating the opportunists' film. An inspection of the left engine revealed that most of its moving parts had been 'shucked like corn from the cob' and were laying in the tail pipe and the afterburner. A recovery crew flew in a spare engine, but the aircraft had also sustained notable damage to the nacelle and to some of the nearby electrical wiring. It was decided that the jet would have to be flown back to Kadena 'low and slow' on 9 October. Frank explained: 'I got airborne and headed off south over the Gulf of Thailand, where I picked up an F-105 escort that led me out over South Vietnam. These changed places with a group of F-4s which covered me and my tanker before they broke off to return to their base. We then made our way via the Philippines, where I picked up another tanker which led me back to Kadena.'

While Frank was dealing with the in-flight emergency over North Vietnam, his attention had been diverted away from switching off the photographic equipment to the more pressing priority of controlling the aircraft. As he turned south, his still-operating camera had taken a series of oblique shots into China. Close analysis of those photos revealed eight tarpaulin-covered objects among a mass of other material along the large main rail link between Hanoi and Nanking. Further photo interpretation ascertained that the 'tarps' were flung over rail flatcars in an attempt to hide 152-mm self-propelled heavy artillery pieces. A great mass of other war materiel in the rail yards had been assembled for onward movement to North Vietnam during the oncoming winter season, when low clouds and poor visibility would hamper US bombing efforts to halt south-bound supply lines. A timely and highly valuable piece of strategic intelligence had therefore been gained on the back of Frank's troubled sortie, which allowed intelligence specialists a unique opportunity to track the further movement of those guns and supplies, which were obviously intended for use in future offensive actions.

DET F-101S AND MORE MISSIONS

Two F-101s from Area 51 were deployed to Kadena as part of Black Shield. They were positioned on the island by Air Force Ferry Squadron pilots and once there they were used to provide the detachment crews with proficiency training. One of their number was lost, together with its pilot, Walt King – the detachment weather officer – when it crashed immediately after take-off. The aircraft was never replaced.

During sortie number BX6732, flown by Denny Sullivan on 28 October 1967, the pilot received indications on his Radar Homing and Warning Receiver (RHWR) of almost continuous radar activity focused on his A-12, while both inbound and outbound over North Vietnam. Among this activity were signals indicating the launch of a single SA-2. Two days later, during the course of sortie BX6743, Sullivan was again flying high over North Vietnam when two SAM sites tracked him on his first pass. On his second pass, while approaching Hanoi from the East, he again noted he was being tracked on radar, then, over the next few minutes, he counted no less than eight SA-2 detonations in 'the general area though none particularly close'. This was the first occasion on which the North Vietnamese had employed a salvo-launch technique. After the aircraft had recovered back at Kadena without further incident, a post-flight inspection revealed that a tiny piece of shrapnel had penetrated the lower wing fillet of his aircraft and become lodged against the support structure of the wing tank – history would prove this to be the only enemy 'damage' inflicted on a 'Blackbird'.

Just 48 hours after the seizure of USS *Pueblo*, Frank Murray conducted the first overflight of North Korea in an A-12. Without the earlier contingency planning that had been done concerning possible North Korean overflights, such a rapid response would not have been possible; indeed, an even earlier mission, launched on 25 January, was aborted owing to aircraft failure. (CIA)

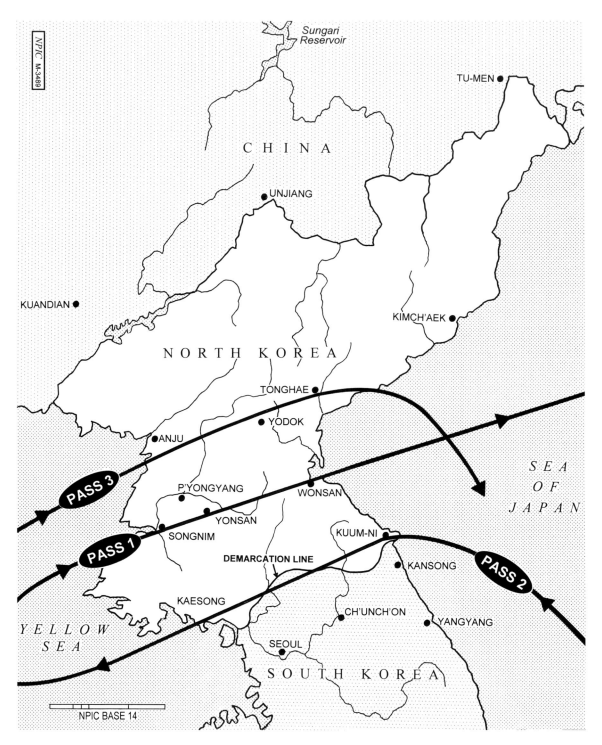

On a later mission, Jack Layton accidentally violated Chinese airspace during a flight over North Vietnam when his INS failed. Since the aircraft was flying on autopilot, Jack did not immediately notice the glitch that resulted in a

This incredible map shows the routes flown by Murray for his three passes over North Korea. The North Koreans apparently remained unaware of the A-12's presence until later being informed by the Chinese that their country had been overflown. Note how pass 1 took the aircraft directly over Wonsan.

Just visible here are the twin fins of A-12 '937, which was surrounded by other aircraft on Wake island after it was forced to divert there on 7 June 1968. (via Frank Murray)

further failure of the autopilot to execute a pre-programmed turn, causing him to 'penetrate the bamboo curtain'. After turning south and getting back to an approximate course toward the ARCP over Thailand, Jack had difficulty finding the tankers. He later recalled that the clouds were low and the visibility was poor: 'I got the aircraft up in a bank to search for the tankers but the visibility from an A-12 is very poor; you can look down and see the ground but you can't look inside the turn because of the canopy roof. I'd just about reached the point where I was about to divert to Takhli due to the lack of fuel when I finally saw the tankers. We got together and I was able to complete the mission even though the INS wasn't working.'

TARGET, NORTH KOREA

During 1967, a total of 41 A-12 missions was alerted, of which 22 were actually granted approval for flight. Between 1 January and 31 March 1968, 17 missions were alerted, of which seven were flown, four over North Vietnam and three over North Korea.

In a CIA document classified Top Secret, which was approved for release in June 2002, the rationale was outlined for Oxcart reconnaissance missions against North Korea. It stated that the belligerent pronouncements by North Korean civil and military leaders and an increase in the number and expanded scope of North Korean probes along the DMZ, coupled with their efforts to establish the structure for guerrilla operations in the Republic, had established a critical requirement for accurate intelligence. It further noted that satellite photo missions had not provided adequate imagery of North Korea to satisfy the requirement and that ground collection of this intelligence was becoming increasingly difficult; taken together, this had made an accurate estimate of capabilities and intentions all but impossible. It continued that the operational concept could now be accomplished on a 24-hour alert basis, using

Oxcart operational Black Shield assets in place at Kadena, without coverage degradation of targets in North Vietnam. Three passes traversing the target areas, east to west or west to east could be accomplished utilising two air refuellings, or two passes of similar orientation could be executed with a single air refuelling. All routes provided flexibility to adjust photographic flight lines to meet changing weather and/or target requirements. It further noted that penetration of denied territory would be accomplished at 76,000 ft (23165 m) or above at Mach 3.1. Emergency or missed air refuelling divert bases would be in South Korea, but in all other circumstances launch and recovery would be from Kadena. In the document's air defence analysis it notes that there were 13 known SA-2 sites in North Korea at the time and that as no airborne jamming would be undertaken by other US airborne assets, the threat of a possible SAM reaction from North Korean SA-2 systems was deemed to be greater than in the skies above North Vietnam. For this reason, Oxcart flight over SAM-defended areas of North Korea was to be conducted above 80,000 ft (24384 m) and at a speed of Mach 3.2 to provide maximum invulnerability. It also noted that there were 30 or more Soviet SA-2 C-band and possibly S-band sites in the Vladivostok area, the furthest known sites to the south of this enclave being approximately 75 miles (121 km) from the North Korean border. In relation to the airborne threat, it stated that there were no aircraft in the North Korean air order of battle that were a threat to Oxcart. However, it noted that the Soviet Yakovlev Yak-28P 'Firebar' had an interceptor capability against the A-12 and that 21 such aircraft were based at Spassk Dalnij East airfield, located approximately 175 miles (282 km) from the closest Oxcart flight path, 125 miles (201 km) north of the North Korean border. In summary it concluded that although a somewhat higher total threat potential existed for the proposed mission compared to North Vietnam, the surprise element could well prevent an effective response, particularly during early sorties. In a final note – especially in relation to any unfortunate

Above: Agency pilots who flew the A-12 operationally were awarded the CIA Intelligence Star for Valour on 26 June 1968. From left to right are Mel Vojvodich (just in shot), Dennis Sullivan, Admiral Rufus Taylor (Deputy Director of the CIA), Jack Layton, Ken Collins and Frank Murray. (via Frank Murray)

Right: The coveted CIA Intelligence Star for Valour. (via Dennis Sullivan)

'incidents' – it noted that in the event that any such sortie required implementation of an official contingency, the aircraft would be described as an unarmed reconnaissance aircraft, engaged in surveillance of activities in the demilitarised zone between North and South Korea and that intentional overflight of North Korea would be denied. On a footnote, at the bottom of a sample route map, it added that photographic resolution would be in the order of one to three and a half feet and that two eastbound and one westbound pass over the north would take a total of just 17 minutes to complete. Despite this, the US State Department vetoed the plan.

In late 1967 DCI Richard Helms requested that the Committee on Imagery Requirements and Exploitation (COMIREX) prepare a briefing document concerning reconnaissance of North Korea. Two earlier pieces of work in this regard had been carried out one – as alluded to earlier, by the Commander US Forces Korea – and the other by the Board of National Estimates, which had recommended: 'increased efforts in the collection

Eight A-12s sat in long-term storage at Palmdale after their retirement in 1968. The two-seat 'Titanium Goose' (towards the rear of the hangar) still sports its two-tone paint scheme. (CIA)

and analysis of political, economic and military information, particularly on the subjects of North Korean intentions toward the South ...'

The Top Secret COMIREX memo, dated 9 October 1967, drew reference to both of these earlier recommendations and also made reference to other reconnaissance assets that had been available for use against North Korea, including, in sub selection a, of paragraph 3, KH-4 Mission 1101 [satellite] during the period 21–28 September 1967 that had provided usable photography of over 85 per cent of North Korea, and in sub section c, of the same paragraph, that noted: 'U-2 – North Korea was last covered by the U-2 Tackle program on 31 July 1965. The program is currently stood down; but even if a U-2 mission were attempted against North Korea, it would now have only limited access because of the SAM sites which protect much of the interior of the country.'

The memo ended by observing that Black Shield could – subject to weather – provide the necessary coverage of the country within a short period of time and that this would be of 'substantial

assistance in correcting the intelligence deficit on the North Korean military posture and in providing a new baseline against which to check other intelligence as may be available'. Yet again, however, no immediate action was taken.

THE *PUEBLO* AFFAIR

In an April 1965 intelligence planning meeting it had been decided to establish a small fleet of Sigint vessels, similar to the Soviet fleet of 40 such ships which operated near the United States and in many other strategic points around the world. That decision received prompt approval from Director of Defense Research and Engineering, Dr Harold Brown, and from Deputy Secretary of Defense Cyrus Vance for the implementation of a two-phase plan.

In Phase One, USS *Banner* was transformed into AGER-1 (Auxiliary General Environmental Research Ship number one), and duly steamed out of Washington State's Puget Sound Naval Shipyard on the first of its planned 16 sea patrols in the western Pacific. Meanwhile, two Army supply ships, FS-344 and FS-389, were re-christened as USS *Pueblo* (AGER-2) and USS *Palm Beach* (AGER-3). By 1 December 1967, the extensive modification programme was complete and *Pueblo* joined its sister ship, *Banner*, in Yokosuka harbour, Japan. By then Banner was a veteran on intelligence surveillance duties. While at Yokosuka, a six-month schedule was drafted covering nine separate missions, five of which were tasked by the NSA.

Pueblo's first sortie was tasked by the US Navy and called for the ship to 'sample the electronic environment off the east coast of North Korea' and to 'intercept and conduct surveillance of Soviet naval units operating in the Tsushima Straights'. The risk estimate was assessed as 'minimal'. A request for final approval was contained in the 'Monthly Reconnaissance Schedule for January 1968', which was maintained by the Joint Chiefs of Staff's Joint Reconnaissance Center (JCS-JRC). On 29 December 1967, approval was received from the proper agencies (the JCS, the CIA, the NSA and the State Department) and from officials (Deputy Secretary of Defense Paul Nitze and the NSC's 303 Committee).

Ken Collins finally made it to Hawaii after innumerable attempts to launch from Wake island. He was attempting to ferry an A-12 back to Groom Lake in 1968, following termination of the Oxcart programme. (Paul F. Crickmore Collection)

On 5 January 1968, the unprotected *Pueblo* sailed as ordered on its maiden voyage for the east coast of a hostile-natured nation, North Korea. Onboard was a crew of six officers, two civilians and 75 enlisted men. Just 18 days later, during the night of 23 January, the ship's radio operator managed to get off an emergency signal. 'We Need Help! We are Holding Emergency Destruction! We Need Support! SOS. SOS. SOS. Please Send Assistance! SOS. SOS. SOS. We Are Being Boarded!' The last sentence clearly stated what was happening aboard the beleaguered vessel, and with one sailor dead and the rest of the crew captured the year-long nightmare for Lt-Cdr Lloyd Bucher and his crew was just beginning.

In response to the incident, President Johnson summoned his top advisors to a meeting at the White House the very next day, to plan a response and agree a course of action. Later that same day, DCI Richard Helms despatched a top-secret memo to Special Assistant to the President Walt Rostow, Secretary of Defense Robert McNamara, Under Secretary of State Nicholas Katzenbach, Deputy Secretary of Defense Paul Nitze and Chairman of the JCS Gen Earle Wheeler, in which he referred to the earlier meeting and confirmed that he was,

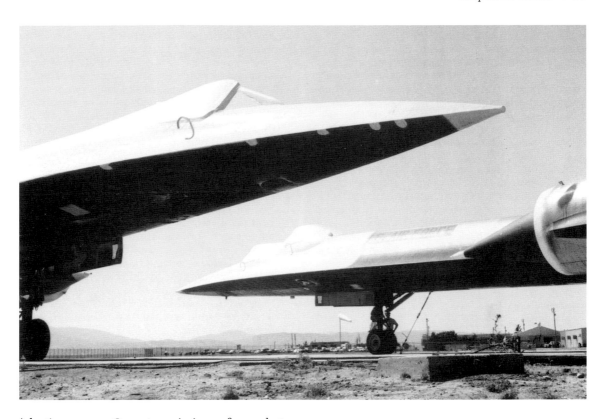

At Palmdale in 1980 these A-12s, including the two-seater, were cocooned and tethered to protect them from the ravages of open storage. (John Andrews)

'alerting an Oxcart mission for photo reconnaissance of North Korea'. It continued that, 'The Oxcart mission has been alerted to take off [deleted] on 25th January at 2100 EST (1100/ 26 January [delete]) and return four and a half hours later. The film will be off loaded immediately and airlifted to Eastman Kodak, Rochester, New York, to arrive at approximately 0430 EST on 27 January. The processed film will be delivered immediately to NPIC with an arrival time of 1440 EST on 28 January.' Point 3 in the memo noted, 'The weather forecast for this mission indicates Category II (25% or less cloud cover) weather conditions for the target area.' Finally, point 4 noted, 'No additional resources or support over and above those normally used on Oxcart North Vietnam operational sorties will be required for this mission.'

The draft CIA plan to overfly North Korea was about to be implemented in full. In total three A-12 sorties would be flown as a consequence of the capture of *Pueblo*. The first of these was attempted by Jack Weeks on 25 January – just 24 hours after the ship was captured; however, a malfunction on the A-12 resulted in an abort shortly after take-off. The next day another attempt was made, this time by Frank Murray, whose task was to complete three passes over North Korea, primarily to establish where *Pueblo* was being held, but also to determine if North Korea was about to embark

upon some form of large-scale follow-up ground action. Frank now recalls A-12 mission BX6847: 'I left Kadena and topped-off to the north of the island. The flight paths were designed to avoid overflying any part of Japan or China. Entry into denied territory was made above 80,000 ft [24384 m] and in excess of Mach 3.1 due to the SAM threat. The first of three passes started at the centre of the west coast of North Korea and with camera on; the direction of flight was basically east, northeast. This pass terminated when the A-12 cleared the harbour area at Wonsan, where it was believed the *Pueblo* was being held. As I approached Wonsan I thought that I could see the *Pueblo* through my view sight. The harbour appeared to be all iced up except at the very entrance, and it looked as though she was sitting off to the right of the main entrance. I switched the camera off and completed a teardrop shaped turn over the Sea of Japan and with camera on, I coasted in for a second pass, heading in a westerly direction with the track displaced to the south of my first pass. Clearing the coast, I again switched the camera off, conducted another turn, this time over the Yellow Sea, before running-in, camera on, for my third and final pass, again on a northeast track, but north of the first pass. This mission was very busy from a pilot's perspective, since there were multiple passes all carried out in close quarters, with several turns made after relatively short camera runs; bear in mind that most Southeast Asia missions consisted of one camera run on a single heading, followed by another pass later, after refuelling on another single heading/pass. The onboard Electronic Warfare System never indicated that the North Koreans detected or reacted against my overflight, although I was later told that the Chinese informed them that they were being overflown. Recovery back into Kadena was without incident and I think that the entire Detachment knew that we'd done a good job. As I taxied back to the hanger, our Det Commander, Col 'Slip' Slater, was waiting and gave me a quizzical look as to how it went. I gave him a thumbs-up and he drank my shot of Pinch mission whisky – he was and remains one of the finest "managers" I've ever met. The National Photographic Interpretation Center (NPIC) rated the imagery gained from the mission as "Very Good". Of the 14 known SAM sites in North Korea, 12 were photographed and their missiles counted'.

As usual, 'the take' was immediately flown to the 67th RTS at Yokota for initial processing, where it was soon established that North Korea was not intending some form of follow-up action – at least not immediately. Just three days after Frank Murray's highly successful mission, Lt Gen Joseph Carroll, Director of the NRO, fired-off a memo to the Chairman of the Joint Chiefs of Staff, noting the following:

'1. CINCPAC and the Defence Intelligence Agency have conducted independent assessments of photography acquired by BX Mission 6847, flown over North Korea on 26 January. From these assessments, it has been determined that while much valuable photography and information were obtained, major deficiencies in our intelligence holdings still remain in the following target categories:

a. Jet Capable Airfields: Current overhead photography is still required of seven major jet capable airfields in North Korea. Included is the important [Ilyushin] Il-28 ['Beagle'] bomber base at Uiju which is the normal operating base for a majority of these aircraft. Of 80 Il-28s currently estimated in the North Korean inventory, only 12 were located by the 26 January mission. The seriousness of this coverage gap was further aggravated [text deleted – remains classified].

b. Naval Order of Battle [OB]: Coverage was not acquired of the naval facility at Mayang Do which normally serves the North Korean submarine fleet, nor was coverage of several

key naval bases in northeastern Korea. The requirement for current naval OB information was emphasized by the identification of three Komor-class guided-missile patrol boats on the recent BX mission. These boats, which were observed at Wonsan, increased our estimate of their holdings to seven. Coverage of the important naval bases in the northeast, therefore, is required to insure our awareness of any important changes to North Korean naval OB in that area.

c. Ground Force Activity: Additional high resolution photography of the areas covered by the 26 January mission is essential to our continued military awareness of significant changes to ground force OB and related installations and activities. In addition, reconnaissance coverage of the North Korean border area adjacent to China as well as most of the northeastern segment of North Korea is still required to establish a high resolution data base by which to measure military activities in these areas.

2. In order to satisfy the outstanding requirement outlined above, CINCPAC has specifically and urgently requested that an additional Black Shield mission be flown over North Korea. Based upon an assessment made within the Defence Intelligence Agency, I concur in the CINPAC position and recommend that the Joint Chiefs of Staff endorse this requirement and seek authority for additional Black Shield reconnaissance of North Korea.'

However, US State Department officials were extremely wary of endorsing a second mission over North Korea after the *Pueblo* event. The diplomatic scars left by the 1960 Powers incident were still sensitive eight years after the event. It was not until Brig-Gen Paul Bacalis had briefed Secretary of State Dean Rusk on the specific mission objectives and assured him that the aircraft would only be in North Korean airspace for seven minutes (two passes or 'photo lines'), that the State Department gave its blessing and the sortie, BX6853, was flown on 19 February 1968.

On 8 May 1968, Jack Layton launched on sortie BX6858 and headed out on the A-12's third mission to North Korea. Unknown to him at the time, his mission was to prove the final operational flight of the Oxcart programme. That sortie also experienced a moment of tension when Jack was on his way back to Kadena having completed a successful mission. After a high-speed flight, 'milky white fingers' began slowly clawing their way across the windshield. Having already experienced this 'white-out' phenomenon to a lesser degree during a stateside training sortie, Jack was aware of the problem, which was caused by frictional heating on

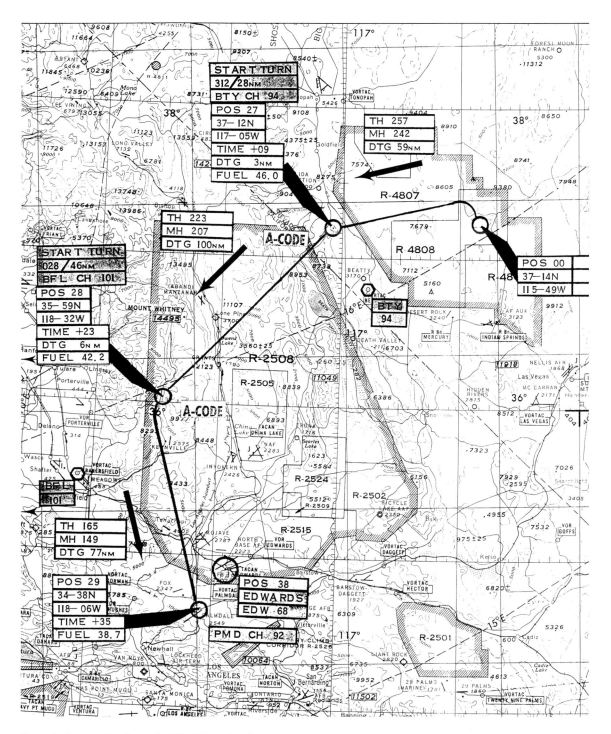

The following data boxes appear on the pilot's chart:

START TURN
312/28NM
BTY CH 94
POS 27
37—12N
117—05W
TIME +09
DTG 3NM
FUEL 46.0

TH 257
MH 242
DTG 59NM

TH 223
MH 207
DTG 100NM

A-CODE

START TURN
028/46NM
BFL CH 101
POS 28
35—59N
118—32W
TIME +23
DTG 6NM
FUEL 42.2

POS 00
37—14N
115—49W

BTY 94

A-CODE

TH 165
MH 149
DTG 77NM

POS 29
34—38N
118—06W
TIME +35
FUEL 38.7

POS 38
EDWARDS
EDW 68

PMD CH 92

the windscreen to the point that the glue between the windscreen's glass laminations became viscous and turned completely opaque. Proceeding on instruments all the way to landing, Jack completed a successful ground-directed radar approach for a safe recovery back to Kadena.

This pilot's chart was used by Frank Murray on the final A-12 flight (made in Article 131), to Palmdale's storage facility from the Ranch. The flight was performed on 21 June 1968, the final shut-down having come very quickly as the SR-71A was coming on line and taking over the A-12's missions. The change in aircraft type brought with it a change in operator, from CIA to US Air Force.

Although the procurement of such intelligence information was not of direct benefit to Lt-Cdr Bueher and his crew, who were beaten and not released by their North Korean captors until nearly a year had passed, such a 'hot-spot, quick-look' capability was considered an early and important achievement of the Oxcart programme, clearly demonstrating the ability of manned reconnaissance vehicles to respond with minimal lead times to international incidents of political and military importance. At the same time, the Pueblo incident ended the Navy's sea borne foray into the world of Sigint trawling, the two remaining AGERs being scrapped soon after *Pueblo's* seizure.

OXCART CLOSE-DOWN

It seems almost unbelievable that during the very month Oxcart was finally declared operational (November 1965), and before the programme had the opportunity of fully vindicating itself, moves were already afoot to close it down. It was during that month that a memorandum was circulated within the Bureau of the Budget (BoB) that expressed serious concerns at the costs of Oxcart and Senior Crown (the SR-71 programme). That BoB memo questioned the requirement for the overall number of high-performance aircraft and doubted the necessity for separate 'covert' CIA and 'overt' USAF operations. Its writer proposed several less costly alternatives, recommending that the A-12s be phased out by September 1966 and that all further procurement of SR-71s should stop. Copies of the memorandum were circulated in certain circles within the Department of Defense and the CIA, together with the suggestion that these organisations explore the alternatives set out in the paper. Since the SR-71 was not scheduled to become operational until September 1966, the Secretary of Defense quite rightly declined to accept the proposal. In July 1966, BoB officials proposed that a tri-agency study group be set up to again establish ways of reducing the costs of the two programmes. After the study was completed, a meeting was convened on 12 December 1966 and a vote was taken on each of the three alternatives that had been proposed:

1. To maintain the status quo and continue both fleets at current approval levels.
2. To mothball all A-12 aircraft, but maintain the Oxcart capability by sharing the SR-71 between SAC and the CIA.
3. To terminate the Oxcart fleet in January 1968 (assuming an operational readiness date of September 1967 for the SR-71) and assign all missions to the SR-71 fleet.

Three out of four votes cast were in favour of option three. The BoB's memorandum was transmitted to President Johnson on 16 December despite protestations from the CIA's Richard Helms, who was the sole dissenting voice in the vote. Twelve days later Johnson accepted the BoB's recommendations and directed that the Oxcart programme be terminated by 1 January 1968.

As the war in Vietnam escalated and the results of Black Shield's outstanding work became apparent to a privileged few, the wisdom of the earlier phase-out decision was called into question. As a result, the rundown lagged and the question was re-opened. A new feasibility and cost study of Oxcart was completed in the spring of 1968, and despite the continuing objections raised by Richard Helms, the original decision to terminate the programme was reaffirmed on 16 May 1968 by the Secretary of Defense. This decision was further endorsed by President Johnson five days later during his weekly luncheon with his principal advisors.

Project officials decided that 8 June 1968 would be the earliest date to begin the redeployment from Kadena back to the States. During the intervening period, sorties would be restricted to those essential for maintaining flight safety and pilot proficiency. Those aircraft back at Area 51 were to be flown to Palmdale and placed in storage by 7 June. Meanwhile at Kadena, preparations were being made for the A-12 ferry flights back to the United States. Mission sensors were downloaded for the final time, and low-time/high-performance engines were replaced with less highly-tuned units. FCFs were flown to confirm each aircraft's readiness for the transpacific ferry flights.

During one such test flight, Frank Murray got airborne on 2 June 1968 and headed out south of Okinawa well away from unfriendly land-based radars. The well-worn test and training route was tear-drop shaped, pointing toward the Philippines, where first a long, shallow, 190° turn was initiated back toward Kadena. This high and fast cruise leg continued over the base, and was followed by a tighter let-down tear-drop pattern which brought the aircraft in towards final approach prior to landing. Having taken fuel from a tanker, Frank flew the full route, but recalled that the right engine would not go into bypass until the aircraft reached Mach 3, as opposed to the normal speed of Mach 2.6. The flight continued without further incident until Aircraft 129 passed over Kadena, where Frank began what was to be a normal deceleration and decent. At that point, he discovered that the right engine would not come out of bypass. As deceleration continued, the inevitable happened. Since the bypass system continued to deliver most of the air to the afterburner section and very little to the combustion section, the engine flamed out. Once

129 was subsonic, Frank restarted the engine and recovered into Kadena without further incident. It was obvious that the right engine would have to be changed to solve this problem.

On 4 June, Jack Weeks left Kadena in 129, with the intention of finishing the FCF. He completed a 34,000-lb (15422-kg) fuel off-load from the tanker, accelerated and climbed away – that was the last anyone ever saw again of either pilot or aircraft. Forty-two minutes into the flight, the Birdwatcher at Kadena received a signal from channel 54, indicating that the starboard engine EGT was in excess of 1,580°F (860°C). Twenty-two seconds later, Birdwatcher repeated the same signal, along with a transmission from channel 7, indicating that fuel flow to the same engine was less than 7,500 lb (3402 kg) per hour. Just eight more short seconds on and a third and final transmission from aircraft 129's Birdwatcher was received, again it repeated the earlier information from channels 54 and 7, this time, however, it also included a signal from channel 3, ominously indicating that the aircraft was now at or below 68,500 ft (20879 m). From this limited evidence, it is reasonable to conclude that some kind of malfunction involving an over-temperature and low fuel flow on the right engine had somehow contributed to what appears to have been a catastrophic failure and subsequent aircraft break-up. Not a trace of wreckage was ever found and it is particularly ironic and an especially cruel twist of fate to lose such a highly competent and professional pilot on one of the very last flights in the Oxcart programme.

The two remaining A-12s on Okinawa (Article Numbers 127 and 131) were to be ferried back to Area 51 before being positioned to Palmdale. On 7 June 1968, Frank Murray boarded 131 for the flight back to the US. He topped-off his tanks near Iwo Jima and then flew a 'hot leg' to Wake Island, where he decelerated for another refuelling. Before 'plugging in', he noticed a high rate of fuel flow on the right engine. Through the small rear-view periscope, he saw that the right engine was leaving an unburnt trail of fuel behind the aircraft. He told the tanker crew that he had a fuel leak and that he would have to dump much of the remaining JP-7 before landing at Wake Island. After the recovery team arrived, the afterburner fuel line was replaced and the aircraft was flight tested. Next, Ken Collins flew 131 at subsonic speed into Hawaii's Hickam AFB for a full service prior to flying the final leg home. It was found that the airframe-mounted gearbox was out of alignment and was vibrating so badly that it caused fuel lines to break. From Hickam, it took Frank Murray three more attempts before he was able to coax the reluctant A-12 back to the 'Ranch'. Meanwhile, Denny Sullivan had flown the last remaining Oxcart aircraft back from Kadena to Nevada on 9 June in just five hours and 29 minutes.

After it was all over, Maj Bill Wuest, the poetic weather officer at Area 51, penned the following rhyming couplets in honour of those two record-breaking return trips.

Congratulations from the Bard of Beatty [a settlement near Area 51]– 19 June 1968
When Denny rushed across the Pond in Five-plus-Twenty-Nine,
All hopes had sunk for Ken and Frank to break the record time.
But nothing daunted, that slow pair conspired to save the day,
With greatest skill and cunning broke a record anyway.
Eleven days it took them both to make that ocean trip.
The slowest 'Record', high-speed flight was now within their grip!
That Record time they'll surely keep until the final day.
For Beale's crews will never want to take their TIME away!

The final flight of an A-12 took place on 21 June 1968 when the last remaining Cygnus, number 131, was ferried from the 'Ranch' to Palmdale by Frank Murray. When the aircraft reached the Lockheed plant, company maintenance technicians drained all its fuel and hydraulic lines, and Mel Rushing skillfully interwove all nine remaining Oxcart aircraft into a tightly-regimented, sardine-like parking array in a corner of one of the large hangers. Here they remained for more than 20 years, before being dispersed to museums.

On 26 June 1968, Deputy Director of the CIA, Vice-Admiral Rufus Taylor, presided over a ceremony at Area 51 where he presented the CIA Intelligence Star for Valour to Ken Collins, Jack Layton, Frank Murray, Denny Sullivan and Mele Vojvodich for their participation in Black Shield. The posthumous award to Jack Weeks was accepted by his widow. The Legion of Merit was presented to Col 'Slip' Slater and to his deputy, Col Amundson. In addition, the Air Force Outstanding Unit Award was presented to members of the Oxcart Detachment, the 1129th Special Activities Squadron, also known as 'The Road Runners'.

The long-standing debate concerning whether Oxcart or a programme known as Senior Crown should carry forward the strategic-reconnaissance baton, had, after three years, been resolved and the former was vanquished. In early March 1968, SR-71s began arriving at Kadena to take over the Black Shield commitment.

Table of operational missions flown during Black Shield

Date	Mission number
31/05/67	X001
10/06/67	X003
20/06/67	BX6705
30/06/67	BX6706
13/07/67	BX6708
19/07/67	BX6709
20/07/67	BX6710
21/08/67	BX6716
31/08/67	BX6718
16/09/67	BX6722
17/09/67	BX6723
04/10/67	BX6725
06/10/67	BX6727
15/10/67	BX6728
18/10/67	BX6729
28/10/67	BX6732
29/10/67	BX6733
30/10/67	BX6734
08/12/67	BX6737
10/12/67	BX6738
15/12/67	BX6739
16/12/67	BX6740
04/01/68	BX6842
05/01/68	BX6843
26/01/68	BX6847 North Korean mission
16/02/68	BX6851
19/02/68	BX6853 North Korean mission
08/03/68	BX6856
06/05/68	BX6858 North Korean mission

TAGBOARD AND SENIOR BOWL
Chapter 3

Following on from the 'political fall-out' of the U-2/Gary Powers shoot down, a meeting between Kelly Johnson and Dr Eugene Fubini of the DoD's Office of Research and Engineering took place early in 1962, during which Kelly was asked if it would be possible to develop a small-scale version of the A-12 that could be droned, carry a reasonable reconnaissance payload and possess similar performance characteristics to that anticipated for the full-size manned A-12. Fubini believed that were such a parallel development possible, it would afford the President a choice between a manned or unmanned platform from which to conduct 'reconnaissance of critical denied areas'.

Perhaps not surprisingly, Kelly responded that such a development was entirely feasible and that its development timescale would be compatible with that of the full-scale platform. He further suggested that the drone could be launched from a modified Oxcart vehicle. In a memo to Secretary of Defense McNamara, dated 26 September 1962, Dr Joseph Charyk, Director of the National Reconnaissance Office, noted that the projected

A single broad-chord, low aspect-ratio pylon supported the D-21 drone above the M-21 mother ship, as seen here on the first combination prior to the first D-21/M-21 flight from Groom Lake. A bottle of compressed air in the pylon aided drone separation. (Lockheed ADP)

drone, now known as Project Tagboard, 'appears to offer an alternative means to the A-12 and satellite systems for the purpose of overflight photography, but' he went on, 'It seems to me that the drone would provide no better overflight capability than the A-12 will provide and, from my assessment, the political considerations in sending a drone on this type of mission are not significantly different from the political considerations in manned overflight'. He did, however, recognise that a scaled-down version of the A-12 would result in a vehicle with an equally reduced radar cross section, making the enemy's task of tracking the drone during clandestine overflight operations more difficult to achieve.

During a meeting between McNamara and DCI Allen Dulles, on 5 October, it was agreed to proceed with the initial stages of Tagboard. However, in view of the system's technical uncertainties, it was further agreed that the programme would be carefully reviewed after an initial study and feasibility phase had been completed. A subsequent meeting between Dr Charyk and Dr Herbert Scoville, CIA Deputy Director (Research), determined that management responsibility for the project should, as in the case of Oxcart, lie with the CIA and that the DoD should assign an individual to the Agency who was both 'knowledgeable and enthusiastic' for the programme.

On 9 October 1962, Kelly provided a written proposal for a feasibility study of the project to the Assistant Director, OSA, and a completion date for the work was set at 2 January 1963. In a memo to

Initially, large aerodynamic fairings were used to cover the drone's intake and exhaust nozzle, with the intention that these should be jettisoned prior to launch. This shedding process proved so difficult to master, however, that the fairings were omitted for the four flights in which drone separation was to be attempted. The M-21 shown here is Article 134, which survived the programme and is on display at the Museum of Flight in Seattle. (via Lockheed)

Herb Scoville dated 17 October, Dr Charyk stated that: 'NRO management responsibility for this development is assigned to the Director, Program B (AD/OSD)', and that he, Dr Charyk, 'was prepared to assign Lt-Col Henry Howard from the NRO Staff to the Director, Program B, for this important task' (in a classified memo to the DCI, from Herb Scoville and dated 12 June 1963, the later noted that: 'Nothing further was heard from the NRO Staff on Colonel Howard's nomination to this Agency' – an indication of the friction that had developed between the NRO and the CIA at this time). Nine days later, Scoville responded to Charyk's memo, and confirmed that: 'Colonel Jack C. Ledford, USAF, Director, Program B, has assumed managerial responsibility for the AQ-12 drone project'.

While Lockheed was conducting Tagboard's feasibility study, the OSA was busy soliciting camera proposals for the AQ-12 from likely manufacturers. On 3 December 1962 firm proposals were received from Eastman-Kodak, Perkin-Elmer Corporation, ITEK Corporation and the HYCON Manufacturing Company.

Both Charyk's and Scoville's respective departments closely analysed Kelly's feasibility

Above: Both M-21s were finished in a combination of black paint and bare titanium. The D-21was finished in a similar fashion, although when the programme became Senior Bowl and the B-52 became mother ship, the D-21B drones were generally painted black overall. (via Lockheed)

studies and recommended that the development of Tagboard should proceed, a decision further endorsed by both the Secretary of Defense and the DCI during a subsequent meeting. Consequently, on 28 February 1963, Lockheed was given the go-ahead for the procurement of 20 drones and for modifications to be made to two A-12s into drone-launch configurations; this was confirmed in an official letter from the CIA dated 20 March 1963. However, ill feeling between the CIA's deputy Director for Research, Herb Scoville, and the NRO's newly appointed Director, Dr Brockway McMillan, continued to deteriorate as the latter attempted to wrest control of Tagboard away from the CIA and over to the USAF. During the afternoon of 4 June 1963, Dr McMillan signed a memo to Herb Scoville, and the Director of Program D, assigning responsibility for conducting Project Tagboard to Col Leo Geary, USAF, Director of Program D! The gloves were off and the fight was certainly set to continue.

Earlier that year, Bob Murphy received a telephone call from his boss Robert Pouc, who informed him that he intended to promote 'Murph' to superintendent. Lockheed was carrying out modifications to Air Force U-2s which would enable them to utilise the more

powerful J75 engine, and 'Murph' was to head-up the programme. Delighted by the news, he soon received yet another phone call, this time from Kelly's secretary requesting his presence. Kelly said, 'Murph I'm going to promote you to superintendent', to which Bob replied, 'Yes, I know'. 'How do you know? I've only just told you'. It was his second promotion that day!

But what Kelly had in mind was something radically different from 'Murph's' earlier promotion. The ADP boss showed his newest superintendent some sketches of an altogether strange-looking beast, designated D-21. Johnson instructed 'Murph' to 'find a building for housing the necessary engineering and build them'.

Initially the Lockheed programme manager for Tagboard was Rus Daniel, but when he became involved in the development of the RS-12, responsibility for the D-21 became the purview of Art Bradley. Construction got underway in building 199 at Burbank and by June 1963 a D-21 had been mated to its mother ship. The launch platforms were A-12 serial numbers 60-6940 and 60-6941 and to avoid confusion with the single-seat reconnaissance version they were referred to as M-21s (the 'M' standing for Mother).

Built primarily from titanium, the D-21 had a frontal area RCS of just 2.15 sq ft (0.2 m²) at a 15° depression angle. It had a range of 1,250 nm (1,439 miles; 2316 km), cruised at Mach 3.3 and possessed an altitude capability of 90,000 ft (27432 m). It was powered by a Marquardt RJ-43-MA-11 ramjet and, once released from the modified A-12 by a Launch Control Officer (LCO)

Inflight refuelling remained an important part of operations, even with the D-21 attached., a refuelling hook up being used to position the combination prior to drone launch. (via Lockheed)

sitting in what had been the aircraft's Q-bay, the drone flew its sortie independently. The D-21's INS had programmed into it the desired track, flight profile, camera on and off points and bank angles, allowing it to satisfactorily execute the perfect photo-recce sortie. COMIREX controlled the classification of film for Tagboard, Oxcart and other blackworld reconnaissance projects. For the Tagboard programme, each mission would be classified Top Secret, with the handling caveat 'No Foreign Dissemination'. To further protect the platform's code name (Tagboard), each frame was allocated the random, non-aligned code word Chess. With its camera run completed, the drone's INS sent signals to the autopilot system to descend the vehicle to its 'feet wet' film collection point. The entire palletised camera unit was then ejected

and allowed to parachute towards the ground. As the drone continued its descent, it would be blown apart by a barometrically activated explosive charge. The camera unit containing the valuable film would be retrieved by a Lockheed C-130 Hercules equipped with a Mid-Air Retrieval System (MARS) and flown to a base for processing and analysis.

During the early development stages of the D-21, tests were conducted at Area 51 utilising a MARS-equipped C-130, in order to validate recovery techniques for the reconnaissance pallet. The pallets were air-dropped from a B-66 flying at maximum altitude and the C-130 took-up a race-track holding pattern in readiness to catch the pallet. It was deemed necessary to document these events on film, so a photo-chase platform capable of flying in formation with the C-130 at about 24,000 ft (7315 m) had to be identified. Neither the Area's F-101s nor its T-33s were up to the task – the C-130 would be flying with its flaps

The M-21 was a two-seater; the aircraft's erstwhile Q-bay was converted into accommodation for a Launch Control Officer. Taking responsibility for launching the drone, the LCO was provided with a window to each side of his position, which modification gave the M-21 something of the look of the SR-71A. This may be the only photograph of M-21 60-6941, the aircraft that was lost on 30 July 1966. (Paul F. Crickmore Collection)

Senior Bowl saw the D-21 in use with the B-52H, as the modified D-21B – there was no D-21A. In order for the drone to reach a speed at which its ramjet could function, a rocket booster was required to accelerate it to Mach 3.2 from the relatively slow speed of the B-52. A number of operational launches was attempted, but the results obtained were disappointing compared to the investment swallowed by the programme. (Lockheed ADP)

down. Similarly, the U-3B was not a chase candidate either. As the Instructor Pilot (IP) for the Cessna 210, Frank Murray volunteered to attempt to take that aircraft up to 24,000 ft to see if it was capable of performing the job, as he now explains: 'I loaded our trusty Lockheed movie photographer on board and took off to see ... Bearing in mind that the 210 had the most rudimentary oxygen system, just a plastic mask of sorts and a small oxygen cylinder. The Cessna's handbook indicated that flight at 24,000 ft was possible and I managed to get it up to that altitude and about 125 kt (144 mph; 232 km/h), thanks to the turbocharger. We returned to base with the good news and were scheduled on the next MARS mission. I took off first, rendezvoused with the '130 and the game was on. The "Herky-bird" acquired the radar beacon on the pallet when the chute was deployed on descent; it flew a race track pattern over the intended drop zone, and I followed a bit higher, so that I could manoeuvre into position and dive-off a bit of altitude if I needed to be in position for the pallet pick-up. It was planned that the MARS C-130 would make repeated passes at the descending pallet's chute until he either caught it or had to quit trying due to getting too low. If I remember correctly, the first attempt did not result in a catch, so the pallet let down all the way to the lake bed, north of the Area, in the vicinity of the A-12 refuelling track in

the SOA. So we flew home without much except for some pictures of him trying to capture the thing. Interesting flying really, but then I had all kinds of interesting flying in my five years at the area and elsewhere. Another MARS sortie was scheduled shortly afterwards and off we went again. The tactics of the first mission had worked, so nothing was changed in either my plan or theirs. After a while the '130 reported that he had contact with the beacon, so he adjusted his pattern to suit the catch. As usual, I'm behind and a little higher than him. Soon we both see the pallet and shout, he heads in; I'm slightly out of position and behind him, so I let down towards him in a turn calculated to cut him off and be in a position for filming. But at about this time I fly through his turbulent wake path and the poor little 210 gets tossed around like a rag doll. At one point I saw the big 24 volt battery that powered the movie camera right next to my head, it had been sitting on the floor at the back of the 210; luckily it came to rest on the seat in the back and we just barely got our pictures – the MARS was also successful this time'.

The maiden flight of the so-called 'Mother/Daughter' combination took place at Area 51 on 22 December 1964. Take-off time slipped because of delays brought about by the late arrival of senior Lockheed executives, who had already attended the maiden flight of the SR-71 down at Palmdale earlier that day.

Lockheed test pilot Bill Park piloted all the M-21/D-21 mated sorties. The monumental problems concerning platform and systems integration that Tagboard had to overcome cannot be overstated. By 1966 the programme had progressed to the point where vehicle separation was to be performed. The mission profile during this critical stage called for Bill to fly the aircraft at

This D-21 was photographed sitting on its handling dolly in the 'desert boneyard' at Davis Monthan AFB, Arizona, in December 1979. (Ben Knowles via Chris Pocock)

Mach 3.12 and commence a slight pull up at 72,000 ft (21946 m), then push over to maintain a steady 0.9 *g* on the highly sensitive *g* meter fitted in the M-21. With controllability checks on the D-21 drone completed, and its ramjet 'burning', Keith Beswick in the Launch Control Officer's (LCO's) position initiated vehicle separation by throwing the switch that fired off a blast of compressed air from a cylinder fitted in the M-21's pylon – it was without doubt an extremely dangerous series of manoeuvres.

This pioneering work achieved its first successful separation on 5 March 1966; however, drone number 503 was lost just 120 miles (193 km) from the launch point. A second launch was completed by Bill Park and Ray Torrick on 27 April, drone 506 adhering to its preprogrammed course to within half a mile during a flight of 1,200 nm (1,382 miles; 2224 km). It reached an altitude of 90,000 ft (27432 m) and Mach 3.3, before finally falling out of the sky and into the Pacific Ocean after a hydraulic pump burned out – the whole flight having been followed from the ground by Kelly who had flown into Point Magu, California, for the event.

A second batch of D-21s was ordered on 29 April and the following month Kelly made a formal proposal to SAC to launch the new drone from Boeing B-52Hs, on the basis of greater safety, lower cost, and greater deployment range. On 16 June, drone 502 successfully completed a third launch from the M-21, as Kelly noted in his diary: 'It flew about 1,600 nm (1,842 miles; 2964 km), making eight programmed turns, to stay within sight of the picket ship. It did everything but eject the package, due to some electronic failure.'

LAUNCH ACCIDENT

The fourth launch was to take place on 31 July 1966. Bill and Ray left Area 51 with drone number 504, in M-21 '941, and headed for the launch area, some 300 miles (483 km) west of the naval air station of Point Magu. On this occasion, accompanying them as chase in M-21 '940, were Art Peterson and Keith Beswick. The test card called for '941 to launch the D-21 at precisely 1 *g* and at a slightly faster speed. This revised launch profile would hopefully be easier for the operational pilots to follow. In addition, for the first time ever the D-21 was carrying a full fuel load.

Everything was progressing well, and a systems check of the drone revealed that its fixed inlet was feeding the Marquardt with the correct volume of air. At Mach 3.2+ and exactly 1 *g* Ray effected drone separation, after which everything went horribly wrong. A combination of factors caused an unstart on the D-21, which slammed down onto the aft section of the M-21's launch pylon. The impact caused a violent pitch-up that was well beyond correction by the pilot through the manipulation of the aircraft's flight controls. The large underside chine area of the M-21 was subjected to the immense pressure of a Mach 3.2 airstream, which quickly ripped the fuselage forebody from the wing planform, trapping its two-man crew through the incredible *g* forces inside the shattered cockpit. With their life support pressure suits inflated, the crew was subjected to high levels of positive and negative *g* as the forebody tumbled through the sky. Although these forces loosened the seat harnesses, the pilot and LCO remained firmly stuck in their cockpits. Bill determined that despite their altitude and speed, their chances of survival were better outside. Both he and Ray ejected and made a 'feet wet' landing in the ocean. Soon afterwards, Bill was picked up by a helicopter. Although both men incredibly survived the collision, Ray Torrick had tragically drowned before he could be brought aboard a US Navy vessel.

Kelly Johnson was desperately upset by the loss of one of his team, and cancelled the M-21/D-21 programme despite pleas from many of his engineers that the concept was basically sound and could be made to work.

Instead, the D-21s were modified to incorporate a less sensitive inlet and were launched from two B-52Hs – airframes 60-0036, nicknamed *Tagboard Flyer* and still operational with the 419th FTS at Edwards and 61-0021, nicknamed *Iron Eagle* and currently operational with the 93rd Bomb Squadron, Barksdale AFB, LA. The B-52H unit was initially designated as 'A' Flight. It later became the 4200th Support Squadron and operated out of Beale AFB. This new operation, code-named Senior Bowl, produced its own array of problems. Launched from a slower, lower platform, the D-21 was accelerated to its operational Mach speed and altitude by a rocket booster fitted to the underside of the drone, which separated from the vehicle at cruising speed. The booster had a length of 44 ft 3 in (13.49 m), a case diameter of fractionally over 2 ft 6 in (0.76 m), a weight of 13,286 lb (6027 kg), an average thrust of 27,300 lb (121.41 kN) and a burn time of 87 seconds. It was ignited shortly after the drone was released at about 38,000 ft (11582 m) and accelerated the D-21 out to Mach 3.2, at which point the now functioning ramjet would take over. Thermodynamic stresses on the D-21 during the launch sequence were severe since the platform was blasted rapidly from an ambient temperature state of circa -58°F (-50°C) to its cruise speed and airframe temperatures way above 428°F (220°C).

Between 6 November 1967 and 10 July 1970, 11 Senior Bowl flight-test sorties were flown, all utilising the Pacific Missile Range (PMR), located off the coast of California. Critical to the success of any operational mission would be the recovery of the drone's hatch containing the Hycon Manufacturing Company's camera and its Kodak film and during five of the test sorties the hatch was successfully recovered, once from the ocean and the remaining four times in mid-air by a Lockheed JC-130.

On 10 November 1970, the first operational mission was attempted. The collection area was to be southern China, where, according to a classified memo (written eight days after the attempted sortie), from the Chairman of the Imagery Collection Requirements Subcommittee to COMIREX, the desired frequency of coverage in the region had fallen consistently short of requirements. It continued that the Tagboard mission track would access 43 of the 84 priority targets, 18 of which had not been covered throughout 1970 and that, if successful, such a mission would impact favourably on the standing intelligence requirements for the South China area.

To maintain tight security, the B-52, hauling its unique payload, departed Beale at night and lumbered westward to the Pacific island of Guam. Just before dawn the next day the flight resumed, the bomber departing Guam and heading for the launch point. After vehicle separation, the 'BUFF' – for 'Big Ugly fat Fucker' – made its way back to Guam, while the drone climbed and accelerated on course to China, ready to begin a day-time reconnaissance run. During the sortie, both the launch and boost phase were successful and the drone attained its programmed altitude of 84,000 ft (25603 m) and a cruise Mach of 3.27. The NSA reported that despite the drone's telemetry being turned off just 50 miles (80 km) off the Island of Hainan and 80 miles (129 km) from the Chinese mainland – well within the range of coastal air defence radars – no Sigint activity could be correlated with the mission. However, computational errors in the drone's INS prevented it from flying the pre-programmed route. It is believed that D-21B number 517 continued on its initial track, which carried it far into the wilderness of the former Soviet Union before its self-destruct charge was triggered automatically upon descent after the craft's fuel supply had been exhausted. Interestingly, many years later, during a visit to Moscow, Ben Rich (then retired president of Lockheed's Skunk Works) recalled being presented by the KGB with what it believed were the remains of a 'stealth' fighter that had crashed in its territory – checks on arrival back home indicated that in fact the 'trophy' consisted of remnants from drone 517!

On 20 February 1970, drone 521 completed a flight test sortie into the PMR. Fail-safe modifications to the INS software were validated, the hatch was air-recovered by a JC-130 Hercules and once again it was time to attempt another operational mission. This second operational mission was undertaken by D-21B number 523 on 16 December 1970. This drone completed its 2,648-nm (3,049-mile; 4907-km) sortie, only to lose its payload at sea following a partial parachute failure.

During operational mission number three, flown by drone 526 on 4 March 1971, the 2,935-nm (3,380-mile; 5439-km) flight was completed flawlessly. The recce pallet was ejected and its chute fully deployed, but unfortunately the JC-130B missed the aerial recovery and the valuable payload splashed into the Pacific. Procedures, however, for such an eventuality had been pre-briefed and with a US Navy recovery ship on station, all was not lost. The vessel failed to recover the pallet on its first pass, so a Navy SEAL team went over the side to render assistance. The problem was that the pallet was still attached to its parachute cables. These were reinforced with stainless steel wire and the SEALs could not cut through them. Even worse, the drone's parachute now acted as a sea anchor, so that when the vessel made a second attempt at recovery by positioning up-wind and drifting towards the floating pallet, it drifted over the top, keel-hauling it and consigning it forever to Davy Jones's Locker.

The forth and final mission was flown just 16 days later by number 527, on 20 March 1971. Those directly connected to Senior Bowl believe that following some form of malfunction the drone was shot down in the vicinity of Lop Nor, the People's Republic of China nuclear weapons test facility, tucked away in remote west-central China.

During the course of some of these sorties, intelligence sources have stated that Chinese radar controllers managed to track the occasional D-21 over their territory, incorrectly identifying it as 'The Big One', their adopted term for the SR-71. At least one incident resulted in Peking protesting to Washington that SR-71s were violating its sovereign airspace, and this and similar incidents formed the basis of rumours that have persisted ever since. Indeed, President Richard Nixon perpetuated such rumours when, during the course of his state visit to China in February 1972, he promised that: 'all SR-71 over-flights of China would be halted'.

On 23 July 1971 the Senior Bowl programme was cancelled. At a cost of $5.5 million (1970 dollars) per mission, it had failed to produce a single image of denied territory, despite the best efforts of an outstanding team. One observer summed up the programme as 'an overhead mission with airborne technology that just didn't run long enough to make it'.

THE YF-12
Chapter 4

During the late 1950s a specification was drawn up to provide a fire-control and missile system for the North American F-108 Rapier interceptor. This so called Improved Manned Interceptor (IMI) was to be Mach 3.0 capable and its ASG-18 pulse-Doppler radar system, developed in parallel with the GAR-9 missile by Hughes, would have a look-down/shoot-down capability for head-on attacks. Furthermore the system considerably advanced the maximum range of contemporary airborne intercept monopulse systems then in use, from 40 miles to 120 miles (64 to 193 km).

As development of both aircraft and avionics progressed, a Convair YB-58 Hustler (55-665) was

As an Improved Manned Interceptor the North American F-108 Rapier was killed off by its development costs, but it did much for the YF-12A, which inherited the Rapier's weapons system. When the YF-12A was also struck by cancellation, elements of the system, including radar and missile technologies, were passed to the abortive General Dynamics/Grumman F-111B and superlative Grumman F-14 Tomcat naval interceptors. (Rockwell International).

bailed to Hughes to act as a systems test bed. Delivered to the Hughes main plant at Culver City, California, it was on the ground in excess of a year while re-configuring work prepared it for the missile and fire-control system (FCS) flight test programme. While this was being undertaken, Hughes engineers were using high-speed film techniques and a 9-ft (2.74-m) deep pit filled with foam, to analyse separation and pitch characteristics of the 818-lb (371-kg) missile. Missile/vehicle separation was provided by two thrusters, one located at each end of the missile. On firing, these propulsive charges unlocked the missile from its rail then forced the missile down, clear of the aircraft. At a finite time, the weapon's rocket motor ignited and the GAR-9 sped away; but who would fly these high-speed test flights?

JAMES D. EASTHAM

James D. Eastham, a native of El Dorado, Kansas, began his aviation career in 1942. Having graduated as a primary flight instructor, he was called to active

duty two years later, completing his US Army Air Force pilot training in class 45-1; he graduated and received his commission at Luke Field, Arizona. One of the original Berlin airlift pilots, Jim flew various aircraft types, including F-84s with the 31st Strategic Fighter Wing, during the Korean War. Released from active duty, he gained a mechanical engineering degree from Georgia Tech in 1955 and became a production test pilot with the McDonnell Aircraft Corporation on the F2H Banshee and F3H Demon. However, it was Jim's next move that set him up as 'Mr Missile' when, in October 1956, he joined the experimental flight test department of the Hughes Aircraft Company and was assigned as project pilot on the Falcon missile programme at White Sands Missile Test Range, New Mexico. Over the next four years, Jim flew nearly 800 test missions in Convair's F-102 Delta Dagger and F-106 Delta Dart, firing over 350 missiles in the process – a record for any one person!

In 1961, with work progressing well at Culver City, Jim attended the B-58 combat crew training school at Carswell AFB, Texas, where he graduated first in his class, thereafter becoming the Hughes project test pilot flying a YB-58 ASG-18/GAR-9 programme. Hughes also provided the Fire Control Operators (FCOs), two of whom would occupy the tandem positions behind Jim. Their task was to monitor the entire system and fire the GAR-9. During the course of this programme Tony Byline, Lyn Gear, John Moore, Jess Le Van, John Archer and, later, George Parsons and Ray Scalise all became intimately familiar with these duties.

AN/ASG-18 AND GAR-9

The AN/ASG-18 employed a high average-power, liquid-cooled, travelling wave tube transmitter chain, that consisted of two travelling wave tube amplifiers that were set in tandem to provide the desired gain and analogue circuitry for generating and processing of a coherent high-pulse repetition

Snoopy was YB-58A Hustler 55-0665, one of eleven production prototypes of Convair's impressive four-engined supersonic bomber, modified for use in the AN/ASG-18/GAR-9 trials. The Hustler had been designed to carry its nuclear payload in external pods and a specially-configured pod was used for the trials, housing a single GAR-9 in a bay covered with a set of double-folding doors, as well as telemetry and tracking equipment. Streamlined pods mounted beneath the outer engine nacelles housed high-speed cameras for recording missile launches, while the aircraft gained its nickname from its grossly enlarged nose radome. The radome added 7 ft (2.10 m) to *Snoopy's* pre-modification length and was wide enough to house the 40-in (1-m) diameter antenna of the AN/ASG-18 radar. (Paul F. Crickmore Collection)

frequency (PRF) wave form. This entire package included a solid-state digital computer for navigation, attack and BIT; integrated controls and displays; missile auxiliaries; an analogue attack steering computer; and an infra-red search and track (IRST) set capable of cooperative use with the radar.

The effective range of the IRST depended upon the point where its view either traversed over the horizon or something got between the target and the system. All early IR systems used an uncooled lead sulphide sensor cell and operated in the short wave length of 2.0–2.5 microns. This generated countless discrimination problems, however, so Hughes continued development work in this field, utilising the F-102 that Jim Eastham flew out of Holloman AFB, and eventually produced a long-wavelength sensor cell utilising an indium antimonide cell, cooled by liquid argon. This worked in the 3–5 micron range and had an outstanding discrimination capability, The IR system installed in the YB-58 and later in the AF-12, was yet another development and it utilised a lead selenide cell which was cooled by liquid nitrogen; however, extensive testing of this system was never carried out.

On completion of modifications to the YB-58, the programme was moved to the Hughes facility on Contractors Row at Edwards. Despite the cancellation of the F-108 programme on 23 September 1959, Department of Defense Officials decided that the outstanding FCS and missile development programme should continue on a stand alone basis.

With its FCF completed satisfactorily, the next order of business was to undertake a BIT check flight of the ASG-18 in the YB-58. During the following missions, the test crew was tasked to monitor the tracking capabilities of the FCS against both Titan and Atlas ballistic missiles, following their launch from Vandenburg AFB. Jim recalls: 'The mission against the Titan was only partially successful because a problem developed

The YF-12 featured a conical nose radome to house the AN/ASG-18 radar scanner, as well as cut-back chines which terminated in line with the leading edge of the windscreen. At the point where the chines began their curve back into the forward fuselage a pair of IR sensors was housed, one on each side. Ultimately these might have allowed passive target acquisition and tracking. Note also that the forward left missile bay doors are open here. (Hughes)

in the velocity gate of the ASG-18. But during the next sortie, against the Atlas D, we acquired the missile and tracked it with the ASG-18 until the antenna hit the bumper ring. The IR tracker was slaved to the radar and it also acquired the target and tracked it until its antenna hit the IR bumper ring. This, however, was purely academic, because we didn't have an IR version of the GAR-9 missile'.

But progress was slow during this first year, with B-58 accidents throughout the SAC fleet causing numerous groundings of '665. During this off-and-on testing time, a question arose concerning the effectiveness of the ASG-18's ability to detect an extremely low-altitude target. It was soon put to rest, however, when the system actually locked onto and tracked a B-57 at long range as the target completed a touch-and-go landing at Edwards.

KEDLOCK

Undoubtedly spurred on by the earlier success of his A-12 design with the CIA, Kelly Johnson discussed the possibility of building an

Its titanium and black finish bestowing a somewhat more angular appearance upon it than was the case, 60-6934, the first YF-12A, is shown here with high-speed camera pods mounted beneath its engine nacelles. This aircraft was used in unsuccessful speed and altitude record attempts and later went on to become the SR-71C trainer. The 'porthole' aft of the RSO's cockpit canopy was painted on to disinform observers. (Lockheed)

interceptor version of the A-12 for the Air Force, on 16/17 March 1960, with Gen Hal Estes of Air Force Systems Command and Dr Courtland Perkins, the Air Force Secretary for Research and Development. Kelly's ideas for what he referred to as the AF-12 were keenly received and subsequently forwarded to Gen Martin Demler, at Wright-Patterson, for further discussion and analysis. During late October 1960, Lockheed received a letter of intent for $1 million and was directed to, 'go forward with Plan 3A' and produce an interceptor version of the A-12, equipped with the Hughes ASG-18 FCS and the GAR-9 missile system. The programme was accorded the classified code name Kedlock. Kelly appointed Rus Daniel to become the project engineer and the seventh A-12 was nominated to become the AF-12 prototype. In December 1960, a second project group was organised at the Skunk Works and in order to maintain security it worked independently of the Oxcart team.

A considerable amount of work was necessary to convert the reconnaissance platform into an interceptor – although it is fair to say that most of this was focused around the forebody of the aircraft. Initially these external changes were typified by the creation of a second cockpit in what was the A-12's Q-bay. The fuselage chines were cut back to incorporate a radome that housed a 40-in (1-m) diameter scanning dish, and four weapons bays were cut into the underside of the chines. These would house the FCS – in the right forward bay – and three GAR-9 missiles, two in the left bays and the third in the right rear bay.

On 23 and 24 January 1961, the first meetings with the Air Force's weapon system project team took place at Burbank and it was briefed on Skunk Works design and development philosophy. On 31 May, some 15 Air Force officers returned to the plant and completed a review of the mock-up. All seemed to be progressing

extremely well. However, by June wind tunnel tests had revealed serious directional stability problems that resulted from the re-configured nose section and the slightly raised second cockpit. To alleviate these problems, further external modifications were necessary, this time to the rear of the aircraft, where two fixed ventral fins were installed on the underside of each engine nacelle. In addition, a large folding fin was mounted at the rear, on the aircraft's centreline. Retraction and extension of the folding ventral fin worked out of phase with the cycling of the landing gear. In short, when the gear was retracted, the fin extended and vice versa.

One evening early in 1962, Jim Eastham was at his home in Lancaster, Nevada, when his doorbell rang. He answered to find Lou Schalk – a long-standing friend – at the door. Jim recalls: 'At first I thought that Lou had swung by on his way to visit his children and wife, who also lived in Lancaster, but he said no, he'd come to visit me! I invited him in, poured a couple of "cold ones" and asked what was on his mind. He said he wanted me to go and work for him. But when I asked him what I'd be doing, he said he couldn't tell me. I responded by saying, "Lou, I'm flying the B-58, it doesn't get any better than that!" And Lou said, "This is a hell of a lot better than that!" So I replied that I was definitely interested! I suspected that Lockheed were developing a new interceptor and that it would be using our weapon system and missile. He arranged for me to have a meeting with Kelly Johnson and I drove down to Burbank. When

Here '934 has its ventral fin extended in the flight position. It also features an Air Force Systems Command badge on its starboard dorsal fin, as well as an all-black finish. (Lockheed)

I got there, Johnson put his fat finger in my face and said, "You'll continue to do what you're doing and we'll find something for you to do around here". And that is the origin as to how I ended-up working simultaneously for two companies! I would hasten to add I didn't receive two base salaries; for the next two years, my primary pay continued to come from the Hughes Aircraft Company.' Once an extensive security check had been completed, Jim began spending time with Skunk Works engineers at Burbank, familiarising himself with the location of switches and other specialised equipment in the AF-12 mock-up.

His second year of flight testing with the YB-58 involved integrating the missile onto the aircraft and tailoring it to work with the radar system. This extremely complex task was carried out under the direction of Mr Clare Clausen, the programme manager, and involved some of the finest electrical engineers in the Western world. First of all captive flights were flown. These involved making runs against manned aircraft and checking out both the radar and missile system to the point of launch. Subsequent analysis of this recorded data would isolate problems that were apparent to the flight crew during the sortie. Then, after missile separation tests – which included some unguided firings – about six live, guided firings were made by Jim and his team in the B-58 over the White Sands missile range.

By 2 August 1962, Air Force funding had been increased to allow for the modification of three A-12s and the major elements of the prototype,

assigned the Article Number 1001, were in the jig at the Skunk Works. As the manufacturing effort continued from December 1962 through to the spring, reservations were muted in some quarters about the security of the Oxcart programme and that of its fighter stablemate, particularly in relation to the latter's fast approaching flight test programme. Edwards certainly appeared to offer the best option, but in the event 1001 was crated-up and trucked to Area 51.

With Jim now spending an increasing amount of time at Area 51, Lou Schalk and Kelly agreed that Jim should be the first pilot to fly what had by now been designated YF-12A by the Air Force. Consequently, in March 1963, Jim began writing the flight handbook – or Dash 1 – for the aircraft. This rather complicated volume consisted of 12 sections that covered every aspect of both normal and emergency operation and necessitated moving in with each engineering section concerned with that particular sub-system. A good deal of time was also spent with the aerodynamicists. Having earlier flown the A-12, this outstanding engineering test pilot was anxious to learn the differences between the two Skunk Works' birds.

OUTLINE DESCRIPTION

The YF-12A was 101 ft 8 in (30.99 m) long, stood 18 ft 4½ in (5.60 m) high, had a wing span of 55 ft 7½ in (16.95 m) and a wing area of 1,605 sq ft (149.10 m²). The wing featured a leading edge sweepback of 61° 15' with no dihedral, and its angle of incidence was 1° 2'.

Empty gross weight of AF-12 Article 1001 was 60,730 lb (27547 kg) and maximum take-off weight was 127,000 lb (57607 kg). While on the ground the aircraft was supported by a tricycle undercarriage, which had a wheel track of 37 ft 9¾ in (11.53 m). The aircraft's cg limits were between 16 and 29 per cent of the mean aerodynamic chord (MAC) and its g limits were -1 to +3.6. Interestingly, the aircraft's maximum allowable airspeed and its design speed were one and the same, 450 KEAS. The expression KEAS was used throughout the A-12/YF-12 and SR-71 programmes when speed criteria needed to be followed, because aircraft are structurally designed using KEAS and it also enabled one airspeed limit to be specified for all altitudes. Prohibited manoeuvres were spins and roll rates in excess of 120° per second, and take-off rotation had to be limited to less than 14°, or the engine nacelle ventral fins would contact the runway.

FUEL SYSTEM

The YF-12 used a fuel referred to in the flight manual as PWA 523B. Possessing a high flashpoint, it also contained a liquid Teflon

additive to lubricate the engine hydraulic pumps and various engine accessories. The fuel density averaged 6.4 lb per US gal (0.77 kg per litre) and the fuel tank capacities were:

Tank 1	5,990 lb/ 2717 kg	936 US gal/ 3543 litres
Tank 2	7,872 lb/ 3571 kg	1,230 US gal/ 4656 litres
Tank 3	9,504 lb/ 4311 kg	1,485 US gal/ 5621 litres
Tank 4	13,645 lb/ 6189 kg	2,132 US gal/ 8070 litres
Tank 5	13,702 lb/ 6215 kg	2,141 US gal/ 8105 litres
Tank 6	12,480 lb/ 5661 kg	1,950 US gal/ 7382 litres
Total	63,193 lb/ 28664 kg	9,874 US gal/ 37377 litres

Fuel was moved from one tank to another using 16 200-volt, 400-cycle booster pumps. Four pumps were located in tanks one and six, while the remaining tanks each had two pumps. Tanks one, three, four and six fed the left engine while

The pilot's instrument panel was very much that of a typical late-1950s/early-1960s twin-engined combat aircraft, as shown in this 1964 image. Note that the control column is relatively uncluttered and that the vertical scale to the left of the aircraft attitude indicator in the centre of the panel is a combined Mach/knots display. (Lockheed)

The pilot's starboard console panel contained switch gear for a number of systems, including the SAS, autopilot, canopy seal and TACAN. The cylindrical item connected to the cockpit wall to the righthand side of the image was a positionable cockpit light. (Lockheed)

tanks one, two, five and six, fed the right. Fuel could be used in either engine using the cross feed control. A jet pump system removed any residual fuel from a tank that had stopped pumping into the feeding tank. For example, when tank one stopped pumping, a jet pump in tank two pumped any remaining residual fuel in tank one into tank two.

ELECTRICAL SYSTEM

The YF-12 had an awesome electrical system – it had to – the ASG-18 alone required 40 KVA to operate! To satisfy this voracious appetite the aircraft was equipped with two 60 KVA alternators, one a 400-cycle, 200-volt, three-phase unit, the other a 400-cycle, 115-volt, single-phase unit, each delivering 175 amps. They were driven by a Sundstrand constant speed drive turning at 8,000 rpm. Two transformer rectifiers supplied dc power to the aircraft, while a small silver zinc battery, located in the nose wheel well, provided 15 minutes of emergency dc electrical power. There was only one inverter in the YF-12 and this supplied emergency instrumentation power and lights for about 15 minutes. During normal operation, the inverter furnished power to correctly

functioning systems, but during emergency operations this dropped off, as power was fed to the critical systems which most needed it.

To cool the mighty ASG-18, an oil-cooling package was provided. Driven by a 40-hp (30-kW) freon compressor, this had an initial current that ranged from 500 to 600 amps and a running current of 100 amps.

COMMUNICATIONS EQUIPMENT

For communication (comms), the YF-12 was equipped with two Collins ARC-51 UHF radios that provided 1,750 channels, two Collins 618-7 HF single sideband radios and an AIC-18 intercom. An ITT-manufactured ARN-52 with 128 channels provided a TACAN capability; an ARN-58, built by GFE, equipped the YF-12 with the air component of an instrument landing system (ILS) and, finally, APX-46 identification friend or foe (IFF) equipment was located in the rear cockpit.

HYDRAULIC SYSTEMS

There were four hydraulic systems designated Left, A, Right, and B; they utilised a hydraulic fluid known as SP-302, which was a highly de-waxed mineral oil. Nine Vickers pumps were used on all four systems and they each produced a pressure output of 3,350 psi (23095 kPa). There was one reservoir for each system, located in the main wheel well. In addition, a reserve hydraulic reservoir with a capacity of 10 US gal (38 litres) at

The port console panel in the YF-12A's forward cockpit was dominated by the twin-throttle quadrant for control of the aircraft's J58 engines. Other switchgear related to the cockpit environmental controls and other systems. (Lockheed)

500°F (260°C), provided a standby for the A and B system reservoirs when either dropped down to the 1 US gal (4 litre) level.

PREPARATIONS FOR FLIGHT

Once Article 1001 had arrived at Groom Lake, several weeks were spent assembling the aircraft and equipping it with new J58 engines. Little in the way of a fire-control system was installed at this stage and after a few wrinkles in the electrical system were ironed out, engine runs were made. The hydraulics were checked to ensure they functioned correctly and were leak free. The SAS was brought on line and checked to ensure it would engage and function properly. Further ground tests on the J58s involved operating at full power to ensure that their output agreed with Pratt & Whitney's performance data schedule.

Early taxi tests uncovered a slight problem in the brake and damper systems. Once these problems were resolved, a high-speed taxi test was undertaken to near take-off speed, whereupon the power was chopped and the brake chute was deployed. Having satisfied all the ground requirements and determined that all instrumentation and communication equipment functioned properly, the YF-12 was deemed to be ready for its maiden flight.

On 7 August 1963, Jim Eastham climbed aboard Article 1001 (60-6934) for a first flight which he later modestly characterised as a typical production test flight. He was chased by Lou Schalk flying an F-104. On that smooth flight, the YF-12's powerplant, control system and SAS were first checked for proper operation and then the electrical, hydraulic, environmental and pressurisation systems were checked as satisfactory. Finally, the vertical instrument indicating Mach number and KEAS functioned well. This kind of instrumentation was later vetoed by the bomber-minded generals at SAC for the SR-71 in preference for 'old-standard' round dials. Some minor handling quality checks were conducted followed by an appraisal of the aircraft's static stability. Checked in all three flight axes, the YF-12 appeared, at least subsonically, to be 'much the same as its blackworld stablemates'. Because of its stability, Jim was of the opinion that the aircraft 'carried enough tail'. With all systems functioning well, the power levers were advanced into full military power and the aircraft went supersonic. This venture presented no problems in either the transonic or low supersonic regions, where handling characteristics were once again assessed as identical to those of the A-12. After deceleration to subsonic speed, the aircraft was prepared for landing back at Area 51. With the gear lowered, a cockpit light indicated that the ventral fin had retracted – this was visually confirmed by Lou Schalk. The approach phase was characterised as identical to that of the A-12.

Concern over available ground clearance of the ventral fins during flare prior to touchdown proved unfounded and the near perfect 'squawk-free' test flight ended with the successful deployment of the drag chute.

Kelly would later note in his AF-12 log: 'It is the first airplane I've ever worked on where the fire control system was checked out prior to the first flight'. However, with the YF-12A having completed its first flight with flying colours, there was little urgency in getting it out to design speed, since the full speed envelope had already been achieved with Oxcart. Instead time was spent installing the fire control system, ensuring that it integrated into the YF-12, and testing the inertial navigation system.

In the rarely seen FCO's cockpit, the instrument panel was dedicated to the control of the aircraft's formidable weapons system. Three displays provided target, ranging and position data, with radar control panels to the left of the square displays, armament controls below these, radar and IR controls opposite to their right and computer controls above these. The FCO was provided with airspeed and altitude readings via the vertical scales to the left (knots) and right (feet), respectively, of the central displays. (Lockheed)

GOING PUBLIC

With the Oxcart flight-test programme now in full swing, and a notable increase in Cygnus test and training sorties, questions were being raised as to how much longer the project could remain hidden. In a curt, top-secret memo dated 20 May 1963, addressed to Director, National Reconnaissance Office (Brockway McMillan) and written by Herbert 'Pete' Scoville (CIA Deputy Director for Research) titled *Proposal for Surfacing an LRI* [Long Range Interceptor] *Prototype as Cover for the OXCART Program*, it noted in point 3: 'The purpose of this memorandum is to restate the grave concern expressed in our previous memorandum with regard to the possibility of an untoward incident which could result in an uncontrolled surfacing of the OXCART vehicle. Since that paper was written, there have been several minor incidents involving mechanical malfunctions and sightings of the A-12 which might have developed into serious problems had fortune not otherwise dictated. In addition, during this period, escalated activity in the R-12 [a pure reconnaissance version which evolved into

Hughes' GAR-9 or AIM-47 radar-guided air-to-air missile never entered service in its original form, but provided so much technology for the subsequent AIM-54 Phoenix, that it acted as a test bed for that weapon. AIM-54 was developed for the Tomcat, which can carry a theoretical load of six, while the F-12 would have carried just three of the AIM-47. (Lockheed)

the SR-71A] procurement program has, as we anticipated, generated increasing speculation both in the industry and in the Air Force regarding many facets of the programme'. In point 4, the final paragraph, Scoville continued: 'In light of the foregoing, I feel that it is not only appropriate but essential at this time, to request a reconsideration of this problem by the NRO with a view toward making recommendations to the Ad Hoc Cover Committee and higher authorities as to whether we should continue with the current contingency plan or take action to implement the proposed LRI surfacing …' This contentious issue needed to be resolved and undoubtedly Scoville's tenacity ensured that minds remained focused on the problem at hand. Sure enough, things began to

Several live GAR-9 firings were made, most with great success, as demonstrated by this target drone. The weapons system had an impressive look-down/shoot-down capability well in advance of comparable systems of the time. (Lockheed)

move. The first stage was the transfer of all management functions relating to Program D – the AF-12 programme and the R-12 – to the Air Force; this brought with it a change in security. Another secret memo dated 11 July 1963 addressed to Eugene Zuckert, Secretary of the Air Force and 'penned' by Gen Schriever, Commander USAF Systems Command, noted: 'The change in security would publicly disclose (2d level) the existence of the development of the AF-12 and/or R-12'. But concerns continued, as witnessed in point 10 of a classified CIA diary note dated 27 September: 'At

With its giant antenna, AN/ASG-18 is among the largest radars ever fitted to a fighter. As well as revealing details of the radar installation, this image also shows that a 35-mm camera was mounted on the lower right frame of the pilot's cockpit canopy in order to record images of the instrument panel in flight. As servicing work is being carried out here, both left side weapons bays have been opened. (Hughes)

the executive meeting this morning the Director reported that Mr Hotz, the editor of *Aviation Week*, had been to see General Carroll. He told General Carroll that he had good information that another airplane, a follow-up for the U-2, had been developed. Carroll apparently told Hotz that it would not be in the national interest to print anything on this, in response to which Hotz said that he was willing to sit on it provided everyone else did. In other words, he was not about to be scooped. The Director is seriously concerned that OXCART is going to blow sooner or later …'

On Friday 29 November 1963 (one week after the assassination of President Kennedy) the new president, Lyndon B. Johnson (LBJ), convened a meeting of the National Security Council (CIA Director John McCone, Secretary of Defense Robert McNamara, Secretary of State Dean Rusk, Special Assistant McGeorge Bundy and FAA Chief Najeeb Halaby). The main question on the agenda was whether to, or how to 'surface' the technological triumph of Oxcart. McCone counselled delay, but was in favour of some sort of press release in connection with the planned

development of a Supersonic Transport (SST). Halaby agreed. McNamara was in favour of total exposure because the Oxcart aircraft would weaken the case for the B-70 programme and other expensive Air Force projects, which he did not like. At that point Lyndon Johnson was informed by Bundy that Kennedy had been opposed to the early release of information pertaining to Oxcart, preferring instead to hold off its public debut until the following year so as to strengthen his re-election campaign. Bundy was attuned to the politics of 'high-tech projects', and spoke against early release because of potential criticisms likely to be levelled at the new president for attempting to make political 'capital' out of a great intelligence secret. Consequently, LBJ decided to 'keep his powder dry' until the run up to the 1964 elections. However, after Republican candidate Senator Barry Goldwater accused the Democrats of failing to sponsor new aircraft projects, Johnson concluded that the earlier than planned release of some form of statement was inevitable, and directed his advisors to prepare a formal announcement about the hitherto blackworld project. Kelly was asked to work on the draft that would be used by Johnson and noted in his diary on 25 February that he: 'proposed the terminology "A-11" as it was the non-anti-radar version' – referring back to the series of A-designated projects which originally led to the A-12.

BACK AT AREA 51

Meanwhile, as all of this politicking was taking place in far away Washington DC, Jim Eastham and Flight Test Engineer (FTE) John Wallace got airborne in 60-6936, the third YF-12A, for yet another test sortie. The date was 3 February 1964 and this time the test card directed that they should complete the very first heat soak of a 'Blackbird'. To achieve this, the flight was to be conducted at Mach 3.16 for precisely 10 minutes. The test procedure was followed to the letter; however, on recovery back at 'the Ranch', an inspection revealed that due to an error in the

pitot/static system, Jim had exceeded Mach 3.2! Consequently, the aircraft had encountered considerably higher stagnation temperatures than intended. These had incinerated practically all of the electrical wiring. It would be several months before '936 would fly again and during the intervening period events on Capitol Hill caught up with the programme.

On 29 February 1964, just four days after Kelly's diary entry concerning his work on a draft statement, President Johnson made the following announcement: 'The United States has successfully developed an advanced experimental aircraft, the A-11, which has been in sustained flight at more that 2,000 mph and at altitudes in excess of 70,000 ft. The performance of the A-11 far exceeds that of any other aircraft in the world today. The development of this has been made possible by major advances in aircraft technology of great significance to both military and commercial applications. Several A-11 aircraft are now being flight tested at Edwards Air Force base in

JQB-47E 53-4256, formerly with the 3214th UMS at Eglin AFB, Florida, was placed into storage on 20 August 1968. Mission markings on the aircraft's nose record three missions against the YF-12A, as well as other missile tests. At least one QB-47 suffered damage during the YF-12A programme. (Norman Taylor)

California. The existence of this programme is being disclosed to permit the orderly exploitation of this advanced technology in our military and commercial planes. This advanced experimental aircraft, capable of high-speed and high-altitude and long-range performance at thousands of miles, constitutes the technological accomplishment that will facilitate the achievement of a number of important military and commercial requirements. The A-11 aircraft now at Edwards Air Force base are under extensive tests to determine their capabilities as long-range interceptors. The development of supersonic commercial transport aircraft will also be greatly assisted by the lessons learned from this A-11 program. For example, one of the most important technological achievements in this project has been the mastery of the metallurgy and fabrication of titanium metal which is required for the high temperatures experienced by aircraft travelling at more that three times the speed of sound. Arrangements are being made to make this and other important technical developments available under appropriate safeguards to those directly engaged in the

supersonic transport program. This project was first started in 1959. Appropriate members of the Senate and House have been kept fully informed on the program since the day of its inception. Lockheed Aircraft Corporation, at Burbank, California, is the manufacturer of the aircraft. The aircraft engine, the J58, was designed and built by the Pratt & Whitney aircraft division, United Aircraft Corporation. The experimental fire-control and air-to-air missile system for the A-11 was developed by the Hughes Aircraft Corporation.

'In view of the continuing importance of these developments to our national security, the detailed performance of the A-11 will remain strictly classified and all individuals associated with the program have been directed to refrain from making any further disclosure concerning this program.

'I do not expect to discuss this important matter further with you today but certain additional information will be made available to all of you after this meeting. If you care, Mr Salinger will make the appropriate arrangements'.

This statement effectively split the programme in two, and in order to back-up the president's announcement the YF-12 element was moved away from Area 51 and into the white world just a few hours prior to the President going on-air. The two flyable aircraft, 60-6934 and 60-6935 were positioned to Edwards AFB by Lou Schalk and Bob

This dramatic shot shows the demise of a QF-80 target drone after a GAR-9 struck an augmentation pod slung from the aircraft's right wing pylon. The GAR-9/AN/ASG-18 combination demonstrated lethal ranges in excess of 60 miles (96 km) and would almost certainly have shown an even longer reach in a production version. (via Jim Eastham)

Gilliland and the event was witnessed by just a few dozen maintenance staff who happened to be at work that Saturday morning. Lou Schalk remembers taxiing to the assigned hanger as eyes bulged and heads shook in utter disbelief at the sight of the two sleek aircraft, the like of which had not been seen before by anyone outside the programme, with the possible exception of a few desert dwellers and incredulous airline crews. Lou continues: 'Our supposed low key, rather laid-back positioning flight lost a touch of elegance when, to aid push-back into the hanger, we turned the aircraft through 180° at the entrance. This turn-around manoeuvre sent hot engine exhaust gasses into the hanger that caused the overhead fire extinguisher valves to open. These valves were big – like the flood valves on the hanger decks of aircraft carriers – the desert hadn't seen so much water since Noah's embarkation!'

Once its re-wiring work had been completed, aircraft 60-6936 joined its two stablemates at Edwards and the now overt programme continued in a totally new environment. Suddenly, it appeared that the US Air Force had virtually matched, man-for-man, all the contractors involved on the programme and it began to look to the civilian test force that the Air Force was trying to take over the entire project. The move also caused logistical headaches, since most of the expertise was still based at Area 51. Several people intimately involved in the project have said that the YF-12 was considered the stepchild of the 'Blackbird' family, and received neither the emphasis nor the backing from Lockheed Management enjoyed by the two reconnaissance variants. Notwithstanding these 'ripples on the mill pond', one of the first tasks after arriving at Edwards was to install and make operational the new electrically-controlled air inlet system. Once it had been installed, it took Jim Eastham just three months to complete the envelope-extension programme.

Jim flew all of these flights in the Lockheed-operated prototype, 60-6934. A minor problem occurred as the aircraft approached its design speed of Mach 3.2, which resulted in a directional oscillation. This discrepancy was noticed immediately and acceleration terminated. On return to Edwards, the cause was found to be instability in the inlet controls – as the aircraft yawed in one direction both spikes reacted to the change as a function of the Beta (yaw) angle. With the problem identified, Jim attained design speed during the next flight.

HIGH-PROFILE SORTIES

One of the favoured 'watering holes' frequented by several test pilots involved in various programmes in the Edwards area at this time was Hernando's, in the vicinity of Palmdale. The XB-70

Valkyrie was a big whiteworld programme, rivalling the YF-12A certainly from the prospective of procuring funds. By mid-1964, the big bomber was slowly beginning to rack up high-Mach flight time, although concerns were being muted about the aircraft's propensity to lose large pieces of structure in the process. Notwithstanding, the XB-70's positive accomplishments where trumpeted at every opportunity by its crews and support staff. One evening at Hernando's, Al White (the XB-70 Chief Test Pilot) was loudly boosting about his high-Mach time, when his remarks were overheard by Jim Eastham, who turned to White and said: 'Al, we do more Mach-3 time during a single YF-12 mission than you guys have flown in your entire programme'. Al then looked over at Jim and without hesitation retorted: 'Yes that's true Jim, but we lose bigger pieces than you fly!'

In April 1965, Jim Eastham flew a number of profile proving sorties that would later allow Air Force crews to fly the YF-12 into the record books. By no means a coincidence, the date chosen to establish these records was 1 May 1965; five years to the day since Francis Gary Powers had been shot down by a Soviet SA-2 missile. In this very public manner the United States was able to aptly demonstrate that over the intervening period it had been far from asleep and that it once again ruled the skies. Col Robert L. 'Fox' Stephens flew YF-12A 60-6936 to a new absolute altitude record of 80,257.86 ft (24390 m) and Col Walter Daniel took the absolute speed record over a 500-km (311-mile) closed course and also obtained the 1,000-km (311-mile) 621-mile) closed course record.

Later, Lockheed test pilot Bill Weaver found himself in the unenviable position of flying a YF-12 with a ventral fin that stubbornly refused to retract. Demonstrating great piloting skill and determination, he successfully landed the aircraft and saved an extremely valuable piece of hardware – but the fin's profile was considerably modified by the incident.

With much of the 'pick and shovel work' completed in the B-58, the ASG-18 and the GAR-9 missile were quickly integrated into the YF-12, where the system transcended its predicted performance figures. In operational service, three GAR-9s were to have been hauled aloft by the F-12B; however, the highly instrumented test aircraft never carried a full missile load.

During the first missile separation test, onboard cameras showed the missile incorrectly aligned. Had the rocket motor ignited, the missile would probably have ended up in the front cockpit. Adjustments were made and the remainder of the test programme proceeded extremely well. In all, approximately 12 live missile firings were made from the YF-12. Seven were flown by Jim, the remainder by Air Force crews. An indication of the system's operational potential can be gauged from a test flight flown on 25 April 1966, in '934, from Eglin AFB, Florida, over the Gulf of Mexico. As Jim Eastham now recalls: 'Following take-off, we accelerated in a general southwest direction and made a right turn on to an east-bound heading for the "hot run". George Parsons, my FCO, acquired the target, which was at about 1,000 ft [305 m], Mach 0.6 and heading west at a range of 130 nm [150 miles; 241 km]. At that time we were at Mach 3.2 and 75,000 ft [22860 m]. Even though we were being vectored, we also ran the mission utilising the modified close-control feature of the ASG-18 weapon system and tracked the target at the exact 12 o'clock position. Our closure rate was Mach 3.8 and essentially we had an altitude differential of 75,000ft! We went through the mission prep stage and the launch was made at approximately 53 nm [61 miles; 98 km]. The missile guided to impact on the left horizontal stabiliser of the QB-47. At the time of impact we were looking down 73° at the target!' The unarmed missile hit and destroyed approximately four feet of the QB-47's horizontal stabiliser. It seems that all but one of the seven launches made by the Lockheed crew were deemed to be a success – the failure of one of the sorties was attributed to a missile gyro system failure. Perhaps not surprisingly, the Air Force was extremely impressed. Aerospace Defense Command (ADC) calculated that it would require 96 of the production version of the big fighter – designated F-12B – to replace its fleet of F-102 and F-106 interceptors. With a force this size, ADC officials were confident that they could provide protection to the entire United States against incoming high-speed, low-level bombers by stationing three squadrons of sixteen aircraft on the east coast at Otis AFB, Maryland, and another three squadrons of sixteen at Paine AFB, Washington, to protect the west coast. Another important facet of the F-12B was its re-attack speed, which was much faster than, for example, the Convair F-106, which required double the time to reposition itself on a subsonic bomber compared with the F-12. In the case of a supersonic bomber, the F-106's time requirement was four times greater. But it was not to be. Instead, political shenanigans and a long-simmering feud over the appropriation of defence funds between Robert McNamara and the Air Force deteriorated into a bitter fight.

The war of words between the Air Force and its political masters had begun in April 1964, when the head of ADC, Gen Herbert B. Thatcher, said that he would like to have a large IMI fleet operational by 1967. The root of these comments was engrained in his observations that the Department of Defense had decided not to proceed with such a programme despite giving the impression that such a development was under way via the YF-12A. In truth, McNamara preferred the F-106X proposal after a national intelligence estimate showed it to be the most cost effective answer to the predicted Soviet bomber threat. As a result, on three separate occasions over three years, he took the unprecedented step of actually denying the Air Force access to $90 million worth of funds that had been appropriated by Congress to begin F-12B production. Questioned during the joint hearing of the Senate Armed Services Committee and Appropriation Defense Sub-Committee McNamara said: 'I feel quite confident that it is not necessary to appropriate money that can't be justified for the weapon system itself, simply to keep the production line open'. These flagrant delaying tactics undoubtedly protected funds earmarked for the B-70 bomber and the F-106X – the latter metamorphosed into the F-15 Eagle.

Consequently, in July 1966 Kelly Johnson was directed to 'give up further flying of the YF-12As'. Things continued to deteriorate and on 5 August 1966 Kelly noted in his log: 'We have laid off half of our test crew on the YF-12A and are maintaining only enough people to store the airplane or send it to Burbank. We are very near the end of this program'.

Despite this rather bleak outlook, Kelly still remained hopeful that F-12B production would be re-instigated and even as late as 27 January 1967 he was still awaiting a final decision from the Air Force. In March of that year, Kelly's optimism seemed justified when Col Ben Bellis led him to believe that the F-12B proposal had been accepted by the Air Force. On 13 November 1967 Kelly was asked to carry out studies into converting the ten now retired Oxcart A-12s and also ten SR-71s into fighters. These studies envisaged the installation of Sparrow missiles and a Westinghouse radar, but nothing further came of this. Then, in late December, Kelly received a call from the SPO instructing him to shut down all AF-12 studies immediately and cancelling all other ADP air defence programmes with the exception of a vulnerability study that was to be transferred to the SR-71. On 5 January 1968 the Skunk Works received official notification from the Air Force, closing down the F-12B. The YF-12A programme formally ended on 1 February. This was followed four days later by a letter from the Air Force instructing Lockheed to destroy all A-12/F-12 and SR-71 tooling. Consequently the large jigs were cut up and duly sold for scrap at seven and a half cents per pound. As Kelly noted in his log: 'Ten years from now the country will be very sorry for taking this decision of stopping production on the whole Mach-3 series of aircraft in the USA'.

After the test programme was halted all three YF-12As had been placed in storage at Edwards,

however, this was not quite the end of the story. The loss of SR-71B 64-17957 prompted an interesting piece of aviation surgery. After ablation of the fuselage forebody, the rear section of Article 1001, the first YF-12A, was grafted onto a front fuselage static-test specimen to create 'The Bastard', 64-17981. This so-called SR-71C replacement trainer first flew on 14 March 1969. Three test flights were made in just two days

With all hopes of a production contract dashed, 60-9635, the second YF-12A, was delivered to Wright-Patterson Air Force Base for permanent display. It remains at the USAF museum as the only surviving example of its type. (Lockheed)

before the aircraft was then delivered to Beale, where it was used as a stand in whenever the surviving trainer, serial 64-17956, was undergoing extensive maintenance.

SR-71 TECHNICAL BRIEFING
Chapter 5

The ambitious nature of Oxcart cannot be overstated. When E. M. Land of the Polaroid Corporation presided over those six historic meetings between 1957 and 1959 that led to the A-12, the highest-performing front-line fighters of the day were jets like the F-100 Super Sabre and F-101 Voodoo.

In a single bound, it was proposed that the A-12 would operate routinely at two or three times the performance parameters of these contemporary fighters. In addition, the designers and engineers had to master not only the many daunting problems associated with high-altitude, high-Mach flight, but they also had to employ the latest techniques and materials to reduce the A-12's RCS to produce what can now be regarded as the world's first operational 'stealth' aircraft.

GENERAL LAYOUT

The exterior of the SR-71 was characterised by an aft-body delta wing with two large engine nacelles, each mounted at mid-semi-span. An all-moving vertical fin was located on top of each nacelle, canted inboard 15° from the vertical to reduce the aircraft's radar signature and to aid in controlling excess offset yaw-thrust during single-engine flight. A large, aft-moving inlet spike, or centrebody, protruded forward from each engine nacelle, helping to regulate mass airflow to the two Pratt & Whitney J58 engines. Mission sensors were housed in a detachable nose section and in equipment bays located in the underside of the chine (a boat-like hull form) that extended along both sides of the long fuselage forebody. The two full pressure-suited crewmembers, a pilot and a Reconnaissance Systems Officer (RSO), sat in tandem.

The wing was arranged in box sections, one outboard of the engine nacelle and two inboard. The inboard sections were positioned one forward and one aft and were separated by a 3 ft 3¼-in (1-m) wide compartment housing the main gear bay. The front and rear beams of the inboard box sections provided support for the main gear.

The unmistakable planform of the SR-71 was characterised by its aft-body delta wing, two large engine nacelles and forward fuselage chine. (Ministry of Defence)

Some 5° of conical camber was applied to the outboard wing leading edge to reduce bending movement and torsion, moving most of the aerodynamic load in this section to the rear of the nacelle. The nacelle, considered an integral part of the wing, acted as a chordwise beam and torque tube, transmitting aerodynamic loads forward and redistributing them, via the nacelle rings, to the forward and aft box sections. The thin biconvex wing had a leading-edge sweep of 52° 37' 12" and a trailing-edge forward sweep of 10° and it joined the mid fuselage with a slight negative incidence. The aircraft's loaded gross weight varied from between 135,000 lb (61236 kg) to over 140,000 lb (63504 kg) and zero-fuel weight varied from 56,500 lb (25628 kg) to over 60,000 lb (27216 kg).

The fuselage can be described in three sections. First the forebody. Since the nose section was interchangeable for mission flexibility and structurally independent of the fuselage, the forebody can be said to extend from the tip of the forward cockpit to a point perpendicular to the intersection of the leading edge of the wing – a point known as fuselage station 715. Its structure consisted of a ring-stiffened cylinder, fitted with longerons at the top, bottom and side and modified to the extent necessary to accommodate the cockpit, equipment compartments, nose gear well, air refuelling receptacle and two fuel tanks. The mid-section, which extended to the main undercarriage well, contained fuel tanks that stretched laterally into the forward wing box area. The main gear bay dissected the forward and aft wing boxes and formed two structurally independent elements. Inboard, aerodynamic and bending loads at the root were carried by the fuselage longerons located at the top and bottom of the centreline, whereas outboard loads were borne by the wing attaching structure.

The aft fuselage section began at the rear of the main gear bay and tapered into the tail, but excluded the brake chute receptacle. This entire area, together with the aft wing section, was used to provide two more large fuel compartments. To reduce trim drag at high Mach numbers the nose section canted upwards some 2° 30'. Fuselage structural rigidity was enhanced by the use of ring stiffeners, while fairings fitted between the fuselage and wing root, although not part of the structure and supporting local air loads only, provided a convenient cavity within which to house electrical and plumbing lines.

An inherent aerodynamic design characteristic of delta-winged aircraft, resulting from their large root chord, is a major rearward shift of the centre of pressure (CoP) during acceleration from subsonic flight. This results in the pilot having to apply an increasing amount of drag-inducing elevon, to trim the aircraft and reduce the pitch moment. A key aerodynamic asset in reducing trim drag in the SR-71 was its chine. The chine acted as a fixed canard surface, producing lift as a function of the square of its speed, thereby becoming more effective with increasing Mach number. This, when combined with the long moment arm of the forebody in relation to the

Five degrees of conical camber was applied to the outboard wing leading edge, reducing bending movement and applying most of this movement's aerodynamic load to the rear of the nacelle. The nacelle then redistributed these loads to the forward and aft wing box sections. (Paul F. Crickmore Collection)

centre of gravity, greatly reduced the rearward translation of the CoP, which in turn reduced the amount of elevon necessary to balance these forces and so reduced trim drag. The chine also offered the SR-71 additional benefits when manoeuvring at low speed. As incidence increased, there occurred an increase in suction over the upper surface, particularly at the leading edge wing tip. This created an adverse pressure gradient behind the leading edge that then separated and rolled into a vortex and turned downstream to be shed at the wing tip. As incidence further increased, the separated flow moved inboard until the entire leading edge inherited a continuous vortex. This allowed for both a lower approach speed and the use of smaller vertical surfaces to retain minimum longitudinal stability, while additionally reducing rolling moment due to yaw at high angles of attack (AoAs). The maximum trimmed lift/drag ratio at subsonic speed was approximately 11.5 and at Mach 3 this value was 6.5.

MATERIALS

In the near-vacuum conditions at 83,000 ft (25298 m), the ambient air pressure is about 0.4 psi (2.76 kPa) and the temperature hovers around -67°F (-55°C). However, cruising in afterburner at its design speed of Mach 3.2 – that is a mile every 1.8 seconds and faster than a .30-calibre bullet – there remained enough air resistance to send the SR-71's airframe temperatures rocketing. External to the cockpit areas, these temperatures registered 428°F (220°C) – that is about the hottest setting on a domestic cooker. The wing leading edges became hotter than a domestic soldering iron and the outside nacelle areas adjacent to the afterburner section reached a staggering 1,040°F (560°C). For this reason, thermodynamic factors influenced the design and construction of the SR-71 more than any other aircraft of the time. Only titanium and stainless steel could withstand operating in this 'thermal thicket', and as titanium weighs only half as much as the latter, 93 per cent of the SR-71's structural weight consisted of aged titanium B-120 VCA; the remaining seven per cent – the tail units and the triangular wedges that framed the outer edges of the aircraft – were of composite construction. Made from a mixture of asbestos

As '963 comes in to land, a vortical flow pattern is generated in moist air at the root of the outboard wing section. Note also that a small amount of rudder deflection has been set. (USAF)

The inlet spike has been removed from this SR-71, which was undergoing depot maintenance at Palmdale. Also visible are the radar absorbing material wedges in the wing leading edge and the apertures where some of them have been removed. Some of the thin titanium skin has also been removed, revealing fuel tanks 3, 6A and 6B. (Lockheed ADP)

and epoxy, these provided high-temperature resistance and radar absorbent characteristics in order to reduce the aircraft's RCS.

The decision to use titanium represented a milestone in the continuing evolution of aviation materials and, by necessity, led to the invention and perfection of many new and different airframe assembly procedures. Initially, the titanium ageing process required 70 hours to achieve maximum strength, but careful processing techniques by the Skunk Works reduced this to 40 hours. Over-ageing titanium causes brittleness and some early coupons fell foul of this, shattering when dropped from desk height. Lockheed believed the problem to be hydrogen embrittlement produced during the heat-treatment process, but despite the close cooperation of its supplier, Titanium Metals Corporation, the case remained unproven and

unresolved until Lockheed replaced its entire acid-pickling facility – the acid-pickling technique was used to ensure that each coupon of titanium was perfectly clean and prepared before use – with a unit identical to that used by TMC.

A rigorous quality control programme was introduced. For every batch of ten or more parts processed, three test samples were heated to the same levels that the other parts from the batch experienced on the aircraft. One was then strength tested to destruction, another tested for formability and the third held in reserve in case reprocessing should be required. With more than 13 million titanium parts manufactured, data was stored on all but a few early samples.

Titanium is a metal with several idiosyncrasies and it was not long before Lockheed became well acquainted with all of them. For example, it is not compatible with chlorine, flourine or cadmium and a line drawn on a sheet of titanium with a Pentel pen will eat a hole through it in about 12 hours. Perhaps not surprisingly, all Pentel pens were called in off the shop floor. Early spot-welded panels produced during the summer had a habit of failing, while those put together in the winter lasted indefinitely.

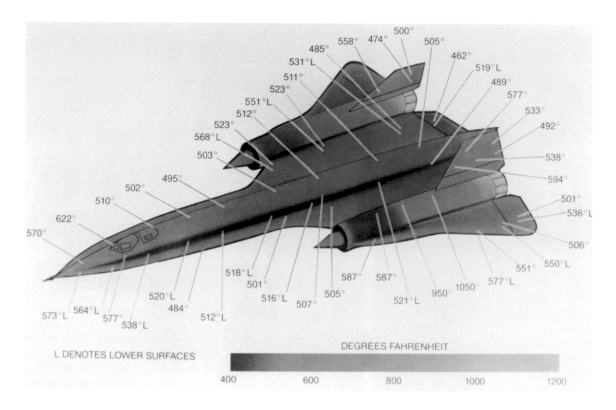

DEGREES FAHRENHEIT

L DENOTES LOWER SURFACES

400   600   800   1000   1200

Incredible airframe temperatures were produced while the SR-71 was cruising at one mile every two seconds at 82,000 ft (24994 m). Such temperatures arose despite outside air temperatures and pressures of -69°F (-56°C) and 0.4 psi (2.76 kPa), respectively. (Lockheed)

Through diligent detective work, it was discovered that to prevent the formation of algae in summer, the Burbank water supply is heavily chlorinated. Thereafter, all the titanium parts were washed in distilled water. During prolonged heat soak tests, bolt heads began dropping off various installations and this, it was discovered, was caused by tiny cadmium deposits left after cadmium-plated spanners had been used to apply torque. Needless to say, all cadmium-plated spanners were removed from tool boxes.

Lockheed awarded the Wyman Gordon Company a $1-million contract to fund a research programme into methods of forming complex structural pieces from titanium, such as the gear legs and engine nacelle rings. The result was a unique hot-forging process that utilised a 50,000-ton press to force the metal to the desired shape. Lockheed designed high-speed cutting tools that were then used to machine the forged metal. Initially, a drill bit could cut just 17 holes in the hard metal before it was ruined; however, by the end of the programme, Lockheed ADP had developed drills that could bore 100 holes and then be successfully re-sharpened. The Skunk

Works even developed a cutting fluid which, as well as eliminating the corrosive effects of many similar fluids, permitted metal removal at double the normal rates. The parts were then pickled. To prevent them from becoming under gauge while in the acid baths, metal gauges two thousandths of an inch thicker than required for the final parts were used. After cleaning, a pre-assembly inspection was carried out and the relevant segments assembled on spot-welding machines. To prevent oxidisation, welding was conducted with the parts placed in specially constructed chambers with a neutral, nitrogen gas environment.

During a test undertaken to study thermal effects on large titanium wing panels, a sample 4 x 6 ft (1.22 x 1.83 m) was heated to the computed heat flux expected in-flight. It resulted in the specimen warping into a totally unacceptable shape. Kelly Johnson overcame the problem by pressing chordwise corrugations into the outer skins. Upon reaching the design heat rate, the corrugations merely deepened a few thousandths of an inch and, on cooling, returned to their original shape. Kelly commented at the time that some accused him of, 'trying to make a 1932 Ford Tri-Motor go Mach 3', but the concept worked well. Another thermodynamic challenge to overcome was the problem caused by the differential heating received by various pieces of interconnecting structure. For example, from a uniform start temperature of 81°F (27°C), eight minutes after acceleration a wing spar cap would reach 171°F (77°C), the spar web 216°F (102°C) and the wing skin 351°F (177°C). It took another 16 minutes before all three components were within 14°F (8°C) of one another. The problem,

Low compression-ratio bypass ducts fed bleed air from the fourth stage of the J58's compressor into the turbine exhaust, an arrangement which allowed the turbojet to perform over the entire speed range of the SR-71. Three of the six ducts can be seen here, as the dog-legged pipework toward the middle of the engine. (Pratt & Whitney)

therefore, was how to attach a thin sheet of titanium to much bulkier sub-structure without the former buckling and tearing. As ever, the Skunk Works developed an innovative solution. A stand-off clip provided the anchor mechanism to the sub-structure, while also creating a heat shield between adjacent components.

The SR-71 was painted black not to make it look sinister or menacing, but in an attempt to further reduce airframe temperatures. As stated in Kirchoff's Law of Radiation, a good heat absorber is also a good emitter, and a good absorber is a black body. Since convective heating decreases

Pratt & Whitney JT11D-20 (designated J58 by the US Air Force) engines undergo maintenance at Palmdale. When the Senior Crown programme was cancelled by General Larry Welch on 22 November 1989, enough engines and spares had been stockpiled to keep the fleet running well into the next century. (Lockheed ADP)

with increasing altitude and heat radiation is independent of altitude, it was useful to harness this radiation component when cruising above 70,000 ft (21336 m). Experiments demonstrated that black paint provided an emissivity value of 0.92 compared to 0.38 for bare titanium. In addition, it was estimated that a black 'overcoat' would actually reduce airframe temperatures by 27–54°F (15–30°C) and this, it was felt, was well worth the 60-lb (27-kg) weight penalty that a coat of paint imposed. Finally, when cruising at the inky-black altitudes of near space, an overall black colour also helped to reduce the aircrafts visually conspicuity when operating over denied territory. Although the aircraft was to be all black, the Air Force was obliged to comply with the rules of the 1907 Hague Convention which stipulated that military aircraft must bear conspicuously placed national insignia (which would necessitate using the non-heat-resistant paint used for such markings as standard). Adding a touch of humour to an otherwise serious matter of international diplomacy, Ben Rich, who was chief

thermodynamicist at the time, asked, 'Who'll be up there to look at them?' Thereafter, expensive red, white and blue paints were developed that would not tarnish after repeated heat soaks.

Another, perhaps more important, problem for Ben and his engineers concerned the air-conditioning system. The challenge was to produce a system capable of cooling down air at up to 806°F (430°C) to a temperature more useful for the air-conditioning job. Eventually, a two-stage system was devised whereby air bled from the 9th stage of the J58's compressor was led through a ram air bleed, air cooled and then fed through a fuel cooler. The result was air-conditioned air at -4°F (-20°C) which was supplied to the cockpit, where it maintained regulated, steady-state temperatures of between 68 and 86°F (20 and 30°C). It was then ducted to various equipment bays and the nose wheel bay, and having reached a temperature of between 140 and 167°F (60 and 75°C), was vented overboard through exit louvres. Since the nose-gear tyres were cooled in this manner, their walls, unlike those of the mainwheels, were not coated with silver alloy powder to help reflect heat. A pressure differential of 1 psi (6.90 kPa) was maintained in the bays to ensure that the flow always vented out.

As fuel was burnt off and the temperature of that remaining increased, a system of smart valves was used to direct hot fuel to the engines and cool fuel back into the tanks to be used for environmental cooling. Thermodynamic heating dictated that the fuel in the wings was used first, due to a high surface area to volume ratio. Fuel tank sequencing was automatic and provided cg control, by pumping fuel from one area to another. In an interview, Ben noted that an interesting side effect of fuel depletion was that differential expansion between the top of the fuselage and the cooler underside, where fuel remained, caused the chines to be pushed downward, marginally changing their aerodynamic characteristics.

POWERPLANT

Two Pratt & Whitney JT11D-20s (designated J58 in US military nomenclature) powered the SR-71, each developing a maximum uninstalled, afterburning thrust of 34,000 lb (151.20 kN) under sea level static conditions. Having its beginnings in a US Navy project that was subsequently cancelled, the engine retained its earlier even-numbered, Navy-style designation – hence an engine with an even designation number was used in an Air Force airframe. The engine was designed for continuous operation at compressor inlet temperatures above 752°F (400°C). Its stretched design criteria – particularly concerning the high Mach numbers it was to operate at and their associated large air flow turn-down ratio – led to the development of a unique variable cycle

engine, later known as a bleed bypass engine – a concept conceived by Pratt & Whitney's Robert Abernathy. To solve the problems associated with high compressor inlet temperatures (CIT), the single rotor, nine-stage, 8.8:1 pressure ratio compressor utilised a bleed bypass system at high Mach. When opened, bypass valves bled air from the fourth stage of the nine-stage compressor and six ducts routed the air around the rear stages of the compressor, combustion section, and turbine. The bled air was then re-introduced into the turbine exhaust around the front of the afterburner, where it was used to both augment thrust and cool the back end. Transition to bypass operation was scheduled by the main fuel control as a function of compressor inlet temperature and engine speed. This usually occurred within a CIT range of 185–239°F (85–115°C) and corresponded to a Mach range of 1.8–2.0. In addition to reducing the effects of high temperatures, the bleed bypass process also sharply reduced airflow pressures across the rear stages of the compressor assembly, preventing them from choking with high-velocity airflow. It also prevented the front stages from stalling, due to low mass airflow. To further minimise the possibility of the front stages of the rotor blades stalling at low engine speeds, the engine incorporated movable inlet guide vanes (IGVs) to help guide airflow to the compressor. During take-off and acceleration to intermediate supersonic speeds, these remained in the 'axial' position in order to optimise air ingestion to the compressor. A change to the 'cambered' position occurred at the same CIT values as those set to activate operation of the bleed bypass process in order to ensure that the CIT remained within limits – the compressor temperature had a maximum limitation of 800°F (427°C) – a failure of the IGVs to transition to the 'cambered' position was a mandatory abort item on the 'Go-No-Go' checklist.

The engine contained a two-stage turbine, discharge temperatures from which were monitored by exhaust gas temperature sensors (EGT). When operating at cruising speeds, the EGT rose to 2,012°F (1,100°C). This presented Pratt & Whitney with one of its greatest challenges, and one that was eventually overcome by Joseph Moore, a materials engineer at the Florida Research and Development Center, who perfected a special high-temperature alloy used in both the first and second stages of the J58's turbine, known as Astralloy.

The main and reduction gearboxes were mounted beneath the diffuser section of each engine and were mechanically linked to the

These J58 engines are sitting on their special transport dollies, minus the afterburner flaps which were a continuation of the rear of the engine nacelle.

engine's compressor section. The main gearbox was connected to an external drive shaft for starting the engine, while the reduction gearbox provided mechanical power to the airframe-mounted Accessory Drive System (ADS), which included a constant-speed drive, linked to a 60 KVA electrical generator, two hydraulic pumps and a fuel circulating pump.

FUEL

The major components of the fuel system comprised the engine-driven fuel pump, main fuel control, windmill bypass valve and variable-area fuel nozzles in the main burner section. The two-stage, engine-driven main fuel pump consisted of a single centrifugal pump that acted as a boost stage, with its second stage made up of two parallel gear-type pumps with discharge check valves. This configuration facilitated continued operation if either pump failed.

The main fuel control metered main burner fuel flow and controlled the bleed bypass, start bleed

valves, IGVs and exhaust nozzle modulation. It regulated the main engine thrust as a function of throttle position, compressor inlet air temperature, main burner pressure and engine speed. Afterburner operation was always at Military-rated engine speed and EGT. The control had a remote trimmer for EGT regulation of each engine. These were always set one-engine at a time, by the pilot, during EGT engine trim-checks prior to take-off to ensure that the temperature remained within limits. The engine was equipped with an eight-can annular combustion section with 48 variable-area, dual-orifice fuel nozzles. These were arranged in clusters of six nozzles per burner.

The extremely high airframe temperatures encountered by the SR-71 and the A-12 during high-Mach cruise completely ruled out the use of standard JP-4 jet fuel as its fuel source, since it would have ignited in the fuel tanks. Instead, a bespoke fuel was used by the SR-71 and known as JP-7 (PWA 535) and PWA 523E. JP-7 and PWA 523E contained additional lubrication to aid fuel pump operation. The fuel was developed by Pratt & Whitney in partnership with Ashland, Shell and Monsanto and remained stable despite the high temperature environment. It was used first as a hydraulic fluid to activate the main and

This incredible shot is a still from a rear-looking movie camera fitted to an operational SR-71 out of Kadena. The camera was intended to capture footage of SA-2 launches, but also provided wonderful images of the intake spikes, fully retracted at Mach 3.2. (via Frank Murray)

afterburner fuel nozzles before being injected into the fuel burners at over 662°F (350°C) and 130 psi (896 kPa). Such high fuel burn temperatures presented the design team with yet another problem – standard electrical plugs were incapable of igniting the fuel. This was overcome by developing a unique chemical ignition system (CIS), using triethyl borane (TEB). This substance is extremely flash sensitive when oxidised and a small tank was carried in the aircraft and used to start or re-start the engines and afterburners on the ground or in the air. To ensure that the system remained inert when not in operation, gaseous nitrogen was used to pressurise the TEB tank and power the piston that injected the material into the burner cans during the ignition process, regardless of engine operating conditions. As fuel was burnt, gaseous nitrogen was used to pressurise the fuel tanks to prevent them from being crushed as the aircraft descended to lower levels to either air refuel or land. For this purpose, liquid nitrogen was carried aloft in three dewars that were located in the front wheel well. Each time the SR-71 air refuelled the nitrogen gas in the fuel cells was vented overboard. Range was therefore governed by the number of times the aircraft could be refuelled before the liquid nitrogen supply became depleted.

Development of a durable fuel tank sealant was an ongoing problem. Cruising at high Mach, it has been estimated that the aircraft expanded 3 in (7.62 cm) in length due to thermodynamic heating. Upon descending to air refuel, the airframe cooled, a process that was considerably speeded-up as fuel at -58°F (-50°C) was pumped

This inlet spike was moved to the fully-forward position during AICS testing on the ground. It makes an interesting contrast with the photograph on the facing page and demonstrates the full range of spike travel. With the spike so far forward, its centrebody bleed slots are also visible. (Paul F. Crickmore Collection)

into the tanks from either a KC-135 Stratotanker or a KC-10 Extender tanker at 5,000 lb (2268 kg) per minute. This cycle of events was repeated up to five or six times during an extended mission and many more times during the period between major maintenance overhauls. The pounding taken by the silicon-based fuel tank sealant invariably led to its cracking, causing fuel to leak from numerous gaps.

OIL SUPPLY SYSTEM
The engine and speed-reduction gearbox were lubricated by an engine-contained 'hot tank' closed system. Its oil was cooled by circulation through an engine fuel/oil cooler, the tank being mounted on the lower side of the engine compressor case. Its capacity was 6.7 US gal (25.4 litres). The oil was gravity fed to the main oil pump and forced through a filter and the fuel/oil cooler. From there it was distributed to the engine's bearings and gears, before being returned to the tank by scavenge pumps. Engine oil temperature was controlled by fuel that was passed through the main fuel/oil heat exchanger.

ACCESSORY DRIVE SYSTEM
An Accessory Drive System (ADS) was mounted forward of the engine in each nacelle. It consisted of a constant-speed drive, an accessory gearbox

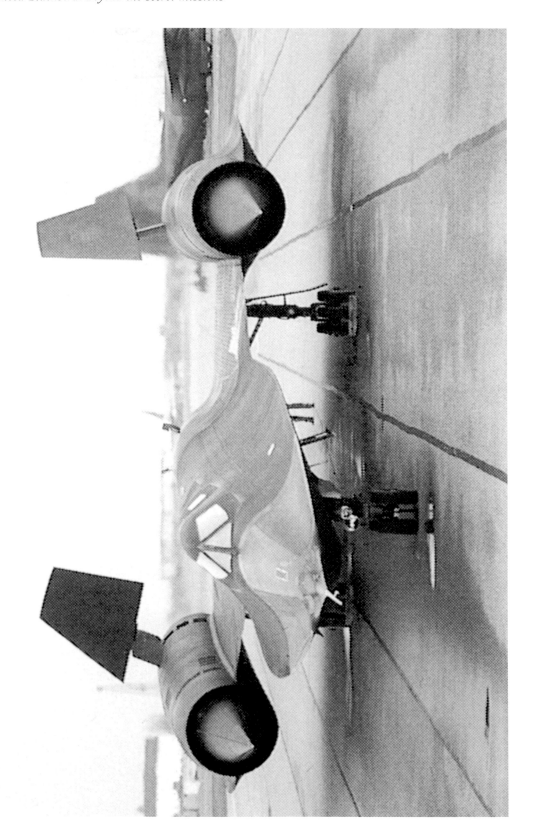

The Bertia company developed the high-temperature hydraulic actuators that powered the all-moving tail fins. (Paul F. Crickmore Collection)

During stateside training sorties, Oxcart pilots used personalised callsigns. DUTCH 21, Ken Collins, was the first pilot forced to eject from an A-12. The incident occurred in aircraft '926 on 24 may 1963. (CIA)

Agency pilot Jack Layton is pictured wearing a David Clark S-901 pressure suit in front of aN A-12. The 'yellow box' to his left is a portable oxygen and environmental control unit. Layton was DUTCH 27 on the A-12, uniquely changing to DUTCH 72 on the YF-12. (CIA)

A-12 '928 was lost during a test sortie on 5 January 1967. Its CIA pilot, Walt Ray, was killed during the incident. (CIA)

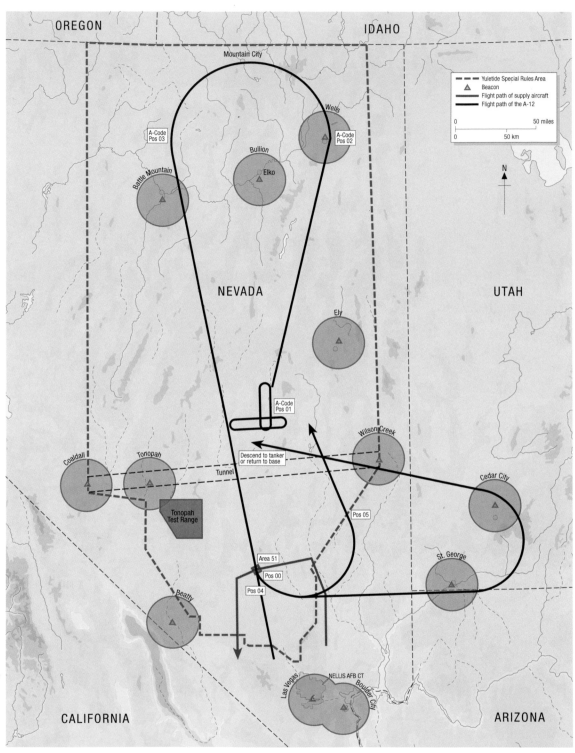

This map shows the Yuletide Special Rules Area, which was maintained for Mach-3 A-12 operations out of Area 51. Roughly north-south/east-west tanker racetracks were maintained to support the A-12s, with standard waypoints and turning points being established at 'Pos' positions. The Yuletide Area extend from 24,000 ft up to 60,000 ft and was bisected at its southern end by the 'tunnel', a civilian airway which extended from 24,000 ft to 40,000 ft altitude and which A-12s were generally required to fly under or over.

Above: Highly modified KC-135Qs of Beale's 903rd Air Refuelling Squadron provided the 'Road Runners' with invaluable AR support. Even though the A-12/SR-71 series served on the front line for the best part of three decades, the aircraft always looked the most modern among its peers. Nevertheless, the longevity of its career saw many other types come and go or evolve into other forms. The tanker illustrated here was modified from one of the original short-finned KC-135As. (CIA)

Below: 60-6927 was the only two-seat A-12 pilot trainer. Known by the designation AT-12, the aircraft was fitted with J57 engines for Mach-2 performance, but was otherwise similar to the single-seater in handling. The instructor's cockpit was raised to provide for an improved forward view, while his space was produced by using the area previously set aside as the Q bay for sensors. It is shown here in a mainly bare titanium finish, with black paint. (Lockheed)

Above: The same three A-12s remained at Kadena throughout the entire Black Shield deployment. Painted 'overall black', at the time their only external markings were five-figure dark red serial numbers sprayed on their twin fins. The completely bogus serials always began with the numbers '77'. One Agency pilot recalls the same aircraft, at various times, carrying the serials ''858', ''835' and ''855'. Aircraft '932, pictured above, which was one of the three Kadena A-12s, was lost with pilot Jack Weeks on 5 June 1968. (CIA)

Below: Lined up sequentially, seven single-seat A-12s, plus '927 (the 'Titanium Goose' two-seat trainer) and two YF-12As, sit at Groom Lake. In the foreground is A-12 '926, which became the first A-12 lost in an accident when it crashed on 24 May 1963. The third aircraft in the line up was lost on 7 January 1967, while '929 was written-off on 28 December 1967. Note how the YF-12As at the end of the line have a distinctly different nose shape to the A-12s, thanks to their large radomes. (CIA)

Above: All nine of the surviving A-12s were moved outside prior to their ultimate disposal. They are seen here clustered together at the Palmdale plant, having benefited from the application of protective coatings. (Lockheed Martin Skunk Works)

Below: The ceramic shells covering the D-21's fixed inlet and exhaust were to have been ballistically removed prior to firing its Marquardt RJ-43-MA-11 ramjet, but in-flight trials showed this to be impossible without causing damage and they were abandoned. (Lockheed ADP)

The first M-21/D-21 combination is shown here flying high above the Nevada desert. Aircraft '940 survived the Tagboard flight-test programme and has been preserved in Seattle. The drone's nose and tail fairings are in place here, the in-flight jettisoning of which damaged the drone's airframe. (Lockheed)

The ceramic nose fairing of the D-21 included a pitot tube. Within the fairing, the intake centrebody of the drone itself featured a separate pitot serving the aircraft's flight control systems once it was in autonomous flight.

Again the first M-21 is shown early on in the test programme. It is accompanied by another of Kelly Johnson's great designs, a Lockheed Starfighter, here in its F-104A form.

NASA carried out invaluable research with the YF-12A. Here the aircraft is equipped with camera pods and a pylon-mounted pod beneath the mid-fuselage to accommodate test packages. For this formation shot with a NASA T-38 Talon, the YF-12A was flown by Fitz Fulton and Ray Young. (Paul F. Crickmore Collection)

Above: The stop-start nature of the end of the SR-71 programme was a poor way to mark the passing of a great machine. This aircraft is shown towards the end of the type's career, wearing minimal red markings over its all-black finish. Dedicated paint was required throughout the Blackbird programme, such were the rigours of high-speed flight on the aircraft's finish. (Lockheed)

Below: The 'space-suited' pilot of this SR-71A can just be seen through the cockpit glazing. The knife-edge to the windscreen centreline is also apparent, as is the extent and shape of the forward-fuselage chines. The aircraft's inflight-refuelling receptacle is positioned just aft of the cockpit, with a retractable red anti-collision beacon aft of that. (Lockheed)

Ben Rich took over as Skunk Works' boss when Kelly Johnson retired. Rich had come to the Skunk Works at Kelly's request as an engineer on the U-2 programme. He was a key member of the SR-71 team, although his greatest achievement at Lockheed was probably the F-117A Nighthawk.

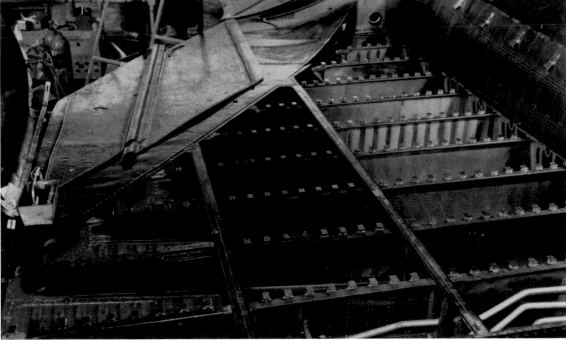

Early problems with airframe heating causing panels to deform were solved by a simple clip. A so-called stand-off clip was developed to sit between the aircraft's skin and the sub-structure beneath. The cleverly designed clip retained structural integrity while also providing a heat shield between the skin and internal structure. (Lockheed Martin Skunk Works)

Above: This production-line shot shows five SR-71As in various stages of completion. The outer wing panels and nacelle halves of the second aircraft away from the camera have been swung upward, while in the foreground a nose section is under construction. A large yellow and red sign at left warns of the dangers of FOD. (Lockheed)

Below: With its afterburner section glowing red, this J58 was undergoing a ground test. The Pratt & Whitney team overcame considerable technical challenges to match its engine to an airframe that delivered hitherto unseen performance. (Lockheed Martin Skunk Works)

Above: At engine start, or when the afterburners were lit, the chemical ignition system dispensed a shot of triethyl borane into the engines' combustion cans. The TEB ignited spontaneously, briefly producing a spurt of green/yellow flame. TEB capacity was one limiting factor on the aircraft's endurance. (NASA)

Below: Engine maintenance was facilitated by the outer portion of each engine nacelle, which was able to be rotated upward, along with its associated outer wing section, to reveal a good two thirds of the engine. Here specialist lifting equipment is being used during an engine change. (Paul F. Crickmore Collection)

Throughout its career the SR-71 was supported by the KC-135Q Stratotanker, the KC-10 Extender only becoming available during the 1980s. As well as a modified fuel system, the 'Q' featured special communications and navigation gear better suited to the sensitive nature of SR operations. Indeed, even when the KC-10 came into service, a KC-135Q might be called upon to act as a 'pathfinder' for a tanker package. (Paul F. Crickmore Collection)

Above: The six BF Goodrich main tyres were 32 ply and filled with nitrogen at 415 psi (2861 kPa). They cost around $2,300 each and were good for approximately 15 full-stop landings. (Paul F. Crickmore Collection)

The navigation readouts on the starboard SR-71 console panel to the the right allow the present latitude of 35° 12' north and longitude of 116° 15' west to be read. The pilot's cockpit below shows that this was an aircraft of 1960s vintage with little in the way of modern cockpit instrumentation. (Curt Osterheld/Paul F. Crickmore)

Left: Since ambient conditions in the nosewheel bay were maintained by the aircraft's environmental control system, the nosewheel tyres did not require the aluminium impregnation of the mainwheel tyres. (Lockheed)

Above: Initially the S-901J pressure suit featured an aluminium coverall, as seen here on the right, but a white coverall was later developed to cut down on reflections within the cockpit. Latterly SR-71 crews wore 'old gold' suits. (USAF)

Suiting up for a Habu mission was something of an arduous operation, requiring the assistance of PSD technicians. After a low-residue preflight meal and medical, the crew began the suiting-up process. Here a strap connected to the front of the helmet is being tested – in the event of suit inflation the helmet could ride up over the wearer's chin and the strap was provided to counter this tendency, which could result in great discomfort for the crewmember. (Paul F. Crickmore Collection)

and an all-altitude oil reservoir. Power from the engine was transmitted to the ADS via a reduction gearbox on the engine and a flexible drive shaft. The constant speed drive within the ADS then converted the variable shaft speed to a constant rotational speed to power the ac generator. Two hydraulic pumps and a fuel-circulating pump were also mounted on the ADS gearbox. The two hydraulic pumps supplied power to the A and L or B and R hydraulic systems, while the fuel-circulating pump supplied fuel to the aircrafts heat-sink system.

AIR INLET CONTROL

The SR-71 boasted a unique, highly efficient air inlet system that supplemented thrust via three components: an asymmetric mixed-compression, variable-geometry inlet; the J58 engine; and a convergent/divergent blow-in door ejector nozzle. The Air Inlet Control (AIC) system regulated the massively varying internal airflow throughout the aircraft's entire flight envelope, ensuring that the two engines received air at the correct velocity and pressure.

To satisfy the J58's voluminous appetite for air during operations at ground idle, taxiing and take-off, the centrebody spikes were positioned fully forward, allowing an uninterrupted flow to the engine compressor. Supplementary flow was also provided through six forward bypass doors, and a reverse flow was set-up through exit louvres on the spike's centrebody and a set of variable-area 'inlet ports' that were regulated by an external slotted band, which drew air in from two sets of doors. The task of operating these doors was initially manually controlled by the pilot, but was later accomplished automatically by a Digital Automatic Flight Inlet Control System (DAFICS) computer. Positioning of the electrically operated, hydraulically-actuated spike was also controlled by the DAFICS. Operating together, the forward bypass doors and the centrebody spike were used to control the position of the normal shockwave, just aft of the inlet throat. To optimise inlet efficiencies, the shock wave was captured and held inside the converging-diverging nozzle, just behind the narrowest part of the throat, thereby achieving the maximum possible pressure-rise across the normal shock.

Once airborne, the forward bypass doors closed automatically as the undercarriage retracted. At Mach 1.4 the doors began to modulate, again automatically to obtain a pre-programmed ratio between 'dynamic' pressure at the inlet cowl on one side of the throat and 'static' duct pressure on the other side. When the aircraft reached 30,000 ft (9144 m), the inlet spike unlocked and at Mach 1.6 it began a rearward translation, achieving its fully-aft position of 2 ft 2 in (0.66 m) relative to its fully-forward position, at Mach 3.2 – the inlet's most efficient speed. As the spike moved aft, the 'capture airstream tube area' increased by 112 per cent, while the throat restriction decreased by 46 per cent of its former size.

A peripheral 'shock trap' bleed slot (positioned around the outer circumference of the duct, just forward of the 'throat' and set at twice the boundary layer displacement thickness), shaved off 7 per cent of the stagnant inlet airflow and stabilised the terminal (normal) shock. This air was then rammed across the bypass plenum through 32 shock trap tubes spaced at regular intervals around the circumference of the shock trap. As this compressed tertiary air travelled down the secondary bypass passage, it firmly closed the suck-in doors and cooled the exterior of the engine casing before being exhausted through the ejector nozzle. Potentially turbulent boundary layer air was removed from the surface of the centrebody spike at the point of its maximum diameter and then ducted through the spike's hollow support struts before being dumped overboard, through nacelle exit louvres. The aft bypass doors were opened at mid-Mach to minimise the aerodynamic drag that resulted from dumping air overboard through the forward bypass doors.

By carefully dove-tailing all the above parameters, the inlet was able to generate internal duct pressures of 18 psi (124 kPa). When this is considered against the ambient air pressure at 82,000 ft (24994 m) of just 0.4 psi (2.76 kPa), it is immediately apparent that this extremely large pressure gradient is capable of producing a similarly large forward thrust vector. In fact, at Mach cruise, this accounted for no less than 54 per cent of the total thrust being produced; a further 29 per cent was produced by the ejector, while the remaining 17 per cent was generated by the J58 engine. If, however, airflow disturbances disrupted this delicate pressure-balancing trick, it is equally easy to appreciate the effects that such excursions would have upon the aircraft. The result was another of the SR-71's unique idiosyncrasies, the unstart. These aerodynamic disruptions occurred when the normal shock wave was 'belched' forward from the inlet throat, causing an instant drop in the inlet pressure and thrust. With each engine positioned at mid-semi span, the shock wave departure manifested itself in a vicious yaw in the direction of the unstarted engine. Sometimes these were so strong that crewmembers would have their helmets knocked against the cockpit canopy framing. Recovery for such an incident involved an automatic, computer-sequenced inlet restart. This involved the spike being driven forwards and the forward bypass doors opening to re-capture and reposition

A titanium shroud was fitted in each main gear bay to protect the tyres from heat damage during sustained Mach-3 flight. It also offered limited protection to hydraulic lines should a tyre explode in flight. (Paul F. Crickmore Collection)

the shock wave. The spike then returned to its correct position, followed by the bypass doors, which reconfigured the inlet to its optimum performance. Unstarts were a regular feature of A-12 and early SR-71 flights, but as computer software improved, the DAFICS was able to achieve near-perfect inlet airflow control that practically rid the jet of its unstart problems.

To improve the duct's diffusion rate, small rounded protuberances – referred to in-house by the design team as 'mice' – were positioned at the rear of the duct. Acting like vortex generators, they changed the area of distribution and thereby improved recovery. Early in the programme, Lockheed engineers also re-christened other assemblies; the free-floating trailing-edge flaps at the end of the nacelles, used to help shape the exhaust plume, were referred to as 'tail-feathers'. Perhaps a little less obvious were the terms 'onion slicer' – used to describe the forward bypass system – and 'cabbage slicer' for the aft bypass system. However, a memo issued from upon high instructed that henceforth, correct terminology would be used at all times.

FUEL SYSTEM

The SR-71 had five individual fuselage tanks, numbered 1A, 1, 2, 4, and 5, and two wing-fuselage tank groups numbered 3 and 6 (tank 6 was further divided into 6A and 6B); interconnecting plumbing and electrically driven boost pumps were used for fuel feed, transfer and dumping. The fuel system moved the aircraft's centre of gravity by automatic tank sequencing to the engine feed manifolds, or manual aft transfer into tank 5 when it was less than full or, manual forward transfer into tank 1.

Tank capacities were:

Tank 1	2,096 lb/ 951 kg	13,770 US gal/ 52125 litres
Tank 1A	251 lb/ 114 kg	1,650 US gal/ 6246 litres
Tank 2	1,974 lb/ 895 kg	12,970 US gal/ 49097 litres
Tank 3	2,460 lb/ 1116 kg	16,160 US gal/ 61172 litres
Tank 4	1,454 lb/ 660 kg	9,550 US gal/ 36151 litres
Tank 5	1,758 lb/ 797 kg	11,550 US gal/ 43721 litres
Tank 6A (forward)	1,158 lb/ 525 kg	7,610 US gal/ 28807 litres
Tank 6B (aft)	1,069 lb/ 485 kg	7,020 US gal/ 26574 litres
Total	12,220 lb/ 5543 kg	80,280 US gal/ 303893 litres

Sixteen single-stage, centrifugal, ac-powered boost pumps supplied fuel to the manifolds. Tanks 1 and 4, which normally fed fuel to both engines, were each equipped with four pumps, while tanks 2, 3, 5 and 6 each had two pumps. Where the pumps were grouped in pairs, either pump was capable of supplying fuel at sufficient pressure to permit engine operation at reduced afterburning thrust if the other failed.

ELECTRICAL SYSTEM

Electrical power was normally supplied by two ac generators, each rated at 60KVA. The generators were mechanically driven, by their respective engines, through the constant speed drive (CSD) units and operated in parallel. They provided 115/200 volt, 400-cycle, three-phase power to five ac buses and to two 200-amp transformer-rectifiers – these energised three 28-volt dc buses. Either generator was capable of supplying the normal ac and dc power requirements of the aircraft.

Two 25-amp-hour batteries provided limited emergency power if both generators were off or inoperative, or if both transformer-rectifiers failed; each battery individually supplied one of the two essential dc buses. The maximum duration of the dual-battery power system was about 40 minutes, provided that all unnecessary electrical equipment was turned off.

HYDRAULIC SYSTEMS

As briefly mentioned earlier, the SR-71 had four separate hydraulic systems, each provided with its own pressurisation reservoir and engine driven pump. Pumps for the A and L system were driven from the left engine ADS. The B and R pumps were powered by the right engine ADS. The A and B hydraulic systems powered the flight controls. The L hydraulic system powered the left engine air inlet system, the landing gear, brakes, air-refuelling door and receptacle, and the nose-wheel steering. The R system powered the right engine air inlet system. If pressure in the L system dropped to less than 2,200 psi (15169 kPa), the R system automatically powered the landing gear retraction cycle.

STABILITY AUGMENTATION SYSTEM

The SR-71's centre of gravity was automatically moved aft during acceleration to high-Mach flight, to reduce trim drag and improve elevon authority in both the pitch and roll axes. The fuselage chines produced lift forward of the cg, which had the effect of destabilising the aircraft in the pitch axis and reduced aft cg travel, resulting in low static margins of stability and safety. Additionally, the

chine had an adverse aerodynamic effect on the aircraft when performing sideslip manoeuvres at cruise AoA (approximately 6° of positive Alpha (AoA)). This, coupled with the low aerodynamic damping which is inherent to flight at high altitudes, conspired to ensure that the SR-71 was only marginally stable in both pitch and yaw at high Mach.

Control in this delicate, but critical, corner of the flight envelope was achieved by the aircraft's elevons and rudders, worked through an automatic flight control system (AFCS), which in-turn was controlled via the DAFICS computers. The AFCS consisted of three sub-systems, a Stability Augmentation System (SAS); an autopilot; and a Mach-trim system. As coordinating system, the AFCS provided pitch, roll and yaw stabilisation via the flight control surfaces. Eight rate-sensing gyros detected divergence from stable flight and together with three lateral accelerometers, also provided motion-sensing signals that were applied to the multi-redundant SAS circuits in the DAFICS. Control over the AFCS was provided to the pilot via 'Pitch SAS', 'Roll SAS' and 'Yaw SAS' switches, located on the right console panel. In addition to responding to the signals from DAFICS, the servos could also be activated by direct stick and rudder pedal inputs.

The autopilot featured two separate 'hold functions': pitch and roll. Pitch control was achieved via the basic attitude hold mode, KEAS 'hold', or Mach 'hold'. In roll mode, control was exercised via the basic roll attitude hold mode, heading hold mode or auto-steering 'Auto Nav' mode. This latter mode was programmed to obey heading commands from the astro-inertial navigation system (ANS). When the autopilot was engaged, the aircraft was held in the roll attitude established at the time of engagement. With 'AutoNav' selected, the autopilot controlled roll to ensure that the aircraft adhered to the predetermined navigation track that the ANS accurately maintained. During operational sorties the aircraft was invariably flown in this mode to ensure that it remained stable and on an accurate track while the onboard sensors were activated.

The Mach trim system provided speed stability up to Mach 1.5, while the aircraft was either accelerating or decelerating – a period during which the autopilot could not be engaged. It compensated, via the pitch trim actuator, for the aircraft's propensity to 'tuck' nose down while

The SR-71's three-wheeled main gear had a hollow axle which enabled any wheel to be changed without removing the other two. The sidewalls of the main tyres were impregnated with aluminium powder to dissipate airframe heat generated at high-Mach cruise. (Paul F. Crickmore Collection)

accelerating through the Mach and to rise nose up, while decelerating.

ASTRO INERTIAL NAVIGATION SYSTEM

The reconnaissance missions conducted by the SR-71 took it to some of the most politically sensitive areas of the world. It was therefore essential that it should be equipped with the most accurate navigation system available, particularly bearing in mind that it would be flying at a velocity of 3,000 ft (914 m) per second! The Nortronics Division, Astro Inertial Navigation System (ANS) designed for the Douglas Skybolt air-to-surface missile, was modified for use in the SR-71, and designated NAS-14V2. Producing a terminal error accuracy of less than half a mile after covering distances the equivalent of more than half way around the world, it was justifiably considered by some to be the most outstanding piece of equipment to come out of the entire Senior Crown programme. The ANS combined data from an inertial platform with a time datum supplied from a chronometer that was accurate to within five milliseconds. Position updating was achieved automatically by astrotracking, at any one time, six of the 52 most prominently visible stars by day or night. The stars were computer-catalogued in an ephemeris memory that could be used for continuous cross-checking for track position referencing. Scanning the celestial bodies sequentially, through a pre-programmed tracker mechanism mounted on a gimballed platform on top of the nav unit, the ANS provided passive, refined location information.

When the autopilot was coupled to the ANS through the AutoNav function switch, the aircraft could be flown automatically and precisely on a predetermined flight path. The pre-planned route (worked out by highly experienced navigators) was electronically loaded via a Milar tape into the ANS's computer memory a few hours prior to take off. Inflight modifications could be made by the RSO using his Control and Display panel. During flight, the computer-sequenced plan directed the aircraft from one destination point (DP) to the next. Two further features of the ANS included ground reference position updating through the forward-looking view sight, and sensor monitoring by reference to Control Point (CP) actions. CPs were pre-determined track points programmed into the ANS that would activate or deactivate reconnaissance sensors and served to alert the RSO that the system was about to turn on, that the system had functioned correctly, and that programmed activities were being automatically carried out.

Latterly, the ANS was backed up by a Singer-Kearfott (SKN-2417) INS that had a CEP of one nautical mile per hour. This had replaced the earlier SR-71 gyro Flight Reference System (FRS) in June 1982. The earlier system had no navigation capability and provided heading and attitude information only. At the heart of the new unit was an inertially stabilised platform (consisting of four gimbals for all-attitude operation, vertical and azimuth gyros and three sub-miniature pendulous linear accelerometers). Located in the 'R' Bay, the gyro-platform provided navigation data to a control panel located in the RSO's cockpit.

MISSION RECORDER SYSTEM

The Mission Recorder System (MRS) was an airborne mission and maintenance data-recording system used to store up to 12-hours of monitored aircraft and system performance information. In addition, the MRS recorded the actions of the reconnaissance sensors and navigation systems, as

Aircraft '967 shows off equipment bay Q, in which the right palletised TEOC, or Technical Objective Camera, was housed. (Paul F. Crickmore Collection)

well as all inter-cockpit and radio voice transmissions. The purpose of this crash-survivable system was to identify failures, impending failures, and sub-standard system performances for maintenance purposes or accident analyses. Data collection was achieved through the use of multiplexing switches within the MRS, which sequentially shared analogue and digitised signals at a sample rate of once every three seconds. Once activated, the system operated continuously and automatically. After a mission, the recorded data was copied from the Unit 500 recorder-assembly on the aircraft using a Mobile Ground Formatter Unit (MGFU), which created a Computer-Compatible Tape (CCT) of non-voice data. A portable Tape Copy Unit (TCU) was used with the MGFU to copy the crew's voice audio recording. The table below summarises the number of signals monitored by the MRS within each aircraft system.

VELOCITY/HEIGHT SYSTEM

A Velocity/Height (V/H) system produced information scaled electrically to represent the

Engine	16
Hydraulic system	13
DAFICS	58
Electrical system	24
MRS	18
ANS	100
ECS	16
Miscellaneous	20

angular rate of motion between the aircraft and the terrain below. Signal sources for the system were the ANS and the V/H indicator in the RSO's cockpit. These signals were scaled at 0.2 volts (dc) per milliradian per second and produced reference information for the various reconnaissance sensors on the aircraft. Another device aiding surveillance interpretation was the sensor event/frame count system. This correlated time, position, altitude and heading when the 'close-look' cameras or Technical Objective Cameras (TEOCs) were in operation. The system used the ANS Mission Recorder System and a signal sensor processor to convert event input signals into six millisecond-wide event-marker pulses, that were

A detachable and interchangeable nose section greatly enhanced the Habu's mission flexibility. As seen here, the entire section forward of the cockpit could be detached. (Paul F. Crickmore Collection)

monitored by the ANS. On receiving an even-marker-pulse, the ANS activated a frame-count register associated with a particular sensor. This data (with precise location information) was recorded by the MRS.

The RSO had the ability to manually operate and control all reconnaissance system sensors, despite the fact that these were normally fully pre-programmed for automatic turn on/turn off, and for changing 'look angles' to many different points, in order to frame hundreds of separate targets of interest. A manual exposure control panel also enabled the RSO to remotely control camera exposure settings in order to take account of various lighting conditions (brightness and reflectivity). This was graduated in degrees of sun angle with reference indices for low, normal, high and very high terrain reflectivity. Such changes were made by regulating dc voltage between 10 and 38 volts for sun angle settings between 5° and 90°.

COMMUNICATIONS AND NAVIGATION

The SR-71's communications equipment comprised of an AN/AIC-18 interphone system for crew intercommunication and crewmember-to-groundcrew interphone communication. A COMNAV-50 UHF radio provided voice transmission and reception on any of seven thousand channels in the P-Band frequency range together with a direction-finding capability. The system operated in two modes, either 'internal' that was compatible with other types of UHF radios, or 'external' wherein coded communication was possible only between other COMNAV-50 radios. Operating in the 'external' mode the system offered a high resistance to jamming in addition to security and a range measuring capability. Two independent UHF radio sets were provided, designated UHF-1 in the front cockpit, and UHF-2 in the rear cockpit. A modem control panel in the RSO's cockpit controlled coding of 'external' mode signals and discrete selection of the ranging partner. An AN/ARA-48 automatic direction finding (ADF) antenna was used in conjunction with the UHF radio system, automatically pointing to emissions emanating from compatible equipment transmitting on the same frequency – ie when the COMNAV-50 was operating in 'external' mode, the ADF function would operate provided that it was within the detection range of a similarly programmed COMNAV-50 – the system had a range of up to 200 nm (230 miles; 370 km).

An AN/ARC-186(V) VHF radio provided AM transmissions and reception from 108.000 to 151.975 MHz. Frequency spacing was 25 kHz and 20 channels could be preset in addition to the emergency (guard) frequency (121.5 MHz). Either narrow or wideband operation was possible, but this had to be preset by maintenance personnel.

The FM capability of the radio was not operative.

For long-range voice communication the SR-71 was equipped with a 618-T and an AN/ARC-190C(V) HF radio. The modes of operation for the 618-T set were single sideband (SSB) or amplitude modulation (AM). The frequency range was 2 to 30 MHz, tunable in 1-kHz steps. The ARC-190 received and transmitted on 280,000 frequencies in a band from 2 to 29.9999 MHz, spaced at 100 Hz. Modes of operation were upper and lower sideband, amplitude modulation and continuous wave. The antenna for both HF radios comprised the aircraft's pitot boom.

A 51RV-1 ILS receiver supplied signals to the bank and pitch steering bars and the glide slope indicator on the Attitude-Director Indicator (ADI) and to the course deviation indicator (CDI) on the pilot's Horizontal Situation Indicator (HSI), to enable him to conduct instrument landings. The receiver operated on 20 frequencies. Localiser frequencies ranged from 108.1 to 111.9 MHz, while glide-slope frequencies ranged from 329.3 to 335.0 MHz. The correct glide-slope frequency was automatically tuned when the localiser frequency was selected.

Viwed through a U-2 viewscope, these technicians are working on an Itek TEOC as employed by the SR-71A. A combination of optical and electronic sensors could be carried for maximum intelligence coverage. (USAF)

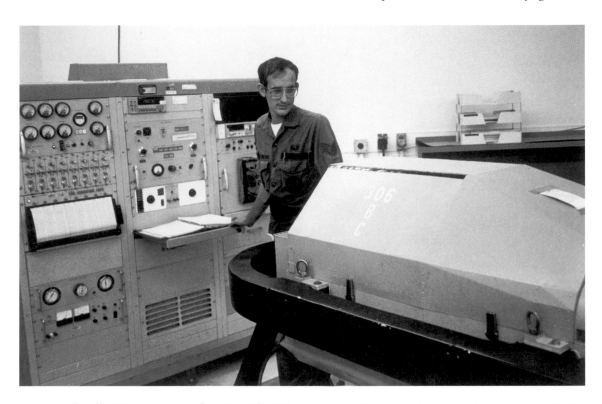

As with all IFF systems, the SR-71's IFF transponder responded to radar interrogation signals in order for its identity to be ascertained. The SR-71 was equipped with two such transponders, an AN/APX-108(V) IFF (W/SB R-2668) and a WILCOX 914X-2 IFF (W/O SB R-2668). The system included altitude reporting (suppressed by the RSO above 60,000 ft/18288 m), selective identification and emergency reporting features. Mode 4 provided an encrypted IFF capability. Two beacons, a G-band and an I-band, were also provided to aid radar tracking when the SR-71 was participating in special tests.

Finally, for non-covert flights the aircraft was equipped with an AN/ARN-118(V) TACAN, which was used with ground stations and co-operating aircraft.

SENSOR SYSTEMS
The first operational Giant Scale SR-71 mission was flown from Kadena, by Majs Jerry O'Malley and his RSO, Ed Payne, in aircraft 64-17976 on 21 March 1968. For this historic sortie the aircraft was configured with a high-resolution radar (HRR) in the nose section. Known as the PIP (Product Improved) radar by the Air Force, the unit had been developed and built in 'the black' and designated by its manufacture, Goodyear Aerospace, as -531 or GA-531, the numbers signifying the block numbers assigned by the company to identify that particular programme's

Encased within its own environmental control system 'jacket', this OBC has been removed from an SR-71 for bench checks. The OBC joined the Habu's sensor suite in 1972. (USAF)

drawings. The antenna received X-band generated, doppler phase information, which was then stored on a recorder housed in the forward right mission bay. This was then transferred onto a continuous, 4-in (10-cm) wide map film, via a ground-based optical correlator. The end result was an image similar in appearance to that obtained by a camera, with a ground resolution of about 6 ft (1.83 m).

In the C-bay, a Fairchild Camera Company F489 Terrain Objective Camera (TROC) was mounted. Equipped with a 6-in (152-mm) focal length lens, this wide-angle mapping camera, operated throughout the sortie, producing a single overlapping exposure of the terrain directly below. Its 663 ft (202 m) of film could photograph a strip 7,800 nm (8,982 miles; 14455 km) long at 55 per cent overlap. Weighing in at 135 lb (61 kg), the developed images enabled photo interpreters to cross-check the aircraft's position and provide additional ground cues in relation to targets photographed by the other sensors.

Next came two close-look Hycon HR-308B TEOCs, which were also referred to as Tech cameras. They were mounted horizontally in bays P and Q and viewed targets below and out to about 45° by tilting a beryllium mirror located in the camera's scan-head. The camera touted a 48-in

The removal of panels on the underside of the aircraft's nose reveals the antenna for the Loral CAPRE high-resolution ground-mapping radar. (Lockheed Martin Skunk Works)

(1219-mm) focal length lens that imaged onto fine grain film producing a 9½-sq in (61.3-cm²) frame Maximum film capacity was 1,500 ft (457 m), producing 1,800 usable frames per camera, per flight, that covered about 2,000 nm (2303 miles; 3706 km) of track; the nominal ground area being photographed was about 2½ sq miles (6.47 km²) per frame. These variable pointing angle, high resolution, narrow-field framing cameras had four modes of operation: Burst Mode took a burst of ten photos at a rate of about one per second; Stepping Mode slewed the camera head back and forth, four digits either side of a commanded look angle, to provide wider coverage of a given area when a target's precise location was unclear or the area of interest was wider than the normal frame width. Finally, two overlap modes were available. One was timed to provide a 55 per cent overlap of each consecutive frame; the other produced a ten per cent overlap between frames. The system was

Left: This incredible photograph of Oakland baseball stadium was reproduced from a first-generation OBC image. It was taken during a routine Stateside training sortie at operational speed and altitude. (Paul F. Crickmore Collection)

activated either automatically by the ANS, or manually by the RSO. The camera was available in two models. The HR-308B and the HR-308C, the B model having two versions, the -11 and the -21. Except for passive vibration isolation, the HR-308B was unstabilised, while the HR-308C was actively stabilised in pitch, roll and, at higher look angles, in yaw.

On that historic first operational mission, aircraft '976 also carried two Itek Corporation HR-9085 Operational Objective Cameras (OOCs). These were mounted horizontally and utilised a mirrored scan head. They were located in bays S and T. These high-resolution, three-dimensional panoramic cameras had a focal length of 13 in (330 mm) and a maximum capacity of 3,300 ft (1006 m) of 70-mm (2¾-in) film that was sufficient to cover 3,600 frames, with alternate forward and aft exposures of the terrain below and to the side of the aircraft's track. Each camera had a lateral coverage of 45° and total track coverage of about

1,500 nm (1,727 miles; 2779 km); they were manually activated by the RSO.

HRB-Singer produced a little known sensor system for the Senior Crown programme, that was successfully flight tested during the aircraft's early years. This was the HRB-454 IR system. Its 100 ft (30 m) of 70-mm film was sufficient to image a strip 12,000 miles (19312 km) long to 45° either side of the aircraft's flight path. Having undertaken its first SR-71 Category (Cat) II flight test on 3 May 1966, it completed 49 IR test flights but was discarded early in the aircraft's operational career.

OBC TEST

At 14:00 hours, on 5 April 1972, Randy Hertzog and his RSO, John Carnochan, launched 64-17980 from Kadena equipped with an Optical Bar Camera (OBC) in its nose section, for the camera's first operational test. This panoramic camera, fitted initially with a 24-in (610-mm) focal length lens (in November 1973, SAC received its first OBC unit fitted with a 30-in/762-mm lens), was built by the Itek Corporation and obtained high quality horizon-to-horizon imagery focused on fine grain black and white film with an ISO rating of just 8. So successful were the results that by the end of the year the SRC directed that the OBC unit should be used whenever weather over Southeast Asia

Robust framework was a feature of the SR-71's glazing, a must for the kinetic heating encountered during cruising flight. The pilot's canopy was reminiscent of that employed by Convair's F-106 Delta Dart. Stencilling on the aircraft's skin provided information for rescue crews in the event of an accident on the ground. (Paul F. Crickmore)

(SEA) permitted and that on days of heavy cloud cover the HRR unit should be substituted – an operation that took maintenance about 16 hours to complete. Having proved its worth, the OBC went on to replace the OOCs as a means of collecting panoramic coverage.

The OBC was mounted on a hatch and located within its own shroud that was provided with refrigerated air supplied by an extension of the cold air supply in the forward chine bay and directed into the shroud above and on each side of the rotating lens system which then exhausted into the nose compartment. To prevent the OBC lens system from being over-cooled, electric heaters in the shroud ensured that the temperature was maintained at approximately 104°F (40°C). The film was supported by air that was ducted through the canopy seal supply line and, although the camera was not stabilised, it was equipped with vibration isolation and a damping system that was compatible with its environment in the nose. The lens system had a fixed aperture and was mounted on an 'optical bar' that accommodated the lens and the two mirror assemblies used to create the folded optical path. When in operation, the optical bar rotated continuously around its longitudinal axis. Film exposure was accomplished via a scanning slit shutter while both the bar and film were in motion. The width of the slit adjusted automatically to compensate for varying degrees of brightness and the velocity/height (V/H) ratio. Full coverage was obtained through a scan angle of 140°, ie 70° either side of the aircraft's track with a field angle along the flight path of

At cruising altitudes the earth's curvature became very apparent, although it has been exaggerated here by a wide-angle lens. Combining high-altitude flight with Mach-3 plus speed, the Habu was able to remain immune from surface-to-air missiles in all its operational theatres. (BC Thomas)

approximately 8°. Aircraft forward motion compensation (fmc) was provided during frame exposure when the V/H ratio was between 35 and 45 milliradians (mr) per second; otherwise the fmc was automatically set at 40 mr per second if the applied signal fell outside that range. A data block in each frame recorded mission information, frame number and camera fore/aft or vertical orientation. The camera's cycle rate was controlled automatically by the frame overlap requirement of the mode selected and by the V/H fmc. The film used was either 3414 or 1414 and three operating modes could be selected in flight.

The final major sensor upgrade intended to become operational on the SR-71 prior to the end of the war in SEA was the Capability Reconnaissance Radar (CAPRE). This improved HRR was designed to replace the PIP. Manufactured by Loral, the prototype received its baptism of fire on 29 August 1972. However, due to various technical problems the anticipated deployment of production units on the three SR-71s participating in the June 1973 deployment to Kadena was delayed and instead PIP units were again used. The CAPRE system was a side-looking synthetic aperture radar and could be used in conjunction with the Radar Correlator

Display (RCD) to produce an in-flight display for navigation purposes. Its main function, however, was to illuminate ground targets that were then recorded onto a film strip on two recorders that were housed in the aft portion of the right forward mission bay. Range marks and data block information were automatically superimposed onto the film and the unit could be programmed to cover a strip either 10 or 20 nm (12/19 or 23 miles/37 km) wide on either side of the aircraft's track, with the near edge of the swathe between 10 and 70 nm (12/19 and 81 miles/130 km) from the aircraft. However, CAPRE could only image during non-turning flight. Two modes of operation were provided. In automatic mode, system operation was controlled by the ANS; in manual mode the RSO controlled the system's operation.

The RCD was a self-contained unit located in the forward portion of the aft cockpit. It operated in conjunction with, but was independent from, the radar recorders. The RCD operated when power was applied to the unit and when the SLAR was in operation, since it was dependent upon SLAR Doppler phase history video to produce the in-flight display for navigation. The display moved downward at a rate proportional to the aircraft's ground speed and was normally some 50 seconds (25 nm/29 miles/47 km at cruise and altitude) behind the aircraft's real-time position. The RCD map display was 15 nm (17 miles; 27 km) wide and had to be stopped by the RSO for target evaluation and the determination of navigation fix-point error.

The final radar system developed and deployed on the SR-71 fleet before programme shut-down was the Loral Advanced Synthetic Aperture Radar System (ASARS). This catapulted radar-generated ground-mapping into a new dimension. First deployed operationally to RAF Mildenhall on 9 July 1983, the system is believed to have had a resolution of less than 1 ft (0.30 m) at nadir from 80,000 ft (24384 m). As a note of interest, all three ground-mapping radars built for the SR-71 emanated from the same production facility. However, its ownership changed several times over the years. As noted, the first system was built by Goodyear, which also built the CAPRE/HRR system. The company was later bought by Loral and under this name ASARS-1 was developed and fielded. However, during the reactivation programme, Lockheed Martin bought Loral, so ASARS-1 was ultimately owned by the latter – all the same people, just with different corporate names paying their salaries.

SIGINT RECEIVERS

In May 1969 the SR-71's electromagnetic reconnaissance system (EMR), built by Airborne Instrument Laboratories, was deployed for operations. The system was interfaced with the

ANS and MRS for data collection and also with the IFF, TACAN, SLAR and DEF system to prevent received intelligence from being masked by aircraft transmissions from those systems. To provide meaningful data, it was necessary that the ANS was fully operational even though the EMR operated independently. Once activated by the RSO, the EMR was an entirely automatic, passive collection system and performed two search functions simultaneously, special search and general search. Special search was based upon pre-flight instructions in the Elint Improvement Programme (EIP) system computer that designated emitters of special interest. When a received signal matched the designated emitter, a monitor receiver was automatically tuned to that signal for a pre-programmed period, and the signal pulses were passed to special detectors and recorded on tracks of the continuous analogue recorder as video signals to be evaluated utilising specialist equipment after landing.

The general search function searched the frequency spectrum from 30 MHz to 40 GHz. This spectrum was divided into six bands, all of which were searched simultaneously. Every emitter signal received in the bands was recorded on the digital recorder by way of time, frequency, direction, pulse width and amplitude.

The continuous analog recorder was a 14-channel Ampex Model AR-1700 wide-band magnetic tape recorder that recorded special search signals, Elint data from the on-board DEF systems, and maintenance data. The recorder

This Habu driver self portrait was taken by BC Thomas, who accrued 1,217 hours 18 minutes in the aircraft – more than any other Habu pilot. (BC Thomas)

could be operated automatically by the EIP system and/or manually by the RSO.

The tape transport operated at 5 or 10 ft (1.5 or 3 m) per second. A 14-in (35.6-cm) reel supplied 9,200 ft (2804 m) of 1-in (2.5-cm) magnetic tape that provided 30 or 15 minutes of recording time per flight.

The increased capability provided by the EIP generated further mission requests from SAC for its Single Integrated Operational Plan (SIOP) and also from the DIA, the Commander in Chief Pacific (CINCPAC), Military Assistance Command Vietnam (MACV) and the Commander United States Forces Korea (COMUSKOREA). These in turn led the JCS to direct SAC to execute peripheral SR-71 Elint sorties of China, the USSR, North Korea, the Taiwan Straits and the Sea of Japan, in addition to overflight missions of all high threat areas of North Vietnam (NV). This increase in aircraft utility was such that on 18 December 1970 another SR-71 was added to the Kadena detachment, and for the next two and a half years it operated four aircraft.

DEFENSIVE SYSTEMS

Defensive (DEF) systems were deployed to defend the aircraft by electronic means and were arbitrarily assigned letters and numbers to identify each system. This equipment was continually evolved to counter Soviet anti-air developments. Not surprisingly, these systems were among the most security-sensitive aspects of the aircraft. In March 1969, System E became operational and was followed by Systems F and G in June and December 1970 respectively.

In April 1972, a Special Elint Beacon Receiver (SEBER), known as System G, was deployed for operational testing on selected Giant Scale missions. It was designed specifically to collect the beacon transponder signals of SA-2 SAMs.

At the close of the Senior Crown programme there were two main DEF systems deployed on the SR-71, namely A2C and H. DEF A2C was an ECM system designed to counter advanced aircraft radars and DEF H was designed to defeat advanced SAMs. The A2 system comprised two sets of receiver antennas located aft of cut-outs on the left and right side of the nose chines and two transmit antennas that protruded slightly from the lower surfaces of the chines, opposite the pilot's cockpit. Gaseous nitrogen was used to pressurise the transmit waveguides. The antennas received signals from emitters below the SR-71 and identified the threat aircraft in the left or right forward quadrants. It seems highly probable that the system utilised either range gate pull-off (RGPO) or velocity gate pull-off (VGPO) deception jamming to mislead the would-be interceptor's missile.

The DEF H system included a transceiver, two transmitting systems, an interface unit, a data processor, an evaporative cooler and two centreline receiver antennas – one tuned to hi-band and the other to lo-band emissions. The system was capable of simultaneous hi- and lo-band jamming from four antennas.

CREW SURVIVAL SYSTEMS

Air Force regulation 60-16 requires pressure suits to be worn when flying above 50,000 ft (15240 m). The reason is that entry into this abnormal environment can cause many physiological problems that, if left unchecked, would kill the crew in minutes. For example, during ascent a reduction in the partial pressure of oxygen will cause hypoxia if a person is unprotected above 25,000 ft (7620 m). Progressive cardiorespiratory and neurological effects trigger such symptoms as euphoria, loss of judgment and impaired memory. Semi-consciousness and unconsciousness will follow if left unchecked, with death resulting four or five minutes later. Also, above 25,000 ft decompression sickness (DCS) develops, due to the reduction of ambient air pressure. It is acquired with increasing rapidity and severity the higher the altitude. The condition results from the evolution of nitrogen gas bubbles from body fluids as the ambient pressure falls (much like the bubbles generated in a carbonated drink bottle when its top is removed). Joint pain (the 'bends'), chest pain, skin itching and neurological manifestations may develop alone or together, the latter being more serious and even fatal.

Gas-containing cavities of the body – the lungs, gut, sinuses, etc – will increase in volume on ascent and contract on descent. Most of these problems are self-righting via the body's orifices; however, gas within the small gut is not free to escape and expansion can cause abdominal pain. To help reduce such symptoms crews ate a high-protein meal prior to flight. In addition, during descent, considerable pain can arise if pressure in the middle ear cavities and sinuses cannot be equalised. For this reason crews underwent routine medicals prior to flight and should a slight cold or throat infection be detected they were grounded until the condition had cleared. Were the crew to be subjected to the outside air temperature prevailing at 80,000 ft (24384 m), they would undoubtedly risk local or general cold injury (frostbite and hypothermia respectively).

To protect the crew from these effects, the cockpit was pressurised and pressure suits were worn. Within the cockpit pressurisation was allowed to fall from sea level to 8,000 ft (2438 m); it then remained constant to 25,000 ft (7620 m). At these altitudes the ambient air pressure falls from

10.9 psi (75.2 kPa) to 5.9 psi (40.7 kPa), respectively, giving rise to a pressure differential of 5 psi (34.5 kPa). This maximum figure was maintained by the aircraft's pressurisation system throughout the flight profile, which ensured that the fuselage was not subjected to unduly high pressure gradients, allowing structural weight to be reduced. However, in the event of rapid decompression or ejection, it meant that the crew must wear full pressure suits to survive.

Like most other systems associated with the SR-71, the pressure suit evolved throughout the life of the programme. The first suit was custom made by the David Clark Company in Worcester, Massachussetts, having been ordered on 7 March 1960. Designated S-901, it was made for Capt Harry Collins, who thoroughly tested it in numerous checks. The second suit, for Subject Number Two, was ordered on 28 June 1962. Designated S-901A, it was made for Lou Schalk, the Lockheed A-12 Chief Test Pilot. Thereafter the suits were developed in parallel with the Oxcart programme, each being tailor-made for its owner and sequentially designated S-901A to S-901H. A culmination of redesign work and development created the S-970 suit, which again was bespoke for its owner and used by both Agency Oxcart pilots and Air Force YF-12 crewmembers.

The first suits designed for the SR-71 programme were designated S-901J. These varied from their forebears, since they were non-custom-built and instead were available in 12 standard sizes. The first of these were produced in 1965. Initially the outer coveralls of these early suits had a layer of aluminum vacuum-deposited on HT-1 material, to provide a level of fire-resistant protection during high-Mach ejection and to help reflect heat away from the crewmember when in the cockpit – the inner surfaces of the windows routinely reached temperatures of 248°F (120°C). The problem with this was that the suit generated unwanted reflections, making it difficult for the crew to monitor instruments. A white coverall was developed that reduced, but did not eliminate, the problem, the drawback here being that the white Dacron material from which the coveralls were made was not fireproof. David Clark therefore developed a material it called Fypro. Its dark chocolate-brown colour killed unwanted cockpit reflections, but did nothing to reflect internal cockpit heat away from the crew. In 1977 the company developed the next generation of pressure suits, designated as the S-1030 series. These featured a high level of commonality between the U-2 and SR-71 programmes. Coloured 'Old Gold' and designated S-1031C for SR-71 use, the suit incorporated state-of-the-art textiles and was more durable and comfortable. Its four layers consisted of an outer coverall of Dacron (a form of

Cotton underwear, including long johns, was worn beneath the pressure suit as a protective layer between the skin and the suit's inner layer. Many crewmembers preferred to wear their underwear inside out to prevent seams rubbing during what could be several hours in the cockpit. (Paul F. Crickmore)

terylene) that was durable, tear and fire resistant. A restraint/joint layer held the suit together through restraint lines and acted as a pressure boundary. A third 'bladder' layer performed rather like a tyre inner tube and was made of polyurethane. Finally, an inner scuff layer protected the all important bladder layer from scuffing against other clothing and the urine collection device (UCD). An optional thermal layer could be worn inside the suit, but this was usually discarded in favour of more comfortable, long, cotton underwear, which was worn inside out, to prevent its seams from pressing into the skin.

Again the suit was built in 12 sizes and assumed the seated position when pressurised in order to aid cockpit mobility. Gloves completed the pressure seal and were attached via wrist hinges. Boots featured heel retraction strips that were connected by cable to the ejection seat on entry to the cockpit. The complete pressure suit system cost about $30,000 a copy and lasted 10–12 years, undergoing a complete strip-down overhaul every five years and a thorough inspection every 90 days, or 150 hours.

ESCAPE SYSTEM

Both crew positions were equipped with electrically-adjustable ejection seats that were activated in an emergency by using the 'D' ring located at the front of the seat. The rocket-powered seats automatically extended knee kickers and feet retractors, and locked the shoulder harness. The minimum safe altitude for use of the seat in the early days was ground level, provided that the aircraft was travelling faster than 65 kt (75 mph; 121 km/h). This automatic system was designed for extreme altitude bailouts, its two-stage chute system consisting of a 6-ft 6-in (1.98-m) diameter stabilising chute that deployed immediately following separation from the seat, provided that the altitude was greater than 17,000 ft (5182 m). At 16,800 ft (5121 m) the stabilising chute was jettisoned by a timer-actuated mechanical release. During this second stage, the main, 35-ft (10.67-m) diameter chute opened at 15,000 ft (4572 m). If bail out occurred below 16,200 ft (4938 m), the stabilising chute sequence was bypassed and the main deployed at 15,000 ft. Oxygen for breathing and inflation of the pressure suit was provided from six 20-cu in (328-cm³) bottles located in the back of the parachute pack and providing enough oxygen for 30 minutes.

The oxygen system in the aircraft consisted of four 875-cu in (14339-cm³) bottles, two for each crew position, and provided sufficient oxygen to last 7 hours 54 minutes. Should this system fail, a back-up source was available utilising that in the parachute emergency system simply by pulling a round green toggle – referred to as the 'green apple'. The crew's pressure suits were ventilated by the aircraft's air-conditioning system and the temperature regulated by an electrical heating element, controlled by the pilot.

DRAG CHUTE SYSTEM

To aid braking after touchdown, a 40-ft (12-m) diameter ring-sail ribbon chute was located in a compartment on the top aft section of the fuselage. This could be deployed at a maximum speed of 185 kt (213 mph; 343 km/h) when the chute deployment switch in the cockpit was thrown. This action opened the two chute compartment doors, the left door pulling out the ripcord pin during the opening process. A spring-loaded 18-ft (5.49-m) diameter pilot chute then deployed, pulling out a 10-ft (3.01-m) diameter parasail, which in turn pulled out the main drag chute. The parasail broke away from the main chute when the brake force exceeded 80 lb (36 kg). The brake chute could then be jettisoned by the pilot moving the chute switch to the jettison position – an action necessary before the aircraft had slowed below 20 kt (23 mph; 37 km/h) to ensure that the heavy chute attachment ball was pulled clear of the rear fuselage in order to avoid possible damage.

FROM RS TO SR AND BEYOND
Chapter 6

During the initial stages of assembling the YF-12 in late 1960, it became apparent to the ADP engineers that the basic interceptor airframe could be adapted to produce a strike bomber. Russ Daniell approached Kelly with the idea and asked if he could write a basic feasibility report. Having reviewed Daniell's resulting B-12 document, Kelly generated an unsolicited proposal that he took to Washington DC in January 1961 and dropped on the desk of the Under Secretary of the Air Force,

Dr Joseph Charyk. Col Horace Templeton, from the Air Development Center, was then summoned from his office, located in the basement of Building 14, at Wright Field, Ohio, to Dr Charyk, and asked to

As the initial grouping of SR-71 crewmembers was being established, the number 10 crew slot was taken by Maj Jerry O'Malley (pilot) and Capt Ed Payne. Both had previously been B-47 crew and they went on to fly the first operational Giant Scale mission from Kadena in 1968. (Paul F. Crickmore Collection)

complete an engineering analysis on the proposal. By April 1961, two different forward fuselage mock-ups were under construction at Burbank, for a strike version, referred to as the RS-12, and a pure-reconnaissance version known in-house as the R-12 (the latter is referred to in a recently declassified memo written by the CIA's Deputy Director (Research), Herbert Scoville, as Project Earning). Pentagon staffing of the initiative became the province of the Chief of Special Activities, Col Leo Geary and Lew Meyer, a Special Projects finance officer. The Air Force selected two competing teams (Westinghouse and Goodyear) to work in isolation to provide radar systems integration for the strike version, and it was proposed that an adaptation of the Hughes GAR-9 missile, carrying a Polaris A-3 single megaton warhead, would provide the platform's punch.

The concept of operations called for the RS-12 to penetrate enemy airspace at Mach 3.2 at an altitude of 80,000 ft (24384 m) (where it would be immune to SA-2s), and use radar to search designated areas to locate, identify and strike selected targets. Each aircraft would haul the four nuclear missiles internally. These would be lowered for firing one at a time, on a hydraulically-operated parallelogram arm (similar to the mechanism planned for the F-12B's AIM-47s). The aircraft's radar and internal guidance system would then transfer details of the target's relative position to the missile and the fired weapon would guide itself to the point of impact using either radar or an optical area correlation system. This guidance concept was thought to be impractical by certain critics, but the ADP team proved that the all-weather radar-guided missile would be capable of hitting its target within a 50 ft (15 m) circular error of probability (CEP), and 20 ft (6.10 m) using an optical system even though it had been launched from a distance of 50 miles (80 km).

There remained, however, important doubters. Secretary of Defense Harold Brown rather pompously proclaimed that the entire proposition was ridiculous and that 'finding a target along a 3,000 mile track, in a swathe 20 miles wide was like quickly locating a single word in the *Encyclopaedia Britannica*.' Viewed in such simplistic terms, target finding and pin-point strike accuracy was certainly an ambitious undertaking, but to simplify matters the aircraft would look for certain en route clues which would lead the proposed B-12 (or RS-12) directly to specific targets. Even Kelly was sceptical. Russ Daniell recalled a conversation with the Lockheed chief designer during a flight from Washington DC to Burbank in the company JetStar, which went along the lines of, 'Do you still think you can hit that garage door down there Russ?' Daniell

Here Buddy Brown, who piloted the first SR-71 to Kadena on 8 March 1968, is being helped into the inner layer of his S-901J pressure suit. (USAF)

replied in the affirmative, adding, 'What you don't do is aim, shoot and forget. Like your car, you don't point it at your garage from the parking lot at work, close your eyes and drive'.

When Dr Charyk flew to Burbank to review 'progress to date', he was directed to the RS-12 mock-up into which a prepared mission tape had been installed. This demonstration consisted of experimental SLAR imagery taken from a B-58 Hustler as it flew 1,200 miles (1931 km) at Mach 2 over six western states. The radar map was then transposed onto a 35-mm film and moved through the back-seater's radar display at a speed that equated to Mach 3. Charyk was briefed on how to work the cursor that would be placed over a target and then 'pickled' to feed information into the weapons system. He was then invited to 'fly' a mission and see at first-hand how, in the words of Secretary of Defense Harold Brown, 'a single word in the *Encyclopaedia Britannica*' could be located when you knew how the system worked. He

Major Ben Bowles was among the first crewmembers selected by Col Doug Nelson for the Senior Crown programme. He later became the first pilot to log 900 hours on type on 12 April 1972. (via Ben Bowles)

emerged from the cockpit 40 minutes later beaming – he had located and 'pickled' all 20 designated targets! The feasibility argument was laid to rest once and for all.

As noted in Kelly's diary on 4 June 1962, the 90-day study that had been granted to the Skunk Works was reviewed by: 'Rus Daniell, Templeton, and a large number of aerial reconnaissance people'. This was concluded satisfactorily, but a firm commitment to move ahead with hardware was not immediately forthcoming. On 20 December 1962, Kelly noted in his diary that he and several of his engineers flew to Washington and: 'Presented our R-12 version, which Templeton and group presented to the Air Force in a closed session the next day. The outcome was that we are proposing too heavy an aircraft, with too much equipment, so we were requested to scale it down to 1,500 lb [680 kg] of payload.' Design refinement of the 'R' model, primarily

under Rus Daniell, continued and on 18 February 1963 the team's tenacity finally paid dividends when the Air Force issued pre-contractual authority to build six aircraft for flight testing, with the understanding that an additional 25 aircraft (which emerged as the SR-71) would be ordered by 1 July. Aircraft production rate was set to be one per month, for 31 months, a target that was met, and the entire static and flight test Categories I, II and III were completed under budget at a cost of $146 million – a great achievement by any standards. A classified memo dated 15 February 1963 to John McCone (DCI) from Dr Charyk, now Director of the National Reconnaissance Office, noted how the new reconnaissance programme would be funded: 'We have recently had approval by the Secretary of Defense for a 138,000 lb, two-place reconnaissance version of the basic A-12 design, to be known as the R-12.

'Your organisation in three previous instances, the U-2, the A-12 and the AF-12 (the long range interceptor version), has acted as a procurement agent for the Air Force.

'Inasmuch as the decision has already been made that the R-12 program will be administered in the black, it is requested that you again perform as the procurement agent for the R-12.

'A memorandum of understanding similar to that existing for the AF-12 program is being drawn up and will be reviewed with the appropriate personnel in Dr Scoville's office in the immediate future ...'

At this point, Col Leo Geary was assigned as Weapon System Program Officer for the RS-12 in the Pentagon, and after a protracted debate, Col Templeton and the AF-12 project group became the project group on the R-12. The Air Force assigned the RS-12 to a post-ICBM 'look and clean-up' role and provisionally incorporated the proposed new aircraft into SAC's nuclear war plan – the SIOP (Single Integrated Operational Plan). However, during this period considerable doubt was being expressed in 'strategic think tanks' as to the long-term value of bombers as delivery platforms for nuclear weapons. The ballistic missile had come of age and more than 1,500 B-47s were on their way out of SAC's inventory. The fallout of such thinking within the Kennedy administration was that Secretary of Defense McNamara never ordered weapons for the RS-12 and the design was left to wither on the vine.

Notwithstanding, it is interesting to note that the likely viability of Rus Daniell's original 1961 B-12 proposal was demonstrated in practical terms just four years later by three YF-12s that achieved the following results firing AIM-47 missiles from high altitude, against much lower moving targets:

Date	Mission number	YF-12	YF-12 speed/ Mach	YF-12 altitude, × 1,000 ft/m	Target	Target altitude, × 1,000 ft/m
18 March 1965	G-11	935	2.2	65/19812	Q-2C	40/12192
19 May 1965	G-13	935	2.3	65/19812	Q-2C	20/6096
28 September 1965	G-15	934	3.2	75/22860	Q-2C	20/6096
22 March 1966	G-18	936	3.15	74.5/22708	Q-2C	1.5/457
25 April 1966	G-19	934	3.2	75/22860	QB-47	1.5/457
13 May 1966	G-16	936	3.17	74/22555	Q-2C	20/6096
21 September 1966	G-20	936	3.2	74/22555	QB-47	terrain

The secret of the aircraft's adaptability to perform such varying tasks was its ability to have a re-engineered forebody, mated to the aft body at joint 715 (a point perpendicular to where the inboard wing leading edge met the fuselage chine).

The aircraft's weapons bays had the capability of housing either four AGM-69 Short-Range Attack missiles (SRAMs) (when launched at Mach 3.2 the SRAM's range increased dramatically to 514 nm/ 592 miles/953 km downrange and cross-range up to 200 nm/230 miles/370 km), or it could haul six strike missiles (each 9 ft 5 in/2.87 m long and with a range of 360 nm/415 miles/668 km), or 12 guided bombs (each 4 ft 7 in/1.40 m in length with a range of 40 nm/46 miles/74 km).

In the late 1970s, Lockheed ADP continued to draft proposals to the Air Force, outlining the platform's suitability as a bomber. One such proposal harnessed greatly increased levels of kinetic and potential energy to inert weapons. Such weapons obviated the need for warheads, thus reducing the cost of the missiles appreciably. For example, a weapon weighing 1,200 lb (544 kg) launched at Mach 3.2 and 80,000 ft (24384 m) on an optimum 0.5 g trajectory, had the ability to penetrate 23 ft (7.01 m) of reinforced concrete. This high-velocity projectile would cause virtually no collateral damage, but considerable damage to a subterranean target (like a bunker or missile silo), as the weapon's kinetic energy transferred to, and throughout, the structure. The same weapon could penetrate hard soil to a depth of about 120 ft (37 m). If combined with a small high-explosive or nuclear warhead, such a missile becomes a highly effective sub-surface weapon, since the explosion causes soil above to collapse, and thus contain fallout in a nuclear scenario. Despite the concept's feasibility and moderate cost, SAC showed little interest in it.

In contrast to the supersonic bomber, the concept of trisonic reconnaissance operations was fully vindicated when, in May 1964, NcNamara cancelled the RS-70 (XB-70) programme – but the R-12 had prevailed. It was an election year in the United States and a time when political disagreements concerning national security were rife. The Republican candidate for president,

Senator Barry Goldwater, was stridently critical of the Kennedy/Johnson track record on air-power issues, contending that the Democrats had not initiated a single, significant advanced aircraft development programme and that they had thereby neglected the defence needs of America. Predictably, the 'bullish' Lyndon Johnson reacted sharply to counter Goldwater's charge, and on

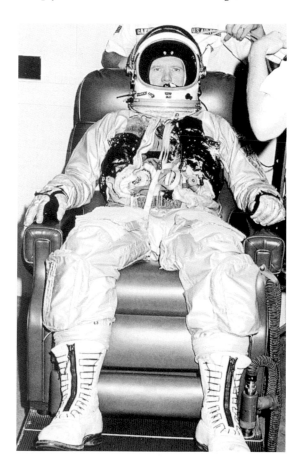

Roy St Martin, shown here during the suiting-up procedure, and John Carnochan both ejected safely from '965 on 25 October 1967 when it was lost following an INS platform failure during a training sortie. (USAF)

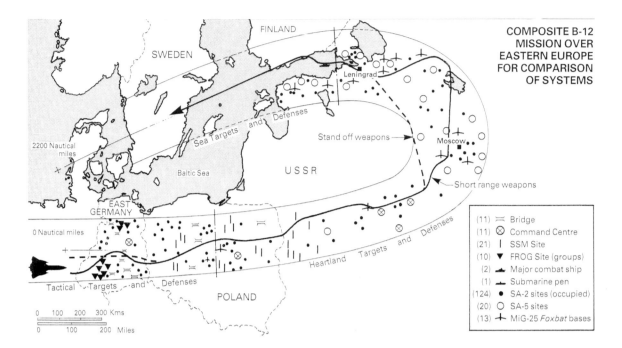

COMPOSITE B-12
MISSION OVER
EASTERN EUROPE
FOR COMPARISON
OF SYSTEMS

(11)	⋈	Bridge
(11)	⊗	Command Centre
(21)	I	SSM Site
(10)	▼	FROG Site (groups)
(2)	⬤	Major combat ship
(1)	⬤	Submarine pen
(124)	●	SA-2 sites (occupied)
(20)	○	SA-5 sites
(13)	✛	MiG-25 *Foxbat* bases

25 July 1964 the White House press office released the following presidential statement: 'I would like to announce the successful development of a major new strategic manned aircraft system which will be employed by the Strategic Air Command. This system employs the new SR-71 aircraft and provides a long-range advanced strategic reconnaissance plane for military use, capable of worldwide reconnaissance for military operations.

The Joint Chiefs of Staff, when reviewing the RS-70, emphasised the importance of the strategic reconnaissance mission. The SR-71 aircraft reconnaissance system is the most advanced in the world. The aircraft will fly at more than three times the speed of sound. It will operate at altitudes in excess of 80,000 ft. It will use the most advanced observation equipment of all kinds in the world. The aircraft will provide the strategic

EFFECTS OF SPEED AND ALTITUDE AS A DEFENSE ON SA-2 *Guideline*

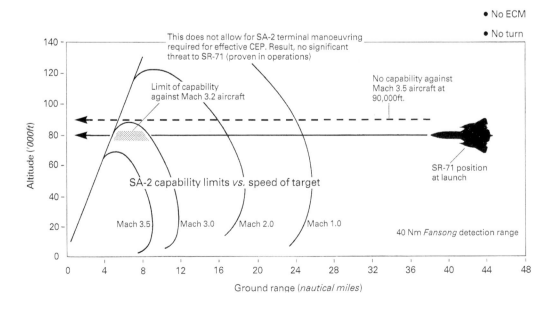

forces of the United States with an outstanding long-range reconnaissance capability. The systems will be used during periods of military hostilities and in other situations in which the United States military forces may be confronting foreign military forces.

'The SR-71 uses the same J58 engines as on the experimental interceptor previously announced, but it is substantially heavier and it has a longer range. The considerably heavier gross weight permits it to accommodate the multiple reconnaissance sensors needed by the Strategic Air Command to accomplish their strategic reconnaissance mission in a military environment

'The billion-dollar program was initiated in February of 1963. The first operational aircraft will begin flight-testing in early 1965. Deployment of production units to the Strategic Air Command will begin shortly thereafter.

'Appropriate members of Congress have been kept fully informed on the nature of and the progress in this aircraft program. Further information on this major advanced aircraft system will be released from time to time at the appropriate military secret classification levels.'

Although the A-12 had flown before, such statements were political fodder for upcoming elections. The overall programme had been conceived during Eisenhower's administration, but the SR-71, as the aircraft had now become and

Here Bob Gilliland eases the first SR-71A into a left turn high over the Sierra Nevada mountains north of Edwards during an early sortie. With Gilliland in the pilot's seat, the aircraft became DUTCH 51. (Lockheed)

which Johnson had just announced, had not yet undertaken its maiden flight. Although the political wrangling continued, the future of the R-12 was certainly assured.

FIRST FLIGHT PREPARATIONS

In August 1964, Kelly phoned Bob Murphy and asked him if he wanted to work on the SR-71 programme. At the time Murphy was a superintendent in charge of D-21 drone production. Drone number one was undergoing final check-out, while another nine were at various stages of assembly. Bob accepted the offer and was immediately briefed by Kelly who said: 'I want you to go to Palmdale and get site 2 away from Rockwell [into which North American had merged]. Hire the people you need. The pieces of the SR-71 will be up to you on November 1st and I want her flying before Christmas. Oh, I also want you to move up there because I don't want you to commute.' This was typical of the way Kelly operated. The next day, Murphy went out to Palmdale and met the base commander, who arranged a meeting between the various parties affected by their activities. 'Murph' recalled: 'Rockwell controlled all three sites; they were using Site 1 and Site 3 for B-70 production. Site 2 housed various other facilities including a paint shop and a huge telephone exchange. The meeting got underway and I began negotiating for various parts of the building that would have to be vacated by specified dates to allow our people to move in. One of the Rockwell people said, "Well we don't have anything from the Air Force that

Colonel Bill Hayes led a highly skilled team of USAF maintenance technicians as they brought the SR-71 into operational service. He chose some of the best crew chiefs and maintenance supervisors in the entire Air Force. (USAF)

says we need to be out of this building". At that point I bluffed a move to get out of my chair and said, "You don't'? Well I'd better call Washington and find out what the heck is going on". The ruse worked and he said, "Wait a minute, we don't have to get Washington involved in this", and I was able to complete the arrangements without having any official orders to do so – although they were probably just around the corner.'

So it was that Lockheed inherited Site 2 at Palmdale. The prototype SR-71A (Article 2001, serial number 64-17950) was delivered in a disassembled form in two large trailers on 29 October 1964 to Site 2 (Air Force Plant 42, Building 210 at Palmdale, California). At that point Bob Murphy's team went into overdrive in an attempt to fulfil the extremely tight deadline set by Kelly.

In the summer of 1964, Kelly had offered test pilot Robert J. Gilliland the post of Chief Project Pilot for the SR-71. It was a position that Bob was admirably qualified for, having gained a great deal of experience as a member of the F-104 and A-12

test teams. In early December, Kelly and Bob flew from Burbank to Palmdale in Lockheed's corporate JetStar to review the progress toward final assembly. Bob Murphy escorted them around Building 210, revealing that Article 2001 was spread all over the hanger floor in the process. During the return flight to Burbank, Bob (who was mindful that a number of Air Force Generals from Omaha, Wright-Patterson and Washington were planning to be on hand at the 21 December maiden flight) told Kelly: 'Maybe we'd better postpone this thing till after Christmas. It's likely to be a little embarrassing to you, me and the Skunk Works if we get them out here and don't go'. Kelly refused to budge, contending that if he postponed schedules everytime he was asked, the aircraft would still be in the jigs.

Dick Miller led the flight test engineering effort for the entire contractor test programme. Once his brief had been decided upon and approved, he became responsible for the implementation of specific tests to be completed on individual flights. During those final weeks leading up to the first flight, Bob Gilliland recalled having to attend frequent meetings which he characterised as being 'tedious and in great danger of causing analysis-paralysis'. There was considerable discussion as to whether the first flight should be

flown at subsonic speeds with the gear down, or whether the gear should be retracted and (if all went well) the aircraft flown supersonically. It was agreed that no dead-stick landing would be attempted if there was a serious problem on the first flight and it was also agreed that the aircraft would not be landed on its belly if the gear failed to extend. Ejection was the preferred option in either case. Kelly and Bob agreed that an attempt would be made to fully exercise Article 2001 on its first flight.

With two J58s installed, Article 2001/'950 conducted its first engine test run on 18 December 1964. Three days later, a 'non-flight' was conducted. All pre-flight checks were carried out as if the flight was really going to leave the ground. This checkout included firing up each engine, checking control movements, and a close scrutiny of all gauges, lights, switches and indicators, and external checks for hydraulic leaks or other abnormalities were performed by ground crews. Finally, after testing the trim movement, cg position and radio operations, Bob taxied out using the brakes and nose gear steering. He did full engine run ups at the end of the runway and took the number one position for take-off as if he was really going to launch. '950 was lined up for take-off, and the test pilot eased the throttles to full military power, checked engines 'in the green' and released the brakes. As the aircraft lurched forward, Bob engaged 'min burner' to fell the asymmetric 'pulse-pulse' of light-up. Accelerating rapidly due to the light fuel load, he snapped the throttles back to idle upon reaching 120 kt (138 mph; 222 km). As he deployed the 40-ft (12-m) drag chute, the deceleration threw him almost as hard against the shoulder straps as a

Aircraft '965 was the second SR-71 lost by the 9th SRW. The aircraft is shown here with a T-33 trainer, a direct descendent of Kelly Johnson's P-80 – later F-80 – Shooting Star jet fighter. Created in record time, the P-80 arrived in the Mediterranean theatre just as World War II was drawing to a close and failed to see combat, but later fought initially as an interceptor and then as a fighter-bomber during the Korean War. Ousted in the interceptor role by North American's F-86 Sabre, the F-80 faded fairly quickly from service, while a few T-33s remained in military use into the 21st century. (Lockheed)

carrier landing. He jettisoned the chute at 50 kt (58 mph; 93 km), turned off the runway and taxied back to the hanger. There were very few write-ups and the team knew that the aircraft was ready for its maiden flight.

On 22 December 1964, Gilliland (using his personal call sign DUTCH 51) got airborne from runway 25 at Palmdale in the first SR-71. The back seat remained empty on this flight for safety reasons. Consequently, many of the functions that would have been carried out by an RSO or a Lockheed systems engineer were 'jury-rigged' onto a special instrument control panel mounted in the front cockpit. After take-off, Bob immediately retracted the landing gear, reduced the afterburners to 'min', turned right and continued his climb northbound over the Edwards test range until he levelled off at 20,000 ft (6096 m) and 0.9 Mach. Lockheed's experienced A-12 test pilot James Eastham (later to become the second pilot to fly the SR-71), flew one of three F-104s which 'chased' '950 to observe and assist if problems occurred. The other two Starfighters were flown by USAF test pilots Col Robert 'Fox' Stephens and Lt-Col Walt Daniel. One of the jets was a two-seater and it carried a photographer in the rear seat.

This historic photograph, taken on 27 May 1967, depicts the initial cadre of the 9th SRW. They are from left to right,front rank: Sgt Dave Gallard, Jack Kennon (Operations Officer), Ray Haupt (1st SRS commander), Hal Confer (Deputy Commanding Officer), Bill Hayes (9th SRW commander), Charles Minter (9th SRW Vice Wing Commander), John Boynton (99th SRS commander), Harlon Hain (Operations Officer) and MSgt Loignon. The pilots in the second rank are paired with their RSOs, who stand behind them in the third rank as follows: Storrie/Mallozzi, Sowers/Sheffield, Hichew/Schmittou, Collins/Seagroves, Bill Campbell/Pennington, Halloran/Jarvis, Brown/Jensen, Dale Shelton/Boggess, O'Malley/Payne, Walbrecht/Loignon, Boone/Vick, Bevacqua/Crew, Watkins/Dempster, DeVall/Shoemaker, Spencer/Branham, McCallum/Locke, St Martin/ Carnochan, Bull/McNeer, Powell/Kendrick, Daubs/Roetcisoender, Bobby Campbell/Kraus, Kardong/Coleman, Maier/Casey, Fruehauf/unknown and Hudson/Ferrell. (USAF)

Immediately after Bob's take-off, Eastham tucked into close formation position on '950's right wing, allowing the two pilots to compare and calibrate the SR-71's airspeed and altitude readings against the F-104's, to verify accurate pitot/static system operations. The test flight instructions called for manoeuvrability and handling checks during 'static and dynamic' stability and control tests. These checks were carried out with the SAS axes 'on' and 'off', both 'individually' and then 'collectively'. Performance comparisons of predicted values of speed versus thrust and fuel consumption were also recorded, followed by a climb to 30,000 ft (9144 m) where cabin pressure, oxygen flow and temperature control were checked. After passing Mojave, Bob turned left to fly on a heading west of NAS China Lake and then northward up the Owens Valley between the Sierra Nevada mountains to the west and the White Mountains to the east (all within the Edwards Special Operating Area). Just north of Bishop (near Mammoth and Yosemite National Parks) Bob completed a 180° turn to the left and rolled out on a southerly track over the spectacular high cordillera of the snow-covered Sierra Nevadas.

It was now time to do a supersonic dash, since all systems were performing well. Just northwest of Bishop, and with Jim's F-104 sticking with the SR-71 like glue, Bob eased the throttles into 'min' burner, checked the engine parameters, and slid the throttle levers on up to 'max'. The light test jet accelerated very quickly to 400 kt (461 mph; 742 km/h) in level flight and on to supersonic speeds quite easily. At Mach 1.2 the 'Master Caution' warning light flashed on, drawing Bob's attention to the Annunciator Panel where he saw a 'read-out' light identifying the problem as 'Canopy Unsafe'. By visually checking the two canopy locking hooks on either side of the canopy, Bob verified that the canopy was really fully locked. The pressure-sensitive microswitches that transmitted the electrical 'unsafe' signal had been activated because an aerodynamic low-pressure area above the aircraft had sucked the canopy up against the locking hooks. The canopy was really safe, but it had risen high enough to complete the electrical circuit which turned on the Annunciator and Master Caution Lights. Bob correctly analysed the situation as safe and pressed on with the test flight. He advanced the throttles once again and continued to climb and accelerate while rigorously scanning his instruments. On reaching 50,000 ft (15240 m) and Mach 1.5, Bob eased the power out of burner into 'mil' and began deceleration to 350 kt (403 mph; 649 km/h) indicated airspeed, whereafter he descended to 20,000 ft (6096 m) to allow the engines to cool down.

As Bob approached Palmdale, he was advised by Test Ops that Kelly had requested a subsonic flyby down the runway. He and the accompanying F-104s streaked by to highlight the successful completion of the first flight. At the far end of the runway, Bob chandelled '950 up onto the downwind leg where he dumped the gear and was most pleased to see the 'three little bright green lights' which indicated that all three of the landing struts were down and locked. He turned onto a wide base leg and set up a long final approach at 185 kt (213 mph; 343 km/h). After making a smooth touchdown on Palmdale's runway 25, he gently lowered the nose and deployed the drag chute. At 50 kt (58 mph; 93 km/h) Bob jettisoned the chute, turned off the active runway and taxied back towards the crowd of USAF dignitaries and Lockheed engineers and technicians who awaited his debriefing.

After congratulations from Kelly and the others, the debriefing took place with more than two dozen engineers and subcontractor representatives present. Bob narrated details of his flight chronologically from start up to shutdown, whereafter Dick Miller's Lockheed engineers and the other companies' technicians asked clarifying questions. Since the session was recorded, Bob's description was prepared in a typescript that was circulated to all concerned. After this 'first quick look' was satisfied, a further analysis was made of canopy-mounted camera recordings that had viewed the instrument panel throughout the flight. All of this data along with data from other 'automatic observer' sensors enabled Bob Klinger's Data Reduction Group to 'reconstruct' the flight for engineering analysis. So ended Bob's pre-Christmas historic and most successful maiden flight of the SR-71.

Following the first three experimental test sorties, Dick Miller flew as 'flight test engineer' on all the development flights except the limited structural tests which were 'pilot only' for safety reasons. Aircraft numbers 64-17951 and '952 were added to the test fleet for contractor development of payload systems and techniques. Shortly after the Phase II Development Test Program had started, four other Lockheed test pilots were brought into the project: Jim Eastham, Bill Weaver, Art Peterson and Darrell Greenamyer.

The concentrated developmental test efforts were matched by those of HQ Air Force Systems Command (AFSC) at Wright Patterson, where Col Ben Bellis had been appointed System Project Officer (SPO) for the SR-71. His task was to structure a Development and Evaluation Program that would 'sound out' the new aircraft for the Air Force. Implementation of this programme would be undertaken by the SR-71/YF-12 Test Force at the Air Force Flight Test Center at Edwards. Air

The 9th SRW lost half of its SR-71Bs when 'Gray' Sowers and Dave Fruehauf 'punched out' of '957 on 11 January 1968. (Appeal-Democrat)

Force Systems Command (AFSC) pilots would work in parallel with their counterparts from Lockheed and ensure the successful development of systems and sensors. Both Phase I 'Experimental' and Phase II 'Developmental' test flying had moved to Edwards where 64-17953, 64-17954 and 64-17955 were to be evaluated by the 'blue-suiters'.

In 1965 the team began SR-71 air refuelling tests (supported by Beale's 903rd Air Refuelling Squadron); the aircraft proved adequate for skilled pilots to refuel. The flight envelope expansion phase proceeded well, as did a host of other tests. On 2 November 1965, Bob Gilliland and Bill Weaver completed the maiden flights of the first two SR-71B pilot trainers (64-17956 and 64-17957). By the end of the year, Kelly Johnson could be justifiably pleased with the progress of his latest evolution of the A-12 family of black trisonic aircraft.

AIRCREW RECRUITING

US Army Camp Beale began its life as a military post in October 1942, when a vast site stretching over 80,000 acres (32376 ha) was named in honour of Gen Edward Fitz-Gerald Beale (a mid-19th century western explorer). Acquired by the newly formed US Air Force in early 1948, Camp Beale was used as a bombing and gunnery range during the Korean War. On 27 November 1951, General Order 77 reduced the bombing range by half and

created Beale Air Force Base, which was later reduced to 23,000 acres (9308 ha). Between April 1957 and August 1958, USAF engineers constructed a 12,000 ft (3658 m) strategic bomber runway at Beale, thus allowing the California base to become home to one of the first B-52 Stratofortress wings in SAC.

The 456th Bombardment Wing operated its B-52s and KC-135s from Beale, along with the 851st Strategic Missile Squadron's (SMS's) first-generation Titan ICBMs. After the 851st SMS was deactivated in 1964, the Air Force informed the Press in October that the SR-71s would be stationed at Beale. Soon after, an $8.4 million construction programme was initiated at the base, which included the installation of an array of specialised technical support facilities and 337 new Capehart houses for the newcomers.

The official announcement of the new SR-71 unit was made a week before the first test flight of the SR-71, when the Commander in Chief SAC (CINCSAC) Gen John Ryan revealed that the 4200th Strategic Reconnaissance Wing would be activated at Beale on 1 January 1965. Three months after the activation of the parent wing, four permanent support squadrons were formed: the 4200th Headquarters Squadron; the 4200th Armament and Electronics Maintenance Squadron; the 4200th Field Maintenance Squadron; and the 4200th Organizational Maintenance Squadron.

Col John DesPortes was the commander of the new wing while construction works were being carried out at the base. This former U-2 Wing Commander was soon promoted to Brigadier

General and given command of the 14th Strategic Aerospace Division, after which Col Doug Nelson took over the SR-71 wing. Nelson was particularly well-suited to his new command, since he had been SAC's project officer for the deployment of the U-2 nine years earlier and, in August 1961, he had been assigned the job of Director of Operations for the Oxcart project. Three years later he received a telephone call from Lt Gen Archie Old (Commander of the 15th Air Force), who informed him that he was to be Director of Plans for the 14th Air Division at Beale, and to take over the new wing when DesPortes' promotion was announced.

Nelson's immediate task would be to select a small group of highly competent sub-commanders and SAC fliers to form the initial cadre of the SR-71 unit. Nelson began the necessary planning for the activation of the world's first trisonic flying wing. After being assured by Gen Thomas Power that he would have top priority for choosing the right people for the programme, Nelson believed that one of his first tasks was to find the best maintenance supervisors, flightline and shop personnel, and the best pilots and navigators. General Old agreed that Col William Hayes (later known as the 'White Tornado') had to be deputy commander for Maintenance. Nelson recalled: 'Bill Hayes hit the ground running and immediately began selecting his team of maintenance supervisors, crew chiefs and system specialists. That Bill clearly realised our goal of putting together a top quality maintenance unit was evidenced by the outstanding results that his guys achieved within the first year'.

At the same time, Nelson was interviewing crewmembers for the flying squadron. He first recruited Lt-Col Ray Haupt, a former U-2 pilot who was serving as Head Instructor and Standardisation Pilot on Oxcart at Area 51. He joined the SR-71/YF-12 test force at Edwards AFB where he became the first Beale pilot to be fully qualified on the SR-71. Ray was to be Beale's Chief Instructor-Pilot (IP) for all new SR-71 fliers.

Steadily, Nelson found the finest officers in SAC for his new hand-picked organisation. The 4200th Medical Group was to be commanded by Col Walt Wright, the most outstanding flight and orthopedic surgeon in the Air Force. Col Clyde Denniston was chosen to supervise all the Category III flight test planning (to prove that the aircraft could really do the mission for which it had been developed). Top rated colonels and field grade officers were picked for unique staff positions and before the end of 1965 the wing had been fleshed-out with the necessary talent to make it all happen. Meanwhile, Nelson was busy visiting the two B-58 units, the U-2 organisation and HQ SAC to review the records of the best

pilots and navigator-bombardiers among many highly qualified SAC aircrew members. Many of those whom Nelson considered were SAC's 'Select' crewmembers – those who had held spot promotions because of their proven status as SAC's best. Most of those considered were young enough to undertake another four years of new-generation flying.

From the start, SAC kept its Senior Crown (SR-71) programme its own exclusive preserve, restricting recruitment to select crewmembers from bombers and U-2s. The only exceptions were graduates from the Air Force Test Pilot School at Edwards. Meanwhile, Nelson selected ten B-58 crewmembers: pilots Al Hichew, Robert 'Gray' Sowers, Charles 'Pete' Collins, Ben Bowles and John Storrie; and navigator-bombardiers Cosimo 'Coz' Mallozzi, Richard 'Butch' Sheffield, Jimmy Fagg, Tom Schmittou and Dave Dempster. They arrived at Beale to begin preliminary training after having successfully completed the tough 'astronaut's medical exam' at Brooks AFB near San Antonio, Texas. Since there were no aircraft at Beale, it was arranged that the ten would undertake a seven-week training course on the SR-71 at the Skunk Works. They would be able to spend their time with key Lockheed engineers including Kelly Johnson and Ben Rich, and would write up lesson plans for a Combat Crew Training School that they would later establish at Beale. They would become the instructor cadre to train the other SR-71 crewmembers who would follow.

At the end of the Burbank course, Doug Nelson (who had been monitoring the progress of all ten) called them together for some good and bad news. Some would go to the 'Ranch' for flying training in the 'Tin Goose' (the J75-equipped A-12 trainer) and other crews would go back to Beale to get the flight simulator programme started and lessons planned for follow-on crew training. Further, he told them that as they were all on a par with one another academically and professionally, he would therefore have to make a purely arbitrary decision based on age. Since John Storrie and Dave Dempster were the youngest, they would get some preliminary flying time at Edwards and Groom Lake prior to returning to Beale.

At the same time many others had applied to join the Senior Crown force. At Air Command and Staff College at Montgomery, Alabama, three former SAC select crewmembers who had flown B-47s and B-52s and one general's aide who had flown B-47s were selected on orders of CINCSAC Gen Joseph Nazarro who instructed his Director of Personnel, Col Lester Miller, to use SAC's best resources to man the new system. Consequently, Maj Jerry O'Malley, Don Walbrecht, Larry DeVall and Capt Connie Seagroves made the early cut without meeting Col Doug Nelson. Since there were no

SR-71s at Beale, these early arrivals formed the flying squadron and managed the early activities at unit level (including mobile control for T-38 flying, providing SR-71 simulator buddy-crew instructor teams, etc). As they had jumped the queue and arrived ahead of all but a few of the B-58 selectees, Gen DesPortes interceded for his U-2 pilots and assigned them earlier check-out numbers than the B-47/B-52 inputs. As a result, U-2 pilots Pat Halloran and Buddy Brown got precedence, as well as test pilots Bill Campbell and Russ Scott. When the final crew list shaped up between late 1965 and early 1966 it read as follows, since Russ Scott had dropped out and others had arrived (all in the order pilot and RSO):

Crew 01: Maj John Storrie (B-58) and Capt Cosimo Mallozzi (B-58)

Crew 02: Maj Robert Sowers (B-58) and Maj Butch Sheffield (B-58)

Crew 03: Lt-Col Al Hichew (B-58) and Maj Tom Schmittou (B-58)

Crew 04: Capt Pete Collins (B-58) and Capt Connie Seagroves (B-52)

Crew 05: Maj Jack Kennon (B-58) and Capt Cecil Braden (B-58)

Crew 06: Capt Bill Campbell (Test Pilot School) and Capt Al Pennington (B-58)

Crew 07: Maj Pat Halloran (U-2) and Capt Mort Jarvis (B-52)

Crew 08: Maj Buddy Brown (U-2) and Capt Dave Jenson (B-52)

Crew 09: Capt Dale Shelton (B-58) and Capt Larry Boggess (B-58)

Crew 10: Maj Jerry O'Malley (B-47) and Capt Ed Payne (B-47)

Crew 11: Maj Don Walbrecht (B-47) and Capt Phil Loignon (B-47)

Crew 12: Capt Earle Boone (B-58) and Capt Dewain Vick (B-52)

Crew 13: Capt Tony Bevacqua (U-2) and Capt Jerry Crew (B-52)

In addition, a number of other officers were on hand, or had been identified for check-out positions some time in the future, but did not have crew identity until later. These pilots were Jim Watkins (KC-135), Larry DeVall (B-52), Bob Spencer (U-2), Roy St Martin (U-2), George Bull (U-2) and Bob Powell (U-2). The RSOs were Dave Dempster (B-58), Clyde Shoemaker (B-52), Keith Branham (B-52), Bob Locke (B-52), Jim Carnochan

(B-58), Bill McNeer (B-52) and Bill Kendrick (B-52).

The first five crews were still at Edwards and the 'Ranch' getting some preliminary flying in T-38s and the A-12 trainer to become the first instructor pilots. Kennon, Braden, Bowles and Fagg stayed on at Edwards with the Test Force.

A typical RSO candidate was spot Maj Ed Payne at Mountain Home AFB who had applied for the programme. His background was similar to that of most navigator-bombardier/RSO applicants at the time. He had joined the USAF only nine years before and had become a Radar-Bombardier on B-47 Stratojets. In 1962 as a 'spot-promoted' captain with the 303rd Bombardment Wing (BW) at Tucson, Arizona, he and his crew had won ten of 22 trophies at SAC's annual bombing competition. In May of 1964 the 303rd BW deactivated, whereupon Ed was given orders to report to the 92nd BW at Spokane, Washington, which was equipped with B-52s.

'My squadron commander urged me to trade the assignment with another bombardier so we could retain our 'spot' promotions to Major a year longer by transferring to Mountain Home, Idaho, where we could continue to fly B-47s. I accepted my boss' advice and moved to Idaho with the rest of our crew.

'One day later at the Standardization Board Office, where our crew was assigned as flight evaluators, a young crewmember beamed, "I know where I'm going, I know where I'm going!" I looked at a copy of a message that told of the qualifications for entry into a strange programme. I talked over such an assignment with my wife Millie and the next day I completed an application for duty as an RF-101 'pilot'. Three weeks later I was notified that I'd been selected for an interview at Beale. The instructions informed me to travel in civilian clothes from Boise Idaho to Yuba City, California. On the final leg of the flight, another passenger asked me if I was Payne, Vick or Jarvis. I admitted my identity, whereupon Larry Boggess introduced himself. "How did you know who I was?", I inquired. "You're wearing a hack watch, Air Force sunglasses, and have a good haircut," replied Larry, "and those two guys up front must be Dewain Vick and Mort Jarvis", he commented.

'The interview at Beale was conducted in an old World War II building. A secretary in civilian clothes first called Dewain Vick into the office for the interview, he was followed by Mort Jarvis and me. Larry Boggess was last in that day. When I walked in and saluted I noted that Col Doug Nelson was wearing an orange-coloured flight suit complete with an RF-101 patch. As the tall, slim Colonel read through my personal records, he said "Welcome to Beale Capt Payne". Looking up he saw my gold majors leaves and apologised for the mistake, to which I replied, "Oh well Sir, easy come, easy go," referring to the temporary nature of SAC's spot promotions. Col Nelson told me he was indeed hoping for an all-spot team. The interview was very short. Nelson asked a few personal questions asking "were all RSO applicants 32 years old with five children, as the other two candidates had also been?" He then asked if I would be prepared to fly over enemy territory, to which I replied, "Of course". I was told that I had passed the interview and was "hired" pending passing the physical examination in Texas.'

Back at Mountain Home, Ed received orders to attend a ten-day medical exam at Brooks AFB, Texas, in April. Prior to the medical exam he completed a 505-question paper asking all about his previous state of health. Ed recalled that the detail was 'incredible'. One question asked, 'Have you ever worked in or around a silo?' Since he had grown up on a Montana cattle ranch, he answered 'yes' and had to see a specialist at Brooks who checked him over for Silo Fever – a condition that a person working everyday in wheat dust might contract from the poor quality air one would breathe. Ed explained that during a summer vacation from school he had worked as a carpenter's helper repairing a silo; such was the detail of the examination, which was the same as that being used by NASA in their selections for the astronaut programme.

He was given a clean 'bill of health' and returned to Idaho. While he awaited further orders, it was announced that the 9th BW was to deactivate on 1 January 1966. On that date, Ed lost his spot promotion and returned to the rank of Captain. He was in contact with Col Nelson at Beale who told Ed that they had no aircraft to commence the training programme, but the 4200th SRW was inheriting the 9th BW's 'historical number', which dated from World War I. The new unit would be called the 9th Strategic Reconnaissance Wing (SRW) after 25 June 1966. On Nelson's instructions, Ed gathered up all of the 9th's heraldic items (pictures, trophies, battle flags, unit histories) and other paraphernalia relating to the wing and its squadrons, the 1st and the 99th, and packaged them for shipment. Another RSO (Capt Connie Seagroves), who was already at Beale, came to Mountain Home in a C-47 to collect the boxed treasures. Ed reported to Beale in April 1966, to team up with Maj Jerry O'Malley who had arrived from Maxwell AFB ten months earlier.

The first two of eight Northrop T-38 Talon trainers arrived at Beale on 7 July 1965. These small and agile white jets (widely used as advanced pilot trainers in Air Training Command) would be used as 'companion trainers' to maintain

overall flying proficiency for the SR-71 crews at a fraction of the cost of flying the main aircraft. They were also to be used as 'pace-chase' aircraft to accompany every SR-71 flight during the first year of Beale operations, observing landing gear positions and giving crew and staff pilots an opportunity to practice formation flying. Because of the T-38's size alongside the SR-71, one of the wives jokingly called the two aircraft 'the horse and the horsefly' when they first appeared together over Beale.

Doug Nelson recalled that the T-38s were obtained only after a long and traumatic battle with SAC Headquarters over the companion trainer issue: 'Even though the need for such an aircraft to augment the SR-71 fleet had been clearly demonstrated in the A-12 programme in Nevada, I had some considerable difficulty convincing some of the senior staff people at HQ SAC and at HQ 15th Air Force. I think the argument that finally won them over had to do with the fact that some of these same people had already been expressing the view that I should consider selecting SAC B-52 bomber and KC-135 tanker pilots for entry into the programme, as well as supersonic B-58 pilots, test pilots, U-2 pilots and former fighter pilots. I agreed that this could probably be done, but was really only feasible if they could be put through a 'lead-in' training course conducted by us at Beale in an aircraft such as the T-38. Other alternatives I suggested included the F-5B, F-101F and F-104B.

Aircraft '977 was left in a sorry state, doused in foam and lying on its belly following its wheel failure. Such problems afflicted the programme early on, but were eventually overcome. (Appeal-Democrat)

They settled on the T-38 as the obvious choice and went all out to obtain eight of them from Training Command'.

In December 1965, Maj Don Walbrecht flew Lt-Col Ray Haupt to Palmdale, where Haupt and Charlie Bock (the USAF acceptance test pilot at Edwards) picked up SR-71B trainer 64-17957 from Plant 42 and test-delivered it a few miles away to Edwards, where it underwent further acceptance testing before it was ready for delivery to Beale. At 14:00 hours on 6 January 1966, Col Nelson and instructor pilot Haupt made the first pass of an SR-71 over Beale to deliver the trainer to SAC's 9th SRW. Soon after, Storrie and Collins would be able to finish their pilot checkouts. Four months later Col Nelson and Maj Al Pennington took delivery of Beale's first SR-71A, 64-17958. From then on, crew training and Category III Operational Testing could proceed in earnest.

SR-71 LOSSES

On 25 January 1966, Bill Weaver and Jim Zwayer took off from Edwards in SR-71A '952. Both were Lockheed test-flight employees. The two main objectives of their flight were to evaluate navigation and reconnaissance systems, and to investigate procedures for improving high-Mach cruise performance by reducing trim drag. This research required that the cg be moved further aft than normal to compensate for the rearward shift of the CoP at high Mach. After in-flight refuelling, DUTCH 64 climbed back to cruising altitude. While the aircraft was in a 30° bank to the right at approximately 80,000 ft (24384 m) and at a speed of Mach 3.1, an inlet scheduling malfunction occurred followed by an unstart of the right engine. The cumulative effect of the inlet malfunctions, cg configuration, speed, altitude and attitude resulted in pitching and yawing forces that exceeded the restorative authority of the flight controls and the SAS. This combination of rapid out-of-control actions led to the break-up of the aircraft, with the entire forebody becoming detached from the main body.

As soon as it became apparent that the situation was hopeless, Bill tried to tell Jim what was happening and that he should try to remain in the cockpit until they were down to a lower speed and altitude, since he did not think it would be possible to eject successfully under such stressful conditions. Unfortunately, as revealed upon subsequent recovery of the cockpit voice recorder, most of Bill's words were unintelligible due to the incredibly high *g* forces that both men were being subjected to at the time. Bill subsequently blacked out and to this day still does not know how he escaped. Indeed, his ejector seat was found inside the cockpit section of the wreckage.

During the break-up of the aircraft, the cockpit canopies were blown off and a combination of *g* forces and air loads blew both men clear as Bill later explained: 'I thought I was having a bad dream and hoped that I would wake up and all this would go away. However, as I began to regain consciousness, I realised it was not a dream and that this had really happened. At that point, I thought I was dead because I was convinced that I could not have survived what had happened. I remember thinking that being dead wasn't so bad after all. I had a kind of detached, euphoric feeling. As I became more conscious, I realised I wasn't dead after all, and that I somehow became separated from the aircraft. I couldn't see anything as my visor had iced up.

'My pressure suit had inflated, so I knew the emergency oxygen supply in the seat kit attached to my parachute harness was functioning. This source provided breathing oxygen and pressurisation essential at those altitudes, and physical protection against the intense buffeting and *g* forces I had been subjected to. It was like being in one's own life support capsule. After realising that I wasn't dead and that I was free of the aircraft, I was concerned about stability and not tumbling at such high altitude. Centrifugal forces sufficient to cause physical damage can be generated if the body tumbles at high altitude where there is little air density to resist spinning motions. Fortunately, the small stabilisation chute designed to prevent tumbling had worked fine.

'My next concern was the main chute – would the barometric automatic opening device work at 15,000 ft [4572 m]? I certainly hadn't made a proper exit – I knew I had not initiated the ejection procedure. How long had I been blacked out and how high was I? I was about to open the face-plate so I could estimate my altitude above the terrain and locate my parachute's 'D' ring. At that moment, I felt the sharp, reassuring tug which indicated that the main 'chute had deployed. This action was a very reassuring feeling, believe me. I then managed to raise my face-plate and noted that the visibility was just incredible. It was a clear winter's day at about three o'clock in the afternoon, and from my vantage point beneath the canopy it appeared that I could see for a couple of hundred miles. But what made everything just perfect was that about a quarter of a mile away was Jim's chute. I was delighted because I didn't believe either of us could have survived, and to think that Jim had also made it gave me an incredible lift.

'I couldn't manipulate the risers to steer my chute because my hands were frozen and I needed one hand to keep my iced-up visor raised (the up-latch was broken). As a result, I could only see in one direction and the terrain wasn't all that inviting. I was convinced we'd have to spend the night out there and I was trying to think of things I had been taught in survival training. I landed okay and was trying to undo my parachute harness when I heard a voice say, "Can I help you?" I looked up and there was a guy walking towards me wearing a cowboy hat and behind him was a helicopter. He turned out to be Albert Mitchell, who I later learned owned a huge cattle ranch in northeast New Mexico, upon which I had landed. He helped me out of the chute, told me he had radioed the police, the Air Force and the nearest hospital and then said, "I saw your buddy coming down, I'll go and help him".

'He climbed into his little helicopter and was back a few minutes later with the devastating news that Jim was dead. I asked him to take me over to see Jim and after verifying that there was nothing that could be done, other than have his ranch foreman watch over the body until the authorities arrived, he flew me to Tucumcari hospital about 60 miles [97 km] away to the south. I have vivid memories of that flight, as well. I didn't know much about helicopters, but I knew a lot about red lines, and the airspeed needle was above the red line all the way to Tucumcari. I thought about the possibility of that little thing shaking itself apart in flight and how ironic it would be to have miraculously survived the previous disaster only to be finished off in the helicopter that had come to my rescue! We made it without mishap and on reaching the hospital I was able to phone Lockheed Flight Test at Edwards. They knew the aircraft had been lost, after loss of radio and radar contact, and just didn't believe that I had survived.'

The solution to reducing the excessive trim drag problem was to move the centre of lift forward, thus reducing static margin and trim drag. This was achieved by Kelly inserting a 'wedge' between the aircraft's forward fuselage and its nose section. The result was the distinctive two-degree nose-up tilt.

During the closing stages of 1966 the SR-71 underwent a series of anti-skid brake trials. Bill Weaver conducted most of these tests and on 10 January 1967 was due to evaluate the system with the aircraft at maximum gross weight. By a twist of fate, he was unable to conduct this particular test because of the funeral of his friend Walt Ray who had been killed a few days earlier in an A-12 accident. Art Peterson was substituting and the RSO position remained empty. As the aircraft entered a flooded test area of the Edwards runway at well over 200 kt (230 mph; 370 km/h), the brake chute failed to deploy properly and the wheel brakes remained ineffective until the aircraft had cleared the test area. Once on a dry surface the brakes locked the

wheels and all six main tyres blew. As momentum carried the aircraft onward, the brakes burned out and the magnesium wheel hubs were consumed on the concrete runway, triggering an even greater fire. Peterson skillfully retained control of the stricken aircraft until he ran out of runway (although it was riding on the main gear stumps). On the overrun one of the main gear legs dug into the dry lake bed, causing side forces to rip the nose-wheel leg off. This sudden breakage simultaneously stopped the aircraft and broke its back. Fire quickly spread to engulf the entire machine, but Peterson managed to extract himself from the cockpit, sustaining back injuries that would ground him for several weeks in the process. It was the end of the line for the SR-71 prototype, Article 2001, which was written off as 'beyond repair'.

In mid-1966 Bill Skliar left the A-12 programme to become Chief of Operations for the SR-71 test force at Edwards. On 11 April 1969, Lt-Col Skliar and Maj Noel Warner lined up SR-71A 64-17954 on runway 04 at Edwards and began a maximum gross weight take-off. DUTCH 60 had just rotated when one of the left main gear tyres blew. The two remaining tyres were unable to support the aircraft's weight and they also failed. Immediately Bill aborted the take-off, but the burning shrapnel from the disintegrating magnesium wheel hubs caused a fire that rapidly engulfed the entire aircraft. He managed to retain control of the SR-71 and brought it to a halt on the runway. The worst of the fire was along the left side as a breeze kept the right side relatively clear. Skliar exited to the right and then assisted Warner exit the rear cockpit as the fire began to billow all around

Another wheel failure caused '954 to be lost following an aborted take-off from Edwards AFB. Lt-Col Bill Skliar and his RSO Noel Warner both managed to escape from a fire which encircled the crippled aircraft. (Lockheed)

Joe Rogers and Garry Heidlebaugh ejected from '953 following an in-flight explosion on 18 December 1969. Both escaped uninjured. (Lockheed)

them. Fortunately, both crew members survived, but '954 never flew again. After the incident all SR-71s had their wheels replaced with less combustible aluminium units, and BF Goodrich beefed up the high-speed, 239 kt-rated tyres.

PITCH-UP ACCIDENT

On 18 December 1969, the Director of the Test Force, Lt-Col Joe Rogers (an experienced test pilot with more than 200 hours on the SR-71) and RSO Lt-Col Gary Heidelbaugh, were scheduled to fly 64-17953 on a routine test sortie. The aircraft had been undergoing extensive modifications to install a new ECM system, and this would be its first flight for many weeks. After completing air refuelling, Rogers initiated a pre-planned acceleration and climb. Soon after transitioning to supersonic flight, the crew of DUTCH 68 experienced an explosion accompanied by a loss of power and severe control difficulties. As the aircraft decelerated, its AoA continued to increase despite Joe pushing the control stick 'hard against the firewall'. After slowing to subsonic speed, the fully-fuelled aircraft was increasingly less controllable and both crewmembers realised that '953 had entered an irrecoverable corner of the flight envelope. Ten seconds after the explosion Rogers knew it was time to go and ordered, 'Let's get out Gary!' Both men safely ejected while the aircraft (in a deep stall) entered a pitch-up from

which it was impossible to regain controlled flight. Soon after, '953 made its crater-grave near the southern end of Death Valley. The cause of the explosion remains unknown.

TRAINING AND CATEGORY III TESTING

Training techniques changed little over the 25 years of the SR-71's useful lifespan. The aircrew curriculum consisted of three phases of progressive activity that readied pilots and RSOs for the move from a variety of other jets into the highest performance aircraft in the world. At first, crewmembers accumulated many hours in the flight simulator before beginning their in-flight training. The pilots, after completing the elongated simulator course, during which they had endured every conceivable emergency procedure and many T-38 flying hours, were then introduced to the SR-71B, which they all recognised as 'friendly'. The B-58 pilots found it particularly easy to fly. Most other aircrew also found that flying the SR-71B was simply an extension of their former jet flying, no matter what principal type they had flown. The new pilots (under the supervision of Haupt or Hichew) found that the first sortie flown in the SR-71B ('957) was 'tame', and it proved easy both to fly and land.

The first training sortie was accomplished at subsonic speeds under the supervision of an instructor pilot, who evaluated the new pilot's 'first performance'. Such a 'first flight' included 20 minutes of air refuelling practice as well as instrument approaches and landings. It also included touch-and-go landings and confidence-building manoeuvres that soon made the aircraft feel like an 'old friend'. Two other three-hour, instructor-supervised sorties followed, consisting of more air refuelling practice, an acceleration to Mach 3.0 and a descent and approach, culminating with GCAs, ILSs and more landings. The fifth flight was a three-hour evaluation sortie which reviewed the student's total performance to assure that the pilots were ready to take their own simulator-trained RSOs on six more crew training sorties before both crewmembers could be declared qualified. Sorties lasted between three and five hours, and consisted of 'combat-oriented' missions which included emergency navigation legs at up to Mach 3.0 to demonstrate that large errors could develop unless headings were held for long distances.

The crew then undertook a simulator check ride. This no holds barred evaluation tested the crew's ability to control serious in-flight emergencies that involved flight judgment and crew coordination of high standards. A few days later, the crew flew a long in-flight profile after which instructors reviewed every voice transmission made during the mission, and the MRS record of flight. Their ability to fly a mission profile 'to the letter' was evaluated by the use of the latter device. When crews were declared combat ready, they then continued clocking-up more hours by performing Category III (Operational) flight tests.

During operational testing, two major areas of concern were focused upon: the aircraft's inlet control system, and the effects of the prolonged heat soaks during high-speed flight. The inlet control system was complex and fault-free operation depended upon accurate sensing of many different parameters of air flow, shockwave position, spike position, bypass door position, aircraft attitude (pitch and yaw) and engine nozzle position. The hydromechanical nature of the inlet control system, combined with the analogue inlet sensor's inability to process data fast enough to trim or bias the signals responsible for triggering various actuators when in the normal automatic mode of inlet operation, served to complicate inlet control further. Crews were often subjected to sharp and distracting unstarts, and an immediate solution to the problem was to operate the inlet system in the manual mode, with the pilot controlling the spike and door positions with switches while reading their changing positions on cockpit indicator instruments. Such manual operations took up an undue amount of the pilot's attention at high speed and resulted in off-optimum inlet operations. Though less efficient, this manual control often allowed new flyers to complete more training missions and accumulate data for the Phase III testing programme.

TESTING PROBLEMS

Many of the problems encountered in testing arose because sustained high-speed flight caused the airframe to undergo prolonged high-temperature heat soaks. Repeated expansion and shrinkage caused the silicone fuel tank sealant to diminish and crack, causing many leaks. This phenomenon was especially apparent when the aircraft was fully fuelled because most of the leaks appeared on the topside of the tanks, which became hotter and drier during high-Mach flight. As a consequence, it was necessary to perform routine resealing and extensive depot-level fuel tank maintenance when an SR-71 was returned to Palmdale (the old sealant was usually stripped away and replaced). It was a problem that remained with the aircraft throughout its operational life.

Heat was also responsible for electrical systems problems, especially in the high-output generators. Heat-related generator failures caused many air aborts during the first two years of training and Category III testing. After the loss of SR-71B '957 to a double generator failure on 11 January 1968, a single generator failure was flagged as a mandatory abort item that meant 'land as soon as possible'. Over the next year, SR-71s with generator failures landed at bases across the US. Various modifications were tried before the problem was finally isolated.

SR-71s were not cleared for top speeds during Cat III test flight training for most of 1966, an initial restriction speed of Mach 2.6 being applied. By mid-year the limit was raised to Mach 2.8, and by December Mach 3.0 was allowed. Finally, in early 1967, all aircraft were cleared to fly at the design limit of Mach 3.2. Since SAC allowed its wing commanders to be fully qualified in their unit's aircraft, Col Doug Nelson teamed up with senior staff RSO Col Russ Lewis and formed 'Staff Crew Number One'. They undertook the full aircrew course at Beale, completing their certification in September 1966. Soon after they flew SAC's first ever Mach-3.0 flight.

As training began in earnest around the western US, the Air Force began receiving lots of sonic boom complaints. Most of the heavy booms were attributed to operations in the ascent and descent phases when the SR-71 accelerated or slowed. The nuisance factor, rather than real damage, caused Congress to instruct the USAF to modify its training routes to avoid flying over large urban areas. The township of Susanville situated just north of Beale on the 006 degree radial of the Sacramento VORTAC, knew a great deal about sonic booms. During the first 18 months of flight operations, SR-71s were cleared by FAA flight controllers to accelerate and climb supersonically on that radial. On reaching FL330 (33,000 ft) and Mach 0.9, the pilot would push the nose below the horizon to quickly accelerate beyond the Mach while descending to FL270 before starting another climb at Mach 1.25. The intensity of a sonic boom is dependent upon the slant range from the aircraft to the ground along the shockwave. Consequently, poor Susanville, which nestled high in the Sierra Nevada foothills, was taking a real hammering.

CREW COMFORT

Prolonged flights in a full pressure-suit could be uncomfortable, especially with a full bladder. For this reason a Urine Collection Device (UCD) was developed for a 'suit-dry' method of eliminating excess body fluids. The urine could be discharged into a condom-like receptacle that was tube-connected to a plastic collector bag that was donned prior to suiting-up. One crewmember

Aircraft '978 was written off in a landing accident at Kadena on 20 July 1972. At that point in its illustrious career '978 sported *Playboy* Bunny symbols on its tail surfaces and was known as the 'Rapid Rabbit'. (Lockheed)

described his pre-UCD in-flight urination experience in the following terms: 'Wearing pressure-suit gloves, undoing several zippers and fighting through four inches of pressure suit wasn't easy'. Maj Dave Dempster was on a three-hour training sortie in April 1966 in '958 with Maj John Storrie when he was confronted with a full-bladder problem. His S-901J pressure suit had not yet arrived from the David Clark Company and he had borrowed a suit from a similarly tall colleague. The demands of nature had become irresistible and Dave mentioned this unpleasant fact to John. Most crewmembers were very reluctant to use the 'jug' because (unlike the later UCD), suit integrity was not maintained and bloodstream re-nitrogenation was likely. John after devoting some thought to Dave's problem, said 'Well, the way I see it, you can either hold it in or let it go in your suit. By the way, whose suit are you wearing?' Dave replied, 'Col Nelson's'. That thought provided him with all the encouragement he needed to wait until he landed!

The first two years of operating the SR-71 at Beale were crammed full of training and testing activity. More and more crews were building up flying time and testing the aircraft's ability to do its intended mission. In November 1966, Capts

Earle Boone and Dewain Vick climbed into 64-17966 for their first flight together. Their families were proudly witnessing the event from the PSD van. They had just cranked engines when one caught alight and fire engines converged on the 'hanger barn' from all points of the compass. The crew evacuated the aircraft and the fire was quickly extinguished with minor damage to the machine, whereupon Earle and Dewain transferred to another SR-71 and were able to complete their sortie together. Similar aircraft switches allowed the crew members to get airborne on their day, while other problems caused the loss of up to 20 per cent of the early training sorties.

Precautionary landings away from Beale were also frequent during this early period. Typical of many diversions were those of Jerry O'Malley and Ed Payne who landed at Hill AFB, Utah, with a generator problem, and then recovered the very same aircraft into Buckley Field, Colorado, a week later with the opposite generator inoperable. A few weeks later they lost a piece of the aircraft shortly after take-off. The errant fillet was found by a resident near Beale, who turned it over to the County Sheriff, who in turn passed the 9-ft (2.74-m) length of black aircraft skin back to the 9th SRW. Base officials identified the missing part as belonging to Jerry and Ed's aircraft. As Jerry prepared to refuel near Walton Beach, Florida, he asked to pull farther forward so the KC-135 crew could look at the rear of his aircraft. The boomer had reported that 'the ass-end of the aeroplane was missing'. Since the aircraft had just transited the US without the slightest indication of a problem, and the boomer had relayed to the crew that 'the panel appeared to merely cover some plumbing', Jerry refuelled with the intention of returning to Beale 'high and hot'. Ed reported the crew's intentions via HF radio to the Beale Command Post whose officer controller passed the information on to HQ 15th Air Force and SAC. In return, Ed got a return call from the 15th Air Force Command Post instructing him to divert into Barksdale AFB, Louisiana. This order was not queried as it came from Lt Gen P. K. Carlton, Commander of the 15th Air Force, himself.

Jerry landed on the southern end of Barksdale's long runway, jettisoned the drag chute at 50 kt (56 mph; 90 km/h) and switched off the anti-skid brakes, as per the checklist. At that point, the SR-71 entered a 1-in (2.5-cm) deep rain puddle and slewed into a sideways skid down the runway. As the aircraft exited the hydroplaning skid and touched dry runway, all six mainwheel tyres blew. It was three days before Jerry and Ed could return to Beale. When they suited up for the flight home, the Physiological Support Division (PSD) technicians accidentally interchanged their 'moon suit' helmets, which caused acute discomfort to Jerry on the four hour slow-flight back to northern California.

FIRST BEALE ACCIDENT

On 13 April 1967, Capts Earle Boone and Dewain Vick were scheduled to fly their ninth training sortie, a night flight which included air refuelling and a Mach 2.8 run over the southern United States. During the preflight medical exam it was discovered that Vick had a cold which precluded him from clearing his middle ear pressure because of a swollen eustachian tube. As a consequence, the flight surgeon grounded him, and 'Butch' Sheffield, the buddy-crew RSO, was substituted. It would turn out to be a very long night for the two fliers. After completing air refuelling near El Paso, Texas, Earle (an experienced B-58 pilot) decided to turn after leaving the tanker to avoid a thunderstorm that lay ahead on their planned track. Earle had started a subsonic climb to perform the 'dipsy-doodle' manoeuvre to hasten the transonic breakthrough, but during the climb in the fully-fuelled aircraft, the airspeed fell below the desired 0.90 Mach profile. To regain lost momentum, Earle lowered the nose of the aircraft below level flight, but when he pulled the stick back, the heavy jet shuddered in an accelerated stall. He fought hard to regain control of '966 but its angle-of-attack became uncontrollable and it suddenly entered a pitch-up rotation from which there was no recovery. Both crew members ejected from the aircraft, which had broken in half and spewed a great shroud of fuel around them. Since Butch ejected first, his ejection-seat rocket ignited the fuel-rich shroud into a fireball, through which Earle ejected a second behind his RSO.

The New Mexico surface winds were gusting at up to 40 kt (46 mph; 74 km/h) when the pilot and RSO hit terra firma, their wild ride across the desert floor eventually ending in a cattleman's barbed-wire fence more than a half mile from initial touch-down. Neither was seriously injured, although for the next few days Earle had blisters along the back of eight fingers, and both crew members suffered considerable bruising and stiffness as a result of their night parasail ride across a part of New Mexico not too far from the site of Bill Weaver's crash in '952.

A great deal was learnt from this accident, which was largely attributable to the pilot 'trying to do too much too soon' in an aircraft which was still being tested. Similar flight conditions were re-flown in the SR-71 flight simulator by the other crews, and it was found that heavyweight

Not all operational missions were flown over hostile territory, this graphic high-altitude 'take' featuring the aftermath of a freight train explosion in Rosville, Sacramento, on 28 April 1973. (USAF)

accelerated stalls were extremely difficult to recover from, and that secondary stalls could induce the dreaded pitch-up phenomenon, particularly at night or in clouds. SAC also began to realise that night training was being undertaken too early in SR-71 transition training. At the same time, it was decided that all flights, including subsonic movements, should be in pressure suits for improved aircrew protection.

Eventually the Automatic Pitch Warning (APW) system was added. This new device was far superior to the original system, and following its installation no further aircraft were lost through stalls.

Another serious incident, which could very easily have resulted in an aircraft being lost, was experienced by Maj Bob Spencer and Capt Keith Branham as they approached the Great Salt Lake on their return to Beale. Bob Spencer began feeling unwell, and before he was aware of the nature of his problem, he started to hyperventilate. In his reduced state of consciousness, Spencer realised that his oxygen supply had somehow been cut off so he yanked the 'green apple' oxygen-flow starter knob on the emergency oxygen supply in his parachute's survival seat pack, which unfortunately fed into the same supply lines through which the main aircraft oxygen flowed. Since he was 'hot and high' he realised that he was getting into deep trouble. The oxygen connections were located low on the right side of the ejection seat but were out of reach. Fortunately the SR-71's cockpit was pressured to 26,000 ft (7925 m), but this still left the Major groggy and suffering from narrowed vision (at a pressure altitude higher than most mountains in the world). Suffering now from hypoxia, he told Keith that he was having some oxygen problems and might need some advice to better control a ragged descent. At that point, he reduced power and adjusted the pitch attitude on his autopilot. As the aircraft began to exceed the KEAS and Mach limits during descent, Bob grunted to open his 'gun-barrel' vision in an attempt to read the TDI instrument, which displayed Mach, KEAS and altitude. For the next ten minutes Keith shouted instructions to Bob to keep him from exceeding the dangerous low or high speed limits that could result in loss of control.

Fortunately, Bob and Keith brought the aircraft down to 15,000 ft (4572 m), where Bob snapped out of his condition, or so he thought. He 'felt so good' from the raptures of hypoxia that he convinced Keith that there was no need to divert into Hill AFB at Ogden, Utah. After Keith computed that they had enough fuel to reach Beale at Mach 0.90, Bob headed for California. Halfway home the right engine flamed out. Bob looked at the fuel pressure warning light, which had not illuminated, indicating that the flame out was not due to fuel mismanagement. He tried

unsuccessfully to restart the engine, which left them in a less fuel-efficient condition since the rate of fuel use on one engine was much higher than normal. At that point they called the Beale Command Post, whose controller ordered a tanker to be scrambled to meet them over Nevada. Twenty-five minutes later, the tanker approached the rendezvous point, but initiated the 180° join-up turn much too late, and Bob and Keith saw their much-needed supply of JP-7 fly straight past them. To rejoin with the tanker, which was now well in trail, would use even more of their precious fuel and they could not risk this. Luck however, was on their side, and they recovered at Beale with little fuel left aboard.

The next day Bob and Keith listened to the voice recording and the read out from their MRS. In his hypoxic state, Bob had been left incredulous to the predicament they faced, and he was stunned to hear his voice recordings. He realised how the lack of oxygen had made his responses sound absurd and he began to wonder if the flame out had also been self-induced due to his mismanagement. The flight was a stark lesson in the dangers of hypoxia. The aircraft's oxygen system was quickly modified so the primary and emergency oxygen supplies were independently routed to the crewmembers.

Russ Scott, a fighter pilot who had been an Air Force Test Pilot School graduate and a Gemini Astronaut candidate prior to being eliminated due to his excessive height, became impatient with the slow progression of SR-71 pilot checkouts, and requested a move to the remnant A-12/F-12 programme. After an Oxcart checkout, he flew the YF-12 briefly then joined Ling Tempco Vought as an A-7 production test pilot. Later he became 'Mister F-20 Tigershark' for Northrop. His departure from Beale in 1966 altered the crew line-up. John Storrie was then teamed up with 'Coz' Mallozzi since they had flown together in B-58s. Dave Dempster inherited a pilot who had been recruited from the tanker squadron into the 1st SRS's staff as Ops Officer. Jim Watkins had been with Beale's 903rd ARS flying KC-135Qs, where he had received all the security clearances to deal with the Oxcart programme. Due to his progressing years, master joke-teller Jim took a lot of good-natured ribbing from his younger squadron colleagues, occasionally wearing a World War II leather flying helmet to reinforce the 'old pilot' image.

Jim Watkins and Dave Dempster flew their first SR-71 sortie together in 64-17959 on 21 February 1967. As they progressed in their training, they flew weekly sorties including a 'Kitty Three' (a sortie conducted over a regular track) training sortie in 64-17972 on 2 July 1967. The mission plan called for them to head east on a standard refuelling course across northern Nevada, accelerate east over Idaho and Wyoming and turn south to Texas, west over New Mexico to make a photo run on San Diego, and north past San Francisco before returning to Beale. On the eastbound leg over Wyoming, their ANS failed, and should have resulted in an abort of the 'high and hot' portion of the flight and a subsonic return to base via airway routes. Since they were aware that the Senior Crown reconnaissance programme would soon be moving to cover the Vietnam War, Jim and Dave were reluctant to lose an opportunity of flying a 'hot leg', especially when they had the chance to attempt emergency navigation training while being backed up by the stateside VORTAC radio navigation system, which told them where they were along the route. They reasoned that should their ANS failure occur when crossing the Pacific, they would have to continue at speed because of fuel considerations.

Consequently, they continued to Mach 3.0 and cruise altitude using the aircraft's Attitude Heading Reference System, its compass systems and ground-based TACAN transmissions for heading and location references. Whilst at Mach 3.0, they failed to note the precession in their magnetic compass, and when ATC at Tucson, Arizona, said: 'ASPEN 21, you are now leaving the state', they did not understand the significance of the message. It was not until Dave checked their position using TACAN and the ground view sight that he realised they had left Arizona, and violated Mexican airspace. Instead of their tracking camera showing images of San Diego's harbour, it featured photographs of Ensenada, Mexico. After a 'chewing out' by 9th SRW officials for violating the 'Go-No-Go' checklist, they joked that they were the first to fly an SR-71 on an 'international sortie'. Before long crews were instructed to practise a transcontinental emergency navigation leg when returning across the middle of the US.

Ten days later, Jim and Dave were airborne in '972 on a routine sortie that was typical of the flights being performed at that stage in the SR-71's development. They had climbed north from Beale into Washington and descended into Montana for refuelling. While climbing back to high altitude there was a loud bang as the left engine unstarted. The aircraft yawed hard into the 'dead' inlet but the SAS and autopilot kicked in right rudder to maintain track. The unstart was so strong and the yaw angle so great that the right inlet unstarted and the engine compressor stalled. Jim fought to maintain control as '972 suffered repeated unstarts and began a descent that finally ended in stable flight at 29,000 ft (8839 m). When '972 returned to Beale, inlet technicians found that the Linear Voltage Transducer within the left spike had suffered a 'hard-over' failure, and was not reacting to voltage signals from the analogue automatic inlet control system. At the time of the first unstart, the left spike had moved forward during the re-capture cycle and remained extended, rendering shock wave re-capture impossible. In the squadron's flight lounge such experiences were shared as 'things to watch out for' when flying this still-to-be-proven aircraft.

ANOTHER LOSS

On the night of 25 October 1967, a black-tie dinner was being held at the Beale Officers Club with Kelly Johnson as the guest of honour. At the same time, Maj Roy St Martin and Capt John Carnochan were flying a night training sortie that included a Mach 2.8 run back towards Beale. As Roy eased 64-17965 into the descent profile over central Nevada, the gyro-stabilised reference platform for the ANS drifted without a failure warning. Since that system provided attitude reference signals to the primary flight instruments and guidance signals to the autopilot, the aircraft entered an increasing right bank while the Flight Director and Attitude Director Indicator instruments showed no deviation from wings-level flight. There was no visible horizon at high altitude over Nevada at 20:25 hours in the late autumn, and the few scattered ground lights merged easily with the stars as night background. An emergency reference, the miniature standby artificial horizon instrument, which used an independent gyro, was working properly but was poorly located well down on the instrument panel, so the pilot did not note the increasing bank.

As the aircraft rolled over from its stable high-Mach run, the nose began to fall far below a safe descent angle. The SR-71 quickly plunged below 60,000 ft (18288 m). The crew first sensed that something was wrong when the speed increased despite the aircraft's supposedly wings-level, slightly nose down attitude as displayed on the flight instruments. At that point, Roy glanced at his standby horizon, which indicated a 'screaming dive and a roll-over toward inverted flight'. He quickly attempted a 'recovery from unusual positions manoeuvre', which had been part of normal instrument training throughout his 12 years of flying, but the nose had progressed so low and the speed built up to such an extent, that the aircraft was unrecoverable, even though they were still 40,000 ft (12192 m) above Nevada.

Although Roy had pulled the throttles to idle and had rolled the wings level toward what would have been the nearest horizon, the aircraft was in a terminal dive well above the speed from which level flight could be achieved without straining '965 to the breaking point. With no options for recovery left, Roy gave the bailout order. The RSO ejected into the full force of a Mach 1.4 slipstream from which he suffered severe strains. Just before he pulled his between-the-knees bailout ring, Roy heard a warning horn blow that indicated to him that he was below 10,000 ft (3048 m) (with the landing gear up) and descending at a very high speed.

Tugging on his ejection ring, the pilot escaped at a tremendous rate of descent. Exactly as programmed, his automatic escape sequence operated. The lap belt separated, the 'butt-snapper' strap in his seat tightened to fling him free of the seat, and the parachute's explosive slug fired it to full length, his canopy deploying just prior to landing at a terrain altitude above 5,000 ft (1524 m). While the ejection sequence was occurring, '965 plunged into the ground near Lovelock, Nevada, like a hypervelocity meteorite creating a ring crater at its point of impact. In a blinding flash almost all traces of the aircraft disappeared deep into the ground.

Luckily both crewmembers survived without permanent injuries, although John was grounded for a year as a result of severe concussion. Roy remembered walking for what seemed like the rest of the night toward the crash site. Meanwhile, Beale's formal dinner had been disrupted with the discovery that Roy and John were missing somewhere over Nevada. Reports soon came in from Oakland ATC Center and from Lovelock that an aircraft had crashed. A search effort was quickly mounted and the crew was recovered at first light.

The accident board established that pilot error was not a factor in the loss of '965 and recommended the following design and procedural changes:

1. Warning lights should be provided to show ANS failure;
2. The standby attitude indicator instrument should be enlarged and placed atop the pilot's instrument panel directly below the windscreen;
3. The pilot's and RSO's attitude instruments should be powered by different sources;
4. The training programme should contain less night flying until crews had considerably more daytime experience in the SR-71.

PREPARING FOR OPERATIONS
As the 9th SRW approached its time for overseas deployment, much talk in the crew lounge was devoted to anti-SAM tactics. The plan was to penetrate enemy airspace at Mach 3. If fired upon, the pilot would increase speed to Mach 3.2 and climb, thereby forcing the missile's guidance system to recalculate the intercept solutions. Some crews considered other 'jinking' options, but such

manoeuvres were discounted as they would also disrupt effective intelligence gathering. One half-baked consideration was to dump fuel to become lighter for a more rapid climb, but Watkins and Dempster ended that argument once and for all on a winter training sortie by dumping fuel for ten seconds high over Montana to see if the afterburner might ignite the fuel trail. The fuel instead turned into an instant ice cloud in the -67°F (-55°C) stratosphere and left a 5-mile (8-km) long contrail-finger pointing directly to the aircraft. Jim reported that he could see the trail for hundreds of miles after they had turned back toward the west.

Yet another accident befell the 9th SRW on 11 January 1968. Lt-Col 'Gray' Sowers (one of the unit's most experienced instructor pilots and the commander of the 99th SRS) was airborne in SR-71B '957 with student pilot Capt Dave Fruehauf on his third training sortie. The aircraft experienced a generator failure near Spokane, Washington, followed by a second failure a few minutes later. They immediately switched off all non-essential electrically-powered equipment to conserve battery power, and made repeated attempts to reset both generators, which would come on-line briefly, only to fail again. Since airfields directly under an SR-71 flying at altitude were as far away as 250 miles (402 km) after the aircraft had descended, most Washington State bases were not considered suitable for a diversionary landing. Portland, Oregon, looked like the best bet, but it turned out to be overcast, so the crew pressed on toward Beale which appeared within easy reach.

As they approached home on a long straight-in descent, their 175-kt (202-mph; 325-km) airspeed placed the aircraft in its natural 10° nose-up angle of attack. That positive attitude allowed some of the dry tank fuel-inlet ports to suck air, which interrupted the gravity flow of fuel to the engine combustion chambers because the fuel boost pumps were inoperative. This caused cavitation, and both J58s flamed out. Gray got each of the engines restarted intermittently, but they flamed out again and again. Since '957 was rapidly losing its last feet of useful altitude, Gray ordered bail out at 3,000 ft (914 m) above the ground. Both pilots watched 'good old' '957 pancake inverted only 7 miles (11 km) north of Beale's long runway as they rode their parachutes safely down.

Two months later, Maj Buddy Brown and Capt Dave Jensen departed from Beale in 64-17978 to cross the Pacific to Okinawa. The 9th SRW's long-awaited deployment to the war zone had finally begun. Meanwhile, more and more new crews were being trained to reach SAC's desired operational strength of two full squadrons.

On 10 October 1968, a new pilot/RSO team began their take-off roll down runway 14 at Beale in the recently delivered 64-17977. Maj Abe Kardong (an ex B-58 pilot) neared his take-off 'Go-No-Go' decision point when a wheel failed, throwing shrapnel up into a fuel cell. The afterburner's flames ignited the leaking fuel, starting a fire that was soon catching up with the fast-moving aircraft. The 'buddy-crew' Mobile Control officers warned Abe that he had 'one helluva fire', whereupon he aborted the take-off at high speed. At that point the remaining tyres on the affected gear truck also burst. The brake chute blossomed and was quickly consumed by the fire. Abe steered the aircraft toward the arresting barrier at the far end of the runway, but since the aircraft crossed the roll-over sensors (which triggered the arresting cable's pop-up) off-centre and with one wing low, the cable snapped up in front of an inlet, whose sharp edge instantly knifed through the barrier cable, rendering it useless.

As the aircraft proceeded on a very hard ride into the rough, the helpless RSO, Maj Jim Kogler, decided to eject. A few moments later he descended safely under a fully deployed chute which had unfurled a few hundred feet up. For a brief moment he thought that he would drift back into the blazing grass fire that '977 had caused. Meanwhile, Abe rode it out for a full half mile before the SR-71 finally ground to a halt, whereupon Mobile Control Crew members Willie Lawson and Gil Martinez dashed into the blaze and extricated the pilot from the wreckage. Jim was unhurt, but Abe hobbled around for a few days from spinal compression, bruising and abrasions from his high-speed ride toward Beale's Main Gate. Yet another wheel failure – fortunately the last one – had resulted in the loss of an SR-71. Despite four 9th SRW aircraft losses between 13 April 1967 and 10 October 1968, Category III Operational Testing ended in December 1968. The 9th SRW was awarded the Presidential Unit Citation for meeting the many great challenges that faced it as it brought the 'most advanced' reconnaissance system of its day to operational readiness.

BEALE OPERATIONS
Chapter 7

On 17 June 1970, Majs Buddy Brown and Mort Jarvis were to fly a special mission to check out a new type of defensive system and to verify some changes that had been made to another high-powered jammer for the SR-71. The test was to be conducted over the Gulf of Mexico in the Eglin AFB Test Range that was instrumented for tracking high-altitude targets. The flight took them around the western US toward a second air-refuelling point near El Paso, Texas, before the planned 'hot and high' run across the Eglin Test Range. The flight, which began at 07:30 hours from Beale, went well until the SR-71 was engaged in its split off-load air refuelling from two tankers. Buddy described what happened next: 'When we

completed the rendezvous, I pulled up into the pre-contact position and waited for the "cleared for contact" call from the boomer. After receiving the call, I flew to the contact position and waited for the boom to be inserted into '970's [64-17970] receptacle. I got the nozzle contact light and started taking on fuel. I remember commenting to Mort on how smooth the air was that morning; there wasn't any turbulence that one sometimes felt on the eastern side of the mountain range

NAS Miramar F-14s took part in intercept trials against SR-71s off the coast of San Diego in the early 1970s. Code-named Tom Too Hot, they were enjoyable exercises that held none of the rivalry which tainted early USAF F-15 Eagle Bait missions. (Grumman History Center)

around the El Paso area in the summer time. During the refuelling, I was following the directional lights on the bottom of the tanker to keep position "in the green" (the centre of the air refuelling envelope). After taking on about 35,000 lb [15876 kg] of fuel, a crewman called over the boom-linked interphone that I had taken the required amount of fuel and that they would initiate a disconnect on the count of three. At the end of the count I felt the disconnect, throttled back, dropped down and back slightly and spotted my second tanker which was to my right.

'I moved to the pre-connect position behind number two, reset my refuelling system for contact and called that I was ready to refuel. The second boomer acknowledged "ready to refuel" and I pulled into the contact position and waited for boom contact. Shortly thereafter the boom made contact, which I again verified by feel and the "contact-made" light on my instrument console, and continued with what I expected to be a routine air refuelling. Two or three minutes into the second refuelling, the aircraft hit a sort of bump and shook as if it had just flown through some turbulent air. I asked Mort, "Did you feel that?," to which he emphatically answered, "Yes". It felt quite unusual because the air had been so smooth that morning. It may have been another aircraft's jet-wash that was laid across our track by an airliner which had passed earlier. Again, there was another disturbance that I corrected with a small stick input. Then it was quiet and smooth again.

Following their record-breaking long-distance flight of 26 April 1971, Tom Estes and Dewain Vick received the 1972 Harmon International Trophy. The award was made on 20 September 1971 in a ceremony at the White House. The personalities present were, from left to right, Senator Barry Goldwater, Lt-Col Tom Estes, President Richard Nixon and Lt-Col Dewain Vick. (USAF)

'Out of nowhere, the nose gave a small pitch down and a hard pitch up. I pushed the stick quickly forward but the nose and canopy struck the bottom of the tanker. The nose section was gone just forward of the cockpit and the canopy had caved in on me. I thought, "I'm inside the tanker; death is imminent!" My next thoughts were about bailing-out so I told Mort to bail out and pulled the "D" ring between my legs. I still thought I would eject up inside the tanker. There was a lot of noise and debris flying around as I was pushed down into my ejection seat by the rocket that was firing me free of the aircraft. Next, I was aware of free-falling in my ejection seat, whose chute is stabilising my descent toward 14,000 ft [4267 m] where the butt-snapper lofted me out of my seat and my pretty parachute opened automatically. I opened my visor to look around the sky for my RSO, the Habu and the tanker. The tanker was making a turn overhead and Mort was about a thousand feet below me in his 'chute. I didn't realise it at the time, but both my legs had been broken during the ejection. They were numb from the break and I couldn't feel a thing. During the descent, I looked at the ground and contemplated my landing. When I hit, I was dragged a few feet before I got one side of my parachute unhooked. I then unhooked the other side, crawled over to my seat kit and got the emergency radio out. I called the tanker and said that I was OK and asked if they had contacted my RSO. The tanker crew responded affirmative to both questions and waited for us to be picked up by a chopper from the Fort Bliss Army Hospital at El Paso, where the doctors checked us over and splinted my legs.

'My aircraft had smashed in to the ground approximately 20 miles [32 km] east of El Paso at 09:15 hours. The tanker flew back to Beale, did an in-flight controllability check with an approach to landing speed and determined it was safe to make a landing. After it rolled to a stop off the Beale runway it was encircled by fire trucks and Beale officials who were amazed at the amount of damage inflicted to the tail of the tanker, and how that tough old bird was able to continue flying with a severely damaged horizontal stabiliser.'

Buddy recovered from his broken legs, was cleared to return to crew duty later that year, and served a full career as a senior staff officer.

EAGLE BAIT

During the early 1970s, an evaluation programme began involving SAC's SR-71s and TAC's new F-15 fighters. Its purpose was to determine the interceptability of the SR-71 by the F-15 Eagle, which had speed and altitude characteristics similar to the Mikoyan-Gurevich MiG-25 'Foxbat'.

Additionally, the very high-altitude intercept training would be very useful for the 'Eagle drivers'. The programme initially got off to a bad start with inter-command rivalries coming into play, as Buddy Brown recalls: 'I was briefed on the particulars of one F-15 intercept training mission the day prior to the flight. The intercept was to take place in the Edwards Test Range area in California. We were to pass on our exact time, heading and altitude as to when we would be at a specific location over the range to assist the intercept as much as possible the day before the sortie. Additionally, we were to let down to 70,000 ft [21336 m] and slow to Mach 2.85, again to assist the F-15's intercept geometry. Just prior to our arrival at the "start of intercept point", I was asked to dump fuel for approximately 15 seconds to mark my position in the sky. I was told that ground radar sites had got the F-15 lined up so that the pilot could make his pull up at the right moment and "acquire" my aircraft on his on-board radar. He called back a successful "kill" on the SR-71. Immediately TAC Headquarters put out the word that they could shoot down an SR-71 because they had intercepted one.

'Well this did not go down well with the troops back at Beale because they had given the F-15

T-38 Talon 59-1606 was lost at Beale on 23 March 1971 when its elevator controls failed on take-off. Maj Jim Hudson, an SR-71 pilot, was killed when he ejected too low for his parachute to fully deploy. Lt-Col Jack Thornton stayed with the uncontrollable aircraft, sustaining back injuries. (Appeal-Democrat)

Colonel Pat Halloran headed the SR-71 detachment at Griffiss AFB, New York. Air Force Systems Command deployed '955 to New York, under the code name Black Knight, to evaluate a new ECM suite. This exercise provided a cover story for a series of 11-hour transatlantic round-robin sorties over the Middle East. (Tom Pugh)

guys everything they needed to make the intercept. We had not even used our DEF system to jam them. Prior to the next mission, TAC asked for the usual information (position, altitude, speed and heading). We replied, "we'll be in the Edwards Test Area tomorrow." An HQ TAC staff officer protested, "but we need the information to make the intercept." Our reply was, "Why? You claim you can intercept and shoot down an SR-71." For the next two missions the F-15 crews were unable to get anywhere near us; we didn't slow down or descend. They retracted the earlier claim, and from that point on we gave them the information they needed to ensure that the mutual training exercises were beneficial to both parties.'

SUPERTANKERS AND LONG FLIGHTS

Gen P. K. Carlton, the commander of the 15th Air Force, became interested in extending SR-71 missions to fully encompass the concept of global reach. In 1970 he initiated two actions which hastened very long-range operations. The first idea was one covering nuclear war reconnaissance. One day he asked his Director of Reconnaissance, Lt-Col Don Walbrecht, to conceive a post-SIOP coverage of the Soviet landmass with SR-71s, assisted by advanced tankers that were not yet programmed into SAC's inventory. In the next few days, Don and his fellow 15th Air Force reconnaissance officers drew up a plan whereby the existing SIOP was covered with lots of tankers and all of the SR-71s. After Don briefed the 'Boss' the first time, P K said 'back to the drawing boards Recce; you're not thinking big'. A few days later, a new plan was briefed which showed that a dozen pre-positioned Boeing KC-747s and a dozen

Beale-based Habus could cover all probable targets less than five hours after the initial ICBM lay-down. 'That's more like it!' he said. 'That'll help advocate the use of the Jumbos'. Soon after, newly-promoted Col Walbrecht found himself assigned to SAC Headquarters, where he was 'advocating new tankers and re-engined KC-135s' as the Division Chief of Advanced Strategic Aircraft Systems.

Aircraft '979 and '964 are pictured in a hangar at Griffiss. T-38 Talon TOXON 01, just in shot to the right, was used to chase '955 on its test flights. (Tom Pugh)

The 1974 Palmdale test crew consisted of, from left to right, Lt-Col Tom Smith, Lt-Col 'Coz' Mallozzi, Maj Tom Pugh and Maj Ron Selberg. (USAF)

6 October 1973 (Yom Kippur Day – the Jewish Day of Atonement), the Egyptians opened an hour-long barrage from 2,000 artillery pieces along their western border. Simultaneously, 240 Egyptian aircraft hit three Israeli airfields and other important targets in the Sinai.

Within 15 minutes the aggressors were advancing along a 130-mile front, employing five infantry divisions, supported by three mechanised and two armoured divisions. As Israeli soldiers prayed in their bunkers in celebration of Yom Kippur, the Egyptian war machine rumbled over ten pontoon bridges that had been thrown across the Suez Canal, stormed the supposedly impregnable Bar-Lev Line, and established bridgeheads on the East Bank. Simultaneously, the Syrian phase of the attack opened in the north with a massive 30-minute artillery bombardment. This barrage presaged the advance of three Syrian infantry divisions and two armoured divisions. To coincide with the advance, an independent attack was mounted by Syrian helicopter-borne commandos on the vital Israeli observation post at Mount Hermon in the Golan Heights.

The speed and ferocity of the Arab attack caught the Israelis off guard. Troops were mobilised from synagogues and Israeli Radio broke its traditional silence during Yom Kippur to broadcast instructions to its threatened population. Most Western intelligence agencies were equally surprised by the joint attack. Three days before the Arab onslaught, the Soviets had launched the low-resolution camera equipped

Cosmos 596 satellite from Plesetsk in the southwestern USSR. This device allowed them to watch the battle on behalf of their Arab allies.

The Israelis regrouped within two days and attacked the bridges over the Canal. In the north, the Syrians continued their push toward the River Jordan and the Sea of Galilee. The Soviet reconnaissance effort was strengthened on 8 October when the USSR launched Cosmos 597; this satellite was able to change its orbit using rockets and, despite the resultant increase in the satellite's speed, its perigee improved photographic resolution. Its path, inclined 65° to the equator, aligned it across both war fronts. The next day Cosmos 596 was recovered, but the ground situation had turned in favour of the Israelis. Syrian efforts in the north had ground to a standstill after a furious battle, and General Sharon's forces in the south had successfully attacked the Egyptians and retaken a second-line fortification that had fallen the day before.

The Soviets launched Cosmos 598 on 10 October to improve surveillance of the war zone. Pitched slightly higher than the preceding Cosmos satellites, 598 was already in orbit when 597 returned its film cassettes to earth. The Soviets were also receiving real-time imagery from 598 via the Yevpatoriya tracking station in the Crimea. As a consequence of the Soviet advantage in reconnaissance, the US decided to step up its intelligence efforts. The SR-71 offered the best hot-spot reconnaissance capability, and plans were drafted to fly missions from Beale to Egypt and recover into Mildenhall. This long-range concept had been validated two years before by the Estes/Vick 15,000-mile test sortie.

CINCSAC General John Meyer ordered Col Pat Halloran to prepare for these missions. At that point, Pat knew that the sorties would attract wide attention within government circles, and that the success of those flights was central to the survival of the entire Senior Crown programme. Due to its importance, he asked the new 15th Air Force commander, Lt Gen Bill Pitts, for permission to 'run the show' himself. Col Halloran put together a maintenance recovery team and left Beale on a tanker for Mildenhall at midnight on the same day as the 9th SRW's alert. He later recalled: 'I was scheduled to go straight to London to brief senior MoD [Ministry of Defence] officials on the plan, but upon my arrival at Mildenhall I was informed that the British government had had second thoughts and denied us authority to operate from the UK. I was then told that Griffiss AFB in New York State would be our operating location. Without rest, we turned the tanker around, and the full complement of planners and maintenance

personnel were reloaded for a quick return trip to the US. Undoubtedly that was the shortest overseas TDY in the history of the 9th Wing!'

It appeared later that the UK's Heath government had denied the Air Force use of Mildenhall so as to guarantee continued oil supplies from the Arabs, a move that would later produce heated exchanges between Europe and the US.

Palmdale's flight-test SR-71 ('955), had already been scheduled to conduct a series of evaluations on its new A-2 electronic defensive systems from

Tom Tilden and JT Vida flew '955 for KC-10 aerial refuelling tests on 17 March 1983. Based on the commercial DC-10 airliner, the KC-10 was the subject of 60 orders and, like the KC-135Q, had to have its tanks flushed to remove traces of the Habu's JP-7, before standard jet fuel could be loaded for subsequent refuelling missions with other receivers. (Lockheed)

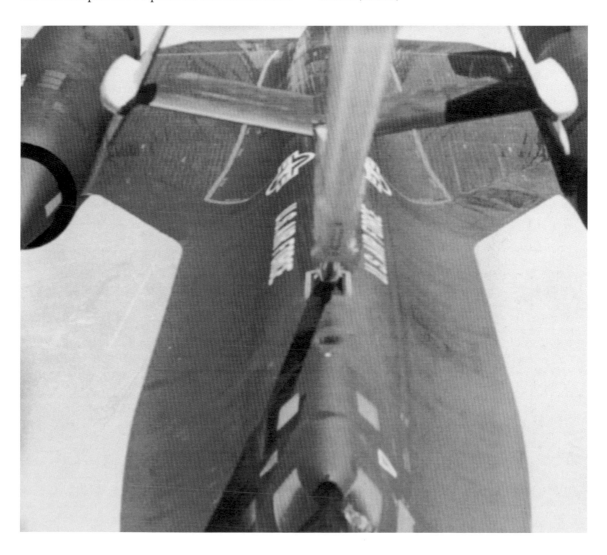

Griffiss AFB from mid-October onwards, so by stationing Beale's detachment at Griffiss at the same time, Halloran would have additional support from Lockheed's technical field support personnel, and a cover story for the secret operations in the Middle East.

As Halloran's new operating location was firmed up and higher Headquarters approved the overall transatlantic plan, crews began serious flight planning for the first mission. Lt-Col Jim Shelton and Maj Gary Coleman got airborne from Beale in 64-17979 at 22:00 hours on 11 October and headed

Between 30 October 1980 and 21 January 1981, '974 participated in ten sorties to evaluate NASA's new TACAN and S-band radio. These systems were designed for the Space Shuttle. (NASA)

for Griffiss. They were met by an angry base commander and three Lockheed tech reps after laying 'a heavy late-night sonic boom track' across the US and down into New York state as they made their descent from altitude. A phone call from Jim Shelton to Al Joersz and John Fuller (who would fly a second SR-71 into Griffiss) advised them to make their descent profile over the Great Lakes to minimise the effects of the boom on the urban eastern states. Fortunately, there were no boom complaints when the second crew made their crossing. The next day's news papers reported a strange phenomenon which was described by one scientist as a probable 'meteoric shock wave'.

The second aircraft developed a hydraulic problem that forced an engine-change, leaving the new detachment down to one mission-ready aircraft until specialised equipment could be flown in from Beale. An hour after the last SR-71 landed, the first tanker arrived carrying Tom Estes (the operations officer), three mission planners and a number of Beale's best intelligence and maintenance personnel. At 06:00 hours a secure teleprinter clattered out the final details of the first sortie which was to be flown 22 hours later.

The first major question to arise when the aircrew met with the mission planners concerned diversionary fields, and no one could offer a satisfactory answer. Later that morning the

Bob Powell, in a chocolate-brown pressure suit, receives his 1,000-hour award from 9th SRW Wing Commander Col Pat Halloran on 10 January 1974. (USAF)

Mildenhall tanker arrived, and the unit's technicians began preparing '979 for the longest operational sortie to date. By mid-afternoon someone suggested that the crew should get some sleep since they had been up for nearly 36 hours, and they would soon be airborne for another 16 hours during the sortie itself. They were directed to an old BOQ (Bachelor Officer Quarters) where their rooms were hot and the beds uncomfortable. Gary Coleman recalled: 'No one could snore like Jim Shelton and I got no sleep at all, but I consoled myself with the thought that my pilot was getting some solid rest!'

The belligerent attitude of some usually helpful allies required JP-7 fuel and tanker crews to be re-positioned from Mildenhall and Incirlik, to Zaragoza in Spain and the quest for emergency landing sites was proving all but impossible. Notwithstanding, Jim Shelton cranked '979's engines on cue and lifted off from Griffiss at 02:00 hours, on the first of nine so-called Giant Reach/Busy Pilot missions. He made good the first of six aerial refuellings (two tankers in each AR track), off the Gulf of St Lawrence (in an area known as Old Barge East). Having topped-off, '979 then accelerated and climbed east, en route to the next cell of tankers awaiting the thirsty Habu off the coast of Portugal (Rota East). Returning again to speed and altitude the aircraft made a high-Mach dash through the Straits of Gibraltar and let down for a third AR south of Crete (Crete East). Due to the SR-71's proximity to the war zone and Libya, the US Navy provided a CAP (Combat Air Patrol), using carrier-based aircraft on station in the Mediterranean.

The SR-71 then resumed its climb and acceleration to coast in over Port Said. Gary Coleman comments: 'There was no indication of anything launched against us, but everyone was painting us on their radars as we made our turn inbound. The DEF panel lit up like a pin-ball machine and I said to Jim, "this should be interesting".' In all '979 spent 25 minutes over denied territory; entering Egyptian airspace at 11:03 GMT, it covered the Israeli battle fronts with both Egypt and Syria before coasting out and letting down for its fourth ARCP (Crete West), which was also being CAPped by the US Navy. The next hot leg was punctuated by a fifth refuelling, again off Portugal (Rota West), but the tankers from Zaragoza had difficulty getting a clearance through the busy offshore airway, which was filled with airliners. They could not request a priority clearance because of the secrecy of the their mission. When approval was at last received, the air traffic controllers hesitated clearing the tanker cell on the requested track because 'unidentified high speed traffic, height unknown', was approaching from the tankers'

12 o'clock position. The tankers could not reveal that the 'traffic' was actually their trade.

Soon after completing his mid-ocean refuelling, Jim climbed and accelerated '979 back up for its final high-speed run across the western Atlantic towards New York. Mindful of his own fatigue, Gary was in awe of his pilot, who completed a text book sixth air refuelling (Old Barge West), before greasing '979 back down at Griffiss after a combat sortie lasting ten hours 18 minutes (more than five hours of which was at Mach 3 or above) and involving support from 14 ever-dependable KC-135Qs, four from Goose Bay, two from Griffiss and eight from Torrejon. Their reconnaissance 'take' was of high quality and provided intelligence and defence analysts with much needed information concerning the disposition of Arab forces (and Soviet equipment) in the region, which was then made available to the Israelis.

The Syrian military situation was swinging in favour of the Israelis by 14 October. The Soviets had stepped up an airlift of military equipment and were aware that the Syrian front was collapsing. Washington had also begun supporting Israel with a huge airlift of US war materials. President Nixon had requested $2.2 billion in emergency aid for the Israelis, a request that incensed the Organization of the Petroleum Exporting Countries (OPEC) members Abu Dhabi, Libya and Qatar, which had been meeting with oil companies in Vienna since 12 October. They immediately imposed a complete oil embargo on the US, a move quickly followed by the other OPEC oil producers. To further warn the nations against supporting Israel, OPEC unilaterally announced a 70 per cent rise in oil prices and a 5 per cent per month cut in petroleum production. The decision caused panic in western Europe, which depended on the Arab States for 80 per cent of its oil supply.

Meanwhile, in the Sinai desert the Egyptians launched a 100,000-strong offensive toward the east on 14 October, this attack resulting in one of the biggest tank battles in history. As Israeli forces gained ground, they also established a bridgehead west of the Suez Canal that threatened to cut off the Egyptian army. With the Egyptian military situation becoming more and more acute, President Nixon announced that US forces across the globe had been placed on military alert following the receipt of information indicating that the Soviet Union was planning 'to send a very substantial force to the Middle East to relieve the beleaguered Egyptian Third Army, now completely encircled in the Sinai'.

This tense period in superpower relations was somewhat defused when Soviet Secretary Brezhnev supported a United Nations motion of 24 October that would eventually end the Yom

THE UNITED STATES OF AMERICA

TO ALL WHO SHALL SEE THESE PRESENTS, GREETING:

THIS IS TO CERTIFY THAT
THE PRESIDENT OF THE UNITED STATES OF AMERICA
AUTHORIZED BY ACT OF CONGRESS JULY 2, 1926
HAS AWARDED

THE DISTINGUISHED FLYING CROSS
(THIRD OAK LEAF CLUSTER)

TO

CAPTAIN REGINALD T. BLACKWELL

FOR
EXTRAORDINARY ACHIEVEMENT
WHILE PARTICIPATING IN AERIAL FLIGHT
10 DECEMBER 1973

GIVEN UNDER MY HAND IN THE CITY OF WASHINGTON
THIS   5th   DAY OF   NOVEMBER   19 74

David C Jones
CHIEF OF STAFF

John L. McLucas
SECRETARY OF THE AIR FORCE

Kippur War. Meanwhile SR-71 surveillance missions continued. At 02:00 hours on 25 October, Majs Al Joersz and John Fuller got airborne from Griffiss in '979 and paid a second successful visit to the Yom Kippur war zone. However, owing to protestations from the Spanish government, the second and fifth AR tracks were re-positioned off the coast of the Azores (out of range of Spanish radars) and renamed Lajes East and Lajes West. Since the US intelligence community was concerned that the Soviet Union might deploy personnel and materiel in support of the Arabs, the mission's priority objectives were to monitor port facilities at Latakia and Tartus in Syria and Port Said and Alexandria in Egypt. A third mission was chalked up by the same aircraft eight days later, when on 2 November Majs Bob Helt and Larry Elliott secured more photography of the ports for national intelligence users, in addition to coverage of Cairo International

Above and right: Reg Blackwell was awarded the DFC for his part in the reconnaissance mission flown over the Golan Heights on 10 December 1973.

Airport and the Tura cave facilities, near Cairo, which, it was believed, might contain Soviet 'Scud-B' mobile missiles. Majs Jim Wilson and Bruce Douglas took 64-17964 on its first sortie to the Mediterranean on 11 November. The ten hour 49 minute flight departed Griffiss and terminated, as planned, at Seymour Johnson AFB, North Carolina. The reason behind the detachment's migration to the south was the wish to avoid the New York winter weather. Col Don Walbrecht headed up the new detachment at Seymour Johnson, which had been pre-arranged with HQ TAC by Col Harlon Hain from the SAC Reconnaissance Center. Since the shooting war had died down, SR-71 reconnaissance was now used to demonstrate compliance with the

CITATION TO ACCOMPANY THE AWARD OF

THE DISTINGUISHED FLYING CROSS
(THIRD OAK LEAF CLUSTER)

TO

REGINALD T. BLACKWELL

Captain Reginald T. Blackwell distinguished himself by extraordinary achievement while participating in aerial flight as an SR-71 Reconnaissance Systems Officer on 10 December 1973. On that date, his courageous accomplishments and superior professional skill resulted in the successful collection of significant intelligence vital to the highest national interests. While operating in a hazardous environment and despite conditions which threatened the effectiveness of this flight, Captain Blackwell applied his exceptional airmanship and successfully concluded this unique and important mission. The professional competence, aerial skill and devotion to duty displayed by Captain Blackwell reflect great credit upon himself and the United States Air Force.

cease-fire agreement and provide irrefutable evidence for Secretary of State Kissinger's team, which was leading the delicately balanced withdrawal negotiations between the deeply distrusting Israelis and Arabs.

Fierce fighting broke out along the ceasefire line on 30 November, threatening to destroy the fragile agreement brokered by the US. Jim Sullivan and Noel Widdifield flew '964 across the Atlantic on 2 December to look at the situation. It proved to be a well-timed move, since fighting had begun that same day in the Golan Heights. Further diplomatic pressures put an end to the new skirmishes before Pat Bledsoe and Reg Blackwell went out in '979 on 10 December for another look at the belligerents. They flew their 'clockwork' ten-hour mission, arriving back at Seymour Johnson on the minute of their flight plan. Thereafter, things were quiet for the next five weeks, so the Beale troops went home for Christmas. In January they returned to base to carry on with Sinai surveillance activities.

On 25 January, Majs Buck Adams and Bill Machorek flew another perfect ten-hour sortie, but they returned to Seymour to face a very low cloud ceiling and visibility conditions that mandated a diversion to Griffiss. This would put the 'take' out of position for processing. Don Walbrecht said: 'We had Buck grab some fuel from the standby tanker and jacked the ceiling up a bit (against the complaints of Harlon Hain at SAC Headquarters) and Buck snuck in to a perfect landing at Seymour under the lowest ceiling an SR-71 has ever landed.'

The detachment's spirited high jinks (after each outstanding mission of recognised national importance) annoyed the 4th Tactical Fighter Wing's commander, Col Len Russell, whose fuel stocks had been quickly depleted by the five KC-135Q tankers that supported the SR-71 movements. With a serious shortage of fuel throughout the war, Seymour Johnson had not been re-supplied for fighter training sorties. To further complicate matters, Beale's new 14th Air

This group shot was taken after Lt-Col Roger Jacks' last SR-71 flight. From left to right, top row, the crewmembers are: John Murphy, Joe Vida, Don Emmons, Al Cirino, Tom Allison, John Fuller, Rich Graham (on his own), Buzz Carpenter, Bill Groninger and Bruce Leibman. Standing at the left are Bill Keller, Chuck Sober, Joe Kinego (in the pressure suit to the left) and Roger Jacks; and in the bottom row are Jim Sullivan, Jay Reid and Tom Keck. Standing to the right of the shot are BC Thomas and Pat Bledsoe, who are almost obscured by John Storrie. (Paul F. Crickmore Collection)

Division commander, Brig-Gen Don Pittman, really messed things up by demeaning Col Russell, who was embittered by what had appeared to be SAC heavy-handedness. The fuel embargo imposed by the OPEC nations caused the Air Force to husband its fuel supply and drastically reduce most flying to currency rides only. Because of Russell's complaints to his TAC boss Gen Dixon, headquarters' arbitration was necessary to put things back in perspective. In response, SAC's Deputy Chief of Staff for Logistics came to Seymour Johnson to thank Russell for supporting the Sinai effort and to solve his fuel problem. Within a few days the pipeline flowed with JP-5 for the TAC F-4s and a trainload of JP-7 arrived for the two SR-71s.

The success of international peace efforts soon began to show. On 18 January 1974 a military separation agreement was signed between Egyptian and Israeli defence officials that led to troop withdrawls. By mid-February, the Middle East peace process was beginning to go into overdrive and on the 18th four Arab nations proposed a truce in the Golan Heights, Adams and Machoreko's 25-January mission in 64-17971 verifying the pull-back. There had been a great deal of suspicion on both sides that the opposing forces would not pull back. Consequently, the Habu's photography became the instrument of verification and was shown at the peace negotiations as proof. With the evidence in hand, full diplomatic ties were finally restored between Egypt and the US after a break lasting seven years.

As troop withdrawals continued Majs Ty Judkins and G. T. Morgan flew '979 on the next to last long sortie. Appropriately, this evergreen aircraft also flew the final sortie on 6 April 1974. It had flown two-thirds of the nine 'ten hour' sorties, chalking up a remarkable rate of success, despite the very demanding nature of the missions without ground or air aborts or diversions.

Those nine long-flights represented a pinnacle of operational professionalism. They were a tribute not only to the dedication of the aircrews, but also to that of the staff planners and the small group of top ground technicians who maintained the SR-71s away from home. These sorties stood as a testament to the long reach of the aircraft, and its ability to operate with impunity in a high threat environment.

SIMULATOR TESTS

Capt Maury Rosenberg and another Air Force pilot were instructed to report to the General Dynamics plant at Carswell AFB near Fort Worth, Texas, in May 1976 to help in some research. The two officers were directed to an obscure room in the plant containing two very crude cockpits equipped with a stick, throttles and basic flight instruments. The room was a web of electrical

Habu driver Jim Sullivan chalked-up over 600 hours in the SR-71 as a crewmember with the 9th SRW and as a test pilot with AFLC at Palmdale. He and Noel Widdifield established a world speed record that still stands: New York to London in less than two hours. (USAF)

wiring connected to racks of monitoring apparatus and a computer. The simulated aircraft's capability was Mach 3.0 at 100,000 ft (30480 m) with no armament. The second cockpit was similar, but it also had a radar, a fire control panel and the simulated aircraft carried missiles.

Two basic intercept profiles were flown. The first began with the missile-equipped interceptor being scrambled from an alert pad when the unarmed aircraft was detected 350 nm (403 miles; 649 km) away and a repeat was flown when the target was 450 nm (518 miles; 834 km) away. In the second profile, the missile-equipped aircraft was in an airborne race-track pattern. As the unarmed aircraft entered the area, the interceptor was vectored inbound on various intercept angles: head on, abeam and tail chase.

Four engineers monitored readouts as the scenarios were played out and would stop the proceedings to reset their instrumentation when they changed from one vector to another. It was dull, time-consuming work in which only 12 intercepts were completed in a full day. The engineers asked the pilots lots of performance questions to help verify some relevant flight data that they had already gleaned from another source. It did not take long to abandon the scramble profile and to concentrate on an orbit-vector profile. Pat Bledsoe repeated those simulator flights two weeks later. One of the other pilots involved in the tests was Maj Bob McConnell, who later became an air attaché in Moscow.

Viktor Belenko defected from Siberia to Japan four months later in a MiG-25P 'Foxbat-A'. During his CIA debriefing, he talked about how he was trained to shoot down an SR-71 near Vladivostok, and how the Soviet controllers and pilots had reached the conclusion that their best chance to make an intercept would be to have an aircraft airborne in a holding pattern which faced the track of the high flyer. He admitted that experience against other 'Foxbats' showed that the prospect of getting an SR-71 was quite remote at that time unless one carried a 'nuke' intercept missile.

RECORDS

In 1976 SAC and HQ USAF agreed to show some of the SR-71's capabilities as part of the nation's bicentennial celebrations. The original plan was to set an 'around the world at the equator' speed record. Pat Bledsoe and John Fuller were the senior crew at that time and were chosen to make the flight. Initial planning showed that it could be done in 16 hours and 20 minutes with seven refuellings. The only modification required for the SR-71 would have been an additional liquid nitrogen dewar for fuel-tank pressurisation.

The crew were sceptical of their own physical limitations for a flight of that duration, but

Jim Eastham (left) was the second person to fly an SR-71. He and Ray Scalise are standing beside a YF-12 – an aircraft for which Jim was Lockheed's chief test pilot. (Lockheed)

believed that adrenaline would probably keep them going. Pat recalled: 'Preparations proceeded well until the full plan reached HQ USAF. When the generals saw the cost of deploying the fuel and tankers to forward bases they were aghast. It would take nearly 100 KC-135 flights to carry out the operation safely. The word came back to Beale to "do something more reasonable". Consequently, the 9th set a new series of world speed and altitude records on 27 and 28 July 1976.

THE FALKLANDS

Argentina invaded and captured the Falkland Islands on 2 April 1982. Three days later, a Royal Navy task force set sail from Portsmouth with the objective of driving the invaders out and returning the islands to British rule. Twenty days later Royal Marine commandos recaptured South Georgia island and soon after President Reagan pledged American support for Britain in the crisis. He branded the Argentinians as 'aggressors' and ordered economic sanctions against them. He also offered to supply Britain with 'unspecified' war materials to assist in the recapture.

Seventy-three days after the invasion, British troops completed their objective and the Union Jack flew over the Falklands once again. Did the SR-71 fly over the islands during the conflict? An analysis of the problem took place at the Pentagon. The study showed that SR-71s could have covered the area easily if SAC could operate KC-135s from South American bases; this, however, was politically unacceptable. It was too difficult to operate the KC-135s exclusively from the US because they could not take on fuel in flight. McDonnell Douglas KC-10 Extenders, which could buddy refuel, were not available so the idea was dropped and the task was left to 'other' sensors.

GIANT PLATE AND CLIPPER SORTIES

The origins of US high-altitude surveillance of Cuba can be traced back to 1962 and the now infamous Missile Crisis. With Cuba located just 90 miles (145 km) from the southern tip of Florida, SAC U-2s continued to regularly monitor the island until the task was passed to the SR-71 in September 1974. The reason behind the move was simply the sheer number of commitments undertaken by the U-2 fleet throughout the world – this had recently increased still further to include monitoring the Middle East from the Mediterranean island of Cyprus, after the Yom Kippur War. Headquarters SAC had, as far back as 1 July 1970, prepared a contingency plan for SR-71 operations against Cuba, code-named Giant Plate. The primary objective of these sorties was to collect Photint and about 90 per cent of the Cuban landmass was photographed on every mission. However, in contrast to other SR-71 sorties, it was the JCS that decided when a Cuban sortie would be launched, rather than the SRC. For planning purposes, the JCS initially directed SAC to prepare for such a sortie once every 30 to 40 days, however, throughout 1975 and 1976, the Giant Plate mission rate averaged out at only one every 55 days. To conduct these round-robin sorties from Beale, it was necessary for the SR-71 to undertake three air refuellings (six different tracks had been established in the Caribbean area for this task). A typical mission lasted about five and a half hours, of which about 50 minutes was spent in the collection area. Of particular interest to the JCS was the deployment of any new weaponry from either the Soviet Union or Eastern Europe and the monitoring of Soviet naval task forces that regularly visited the island. Each Giant Plate sortie was carefully monitored and tracked on radar by the Cubans. As a consequence, the SRC varied the aircraft's track on every mission. The first sortie took place on 26 September 1974 and the aircraft was crewed by Maj Lee Ransom and his RSO Maj Al Payne.

Later, in response to a significant adjustment in United States foreign policy made towards Cuba in early 1977 by President Jimmy Carter, the JCS directed Headquarters SAC to end all Giant Plate overflights. As a consequence, on 11 January 1977, the last planned sortie in a series of 18 similar missions was completed by Capt Maury Rosenberg and the same RSO that had conducted the first – Maj Al Payne. Unfortunately for both the crew and photo interpreters, the western half of the island was completely blanketed by heavy cloud cover. In addition, the OBC's film guidance rollers became loose, damaging what little imagery had been clear of cloud.

Despite the Carter administration's best intentions, it soon transpired that in spite of earlier conciliatory rhetoric, Castro had actually accelerated Cuba's export of Marxist revolution to several developing nations of Central America, Latin America and Africa. By the summer of 1978, US State Department estimates suggested that there were no less than 40,000 Cuban soldiers and civilians in 14 black African countries. Then, later that same year, a reconnaissance satellite photographed a Soviet freighter in Havana harbour surrounded by large crates that were being moved to a nearby air base where aircraft were being reassembled. It appeared that 15 Mikoyan-Gurevich MiG-23 'Floggers' had been supplied to Castro's air force, most likely under Soviet control. Such an upgrading of Cuban air strength was worrying. The MiG-23BN 'Flogger-H' model was known to be capable of carrying nuclear weapons, and if it was indeed this variant of the MiG that had been 'exported', then the shipment violated the 1962 Kennedy-Khrushchev accord, in which the Soviets pledged not to deploy 'offensive' weaponry on Cuba.

A decision was therefore made in November 1978 to fly SR-71s over Cuba to identify the MiG variant, and the first of these new missions was flown on 12 November. A lack of surveillance of the island over the intervening 22 months generated an enormous list of targets from national intelligence users, many of which were aimed at proving compliance with the earlier accord, by establishing the absence of weapon systems that would constitute a violation by the Castro regime. On 20 November, President Carter said that the Soviet Union had assured him both publicly and privately that the MiG-23 jets were in Cuba for defensive purposes only. A *Pravda* commentary citing the American press said: 'The presence of such aircraft would run counter to the 1962 agreement'. It went on to say that the MiG reports: 'were groundless and a provocation from beginning to end'. Photographs taken by the SR-71 confirmed the Soviet claims – the aircraft were indeed MiG-23MS 'Flogger-Bs' optimised for the air-defence role.

On 1 December 1978, amid concerns that the classified mission code name Giant Plate had been compromised, SAC HQ assigned a new one, Giant Clipper, according to Frag Order 60-FY-14-01, which governed the execution of all SR-71 Cuban reconnaissance missions.

Bellicose statements, however, together with the reported presence of a Russian brigade, did nothing to reduce US concerns over Cuban intentions in the area and threatened the Senate's ratification of the vital Strategic Arms Limitation Treaty. As a result, the 12 November mission actually set a precedent for flying further SR-71 monitoring sorties over the island and resulted in the JCS directing SAC to conduct ten further sorties in 1979. These took place on 22 and 31 May, 15 and 28 June, 27 July, 20 and 29 September and 5, 16 and 20 October.

The need to build-up a radar intelligence (Radint) data base of the island dictated that the first four sorties flown in 1979 would utilise the SR-71's HRR capability. The Defense Intelligence Agency (DIA) requested that the aircraft's Elint-gathering systems should also be used to collect signals data. The 27 July mission, however, was a photographic overflight and this was used to help evaluate and validate HRR imagery collected during the four earlier Radint missions.

Throughout 1980, just five Giant Clipper sorties were flown, these taking place on 15 January, 2 February, 17 March and 3 and 22 July. The dates on which the SR-71 executed the majority of its Giant Plate/Giant Clipper sorties can be attributed directly to two periods of increased tension between the United States and Cuba. The first was the MiG issue, the second the build up of Soviet troops on the island. The latter led to frenetic behind the scenes negotiations with the Soviet Union, which continued to insist that the role of its people on the island was no different to what it had been prior to 1979. But such statements failed to pacify the Carter administration. As a result, the administration announced the implementation of five policies in response to the brigade's

This photograph graphically illustrates the way that '959's 'Big Tail' unit rotated downward on landing to avoid becoming entangled in the lines of the aircraft's brake chute. Note the calibration markings on the tail section. (USAF)

presence. The first of these was to increase the level of US surveillance of Cuba: the eight Giant Clipper sorties flown between 5 October 1979 and 22 July 1980 were a central plank of this policy. Other measures included reassuring Latin American nations that the US would protect them against any Communist incursions. The country also promised an increase in the number of US military exercises in the Caribbean and provided greater levels of economic assistance to the region, as well as establishing a US Caribbean Joint Task Force, with its headquarters at Key West, Florida.

As a result of this heightened level of tension between the US and Cuba, in early April 1980, thousands of Cubans who were either anti-Communist, anti-Castro, or both, sought political asylum in the Peruvian embassy in Havana. Later that month, after much wrangling, Castro allowed any disgruntled Cuban national to seek asylum in the United States. This resulted in a deluge of people leaving the island on more than 600 small boats owned by Cuban-Americans living in Florida and intent upon transporting their friends and relations off the Caribbean island and to 'The Land of Plenty'. By mid-summer 1980, it was estimated that 125,000 refugees had arrived in Key West. The Giant Clipper sortie flown on 3 July 1980 provided the photo-interpreters with outstanding imagery in which it was possible to establish that the mass exodus off the island had ended. They counted two large merchant vessels, one small merchant ship, 28 fishing boats and one probable factory ship in the harbour, but no people. A merchant ship approximately 185 ft (56 m) long and of the

type that had been used to transport refugees was also tied up at Mariel – its decks clear of both people and cargo. The SR-71's imagery also showed two unoccupied tents, erected on the pier near the merchant ship. The tents had been cordoned off with ropes. The photo-interpreters found no groups of probable refugees in the quay area, the Rio Mosquitos refugee processing site was being dismantled and 31 of the known 45 tents used as temporary accommodation were also gone. To ensure that both SAC HQ and the DIA had the most timely information available, imagery interpreters at the 9th RTS provided them with both telephonic, as well as teletype reports, so that these could be immediately relayed to the White House Situation Room.

Five years later, Cuba was still being watched. Majs 'Stormy' Boudreaux and Ted Ross departed Beale at 04:00 hours on 19 June 1985 in '980 on a Giant Clipper sortie. After their first air refuelling north of Salt Lake City, they turned southeast toward the target area. Castro had always held a belligerent attitude toward the US and his missile crews often spoofed SA-2 firings to annoy the overflyers. Many crews believed it was only a question of time before a SAM was fired their way, so advanced DEF systems were carried to counter such action. Part of the pre-penetration procedure saw the DEFs fully checked out, and the aircraft flown up to maximum speed before being backed off to cruising speed to ensure that the inlets were performing at their best in preparation for SAM dodging.

As '980 reached Mach 3.2 to test full-speed operations, 'Stormy' began backing off to a Mach-3.0 cruise while Ted checked out the new DEF system. At that instant, the nose pitched up more than 10° before Stormy could reach the stick to stop the rise. Since he was flying with his right hand on the autopilot pitch wheel (where the right index finger moved a very small control wheel to adjust fine increments of nose-up or nose-down deflections), his hand was out of position for immediate reaction. He quickly moved his hand to the stick and exerted enough force to stop the dangerous pitching action.

Stormy had been flying fast and was beginning to slow down, and as a consequence the aircraft was in a nose-up trim condition when all three DAFICS computers shut down. The SR-71 was well out of trim and the SAS was not there to help when it was most needed. Without the SAS to dampen 'Stormy's' sharp nose-down input, '980 responded with an equally sharp nose-down sweep of more than 15°. He then jerked the stick back, which caused a sudden up-sweep as 'Stormy' recalled: 'I had little time to analyse what was going on because things were happening so rapidly. Unfortunately, each oscillation was

getting larger. It seemed that I was trying to learn the flight characteristics of a completely new airplane in a few seconds. Certainly I'd never experienced anything like this before. In training we were only allowed to fly the aircraft with either pitch or roll or yaw SAS off, and that was at a benign 25,000 ft [7620 m] at 0.90 Mach. The loss of one channel of SAS was an abort item.

'I tried hard not to over-control the aircraft and to get the nose back on the horizon. As the nose reared up again to an ungodly 20°, I knew that this would probably be the last chance I'd get before the aircraft exceeded the restoring capability of the controls. The aircraft would surely depart the flight envelope and disintegrate. Fortunately, I was still flying straight ahead, though we were still well above Mach 3. We hadn't deviated from our flight path and these oscillations were exposing the aircraft's underside forebody to awesome airstream loads. As the nose came up again, I hit the forward stop on the stick and still the nose kept rising. When it stopped I cranked in just a little forward trim and, by the grace of God, the nose started coming back down! I eased off some stick pressure, just enough to stop it deviating by much more than 5°, from which I could progressively make smaller pitch movements. When I got that bucking bronco back to some proximity of level flight with the pitot tube near the horizon, I tried to maintain that position while I groped around the base of the stick for three red-cover 'guarded' re-set switches for the DAFICS computers. They were low and to the right and I was holding the stick with my right hand and trying with my left to reach around behind the back of the stick to these switches. Unfortunately, the metal cuff ring that secured my gloves to the rest of my pressure suit kept hitting the stick causing the aircraft to pitch and roll. I soon realised that I'd have to change hands. I managed to do that without over-controlling and was finally able to engage the relevant SAS channel. After that success, the rest was easy.

'When we analysed the MRS printout back at Beale, I learned that the inlet restart switch had activated automatically following the DAFICS shutdown. This action caused the spikes to travel forward and had opened the forward bypass doors and that had prevented unstarts which would have added to our woes. Through all of this excitement, Ted remained remarkably calm despite the 6-lb [2.72-kg] checklist ripping free from the two 6 x 6-in [15 x 15-cm] Velcro pads that had held it on his lap. It's during such frightening emergencies that I'm in awe of RSOs who have to read checklists and 'sit it out'. At least the pilots have plenty to keep themselves busy with, and less time to consider their fate.'

'Stormy' aborted the mission and recovered to Beale, where it was discovered that the triple DAFICS computer shutdown was caused by a voltage drop triggered when Ted activated the aircraft's new DEF system (something the engineers said could never happen). The fault circuitry in the computer had detected this power loss and shut itself down.

NICARAGUA

Some months earlier, SR-71s had overflown Nicaragua for the first time. After the downfall of the dictator Samosa, a Marxist government was established which immediately requested Soviet military aid. In the autumn of 1984, a team of US 'crateologists' became interested in a cargo on board a Soviet freighter that had docked in Nicaragua. The photographs taken by a US reconnaissance satellite showed what was believed to be Mikoyan-Gurevich MiG-21 'Fishbed' interceptors. Nicaragua denied that the crates contained MiGs and maintained that the cargo consisted of Mil Mi-8 'Hip' helicopters. After presidential clearance, six reconnaissance sorties were flown over Nicaragua from Beale. The first was flown on 7 November 1984 by Maj Bob Behler and Capt Ron Tabor (this crew flew three of the six sorties over Central America). As a result of their work and correlative intelligence, the MiG-21/Mi-8 wrangle slowly faded from the headlines, along with rumours of a possible US invasion of Nicaragua. Some months later, the world's press confirmed that no MiG-21s had been shipped to Nicaragua – on this occasion the photo interpreters were off the mark.

AIR FORCE LOGISTICS COMMAND

Although not at Beale, the Palmdale facility was also used as an acceptance test centre for the SR-71 programme. An Advanced Systems Project Office (ASPO) was established and each new aircraft was subjected to extensive FCFs before delivery to the Air Force. Each new and pristine SR-71 would then be picked up by a Beale crew and delivered to the 9th SRW. On 31 December 1970 the functions of this unit were transferred from Air Force Systems Command (AFSC) to Air Force Logistics Command (AFLC), and Det 51 was created as the SR-71-specific unit of AFLC. The unit reported to the Sacramento Air Logistics Center and had sub-division offices at Norton AFB at San Bernardino, California, near to the contractors and sub-contractors.

The function of the ASPO was to provide total logistics support to the SR-71 programme, including maintenance support (spares, major overhauls and testing and evaluation of new or upgraded systems). A September 1977 reorganisation placed the duties of Det 51 at Plant

42 in the hands of Det 6. Command of this new detachment was located at Norton, with further lines of command to Wright-Patterson AFB in Ohio.

The two flight test crews of the Det 51/6 Flight Test Division flew missions on dedicated flight-test aircraft, and in addition conducted FCFs on recently overhauled fleet aircraft. All fleet modifications were first extensively flight tested at Palmdale. Such comprehensive testing encompassed all airframe, engine, subsystems and sensor/defensive systems that would ultimately be incorporated in improved fleet aircraft. Apart from modifications to the DAFICS, the SR-71's mechanical systems remained little changed, but virtually all aspects of the aircraft's sensor systems were modified and updated during the course of the programme. At any one time, contemporary and advanced technology systems and capabilities were fielded.

Significant programmes tested at Palmdale included high Mach/high bank angle envelope clearance, a high Alpha warning and protection system, DAFICS, electrical system replacement, stability system improvements and advanced sensor and defensive system qualification. Literally everything, from nuts, bolts, fasteners and paint to newly manufactured and uprated engines, were all extensively tested. The dedicated flight test crews (one crew selected from the USAF Test Pilot School, the other coming from the operational fleet) flew a total of between 150 and 200 hours a year, and were supported by Lockheed ADP maintenance and engineering personnel from 1970 to 1990.

To remain ahead of Soviet missile development, the Air Force asked Lockheed engineers to develop an aft-directed ECM system to be used against advanced missiles. Additional fuselage space was necessary to accommodate the requirement and to allow sufficient space for real-time data transmitters. Design consideration was given to equipment pods and conformally-mounted packages, but an extended tail became the favoured option. Such a modification added considerably more volume, and involved minimum airframe and systems modifications, produced low aerodynamic drag and was relatively cheap. After the Air Force accepted the new design, '959 was transformed into the 'Big Tail' SR-71 configuration.

The proof of the concept began on 20 November 1975 when Lockheed test crew Darrell Greenamyer and Steve Belgeau conducted high speed taxi tests. The new tail unit was almost 9 ft (2.74 m) long,

The high quality images obtained by the SR-71's cameras are perfectly illustrated by this impressive photograph of the Seattle Dome in Washington state, taken while cruising at 82,000 ft (24994 m) and Mach 3. (USAF)

weighed 1,273 lb (577 kg), had an added volume of 49 cu ft (1.39 m³), and could carry a maximum payload of 864 lb (392 kg). To prevent the appendage from contacting the ground during take-off rotation, or the drag chute from fouling the unit during the landing roll, the tail was hydraulically repositioned 8° 30' up or down.

A second test was conducted by the same crew on 11 December. During that first airborne test, Greenamyer accelerated to Mach 1.27 so engineers could evaluate the stresses on the added fuselage section. Eleven flights later, Lockheed handed 'Big Tail' over to Det 51 at Palmdale. On 5 May 1976, Lt-Col Tom Pugh and Maj John Carnochan chalked up the first Air Force test flight in the aircraft. On that sortie '959 was equipped with DEF 'J' and an Optical Bar nose camera. The test series included a Mach-3.0 flight on 4 August, after which the Air Force test crew certificated the modification as having no detrimental effects on the aircraft's handing characteristics, or its maximum Mach, while considerably enhancing the SR-71's overall mission capabilities. To further demonstrate its enhanced mission capabilities, 'Big Tail' was flown with two Optical Bar Cameras, one in the nose and one in the tail. Later the chine bays were deepened to accommodate two further OBCs in each. It was later found that the intercept capabilities of the SA-5 were less of a threat to the

SR-71 than had been anticipated, and it was determined that the fleet would not require the 'Big Tail' modification for an aft-facing ECM suite. After the test series had been completed, Lt-Col Pugh and Maj Bill Frazier flew the unique aircraft on its final Det 51 flight on 24 October 1976.

The primary test airframe for many years had been 64-17955. However, by 1985 this SR-71 had become so highly modified that it no longer represented the fleet configuration. Lt Cols Tom Tilden and Bill Flanagan therefore flew 'ever-reliable' '955 on its 722nd and last sortie on 24 January 1985. Four days later, the same two crewmembers conducted a runway roughness evaluation in the jet and then returned it to the Palmdale storage barn, where it remained for six years. In 1991, '955 re-emerged and was placed on permanent display at the Air Force Flight Test Center Museum at Edwards AFB.

The test role passed to '972, which was fresh out of Programmed Depot Maintenance, its post-maintenance FCF having been completed by BC Thomas and JT Vida on 22 January 1985. Its final flight was on 6 March 1990 when Ed Yeilding and JT Vida delivered it to the Smithsonian National Air and Space Museum, following a record-breaking flight across the US. During its time with the division, '972 flew 417 hours 54 minutes during 163 test sorties.

OL-8 TO DET 1
Chapter 8

Strategic Air Command was both a major command of the US Air Force and a Joint Chiefs of Staff (JCS) specified command. Headquarters USAF assigned SAC the responsibility for all strategic reconnaissance and the command executed its mission under the supervision and guidance of the Chief of Staff, US Air Force. In part, the Commander in Chief SAC (CINCSAC – pronounced 'sink sack') was directed: 'to prepare plans for strategic aerospace reconnaissance for which the Air Force [is] responsible (electronic, weather, visual, aerial, photographic, cartographic reproduction, and related activities) to meet the global requirements of the Department of Defense'. As a specified command, SAC received assignments directly from the JCS, which included photographic and signal coverage of selected areas, together with global upper atmospheric sampling. Requirements for individual reconnaissance programmes were specified and outlined in operations and fragmentary orders and, through its Strategic Reconnaissance Center (SRC), at Offutt AFB, Nebraska, Headquarters SAC exercised operational control over all such missions, supervising their planning, scheduling and execution, unless such functions had been specially delegated in a SAC operational order. In the specific case of SR-71 operations, code-named Giant Elk by SAC, these were planned by specialists in the SR-71 branch at the SRC, in response to taskings by the JCS. Initially, these were in support of the SAC Single Integrated Operational Plan, the DIA, the Commander in Chief Pacific (CINCPAC), the 7th Air Force, Military Assistance Command Vietnam and the Commander United States Air Forces in Korea (COMUSKOREA). Senior Officers at the SRC participated in twice daily meetings, one held at 7:30 am, the other at 3:30 pm, to review current mission tasking, planning and the weather. Once

This jovial group photograph was taken at Beale just prior to the first OL-8 transpac to Okinawa. Conditions at Kadena on Okinawa were very different to those at Beale and the crews were soon thrown into combat missions. (USAF)

On 8 March 1968, Majs Buddy Brown and Dave Jensen left Beale in '978 as the first Senior Crown crew to deploy to Kadena. Here Mort Jarvis (left) is pictured with Buddy Brown after they teamed up later in the programme. (USAF)

the SRC had completed the mission planning process, details were forwarded to the JCS for final approval.

BUILDING 500

For a more detailed, first-hand insight into the workings of the SRC, Frank Stampf, an ex-F-4 WSO and Habu RSO, provides the following eloquent and useful backdrop: 'Headquarters SAC, Building 500, Offutt AFB, Nebraska, was the place where the means to carry out America's cold war doctrines of "strategic deterrence" were planned and directed under considerable secrecy, and even more considerable security. SAC was the keeper of two legs of the nation's nuclear "triad" – the strategic bomber fleet and the intercontinental ballistic missile force. (The third leg was the US Navy's nuclear ballistic missile submarine fleet). As such, SAC had responsibility for developing and maintaining the plans – and capability – to conduct nuclear strikes on thousands of Soviet and Warsaw Pact military and industrial targets, should the President ever determine it was time to

give the order. Consequently, the SAC Headquarters building had more than its share of high-level security measures to protect that capability. Building 500 itself was a cross between a rather nondescript, boxy, brick and glass architecture, and an imposing presence, depending upon how much one knew (or cared) about what went on inside the structure.

To provide a bit of context, it must be understood that any description I give of that building is from the perspective of a crewmember that did not grow up in the SAC environment. At the risk of stereotyping, I don't think aircrews of that generation would argue the notion that Tactical Air Command fighter crews enjoyed having themselves characterised as the "devil-may-care-scarf-flying-in-the-windstream" type of aviators who rarely broke the rules, but generally did everything possible to bend, circumvent, or otherwise "beg forgiveness rather than ask permission". On the other hand, at least in the eyes of the fighter crews, SAC was the realm of the "hardcore-do-it-by-the-book, By God" aircrews who never, ever would even dream of operating outside the tightly defined constraints of SAC's nuclear strike mission guidelines. In retrospect, this was certainly not a bad thing. Remember "Slim Pickens" as the hat-waving cowboy B-52 pilot who rode his atomic bomb like a rodeo bull right down to his assigned "commie ground zero" target in the movie "Dr. Strangelove?" That was definitely a product of Hollywood ... The point is that once one was inside the headquarters SAC building, the atmosphere was pure business, and it was apparent that the business being conducted within those walls was deadly serious.

'Having said all that, SAC Headquarters, even viewed from the eyes of a TAC-bred aviator, was a pretty amazing place. By the early 1980s Building 500 was one of the first military facilities, at least that I saw, that had concrete barriers placed strategically around the building so that a would-be attacker could not (at least not easily) drive a car laden with high explosives into the front lobby or other entrances. Even those personnel assigned to the headquarters had to park quite a distance from the building and walk, winding their way through the maze of barriers (usually, it seemed, in a snowstorm) before reaching the front entrance. Once inside the lobby, you could go no further than the security desk, where you had to show the young airman of the SAC Elite Guard your SAC ID badge. The badge, if properly annotated, authorised the bearer into the building, but did not necessarily give access to all of the building once inside. Each individual's badge was designed to allow access only into those specific areas for which the individual was cleared and had a "need-to-know" regarding the work being carried out behind the doors.

'After being properly identified by the guard and allowed to pass the main desk, you would then slide your badge into the slot of a turnstile barrier, similar to those used in the subway systems of large cities. Your badge would be automatically "read" by the security system to ensure that you indeed were authorised access into the building, and the turnstile would unlock, letting you past the front lobby. For us "recce" types who worked in the Strategic Reconnaissance Center (SRC), that was the last light of day we would see for awhile, since the SRC was located in the lower depths of Building 500. A few feet after passing through the turnstile we would begin the descent down the several flights of stairs taking us to the basement "vaults". Once downstairs, a short walk would put us in front of the secure entry door to the SRC. Again, the ID badge was run through a slot and if all was correct, the door would open to let you into the world of strategic reconnaissance.

'As you entered the SRC your first sight was the operations desk, which was manned 24 hours a day, 365 days a year. Behind the desk were two duty officers, both former strategic reconnaissance crewmembers, and an enlisted operations specialist, who assisted the duty officers in keeping track of all the recent, ongoing, and upcoming reconnaissance missions flown by Boeing RC-135, U-2/TR-1, and SR-71 aircraft all over the globe. Needless to say, the level of activity behind the desk was pretty constant, with secure phones and other communications media in a regular state of cacophony, reporting the status of "real world" reconnaissance sorties flying from operational detachments around the world and around the clock. Well before the days of high-tech computer capabilities, all those sorties were tracked and displayed on nothing more than a large black, back-lit grease board using varying colours of grease pencils to annotate sorties scheduled, airborne, complete, delayed, or cancelled; and guess what – even without the technology it worked just fine ...

'Turning left from the ops desk took you into the offices and planning areas for the RC-135 fleet. Turning right would take you through the SRC briefing room, decorated with photos of strategic recon aircraft dating back to the early days of the Cold War. Passing through the briefing room led to "high-flyers" country. This was the area occupied by the U-2/TR-1 and SR-71 folks. After passing the office of the colonel in charge, the short hallway opened up to the large mission planning area shared by the U-2/TR-1 and SR-71 planning and operations staffs. The space was divided longitudinally by an oversized planning table, peaked along the top with sides sloping to either side, one facing the U-2/TR-1 troops and the other the SR guys. The large slanted surfaces, very much like drafting tables, gave us a place to lay out the navigation charts we used to review and/or plan the sorties being flown at our operational locations worldwide. Although the majority of the more "routine" missions were planned at the operational detachments, SRC staff still assisted the det planners in preparing for high-priority sorties that were out of the ordinary. Each of the SRC staff members also had a desk in the room, which allowed us to pass information easily among ourselves (or just shoot the breeze in the rare "slow" moments). The entire area, from the point you opened the door to entering the SRC near the ops desk, was specially designed and built as a Special Compartmented Intelligence Facility, or SCIF. Therefore, it was permissible to have highly classified information and materials out in the open, and to discuss classified mission details with other staff members. This greatly simplified the planning and coordination process. Underneath the planning table was row upon row of sectional navigation charts covering every area of the world. These were the days before sophisticated flight planning computers and Global Positioning System technology were in use.

Consequently, the slim tolerances for navigational error when planning an SR-71 mission, to be flown at 2,000 mph [3220 km/h] within tenths of a mile of politically sensitive borders, required extremely accurate planning and execution. Every detail of mission plans, especially for the more demanding and high-visibility sorties, were checked and re-checked by the planners both at the operational detachments and at SRC.

'No description of the SRC could be complete without mention of "The Phone". In a small booth at the far end of the large planning room was a black telephone with a very distinctive (and particularly annoying) ring. It was the secure line with which we communicated secret stuff with anyone we needed to outside of the SRC SCIF. This included our counterparts at the Joint Recon Center in the Pentagon, the SR-71 wing in California, and the operational detachments in Okinawa and England. It also included the folks at the National Security Agency, the Defense Intelligence Agency, and, once in a while, the Central Intelligence Agency.

'All of us at the SRC worked lots of long hours, many nights, and regular weekends. As a result, we all enjoyed those rare moments when everything appeared to be under control, we were ahead of the power curve for any known tasking coming down the pipe, and the generals in the building were (for once) preoccupied with something, or someone, other than us. Every so often, that unique confluence of conditions would occur on a Friday afternoon. As the hours of the day slipped by, we all began to hope against hope that the clock would finally read 17:30, we would be able close up the shop, and at least temporarily leave the reconnaissance world in the hands of the guys at the ops desk. We would plan to slip off to the Officers Club for a well-deserved beer and the opportunity to swap war stories of our longed-for flying days.

'Almost inevitably, just as we were almost tip-toeing toward the door and about to turn off the lights, "The Phone" would blast its annoying clanging ring as if to say, "not so fast, you recce pukes … " And another long night would just be beginning.'

THE STAGE IS SET

When President Johnson endorsed the CIA Director's 31 December 1966 decision to terminate the Oxcart programme, a schedule for the phase-out of the A-12 fleet was formulated to meet a 1 January 1968 deadline. On 10 January 1967, the head of the project advised Deputy Secretary of Defense Cyrus Vance that four A-12s would be placed in storage in July, two more in December, and the last four in January 1968.

In May 1967, Vance directed that the SR-71 assume contingency responsibility to conduct

Cuban overflights in July, and that the Senior Crown programme was also to be ready to cover Vietnam by 1 December 1967. His directive provided for a short overlap between the capability of the out-going covert A-12 programme and the incoming 'overt' SR-71 programme. In the event, the date of the changeover slipped five months, giving Oxcart a brief stay of execution.

Meanwhile, as the 1st SRS neared operational readiness, decisions were made by Col Bill Hayes (the 9th SRW Commander) and Col Hal Confer (the Director of Operations) as to which crews would be the first to be deployed to Kadena Air Base on the island of Okinawa. The eight crewmembers they selected began training for the deployment, flying simulator sorties depicting the oceanic route they would fly.

It was also decided that the crew who ferried the first aircraft to Kadena would fly the first operational sortie over Vietnam. The predetermined sequence would also include a fourth crew in the operational line-up who rode a tanker to Kadena. Each SR-71 departure would be backed up by a spare (with the fourth crew) in the event of the primary aircraft having to abort due to 'Go-No-Go' discrepancies, such as inlet malfunctions. Two days before Glowing Heat – a code name reserved for SR-71 positioning flights – six tankers were flown to Hickam AFB, Hawaii. Air refuelling support for the SR-71 was provided by KC-135Q tankers and SAC code-named this SR-71-specific support, Giant Bear. Initially three units were designated to perform this vital task, the 903rd ARS based at Beale, the 306th ARS at McCoy and the 909th ARS at Kadena (on 1 July 1971, support was increased to four squadrons; the 9th and 903rd ARSs at Beale, the 306th ARS at McCoy and the 70th ARS at Little Rock).

The SR-71 crews agreed to draw straws, leaving the choice of who would go first in the hands of Fate. Dave Dempster held the four straws and the RSOs from each of the other three crews drew one. With the luck of the draw, Dave Jensen's straw decided that he and Buddy Brown would fly the first aircraft across 'the Pond', and would hopefully fly the first 9th SRW ops sortie from Kadena. Jerry O'Malley and Ed Payne would fly the second deployment and Bob Spencer and Ruel (Keith) Branham the third. Dempster was left holding the short straw, so he and Watkins would ride the tanker unless one of the other crews came up with a sick jet.

Command of the Operating Location would be alternated between the 9th SRW's wing commander and vice commander (and later the Deputy Chief of Operations). The first detachment commander would be the vice commander, Col Charles Minter, and Col Carl Estes would be the

Bob Spencer and Keith Branham delivered '974 to Okinawa on Wednesday 13 March 1968. The aircraft was lost 21 years later on a mission from the island, both crew ejecting safely. (USAF)

director of maintenance. With the tankers safely at Hickam AFB, Hawaii, Maj Harlon Hain (the 1st SRS operations officer) set up a down-range radio station on Wake Island to provide emergency radio coverage. All was now ready for Brown and Jensen to make their unofficial record-breaking five-hour flight across the Pacific, the sortie being flown at a speed that was twice as fast as the existing world record.

DEPLOYMENT

At 10:00 hours on the morning prior to their departure, Brown and Jensen (along with their back-up crew, Watkins and Dempster) received their pre-mission briefing. Since this was the 9th's initial operational deployment, the briefing was attended by the wing commander and many others. Mission planners briefed the entire flight profile for the sortie which would begin at 11:00 hours on 8 March 1968. After take-off they would head west from Beale to a point 50 miles (80 km) north of San Francisco, where they would 'light the burners' for a dash to 75,000 ft (22860 m) to check that all systems were functioning normally, before descending to the first air refuelling. With a clean bill of health on the Habu and a top up of fuel from the tankers, Buddy and Dave would race to another refuelling northwest of the Hawaiian Islands, where they would 'buddy cruise' with the tankers for an extra 30 minutes to take them to a point where they would be 'single-engine capable' to the island of Iwo Jima as an emergency landing base.

After a mid-Pacific refuelling from the 'buddy tankers', a third Mach-3.0 dash would take them to their third and final top up west of Wake island, where a maximum off-load would give them enough fuel to reach Kadena and to go to an alternate base on Taiwan should the weather deteriorate over Okinawa. During the briefing they were informed that the weather was expected to be good in the refuelling tracks, at Kadena, and at their emergency landing bases, and that they could expect a comfortable crossing. After a maintenance briefing and some good humour, the two crews began official crew rest.

At 07:30 the next morning the four crewmembers reported to the Physiological Support Division (PSD) for a final weather briefing and a maintenance report on their aircraft. This was followed by the standard preflight physical examination and high protein/low residue breakfast (steak and eggs, and orange juice). After one last trip to the urinal, suit-up began. Two PSD suit technicians aided each crewmember as he donned his full pressure suit. A communications check and pressure suit integrity test confirmed that each garment was functioning properly, and after a ten-minute nap the crews were transported

to their respective aircraft – Brown and Jensen to aircraft '978 and Watkins and Dempster to '980. After 'strapping in and connecting up' they began the normal 'challenge and response' cockpit checklists which would take them through engine start, taxi and pre-take off procedures. With engines revved to full military power and all instruments 'in the green', Buddy released '978's brakes and lit both burners, the SR-71 rapidly rolling down the Beale runway and lifting off into the vivid blue morning sky. He recalls: 'After crossing the coast of California, I started our transonic acceleration climb profile to altitude. This portion of the flight was considered mission critical because the spikes, forward and aft inlet doors, inlet guide vanes, and nozzles all had to check out prior to committing the bird to the Pacific high flight. Everything was "up tight" so we were on our way. Shortly after level off at FL750 we picked up the tanker's ARC-50 radio signals and started getting ranging information to the aircraft, which was about 400 miles [644 km] away. We had a solid lock on so we made the radio-silent rendezvous. We pulled up into the pre-contact position, were waved in, got a contact and started our max off-load to a pressure disconnect. We took on about 60,000 lb [27216 kg] of fuel, said our thanks and goodbyes over the boom interphone, then started on our way to AR No. 2. The second leg was uneventful, although the ARCP was changed slightly due to a line of thunderstorms in the AR track.

'We again accelerated on our next leg to the third and final refuelling. Approximately 20 minutes after level off at 79,000 ft [24079 m], I encountered a problem which could have forced me to land at Johnson Island. My right spike (for no apparent reason) went full forward which caused a very large yaw moment (lots of drag). I checked my cockpit over and found a popped circuit breaker which (when reset) brought the spike back to its normal "bottomed" position for high Mach flight.

'The third decel, AR and climb were also normal, but when we were back at altitude I encountered another potentially serious problem. My left generator went off line and I couldn't reset it. This was a "Go-No-Go" situation which meant I should land as soon as practical. My decision was to continue on because we were less than 1,000 miles [1609 km] (about 30 minutes) from Kadena. I used my coded call sign and contacted 'Mamma' and informed them that, "I was lost, but making good time". We landed at Kadena with the failed generator, but the first SR-71 had arrived and was soon ready to start reconnaissance operations in Southeast Asia, and wherever else the National Authorities might require. We had taken off from Beale at 11:00 and had arrived at

Weary after their long tanker ride, Lt-Col Jim Watkins and Maj Dave Dempster finally arrived on the wet island of Okinawa. Col Charles Minter (the first OL-8 commander) presented the crew with 'Senior Taxi Wings'; Watkins and dempster had taxied out to Beale's hammerhead three times as back-up in '980 to cover the launch of the three other Habus. (Dave Dempster)

Kadena at 09:05 – nearly two hours earlier than take-off time (but in the next day because we had crossed the international date line) – we beat the sun by a good margin.'

Two days later O'Malley and Payne delivered '976 to OL-8 (Operating Location-8) of the 9th SRW at Kadena. They had departed Beale much earlier in the morning and landed at Kadena at 03:30 hours Japan time. Spencer and Branham delivered 64-17974 on 13 March. Three days later the KC-135 carrying Watkins and Dempster arrived at Kadena. It was late in the evening and raining hard when the tanker unloaded its weary passengers. As the last two SR-71 crewmembers (who had made the long Pacific trip 'the hard way') stepped from the tanker to what should have been a rapturous welcome from the others, they were met by a junior NCO who was there to drive them to their Visiting Officers Quarters in a blue Air Force maintenance van. The newcomers felt deflated as the NCO murmured a weak apology

for the sparse turnout, dismissing it as 'high work load due to operational requirements'. As they opened the door to their Visiting Officer's Quarters (VOQ) room they were greeted by the entire gang of crewmembers and senior staff who cried out the raucous wartime welcome, 'Hello Assholes. What took you so long getting here?' OL-8 was now fully manned and it was time for a little celebration.

The Kadena detachment was known as OL-8, following the numerical designation pattern of SAC's overseas reconnaissance locations. It was redesignated OLRK (Ryuk-yus – the name of the island chain which includes Okinawa) on 30 October 1970. It became OLKA on 26 October 1971, changing yet again to Detachment 1 of the 9th SRW in August 1974, a title which it retained until 1990 when the SR-71 fleet was retired. The operational deployment of the SR-71s to Okinawa also gave the aeroplane the nickname 'Habu' after a dark poisonous pit viper indigenous to the Ryukyu island chain. Although the nickname 'Blackbird' has long been publicly associated with the SR-71, that title has been shunned by the crewmembers and others closely connected with the Senior Crown programme, who favoured the serpentine moniker. The name Habu stuck permanently and Dave Jensen designed the

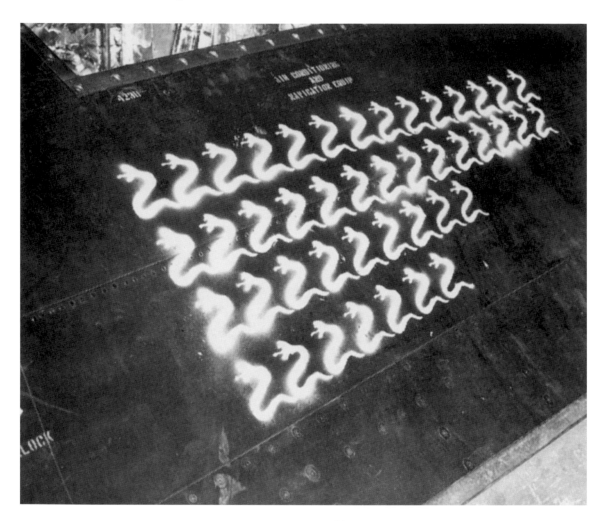

As North Vietnam sortie rates increased, the three Kadena-based SR-71s began to notch up an impressive number of Habu mission marks. (Lockheed ADP)

colourful detachment flight jacket patch, with the snake interlaced around the figure eight.

Col Charlie Minter was the chief architect of most of the operating procedures for OL-8's crews. Those procedures proved so sound and well structured that most of them remained unchanged throughout the entire 22-year life of the Kadena operation. The maintenance teams from the 9th SRW that manned OL-8 were the best at their jobs and were considered the cream of Air Force maintainers. Col Carl Estes' hand-picked Habu technicians had done high-priority work on the three jets as they arrived and had all of them ready for operations by 09:00 hours on 15 March 1968, when the unit was declared fully OR (Operationally Ready).

On Monday 18 March, OL-8 was ordered to fly its first operational sortie. As previously agreed, Buddy Brown and Dave Jensen began preparing themselves for the mission. As a hedge against crew illness or aircraft system failures, every operational sortie was backed up by a spare aircraft and a suited-up aircrew who were equally prepared for take-off orders. The standby crew on this occasion was Jerry O'Malley and Ed Payne. Although everyone was all set for the mission, it was cancelled by higher authorities and Buddy and Dave flew a so-called 'Cathy' training sortie. As previously agreed back at Beale, the next crew to fly was Jerry and Ed.

TO WAR

On the morning of Thursday 21 March 1968, Maj Jerry O'Malley and Capt Ed Payne were driven out to the Little Creeks Hangar near the middle of the base. Precisely 50 minutes before take-off the rear doors of the white PSD van opened and the two USAF fliers emerged wearing full pressure suits, 'space' helmets and 'moon boots'. The two crewmen walked into the old hangar, which was filled with all manner of high-tech support gear, surrounding one of the world's most advanced operational military aircraft.

After shaking hands with Col Charles Minter (the detachment commander), the four other SR-71 flight crewmembers present, key ground crewmen and finally each other, O'Malley and Payne climbed the gantry ladder that took them up to the cockpits of SR-71A serial number 64-17976 (which now rests in the USAF Museum at Dayton, Ohio). Carefully lowering themselves into their respective cockpits, the crew were assisted by white-coveralled PSD specialists who swiftly connected them to their life-support gear, intercommunication leads and escape systems.

The exterior and interior preflight checks had already been completed by the buddy crew who had 'cocked' the aircraft while the prime crew was suiting up. Half an hour before the scheduled take-off time, Jerry turned his attention to the pre-start checklist, reviewing certain important switch-positions on his consoles and instrument panel. Those pre-start checks verified liquid oxygen and nitrogen quantities, and the positions of the switches which controlled aircraft-specific systems such as the left and right aft bypass doors, the inlet centrebody spikes and forward bypass doors, suit heat, face heat and refrigeration for the cockpit and sensor bay environment control system. In addition, the moving-map projector was checked to ensure that it was loaded properly, the Stability Augmentation Systems (SAS) switched on and the TEB counters were each seen to display 16 units. Although some of these checks were unique to the SR-71, many others were standard for conventional jet aircraft. Much of the challenge-and-reply system of formal checklist reading was carried out for the purpose of putting on record (on the cockpit voice recorder) that the many standardised procedural steps had indeed been performed.

While Jerry was doing pilot tasks, Ed was also at work in his 'office' performing HF and UHF radio checks, INS alignment and aircraft DEF checkouts. Other checks embraced checkouts of the TACAN radio-navigation system, camera exposure control systems, ANS and the forward down-looking view-sight. Ed's final checks were concerned with the various reconnaissance sensors, the canopy seal, the Radar Correlator Display system, various camera controls and finally the RSO's moving-map projector, which showed the entire pre-planned mission in considerable detail along a flight-sequenced photo-strip of a standard jet-navigation chart.

During the aircrew's inter-cockpit checklist conversation, the crew chief was also plugged into the aircraft's interphone system (with head-set and microphone) through a phone jack-plug receptacle located in the nose-wheel bay. Through the use of this simple system he was able to monitor their checks and responses prior to them commencing the engine start sequence. 'Interphone' – 'Checked'; 'Bailout Light' – 'Checked'; 'Triple Display System' – 'Checked'; 'Fuel Quantity' – 'Checked'; 'CG Limits' – 'Checked'. As the clock ticked down to one minute before engine start, Ed called out the last four items. 'Oxygen Systems' – 'On and Checked'; 'Baylor Bar' – 'Latched and Locked'; 'Exterior Light Switches' – 'On'; 'Brake Switch Setting' – 'Checked'.

The two Pratt & Whitney J58 engines were fired up by revving each power-plant up to 3,000 rpm through the use of two Buick-powered start carts, which were spline-gear connected to a direct drive shaft in each engine's gear box. The cart's 400-bhp (298-kW) V8 Buicks (working in series) sounded like racing cars when they were accelerated to high rpm during the J58's rapid spooling-up.

At the designated moment, Jerry said, 'Crank number two chief,' and the Buick roared to life with an ear-splitting din in the confines of the Little Creek Hangar. Cocooned within the sound-proofed protection of his helmet, Jerry smiled as the rpm increased on the right engine, the steady climb levelling out as he eased the throttle forward into the 'IDLE' position on the quadrant. The fuel flow into the engine was timed to meet with a 'thimble-full' of TEB, the successful use of which could be verified by a momentary flash of green flame in the tailcone of the starting engine, and by a visible down-click on the right TEB counter (indicating one shot of TEB used) within the cockpit. Less than ten seconds after the Buick had begun cranking, the engine was idling smoothly at 3,975 rpm. Once the other engine was 'turning and burning' after-start checks were performed. 'EGT, Fuel Flow and Hydraulic System Pressures' – 'All Checked'; 'Flight Controls' – 'Checked'.

As the cockpit canopies closed, minor problems appeared which threatened to jeopardise the mission. Firstly, Ed had no indication of cockpit pressurisation. That glitch was remedied by simply advancing the engine rpm, which duly inflated the canopy seals. As Ed searched through the 'Go-No-Go' checklist to determine the importance of the other minor discrepancies, Jerry said, 'Well Ed, do you want to be the first guy to abort an operational sortie, or the first to fly one?' Ed's response was predictable. 'Kadena Tower, this is BEAVER FIVE-ZERO, radio check.' To which the tower operator answered, 'FIVE-ZERO you are loud and clear, and cleared to taxi.' Ed acknowledged with two unspoken clicks of his mic switch – a standard procedure used to minimise radio emissions on unguarded frequencies that could be monitored by Soviet trawlers that often lurked in international waters just a few miles off the coast.

Prior to the SR-71 moving out from the hangar, a ground technician released the scissor switch on the nose-wheel knee and hand-guided the aircraft backward via a nosewheel tow bar. Slowly, '976 was pushed by a tractor (back end first) out of the hangar under the control of a tug operator clad in an aluminised fire-protective 'fear naught' suit. As the ground crew re-secured the nosewheel scissor switch and re-chocked the wheels, Ed called out the last checklist items. The crew chief disconnected his intercom link, removed the wheel chocks and signalled Jerry that he was all clear to move out. The pilot then eased '976 forward and checked the brakes in the first few feet of the roll out, after which he steered the jet down the taxiway to the hammer-head run-up area adjacent to the end of the active runway.

Ed got a 'starlight' from the ANS, indicating that the system had already searched and successfully acquired three stars for triangular position referencing. His Present-Position Indicator confirmed that everything was working fine and that they were within 100 ft (30 m) of track at runway end. In the pre-launch engine run-up position the wheels were tightly chocked, the brakes held firmly and engine trim checks completed. Once more, fuel sequencing, brake switches, pitot heat, battery and inverter switches were checked. The INS's reference altitude was updated, and the crew sat ready to taxi forward to the number one position on the active runway for an on-the-second take-off roll.

All eyes on or around Kadena were fixed upon the black jet. A few minutes before take-off the mobile control car was driven onto the runway by the spare crew, who then proceeded to conduct a runway-length foreign object check for debris that might damage the tyres or engines during launch. The ground crew then sledge-hammered the chocks free from the wheels and stowed them in the back of their ground-support 'bread vans', before sending '976 on its way with a crisp salute. As the final countdown moved towards brake release, Kadena Tower called, 'FIVE-ZERO, you are cleared for take-off'. Ed answered 'Click-Click', and Jerry, who had eased the throttles forward to 7,200 rpm, released the brakes and said to Ed: 'Military Power – Set; Tachometer, EGT, Nozzle Position and Oil Pressure – All Checked. We're on our way Ed.'

The pilot then moved the throttles forward to the mid-afterburner position, which resulted in a left-right yaw movement as each afterburner lit, accompanied by a tongue of flame glinting from the rear of each engine. 'Throttles to Max A/B,' Jerry said as the Habu's take-off roll accelerated,

followed by, 'Decision Speed–looks good. No Problems,' ten seconds later. As '976 approached 180 kt (207 mph; 333 km/h), O'Malley gently pulled back on the stick, whereupon the nose rose smoothly to 10° above the horizontal. At 235 kt (271 mph; 436 km/h) he murmured, 'Lift-off,' and 'Wheels up,' and retracted the undercarriage immediately to ensure that the 300-kt (345 mph; 555 km/h) gear-door limit was not exceeded. In less than 25 seconds Kelly Johnson's masterpiece was airborne on its first operational mission.

Once airborne, Jerry reassured Ed that all systems were looking good, and that the engine instruments were checked. Almost immediately Kadena Tower called, 'BEAVER FIVE-ZERO. Contact Kadena Radar.' Ed replied with two clicks on the mic, and selected Radar's frequency. 'BEAVER FIVE-ZERO, this is Kadena Radar. Squawk 2107.' Ed dialled the code on his IFF panel and pushed the 'Ident' button, whereupon the Kadena controller confirmed that the jet was cleared to proceed on track. Ed then selected an appropriate HF radio frequency for rendezvousing with the KC-135Q tankers.

At 0.5 Mach, Jerry engaged the control surface limiters and observed that the Surface Limiter light on the Central Annunciator Panel extinguished. A cross-check between Jerry and Ed confirmed that both flight-director platforms which powered their flight instruments were operational. Jerry selected the Astro-Inertial Platform Gyro for instrument power and reference, while Ed used the secondary gyro platform for back-up.

Automatic fuel tank sequencing was checked and the altimeter was set to a standard 29.92 inches of Mercury atmospheric pressure above 18,000 ft (5486 m) to insure that all aircraft would have a standard reference for altitude separation. On their way to the refuelling area, Jerry levelled '976 at FL250 and maintained 0.9 Mach, taking up a heading toward the Air Rendezvous Control Point where the KC-135s were orbiting less than 15 minutes away. Ed, meanwhile, had activated his mission sensors.

For its first operational mission, the SR-71 carried a Goodyear SLAR in the nose and a downward-looking, vertically-mounted Terrain Objective Camera in the centre of the fuselage, ahead of the nose gear, and an AR 1700 radar recorder unit in the N bay within the right chine. Behind the cockpits in the P and Q bays were the left and right long focal length 'Close-Look' TEOC, or 'Tech', cameras. Finally, bays S and T held an Operational Objective Camera each.

At this point, Ed was waiting for the reconnaissance systems and sensors to warm up to verify their in-flight performance. It took six minutes for the radar to warm up, two minutes for

Another 'up North' sortie gets underway as a Habu taxies out of its Barn at Kadena. The weather conditions depicted here were not unusual for the island, rain coming as a novelty to the desert-dwelling Habus. (USAF)

the Recorder Correlator Display to function, two minutes for the Electromagnetic Recorder (EMR) to be ready and 20 seconds before the cameras were ready for testing. At that point, Ed pressed the BIT button for the SLAR, but it failed to work. Since it was not a primary sensor for this mission, they decided to proceed without it; the radar also served as a cross-reference for navigation, but they could rely totally on the ANS and Gyro Platform for navigation in any case. Ed then checked the DEF system jammers. First DEF A was turned on, then, two minutes later, when the system had warmed up, the S (standby) light illuminated. This was followed by checks on the other defensive systems, DEF B, C, E and finally DEF G, which was also powered up and declared operational. At that point Ed told Jerry that the DEF System was ready – a definite 'Go' action on the 'Go-No-Go' checklist.

A special covert radio-ranging system known as ARC-50 had been specially developed to allow the SR-71 to rendezvous discreetly with KC-135Q tankers by giving azimuth and distance information to both crews as they approached one another in total radio silence. Linking up with the SR-71 southwest of Okinawa thanks to the ARC-50 system, the KC-135Q started pumping the special JP-7 fuel into the SR-71's tanks immediately after the jet had safely connected with the boom. With an additional 70,000 lb (31752 kg) of fuel now in the tanks, Ed recomputed the aircraft's centre of gravity. The final part of the refuelling was conducted in a near-tropical air mass resulting in the SR-71 responding sluggishly to the military power settings on both engines as it cruised at 350 kt (403 mph; 649 km/h).

To overcome aerodynamic drag and the limited mil-power thrust, Jerry engaged 'min-burner' on one engine and cross-controlled slightly to overcome the off-set thrust – the added thrust made it easy to take on the last 10,000 lb (4536 kg) of the 70,000-lb off load of fuel. At a pre-arranged time and position, and with BEAVER FIVE-ZERO full of JP-7, the boom was disconnected. As the SR-71 dropped back and gently slipped clear of the tanker, Jerry lit both afterburners and pushed the throttles up to 'MAX', accelerating '976 to 0.9 Mach before climbing to FL330.

At 33,000 ft (10058 m) Jerry eased the nose below the horizon into a 2,500 ft (762 m) per minute rate of descent to 'punch through the Mach' in the so-called 'Dipsy-Doodle' manoeuvre that had replaced the 'Whifferdill' of A-12 days to become a standard SR-71 manoeuvre. The jet slid neatly through Mach I and the speed continued to build to 435 KEAS, at which point Jerry applied back-pressure on the stick. At 30,000 ft (9144 m) the descent was changed into a climb and the Triple Display Indicator showed 450 KEAS, which was the standard speed for most of the climb to altitude. Having completed the Dipsy-Doodle, Jerry re-engaged the autopilot and stabilised the climb angle to hold 450 KEAS. On reaching Mach 1.25, the EGT and CIT were noted. At Mach 1.7, inlet parameters and cg trim positions were

monitored, followed by the manual setting of the aft bypass door controls and the locking out of the IGV switches. Finally, the DEF jammer systems were rechecked.

At 60,000 ft (18288 m), Ed switched off the IFF altitude read-out to ensure the security of the SR-71's altitude capabilities. Additionally, the aircraft's red flashing anti-collision beacon was turned off and retracted to preclude heat damage at high Mach, and to reduce the high-flying aircraft's visual signature. Reaching Mach 2.6 with the aft bypass door controls in the 'B' position, Jerry established a KEAS bleed, which resulted in the air speed being decreased by 10 kt (12 mph; 19 km/h) for the gain of each tenth of a whole Mach number.

Their high altitude route took them to the east of Taiwan, north of the Philippine Islands and out over the South China Sea. Skirting the east coast of China, and after passing Hainan Island, the auto-navigation function of the ANS and autopilot turned '976 smoothly right in a 35° bank onto a northbound heading and the jet entered the Gulf of Tonkin. Continuing north, Ed peered through his view sight and located a large pier on the west side of Hainan that he had pre-planned as a visual-offset reference point to verify his track position. To his great satisfaction the pier was 'right on the money', the ANS flying the 'black line' within 50 ft (15 m) of its centre. They had been travelling at Mach 3.0 up to that point at a height of 75,000 ft (22860 m).

As they entered the Gulf, Jerry started a cruise-climb to 78,000 ft (23774 m) and acceleration to Mach 3.17, preparing for a 'front door' entry into North Vietnam. Through his view sight, Ed could see ship wakes on the Gulf waters below, and they could both hear the excited chatter of US combat pilots in heavy action way below over Haiphong and Hanoi. With the tracking camera on for after-mission verification of their ground track, and with the Elint and Comint sensor-recorders already running, Ed switched the OOCs on 10 miles (16 km) prior to 'coasting in'.

Following a heading of 284°, they crossed Haiphong at 78,000 ft (23774 m), immune from any form of interception as they travelled at the rate of a mile every two seconds. All the North Vietnamese could do was watch on their radars. The DEF systems aboard '976 indicated that they were being tracked from the moment they crossed the coast by 'Fan Song' radar units co-located with SA-2 'Guideline' SAM batteries. Ed put out the correct ECM response and the radars failed to

Dave Dempster (left) and Jim Watkins came close to being OL-8's first casualties when Jim became hypoxic during a sortie on 13 May 1968. (USAF)

lock-on. The weather below was perfect for a photo run, and as they flew over the harbour at Haiphong, Phu Kin airfield, Busundi Airport and dozens of other targets in the vicinity of Hanoi, the exposure counters clicked down, indicating to Ed that the sensors were working as advertised – it was going to be a perfect 'take'.

In just 12 minutes they had completed the first phase of the sortie as per the scheduled mission brief. Ed got ready to read the pre-descent checks to Jerry as they exited North Vietnam. Crossing the Red River (which is really brown), Jerry flicked the IGV switches to 'Lockout' and Ed called out the checklist items. 'LN-2 [liquid nitrogen] quantity' – 'Checked'; 'Inlet Controls' – 'Auto and Closed'.

Jerry eased the throttles out of afterburner and set the EGT reading to 720°C (1,328°F), the airspeed being allowed to decrease to 350 KEAS before starting the long gradual descent into Thailand. Carefully monitoring fuel tank pressure so as to avoid inflicting crush damage on the tanks as the jet descended into denser air, the crew reached 70,000 ft (21336 m) 100 miles (161 km) after commencing their descent profile. Now at Mach 2.5, Jerry was able to further retard the throttles to 6,000 rpm to hasten their descent.

The TACAN's Distance Measuring Equipment (DME), as well as the ARC-50's DME ranging element, rapidly 'clicked' down the distance between '976 and the waiting tankers, which were orbiting near Korat Air Base ready to pass 'gas' to their 'hot and high' receiver. Below Mach 1.7, Jerry turned the forward fuel transfer (to maintain longitudinal stability), pitot heat, and exterior anti-collision beacon light switches on. At 42,000 ft (12802 m) and slowing through Mach 1.3 he checked the inlet controls, clicked the IGV switches to 'Normal' after making a slight throttle adjustment. Jerry then turned off the forward fuel transfer, and prepared for refuelling.

Craven 'Gibb' Gibbons, flying the lead tanker, timed his turn to perfection just as '976 arrived at 25,000 ft (7620 m) a few miles behind and 1,000 ft (305 m) below the two KC-135Qs. Sitting slightly to the right and a few hundred feet below in the pre-refuelling observation position, Jerry noted the boom was extended and the boomer was nodding it up and down to indicate that he was ready for a radio-silent contact. Jerry slipped smoothly in behind the trailing boom and stabilised in the pre-contact position, before moving forward. Once the nozzle was plugged in, a secure inter-phone link-up was established between the KC-135 and the SR-71, and while the much-needed fuel was being pumped into the thirsty receiver at the rate of 6,000 lb (2722 kg) per minute, hearty words of congratulations were offered to the two Habu crewmembers. Jerry took

40,000 lb (18144 kg) of fuel from the first tanker and topped off from the second; a third aircraft was standing by to act as an emergency spare should either of the primary tankers be unable to off load its fuel.

After each refuelling, Jerry thanked the tanker crews. At the prescribed time and location, '976 left the KC-135s and headed out for another run to the north. Jerry repeated the climb and acceleration routine up to their prescribed altitude, on track for the second and final 'take' for the mission. This run was to be flown over the Demilitarised Zone (DMZ) between North and South Vietnam, with a primary objective of finding the truck park that supported the transportation of supplies and troops down the north-south Ho Chi Minh Trail, and to the heavy guns that had been pounding Khe Sanh. For this run the primary sensor was to have been the SLAR, which could penetrate the heavy jungle canopy. However, since the system had failed its BIT-test earlier, its serviceability was questionable. Ed concluded, however, that no damage could be done to the system if he positioned it manually and took some shots on the off chance that it would find something. Soon after, the jet exited the 'sensitive' area and they made their way back to Okinawa.

Feeling justifiably proud of how well their mission had gone up to that point, Jerry started his deceleration and descent back towards Kadena with the expectation of a 'proper' first-flight, mission-success party at the BOQ. On contact with Kadena Approach Control the crew were dismayed to find that the base was completely fogged in. Jerry talked to the tower controller and then to Col Charlie Minter, who agreed to allow them to attempt a low-visibility approach for a visual landing. Using Ground Controlled Approach (GCA) radar assistance, Jerry descended as low as was prudent into the fog, which the crews on the ground later reported was below the tops of the tanker tails, only 30 ft (9 m) above the ramp. Although the approach was good, Jerry never saw the runway and pushed the throttles forward to go back 'upstairs' to contemplate further options.

Low on fuel, he called for the standby tanker that had been launched earlier just in case the weather at Kadena had turned nasty. After link up, he took on 25,000 lb (11340 kg) of fuel while Ed copied a two-figure encoded number which told them their divert airfield location – Ku Kuan on the island of Taiwan. Two additional KC-135s were launched to accompany '976 to Nationalist China, the SR-71 adopting a tanker call sign as the number two aircraft in a three-ship formation. This deception was undertaken to hide the inter-island diversion from Sigint monitors on the Chinese mainland. As the SR-71 made its way 'low

and slow' with the tankers, the destination airfield's non-directional beacon returned the unexpected Morse code identity signal of 'CCK'. A tanker crew soon resolved this problem, however. It turned out that Ku Kuan had recently been re-named Ching Chuan Kang!

Jerry asked the CCK tower for permission to land and made a straight-in visual approach at 175 kt (202 mph; 325 km/h) before performing a smooth touchdown. After clearing the runway and lining up behind the lead tanker, Jerry sandwiched '976 between the two KC-135s as they taxied to the parking area. This unusual sight caused considerable confusion among the tower personnel, particularly when one controller asked for the call sign of: 'the little black aircraft between the two tankers, which had replied with a tanker call sign'. While Ed was talking to the tower people, Jerry dialled up the radio frequency of the SAC Command Post that had recently opened on CCK. He asked for the aircraft to be hangared (for security reasons).

Since CCK was a PACAF (US Pacific Air Force Command) joint-tenancy base with the Chinese Nationalists, most of its hangars were already filled with C-130 Hercules transports. To clear a secure spot for the SR-71, a C-130 up on jacks had to be rapidly lowered back onto its undercarriage and rolled out of a hangar. That action took 30 minutes to perform, which left the SR-71 standing in full public view close to the base perimeter fence, with its engines still running. A crowd of at least 500 Taiwanese gathered 10- to 15-deep along a 300-yard section of the fence, all of whom were fascinated to see such a futuristic jet standing on their airfield almost within touching distance.

Once '976 was safely hangared, and a security cordon thrown up around the area, the first order of business was to download the 'take' and get it to the various processing facilities so that the 'goods' could be fielded to the intelligence community as quickly as possible. The next priority was to get the aircraft and its crew back to Kadena. To accomplish that, a recovery crew was sent over in a KC-135 from Okinawa the following day. Meanwhile, the raw intelligence data was dispatched to Yokota Air Base in Japan for processing by the 67th RTS. This unit continued its work until 29 March 1971, after which the 548th RTG, a PACAF unit at Hickham AFB, Hawaii, assumed this responsibility. The SLAR imagery was sent to Beale Air Force Base in California for processing by the 9th RTS, before being sent on to Washington DC for analysis by national-level agencies.

Meanwhile back in Taiwan, Jerry and Ed endured a night in CCK quarters that the RSO described as, 'remedial at best'. Having no proper evening clothes

All top-priority operational missions were 'spared' as a hedge against an air abort. Here the primary and back-up aircraft wait at the hammerhead at Kadena. (USAF)

other than 'moon suits', they borrowed ill-fitting flight 'grow bags' and went to dinner wearing their white 'moon boots'. Things took a turn for the better the following day however, with the arrival of their ever-resourceful Ops Officer, Lt-Col 'Beep-Beep' Harlon Hain, and his recovery team. He brought with him a full set of 'civvies' for both Jerry and Ed, and got them booked into a first-rate hotel near the base. After two nights at CCK, '976 was ready for a ferry flight back to Kadena. The unrefuelled hop was uneventful, but the reception by their friends and colleagues back at the Little Creek Hangar was superb.

The post-mission intelligence results were also quite stunning. The SLAR that Ed had manually programmed had indeed worked. Its 'take' revealed the location of the heavy artillery emplacements around Khe Sanh, and a huge truck park which was being used in support of those guns; both sites had so far eluded US sensors on other recce aircraft. Within the next few days air strikes were mounted against both targets, reducing their effectiveness dramatically. After a 77-day siege, Khe Sanh was at last relieved on 7 April 1968 (two weeks after '976's 'discovery' sortie). As a result of their significant contribution to this highly successful mission, Maj Jerome F. O'Malley and Capt Edward D. Payne were each awarded the Distinguished Flying Cross. On its very first operational sortie, the aircraft had proven its value, as it would on thousands of other occasions over the coming years.

EYES AND EARS

Shortly after their arrival on Okinawa, the crews were summoned to a briefing in a secure room where they heard of local efforts to observe their activities. Since the primary building material of Japanese houses was wood, tall watch towers had been built in numerous locations on Okinawa to detect fires in their earliest stages so the local fire departments could quickly contain them. One such tower existed just outside the perimeter fence on the north side of Kadena Air Base, near Kosser Circle. The so-called fire guards had unrivalled views of the entire base from its commanding platform.

During the year of A-12 operations, intelligence officers had correlated positively that whenever an A-12 emerged from its hangar, a red flag was run up the watch tower's flagpole. In addition, it had been ascertained that within five minutes of the flag's lofting, a Soviet 'trawler' (on radar picket duty just beyond the 12-mile (19-km) limit of territorial waters off the coast of Okinawa) switched on its radar and this remained on as long as the flag remained flying from the tower. All along the China coast to the Gulf of Tonkin the Soviets had positioned a string of such 'trawlers' to relay tracking information on the Vietnam-bound A-12s and, later, Habus. An RSO later commented that it was almost like radar coverage back in America, but instead of FAA air traffic centres handing you off from one ATC centre to another, the Soviets were monitoring every move. The coordinated tracking was also supported by Chinese 'Tall King' surveillance radars along the China coast and on Hainan Island. As an A-12 or SR-71 penetrated North Vietnamese airspace, the first SA-2 target-acquisition radars would lock on at a slant range of approximately 80 miles (129 km). Such monitoring activities caused one crewmember to contemplate a radio transmission on the emergency frequency, saying 'Good Morning, Comrade' in Russian.

What these crews were not told was that US intelligence services had broken the Communist's communications codes. Lacking landlines for point-to-point telephone contacts, the Vietnamese had to transmit Habu tracking data to their command centres via broadcasted radio frequencies, which were immediately intercepted by US listeners on Okinawa, Taiwan, South Vietnam and Thailand, as well as by EC-130 airborne listening posts flying over the Gulf of Tonkin. Fluent Russian and Chinese linguists working at these stations would translate the broadcasts into English for secure onward transmission to various allied agencies.

Back at Kadena, a handful of senior officers were privy to that information and could indirectly monitor their Habu's progress via the enemy's conversations. As an A-12 or SR-71 departed Kadena on an operational sortie, the commander and a few of his key staff members would meet in the Special Activities Office, where a secure teleprinter known as a 'Dingy Whopper' would 'tell them about the sortie'. As one officer described this 'mail reading' exercise, 'We were able to listen to them, while they watched us'.

CANCELLED OPERATIONS
Fate was to intervene and frustrate the other Habu crews who prepared to fly their own first operational sorties – each being cancelled and replaced with a training sortie instead. On 10 April 1968, Brown and Jensen were once again set as primary crew. O'Malley and Payne were suited up as back-up. Buddy cranked '974's engines precisely on time and taxied out of the Little Creek area to run-up near the end of the runway. Jerry and Ed were sitting in '976 waiting to hear that Buddy and Dave were off and running. Instead, Crew Chief Tech Sgt Bill Campbell told them that '974 was taxiing back to the hangar. While Jerry and Ed were getting ready to roll, Buddy and Dave parked '974 nearby, the stricken jet being duly swarmed over by most of the OL-8 maintenance force. Even Col Estes clambered on top of the jet with his ANS specialists and 'was working like a GI mechanic' to help replace the astro inertial navigation set. Meanwhile Ed and Jerry were ready: 'We got out there and were running a fast checklist and I happened to look up and here comes Buddy taxiing like a bat out of hell. It must have been a world record ANS change, but I was certain that Dave hadn't had time to get a 'star light' because the system hadn't had time to go through all of its BIT checks yet. Charlie Minter who was in the mobile control car, obviously was thinking the same thing. Since it was his duty as OL Commander to put the best aircraft over the target, he leapt from the car and wrote "YOU GO" on an 8 x 10-in pad which he held up to Jerry and I, and "YOU STAY" on the other side which he showed to Buddy and Dave.'

As they climbed away, Jerry and Ed elected to adopt the primary aircraft's call sign since they had made that aircraft's take-off slot. They reasoned that the tankers would be expecting that call sign and that they would minimise confusion by keeping '974's identity. Unfortunately, the call sign change did not help Bill Boltersiders in the Command Post, who had to dispatch a coded report to HQ SAC immediately after take-off. In his uncertainty as to which aircraft actually departed, he had to wait for Col Minter's return

from the flight line before having the necessary details to set HQ SAC straight. The mission got off to a good start and Jerry and Ed were again on their way toward Vietnam on the second SR-71 combat sortie.

They coasted-in near Saigon, made a shallow turn to the right to fly northbound across the DMZ towards Vinh and then on to Hanoi. There was no shortage of high priority targets: Phuken and Ying-By airfields, the steel works, and dozens more. Unknown to the crew, President Johnson had stated that day in a broadcast that no US strike aircraft would fly further north than the 19th parallel. His decision had caused confusion within military circles as to the meaning of 'strike aircraft'. The 'ground pounders' at higher headquarters decided to play it safe and sent out an HF Radio message intended to withhold the SR-71 sortie from overflight. Ed actually received a coded message from Sky King on the Giant Talk network, but was too busy flying at 33 miles (53 km) a minute over the prime target area to take time to decode the message, which instructed them to turn left and abort the mission. Some moments later the autopilot initiated a programmed turn that started them back toward the south. With a few moments between high workload events, Ed told Jerry of the abort order. After completing the turn, they exited North Vietnam near Dien Bien Phu and prepared for descent toward their air refuelling rendezvous over Thailand.

The two fliers' spirits had been high throughout the sortie, particularly since their good luck had enabled them to fly both operational missions performed so far. The mission had been a piece of cake so far, or so they thought until Jerry eased back the throttles to the pre-assigned descent RPM. At that moment both engines rumbled slightly in a compression stall and immediately flamed out.

An air start required 450 KEAS and 7 psi (48 kPa) on the compressor face to get things 'turning and burning' again. That meant getting down to denser air where those higher values could be achieved. Jerry pushed the nose down hard and Ed recalled seeing the artificial horizon instrument showing all blacks. As they rode the aircraft down to lower altitudes they decided that if Jerry could not get an air start, Ed would call 'Mayday' at 23,000 ft (7010 m) and they would 'punch out' at 14,000 ft (4267 m). At 40,000 ft (12192 m) Jerry gave the throttles a nudge, which gave the engines positive fuel flow and a shot of TEB for ignition. There was no response. He tried again as they were passing through 30,000 ft (9144 m). Still nothing. Ed recalled further: 'By now we were both getting a little anxious. I saw the altimeter go through 26,000 ft [7925 m] and I was getting set to say, "Mayday! Mayday! Mayday!" I got the word "May" out when I felt the aircraft shake a little. Realising that Jerry had finally got something going, I didn't finish the rest of the message. A glance at the altimeter showed us just below 23,000 ft and still descending quite rapidly. Just then Jerry said, "I've got one of them started." Shortly afterwards he got the second engine fired up and when we hit 20,000 ft [6096 m] we had both engines running fine.'

Having received the 'May' of Ed's message, the tanker crews knew that all was not well with the Habu. This realisation was confirmed as they monitored the air-to-air TACAN's DME ranging. Ordinarily the SR-71 would make a 'hot' rate of supersonic closure on the tankers, slowing notably only in the final 30 miles (48 km). The DME meter would normally be clicking over between 20 and 30 miles (32 and 48 km) per minute during the early part of the deceleration. Instead it quickly slowed to a closure rate of about 8 miles (13 km) per minute. That speed meant the Habu was 'low and slow' well before intended, and way up in 'bad guys' territory. Ed remembered: 'We got our act cleaned up and the first transmission we received from the tankers was, "Are you guys okay?" I answered, "No". They asked "What can we do?" I answered, "Turn North". The double-engine flameout and rapid descent profile left '976 down at a 'gas-gobbling' 20,000 ft [6096 m] over northern Laos, some 300 miles [483 km] short of our planned ARCP. We climbed back to 26,000 ft [7925 m] and headed south. I recall that the lead tanker navigator was a woman. I'm sure they must have violated operating procedures coming that far north without some form of fighter cover, but we were damn glad to see them. By the time we reached the tanker, '976 was below 8,000 lb [3629 kg] of fuel. The tanker turned in front of us and the boomer plugged into our AR receptacle in a heartbeat. We drained 80,000 lb [36288 kg] of JP-7 out of two tankers and even used a little from the spare – perhaps a record off-load. We used the extra gas because we had to lengthen the air refuelling track from Laos to mid-Thailand. Had we just filled up and climbed for home we wouldn't have been able to fly the profile properly, so we just stayed behind those beautiful tankers until we reached the originally planned disengagement point.'

While Jerry and Ed were refuelling, they discussed what might have caused the double engine flameout and what would be the preferred action to get home safely. Ed was in favour of staying with the third KC-135 and flying all the way back at around 0.8 Mach to meet some Kadena-launched spare tankers. Jerry, on the other hand, determined that they should fly a normal profile to help determine the cause of the

problem. Jerry discussed at length what data he wanted Ed to record and just prior to the final decel back into Kadena, he began reading out RPM, EGT and fuel flow information. He eased back the throttles and the engines spooled down normally. They recovered into Kadena without further incident, thus ending the second operational sortie of the SR-71's reconnaissance career. That double flameout foreshadowed a spate of similar problems which would follow over Laos, and would earn the Habu the nickname of 'Lead Sled' back at the SAC Reconnaissance Center.

With the first two ops missions under their belts, Jerry and Ed were relegated to flying test hops for the duration of their tour to ensure that the other crews had an opportunity to accumulate some combat time. The following week, Buddy Brown and Dave Jensen were scheduled to fly a 'double looper' over North Vietnam. After getting airborne in '978 at 11:00 am on 18 April, all went well until it was time to decelerate for their first Thailand refuelling. The tanker had notified them that the ARCP had been moved due to thunderstorms in the AR area, and as they began to decelerate the left gencrator went off line and could not be reset. This failure was followed by a double engine flameout. Dave transmitted the necessary codes stating that they were going to make a precautionary landing at Takhli Royal Thai Air Force Base (RTAFB), since generator failure was a 'land as soon as practicable' abort item. Without power they lost cabin pressurisation and their 'moon suits' inflated, which made cockpit movements awkward. As they descended toward an altitude where the engines could be restarted, Buddy requested that the tankers come north to give them additional fuel after the early and rapid descent. At 35,000 ft (10668 m) he was able to restart the engines. He then adjusted the aircraft's centre of gravity for subsonic flight and called Takhli Approach Control, informing it of his impending arrival. The tower controller told him that the tankers had already alerted the Command Post and that Takhli was ready to receive the SR-71. On approach, the nose gear's down-lock light failed to illuminate, but Buddy made a low pass by the tower to have the gear visually checked 'down' and then circled to an uneventful landing.

Since the CIA had a secure compound on the airfield from where it conducted U-2 operations, Buddy was able to use one of its hangars. A recovery team then arrived from Kadena and readied the SR-71 for a return to Kadena. Later, as Brown and Jensen were preparing to depart, the head of the Agency's detachment told Buddy, 'If you don't tell anyone you were here, I won't either'. Buddy laughed at this 'typical cloak and dagger' remark and thanked him for the first-rate support they had received on their interrupted Habu mission.

On 27 April Buddy and Dave flew their second ops sortie, this time in aircraft '976. As they started their descent into Thailand, they experienced another double engine flameout and another failed generator. As they taxied back into the Agency's hangar at Takhli yet again, Buddy insisted he had not come to join the CIA, but to enjoy their hospitality. On leaving the Thai base two days later, Buddy saluted the CIA with a 'max burner' climb out that 'left them all smiling' as the lightly-fuelled Habu climbed steeply away from its new-found second home in Southeast Asia.

Following cancellations and disappointments, Jim Watkins and Dave Dempster finally got airborne on 19 April in '974. They topped-off their fuel tanks near Kadena and headed out for North Vietnam. Arcing around Hainan Island on their right, they entered the Gulf of Tonkin and reversed left onto their penetration track. This 'front door' entry took them over Haiphong and Hanoi, exiting via Dien Bien Phu. As with the recent flights, everything went well until it was time to come down for aerial refuelling. As soon as Jim slid the throttles out of burner, there was an enormous bang, followed by another double engine flameout. He got both engines started up again after wiping 50,000 ft (15240 m) of altitude off the altimeter's reading. The tanker crews responded immediately to the resulting emergency call, heading north without fighter escort back into the 'bad lands' of northern Laos.

While the Habu was on the boom and taking on three tons of fuel a minute, Jim had time to reflect on the incident that could have ended in disaster. At that point he said to his RSO, 'Davey, I think I might know what happened and if I hold a couple hundred more RPMs above what it says in the checklist the next time I come out of burner, I might be able to keep the engines alive and we can complete the mission. What to you think?' Dave replied, 'Let's give it a try and do the next run.'

It seems that 'cowboy' Jim Watkins had the first glimmer of an idea that would later be proven when Don Walbrecht and Phil Loignon flew Vietnam to Thailand descents without a problem.

In 1968, OL-8's operational mission rate was approximately a mission a week. Jerry O'Malley and Ed Payne rotated home earlier than originally planned and were replaced by Maj Larry DeVall and Captain Clyde Shoemaker. Majs Bob Spencer and Keith Branham flew their first operational sortie in aircraft '974 on 22 April. It was a 'double-looper' over North Vietnam lasting five hours 30 minutes. They were airborne again on 5 May, flying another 'double-looper', this time in '978, and yet again the duration was five hours

30 minutes. The third and final operational flight of their first tour took place six days later.

On 13 May 1968 Jim Watkins and Dave Dempster flew '974 on a two-loop route over North Vietnam using side-looking radar. While on the KC-135's boom during the final air refuelling before the flight back to Kadena, Jim set the cabin pressure altitude switch to 10,000 ft (3048 m). He told Dave he was raising his face-plate for a drink of water – this was certainly an unusual procedure, momentarily breaking the old flying rule 'oxygen over 10,000ft'. After a refreshing libation, Jim closed his visor and informed Dempster that he was ready for the flight back home.

Dropping off the boom, he lit the burners and headed up into the darkening tropical night sky. When he had established an accelerating supersonic climb, Jim engaged the autopilot's 'Auto-Nav' function as the Habu headed North East over the South China Sea. It was during this stage of the climb that Dave first perceived that all was not well with his pilot. Jim's words were beginning to become slurred, but as far as Dave could tell, his actions were still okay. However, having trained with Jim as a crew for well over 100 hours, the RSO was becoming increasingly concerned.

As the climb continued, Jim's speech deteriorated even further. Then the gut-twisting reality of the situation hit Dave with full force – his pilot was hypoxic and the RSO had no flight controls to overcome impending disaster. In a matter of minutes Jim would lose consciousness and shortly thereafter (unless Dave could get oxygen into his pilot's lungs), Jim would die and Dave would have to bail out in the vast South China Sea. The latter was not a realistic option for the RSO, and he wondered how he could get Jim's attention; he certainly could not get into the front cockpit where the flight controls were. Luckily the autopilot and 'Auto-Nav' functions were engaged which allowed Dempster to exercise the only control inputs that an RSO had in the back seat of an SR-71, lateral steering using 'Nav' steering commands, but absolutely no pitch controls. Dave dialled up 7700 on his IFF panel and squawked 'emergency' to alert the radar watchers in South Vietnam who were monitoring the flight that all was not well.

One option Dave considered was to turn the aircraft towards Cam Ranh Bay (the large PACAF base on the coast of South Vietnam). He dismissed this idea almost immediately, however, for in a turn there was a greater chance of an inlet unstart and it was very doubtful if Jim could control the

Tony Bevacqua and Jerry Crew were the first OL-8 crewmembers to be positively fired upon by SA-2s, an event which occurred over Hanoi on 26 July 1968 in SR-71A serial 64-17976. The white exhaust trail across this image marks the path of the SA-2 missile. (USAF)

aircraft in his current state of consciousness, which had become further degraded during the last minute of flight. Turning towards Vietnam would have taken the aircraft closer to the 'bad guys' and Dave was determined that he would not leave his pilot or allow any part of 'his' SR-71 to fall into enemy hands. By now Jim was on the edge of unconsciousness. There was perhaps one possible remedy to this unbelievable situation. Dave summoned up every ounce of command authority in his voice and yelled over the intercom in a clear deliberate manner that, 'We are now at the "Start Descent" checklist. Inlet Guide Vane switches to Lockout.' Surprisingly, Jim flicked the switches. 'Inlet Controls–Auto and Close.' Jim complied. 'Throttles, 720 degrees.' Again Jim carried out the RSO's instructions. Slowly '974's altimeter began to unwind. Dave recalled: 'Jim was one hell of a pilot. All of those thousands of hours of flying and training (and here he was

about to pass out) and yet he was doing exactly what he was instructed to do. He came out of afterburner; he set the correct RPM and then threw the right switches for the bypass doors. Luckily, we didn't flame out or unstart, and, thank God, he didn't disconnect the "Auto-Nav" system so it was still steering us very accurately. On the way down, I monitored my Triple Display Indicator (Mach, KEAS and Altitude) readings and by using the profile card that we used to rendezvous with the tanker, I was able to give Jim additional commands like, "Okay, Jim you're doing great, just ease it down a little bit, ease it down. Adjust your RPM slightly. Okay, you're right on profile." He was a disciplined flier and seemed to respond to those commands, and by the help of God, we raggedly descended and decelerated all the way down to subsonic speed, and he didn't pass out.

'We levelled off at about 25,000 ft [7620 m] and cruised at that altitude for a while, where Jim regained a bit of his normal consciousness. Slowly, Jim's voice began to return to normal and he suddenly said, "What the hell are we doing at this altitude?" I said, "Okay, Jim, the first thing I want you to do is to open your faceplate and to close it again and to check that your bailer arm is down and firmly locked." He did exactly what I instructed and then started swearing at himself because the picture was beginning to return to him what had happened in the last ten minutes. We stayed "low and slow" until he appeared clear and sharp again.

'I calculated that we had enough fuel to fly subsonic all the way back to Taiwan, but Jim convinced me that everything was fine and that he clearly understood what had happened to him, although he had no real recollection of what had transpired during the ten-minute descent. Feeling comfortable that Jim now knew what was going on, I took the IFF out of emergency and he lit the burners and we flew supersonic to Kadena. One thing is for sure, you don't fly anywhere at Mach 3.0 and arrive at your destination fifteen minutes late without an explanation.'

Col Minter and a few of the other SAO watchers knew that something had happened, but no one knew what it was until the debrief (behind closed doors) when the problem was discussed in detail.

The initial rebuffs aimed at Jim soon gave way to more constructive dialogue when those who had not flown began to realise just how fortunate the crew of '974 had been. If Jim had not responded exactly as he had to Dave's instructions, the aircraft and crew would have

Maj Don Walbrecht (illustrated) and Capt Phil Loignon had little trouble with their first set of eight sorties from Kadena. However, they did encounter the worst of the region's weather. (USAF)

Maj Dan House rests in the PSD van prior to an operational sortie. The bulkiness of the pressure suit and its helmet is clearly evident. (Paul F. Crickmore Collection)

Maj Blair Bozek relaxes in the PSD van on the flightline. Once the crew was suited up, their movements were kept to a minimum. (Paul F. Crickmore Collection)

vanished into the sea and the Habu loss may have remained a mystery. It was therefore agreed that no disciplinary action would be taken and the story would be suppressed (which it duly was for 25 years).

As the experience of triplesonic reconnaissance continued, crew changeovers brought other pioneers into the combat line-up at Kadena. In early May 1968, Maj Don Walbrecht and Capt Phil Loignon arrived to make their mark on operational flying. Their eight sorties from Kadena were typical of those flown at the time, and, in contrast to most of the initial missions flown in March and April, went quite smoothly. Like all crews, they started off with a two-hour training flight south of Okinawa in '976 on 19 May 1968, to get the feel of the vast oceanic area of the western Pacific.

Six days later they were airborne in '978 on their first North Vietnamese sortie that lasted five hours 15 minutes. Completing the standard post take-off refuelling, they were determined not to abort their mission unless 'a wing fell off'. Back in the US, Don and Phil had experienced few inlet unstarts, but on their first important ops sortie

while approaching Mach 2.4 and 55,000 ft (16764 m) one of the inlets let its shock wave go with an almighty bang. Phil asked: 'Isn't that a mandatory abort item?' 'Isn't what an abort item?', replied Don. Pressing on to 75,000 ft (22860 m), the inlets kicked and bucked a few more times, but all was as smooth as glass when they arrived at Mach 3.0. After entering the Gulf of Tonkin, Don pressed on to Mach 3.2, which gave the Habu another 4,000 ft (1219 m) above the enemy SAM shooters.

Coasting in over Haiphong at 79,000 ft (24079 m), they cruise-climbed to 81,000 ft (24689 m), where Phil noted a SAM target-acquisition radar locking on. Immediately his ECM equipment nullified the threat and no missiles were fired. After crossing Hanoi and flying close to China, they exited North Vietnam over Laos, where Don eased the throttles out of burner for his descent (well aware of O'Malley, Brown, Watkins and DeVall's double flameouts). Immediately there was a low rumble (the onset of an inlet-airflow mismatch which had probably caused the spate of flameouts). Instinctively, Don eased the throttles slightly forward, adding

200 rpm to the engine speed. The rumble instantly disappeared and the engines remained alight for a notably smooth descent.

After refuelling, Don accelerated and climbed the *Playboy* Rabbit-adorned '978 on a southerly heading, rounding South Vietnam for another northbound run. He charged back up the Gulf of Tonkin, offset from his first pass to make another uneventful run and a smooth deceleration at the slightly higher power settings, the mission terminating (after refuelling) in an uneventful recovery back to Kadena. The crew was airborne again the next day, taking '978 on a functional check flight to verify inlet performance and again on 8 June in the same jet to maintain aircrew currency. Walbrecht and Loignon completed their second operational sortie in '974 a few days later – a four-hour 30-minute 'single looper' over North Vietnam.

Their third mission was again flown in '978, on 30 June (a 'two-looper' lasting five hours 30 minutes), for which they were each awarded the Distinguished Flying Cross. Don explained: 'Phil and I flew this important sortie in the face of a great typhoon, which was positioned off the southeast coast of Vietnam. It was extremely impressive to see from high altitude, easily visible from more than 500 miles (805 km) away. Phil and I completed our two passes over denied territory and were heading back towards Kadena. By this time the typhoon had moved closer to the land mass of Vietnam and had pulled a great deal of moisture into its system. It was a remarkable sight, this enormous boiling maelstrom of great clouds stretching out before us, with vast columns of thunderstorms forced upwards on convective currents of air rising along its forward spiralling arms.

'The exceptionally tall storms looked like giant turrets which were guarding this mass of moving energy. Unable to see the storms that were lined up ahead of us, Phil was concerned that we might have to fly through the tops if they reached above 70,000 ft [21336 m]. When we got closer we could see that we had the better of them by at least 5,000 ft [1524 m]. Flying at Mach 3.0, 15 miles [24 km] up, one rarely approaches any other object closely enough to feel the spectacular sensation of great speed. The typhoon had acted like a giant vacuum cleaner, drawing moist air away from the land mass and into the storm. The result was high-quality, clean air over all of the target areas, allowing us to obtain outstanding resolution of the 400 important targets Phil's cameras photographed.'

Don and Phil were especially proud of having been able to provide such a high quality 'take', but they modestly maintained that it was just good fortune that they happened to be airborne on such a good day, and that any crew back at the OL could have brought home the 'goods'. Thanks to the typhoon, Vietnam, China and Laos were all unusually clear and they got the 'good-goods', which saturated the attention of photo interpreters at all the national and theatre intelligence centres.

On their final ops sortie in the 'always-in-the-green' '978 on 23 July 1968, Don and Phil flew another important 'double-looper' lasting five hours and which yielded yet another superb quality 'take' due to the proximity of the granddaddy of all thunderstorms which squatted over Haiphong. Don explained: 'Phil and I came zipping back up the Gulf clearly seeing all of Hainan and a great piece of China on our right. To our dismay, it appeared that too many clouds loomed ahead for a good run. I could see a great mass of high clouds standing over our target with a storm-pillar billowing up out of its middle – it was the "superdome" of a single massive semi-tropical thunderstorm. I said to Phil, "it looks as if our sortie is going to be ruined by all of the undercast." We pressed on hoping for the best, accelerating and climbing to Mach 3.2 and 80,000 ft [24384 m] to make the run. By the time we topped out, we were beginning to cross over the storm, just barely above it.

'My attention was riveted on the billowing top, which must have extended up to 79,000 ft [24079 m] – surely one of the highest cloud formations ever reported. We made a slight turn to the left to stay on track and went right over the top of the grand storm at an absolutely incredible rate of passage. Momentarily, I could feel the disturbing effects of the rising atmosphere's convective instability that made the Habu wallow around more than I'd ever experienced at that high an altitude. As we shot over the top of it, the landmass ahead was sparklingly clear with perfect visibility all the way to mid-China. Phil photographed all of North Vietnam and much of southern China, and we turned south over Laos descending on our usual tanker track near Korat, Thailand. Again there were lots of medium-sized thunderstorms over Thailand but we found the tankers right where they were supposed to be.

'The tanker's boomer plugged into '978's receptacle immediately and the pilot started dodging all over the sky to avoid thunderstorms. It seemed we were heading west much longer than normal because of the sun's position and I recall looking out during a turn and asking Phil, "What's all that water down there?" He replied that it was the Andaman Sea, near Rangoon in Burma. We finally headed back to the southeast and after filling our tanks I asked the tanker's navigator for a heading that would take us clear of the thunderstorms, to which he replied, "There

CMSgt Bill Gornik performs his famous neck tie cutting ceremony on Lt-Col Pat Halloran in June 1968. A neck tie was worn on first operational missions from Kadena and severed as soon as the crewmember returned to base. (USAF)

isn't one. You'll just have to take your chances." We climbed and accelerated, luckily missing all of the very turbulent thundercells. After we got above 50,000 ft [15240 m] and over the tops of most of the storms, we were in a continuous shroud of high thick cirrus which extended to the mid-sixties.

'We were moving at Mach 2.6 when we blasted from the cloud tops. It was like being shot from a rocket as we bolted from the high tropopause into the clear stratosphere. We did another fast circuit of North Vietnam to see that the great single storm had already entered the post-mature phase with its anvil top flattened out farther below. We then descended back into Thailand where the other storms had been. We were pleased that they had softened and moved further west. Having completed our third refuelling, we raced back to Kadena for an uneventful landing. We flew our final Kadena training sortie, again in '978, shortly afterwards and redeployed back to California in the weekly Beale tanker.'

At just after 9:00 am on 26 July 1968, Majs Pat Halloran and his RSO Mort Jarvis launched in '974 for what was to be their first operational sortie. However, during the course of conducting a BIT check on their DEF suite, Mort detected a systems failure. As mentioned earlier, this was a 'Go-No-Go' item on the checklist, so he continued to recycle the equipment repeatedly in the hope that the problem would clear, but to no avail. With time running short, the crew finally had to admit defeat and literally just five minutes short of their mandatory time to call for the spare to launch, they had no option and made the abort call. Consequently at 10:08 am Majs Tony Bevacqua and Jerry Crew launched in '976 to replace Pat and Mort on the planned 'double-looper' over the 'North'. On their first pass, Jerry warned Tony that a SAM fire-control radar had locked-on them. Almost immediately he said, 'We've been fired upon'. The defensive systems performed as advertised, but Tony was unable to see the missiles, which ended up well behind them. During refuelling Jerry asked Tony if he intended to complete the sortie since their next track would again take them right back over the position from which they were fired upon. Tony replied, 'Why Not? They missed us.' On the next pass there was no reaction from any SAM battery. Back on the ground at Kadena, Tony recalled: 'As we got out of the aircraft we knew that the commander already knew about the incident. The first thing he asked was, "Did you see anything?" We said we hadn't, but we knew that it was for real. We were later told that the nearest of the two missiles was about 1 mile [1.6 km] away.' It was the first occasion that an SR-71 had definitely been fired upon, and by chance, the terrain-tracking camera took a picture of the SA-2s, recording Tony's 'first' for the record books. Pat and Mort launched again in '974 two days later and completed their first ops sortie – a five-hour 18-minute flight – flawlessly.

TRADITIONS AND ANTICS

'All work and no play makes John a dull boy.' Habu crew members certainly knew how to work and to get their job done, and they most definitely could not be accused of being dull, especially John Storrie, Buddy Brown, Larry DeVall and some of the more notorious pranksters. There was usually a genteel Sunday afternoon daiquiri party in the commander's quarters, which were only about 100 yards from the 'O' Club, where many evening activities began. The favourite brew that one party group adopted was titled 'Velvet Punch', so-called because it could knock you out gently. Craven Gibbons (a tanker pilot of Habu renown) was the undisputed master brewer of this 'smoothly lethal concoction', whose main constituents were three parts concentrated frozen lime juice, two parts beer and one part 'Everclear'. Light yellow-green in colour, 'Velvet Punch' was mixed in a stainless steel bowl that had been liberated from the kitchen. For the benefit of visitors, a clean jock and a pair of athletic socks were added. The stainless steel 'tanker bowl' was refuelled throughout the night until there was no one left capable of restocking the bowl.

At the south end of BOQ 310 (the Habu home away from home) was a kitchen where the crews had their preflight (high-protein, low-residue) meal. Next to the kitchen was Doc Malley's room, where the crews received their preflight physical exam. The Habus (under Buddy's leadership) convinced the Doc to give up his office for a crew lounge. They quickly set to work blanking out the entrance door and cutting an entry door into the now isolated room through the kitchen's broom closet. A proper bar, fancy light fixtures, a music system and a refrigerator were added, and the walls were padded. The bright red decor of the 'Secret Bar' would have been more appropriate in a bathhouse. After the party room's reputation spread it became the envy of non-members, one of whom told the base commander who would not tolerate Habu high jinks.

Intelligence gathering was, of course, OL-8's livelihood, so it was not surprising that they learned of the impending visit before the actual inspection. The 'Secret Bar' was quickly and quietly dismantled one night. The old entrance was reopened and the room returned to its former state. When the base commander conducted his 'surprise' visit the next day, he was surprised he could not find what had been reported. Soon after the inspection, the room was again transformed into the 'Secret Bar' and it was business as usual.

Partying with the Habus was great fun and in no time they were frequented (on John Storrie's leadership) by transiting airline crews who passed through Kadena on their way to and from Vietnam and Thailand, and by some of the unattached civilians who worked on base. One scatty blonde was given a meteorological nickname of 'high-thin-scattered', while another, with a narrow-shaped and longer-than-average face and nose was known as 'hangar doors' because the 'giver of nicknames' thought that she had been caught between them at some point in the past.

On the night of 29 May 1968, the Habus held a dinner at the Kadena Officers Club honouring Col Bill Hayes (the 'White Tornado'), who had just completed his 30-day tour as OL commander and would return to Beale on the transpacific tanker in a few days. After dinner the party moved into the less formal 'Stag Bar', where Chief Master Sergeant Bill Gornick and two other senior NCOs crashed the party to say farewell to the colonel. Amid much hilarity, Bill Gornick produced a pen knife and severed the neckties of Bill Hayes and all the Habu crew members. The next day he mounted the ties on a Native American ceremonial pole, just like the battle streamers on a command standard, or the feathers on an Indian ceremonial pole. At that moment a new tradition had been born.

In response, Don Walbrecht and Phil Loignon purchased a miniature Samurai sword and took it on a Mach 3.2 Hanoi flight before presenting it to Bill Gornick, the 'Chief-Master Necktie Cutter'. Thereafter, all crews flying their first operational mission from Kadena would wear a necktie inside their pressure suit. On completion of their sortie, they would emerge from the cockpit and have their tie ceremoniously cut off by Chief Gornick. Approximately 300 aircrew neckties, all properly embroidered with names and dates, and hanging from Bill Gornick's 'Command Standard', which dates from 30 May 1968, are now displayed at Beale's Habu museum.

GLOWING HEAT

By the autumn of 1968, airframes '974, '976 and '978 had each amassed close to 300 flying hours at Okinawa. In so doing, they had easily validated the concept of long-range, triplesonic, high-altitude strategic reconnaissance within hostile airspace. Their sensor systems had acquired intelligence data of national significance that had directly influenced the conduct of many air and ground operations. The dedicated professionalism of the maintenance teams working for Col Estes, and the high-quality systems maintenance done by specialist company technical representatives, kept these deployed aircraft in top condition, but there were nevertheless certain 'heavy' depot-level maintenance tasks which lay beyond the capability of OL-8. To carry out deep maintenance tech-order modification work, the original three aircraft had to be returned to Lockheed's Palmdale Plant 42. A complex every-other-day swap-out exercise code-named Glowing Heat was effected in late September, '974, '976 and '978 being replaced one at a time by 64-17962, '970 and '980 – these aircraft were similarly replaced in April 1969 by '971, '975 and '979.

Newly promoted Lt-Col Tony Bevacqua and his new RSO were participants in a Glowing Heat deployment from Beale to Kadena in '974 in September 1969. They had just completed refuelling in the vicinity of Wake Island when one of the 'generator-out' lights illuminated on the Central Annunciator Panel. It was a mandatory abort item, so they dumped much of the fuel load that they had just taken on and diverted into the tiny island.

Wake is a renowned breeding ground for the Albatross. Luckily these large birds had all left the island a few days prior to Tony's arrival and he landed without incident (many of these creatures rest on the runway and are often hit by landing aircraft). Since Tony led off on the deployment, he was stuck on the island until all the other Habus had been exchanged. A recovery team then came over from Kadena to solve '974's problem after all the other aircraft had been moved. Tony explained: 'The place was all Navy. Our BOQ was a cement-block building with no air-conditioning and equipped with the world's most uncomfortable bed. To make matters less tolerable on this tiny island in the middle of nowhere, the 'O' Club didn't open until 16:00 hours and we had to sit it out there on 'the rock' for ten days while our friends were laying sonic booms on us as they shuttled their Habus back and forth across the Pacific. While there, I had the pleasure of meeting Judy Sides, a nationally-recognised and respected artist of the Gooney Bird.

'By the time '974 was ready to complete its trip to Kadena, she had painted a Gooney Bird symbol on each wheel-well door, applied another to each of the tails and another on the left side of the fuselage, near the cockpit where the white Habu-snake mission symbols were normally painted'. This short-lived artwork won the approval of the Habus at Kadena, and constituted a new kind of first in aviation art.

The escalation of the Vietnam War generated an increase in the demand for timely, high-quality reconnaissance imagery. OL-8's SR-71 establishment was therefore increased in the spring of 1970 from three to four aircraft (64-17969, '972, '973 and '974). The next three years would prove in many ways to be the detachment's Golden Era.

MISSILES

On 20 September 1968 Majs Dale Shelton and Larry Boggess completed their first operational sortie in aircraft '980. However, 30 minutes into their second operational flight on 4 October they were just approaching the KC-135 to top off after take-off, when a coded message came through on HF radio from Sky King, SAC's Giant Talk network, telling them to abort their mission and return to Kadena. Larry checked the authenticity of the message but could not retransmit on HF since Dale had already started refuelling. Larry recalled: 'When we didn't answer immediately, we got a curt UHF Radio call from the Kadena Command Post asking us if we'd received an earlier HF message transmission. We disconnected from the boom, dumped some fuel and recovered aircraft '970 back to Kadena.' It seems that intelligence sources had discovered that the enemy knew of the Habu's intended route, which would take the jet directly over the top of an

active SAM site. Although SR-71s had been fired upon on an earlier sortie, it was deemed that the prior knowledge offered the Vietnamese too much of an advantage on this occasion.

With a full-scale war raging in Southeast Asia, more and more crews got their chance to get their first TDY tour of duty at Okinawa, which was a great place to fly the Habu from because it was a much more secure location than bases in Vietnam. Majs Bobby Campbell and Jon Kraus flew their first sortie over Vietnam on 21 November 1968. It was a 'double-looper' flown in '970 which lasted five hours 30 minutes. Majs Bob Powell and Bill Kendrick flew their first ops sortie in '980, on 29 December 1968 (again a 'double-looper' flight lasting nearly six hours) in which they were fired upon by two SA-2s. They brought back an especially high-quality 'take' by flying straight through their target run despite the rising missiles. They each earned a Distinguished Flying Cross for this mission. One Habu driver later remarked to the author: 'Flying an SR-71 over the war at eighty-odd thousand feet was almost unreal. The "Thud" drivers were right down there in the middle of things while we were passing high overhead safely out of reach of the Soviets' best weapons. On a clear day, you'd see (and hear) the war going on 15 miles below. We could sometimes see flashes of fighter aircraft charging about and could often hear the excited radio conversations on guard channel, especially if an aircraft was down. We were only at risk for 15 minutes on both passes because we could cross North Vietnam in less than eight minutes flat. We always knew, however, that we'd really be in for it if we ever had to bail out over enemy territory for we would certainly have been a propaganda prize in our silver moon suits. We also had the advantage that in just a few hours we could be several thousand miles away back at the "Secret Bar" sipping a glass of Chivas Regal.'

Some of the crews who were fired upon by SA-2s spoke of seeing the SAMs through the RSO's view sight and the pilot's rear-view periscope. The missiles had to be fired 30 miles (48 km) ahead of the jet to achieve the SR-71's altitude by the time it had arrived. Two white trails would appear well ahead of the Habu, but were normally not seen by the pilot since the aircraft's nose blocked his ground view ahead. As the missiles approached the RSO could see them rising by looking through his down- and forward-looking view scope. When the missile exploded (usually above and behind) the pilot could get a quick glimpse of the explosion, which would first appear to billow out and then implode on itself. That visual effect came about because of the rate of speed at which the jet raced away from the point of detonation. It was very strange to see, but the crews reported that it was also very comforting to know that the SAMs were ineffective because of the very long firing lead the missile shooters needed to boost the SA-2 to altitude to point-intercept the 3,000 ft (914 m)-per-second target.

AIRCRAFT LOSS

Throughout the early 1970s, OL-8's Vietnam sortie rate averaged two flights per week. The nature of high-speed flight ensured that those combat sorties would never become 'routine to the point of indifference'. OL-8 lost its first Habu after more that two years of Kadena operations, which included over 200 operational and training sorties, on 10 May 1970. Majs Willie Lawson and Gil Martinez had completed one pass over North Vietnam and had refuelled '969 near Korat RTAFB. Willie had initiated an afterburner climb to prepare for a transonic 'dipsy-doodle'. Unfortunately, thunderstorms had built up rapidly across Thailand and no matter where they looked, a solid bank of clouds enshrouded the heavy thundercells which towered up to 50,000 ft (15240 m).

Even an SR-71 needed climb distance to get above the clouds, and the dip-manoeuvre gave the aircraft a head-start on achieving the airspeed and Mach needed for a higher rate of climb. The 0.9 Mach preliminary climb was sluggish with a full fuel load, and Wille eased '969 into a slightly steeper climb to zoom up over the notch of a 30,000-ft (9144-m) saddleback of connecting clouds between vertical storms, in order to stay clear of the cells ahead. At that moment, the aircraft entered turbulent clouds and both engines flamed out.

In heavy turbulence, without engine thrust, the aircraft's angle of attack increased. Suddenly the nose rose up into the dreaded pitch-up from which there was no recovery. Both crewmembers ejected safely and landed in the vicinity of U-Tapao. Resplendent in their silver moon suits, they recruited the aid of a Thai who was driving a Saamlor (a three-wheeled vehicle common to Thailand) and were driven back to U-Tapao and then flown back to Kadena in a KC-135. On their arrival, Col Hal Confer (the Det commander) and the entire unit had gathered to welcome them back. It was sad to lose a trusty Habu, but it was great to get the crew back. Overall, the pitch-up problem cost four aircraft in the 26 years of the SR-71 programme.

KINGPIN

Son Tay prison camp was located 23 miles (37 km) west of Hanoi, and it had gained notoriety for housing dozens of US PoWs. It was the subject of numerous SR-71 'takes' that endeavoured over two years to establish the number of prisoners held within its stockade. On 10 June 1970, a

Majors Charles 'Red' McNeer – RSO and former B-52 crewmember, to left – and George Bull – previously on U-2s – are shown here during a stint of combat operations from Kadena. (USAF)

feasibility Study Group was convened by the Special Assistant for Counterinsurgency and Special Activities (SALSA), to look into the possibility of springing the Son Tay inmates. A further planning group was established in early August to review reconnaissance imagery provided by Teledyne-Ryan's Buffalo Hunter reconnaissance drones and SR-71s. The low-flying drones were used sparingly over the target area for fear of alerting the North Vietnamese to the possibility of a future raid. The SR-71, with its long-axis camera capability, was an ideal vehicle for obtaining spot photographs of the camp.

In the last ten days before the planned raid, intense reconnaissance efforts were conducted, but every attempt was thwarted by poor weather. Continuous cloud cover had concealed Son Tay's targets from the Habu's high-altitude cameras, and two low altitude drones never returned. Nevertheless, a bold raid was mounted in the morning darkness of 21 November 1970 employing Florida-trained US Special Forces troops who used five Sikorsky HH-53 Super Jolly Green Giant helicopters in an attempt to rescue the 65 inmates thought to be at Son Tay. Unfortunately, the camp was completely empty. It was first thought that there may have been an intelligence leak at Hurlburt AFB, Florida, where a mock prison had been constructed for rehearsing the raid's swift action. However, it later transpired that the camp had been empty for some time due to the threat of flooding from a nearby river. The lack of timely photo-intelligence was a great embarrassment to Brig-Gen LeRoy Manor's Son Tay raiders.

MORE IMPORTANT SORTIES

Flying time in the SR-71 (especially combat flying) was always considered a premium commodity among the 20 crews, who would wheel and deal with the staff schedulers for additional sorties. Although Southeast Asian sorties accounted for the majority of OL-8's flight hours, that area was not the exclusive domain of the Habu. Majs Bob Spencer and Butch Sheffield were particularly pleased to be selected for one such prize sortie on the night of 27 September 1971. After completing the ritual post take-off air refuelling in '980, they climbed away from the tankers on a northerly track opposite to the standard route down south into Vietnam. US intelligence had obtained details of the largest ever Soviet naval exercise to be held near Vladivostok, in the Sea of Japan. Undoubtedly, such an event could provide a rich source of intelligence data, and an SR-71 was the ideal vehicle with which to stir the Soviet fleet's defence systems into action.

National security officials were especially interested in obtaining fresh data on the signal characteristics of the Soviet's new SA-5 SAM system, code-named 'Gammon'. If technical details of signal characteristics like its radar's frequency, modulation, PRF, pulse-repetition interval (PRI) and other factors could be measured, it might be possible to develop an effective ECM device to reduce or even negate the SA-5's highly-touted capabilities. The main problem was that the various Elint recorders carried on the SR-71 filtered the vast range of electromagnetic emissions transmitted from all sources and actuated special recorders when receiving only certain signal types. Maj Jack Clemence (an inventive Electronic Warfare Officer) who worked in the 9th SRW's Electronic Data Processing Center (EDPC), jury-rigged one of the Elint sensors by electronically cutting and splicing the pulse receiver's filtering system, which allowed it to receive a continuous-wave signal.

The possibility of night disorientation (caused by inlet unstarts and other hazards) over the dark northern Pacific, led the mission planners to restrict most turns to a 25° bank limit while night flying at Mach 3.2. Spencer and Sheffield were concentrating their attention on the naval target area just off Vladivostok as they sliced '980 through the night in full afterburner. If they maintained their current inbound track toward the Soviet port and turned at a 25° bank, they would overfly the USSR, crossing high over the Khrebet Sikhote Alin, and exit the area into the Sea of Japan, before returning to Kadena. As they bore down on the target area, dozens of Soviet radars were switched on to record what appeared to be shaping up as a certain violation of sovereign Soviet airspace. The deception worked well as '980 turned at the precise moment and failed to violate Siberian airspace due to it being programmed to roll into a full 35° bank, instead of the previously recorded 25° banks.

On the approach to the target area, Bob noted to his great dismay that the right engine's oil pressure was dropping. Nevertheless, he pressed on. When they had completed their target run and were heading south toward home plate, he rechecked the critical oil pressure gauge. By then its reading had fallen to zero, which was bad news indeed. After a brief consultation with Butch, he shut the engine down. Having already stirred up a hornet's nest of defence activity with their feinting pass over the Soviet's Pacific Fleet, they were now forced to descend and continue the rest of their flight at subsonic speeds, where they would be sitting ducks for any fast jets that might be scrambled to intercept the oil-starved Habu. To make matters worse, they encountered extreme headwinds that rapidly depleted their fuel supply. Butch calculated that a recovery back to Kadena was completely out of the question – they would have to divert into South Korea.

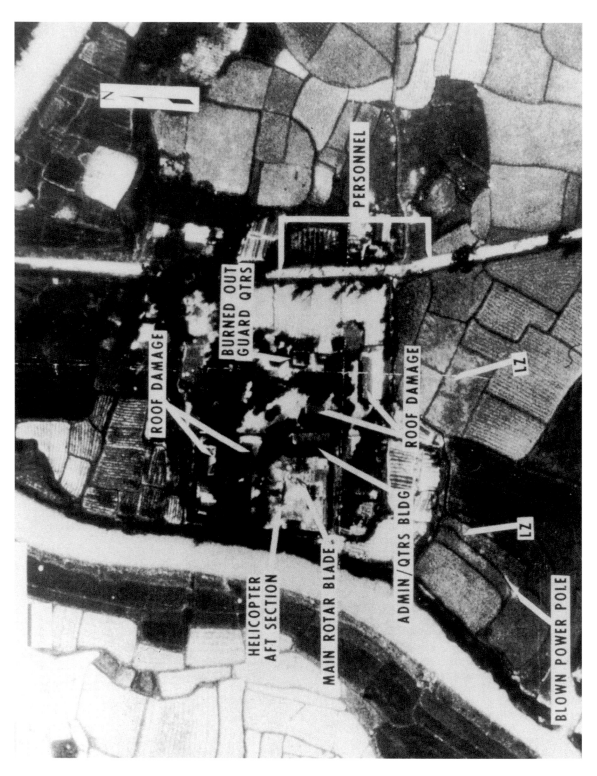

An OL-8 SR-71 was sent north following the unsuccessful Son Tay raid to obtain photographs of the damaged camp. After training at Hurlburt Field, Florida, US special forces used HH-53 helicopters to assault the PoW camp, which turned out to be empty owing to the threat of floodwater. This Habu image has been annotated by photo interpreters. (USAF)

The OL commander had been monitoring '980's suddenly-slowed progress and as the Habu neared Korea, US listening posts reported the launch of several MiGs from Pyongyang, North Korea, on what appeared to be an intercept attempt. USAF F-102 Delta Daggers were immediately launched from a base near Hon Chew, South Korea, and vectored into a position that put them between the MiGs and the SR-71. It was later established that the MiG launch had been unconnected with the Habu's descent. Bob recovered '980 into Taegu, South Korea, where the base commander had already received a call concerning his special visitor and was ready to receive the SR-71 and its crew. Their EMR 'take' turned out to be monumental. In all, Bob and Butch had sniffed out emissions from 290 different radars. Of even greater significance to Western intelligence analysts were the 'beautiful' SA-5 signals that they had successfully captured – the first ever detected by Western observers.

MPC'S BLUE BOXES

On 5 April 1972, Lt-Col Ed Payne (by then OL-8's Chief of Intelligence) received a phone call from a friend at Norton AFB, California, who spoke in indirect references about 'some blue boxes that would soon make Ed's job easier'. The call was so obscure that he did not know what his Norton contact was trying to tell him until a week later when he received a top-secret message. The president had just signed the Defense Appropriation Bill, within which provision had been made for the OL to be equipped with a Mobile Processing Center that could perform post-mission processing at Okinawa, rather than having to send the material to Japan or the US. The computer portion of Mobile Processing Center 1 (MPC 1), contained in eight vans, had been dispatched from Beale to Kadena in time for the arrival of the first three SR-71s deployed to the island in March 1968. Contained within these was the CDC-3200 computer equipment needed for SR-71 mission planning, programming the aircraft's sensors and providing an initial scan of the SR-71's Elint collection. The remaining 15-van portion contained the additional equipment necessary for processing the SR-71's HRR and photo-reconnaissance collections and for preparing a detailed analysis of the aircraft's Elint collection and these were airlifted in by two Military Airlift Command (MAC) Lockheed C-5 Galaxys. The AGT-30, Adage Graphics Terminal was shipped aboard a MAC Lockheed C-141 StarLifter, from Travis AFB.

Just before the arrival of Ed's 'blue boxes', an area of Kadena was rapidly prepared for the MPC's many new vans. The blue trailers were quickly unloaded and towed to the newly-prepared area

Butch Sheffield (left) and Bob Spencer stirred up a hornet's nest on the night of 27 September 1971. In doing so they acquired the first detailed signal characteristics of the Soviet SA-5 'Gammon' SAM. (USAF)

where they were interconnected to function as an in-theatre recce-technical unit. At 18:45Z on 18 April 1972, Ed was on the phone to the National Photographic Interpretation Center (NPIC) informing them that he was ready for quick response intelligence processing. The OL could now process Elint, Comint, and black-and-white imagery. With the MPC up and running, imagery was fast processed as soon as the Habu landed, and was 'wet read' by the photo interpreters who supplied an Initial Photo Interpretation Report (IPIR) on the highest priority targets. Before the full MPC had been deployed, SAC had had to fly the SR-71 film to the 548th RTG at Hickham AFB, Hawaii, for processing and a preliminary readout, a process that took on average 40 hours. With the MPC in operation, this was cut to 11 hours.

This intelligence would be communicated in plain English on a secure telephone to appropriately cleared persons on Henry Kissinger's staff who could, if necessary, provide a report to the President within a few hours of an SR-71 overflying key targets. Such direct reporting of hot intelligence was a remarkable achievement for the time. Duplicate sets of photographic negatives were immediately produced, with a set then being flown to Eielson AFB, Alaska, where it was transferred to another courier aircraft and flown to Washington DC to be sped onward to the NPIC. Another courier would deliver a set of negatives to the 12th RTS at Saigon for the next day's air strike planning. Other high-priority recipients were: Fleet Intelligence, Pacific (FINCPAC); the 532nd RTS at Udorn RTAFB; the 544th RTS at Offutt AFB, Nebraska; SAC's B-52 force in Southeast Asia; the DIA; the JCS; and the president and the National Security Council.

The MPC also accomplished an initial Elint scan for high-threat signals within three hours after the SR-71 had returned. The complete Mission Intercept Report Electrical (MIRE), was produced within 20–24 hours, but final, follow-on technical Elint reporting was still conducted by the 9th RTS, at Beale.

BOOMING THE 'HILTON'

During the late spring of 1972, a number of intriguing and highly-classified sorties were flown from Kadena to North Vietnam on 2 May, 4 May and 9 May. Each mission comprised two primary aircraft and an airborne spare. The mission's objective was to lay down two sonic booms within 15 seconds of one another as a signal to key prisoners of the notorious 'Hanoi Hilton' PoW camp.

As an example, during the sortie flown on 4 May, Majs Tom Pugh and Ronnie Rice approached the target area in aircraft '968 at 75,000 ft (22860 m) from the south, while Majs Bob Spencer and Butch Sheffield maintained 80,000 ft (24384 m) in '980 and flew across the target from the southeast. Meanwhile Lt-Col Darrel Cobb and Maj Reggie Blackwell were the airborne spare in '978; they were to cross the 'Hilton' at 70,000 ft (21336 m) from the west should either of the primary aircraft have to abort. The mission and the timing of the two booms were so critical that Darrel and Reggie flew all the way to the target area. A pre-arranged code word had been established which would indicate that their services would not be needed. When that word was transmitted, Darrel broke off his run short of the target area.

All three missions were termed 'entirely successful' and accomplished their objective within the very tight time constraints – reconnaissance gathering was of secondary importance to the signal. More than three decades after the event, it is still unclear as to why these sorties were flown, or what the double booms were meant to signify to the PoWs.

On 15 May 1972, Majs Tom Pugh and Ronnie Rice were airborne in '978 on Tom's 236th SR-71 sortie. They were flying a routine Giant Scale sortie, scheduled to be a 'double-looper' up through the Gulf of Tonkin for a 'front door entry'. Just short of Haiphong, Tom's concern over a strange cyclical hum in the interphone system was relieved when the generator bus tie circuit split, allowing independent operation of each of the 60 KVA AC generators, one of which had been responsible for the varying frequency, hence the hum. Freed of the AC bus load sharing, the system seemingly returned to normal. The 'Go-No-Go' checklist allowed the mission to proceed. While Tom was maintaining Mach 3.18 at 79,500 ft (24232 m), a generator failed. That failure was a mandatory abort item so the crew began making provisions to divert into Thailand.

Just over a minute later the other generator failed and they were in real trouble. Emergency AC and DC power did not come online and the fuel boost pumps stopped pumping JP-7 to the engines. Without electrical power the SAS cut out, and lacking boost pump pressure the fuel-flow to both engines stopped, causing them to flame out. To add to their grief, the inlet spikes went full forward and, as '978 began pitching and rolling rapidly, Tom knew the aircraft was approaching the limits of its supersonic flight envelope. Tom instructed Ron to, 'get ready to bail … ' but the intercom system failed before he could finish the statement. He held the stick gently while struggling to control the jet (without causing further pilot-induced oscillations), and while also trying to reach the all-important 'Stand by Electrical Switch' located on his right-hand panel. To reach that critical switch he had to move his left hand off the throttles and on to the control stick in order to free his right hand so he could restore some electrical power to the aircraft. This accomplished, Tom initiated a gentle 'needle-ball and airspeed' turn towards a 'friendly piece of concrete'. Having descended to 41,000 ft (12497 m) and slowed to just Mach 1.1, he managed to get one generator back online and both engines relit. He then reaccelerated '978 to Mach 1.7 to exit the area as quickly as possible. Tom crossed Laos to recover '978 into Udorn RTAFB without further problems.

The serious nature of the malfunction necessitated that they return to Kadena subsonically. As they set off with two tankers (one carrying the recovery team), they heard another SR-71 diverting into U-Tapao RTAFB. The tanker with the maintenance team peeled away from '978 and headed back to Thailand to recover the other aircraft. At their post-flight analysis, Tom and Ron learned that they had overflown Hanoi at 41,000 ft. They had been extremely lucky

This group, enjoying 'sun-downers', comprises, from left to right: unknown, Bruce Leibman, Bill Orcutt, Jack Madison, Russ Szczepanik, Don Emmons, Tom Alison, Joe Vida, Duane Noll, Tim Tilden and Jim Jiggens. Joe Vida and Tom Tilden joined their Det 1 hosts on a TDY deployment to conduct flight checks on a DAFICS-equipped SR-71 in tropical conditions. (Paul F. Crickmore Collection)

considering the number of SAMs that encircled the city. It appeared that the Vietnamese radar operators and their Soviet advisers had been asleep at the switch during '978's mid-altitude pass over one of the best-defended cities in the world. The 'Bunny' had pulled off a lucky escape from what appeared to be an easy shoot-down situation. Two days later, '978 had been repaired and the two intrepid aviators returned the aircraft to Kadena. Tom and Ron were each awarded Air Medals for Meritorious Achievement in 'the successful landing of their disabled aircraft'.

On 30 May, '978 was at the centre of yet another scary episode. Majs Bob Powell and Gary Coleman were approaching Hanoi on a 'front-door' entry when the SAS failed. They had just entered a 30° bank at Mach 3.2 and 81,000 ft (24689 m) when the aircraft started porpoising. As Bob struggled to master the destabilised flight characteristics, he found that he had to decelerate and descend to an altitude where the aircraft would be more manageable. Gary radioed the tanker with a delayed rendezvous time because they would be approaching at subsonic speeds. Bob completed a somewhat ragged aerial refuelling and trailed a spare tanker to the east coast of Vietnam, where they filled the tanks and slogged their way back to Kadena at 0.9 Mach (logging six hours 30 minutes flying time).

FAREWELL TO THE 'BUNNY'

On 20 July 1972 'The Rapid Rabbit's' luck finally ran out. While returning from an operational mission, Majs Denny Bush and Jimmy Fagg approached Kadena to learn of excessive cross-wind landing conditions. On touchdown, Denny deployed the aircraft's large braking parachute in a rapid-deploy jettison technique to prevent '978 from weathercocking sharply into the wind and running off the side of the runway. Unhappy with the first touchdown he jettisoned the chute, pushed up the power, and 'took it around' for another landing approach. Although he successfully touched down on the second attempt, the crosswind was so strong that he was unable to keep the weathercocked aircraft on the runway. During the resulting off-runway landing roll-out, one set of main wheels struck a low concrete structure, severely damaging the landing gear and causing substantial additional damage to the aircraft. Both crewmembers clambered out unscathed, but '978 was written-off. The pieces that were salvageable were transported back to Norton AFB in a C-5 Galaxy, and were later used as spare parts for the other SR-71s. The remaining sections of the airframe were scrapped in Okinawa.

HABU SUPPORT OF THE B-52

The 'flexible response' strategy adopted by the Kennedy Administration to fighting the Vietnam War caused SAC to examine the tactical potential of its Stratofortress strategic bombers in that war. By mounting two multiple-ejector racks on wing pylons of some B-52Fs, a further 24 750-lb (340-kg) bombs could be carried to supplement the 27 bombs that could already be hauled internally, thus nearly doubling the aircraft's bomb load. As the situation in South Vietnam worsened, the JCS decided to deploy the modified B-52Fs to Andersen AFB, Guam, in February 1965. Under operations code-named Arc Light, the aircraft could be used to strike targets in North Vietnam in reprisal for terrorist action against US personnel in the south. Meanwhile, an ineffectual bombing raid was mounted by a large number of fighter-bombers against Viet Cong base camps near Black Virgin Mountain on 15 April 1965. Soon after, General Westmoreland obtained permission from Secretary of Defense McNamara to use B-52s in support of tactical operations in South Vietnam.

Majors Ronnie Rice (left) and Tom Pugh overflew Hanoi in an SR-71 at just 41,000 ft (12497 m) on 15 May 1972. Amazingly, they got away with it. They are pictured wearing S-901J pressure suits. (USAF)

The first big strike took place on 18 June 1965 when 30 B-52s flew a 12-hour/5,500-mile (8851-km) round trip from Guam to the Ben Cat Special Zone in Binh Duong Province northeast of Saigon. As these Arc Light sorties continued, a modification programme known as 'Big Belly' got underway back in the US. Between December 1965 and September 1967, 82 B-52Ds received new radar transponders for ground-directed bombing and further bomb-rack mods, that increased their carrying capacity from 27 500-lb (227-kg) bombs carried internally to 84. These, plus 24 500-lb or 750-lb weapons on the wing pylons, could bring the total load to a staggering 108 bombs weighing 60,000 lb (27216 kg).

On 1 April 1966, the 28th and 454th Bombardment Wings deployed to Guam and began flying regular Arc Light sorties. In addition to the great increase in firepower that these 'Big Belly' bombers represented, the sortie rate was increased from 450 to 600 flights per month. Seven ground sites for bombing-director radar – called Combat Skyspot – were established, the first one coming on line at Bien Hoa in March 1966. These sites, working in conjunction with the B-52s' new radar transponders, helped to improve bombing accuracy. On 11 and 27 April 1966, B-52s struck North Vietnam for the first time, hitting targets in

the Mu Gia Pass, which was the keystone of the notorious Ho Chi Minh Trail's supply network. The B-52 sortie rate increased as the ground war continued to deteriorate and by February 1967 it had reached 800 flights per month. Meanwhile, Guam had reached its saturation point in regards to the number of B-52s that it could support. Thereafter, additional aircraft were deployed to U-Tapao RTAFB at Sattahip, Thailand.

A year later McNamara approved yet another increase to 1,200 and then, finally, 1,800 B-52 sorties per month. On 1 November 1968, President Johnson called a halt to the Rolling Thunder bombing operations against North Vietnam. The emphasis for the B-52s then changed to targets under the Commando Hunt heading, in an effort to stem the tide of personnel, equipment and fuel being infiltrated into South Vietnam via a supply network in Laos. Nevertheless, eight months after the election of President Nixon, Secretary of Defense Melvin Laird cut the B-52 sortie rate to 1,400 per month. Two years later the monthly rate was further reduced to 1,000 sorties and many aircraft and crews were returned to the US.

In early 1972, however, an enemy build-up along the Laotian trail network indicated the prospect of an imminent offensive. Gen Creighton Abrams and Adm. John McCain (CINCPAC) requested additional Arc Light sorties to forestall this rising threat. On 8 February the JCS authorised 1,200 monthly sorties and ordered 29 more B-52s to Guam. In a major invasion effort on 30 March 1972, the enemy hit South Vietnamese positions in Quang To, Kontum-Pleiku and Binh Long Provinces. As a result, President Nixon ordered a resumption of the bombing of North Vietnam – a policy that had been in abeyance since 1 November 1968. As the situation worsened on all three fronts, B-52Gs were deployed for the first time. This increase brought the bomber force to 133 aircraft, which could fly as many as 2,250 sorties per month. In an operation code-named Linebacker, five B-52 strikes were launched, the first on 9 April against petroleum storage facilities and the rail yard at Vinh. This was followed by a raid code-named Freedom Dawn on 12 April that hit Bai Thuong airfield; four days later, Freedom Porch Bravo targeted petroleum, oil and lubricant facilities around Haiphong. Then, on 21 April, Freighter Captain launched strikes against Hamn Rong, the transshipment point and the Thanh warehouse area. Two days later, Frequent Winner re-visited the same target list as that hit on 21 April. Linebacker saw B-52s venturing into the heavily-defended Hanoi-Haiphong area for the first time, and they came away unscathed.

SAC was requested to increase the number of SR-71 reconnaissance sorties to obtain imagery for bomb damage assessment. On 8 May, as the war continued to escalate, President Nixon ordered that routes into and out of North Vietnamese harbours should be mined. The next day, in an operation code-named Pocket Money, the JCS directed that drones and the SR-71 should photograph, on a daily basis, the ports of Haiphong, Hon Gai, Gam Pha, Dong Hoi, Quang Khe, Vinh and Thanh Hoa, to identify the enemy's shipping channels in readiness for US Navy mining operations. One week into the operation, the JCS designated the SR-71's High Resolution Radar as an acceptable sensor for this purpose. This was the first occasion that the JCS had specifically directed that the HRR should cover a predetermined intelligence target and in so doing, it signalled that the technology had officially come of age.

In June, the JCS additionally required the SR-71 to photograph communication and logistics supply lines between North Vietnamese ports and the Chinese border areas. Throughout this time the SR-71 also used its sophisticated EMR system to collect Elint, as part of SAC's Combat Apple Sigint collection operation in Southeast Asia that also utilised U-2 and RC-135 platforms. As the situation on the ground deteriorated further, additional B-52s were deployed to the region and, by late June, 200 of the giant eight-engined bombers had been deployed to the region and were chalking up over 3,100 sorties per month. They were also having a decisive effect on the North's invasion.

On 21 April 1972, AFLC, in conjunction with the SR-71's Advanced Systems Program Office, began flight-testing a prototype Capability Reconnaissance Radar (CAPRE). Manufactured by Loral, the new unit promised a significant increase in resolution over the earlier Goodyear GA-531 installation then operational on the SR-71 fleet. The 12 evaluation flights conducted within the United States on the radar prototype were successfully completed by AFLC on 15 July 1972, and on 11 August Majs Bob Powell and Gary Coleman flew aircraft '975 to Kadena, as part of the autumn Glowing Heat aircraft rotation. Onboard was the new radar, deployed for the first time to undertake its operational evaluation (opeval). The first of these opeval sorties was launched at 15:45 the very next day, the crew consisting of Bob Cunningham and his RSO George 'GT' Morgan. By November the new system had demonstrated capabilities that far exceeded those of the earlier PIP radar and, accordingly, HQ SAC directed that the prototype CAPRE unit should be retained by the detachment until production sets became available for operational use.

In total, five other CAPRE units had been contracted for by SAC and plans called for the final unit to be delivered by May 1973. However,

THE UNITED STATES OF AMERICA

TO ALL WHO SHALL SEE THESE PRESENTS, GREETING:

THIS IS TO CERTIFY THAT
THE PRESIDENT OF THE UNITED STATES OF AMERICA
AUTHORIZED BY EXECUTIVE ORDER, MAY 11, 1942
HAS AWARDED

THE AIR MEDAL

(EIGHTH OAK LEAF CLUSTER)

TO

CAPTAIN REGINALD T. BLACKWELL
UNITED STATES AIR FORCE

FOR

MERITORIOUS ACHIEVEMENT
WHILE PARTICIPATING IN AERIAL FLIGHT

27 DECEMBER 1972

GIVEN UNDER MY HAND IN THE CITY OF WASHINGTON
THIS   17TH   DAY OF   DECEMBER 19 73

JOHN C. MEYER, General, USAF
Commander in Chief
Strategic Air Command

ORM 22.12. JUL 70

SECRETARY OF THE AIR FORCE

B-52 strikes in Cambodia, in addition to ascertaining the status of various North Vietnamese-occupied airfields. These included Tchepone in Laos, together with Cam Lu and Kham Doc in South Vietnam. The Plaines De Jarres in Laos also received regular visits from the SR-71, in order to monitor the infiltration of personnel and materiel moving from North to South Vietnam.

On 17 February 1973, Bud Gunther and Tom Allocca departed Kadena at 13:00 hours on mission GS696, a four-hour operational stand-off sortie in aircraft '975. Of particular interest on this mission was the area around Khe Sanh airfield and, as it transpired, the intelligence community was extremely pleased by the 'take' once it had been processed. It revealed that adjacent to the

Above and right: Lt-Col Darrell Cobb and Capt Reg Blackwell were awarded Air Medals for providing ECM support to B-52s taking part in operation Linebacker II on the night of 27/28 December 1972. (USAF)

airfield AAA emplacements had been built; a new, unnumbered supply route and truck park was also discovered, together with a probable cave storage area and two operational SA-2 sites – the first to be discovered in this area since the late spring of 1972. Such a high-level of activity documented by '975's cameras led the analysts to conclude that the occupying Communists intended to make Khe Sanh a permanent control point for operations in the south of the country.

To ensure that the Communist North was adhering to the terms of the Paris accords, the JCS directed that two SR-71 sorties were to be

CITATION TO ACCOMPANY THE AWARD OF

THE AIR MEDAL
(EIGHTH OAK LEAF CLUSTER)

TO

REGINALD T. BLACKWELL

Captain Reginald T. Blackwell distinguished himself by meritorious achievement while participating in aerial flight as Reconnaissance Systems Officer on 27 December 1972. On that date, while operating from a forward location, his courageous accomplishments resulted in the acquisition of significant intelligence vitally important to the United States and the security of the free world. Despite the hazardous environment and the demanding conditions which threatened this mission, Captain Balckwell demonstrated his exceptional airmanship and brought this flight to a successful conclusion. The professional ability and outstanding aerial accomplishments of Captain Blackwell reflect great credit upon himself and the United States Air Force.

conducted in April. The first of these, GS722, was flown by Majs Buck Adams and Bill Machorek in aircraft '971 on 19 April 1973. However, due to heavy cloud cover, the intelligence obtained during this sortie was almost entirely generated by the CAPRE high-resolution radar. It proved that the Viet Tri rail and road bridge, located 30 miles (48 km) northwest of Hanoi, had been interdicted since the imagery collected by Bob Cunningham and Jimmy Fagg in SR-71 '975 during their 23 January mission. Photography collected during that earlier sortie had also caught 11 MiG-21s parked on the western alert apron at Phuc Yen airfield. However, analysis of the HRR imagery obtained on the 19 April sortie suggested that no aircraft were then on alert. Photo interpreters noted that a similar situation had prevailed earlier at Phuc Yen, during Linebacker II, when the MiGs had been moved off the base's apron areas and into cave storage facilities.

However, after the bombing halt and the signing of the peace accords, the MiGs were once again parked on the alert aprons. Intelligence specialists therefore concluded that the absence of interceptor aircraft at Phuc Yen on the 19 April was consistent with an increase in their alerted air defence posture.

Clearing skies enabled a conventional camera configuration to be carried on the second monitoring sortie; this would enable analysts to crosscheck the HRR imagery obtained five days earlier. Consequently, Giant Scale flight GS725 got under way on 24 April 1973, when Majs Pat Bledsoe and Reggie Blackwell left Kadena at 11:45 in aircraft 64-17963. Additional targets covered by this five-hour 30-minute flight were the Ben Thuy transshipment point and the petroleum products storage facilities at Vinh and Bai Thuong airfield. Yet again the SR-71 proved its worth. At Bai Thuong airfield, located 77 miles (124 km) southwest of Hanoi, '963's cameras caught large amounts of material, equipment and vehicles, and bomb craters on the main runway and parallel taxiway had been repaired. Three coastal petroleum barges were noted in the vicinity of the Vinh bunkering pier and a moderate amount of activity was also recorded at the Ben Thuy transshipment point, located about four miles east of Vinh.

Parallel with the activity detailed above, within two weeks of the Vietnam ceasefire, the Pacific Command Elint Center requested SAC to provide increased electronic reconnaissance of various signal threats emanating from Laos. On 9 February 1973, SAC requested the SRC to schedule two SR-71 Elint missions per week against Laotian objectives throughout the remainder of the year.

SS *MAYAGUEZ* INCIDENT

On Monday 12 May 1975, the US-registered freighter SS *Mayaguez* was stopped by a number of Khmer Rouge gunboats as it steamed in international waters some 60 nm (69 miles; 111 km) southwest of Cambodia, near the Paulo Wai Islands in the Gulf of Thailand. The merchant ship was boarded and the next day, under the control of its captors, the *Mayaguez* was moved to a point about two miles off the northeastern tip of Koh Tang Island.

The ship was initially located by two General Dynamics F-1lls diverted from a routine training mission the day after the vessel's seizure. Thereafter, a round-the-clock surveillance plan was put into operation to monitor the *Mayaguez's* movements. Just before dawn on 15 May an initial Marine Corps assault was launched on two beaches at the northern tip of Koh Tang and a search was made of the vessel in a bid to release the ship's crewmembers. However, a small Thai fishing boat had been used to move the crew to the Cambodian mainland the day before, and the Marine boarding party found the freighter to be empty. Having been put ashore, the assault force encountered stiffer resistance than had been anticipated from a much larger and better fortified group of Khmer troops. To make matters worse, during the assault on Koh Tang, which lasted 14 hours and resulted in 15 US Marines being killed, three Missing In Action (MIA), 50 wounded and four H-53 helicopters shot down, the same Thai fishing boat returned the ship's crew unharmed to the destroyer USS *Holt* in a gesture which seems to have been unconnected with the battle for their release.

The importance of this assault resulted in an SR-71 mission being scheduled to monitor the strike on Koh Tang. It was flown on 19 May by Capts Al Cirino and Bruce Liebman in aircraft 64-17961 to monitor the after-effects of the raid

four days earlier. Their 'take' was to prove extremely useful during subsequent debriefings.

Despite the war in Southeast Asia having ended in August 1973, SR-71's from OLKA continued to conduct occasional overflights of Cambodia. Although not officially admitted at the time, the large numbers of US troops listed as MIA continued to be a source of concern for the US government. This, together with occasional 'sightings' of MIAs and rumours of isolated prison compounds in inaccessible jungle areas, proved a strong enough reason for various US intelligence agencies to request that such flights be sanctioned.

One such mission was flown by BC Thomas and Jay Reid in '976. The 5-hour 48-minute flight was conducted on 24 November 1980 – seven years after the cessation of hostilities. Unfortunately for the relatives of those left clinging to such hope, no substantive evidence was produced by the aircraft's sensors to back-up any speculation.

GIANT SCALE II

In May 1978, Vietnam began a series of border skirmishes with Kampuchea and in late December these escalated into a full-scale invasion. Following the fall of Phnom Penh on 7 January 1979, the Vietnamese-backed rebel forces declared Pol Pot and the infamous Khmer Rouge to be overthrown and formed a government. However, fighting between the rival factions continued in the west of the country, creating thousands of refuges who fled into neighbouring Thailand. Concerned that an estimated Army of 200,000 Vietnamese regulars in Kampuchea might turn their weapons on the Thais, the Thai government requested reconnaissance coverage of the area from its long standing ally, the United States. In total, five SR-71 sorties were flown in support of this request, the first by Tom Keck and Tim Shaw in aircraft '979 on 17 February 1980. This sortie was followed by Rick Young and Russ Szczepanik, again in '979, on 3 May; Gil Bertelson and Frank Stampf completed a six-hour 12-minute sortie in '976 on 3 August; Bob Crowder and John Morgan chalked up a mission in '960 on 22 November and BC Thomas and Jay Reid completed the series of sorties code-named Giant Scale II by SAC, in '976, on 24 November. Each round-robin sortie from Kadena covered approximately 6,500 miles (10460 km) and required three air refuellings, one over the Philippine Sea and the other two over the Gulf of Thailand. All five were Photint missions with the aircraft configured with an OBC unit in the nose and TEOCs in the chine bays. Four of the five sorties secured standard black and white imagery of the target area. However, the JCS directed that the cameras for the mission flown in '960 should be loaded with Kodak SO-131

camouflage detection film. This film coloured healthy vegetation red and dead or dying vegetation various shades of grey and white. This effect was used to gauge the probable yield of the rice crop, since Kampuchea had become a member of the United Nations in September 1980. After processing, the imagery was forwarded to the DIA where it enabled it to help plan the US contribution level to the food relief programme for Kampuchea. The rest of the reconnaissance imagery collected during the other four sorties failed to reveal any large concentrations of Vietnamese forces or equipment along the Thai border and, after being sanitised, the photography was passed, via the US Embassy in Bangkok, to high-level officials in the Thai government.

GIANT COBRA AND GIANT EXPRESS

The Horn of Africa is an immensely important strategic location, guarding the Red Sea approach to the Suez Canal and overlooking the oil arteries of Saudi Arabia, Iraq, Oman, Kuwait, Djibouti and the United Arab Emirates as they fan out from the southern entrance to the Red Sea. In August 1977 a war broke out between communist-governed Ethiopia and its neighbour, Somalia. In November that same year, the Soviet Union began airlifting arms to Ethiopia and this action was backed-up by Cuban troops, sent by Fidel Castro. By March 1978, it was estimated that approximately 11,000 Cuban troops were in-country, and two Soviet Generals were directing the ground war against Somalia. Accordingly, the JCS directed that SAC should position a Kadena-based SR-71 to Diego Garcia, a small British-owned island in the Indian Ocean, and plan a round-robin Photint reconnaissance mission over the area to monitor the extent of Soviet and Cuban presence. In response, the SRC prepared a track for such a sortie and the JCS directed that the flight should

Aircraft '972 taxies out to the hold at Kadena AB. As well as seeing combat service over Vietnam, 64-17972 was flown in a series of records in 1974 and 1990 and is now displayed by the Smithsonian Institution. (L. Peacock)

launch on 12 March 1978. However, the theatre situation changed dramatically earlier in the month when Somalia suddenly withdrew its troops from Ethiopia and agreed to keep them out, provided that all foreign troops also consented to leave the region. As a result, the mission was cancelled even before the SR-71 had been positioned on the tiny island. The event, however, proved to be a catalyst in preparing Diego Garcia to support SR-71 contingency operations in the Indian Ocean area. In just three weeks from mid-February, an SR-71 shelter at Beale had been dismantled, transported to and re-erected on Diego Garcia. A water demineralisation plant, rations and a number of 376th Strategic Wing, KC-135Qs with JP-7 fuel had also been positioned. The fragmentary order for any such contingency operations in this theatre was initially code-named Giant Cobra. But as the region slipped into further political upheaval, with the rise to power of Ayatollah Khomeini and his brand of Islamic fundamentalism in Iran, and Soviet involvement in Afghanistan, it was decided to further bolster facilities on Diego Garcia in the event that the needs of national intelligence users required more extensive coverage of the area. On 2 April 1979, the JCS directed SAC to create a permanent SR-71 fuel storage facility on Diego Garcia. Initially, two 50,000-US gal (189270-litre) polyurethane fuel storage bladders were deployed and filled by ten Kadena based KC-135Qs in an operation code-named Giant Ace. On 1 May 1979 a follow-on fragmentary order code-named Giant Express took cognisance of the deteriorating situation and included not only the Indian Ocean area, but also Africa and southwest Asia as potential theatres of operation from Diego Garcia. Further developments on the island by the US Navy eventually freed-up a 1.26 million-US gal (4.76 million-litre) fuel tank for prospective SR-71 operations. This was filled with JP-7 delivered by ocean tanker. During the summer of 1980, the JCS approved a plan to exercise the newly created SR-71 facilities. Consequently, on 1 July, Bob Crowder and Don Emmons completed the 4-hour 24-minute flight to the island from Kadena, in '962. The flight included three air refuellings, two from KC-135s operating from Kadena and a third from tankers that had been deployed a week earlier to Diego Garcia. The aircraft and crew returned to Kadena on 4 July, but despite validating the facilities and subsequent sorties being flown in the region, SR-71s never returned to the tropical island.

CHINA AND THE SOVIET UNION

The aftershocks of the Gary Powers incident ensured that A-12 or SR-71 overflights of the Soviet Union remained politically unacceptable. Some extremely useful intelligence had, however, been obtained of Communist China by Chinese Nationalist pilots flying U-2s loaned from the CIA. The cost in pilots and machines had been high in that programme, however, with a number of aircraft being shot down by SA-2s. The only Peacetime Aerial Reconnaissance Programme options open to the United States when it came to gathering intelligence data over these enormous countries were satellites and stand-off viewing — OLKA and Det 1 performed the latter mission successfully over both countries.

Despite the fact that these stand-off flights were being conducted in international airspace, the Habu crews that flew them remained convinced that, given the opportunity, Soviet fighters would attempt a shoot-down and would argue about the aircraft's position afterwards. There can be little doubting the acute irritation that such flights caused the Soviet leadership, especially when taking into account that the aircraft at the root of this irritation was over twenty years old and that the USSR was unable to match its technology.

On 29 October 1979, Majs Rich Graham and Don Emmons were airborne from Kadena in '962 on just such a stand-off flight. Nearing Petropavlovsk (on the east coast of the Kamchatka peninsula) they observed two medium-altitude circular contrails ahead of them. As they continued, the two contrailing MiGs attempted a snap-up manoeuvre, but were unable to get close to the Habu. Rich and Don later observed four more contrails belonging to MiGs whose pilots were waiting to attempt a similar intercept. Rich said to Don, 'Let's show them that we know they're there

and that we don't care.' Rich then dumped a small burst of fuel that created a high, fast vapour trail. No attempt was made by the MiGs to intercept the 3,000 ft per second target that passed high above them. Such potential intercept actions were typical of the activity that greeted many stand-off flights during the Cold War.

There were not many possible track variations for a stand-off sortie. One can only fly up or down a coastline or fly toward it and break away to the left or right. To keep the Soviet defence controllers guessing, Lt-Col Tom Alison, at the time the Det 1 Commander, thought up an innovative sortie with a difference. On the morning of 27 March 1984, Majs 'Stormy' Boudreaux and Ted Ross got airborne from Kadena in '964 and headed northeast towards Vladivostok. Back at Beale AFB, Lt-Col Les Dyer and Maj Dan Greenwood launched in '973 and headed for deployment to Kadena, via Vladivostok. In a masterpiece of co-ordination and choreography, code-named Busy Relay, the two aircraft streaked towards one another from opposite directions at a closure speed of Mach 6, flashing by each other only 3 miles (5 km) apart. Stormy and Ted then turned right to trace Les and Dan who preceded them south and then west across Korea, just south of the Demilitarised Zone. As expected, the appearance of two SR-71s off Vladivostok triggered a series of atypical reactions from the region's numerous radar sites and the Elint collecting systems of both SR-71s and an RC-135 also sent to the area yielded a rich Sigint harvest.

ANOTHER LOST HABU

After more than 21 years of operating from Kadena, and 17 years without the loss of a single Habu at all locations, '974 crashed near the Philippines on 21 April 1989. Lt-Col Dan House and Maj Blair Bozek had departed Kadena and headed straight out to speed and altitude without a top-off air refuelling, ready to perform a routine stand-off sortie off the coast of Southeast Asia. After Dan levelled off at 75,000 ft (22860 m) and Mach 3, the aircraft began yawing to the left. Blair asked Dan, 'Is that an unstart?' Dan replied, 'I don't know.' It did not appear to be a typical unstart and the inlet had not re-cycled. Dan continued to monitor his instruments and saw that the left engine's gauges were winding down. He told Blair that the left engine had quit. By then there was no RPM, no EGT or oil pressure and the pressure gauges for the 'A' and 'L' hydraulic systems indicated zero. The left engine had seized!

It had been a surprisingly gentle process, but it was nonetheless an immediate abort item. Consequently, the crew began to plan for a diversionary landing base, especially since four SAS channels had also been lost, while

Wonsan harbour, North Korea, as seen from the cockpit of an SR-71 during an operational mission at speed and altitude. (Paul F. Crickmore Collection)

following-up on their engine-out procedures. At that point, the right engine went through four unstarts, during which another of the flight control's SAS channels failed, leaving them with only one out of six. As the aircraft lost speed and altitude, it entered a series of lateral gyrations that threatened to take it beyond the limits of its flight envelope. Dan described the whole incident as follows: 'It felt like we were experiencing a series of falling-leaf manoeuvres. We were "wrapping up" from one side to the other. I was ramming the stick through full-throw, back and forth, as quickly as I could but the aeroplane was doing pretty much what it wanted. That got me quite excited because from Mach 3 to Mach 2.5 I felt that I had no control whatsoever over the aircraft. I was most concerned because I didn't understand its cause. Well, somehow or other we flew out of that wild series of gyrations and I decided to divert into Clark AFB in the Philippines. We continued to descend and slow to subsonic speed on one engine and completed all our obligatory radio calls. Just when things appeared to be getting better, they suddenly got worse. I told Blair, "We've now got a 'B' Hydro Light," which meant that our remaining hydraulic system was getting low on fluid. By then we were at 400 kt [461 mph; 742 km/h] and 15,000 ft [4572 m] and the 'B' system's pressure gauge started to fluctuate. Our situation was now really deteriorating. I quickly updated Blair on the potential failure of my flight controls and told him to hang on.

'We were just off the north coast of the main Philippine island of Luzon and we agreed to remain over water as we proceeded toward Clark because if we had to leave the aircraft, we didn't want it dropping on peoples' heads, and we didn't want classified material falling into the wrong hands. So we turned left into the dead engine, as that was the easiest way to turn, and flew along the coast looking for anywhere suitable to land. Blair thought he saw a field and asked me if I could still control where I was going. At that point, I was holding full left rudder and saw that the "B" hydro had zeroed. As I replied to Blair, "No, I can't any longer," poor old '974 began wrapping up to the right very rapidly. I shouted, "Bail Out! Bail Out! Bail Out!" and pulled my ejection seat's "D"-ring. I remember hitting the stop and the sensation of light coming into the cockpit as the canopy blew off. The next thing I recalled was the reassuring tug as my chute opened. We'd gone out at about 400 kt and 10,000 ft [3048 m]. The elapsed time from the initial yaw to ejection was about 16 minutes. I checked the chute which was fine and then started looking for Blair, whom I could not immediately spot. It seems he'd gone out after me because he wasn't in the correct sitting position for a safe bailout. Therefore, he was ahead of and above me. When I finally located him, I started looking for '974, which was under me, falling straight down in planform. It happened to be upside down and was not pitching or tumbling. As she hit the water, there was a splash and a brief fireball. Then all was gone.

'I readied myself for a feet-wet landing. My descent rate under that 35-ft [10.67-m] wide canopy was very slow, so I had plenty of time to look around. It was a sunny morning, there was no wind, the vegetation on the island was lush and green and the calm blue ocean which I was about to enter was flat with no waves. I could see fishing boats turn toward me and by the time I'd cleared my chute, a Bonka boat had arrived next to my position in the water. A Bonka boat is a 20-ft [6-m] dugout canoe with outriggers on either side and it's powered by the noisiest internally-mounted, two-stroke engine I have ever heard in my life. Two Filipino fishermen offered to lift me into their boat, and since one of my life rules was to never give up a free ride when you're shark bait, I gladly accepted. They retrieved all my life-support gear and lifted the parachute aboard their little boat and then we went over to where Blair was waiting. He'd gotten into his life raft and was just climbing into another Bonka boat that had raced toward him as he descended. He tried the survival radio but couldn't hear anything because the search and rescue forces were still too far away. We went to the scene of the aeroplane's impact where there were only a few pieces of debris and some fuel floating nearby.

'We then asked the Filipino fishermen to take us ashore. They told us that the area opposite was controlled by the New People's Army (Communist insurgents who occupied the island), so they took us instead to a nearby town which was a two-hour ride to the east. After they'd handed us over to an officious policeman who was a member of the local militia, we tried to call Clark Air Base, but no one knew the phone number. Next we asked to talk to the US Consulate in Manila, but we had to wait our turn behind about 30 other people waiting to use the one phone. They eventually decided to take us to some local officials who could certainly help us. We'd taken our pressure suits off and were wearing the dark green nylon lining over our long underwear.

'We entered a large building carrying our survival gear and parachutes and were introduced to the mayor and Town Council. They were very concerned for our well being and asked if we needed to see a doctor. When we told them that it wasn't necessary, they invited us to have lunch with them. We had a wonderful meal of rice, pork, vegetables, pickled squid, and the best ice-cold bottles of Coca-Cola we'd had in our lives. The mayor then insisted that we take coffee with him at his home. While our survival radios were sending out their radiant signals, "come save us, come save us", we were enjoying coffee on the mayor's lawn. We had asked if there was a radio transmitter anywhere. Eventually they agreed to take us to one. As we were en route, a Lockheed P-3 Orion flew overhead. We stopped the truck and made contact but our radio reception was not very good. On reaching the short-wave radio, we identified ourselves to the Orion crew and were told that a helicopter was on its way to pick us up. We drove back to the mayor's house and Blair positioned himself in a dried-up rice field to greet the helicopter's crew. Meanwhile, I went back to the mayor's house for a final cup of coffee and to thank him and his countrymen for their wonderful hospitality. I also picked up our mission gear which we'd left on the patio.

'The HH-53 Super Jolly Green Giant took us back to Clark Air Force Base. The crew was superb and wanted to take us to the "O" Club for a few "coolers", but post-accident rules dictated that they had to hand us over to the medics for a physical examination. After this rather wild five-hour adventure, we were strapped to a stretcher by four medical corpsmen who put us in an ambulance. I had not been so helpless since '974 underwent the falling-leaf gyrations. Once we were in the ambulance, the doors were closed and the driver backed up no more than a hundred feet before the doors were flung open once again and they carried us into the hospital. Other than our bad attitudes for their seemingly stupid procedures, they found nothing wrong with us and after 24 hours of "observation" they released us.'

Side-scanning sonar operations of the crash site took place on 29 and 30 April and it was not long before the debris field of '974 was located. The 280-ft (85-m) long salvage vessel USS *Beaufort* was despatched to the site to lift the wreckage with its 10- and 15-ton cranes, fitted on the bow and stern of the ship, respectively, and to find the sensors and defensive systems. Due to the proximity of the Communist New People's Army, a number of Navy SEALs (special forces) were onboard *Beaufort* to provide protection to the divers and crew. An order for General Quarters was sounded at 04:00 hours one morning during the search. Crewmen rushed to their action stations in readiness for an immediate confrontation. They saw a large number of small vessels (which had been detected on *Beaufort's* radar) making for the ship. Tension mounted until it was discovered that the would-be attackers were really fishing boats that had come toward the bright lights of the naval vessel because a very large school of fish had congregated around it! The local fishermen were expecting to take full advantage of the unique situation.

When the inverted '974 had impacted the water, both engines smashed the sensors and other on-board equipment through its upper surfaces. Those objects were scattered on the ocean floor at varying distances away from the main wreckage. On the evening of 1 May, wire hawsers were attached to one of the J58 engines. The late evening movements dislodged the TEB tank and caused a small leak which released tiny amounts of the chemical throughout the night. As a result, tiny amounts of the volatile chemical were released and bubbled to the surface, where they mixed with ambient air and exploded in small green puffs. The 'magic' of the 'Yankee' engineers caused quite a stir among the native fishermen who saw the eerie 'TEB-bubble show'.

The next day both engines were lifted and brought aboard *Beaufort's* fan-tail and two days later many of the sensors were also recovered. When the ship's crew attempted to lift the main section of the aircraft, however, the crane operator found that the large delta-shaped wing planform greatly exceeded the lifting capacity of his crane, and the wreckage refused to budge an inch. A yard-derrick was then sent from Subic Bay and the forward fuselage section was recovered on 7 May, while the main structure was lifted aboard *Beaufort's* fan-tail the following day. The black wreckage was a sad end for a once proud aircraft, despite Dan's skilful and valiant efforts to save it.

CONFRONTATION NORTH KOREA

A total of three reconnaissance sorties was flown over North Korea by Oxcart pilots in 1968, but their short-lived efforts passed to SAC as a long-term role in early 1968 when the 9th SRW's OL-8 inherited the CIA's facilities at Kadena. The principal objectives of these Western Pacific, or WESTPAC, missions were to provide advanced warning of North Korean intentions by examining 'indications and warning targets', and they were conducted from Kadena, with most of the operational objectives being achieved from international airspace, by either flying off the North Korean coast or over the Demilitarised Zone (DMZ). Such missions were launched to satisfy the requirements specified primarily by the Commander in Chief, Pacific, on behalf of the intelligence users who operated under his jurisdiction. The most important of these were the Commander, United States Forces, Korea (COMUSK); Commander in Chief, Pacific Fleet (CINCPACFLT) and the Intelligence Center Pacific (ICPAC).

The justification for designating this region as a principal area of operations was based upon the fact that by 1977 North Korea had an army of 450,000 men (by mid 1978, the DIA and CIA believed that this number had increased to between 550,000 and 600,000), making it the fifth largest army in the world. In addition, the country's unpredictable dictator Kim Il Sung was committed to reunification of the peninsula under his form of communism. Admiral Maurice Weisner, who at that time was the Commander in Chief, Pacific, believed that given the sophistication of North Korea's weaponry and the level of training undertaken by its troops, the North could order an attack across the DMZ at virtually anytime. He therefore requested the JCS, which in turn directed SAC, to increase the number of monthly SR-71 monitoring sorties to the area from eight to 12 per month. The SRC then scheduled the SR-71 to be configured with cameras on two of the sorties and to gather Radint – using its HRR, and Elint sensors – on the remaining ten missions. The Photint provided a reference base for intelligence specialists to use when interpreting the HRR imagery.

North Korea's propensity to relocate or reinforce its military units and installations along the DMZ at night, prompted further requests from US theatre commanders that the majority of these SR-71 'indications and warning' sorties be conducted at night. This was communicated by the JCS to the SRC, and at 21:05 hours, on 19 September 1977, Jack Veth and his RSO Bill Keller left Kadena in 64-17960, returning 4 hours 6 minutes later, having completed the first night monitoring sortie of North Korea. Four additional Radint/Elint night sorties of North Korea were completed before the end of the year (27 September by Kinego and Elliott in aircraft 64-17967, 16 and 25 November by Alison and Vida in '967 and '960; and finally on 13 December by Carpenter and Murphy, again in '960). The crews that flew these important missions were, however, less than impressed by their nocturnal forays, noting that the aircraft's cockpit lighting was uneven, causing reflections that made monitoring instrumentation extremely difficult and potentially dangerous – especially during the descent phase to rendezvous with a tanker. This situation could be further complicated by a lack of horizon. Such conditions could well trigger vertigo and pilot disorientation, leading to the loss of an aircraft. Therefore, after the first two sorties in September, the mission profile was amended and the number of air refuellings reduced from two to one. The impact of this decision was to also reduce the number of passes made through the sensitive area, again from two to one, which also reduced the flight time needed to execute such missions from just under four hours 30 minutes to approximately two hours 30 minutes. Finally, in a further move to alleviate the problem, these missions were flown at Mach 2.8 and bank angles restricted to a maximum of 35° (the situation was finally rectified in 1982, when the cockpit lighting was improved and Peripheral Vision Horizon Display (PVHD) units were fitted in the SR-71 fleet. These units projected a thin red line of light across the aircraft's instrument panel to produce an artificial horizon that responded to changes in pitch and roll, thereby duplicating the behaviour of a natural horizon).

In April 1981, SR-71 flights began collecting Elint cuts and other raw data on a suspected SA-2 site which was under construction on the island of Choc Tarrie in an estuary near the western end of Korea's DMZ. In July and August of that year, Maj Maury Rosenberg and Capt ED McKim flew several passes over Korea to check on the progress of Choc Tarrie's SAM site. Before each flight, Det 1's intelligence officer briefed the crews about the most recent developments since it was increasingly apparent that the North Koreans were about to embark upon another adventure in belligerence.

On 25 August, Maj Nevin Cunningham and Geno Quist climbed into '967 for a similar two-loop sortie of the 'Z' area to those which had previously been flown. Although it was a clear day over the target area, the primary sensor for this four-hour sortie was the SLAR. During its fourth and final pass over the DMZ, the SR-71 was still carrying excess fuel so Nevin flicked his fuel dump switch in quick Morse-code bursts, which spelled out a four-letter expletive for the benefit of the North Korean ground trackers who were attempting to follow the SR-71 visually. Their humour was probably lost on the enemy, but it brought lots of laughs back at the Habu bar at Kadena.

The next morning, Maury and ED were briefed for their mission, which entailed three passes along the DMZ. Once again they were briefed about the suspected SA-2 site about which Maury asked the intelligence officer, 'Who determines when a suspected site becomes a confirmed site?' He was told that the Defense Intelligence Agency made the final call on such issues and added, 'So what do we have to do before we can confirm it? See a missile?' The intelligence officer replied, 'Well, that would surely help.'

Maury and ED launched in '976 on their 'Z' sortie and headed for their first air refuelling. After tanking they flew through the Straits of Formosa and made their first high pass from west to east along Korea's DMZ. They then turned south and flew down the east coast of South Korea toward their second refuelling. Thereafter they reversed course and after reaching operational altitude off the west coast of South Korea, they repeated their west to east run across the DMZ. Coasting out to the east, Maury made a right and left 90°/270° turn which put '976 on an east-to-west pass. While approaching the western side of Korea at Mach 3 and 77,000 ft (23470 m), ED remarked that he was getting some DEF activity and that everything was 'turned on'. In the next breath, ED exclaimed, 'Wow! It looks like

we've had a launch.' Maury accelerated to Mach 3.2 and told ED, 'I see a contrail! I'll be damned, it's coming right at us.' Maury made a slight turn to the left to turn away from the rising contrail which took them further into South Korean airspace and watched as the SA-2 missed by a good 2 miles (3.2 km), exploding behind and to the right of them at about 80,000 ft (24384 m).

Always mindful of the sensitivity of such sorties, the US authorities monitored these SR-71 flights very closely. Almost as soon as '976 came off track, ED received an encoded HF message from Sky King concerning the track deviation. There was no mention of the hostile missile firing. The RSO responded with the appropriate messages but found there was not a specific coded message that could be sent alluding to the missile incident. As a result of this mission, a coded message format was later added should a crew find themselves in similar circumstances. It was not until the Habu crew arrived back on 'the Rock' that they could inform the staff that they had been shot at.

The incident was of such importance that a coded message was despatched to all interested agencies including the National Security Council. Secretary of Defense Casper Weinberger informed the president of the firing, after which a series of high-level briefings followed. Deputy Secretary of Defense Charles Carlucci recalled that President Reagan was 'furious' over the incident. Meanwhile, Dean Fischer, a spokesman for the State Department said: 'The Reagan Administration roundly denounces this act of lawlessness,' adding that the attack 'violated accepted norms of international behaviour.' Despite faultless photographic evidence of the North Korean missile firing at an aircraft over South Korea, the North Korean government denied the missile charge. While the diplomatic rhetoric continued, Det 1 was told to move the reconnaissance track flown by the SR-71 even further to the south. Six days later, Nev Cunningham and Geno Quist flew a typical four-hour, two-loop sortie along the 'Z' in '976 with little reaction.

Majs BC Thomas and Jay Reid arrived at Kadena during the period of high-level interest in the Det's Korean activity. On 26 September, Deputy SECDEF Frank Carlucci visited the island and was briefed on its operations and shown an SR-71 for the first time. Carlucci met with the Habu crewmembers and explained that the DMZ route package had been moved further to the south for the moment but that they would return to their former DMZ routes after 'certain preparations' were made. He did not explain what those preparations were but seemed angry about the attempted shoot-down. He added that the US government viewed such hostile actions with

serious concern, and emphasised that the President would not stand for a repeat.

On Friday 2 October, BC and Jay flew '967 on a sortie off the eastern coast of China, North Korea and the USSR. They reported an unusual massing of ships off the coast of North Korea. The next day, Lt Gen Mathis (Assistant Vice Chief of Staff) held a special briefing for the Det's crewmembers in which he told of four special category missions which were to be flown on routes which would follow the same triple-pass track that Maury had flown when he was shot at on 26 August. He emphasised that the timing would be extremely important and that the Habu was to be over the earlier mission's firing point within 30 seconds of their mission's preplanned timing. Timing-control triangles would be built into the flight track after the second air refuelling to ensure that the precise timing constraints were met. One of the pilots asked why timing was so important. General Mathis explained that Wild Weasel anti-radar aircraft would be poised to hit any North Korean SAM site within 60 seconds of a launch against the SR-71. The time constraint would ensure that the attack aircraft were headed in the right direction at the moment a missile was launched. President Reagan had personally approved the plan.

Operational sorties to the 'Z' continued to be flown along the amended route until Monday 26 October 1981. Following extensive mission planning and detailed briefings, BC Thomas and Jay Reid took-off from Kadena exactly on time in '975. All four of these high-priority missions were ground-spared as insurance against an abort of the

Tensions were strained to almost breaking point on 26 August 1981, when North Korea fired two SA-2s at an SR-71 conducting a PARPRO mission in international airspace. The RSO and pilot of that flight were ED McKim and Maury Rosenberg, respectively; the latter is pictured second from the left. (Paul F. Crickmore Collection)

primary aircraft. BC recalled: 'We had to employ the timing triangles to lose a few minutes of "pad"; we also delayed with the tanker all the way to the end of the second air refuelling for the same reason. We flew over the critical point within ten seconds of the designated time feeling very proud of ourselves.

'We all felt this mission, which had such importance attached to it, and all of the preparation that had gone into it, was the pinnacle of our professional efforts. Even though there was no firing, I experienced the greatest sense of well being, knowing we did the whole operation "exactly as planned". I must admit that I'd hoped that the North Koreans would fire at us. Their missile capability never bothered us, and I believe that it is fair for me to say that by immediately smashing their launch facility, our national resolve would have been most graphically demonstrated.'

For whatever reason, the North Koreans chose not to launch a missile at this or any other trawling mission, and BC, and all who followed him, recovered safely after each four-hour flight.

The flight profile devised to monitor North Korea meant that crews new to the Senior Crown programme would initially cut their first operational teeth in this theatre, rather than in the more constrained airspace over Europe. Major

Curt Osterheld, an RSO, eloquently describes an incident that occurred during his first operational tour as a Captain in aircraft '976, on 23 January 1984. 'There were many rewards of being a crewmember in the SR-71. After the long first year of initial training, one of the biggest rewards was to embark on your first operational tour to Kadena Air Base, Okinawa, Japan. This was where you would finally win your Habu patch, as well as experience the many hallowed traditions of the island paradise.

'I was privileged to fly with Joe Matthews as my front seater and accomplice in numerous adventures. Joe was a superb pilot. We'd served together before in RF-4C Phantoms, an aircraft which is deserving of its own book of flyer's tales.

'We'd had our share of emergencies during our training at Beale, but that really is to be expected. The simulator and student sorties were intended to build not just your knowledge of the jet but confidence that you could handle whatever the airplane had in store for you. It's only fair to reiterate that since each SR-71 was "handcrafted", each aircraft had something different up its sleeve for the unwary.

'Our first couple of sorties from Kadena were the perfunctory island orientation ride, then a "single-loop" mission just south of the Korean Demilitarized Zone (DMZ). The latter qualified us for the Habu patch, so now we could savour the accomplishment of being fully operational SR-71 crewmembers.

'The "savouring" dissipated slightly during our next operational mission, as we were challenged with a series of malfunctions that left us, for a time, completely mystified.

'The mission objectives were to perform electronic intelligence gathering over the Yellow Sea, then make a standard photo run over the Korean DMZ. Everything was pretty routine through the first air-to-air refuelling. Then, during the climb to operating speed and altitude, we began to encounter some moderate clear air turbulence. From the cockpit, this feels much like sitting on the end of a diving board as it oscillates up and down. At approximately 45,000 ft [13716 m] and Mach 1.4, there was a severe jolt that knocked our helmets against the canopy. After that, the air seemed to smooth out and we continued the climb/acceleration.

'At Mach 3 and 79,000 ft [24079 m], we seemed to be well on our way when, for seemingly no reason, the autopilot disengaged. Our centre of gravity was not where it was supposed to be, and fuel readings were erratic. Joe was fighting with the pitch trim and the autopilot would "kick off" just as soon as it was engaged. I was using the manual circular computer to "spin" the cg over and over again, not believing the calculations.

'Now we were 4,000 lb [1814 kg] down on the "fuel curve", or our planned amount of fuel for a specific point in the mission. Then 5,000. Then 6,000. Joe was using the small periscope to scan behind the aircraft for fuel leaks, but with its very limited field of view, could see nothing abnormal. Again the autopilot kicked off. And now the nitrogen that served as our inerting atmosphere for the fuel tanks was depleting rapidly.

'Our options became very limited. With our remaining fuel, we couldn't continue with the mission and had to abort back to Kadena. Truly a disappointing choice to make, as you are admitting failure. I made the required abort calls over the HF radio, telling the whole world we were heading home a lot sooner than planned.

'The descent was spiced up with a couple of unstarts, but finally we were subsonic and only 80 miles [129 km] away from Kadena. The mysterious fuel loss had stabilised and it seemed that now we could make a normal recovery. There were a few brief moments for Joe and I to discuss "what the hell was all that?" and other topics, before talking with approach control. Both of us were wondering what we had done wrong, and what would be the Detachment Commander's reaction.

'Joe made a great landing which was followed quickly by an expletive over the intercom and news that the drag chute had not deployed. Some judicious use of the SR-71's powerful brakes got us stopped and we didn't have to use the emergency barrier. The barrier was a large diameter cable that pops up from the runway and catches the two main gear struts. I imagine the effect on the landing gear doors would have been very ugly.

'Taxiing in we ran the appropriate checklists and wondered, "what next?" As we pulled into the hangar, a number of the maintenance folks were pointing, wide-eyed, to the back of the aircraft.

'After shutting down the engines, we had a large contingent of folks swarming over the airplane. Joe and I climbed out, took off the Lockheed ejection-seat "spurs" from our boots and put on protective boot covers. On the right wing, near the fuselage, was a jagged 10-in [25-cm] gash that looked like it had been made with a can opener. The drag chute that hadn't deployed on landing was missing all together, as was the right drag chute compartment door from the top of the fuselage.

'So we began to piece the mystery together. That jolt of clear air turbulence we felt at 45,000 ft popped the right drag chute compartment door open and, once in the slipstream, punctured the right wing and fuel tank No. 6 as it departed the aircraft. The drag chute was then sucked from its shallow tub along the top of the fuselage. The genius of Kelly Johnson's engineering was evident

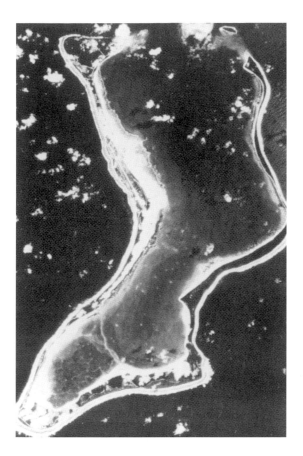

SR-71 64-17962 took this photograph of Diego Garcia in the Indian Ocean. The island was prepared for SR-71 operations, but in the event no missions were launched from this British territory. (USAF)

here. The large drag chute was connected to the aircraft by a ball-and-jaws type joint. The jaws only closed around the ball when the pilot pulled the drag chute handle. Therefore, when the drag chute compartment door opened accidentally, the drag chute, still in a bundle and not attached to the jet, could fall away free from the aircraft. One can imagine the aerodynamic loads placed on the aircraft, even for a brief time, if the chute deployed at supersonic speeds connected firmly to the middle of the aircraft!

'The gash in the wing/fuel tank explained the rest. Approximately 6,000 lb [2722 kg] vented through this hole, along with the nitrogen. This upset the delicate balance of the centre of gravity and caused erratic readings as the fuel transfer system attempted to fix the imbalance. This would cause transients in the pitch trim, which in turn would automatically disengage the autopilot. All very logical when you're standing on the ground.

'This whole experience did have an upside. The instructors in the simulator now had a baffling new scenario with which to humiliate their students. Joe

and I received little pink bunnies from our senior crew, to provide us with four "lucky" rabbit's feet so something like this wouldn't happen again. And we were beginning to feel like experienced Habus. Even if it was just our first tour.'

US EMBASSY HOSTAGE CRISIS

In the face of a resurgence in Islamic fundamentalism, the pro-US Shah of Iran was driven into exile on 16 January 1979. Iranian anti-US feelings grew progressively worse and when, in October, the exiled Shah was operated on in a New York hospital and diagnosed as suffering from cancer, Ayatollah Khalkhali urged Moslems to 'drag him out of his hospital bed and dismember him.' Worse was to follow on 4 November 1979 when the clerics' fanatical followers stormed the United States Embassy in Tehran, brushed aside Marine guards and occupied the building, taking nearly 100 embassy staff and Marines hostage. Over the next few weeks non-US citizens were released and on 25 April 1980, in an operation code-named Eagle Claw and mounted by America's crack Delta Force, an attempt was made to free the remaining 53 diplomatic hostages. Alas, the audacious raid went catastrophically wrong and eight would-be rescuers were killed in the desert 200 miles (322 km) southeast of their objective. For President Carter it was an international humiliation.

The collection of intelligence concerning the hostages was code-named Snowbird, and this continued, as did military planning for another possible rescue attempt, code-named Double Star. But the only substantial intelligence assets available to the US after the aborted April rescue attempt were satellites. Various other actions were contemplated, including leaflet dropping, although it is still not apparent what such an activity was hoping to achieve. Subsequently, on 26 June 1980, a feasibility study and cost estimate schedule was requested from Lockheed ADP to provide an SR-71 with such a leaflet capability. This was provided by Lockheed on 9 July wherein it was envisaged that the system would be designed for internal installation in the existing TROC camera bay, and capable of dispensing 10,000 leaflets, with the system being activated by air-charged initiators and powered by 1,000 lb (4.45-kN) force actuators. Four systems, it noted, would be built, two flight-tested and two made available for operational use, at a cost of $2.2 million. Nothing ever came of the idea, however.

The other plan involved US use of certain airfields near Tehran, from where a second rescue attempt would be launched. However, when it was learned that the Iranians might be attempting to block the runways of these airfields, the JCS requested that action be initiated to investigate the

Majors Mike Smith and Doug Soifer were the first to fly a Persian Gulf sortie, on 22 July 1987. The aircraft used was '962, after a last-minute change when '975's ANS failed, and the mission lasted more than 11 hours. (USAF)

feasibility of an SR-71 overflying, using its HRR to define such obstructions. In response, an SR-71 mission was flown over Condron Auxiliary Air Field, White Sands, New Mexico on the night of 27 June when its runway was clear. A second sortie was flown over the same airfield on the night of 30 June, after a combination of vehicles, steel drums, tires, rocks, wire cable, logs and dirt piles had been heaped along the runway's edge. A qualified photo interpreter then completed an analysis of the SR-71's HRR imagery to ascertain what level of obstruction could be detected. In a memo for the record, classified Top Secret and dated 9 July 1980, it was decided that the CAPRE system then equipping the SR-71 fleet was, 'capable of detection of runway obstructions expected to be of concern for project Double Star … '

On 3 November 1980, Maj-Gen James B. Vaught of the JCS submitted a Top Secret memo to the Joint Reconnaissance Center, the subject: SR-71 Mission Request. It set out the following:

'1. Request consideration be given to conducting several SR-71 surveillance missions of the Persian Gulf during the next 3–6 weeks.

'2. Purpose of mission is to determine locations of major oil-rig concentrations and typical flow pattern of Gulf shipping to assist in selection of low-level air penetration routes.

'3. Recognize that missions could raise Soviet/Iran/ME speculation; however, given irregular scheduling, direct association with any US military planning will probably be low. On the other hand, periodic SR-71 missions would provide "reason" for increased tanker support in the area prior to the execution of any US military contingency action.'

Despite the request, immediate action was not forthcoming and Det 1 was not tasked to perform these sorties – operations into this area would have to wait for another seven years. So with the request on the backburner, diplomatic efforts intensified, and finally come to fruition on 21 January 1981, when the remaining 52 hostages were released after a mammoth 444 days in captivity.

IRAN-IRAQ WAR

On 24 September 1980, a simmering border war between Iraq and Iran flared into full-scale hostilities when Iraqi troops and tanks crashed across the border. Their dawn attack set the world's largest oil refinery, and many of Abadan's oil storage tanks, ablaze. The Iraqis quickly seized the port of Khorramshahr, as they advanced 10 miles (16 km) into Iranian territory. Despite initial successes by the Iraqi army, the war turned into a stalemate with both sides digging in and fighting a long and bloody trench war, not too dissimilar to the battles fought in Flanders and Verdun some 65 years earlier.

Both the USSR and the US made it clear that they would not get involved and that they would remain strictly neutral. However, the US intelligence community fully understood how easy it would be for Iran to exploit the 'oil pressure point.'

On 24 May 1984, two Iranian aircraft attacked an oil tanker off the Saudi Arabian coast. As countercharges continued over the next few years, Iraq's jets attacked the key Iranian oil terminals on Kharg Island and the Iranians attacked oil-laden supertankers bound for the West from Kuwait, Saudi Arabia and Bahrain. To offer greater protection to these unarmed vessels, the US government planned to reflag such vessels as American ships and to escort them through the choke point at the Straits of Hormuz.

On 18 May 1987, two Iraqi Dassault Mirage F1s, each carrying an AM39 Exocet anti-ship missile, locked onto a surface target in the waters north of Bahrain. They both fired their sea-skimming missiles 12 miles (19 km) from the target; fortunately the warhead on one of the weapons failed to explode. The other missile, however, worked with devastating effect, hitting the frigate USS *Stark*, killing 28 sailors and leaving the sleek warship disabled and burning. President Reagan immediately demanded an Iraqi explanation for the attack, which a Baghdad spokesman said was due to the pilots identifying the frigate as Iranian.

The situation, particularly in the Gulf, continued to escalate, and on 22 July 1987, Majs Mike Smith and Doug Soifer were the first to fly four very long, non-stop SR-71 reconnaissance missions from Kadena into the Gulf region. Majs Ed Yeilding and Curt Osterheld backed them up as the spare crew in '967. As the primary crew stepped from the PSD van toward their aircraft, serial 64-17975, Col Tom Alison and Lt-Col Tom Henichek (the Det commander and ops officer, respectively) informed them both that '975's ANS had not checked out properly and that they would have to take '967 instead. Ed and Curt would follow in '975 after its ANS problem was resolved.

The 11-hour sortie would involve two refuellings on the outbound leg and three on the return. As Mike and Doug approached their second aerial rendezvous, Doug called Ed and Curt, who were two hours behind in '967 and told them that everything was progressing well and that their services would not be required that day. The most distant second and third tankings were to be carried out by three KC-10s before and after '967 had flown over the 'cuckoo's nest'. The KC-10s were able to extend their own ranges by buddy refuelling, something which the KC-135Q was unable to do. As a result of this, Mike was able to take on distant pre- and post-target split onloads from the two tankers during each AR.

The cloud cover had been almost continually undercast since they left Kadena, and as '967 was equipped with Technical Objective Cameras and an Optical Bar Panoramic Camera, it looked as if the mission could prove to be a very expensive failure. After much 'gas guzzling', they headed out 'hot and high' to boom the Gulf region, when suddenly the undercast disappeared and conditions were perfect for their high-resolution cameras to do some of their finest work. Their fifth and final AR was completed ten hours after take-off. This night refuelling was complicated by the failure of one of the KC-10's boom lights, which made proper formation flying (in the close-in contact position) very difficult. Despite that added strain to an already tiring flight (at the near limit of an SR-71's and an aircrew's flight endurance), Mike landed an almost 'zero write-up' Habu back at Kadena after a flight lasting 11 hours and 12 minutes.

On 9 August, Majs Terry Pappas and John Manzi left Kadena in '975 and headed out for the first of many aerial refuellings. After clearing the first tanker, they climbed and accelerated toward Southeast Asia and then on south of India toward a second refuelling and their distant target area. Five hours after take-off they neared the collection area in the Persian Gulf. Everything had worked exactly as planned and soon they were heading eastbound on their long trip back to Kadena. It had not been a simple, straightforward mission by any stretch of the imagination, however. Bad weather during two of the refuellings and a boom malfunction dictated that Terry had to maintain his contact position with the tankers for three hours 30 minutes during the mission. To make matters worse, nine hours into the sortie he became temporarily blinded by the combined effects of pure oxygen and an overheat condition which had affected his 'moon suit's' faceplate. The simple task of reading his instruments appeared almost impossible without opening his helmet visor, but such action was out of the question due to the greater dangers of decompression and hypoxia. Terry recalls that by squinting hard he could produce tears. That small bit of moisture revived his vision enough to continue the long mission. He finally completed the sortie with a smooth night landing back at Kadena after flying for more than 11 hours.

Later in the summer of 1987, US intelligence believed that the Iranians had acquired a consignment of land-based 'Silkworm' (HY-2) anti-ship missiles from China. The weapon had a maximum range of about 60 miles (97 km) and employed active radar homing to locate its target. In September 1987 the Iranians began launching the weapons from the Al Faw peninsula at Kuwaiti oil terminals about 50 miles (80 km) away. Initially the weapons missed their targets and fell on uninhabited parts of the coastline, but on 22 October a 'Silkworm' slammed into a Kuwaiti oil loading facility at Sea Island. Its 1,100-lb (499-kg) warhead caused extensive damage and triggered a major fire. Just four days after this attack, Majs Warren McKendree and Randy Shelhorse completed their first Gulf sortie in aircraft '967.

Utilising surveillance information gathered from these flights and by satellite, US intelligence was able to determine the most likely positions from where future deployment of the Iranian 'Silkworms' could threaten the Kuwaiti oil terminals. A brilliant civil servant who was an expert in decoys and worked at the Naval Research Laboratory in Washington DC devised a simple and cost effective solution to the problem by placing large corner reflectors on barges. Utilising the available imagery, these barges were then anchored between the likely launch sites and the potential targets. On 7 December the Iranians launched a 'Silkworm' against a Kuwaiti oil pumping station. The decoy worked as planned, the 'Silkworm' struck one of the barge-mounted reflectors, its short fuse delay detonating the warhead and blowing the unit off the barge. The missile's target was completely unscathed, no one was injured in the attack and afterwards no further 'Silkworms' were launched against the oil terminals.

Majs Dan House and Blair Bozek completed the last of these long-duration, high-priority missions in aircraft '974, on 30 April 1988. In addition to revealing the presence of Iranian 'Silkworms', the sorties also gathered extensive intelligence about the masses of military equipment in the Gulf. Thus, intelligence services were able to forewarn the US Navy of the 'Silkworm' threat, and diplomats were able to bring pressure to bear on Iran. The SR-71 had again performed its intelligence-gathering service in a distant part of the world.

In earlier times, the crews would surely have received Distinguished Flying Crosses for these unique and important missions, but these sorties were being flown at the very time when the Chief of Staff, and other key SR-71 detractors, were undermining the Senior Crown programme because of its costs. The last thing they wanted were 'Habu Heroes'. Therefore, the crews were only awarded Air Medals.

Wearing the later model pressure suits, this Habu crew demonstrates the aircraft's tandem-cockpit layout. The RSO's position occupied what had been the Q bay in the A-12.

Palmdale's 'evergreen' '955 completes yet another test hop. By the time this jet was retired it had accumulated 1,993 hours 30 minutes of flying hours during 712 sorties. It was last flown on 24 January 1985 by Tom Tilden and Bill Flanagan. (USAF)

DUTCH 51, Bob Gilliland, was Lockheed's chief SR-71 test pilot. Here he is seen in one of the earliest S-901 pressure suits inside an SR-71 cockpit. The large 'RESCUE' marking is noteworthy, as is the red seat headrest and the very robust hydraulic ram holding the canopy open. (Lockheed Martin Skunk Works)

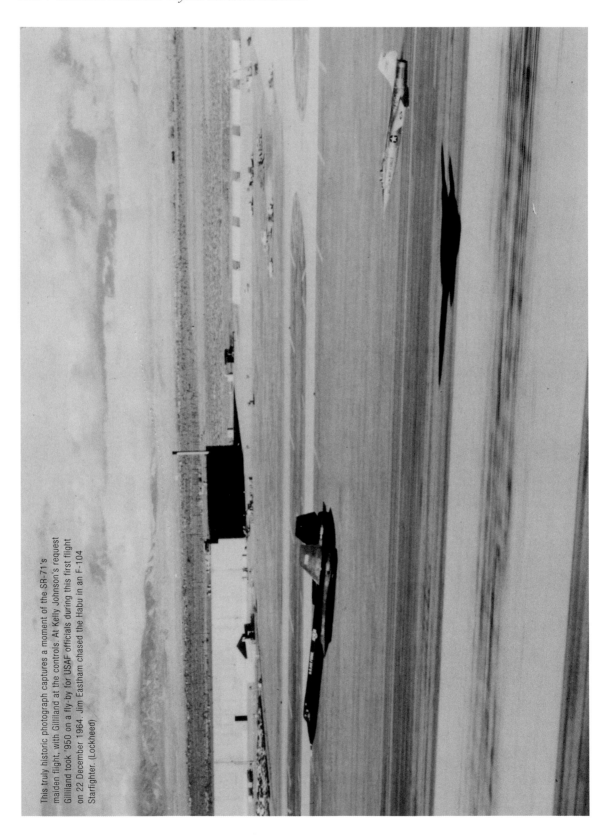

This truly historic photograph captures a moment of the SR-71's maiden flight, with Gilliland at the controls. At Kelly Johnson's request Gilliland took '950 on a fly-by for USAF officials during this first flight on 22 December 1964. Jim Eastham chased the Habu in an F-104 Starfighter. (Lockheed)

The raised cockpit of the SR-71B was very prominent, but had little effect on performance, apart from the reduction in directional stability that was solved by the addition of ventral fins. Tanker support was required in vast quantities for SR operations – both peacetime training missions and operational sorties – as the ranks of KC-135s in the background attest. The smaller, twin-engined jet immediately behind the Habu was the first twin-engined JetStar prototype. It was maintained by Lockheed for corporate communications for several years. (Lockheed)

64-17954 was lost on 11 April 1969 to a take-off accident at Edwards AFB. The aircraft had flown for the first time on 20 July 1965 and pilot Lt-Col Bill Skliar and RSO Maj Noel Warner escaped unhurt from the accident that finished its career. (USAF)

Aside from crew fatigue, the ultimate limiting factor on SR-71 mission endurance was nitrogen capacity. Gaseous nitrogen was used to pressurise both the TEB and fuel tanks as they became depleted, otherwise the part-occupied tanks would be crushed by increasing atmosphericpressure as the aircraft descended from cruise altitudes. (Lockheed)

A view from dead ahead was always likely to catch the Habu at its most sinister. Here the conical camber of the outer wings is very obvious, as is the inward cant of the intake spikes. The protrusions above the fuselage are the open brake chute bay doors. (Lockheed)

In the course of its service life, a military aircraft might be expected to wear a number of colour schemes; the KC-135Q illustrated here might well have gone from natural metal to Air Defense Command grey to this drab green over grey scheme. The SR-71, however, was different. Its very particular flight regime was extremely demanding on paint, the only formulation that worked being the familiar black colour. This proved expensive to develop, as did the red, white and blue paints for national insignia and US Air Force titles. Indeed, some sources report that NASA wanted to paint its SR-71s white in keeping with the rest of its fleet, but balked at the difficulties and expense of creating a white paint able to do the job. (Lockheed)

Palmdale's test aircraft, '955, caught in landing configuration, shows the Habu's snake-like forward fuselage contours to advantage. Again the Skunk Work's motif is visible on the aircraft's fin. (Lockheed)

The 'Big Tail' modification would have allowed additional countermeasures systems to combat newly-evolving radar-guided SAMs. Interestingly, no attempt was ever made to mask the Habu's IR signature, a fact which might well have proved to be its downfall had it encountered expertly flown MiG-25 or MiG-31 interceptors armed with IR-homing air-to-air missiles specifically developed by the USSR for 'Habu killing'. (Lockheed)

Before aircraft '974 was rotated back to Beale after a stint at Kadena, it was painted with tail art by its Crew Chief Don Person and his assistant SSgt Don Campbell. The aircraft was decorated in honour of the fact that at the time it had flown the most operational missions and its artwork took the form of a Habu snake entwined around a number '1' (for Det 1) and the wording *ICHI BAN*. Although applied unofficially, the artwork reportedly won the approval of Lt-Col Halloran when it was first seen at Beale. (Paul F. Crickmore Collection)

An SR-71 take-off was always a noisy affair, with the J58 turbojets in full afterburner and producing distinctive shock patterns in the aircraft's exhaust flame. At low speeds and altitudes the Habu's engine configuration was relatively inefficient, being optimised for high-speed, high-altitude cruising. Under optimum conditions, clever intake and nacelle design, using the variable intake spikes and bleed/bypass systems allowed much greater efficiency. (USAF)

Unlike the *ICHI BAN* artwork applied to '958 at Kadena, this rather more pointed artwork did not meet with official approval and was quickly removed. It was applied to '962's fin to mark the shutdown of Det 1. (via Don Emmons)

Below: Despite the prolonged and courageous efforts of Dan House and Blair Bozek to save '974, this aircraft has the dubious distinction of being the last SR-71 to be lost. (USAF)

SR-71A 64-17964 was flying a Barents Sea/Baltic Sea sortie on 6 October 1981, as MINTY 23, when this photograph was taken. After the tanker's 'boomer' had retracted the refuelling boom's nozzle from the Habu's receptacle, it was common for fuel to stream back along the Blackbird's uppersurfaces after a full top up, as has clearly been the case here. (Paul F. Crickmore)

A surprisingly large number of colourful artworks and badges was applied to various SR-71s over the years. From 24 October to 16 November 1977, '976 displayed large 9th SRW badges on its fins while detached to RAF Mildenhall. (L. Peacock)

DET 4 OPERATIONS
Chapter 9

GIANT REACH

Giant Reach was SAC's code name for the contingency planning of Europe-based SR-71 Photint and Elint gathering operations. The original plan was to split this coverage and conduct both Photint and Elint of the Middle East and purely Elint of Eastern Europe, weather conditions in northern latitudes usually being hostile to the collection of photographic imagery. In order to execute these preliminary proposals, first published by HQ SAC on 6 April 1970, it was envisaged that five KC-135Qs would be deployed to Incirlik AB, Turkey, and an SR-71, together with three KC-135s and support personnel would be assigned to Torrejon AB, Spain, on a 30-day TDY basis. However, the Spanish prohibited overt reconnaissance flights from originating from or recovering into their country consequently, that element of the proposal was modified and instead the SR-71 would be based at RAF Mildenhall, England. During these early planning stages it was thought that the SR-71 would conduct between six and eight sorties during each deployment and the photo-product would be processed by the 497th RTG, at Shierstein, West Germany, while the Elint and HRR 'take' would be ferried back to Beale and analysed by the 9th RTS. However, additional funds to support such operations were not initially available. Despite this, HQ USAF directed SAC to spend $50,000 from its Operation and Maintenance Budget on alterations to the apron adjacent to Hanger 538 at Mildenhall, as a precautionary measure in case the JCS directed that SR-71 sorties should go ahead; this construction work was duly completed in 1971.

The first operational requirement for Europe-based SR-71 sorties occurred on 6 October 1973, with the outbreak of the Yom Kippur War, but the UK government denied the Air Force the use of Mildenhall in what ultimately proved to be a futile attempt to secure the continued supply of Arab oil. As a consequence it was not until 1 September 1974 that the first Habu visited England. On that historic day, Majs Jim Sullivan and his RSO, Noel Widdifield, flying SR-71 '972, established a transatlantic world speed record between New York and London of less than two hours – a record that stands to this day. Four days later, Capt 'Buck' Adams and Maj Bill Machorek set a return trip record to Los Angeles, in the same aircraft, of less than four hours.

To underline the partnership status of any future SR-71 deployments to the United Kingdom, Secretary of State Henry Kissinger instructed Mrs Anne Armstrong, the US Ambassador to Britain, to inform Her Majesty's Government that the US: 'would of course be prepared to share with the British information produced by [such] SR-71 missions.'

Detailed route planning for any future SR-71 deployments to the UK was conducted by the Strategic Reconnaissance Center, which then sent details of three proposed tracks to the 98th Strategic Wing (SW) at Torrejon, Spain, as this unit was responsible for SAC operations from Mildenhall. Detachment 1 of the 98th SW, stationed at the UK base, then coordinated all necessary prior actions and notifications with the appropriate British officials.

On 20 April 1976, two KC-135Qs and the same SR-71 that had established the transatlantic speed records – aircraft '972 – returned once again to the UK, but this time the trip was made without the media coverage that accompanied its earlier brief visit. Using the call sign BURNS 31, Majs 'Pat' Bledsoe and John Fuller completed the flight from Beale to RAF Mildenhall in 4 hours 42 minutes. The key objective of this deployment was for the aircraft to complete two training sorties. The first was to be flown over both the North Sea and the Norwegian Sea and the second was to be conducted over the English Channel and the Bay of Biscay. These flights would both exercise the aircraft's base support facilities and help to shape the aircraft's flight profile and the operating procedures that would need to be adopted when flying in the cramped airspace of Northern Europe. Such actions would pave the way for future SR-71 participation in NATO training exercises, the first of which was scheduled for later that same year.

Three days after the Habu's arrival, the first evaluation sortie got underway when Capts Maury Rosenberg and Don Bulloch engaged both burners and departed the base. However, when they were to the west of Norway at 72,000 ft (21946 m), Bulloch discovered that the outside air temperature was 54°F (30°C) warmer than anticipated. After quickly recalculating the aircraft's performance values in this sub-Arctic environment by cross-correlating exhaust gas temperature against inlet door position and interpolating the aircraft's true airspeed from the astro-inertial navigation system, the crew were alarmed to learn that their computed fuel specifics were way off the mark, and their actual fuel burn considerably higher than that calculated by the nav-planners back at Mildenhall. In fact '972 was going to be 8,000 lb (3629 kg) lighter by the time they arrived at their air-refuelling control point, which meant that they would barely be able to reach their tankers. The crew prudently decided to abort the mission and return to Mildenhall. The second training sortie was completed by Bledsoe and Fuller on 28 April and two days later, using the call sign KABAB 31, Rosenberg and Bulloch returned '972 to Beale.

COLD FIRE AND TEAMWORK

Two large NATO exercises kicked-off in the autumn, Cold Fire '76, a land and air operation running from 7 to 10 September and conducted in West Germany, and Teamwork '76, a land, sea and air exercise to be held in the North and Norwegian Seas from 10 to 23 September. Headquarters European Command was keen that the SR-71 should participate in both exercises, pointing out that not only would this provide valuable training and logistical experience, but that it would also demonstrate 'positive US resolve in support of NATO'. Such participation would of course require authorisation from several command authorities, as well as the UK Ministry of Defence (MoD), the JCS, United States Air Forces Europe (USAFE) and NATO member nations. Luckily, negotiations to obtain prior approval for the SR-71

to overfly NATO countries and enter their airspace began early. As it turned out, the process was far from straight forward and took several months to complete – Denmark took it right to the wire and was the final country to grant its approval, in early September.

The deployment of aircraft '962 began on 2 September 1976, but Al Cirino and his RSO Bruce Liebman had to divert into Goose Bay, Labrador following engine trouble over the central United States. An emergency maintenance team was dispatched from Beale and the flight to Mildenhall was completed by Al and Bruce four days later. Majs Rich Graham and Don Emmons flew the following day in support of Teamwork '76 and incorporated lessons learned from the previous deployment. They successfully completed their mission over the North and Norwegian Seas before recovering safely back to 'The Hall'. Then it was Al and Bruce's turn. They were tasked to fly into West Germany in support of Cold Fire '76 and again '962 completed the mission satisfactorily. In total six sorties were flown and both HRR imagery, photography and Elint was collected from the exercise areas before Rich and Don returned the aircraft home after a European tour lasting 19 days.

Before the next Habu deployment to the UK, a change in SAC's European reporting structure took place following Senate ratification of a new treaty with the Spanish government in January 1976, which stipulated a reduced American military presence in that country. Consequently, on 31 December 1976 the 98th SW was deactivated. Command was transferred to the 306th Strategic Wing, which had been activated four months earlier and co-located with Headquarters USAFE at Ramstein AB, West Germany. General Richard Ellis, Commander in Chief, USAFE and CINCSAC, Gen Russell Dougherty – whom Gen Ellis succeeded as SAC Commander on 1 August 1977 – had had extensive

Resplendent with a 9th SRW badge emblazoned on its tail, aircraft '972 arrives at RAF Mildenhall on 9 April 1980 for 30 days of European reconnaissance service. (Paul F. Crickmore)

discussions in the months leading to this command restructure and had formulated a plan that would have a profound impact on the build-up of SAC assets in Europe.

It had been decided that the 306th SW commander would report directly to CINCSAC and his staff and that he had 'delegated authority' to exercise the CINCSAC's command responsibilities for all present and future SAC European operations. These related to the European Tanker Force and the RC-135s that were on TDY with the 306th SW's detachments at Mildenhall and Hellenikon AB, Greece, as well as any future B-52 or U-2R/SR-71 deployments.

The desire to increase SAC's presence in Europe had its roots in the changing nature of the Soviet/Warsaw Pact threat facing NATO. General Ellis wanted B-52s to deploy periodically to England, together with their support tankers, in order to train such a force to a level that was capable of performing a wartime tactical mission. This, he envisaged, would consist of interdiction both in the vicinity of the battle area and beyond its forward edge, airfield attack, defence suppression, sea surveillance and anti-shipping. It followed therefore that if B-52s were tasked to perform a mission similar in nature to that which they had flown for eight years in Southeast Asia, the U-2R and SR-71 would again be required to provide complementary pre-strike and bomb damage assessment imagery in addition to Sigint warning information. An additional issue of particular concern to Gen Ellis was the unprecedented level of sophistication that accompanied the twice-yearly Soviet/Warsaw Pact exercises that had begun on 31 December 1976. Specifically he noted: 'Of particular interest to us at SAC is their coordinated and extensive use of airborne command posts as alternate command centres and their ability to control forces when required, particularly during/after a global nuclear exchange.' On balance therefore, it is perhaps not surprising that as far as the General was concerned, it was 'most desirous' that the SR-71 and U-2R deploy to RAF Mildenhall to monitor these exercises.

The third SR-71 training deployment was completed by '958, which arrived as RING 21 on 7 January 1977. Again Rich Graham was at the helm with Don Emmons 'in the back'. In support, two KC-135Qs transported 65 maintenance, operations and logistics specialists, together with 80,000 lb (36288 kg) of equipment. Col John Storrie, the 9th SRW commander, also accompanied the deployment to inspect for himself Mildenhall's support facilities. This ten-day deployment was timed to coincide with the approximate date of President Jimmy Carter's inauguration and it would thereby underline the United States' continued support of its NATO allies. Two training sorties were again flown by the SR-71, covering the same sea areas as the April 1976 deployment. Majors Tom Alison and his RSO JT Vida, made up the second SR crew on this deployment and it was them that repositioned the aircraft back to Beale as PAVER 86.

In late February 1977, Headquarters SAC proposed to the JCS that it seek approval for the SR-71's first-ever operational deployment to Europe. It was proposed that the 17-day tour should consist of one training sortie, similar to the two completed in January 1977, and two Peacetime Aerial Reconnaissance Programme (PARPRO) missions; the first of these would be a coordinated sortie with a Mildenhall-based RC-135V and flown along the Barents Sea periphery, while the second sortie would be flown over West Germany. SAC requested that both of the PARPRO missions be approved to collect Elint and HRR imagery, since it was particularly anxious to demonstrate the unique characteristics of the latter to other potential national intelligence users. While the proposal navigated its way through the JCS evaluation process, the SRC worked on preparing the aircraft's tracks in anticipation of receiving an affirmative for the deployment. The JCS duly issued SAC with the necessary authorisation to proceed on 6 May 1977; it was instructed that the SR-71 was to adhere to tracks prepared earlier in the year by the SRC, as these had been used by the State Department to coordinate and obtain the necessary clearances from five NATO nations through whose airspace the SR-71 would fly. The JCS also went on to direct Headquarters SAC to deploy to Mildenhall a Mobile Processing Center held in storage at Beale. This last instruction was issued in response to a request from Gen Ellis, and as such had been anticipated by SAC.

MPC

In 1977 two MPCs existed. In addition to the one alluded to by the JCS, the other (MPC 1), was in caretaker status at Kadena AB. Each MPC consisted of 24 trailer-like vans that measured 8 × 8 × 40 ft (2.44 × 2.44 × 12.19 m) and collectively contained all the equipment necessary to process raw intelligence data collected by the SR-71's HRR and cameras (MPC 1 was also equipped with an EMR formatter that processed the Elint tapes. At a cost of over a $1 million each (mid-1960s values), it had been decided that only one MPC would have this additional capability). The MPC could be deployed overseas in various tailored packages or van combinations to support different levels and types of reconnaissance operation. The complete package was designed to support one SR-71 mission per day and required an operating staff of 60 officers, airmen and civilian contractors. Dependent upon the amount of data collected, typically photography and HRR imagery was available to the interpreters four hours after the Habu had landed (MPC 1 also afforded top-line Elint signals ready for first-stage analysis in about three hours). The entire 24-van package of MPC 2, destined for Mildenhall, weighed in at 290,000 lb (131544 kg) and was transported to the UK in two C-5s and four C-141s. The transportation costs were picked up by USAFE, but manpower and payment for expendable supplies came from SAC monies already allocated. On arrival in the UK, MPC II was located inside a secure compound, within Hanger 538, and at great credit to all involved, the facility was operational when INDY 69, aircraft '958, touched down at the UK base on 16 May 1977.

FIRST OPERATIONAL DEPLOYMENT TO UK

'Buzz' Carpenter now describes the positioning of INDY 69 to the UK for that historic first deployment: 'John Murphy, my RSO, and I, had just completed our first tour overseas at Kadena AB, where we had flown our first operational SR-71 missions. This is where all crews first went after they had completed their year of training at Beale AFB and where you were closely supervised and guided through your first few missions, both training and then operational.

'Returning from Kadena we felt we were too junior to be eligible to deploy to England for these missions. Precedent had always been that the senior crews executed these missions from Europe or any other new locations. However, Col Willie Lawson, then Director of Operations for the 9th SRW, decided that to keep the SR-71 crew force balanced in experience and time away from home, he would allow newer crews who had completed their first Kadena tour to be in the pool to meet these new tasks.

'John and I were delighted and honoured as the most junior crew when we were told we would fly the SR-71 to Mildenhall and stay there for this deployment. We were both excited about this opportunity and most appreciative of the confidence Col Lawson had put in us.

'The mission to England was not any longer than any mission we had already flown with two refuellings. Differences lay in the arrival procedures for the SR-71 entering the United Kingdom and the airfield familiarity of Mildenhall itself. Because of English weather conditions we normally departed California at about 2:00 am, which, after two refuellings and two hot legs in the four-hour flight, got you into England in the middle of the afternoon.

'These missions were supposed to be secret and had been coordinated through the special offices in each of the FAA regional centres we would fly through until entering Canadian airspace. Canadian air traffic centres provided this same level of special support. This idea was to protect our route of flight and also to keep our destination

SR-71 '974 arrived in England on 30 April 1982 for an eight-month stint of European service. The aircraft had been one of the initial cadre of three SR-71s deployed to Kadena and was lost from that base in 1989. (L. Peacock)

unknown. Secrecy was supposed to be a very important mission factor. We went into work the day before departure as always to mission plan and to get everything checked out. Later in the afternoon, we each took a sleeping pill to ensure we got the required crew rest. Around 11:00 pm we awoke and headed to the Physiological Support Division for our preflight physical, pick-up our mission materials, have our preflight meal of steak and eggs and meet with the back-up mobile crew to determine the status of our aircraft. Suiting up started around 1 hour before take-off so that we could arrive at the aircraft about 45 minutes before our 2:00 am take-off slot.

'As I remember everything went smoothly until I discovered that my helmet face heater was not working after I had been strapped into the aircraft, this caused my glass faceplate to completely fog over. Spares were normally available and a replacement helmet was quickly found and installed on my pressure suit. We then blasted off into the darkness at exactly the prescribed time of 2:00 in the morning. About 150 miles [241 km] from Beale out over the Nevada desert we hooked up with our awaiting tankers at 25,000 ft [7620 m]. During the refuelling we took on about 60,000 lb [27216 kg] of fuel (8,000 US gal/30283 litres plus) and dropped off the tanker over northern Utah and started our climb and accel. Passing through 60,000 we would routinely call the air traffic centre, as we turned off our electronic altitude reporting at this point. Salt Lake Center said, "Roger INDY 69, have a great time in Jolly Old England." So much for mission security! We had not said anything, so we felt we would be exonerated. Cruise leg was uneventful as we passed over the northern United States and into Canadian airspace at Mach 3.0 and above 75,000 ft [22860 m]. I remember it was a moonless night, which when flying over areas thinly populated gives you an opportunity to see a vast array of twinkling stars that you don't see on the ground because of their lack of intensity and the atmosphere filters them out.

'As we approached the Canadian east coast near Goose Bay, Labrador, the sun was starting to rise as we were descending and decelerating. This particular condition was wonderful to view from 75,000 ft, yet one of the most difficult for refuellings, because as you were under the tanker, at 25,000 ft, trying to maintain your position and monitor the tanker refuelling director lights on the belly of the aircraft, the sun was just above the horizon and right in your eyes. It blinded you, even with your helmet sun visor down. With the refuelling done, we then separate from the tanker again and start our climb and acceleration eastward over the Atlantic and on into Scotland. As we crossed, Greenland was partly visible and a

couple of huge icebergs were seen slowly floating south. Iceland was completely shrouded in clouds, as usual, and the weather in England was going to be overcast with rain.

'Our descent and deceleration was normal and brought us over England subsonic and we proceeded south and east to Mildenhall. About 50 miles [80 km] out we made contact with our mobile crew for recovery, Tom Alison and JT Vida. They advised us of the weather and to look for the birdwatchers. Initially John and I were puzzled by the "birdwatchers" remark. As it turns out, about half an hour before our arrival, a couple of hundred "aircraft birdwatchers" showed up with their cameras to photograph our arrival! Again, so much for security involving our flight over. The "birdwatcher net" sure trumped our security plan.

'Arrival was uneventful and after a precision approach I choose to take the aircraft around for one visual approach. One could see "birdwatchers" with their cameras at all the opportune spots around the airfield fence. Some even waved to us as we taxied to our parking hangar!'

On 18 May '958 satisfactorily completed the JCS-directed training sortie over the North Sea. The aircraft was configured with the same sensor package that it would carry aloft during the two operational missions, namely the nose mounted HRR, Elint sensors in the two aft mission bays (bays S and T) and a full DEF system.

20 MAY 1977

Tom Alison now recollects that historic first operational mission from Mildenhall: 'JT Vida, my RSO, and I arrived at RAF Mildenhall via a KC-135Q along with the TDY Detachment Commander, Col Willie Lawson, and the Nav/Planner, Lt-Col Red Winters. This particular mission was tasked at the Top Secret level using High Resolution Radar imagery and Elint sensors against the Soviet Union's submarine base at Murmansk on the coast of the Barents Sea, it was also scheduled as a coordinated mission with an RC-135V Rivet Joint.

'It was a little unusual for a PARPRO mission to be classified Top Secret, but JT and I just thought that was because it was a coordinated sortie and one of the first to go in the area around Murmansk. It may also have been due to the fact that the Soviets had deployed the SA-5 surface-to-air missile in the Murmansk area and it would be one of the first occasions that the SR-71 had been used in an area where there were known SA-5s, a much more capable SAM than the SA-2, which was widely deployed and was not considered an extreme threat to the Blackbird.

'During the mission planning session the day before, it was discovered that the Soviets had

Majs Jack Madison and Steve Lee stand in front of Det 4's very 'Anglophied' emblem at RAF Mildenhall. As a British base in use by American forces, Mildenhall retained the RAF title of its 'owners'. (Paul F. Crickmore)

issued a Notice To Airmen (NOTAM) warning of surface-to-air missile test firing from the surface to in excess of 100,000 ft [30480 m]. The coordinates of the area were off the coast of Murmansk and bracketed very nicely the only place on the mission where we would fly through the same area twice, going in and coming out. We were always concerned about prior awareness relating to SR-71 missions and this seemed like a highly improbable coincidence. Maybe, somehow, the word about our mission had leaked.

'Although at the time JT and I were not really aware of it, it seems that in some quarters this possible security leak caused quite a bit of concern. Apparently there were several secure phone calls made between RAF Mildenhall and the SAC Strategic Reconnaissance Center and the discussion centred on whether or not to cancel the mission based on the NOTAM. It should be noted that the mission track was planned entirely in international airspace. If we stayed on the "black line" we would never enter Soviet airspace. However, that said, the mission was planned to obtain maximum information concerning the submarine activities and area defences. At one point during the second pass through the area the Blackbird was planned to be heading directly at the submarine base, perpendicular to the coastline at Mach 3.15. At a certain point we began a high bank turn that would put us parallel to the coastline headed out of the area. That point was right in the centre of the "missile-firing box" outlined by the NOTAM.

'The concern centred on whether the Soviets would actually fire an SA-5 against an aircraft in international airspace. "Intent" was always a key word in a situation like this. Another concern was that the SA-5 was still relatively new and unknown in terms of RF indications and performance. We were later told that Kelly Johnson was actually part of the conference and his position was that we should not fly the mission as scheduled. In the end though, it was

BC Thomas, on the left, and Jay Reid were the first crew to land an SR-71 on a Continental European base. On 12 August 1981 they diverted '964 into Bødo, Norway. (via BC Thomas)

determined that the sortie would be flown as scheduled.

'The following day we all got airborne on time, the RC-135, the "Q models," and the Blackbird. Our mission profile was normal through the refuellings, but as we began our climb and acceleration to Mach 3+ cruise prior to entering the target area it became obvious that the outside air temperature was much higher than we expected and were used to. This causes the climb/accel to be slower than normal. It was so hot, and our performance so degraded, that at the point where we should have been level at Mach 3.15 and 75,000 ft [22860 m], we were just passing 60,000 ft [18288 m] and still climbing, and we were only accelling through about 2.8 Mach. JT and I were discussing our situation and he mentioned that the radar sensor had just come on. We had never had it come on while we were still climbing before. Additionally, the slower performance caused us to be well below the planned fuel curve. Decisions, decisions.

'We decided to press on and finally got levelled off and up to our desired cruise speed. We actually pushed the Mach up a little to try and help ourselves get back on the fuel curve. Although I knew we would never be able to make up all of it, I was comfortable that we would be able to get back to the tankers for the next air refuelling – if nothing else went wrong. And, in fact, that is just what happened. We completed both passes through the target area, and the missile firing warning area, with very little reaction noted on our defensive systems. The last air refuelling and the trip back to Mildenhall were uneventful. Just the way we liked it.

'During the debriefing following the flight we received word that we had already had a very successful mission, and our "radar take" had not even been processed yet. It seems the RC-135 Rivet Joint, which was in the target area for sometime before we arrived, had quite a bit of Soviet company in the form of interceptors. At the point in time where we were beginning to enter the area the "RC" crew became aware that the interceptors abruptly departed and the linguists monitoring the radios overheard the Soviet GCI trying to vector the interceptors to the SR-71. At least one interceptor pilot was heard to say, "I can see the contrail above and ahead. It is climbing at a very high speed and I will not be able to catch it." Heck, we already knew that!

'Further adding to the initial success of the mission was the first ever capture of the RF signals associated with the most recent SA-5 version, which was picked up by both our systems and the systems on the "RC". JT and I had spent 45 minutes in the "denied area," most of it at a little in excess of Mach 3 – just another day at the office.'

24 MAY MISSION

Buz Carpenter now recounts the second operational mission: 'Next flight up was for John and I to fly the tricky German mission. Like the Baltic mission one could not fly the aircraft at Mach 3.0 and make the turns to stay within the country border limits imposed upon us. In both cases while flying at Mach 2.8 a maximum 45° bank high-angle turn was required to stay within the confines. Because of aircraft energy management, a slight descent was sometimes required to maintain the 45° of bank and 2.8 Mach. These turns were planned for 42°, which gave you an additional 3° to utilise to maintain your critical ground track. The problem was, the steeper the bank, the more likely the loss of altitude in the turn. If you were flying in warmer than standard air temperatures, it further aggravated this energy management balance. Often we would descend a couple thousand feet just before the turn to give ourselves an energy advantage.

'To provide as much secrecy as possible, the mobile crew would reaffirm our take-off time and that our flight clearance was ready. With this check complete, we would initiate our engine start and aircraft systems check, without any radio calls, about 30 minutes prior to take-off. The Mildenhall control tower would flash a light to signal our clearance to taxi and to enter the runway for take-off. With the UK airspace deconfliction completed, a green light would be flashed to us from the tower and a radio-silent take-off would then occur.

'Traffic had been cleared from our path and we climbed unrestricted to 25,000 ft [7620 m] and headed out over the North Sea to meet our tankers. When the refuelling was completed, we executed a right turn to the southeast and initiated our climb and acceleration.

'Our entry target was to cross the German coast near Wilhelmshaven at Mach 2.8 above 70,000 ft [21336 m]. Our heading was almost due south, towards Kaiserslautern avoiding over flying major population areas. Below us most of the ground was covered with low clouds. This track was followed by a 30° bank turn to the southeast, passing southwest of Stuttgart and heading into Bavaria. Here the cloud cover broke and the landscape was a wonderful patch work of little villages, agricultural fields, and mountainous terrain; but now came the difficult manoeuvre to ensure that we maintained our track inside of West Germany, while flying south around Munich while executing a 45° high-bank turn. Luckily, during his particular day there were some clouds below and the cooler than standard upper air temperatures enabled us to maintain our altitude. During these turns, as much as one would have liked to have taken advantage of the spectacular views out of our down side turn window, full concentration was required to make sure one executed this high bank turn exactly as planned. Maintenance of the ground track was paramount, as this had been promised to America's national security leadership. Bank angles, Mach stability, engine performance, absolute ground track, and all other aircraft parameters had to be intensely monitored to start corrective actions if deviations become apparent. Nothing would be said in the turn unless it was essential to this turning process. The 180° plus turn placed us north of Nuremberg flying northwest beside the inner German border.

'Basically our sensors ran the whole time along the inner German border objective area. Once abeam Frankfurt, passing to the north, a turn north was completed to align us to depart Germany in the same coastal vicinity we had entered less than an hour earlier.

'Once clear of the coast, we started a 30° descending turn to the southwest. It took over 200 nm [230 miles; 370 km] to start a descent, decelerate and level off at 25,000 ft inbound to England. There was not much margin for error or any type of delay in the close confines we were operating in. This all happened very quickly and descents were another high activity time period to make sure the aircraft maintained those narrow flight parameters to allow for a safe descent. Engine compressor stalls could occur with engine flameouts if your tight descent profile was not maintained. Once below 2.4 Mach the profile became more flexible and at 1.8 Mach, with the inlet spikes full forward, there was even more latitude. This whole descent was designed to be ready to enter the UK landmass subsonic. Approaching England we would then break radio

silence and contact Northern Radar and follow their guidance for an instrument recovery back at Mildenhall. UK Air Traffic Control sector radar controllers and, when required, their precision radar approach controllers, were superb. This in part, maybe because of all the practice they receive with the UK's notorious weather!

'From operational missions a single approach full stop landing was always planned. After landing and deploying our huge orange drag chute, slowing was closely monitored and once below 80 kt [92 mph; 148 km/h], the drag chute would be jettisoned if there was not a severe cross wind. As we taxied in front of our parking hangar, the sensor crews were already in place to immediately download the sensors and process what we had collected, after we had stopped. As the engines were shut down the sensor crews were already under the aircraft opening hatches and by the time John and I stepped from the cockpit most of them had already been downloaded. Aircraft systems and anything unusual from the mission were debriefed at planeside before we were driven back to the PSD building and de-suited. This would be followed by extensive debriefs and then it was our turn to assume the mobile back up position for Tom and JT for their next scheduled mission.

'As a postscript, about two weeks later we were informed that our TDY at Mildenhall had been extended to support the Air Tattoo celebrating the Queen's Silver Jubilee. A two-day open house would attract well over 100,000 visitors and the SR-71 would be on its first UK public display since setting the speed record from New York to London in 1974.

'The SR-71 would be part of the static display, but roped off, so people could not touch the aircraft. We had been advised to watch for representatives from the Soviet Union and eastern satellite countries, trying to get too close to the aircraft and securing material samples. To prevent the Russians or anyone else from exploiting the display, no sensors were left on the aircraft, all fuel had been removed from the tanks and the aircraft was heat soaked to ambient temperatures to prevent infra-red cameras from discovering the secrets of the aircraft's internal structure and support systems. As we four crewmembers were standing around the aircraft answering questions from the crowd, sure enough the Russians showed up in numbers. They took numerous regular and infra-red photos and some of the Russians even had hidden microphones. They were a sight to see, coming up like a covey of quail. It looked like the Salvation Army had outfitted them. Their dress sense was that from a 1930s' movie about American mobsters. Attired in bulky double-breasted suits made from rougher cloth than one normally sees and all clustered around each other waiting for their leader to act. The head of the Soviet delegation, a former MiG-23 fighter pilot, was quite relaxed and talkative in his demeanour and invited John and I to sometime drop in on Vladivostok in the Far East as a gesture of peaceful relationships. We just quipped, "Please forward that request to our State Department." The British open house audiences are much more aviation literate than their American counterparts. Tough aeronautical questions were often asked, as we stood by the aircraft in the static display, but a great time was had by all with wonderful weather and spectacular flying demonstrations.'

On 31 May 1977, Tom and JT redeployed '958 back to Beale AFB using the call sign RESAY 35.

ANOTHER RE-STRUCTURE AND DEPLOYMENT

To improve the command and control of its forces in Europe and to further strengthen liaison between CINCSAC and the US and Allied commanders in Europe, Headquarters SAC activated the 7th Air Division at Ramstein AB, West Germany, on 1 July 1978, as a direct reporting unit. It also moved 'on-paper' the 306th Strategic Wing from Ramstein to RAF Mildenhall, which until this date had been Detachment 1 of the 306th at the UK base.

Even before the Habu's first European operational deployment had begun, planning was underway for a second, which was scheduled to occur in the autumn of 1977. European commanders were anxious that the SR-71 should again participate in exercise Cold Fire. However, recce specialists at HQ SAC were sceptical as to the value of such an exercise, mindful of the limitations imposed upon the aircraft's sensors when forced to adopt a highly restrictive flight profile in order to conform with political considerations based upon Switzerland, Austria and France's decision to deny the SR-71 clearance to overfly.

However, the success of the first deployment ensured that the request of Maj-Gen Earl Peak (SAC Deputy Chief of Staff for Operations) to the JCS for an October/November deployment was approved. The years' second PARPRO deployment was planned to leave Beale on 20 October 1977, fly eastward from Beale over the Arctic Circle and conduct a coordinated intelligence gathering sortie with RC-135U serial 64-14849, in the Barents Sea, before recovering into Mildenhall (this RC-135, a Combat Sent II aircraft, flew 30 operational missions into the Baltic and Barents Sea areas during this, its second, or Papa, deployment to Mildenhall, in 1977). However, due to bad weather at Thule AB, Greenland – the SR-71's nominated emergency recovery base for

this deployment – the mission was delayed for four days and Capt Joe Kinego and his RSO Maj Larry Elliott completed the five-hour 49-minute mission to Mildenhall in aircraft '976 on 24 October. During the sortie, Joe firstly conducted a post take-off top-up near Edmonton, Saskatchewan, Canada. A second AR was completed near Greenland and a third – after the 'take' – off the coast of Norway.

During this tour it was planned to fly several more sorties than on previous UK deployments and consequently two additional Habu crews arrived via KC-135Q tanker, to gain valuable experience in operating in this unique environment; they were Bob Crowder and Jack Veth together with their respective RSOs, John Morgan and Bill Keller. Between the three crews, eight round-robin sorties were flown into West Germany, these occurring on 27 and 29 October and 1, 3, 6, 7, 10 and 11 November. The average mission time for these sorties was two hours 38 minutes and each involved one air refuelling shortly after take-off over the Wash, a large bay like area located off the northern coast of East Anglia. The route consisted of just a single pass along track X-027, which was aligned parallel to the West German/East German/Czechoslovakian borders specifically to monitor the Soviet/Warsaw Pact autumn troop rotation. Headquarters Europe Command (EUCOM) requested that SAC direct the SR-71 to collect as varied an Elint/HRR sampling as possible. Consequently, the 3 November mission launched after sunset and completed a night sortie; a practice seldom undertaken because of noise considerations.

Yet another milestone was achieved during this deployment when, on 16 November, as DEW 49, Bob Crowder and John Morgan returned '976 to Beale. Having left Mildenhall, Bob topped-off over the North Sea. He then completed another coordinated sortie with RC-135U 64-14849; spending 45 minutes collecting intelligence in the constrained geography of the Baltic Sea. He then completed a second AR over the north coast of Scotland and a third off the east coast of North America, before touching down at Beale after a flight lasting six hours 11 minutes. Throughout the deployments in 1977, both the SR-71 and the MPC performed flawlessly.

On 24 April 1978, Jay Murphy and his RSO John Billingsley deployed aircraft '964 to Mildenhall to cover the spring troop rotations. During the 16-day period of its stay, two crews flew the aircraft, Bob Crowder and John Morgan ferrying it back to Beale on 12 May.

US NAVY INTEREST

Bordered by Finland and Norway to the west, the Kola Peninsula extends in a southeasterly

direction into the Barents Sea. This area was of intense interest to Admiral James L. Holloway III, Chief of Naval Operations (CNO), because the five naval bases at Zapadnya Litsa, Vidyayevo, Gadzhievo, Severomorsk and Gremikha were home to the largest and most powerful of the Soviet Union's three fleets – the Northern Fleet. This fleet included two thirds of the entire Soviet nuclear submarine force – over 100 vessels in all – the majority of which was based in the Kola Gulf area, because the warming influence of the North Atlantic Drift meant that these important ports remained ice free all year round.

By the spring of 1978, a group of young US Navy Intelligence analysts had become increasingly concerned at what appeared to be a fundamental shift in Soviet naval strategy. Virtually since the start of the Cold War when the 'Soviet Bear began to swim,' American planners believed that the Soviet Navy was bent on challenging the United States on the high seas and that at war, Soviet attack subs would attempt to sink US shipping re-supplying Europe, just as the German U-boat fleet had done in World War II. However, it now seemed increasingly likely to these analysts that the Soviets were on the cusp of knocking over a cornerstone of US nuclear strategy, since they believed that Soviet 'boomers' were being protected by attack subs and surface vessels and that the powerful Northern Fleet was intent on establishing the entire Barents Sea as a no go area to US and NATO navies. From their ice-free enclave, the subs could slip from their berths at anytime of the year and move into the Barents Sea, from where they could take up firing positions and launch their lethal, 4,800-mile (7725-km) range Submarine Launched Ballistic Missiles (SLBMs) over the Arctic, at targets which included Washington DC and any others within an arc drawn from about South Carolina through Oklahoma to Oregon. It was for this reason that John F. Lehman, President Reagan's Navy secretary, became fond of describing Murmansk and the rest of the Kola Peninsula as 'the most valuable piece of real estate on earth'. But surveillance of the ports from where these

BC Thomas and Jay Reid flew '964 into Mildenhall on 16 August 1980, after their 12 August mission from Beale to the Barents Sea and back ended in an abort into Bødo. (L. Peacock)

powerful subs would sail was particularly difficult, even for satellites, due to the prevailing weather conditions, which for the most part consisted of persistent cloud cover, rain and fog. The long, dark Arctic winters complicated matters further. Even on clear days, the sun angle in the Barents Sea was often too low for the collection of high-resolution photography.

In May 1978, mindful of the SR-71's HRR/Radint gathering capabilities, Admiral Holloway requested that the DIA validate a requirement to check out the submarine force. The DIA's evaluation indicated that seven such missions per month would be required to fulfil the Navy's requirement, but it recommended that the SR-71 should first fly several evaluation sorties. In 1978 the number of Primary Authorised Aircraft (PAA) SR-71As ready for immediate action stood at just eight aircraft and with commitments in the Western Pacific, to SIOP, to the Strategic Projection Force, and the two or three annual deployments to Mildenhall, plus training operations at Beale, it was rightly thought that the level of coverage required by the CNO was well beyond what was possible with the assets then available, so the matter was put on hold.

On 16 October 1978, aircraft '964 again deployed to Mildenhall and was yet again ferried in by the SR-71 Stan/Eval crew of Rich Graham and Don Emmons. The stay lasted 16 days and BC Thomas, together with his RSO Jay Reid, took turns with the Stan/Eval crew to collect Radint and Elint of the troop rotations, but neither ventured into the Barents Sea. Instead, Kadena-based SR-71s collected Radint for the CNO, of the Soviet's Pacific Fleet, based around Vladivostok.

YEMEN

In early 1979, the established cycle of SR-71 European deployments during the spring and autumn, for NATO exercises and to monitor the Soviet/Warsaw Pact troop rotations, was interrupted and increased by the threat of yet another war in the Middle East.

Situated on the tip of the Arabian Peninsula and at the southern approach to the Red Sea, North and South Yemen bordered oil-rich Saudi Arabia. One of the few Arab nations friendly to the United States, Saudi Arabia was the largest foreign supplier of oil to the US.

Throughout the 1970s, South Yemen had received military aid from both China and the Soviet Union. In addition, it had repeatedly tried to undermine the more moderate government of North Yemen. Saudi Arabia had close ties with North Yemen, but not with the left-wing government to the south. On 24 February 1979, while the South Yemeni foreign minister was in Riyadh, pledging that his government would support Arab League arbitration over the problems that existed between North and South Yemen, his country invaded its northern neighbour.

It was an action that caused considerable consternation within the Saudi royal family which feared that a united Yemen, under a Marxist government, would infiltrate and seek to threaten their country's already fragile political stability. So, in response to a Saudi request made through the DIA, the JCS directed HQ SAC to deploy an SR-71 to Mildenhall on 12 March 1979 – one month before the due date to cover the spring Warsaw Pact troop rotation – to conduct a single Giant Reach special mission into the Middle East and secure surveillance relating to events in this latest hot spot.

Despite a 3 March ceasefire that supposedly came into effect between North and South Yemen, intelligence sources advised the DIA that fighting had continued, particularly in the regions of Qatabah and Harib. As a result, the JCS's earlier decision to deploy still stood.

Back at Beale AFB, the saga picked up with the arrival of a SAC Operational Readiness Inspection (ORI) team. The team chief was none other than Brig-Gen Pat Halloran, former 9th Reconnaissance Wing commander, SR-71 pilot and Flight Instructor. Buz Carpenter now eloquently takes up the story: 'For the aircrew members this was normally not much of a challenge, since most of the SAC inspection team members weren't cleared to see the classified aircraft systems and particularly our on-going peacetime missions. During this period we were flying between 10 and 15 operational missions a month, from Beale, Kadena and occasionally Mildenhall.

'So instead, we would take an aircrew bold-face emergency action checklist test: all checklist items had to be from memory and errorless in order to pass. Maintenance had to generate all the aircraft

as if they were to be flown and deployed. We would inspect the aircraft and bring each SR-71 aircraft up to the engine start configuration and then the inspection team would certify the aircraft as generated and ready – other weapons systems had to actually launch their aircraft and demonstrate flying and weapons delivery activities plus their ability to execute their assigned missions; we were scored on the actual success rate on the operational missions we had been tasked for during the previous two years. Our average was always above 90 per cent, which always gave us an outstanding mission execution rating.

'The SAC ORI team arrived on Wednesday as I remember and we completed aircrew testing on Friday, together with acceptance walk throughs on the generated aircraft. An aircrew or two was normally selected to conduct a simulated mission in our incredible computer-supported simulator. For its time it was one of the most advanced mission simulators in the USAF. One did not even need an instructor on the console; as the aircrew executed actions the simulator knew how the aircraft would react and "put the aircraft" into that environment.

'There was going to be an aircrew "solo" party that Saturday night, so a number of us thought it would be fun to go up to the Reno air races on Saturday for the day. Much to our surprise the squadron commander said we needed to stay on base and if we had to leave the base, we had to stay in the local area and in touch with the squadron (this was pre-cellphone days, so it was a much tighter leash for all of us). We thought that this was rather unusual, because basically our part of the ORI was over.

'On Saturday everyone stayed close to base and that night we had the "solo" party. It was customary during SR-71 flight training that as the pilot and RSO first flew together and then completed their first Mach 3+ flight, they would individually host an open bar at Beale's Officers club. This was not an insignificant bill, but one everyone was delighted to step up to, because of what it signified. When the crewed pilot and RSO were far enough along in their training that they were now flying together, they would host a party for the crew force and key staff members. This particular Saturday was one such event. As people were moving around congratulating our newest aircrew and exchanging whatever flying stories of the day, one could detect rumblings of something happening in the background. There was trouble somewhere in the world and an initial planning call must have been made to the SR-71 organisation to get ready for action. Speculation was rife and the same old questions were being asked, "Where is the trouble? Are we officially tasked? Where might we be deploy to and execute

After its unscheduled visit to Norway, '964 was christened *The Bodonian Express*. It is seen here in company with KC-135s and with its new name written on the fin. (Paul F. Crickmore Collection)

these mission(s) from?" and, of course, most importantly, "Which crews are likely to be selected to support this effort?" As bits and pieces of information were revealed a picture and a timeline formed for deployment action probably within the next week ... but the only thing we knew for sure was that we'd be heading east from California to deal with the crisis.

'At about 10:00 pm and with the party in full swing, Col Willie Lawson, the Director of Operations for the SR-71 programme came up to John Murphy, my RSO, and I, stating we needed to come into mission planning around noon tomorrow to look at some maps for potential operations. John and I welcomed this opportunity but it did not mean we would be deploying; that decision was as yet to be made. I remember it was a great party but with little more information than this being learned, John and I, together with our wives, left the party sometime after midnight.

'I was planning on getting up normally for our Sunday routine. I would get the family breakfast and then we would all go off for the Chapel service on base. Well, at 7:30 am I get a call saying that I need to get John and head for the planning shop. I asked can't it wait until noon and the answer was a clear, "It needs to be now." I called John and picked him up about half an hour later and we headed down to the mission planning area. Now we get the Paul Harvey routine ... the rest of the

story. Problem in the Middle East, Yemen and Saudi Arabia are about to go to war over border disputes. Tanks have already started to be assembled and information needs to be gathered as quickly as possible to give the President and the National Security Council, along with the State Department, an opportunity to defuse this building conflict.

'John and I look the mission paths over as the package calls for three missions flown into the Middle East at about two-three days apart from Mildenhall. Our routes to the Middle East from England are known. Once again the French are refusing to let the SR-71 fly across their country for quick access into the Mediterranean Sea and thereby reducing this five-refuelling, almost ten-hour mission by two hours 30 minutes and a refuelling. Major question of the morning is looking for suitable refuelling bases for our tankers. The Special JP-7 fuel was stored at Mildenhall, Incirlik AB, Turkey, and, I believe, at Moron AB, near Seville, Spain. Turkey and Israel said the tankers would not be allowed to operate from their countries. Saudi Arabia was not chosen, but I do not remember why. Finally, Cairo West in Egypt was selected and the tankers would have to pick up fuel from Turkey but not support us from there.

'As one can imagine, the most critical aspect for timing was for the tanker operations to determine their best basing sites and then get the tankers, aircrews and maintenance support heading to these locations. The SR-71 might be able to fly at Mach 3+, but without the tankers that took a while to get to their forwarded deployed locations, the SR-71 was not mission capable.

'At about 11:00 am, John and I were told we'd be part of the advanced party heading to Mildenhall to receive the SR-71 deploying from Beale, which was being flown by one of our most experienced and senior crews, Major Rich Graham and Major Don Emmons. "Oh, and by the way, you'll leave sometime this afternoon or early evening." John and I called home and asked our wives to ready our bags. By about noon the ORI team had stopped all evaluations and was now just watching this magnificent reconnaissance team in action, doing what we are supposed to do for the United States. I kidded Gen Halloran that this is the "best ORI scenario I have ever seen". We both laughed, because this is what it is all about and why so many men and women have so dedicated their lives to serving their nation this way.

'We get a quick trip home at around 1:00 pm to pick-up our bags and say goodbye. We do not know when we'll be back. The families will be given that information as soon as it can be determined, but they aren't told where we are going nor anything about the missions that need to be flown, as that is all classified. A quick stop by the squadron, to pick up our checklists and various deployment materials – we have to secure a special UHF radio and other items to be used by the mobile crew to launch and recover the SR-71 from our deployment base at Mildenhall.

'Early Sunday morning the tankers were already starting to depart before their final destinations – where known. Since their missions involved multiple flight legs, time was the most critical factor in getting them forward and set up to operate. Operational locations, diplomatic clearances, operational concepts would be worked while the tankers were en route. John and I were told we would be leaving around 4:00 pm with a refuelling stop at Pease AFB, New Hampshire, and then on to Mildenhall, arriving an hour or so ahead of the deploying SR-71. It would be tight timing but we needed to get the aircraft on the ground in England so that maintenance could turn it around once the tankers were forward and prepared to support and an execution time was determined. Sensors would have to be prepped and uploaded – some of them needed almost a day to get them mission ready. Primary sensor for these missions would be the Optical Bar Camera

carried in the nose of the aircraft – we called it the 'countries camera', because it was an area camera that took a swath about 70 miles [113 km] wide and thousands of miles long – hence its nickname, because of its remarkable collection capability.

'A last minute delay meant that our tanker didn't depart Beale until nearly 6:00 pm. Time would be really tight now. We flew to New Hampshire at the KC-135's top speed. A quick refuelling turn was a must at Pease so the tanker aircrew called ahead and tried to have everything ready to go for our high-priority mission. Fortunately, it was September and the weather was at its best, an operation such as this in the dead of winter would have added yet another dimension of time risk. But after landing, I remember the operation was a fine orchestration from this Northern Tier Strategic Air Command base. Fuel trucks were standing by to refuel the aircraft and box lunches were ready for the tanker aircrew and all of us passengers. John and I went into base operations and made a few essential telephone calls to update the overall mission status, determine a revised arrival time for the SR-71 into Mildenhall and receive any further instructions. We then rushed back to the tanker and shortly afterwards we were back in the air, heading across the North Atlantic to Mildenhall.

'John and I had the tanker call Mildenhall about an hour before landing to reaffirm that the mobile car would be by planeside as the tanker's engines shut down. On landing, we had, at most, 30 minutes before the SR-71 touched down. We leapt into the car, hot wired the special radio into its electrical system, mounted its external antenna, and proceeded immediately towards the runway to complete our recovery checklists; these included gaining clearance from the tower to access the runway and carry out a visible inspection for any possible FOD (Foreign Object Damage) items that could puncture the SR-71's tyres.

'As we were checking the runway for screws, bolts, panels or whatever John made contact with Rich and Don – affectionately known as "Snake & Nape". They were about 10 minutes out and about to go over to approach control for recovery. We then played about a minute of "Darl'n", a David Allen Coe song that had almost become the theme song for the SR-71 programme at this point in time. It was late in the afternoon as '972, using the call sign AWRY 26 touched down, I recall the weather was pretty good for England. Birdwatchers, as usual, were along the fence to film anything that might be flying on this Monday.

'The tankers were still getting into position and the mission planning team with us worked into the night, planning the three mission-objective routes over the Arabian Peninsula, focusing on the Saudi/Yemeni border.

Nevin Cunningham, who was no stranger to Mildenhall, later became the detachment's commander. He is seen here talking to Lt-Col Joe Kinego, commander of the 1st SRS at that time. (Paul F. Crickmore)

'Refuelling tracks had now been established, with the first off Lands End, England, the second in the Mediterranean Sea, a third over the Red Sea going in and a fourth again over the Red Sea, coming out; the final refueling would be a long drag over the central Mediterranean, abeam Libya, to get us home. Because we were banned from flying over France, the last leg would be critical on fuel – even with the priority handling British air traffic control provided us, fuel would be tight and the English weather was always an additional risk.

'By Tuesday afternoon the tankers were in place and if the weather permitted we could launch the first mission early Wednesday morning. Early departure was required to place the SR-71 over the Arabian Peninsula with optimum daylight for the cameras. Rich and I had already talked about who would fly which missions. I volunteered I would not mind flying these longer missions, so the plan became that as they had brought the aircraft over, John and I would fly the first and third missions – up to 10 hours in length – and Rich and Don would fly the number two mission and then take the aircraft back to Beale … a four-hour flight.

'As I remember, we met at about 3:00 pm Tuesday afternoon and there were representatives from many organisations we did not normally see. This attested to the importance of the mission. We had attaches from our embassy, senior National Security Agency reps, the Two Star USAF Director of Operations from SAC and many others. The USAF two star had questions about our operations, was interested in the route we were

about to fly, potential divert bases and the rules of engagement we were given to operate with.

'Humour entered at this point when we asked if our families knew where we had left for. My answer was no. My wife Nancy knew it was an important mission and her parting comments to me were, "Do good and I do not want to read about you in the paper or see you on the TV!" That was the nature of our business. Our families were truly most supportive.

'The briefing went along fairly well until we got to the issue of possible divert bases if we had trouble. The State Department folks asked what do you mean trouble. "Aren't you guys invulnerable?" Well even the best of aircraft occasionally has a maintenance problem. Israel had denied us any over flight and with Turkey's position of not wanting to support this operation from any of their bases this left us with few options. John and I selected some bases we could use in the Mediterranean and in the objective area. We normally flew our missions radio silent, with a radio listening watch on HF radio for recalls or mission changes. Our tankers would include anything we wanted passed as part of their end-refuelling radio report. One of the great features of the SR-71's refueling capability was the ability to talk with the tanker aircrew through the air-refueling boom, thereby maintaining radio silence. For this mission we were told the president had requested, through the National Security Council, that the SR-71 report operationally normal at the end of each refueling for immediate mission status verification.

'Now started the process of going to bed around 6 to 7 o'clock to be rested before getting-up at 1:00 am for the physical, a breakfast of steak and eggs, mission briefing and then the suiting up process in order to be ready for about a 4:00 am engine start. Wednesday morning we went through all the steps including being installed in the aircraft. John and I were awaiting the thumbs up from Mobile (Rich and Don) to initiate our radio-silent engine start, taxi and take-off. But at 4:00 am word came through of a 24-hour delay, because of weather in the objective area. We got out of the aircraft, talked with maintenance for a while and then tried to figure out what are we going to do until we went to bed around 6:00 pm. Back at our room area we went and broke out some wine and vodka-tonic drinks. The maids showed up at 7:00 am and wondered what these crazy American's were doing having a party at 7:00 am!

'And so off to bed we went on Wednesday night and up again at 1:00 am Thursday. Unfortunately the same routine ends with the same results. At 4:00 am while strapped in the aircraft on a dark wet taxiway, we get another 24-hour delay. It's okay for us, we can go back to our rooms, but for many of our tankers aircrews who had launched hours earlier to be in position, it is another long mission of burning down fuel until a safe landing weight is reached before they can land back at their respective deployment bases. Because of the restrictions imposed upon us, many of the tankers had to fly for a number of hours to be in the refueling track to service us as we flew through. Wednesday had already found them burning down fuel and now the situation called for a repeat on Thursday.

'That evening, I took an early seafood dinner at the Mildenhall Officer's Club. Unknown to me at the time, this would feature later in the story. Early Friday morning we are up at 1:00 am and hoping that this will be the day we finally execute mission number one. The weather is okay in the objective area but not really too good at Mildenhall, light rain and somewhat foggy. We are now at engine start and John and I have our fingers crossed. All of a sudden the crew chief and a Lockheed tech rep storm up the ladder ... this is normally not good. I open my helmet faceplate to determine the problem. By way of a mission remembrance for our maintenance, Intel and photo people, they want me to fly two plastic bags full of SR-71 tie tacks. There is room in my lower suit leg pockets and I stuff the bags in. I re-secure my faceplate and Mobile finally gives us a thumbs up. At last we're off on this adventure. Everything goes as scheduled and we blast off into the night at about 4:30 am and head across England at 25,000 ft [7620 m] towards the southwest and our tankers near Lands End.

'This is quite a change, as we normally head east out over the North Sea and hook up with our tankers fairly quickly. As we fly west I seem to have more intestinal gas than normal. I figure it will pass as we climb and the cabin pressure rises to 28,000 ft [8534 m]. It was very common for us to work on relieving our gas build up as we climb. It takes almost 30 minutes before we are hooked up with the first of our tankers. By now I'm feeling really uncomfortable. John and I discuss our options. We can't proceed if I'm sick, but I sure do not want the mission scrubbed and have it reported to the National Security Council that after two nights of mission slippage the mission was again postponed because the pilot was sick! Well, on the second tanker I have a quick complete diarrhoea attack (seafood special we figure), but afterwards I feel much better. Then comes the next question, are there any adverse effects for "sitting on this stuff" for the next 9 hours. John and I discuss this with the tanker crew and I feel that I'm now fine and we can proceed.

'We drop off the tanker over the Atlantic Ocean and with a full load of fuel begin our climb and acceleration while heading due south. The sun has

come up and we arrive at altitude at 3.0 Mach and about 74,000 ft [22555 m]. A turn east is executed, taking us through the straits of Gibraltar and into the Mediterranean. I now actually feel pretty good and we set up to initiate our descent and deceleration for our second refueling. All is normal from these tankers that came out from Spain and they are extremely glad to see us for what is for them, a third flying day. As directed, at the end of the aerial refueling we call operationally normal and start our next accel and climb. So far there have been no reactions from any potential hostile areas. Now departing the Mediterranean the view of the great pyramids and Sphinx was spectacular! Time to start down once more. John says we're not getting the normal ranging information from the tankers to adjust our rendezvous profile. Unbeknownst to us, the tanker radios are not working and they actually see our contrails as we start down and experience guides them to set-up their turns to roll out in front of us at the right spacing and speed. What can I say ... outstanding teamwork and a typical can-do attitude that makes it all happen.

'The refuelling goes without a hitch, but we are unaware that two Egyptian MiG-23s have followed our tankers out on this third day, to see what's going on. Unknown to us, a picture is taken of us refuelling from the second tanker from above, which, months later, John and I sign and which is then presented to the Egyptian embassy and Egyptian air force, to thank them for their great support. The picture was wonderful, showing three tankers in formation, us refueling under the second tanker and the pair of MiGs about 200–300 yards [183–274 m] in trail.

'With full tanks, we're now off for accel and climb number three, but this one will take us into our objective area. Defensive systems are again checked and all other aircraft systems are functioning normally. Aircraft '972 is performing exceedingly well but now as we pass through 45,000 ft [13716 m] at 2.4 Mach we get a fighter attack-radar indication coming from our right forward quadrant. We determine that a Middle Eastern fighter would not be a threat to us at this speed and altitude (after returning to California I talked with Kelly Johnson about this event, he'd been cleared into any of the missions and occurrences we might see or experience). A turn to the left is initiated as we reach 3.0 Mach and are above 75,000 ft [22860 m]. What a view ... sand for as far as one can see with the occasional interspersed oases. Its incredible to think that people are fighting over this vast open desert that we're flying over. There was a lot of sand blowing around below us making for a hazy scene. Above, the sky was as black as ever. As we fly over the Saudi/Yemeni border area a left turn for a second loop in this objective area is coming up. Hardly a word is spoken between John and I during these intense, high-activity time periods. Just as everything seemed to be working as planned the aircraft tries to make a right instead of the planned left turn. I disconnect the autopilot and get us turning left. John is working to see if he can locate the source of the problem and checking the rest of the objective area to ensure we have maintained route integrity. We are on that mythical black line and swing through for another pass. Now as we leave the objective area we're in a right descending, decelerating turn, looking for our fourth set of tankers. We're a little low on fuel because of the extra manoeuvring, but again the refueling goes without a hitch.

'We're off the tankers again and climbing to start back to England, and after this cruise leg we reach our last refuelling, number five, and then the race home to return just under 10 hours of mission time. This last refueling will be different from the rest as a normal refueling lasts about 15 to 20 minutes and transfers 80,000 lb+ [36288 kg+] of fuel [12,000 US gal; 45425 litres]. The goal is always to reach your end air refueling point with full tanks to begin your accel. Well, for this last refuelling we'll stay behind the tanker for 50 minutes, dragging along subsonically, to give us a closer end air refueling point, assuring extra fuel to deal with potentially bad British weather. This refueling is in the middle of the Mediterranean Sea, North of Libya. Everyone is monitoring closely to see if Libya detects and reacts to our presence. Descent and hook-up go flawlessly. I debate dropping off the tanker a couple of times and re-engaging to top off the fuel in the aircraft, but the decision is made that instead of risking not being able to hook-up again, the easiest action is to stay on the second tanker's boom for about 45 minutes. We see a lot of air traffic over the Med, but none of it is out of the ordinary.

'John and I are ready for this last leg. We have been in our pressure suits now for over 9 hours and I'll later learn that with the normal dehydrating 100 per cent oxygen breathing environment, coupled with my earlier illness, I'll have lost over 8 lb [3.6 kg] even though I have been eating tube food and drinking water throughout the mission. Climb and acceleration are normal and we pass back through the Straits of Gibraltar and start a turn to the north heading home. Prior to descent we learn that the weather at Mildenhall has deteriorated and it's now raining. Descent takes us down to enter the UK landmass subsonically and now we once again drive across the country. Now with radar approach control, we set up for a precision approach, but while running the checklist we determine that the nose gear does not

want to come down. We're now in the rain and have to run the alternate gear-lowering checklist, which involves leaving the landing gear selection handle down, pulling some circuit breakers and then manually pulling a release cable in the front cockpit. During the course of running these actions we have terminated the precision approach and can now take over visually for another approach. After the longest time the nose gear does fall free and into the down and locked position.

'Today we have fooled the birdwatchers, as there are very few around the airfield on this rainy day. Landing, thankfully, is uneventful and as we taxi into our parking position outside of the hangar it seems that all the deployment personnel are standing around cheering our mission completion. John and I feel so honoured to be a part of this great team. Engine shutdown commences and the gantry stand is rolled beside us. I feel pretty good but a little weak. I try to tactfully tell the gang to not get too close and there is a pervading odour. Unknown to John and I, the first tanker had relayed our problem back and during the flight the team had organised a little ceremony. At the foot of the ladder the 9th Vice Wing Commander, Col Dave Young, met me to get a quick debrief, but more importantly to present me with an SR-71 tie tack that they have painted brown and the accompanying certificate attesting that on this date I was the first "surely not true but funny" supersonic turd. What can I say … laughter came from everywhere. I felt pretty good, so the Physiological Support guys gave me my customary after flight refreshing beer – re-hydrating was also a critical part of this high flight.

'As it turns out, our mission would be the only one flown into the Middle East for this crisis. All the data required by the National Security Council had been collected, meeting presidential needs. On 12 March, John and I launched "Snake & Nape" into the air as INPUT 62, taking '972 home. Rich to this day kids me about tricking him into having the Chief of Standardization Aircrew act as a ferry crew for us. Such is the luck of life.'

A SECOND DET IS FORMED

Such was the proven success of the Habu in the European theatre, that a permanent detachment of the 9th SRW was now set up at Mildenhall. Thus, on 31 March 1979, Det 4 was established as the European SR-71 and TR-1 operating unit.

Surveillance of the spring 1979 troop rotation was conducted by Bill Groninger and Lee Shelton, together with their respective RSOs, Chuck Sober and Barry MacKean. Aircraft '979 arrived at Mildenhall as FERN 29 on 17 April and departed on 2 May. In response to the CNO's requests for Radint of the Barents Sea, the very first round-robin mission into the region was flown

On 9 July 1983, Maury Rosenberg and ED McKim touched down at RAF Mildenhall in aircraft '955. Its serial number had been changed to '962 to prevent unwanted attention from base-side aircraft enthusiasts. Here BC Thomas carries out post-flight checks on the aircraft at Palmdale. Note the bulbous 'duck-bill'-like nose, which was a characteristic of an ASARS-1 equipped aircraft. (USAF)

from Beale on 13 July 1979, in support of a SAC worldwide nuclear readiness exercise entitled Global Shield '79. The ten-hour four-minute mission obtained high-resolution radar imagery of the targeted area and two similar missions were conducted in 1980.

The autumn troop rotation of 1979 was covered from 18 October to 13 November by Rich Young/Russ Szczepanik and Joe Kinego/Bill Keller in aircraft '976. The same aircraft returned for the 1980 spring rotation on 9 April and three Habu crews flew the aircraft during its 30-day deployment. Aircraft '972 arrived as CUP 10 and covered the autumn rotation between 13 September and 2 November – four crews sharing the missions. However, due to work on Mildenhall's runway, the aircraft was positioned to RAF Lakenheath during the course of its deployment, from where it continued to operate until being flown back to Beale as ROOM 60.

On 12 December 1980, a third SR-71 deployment to Mildenhall occurred. This time the JCS had directed that the deployment should take place in response to a request from the Commander in Chief Atlantic (CINCLANT), who was concerned at the possible intervention of Soviet military forces to quell rising decent in Poland. Rich Young and Russ Szczepanik duly arrived in aircraft '964, having collected an HRR/Elint take on their inbound leg to Mildenhall. This was to prove a milestone deployment, with the aircraft staying in the UK for four months and being replaced the day before its return to Beale by '972 on 6 March, which in turn stayed for two months, eventually departing on 5 May 1981 as YAPPY 22.

Not all round-robins were flown as planned; the mission scheduled on 12 August 1981 was planned from Beale to the Barents Sea and back to Beale. On that flight Majs BC Thomas and Jay Reid took off from Beale at 22:00 hours to fly the ten-hour 30-minute sortie with refuellings over Idaho and Goose Bay, twice over the North Sea and again over Goose Bay, before returning to Beale. Between the two North Sea refuellings they would make a run over the Barents Sea, where their side-looking HRR would pick up Soviet submarine targets for the US Navy.

The mission went like clockwork until they were in the 'take' area when BC noted that the left engine 'low oil quantity' warning light was flashing on and off. After completing the important radar run, he hooked '964 up with one of the KC-135Qs and began taking on board much needed fuel. It was during this refueling phase that he noted the oil warning light was now shining continuously. That situation was a 'mandatory abort' item on his emergency procedures checklist, because prolonged flight under such degraded conditions could easily result in engine seizure. There were two preferred bases in northwest Europe for diversionary aborts: Mildenhall, a two-hour 30-minute subsonic haul, or Bødo in Norway, which was just 20 minutes away. BC decided that caution was the better part of valour on this occasion and diverted into Bødo. Once there, he was greeted by the base commander, Gen Ohmount, who, as BC recalled, was very polite but very nervous. It later transpired that Ohmount had been a young Lieutenant at the base in 1960 when Gary Powers had been shot down. After it became widely known that the intention was for the CIA pilot to have landed at Bødo, the Norwegian government disclaimed any knowledge of the plan and fired Ohmount's 1960 boss – an event still strongly etched on his memory.

Having notified the SAC Reconnaissance Center of his intentions to divert, BC was anxious to provide 'home plate' with other details. The Norwegian general directed the Habu pilot towards his underground command post, a very impressive place built into the side of a mountain, from where BC could tell Col Dave Young (the 9th SRW commander) of the nature of '964's mechanical problem. Young asked at what stage the decision had been made to abort, to which BC gave the total mission time and the third air refuelling plus time. From that answer, Col Young was able to ascertain that the aircraft had the reconnaissance 'take' on board, and that certain specialists would need to accompany the recovery crew to download the data.

Two officers were then assigned to each of the US fliers – BC recalled that his 'minder' was Lt Roar Strand, a 331st Fighter Squadron F-104 pilot. The two Norwegian pilots didn't let their charges out of sight, and even slept in the same rooms. The recovery team, headed-up by Lt-Col Randy Hertzog, arrived in a KC-135Q on 15 August. Gen Ohmount had requested that the recovery team wear military uniforms and not civilian clothes to ensure that all was kept above board. Unfortunately this message didn't reach the new arrivals, who were quickly ushered back onto the tanker and instructed to don their fatigues.

With a million members of the Polish Solidarity movement going on strike on 7 August, and mounting tension between communist state officials and the rest of the Polish population, it was decided that '964 should remain in Europe to monitor any possible Soviet response.

Consequently at 13:42 hours on 16 August, BC and Jay departed Bødo in the company of their trusty tanker for a flight to Mildenhall, which was performed without fuss at subsonic speed. Now christened on its twin tails *The Bødonian Express*, '964 touched down at 14:52 hours. The crew was met at the bottom of the gantry platform by two other Habu crew members, Majs Jerry Glasser and Mac Hornbaker, who would fly the next *Bødonian Express* sortie into the Baltic, near Poland, on 22 August. One week later, it was BC and Jay's turn. A third sortie to the same area was flown by Capts Rich Young and Ed Bethart on 31 August and finally, on 2 September, BC and Jay returned to Beale by tanker. Their scheduled ten-hour sortie had lasted 21 days! Aircraft '964 continued flying operational sorties from Mildenhall until 6 November, when it too was returned to Beale.

The political situation in Poland continued to deteriorate as the clamour for reforms and democracy gathered momentum. By early December the situation had reached breaking point. Late in the night of 12 December 1981, the communist leader, Gen Jaruzelski, cut all communication links with the West and deployed troops and armour to set up road blocks and occupy strategic installations. He then declared a state of marshal law and appeared on television to announce the formation of a Military Council of National Salvation. He claimed that strikes, protest demonstrations and crime had brought the country 'to the border of mental endurance ... the verge of an abyss'. Two days later it became apparent that at least 14,000 trade union activists had been rounded up and arrested; seven had been shot in the Silesian coal fields while resisting marshal law. Would Jaruzelski turn to the Soviet Union for help in his struggle to retain control of Poland? Or would President Leonid Brezhnev commit Soviet troops to crush the uprising as he had done in Czechoslovakia on 21 August 1968? Clearly, the Reagan Administration needed some answers, and fast, and as ever Det 4 crews were on hand to provide them.

Majs Gil Bertleson and Frank Stampf were on the roster for this important sortie. The significance of their mission dictated that it was to be backed up by a spare aircraft. Consequently, Majs Nevin Cunningham and Geno Quist (known within the crew force as 'Neno' and 'Geno') were also suited up as spares. As Gil and Frank disappeared with their SR-71 into the cold, wet night, Nevin and Geno waited at the end of the runway in '958 for the code words which would either send them 'back to the barn' or on their way on a long mission over much of the North Atlantic and northern Europe. Soon after, Frank called back to Geno on their discrete HF radio frequency saying simply, 'Your guys have got it,' to which both spare crewmen simultaneously said, 'Oh shit,' and off they went. The weather in the first air refuelling area over Nevada and Utah was so bad that it was all the Habu crew could do to find the tanker in the thick clouds. When they finally located it, and were on the boom, it proved extremely difficult for Nevin to maintain the connection due to the heavy turbulence. The updrafts bounced the KC-135 around the sky to the degree that its autopilot was unable to react fast enough to the unstable conditions. This refuelling was therefore one of the most difficult experienced by both the tanker and SR-71 crews. Nevin asked the tanker pilot to forget autopilot and 'go manual' to achieve a better 'hook-up platform'. Meanwhile, the transfer operation was enshrouded in Saint Elmo's Fire, which lit up both aircraft like glowing Christmas trees.

After finally completing the ragged refuelling operation, Nevin lit both burners and pressed on to the second ARCP over the sea off Canada. Again the weather did its utmost to make the operation as uncomfortable as possible. After quickly crossing the 'oily-black' Atlantic, the crew headed towards their third refuelling track off the west coast of Norway. Here they were sandwiched between layers of cloud, but the air was smooth in the Arctic twilight and the top-off went smoothly. The long Atlantic crossing meant that they now required a split off-load from two tankers. After taking half of his load from one KC-135, Nevin looked for the other tanker. As he closed in on the second aircraft, he discovered he was joining up with what turned out to be a Soviet Ilyushin Il-20 'Coot' Elint aircraft! Nevin flew '958 up to the 'would be' tanker, which was no doubt equally startled by the presence of a mysterious Habu. Nevin and Geno quickly dropped back to find the second tanker, and after they had topped-off, the pilot lit the burners for the next 'hot and high' run. At 72,000 ft [21946 m] they headed into the 'take' area, where it was especially dark at altitude (it seemed that the only source of light was from the two J58 afterburners 100 ft/30.48 m behind them). Having completed an inner 'loop' around the Baltic Sea, they were on their way back down to the fourth refuelling when the sun popped back up over the horizon.

To further complicate matters on this long and difficult mission, Geno was unable to make radio contact with the tankers. Fortunately, Nevin spotted contrails well below and ahead of them, and simply followed the aerial 'railroad tracks' for a join up. While on the boom, Geno broke further bad news to Nevin about their ANS, which had failed. Clearly it would not be possible to return to Beale since 'ANS Failure' was a mandatory abort item. They therefore settled into formation with the tankers, which led them to Mildenhall, where

snow and ice covered the runway and taxiways. Finally, after what had turned out to be a very entertaining mission, '958 slithered to a halt outside the dedicated SR-71 barn, and Nevin and Geno climbed out after their eight-hour 30-minute 'fun filled' mission – their 27th sortie together.

Back at Beale AFB the Californian weather was less severe. As BC Thomas and Jay Reid climbed from the tandem cockpits of a T-38 on completion of a routine training flight on Wednesday 16 December, they were met by Col Randy Hertzog, the wing DCO. He instructed them to go home and grab whatever they needed for an indefinite deployment to RAF Mildenhall. The KC-135 carrying them and a maintenance team departed Beale at 19:30 hours and arrived in England at 07:30 hours the next morning. Nevin and Geno had just flown aircraft '958 on a second sortie around the Baltic on 18 December, and another mission was planned for BC and Jay as soon as they were crew-rested from their transatlantic ride. An analysis of Geno's 'take' had revealed that the Soviet Union was not making preparations to intervene militarily to quell Poland's political unrest. On Monday 21 December 1981, BC and Jay departed Mildenhall in '958 and headed out over the North Sea for the first of five air refuellings.

Their first flight was also tasked to monitor the Soviet/Polish border situation, from a stand-off position in international airspace over the Baltic Sea, and to include a long northern run around the coast of Norway along Russia's north coast. Jay activated the sensors as they cruised at Mach 3 on their northern loop, which exited the 'take' area near Murmansk on a westerly heading toward the fourth refuelling. Out over the North Atlantic, the right generator cut off, but BC managed to get it reset. After the fifth tank near Goose Bay, Labrador, another problem arose that would limit their cruise speed inbound to Beale. During acceleration BC noted that '958's supply of liquid nitrogen had been depleted, and that the fuel tanks could not be pressurised to inert the fuel fumes within at high Mach. He therefore limited the cruise Mach to 2.6 in accordance with emergency operating procedures and made his final descent into Beale, somewhat low on fuel, after a flight of almost ten hours. The series of Baltic sorties not only obtained invaluable intelligence at a time of high international tension, but also vividly demonstrated US resolve to stay actively engaged in the situation by using key surveillance assets in the NATO/Warsaw Pact theatre of operations.

Det 4's capability was doubled during the closing stages of 1982 when two SR-71s were based 'permanently' at Mildenhall for the first time, the aircraft being manned by a number of crews on 30 day deployments and flying a succession of 'routine but highly productive missions' across the North Sea and along the border with eastern Europe. After '972 had been deployed for seven months, it was ready to be returned to Beale for periodic heavy maintenance, which included replacing the fuel tank sealant that tended to burn away after repeated high-Mach flights. Nevin and Geno got the big redeployment sortie and left Mildenhall at 10:00 hours on Tuesday 5 July 1983 via the Barents/Baltic Seas, and returned across the North Atlantic to California. After completing their first 'take' run on a 'northern loop' over the Barents Sea, they decelerated into the Viking North air-refuelling track in international airspace west of Bødo, Norway. Topped off, they climbed back to altitude and entered their second collection area within the narrow Baltic corridor to complete the reconnaissance portion of the mission. Preparing to head home, they again decelerated and descended into the Viking North ARCP over the Norwegian Sea. Back at high altitude, Geno calculated that Nevin would have to accelerate to maximum Mach to improve the aircraft's range to ensure that they would have enough fuel to reach the next set of tankers near Labrador.

During this 'hot and high' phase of the flight, the left engine's exhaust gas temperature indicator showed that the EGT had become uncontrollable and that '972 should not be flown faster than 3.05 Mach to ensure that engine damage would not occur. By flying at this less than optimum speed the SR-71 would not be able to reach the KC-135s. Trying manual control of the inlet spikes and doors only made matters worse and they were only able to maintain Mach 3 in this configuration. Slowing to subsonic speeds would further exacerbate their low fuel predicament and they found that they had insufficient fuel to go back to Bødo. Therefore, they had to press on toward their tankers in the hope that they might be able to improve their fuel-flow rate or to divert into Iceland. For the next 45 minutes Nevin flew at 3.09 Mach before slowing to 3.05 to allow the EGT to drop back into the 'green'.

As they approached the point of no return off Iceland, Geno recalculated the fuel situation, which had improved slightly. Nevin decided to press on and told Geno to get the tankers to fly toward them to further shorten their distance to hook-up. After completing a hook-up in record-breaking time (much to the crew's great relief), the fuel streamed into '972 at more than 6,000 lb [2721 kg] per minute. Back at Beale after another seven hours of SR-71 excitement, neither crewmember would admit to how much (or how little) fuel they had remaining before they made contact with their ever-faithful friends in the tanker.

AIRCRAFT '955

In May 1983 it was decided by HQ SAC and Air Force Systems Command officials to demonstrate Goodyear's Advanced Synthetic Aperture Radar System-1 (ASARS-1) on an SR-71 before upgrading the rest of the Habu fleet with this new high-definition, ground-mapping radar system. After aircraft number '955 was equipped with the new system, BC Thomas and John Morgan were assigned the task of conducting the first operational test flight from Palmdale. On 1 July 1983 they made SAC's first ASARS familiarisation flight, lasting just over five hours, during which John learned ASARS 'switchology' and operating techniques. Five days later Maury Rosenberg and ED McKim also flew the modified SR-71 on a five-hour sortie, recovering into Beale AFB, rather than Palmdale. On 9 July, Maury and Ed deployed '955 on a seven-hour flight to Mildenhall, via the Barents/Baltic collection area.

British planespotters peering through binoculars and telescopes from various off-base vantage points excitedly recorded the Habu's arrival, some noting the slightly bumpy ASARS nose, but an 'already familiar' tail number which many people lovingly kept in their log books. On that occasion, all of them logged a false serial since a cover-number was being used to conceal the fact that the test bird was overseas. Since '955 was already known by military aviation enthusiasts as 'the Palmdale test ship', it had been decided by the maintenance folk back at Beale to temporarily rechristen '955 as '962 for this deployment. The latter jet had visited Mildenhall earlier, and would not therefore draw unwelcome attention and speculation to the unique test deployment.

Nine days later on 18 July 1983, BC and John took the aircraft on a two-hour 36-minute ASARS operational test sortie to monitor military installations in East Germany. On 21 July, Maury and Ed took their turn on a four-hour mission. The next day BC and John flew '980 to Greenham Common to help raise money for the RAF's Benevolent Fund. Among the many thousands of people who came to see the aircraft were some of the 'Greenham Women', who had long been demonstrating against many political issues, and who had been camping outside the base to gain public recognition. The day before the SR-71 was due to return to Mildenhall, some of the demonstrators managed to daub white paint on the Habu. They were quickly arrested for causing a disturbance, and for possible damage to the aircraft's titanium, which later laboratory analysis proved was unharmed.

Several days later Maj Jim Jiggens and Capt Joe McCue performed an unforgettable departure from the base. After a morning take-off on 26 July for the short flight back to Mildenhall, Jim (an ex-'Thunderbirds' air show demonstration pilot, who had obtained prior permission from the base commander to do a farewell flyby) flew a wide circular pattern at 250 kt [288 mph; 463 km/h] towards the Greenham Peace Camp. As '980 reached a strategic point, Jim pushed both throttles to full afterburner, whereupon the SR-71 thundered over the encampment at a very low altitude. Applying sharp back-pressure to the control stick and lofting the Habu into a spectacular climb, Jim allowed his sleek aircraft to trumpet the 'sound of freedom' as only an SR-71 could.

The final ASARS demonstration flight was conducted on 30 July when BC and John flew '955 on a seven-hour 18-minute flight back to Beale, via the Baltic and Barents Sea. The series of tests was extremely successful, proving that ASARS-1 represented a quantum leap in radar resolution and capability for reconnaissance purposes. Capts Gary Luloff and Bob Coats ferried the aircraft back to Palmdale on 2 August, where further tests were conducted prior to an initial order for two production radar sets for the operational fleet.

PERMANENT DEPLOYMENT

Although the 1983 deployment to Mildenhall was still called a 'temporary operation', two SR-71s remained at the base throughout the year (apart from a period lasting 33 days early in the year, and three days in the autumn). As early as 1980, SAC had begun planning changes in the SR-71's European operations to cut the cost of deployments and to increase the frequency of surveillance flights. Such changes required actions of 'air diplomacy' on the part of HQ 3rd Air Force, and USAF and SAC staff specialists. On instructions from the JCS, HQ USAF and HQ SAC, Col Don Walbrecht of the Third Air Force (accompanied by Lt-Col John Fuller and Lt-Col Dwight Kealoa of HQ USAF/XOXX (Protectorate of Plans and Policy) and Lt-Col Kenneth Hagemann of HQ SAC/XP (Deputy Chief of Staff Plans)) proposed to Assistant Secretary Martin Scicluna, and to Gp-Capt Frank Appleyard, Deputy Director of Operations in the RAF's Directorate of Organisation (DGO/RAF), that SR-71 operations at Mildenhall should be bedded down on a more permanent basis.

Scicluna (Head of the MoD's 5-9 (AIR)) led the British contingent who reviewed the proposal. Although he thought that the SR-71's high visibility image might cause 'political difficulties' at some senior levels, he took the issue forward to Secretary of State for Defence, Sir Francis Pym, who agreed to consider it. After specialised briefings to a few MoD 'insiders', which included certain intelligence officers who had 'special access' to US reconnaissance information, recommendations were taken to Pym who agreed

to the initiative. Another meeting held three days later worked out the politics of the proposal. The following week, each member of the US team briefed his respective CINC or Deputy Chief of Staff in Ramstein, Omaha, or Washington, that the programme was on track in Whitehall. Soon after, Prime Minister Thatcher's approval was noted as a simple 'change of mode of operations' from temporary deployments to a permanent presence at RAF Mildenhall. U-2 operations were to be moved from Mildenhall to Alconbury as both bases were beefed-up for their expanded intelligence roles.

During the next two months, Walbrecht made regular trips to London to answer questions from MoD officials who prepared authority documents for ministerial signature. Scicluna later confided that the SR-71 initiative went down very well because of long-standing intelligence sharing connections, and because one of his junior staff officials had suggested calling the proposal a simple 'change of mode' of current operations from intermittent to permanent basing. The permissive loop was then closed and the SR-71s could come to England, where they would remain the planespotters favourite attraction for many years.

On 5 April 1984, Prime Minister Thatcher announced that a detachment of SR-71 aircraft had formed at the Suffolk base. A blanket clearance to operate two Habus from the United Kingdom had been granted by the government, but certain sorties would still require prior high-level approval from the MoD. Moreover, those especially sensitive operations would require 'a clearance' from the PM herself.

Anglo-American co-operation extended into SR-71 missions themselves, Habu sorties venturing into the Barents and the Baltic areas was sometimes being coordinated with the RAF's small fleet of Hawker Siddeley Nimrod R. Mk 1 Elint aircraft, operated at that time from RAF Wyton, Huntingdonshire, by No. 51 Sqn. Such co-operation also extended to the German Marineflieger, which used Breguet Atlantics in a similar role to that of the Nimrods. During such sorties, the SR-71 took on the role of provocateur, with the timings of both aircraft controlled to within seconds, to ensure that the slower Elint platform was in the optimum position to take full advantage of signals that were not usually forthcoming from the Soviet side.

FIGHTERS

Immediately after World War II, it was clear that two geopolitical systems would dominate the world. Inherent in both was their mutually abiding mistrust of one another, which sowed the seeds for an arms race that would continue until one system achieved dominance over the other. The emergence

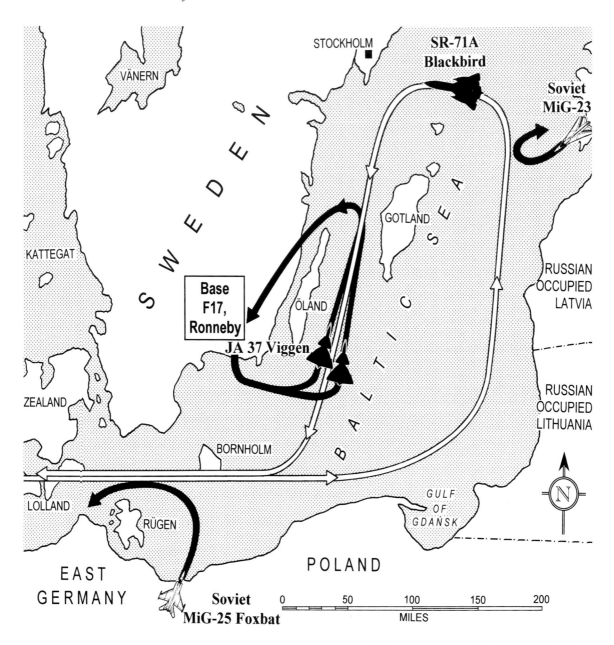

This map shows the SR-71's standard route around the Baltic Sea, with the typical 'engagement' zones of Soviet air force MiG-25 and MiG-31, and MiG-23 fighters, as well as the area of operations of the Swedish air force's JA 37 Viggen, against the Habu.

of the Convair B-58 Hustler, the Lockheed A-12 and SR-71 and potentially the North American B-70 Valkyrie and Lockheed B-12, inevitably provoked the self-perpetuating cause and effect response within the opposing power bloc when, as early as 1960, the Mikoyan-Gurevich Opytno-Konstruktorskoye Byuro – OKB design bureau – was tasked to develop a multi-role

supersonic interceptor, capable of defeating these new and emerging threats then under development in the United States.

The result was the development of its first 'big MiG' – the spectacular MiG-25. The type officially entered service following a directive dated 13 April 1972; the first PVO (air defence forces) MiG-25P units were stationed near Moscow, Kiev, Perm, Baku, Rostov and in the North and Far East. By the mid-1970s, the MiG-25P constituted the backbone of the Soviet air force's interceptor inventory and soon after converting to type, PVO units stationed near

Soviet border areas were carrying out intercepts on SR-71s involved in peripheral reconnaissance missions of the Soviet Union.

On 6 September 1976, Lt Victor Belenko, a PVO pilot based at Chuguyevka air base, located to the north of Vladivostok, defected to the West via Japan in 'his' MiG-25P, providing the US intelligence community with a windfall. The aircraft was virtually dismantled by US Air Force intelligence staff and although later returned to its country of origin, it was obvious to Soviet officials that the aircraft's capabilities were now severely compromised and, unless the design was drastically upgraded, the type's combat efficiency would be enormously degraded.

In a joint effort that involved the Ministry of Aircraft Industry and military experts, the Mikoyan-Gurevich OKB embarked upon a comprehensive upgrade programme. The earlier monopulse, low-PRF Smerch-A2 (Izdelye 720M) radar was replaced by the much-improved Sapfeer-25. This new radar unit was lager than its predecessor and required a modest amount of fuselage stretch forward of the cockpit to facilitate its accommodation; its improved capabilities enabled detection of targets with an RCS of 16 m^2 (172 sq ft) at a range of over 100 km (63 miles). An IRST system was developed which, when coupled with the radar, made the weapons system less susceptible to the effects of enemy ECM; it also provided the platform with the capability to perform 'sneak attacks', without switching on its radar. The upgrade also included installation of the BAN-75 target indication and guidance system, that acted in concert with the ground-based Luch-1 ('Ray') guidance system to align the optical axis of the aircraft's radar with its target. This also ensured that the MiG-25's radar was less sensitive to jamming. In addition, a new IFF set and ground-based command system was also provided (the latter replaced the Vozdookh-1M and incorporated a jam-proof aircraft receiver). R-60 (AA-8 'Aphid') air-to-air missiles (AAMs) would be carried, as well as R-40TD (AA-7 'Acrid') IR-homing or R-40R active-radar homing AAMS. Finally, and perhaps not surprisingly, the upgraded platform would be powered by newer engines, two R-15-BD-300s. Work progressed rapidly on the design, designated MiG-25PD or Izdelye 84D (D for Dorabotannyy, modified or upgraded) and given the ASCC reporting name 'Foxbat-E', and by the end of 1982 the entire fleet had also undergone a mid-life update programme, leading to the designation MiG-25PDS (Perekhvatchik, Doralotannyy v Stroyou, or field-modified interceptor).

There now follows a fascinating insight into MiG-25PD operations as conducted by the 787th IAP against Det 4 SR-71s flying over the Baltic Sea.

It is reproduced here by courtesy of Lutz Freund, editor of *Sowjetische Fliegerkrafte Deutschland 1945–1994*: 'Between 14 July 1982 and 10 August 1989, the 787th IAP (Istrebeetel'nyy Aviapolk, or Fighter Aviation Regiment) operated the MiG-25PD. This was more or less the same period of time that the SR-71 operated out of Mildenhall, UK. With the retirement of the SR-71 from the UK, the MiG-25 was replaced by the MiG-23 and MiG-29.

'Around 1980, the Warsaw Pact's air defence forces (PVO) introduced a new alarm call – "Jastreb" (hawk). It meant that a US Lockheed SR-71 Blackbird is approaching! Later on it became the standard alarm signal for all high and very fast-flying targets.

'Under normal circumstances the alarm call came several minutes before an SR-71 with its typical flight parameters at an altitude of 20–25 km [65,617–82021 ft], flying at some 800–900 m [2,625–2,953 ft] per second, entered the range of Soviet and GDR (German Democratic Republic) radar air surveillance and radar guidance troops. In parallel, this alarm started action at Finow air base, resulting in scrambling a MiG-25PD from the 787th IAP. The MiG took off and approached the intruder by flying a wide curve on a parallel course with a separation of a few kilometres. For this MiG-25 manoeuvre, either the whole northern or southern part of the GDR had to be used. On all military maps the MiG-25's flight path was shown as a big circle.

'Depending on the weather situation, SR-71s flew reconnaissance missions once or twice a week along the Warsaw Pact border. During military manoeuvres flight frequency could rise up to two missions per 24 hours. For all of these SR-71 flights there were two standard routes. The approach towards GDR air space was from Denmark. Over the West German city of Kiel the flight path continued either to Aufklärungsstrecke 2 (reconnaissance route 2) which was along the Baltic Sea coast line to Leningrad (now St Petersburg) and back, or to Aufklärungsstrecke 5 (reconnaissance route 5) along the GDR's western border. Such missions normally lasted some 60 minutes. The distance between the SR-71 and the border varied due to the aircraft's high velocity. It was unable to follow the exact border line. Sometimes an SR-71 closed up to within a few kilometres of the GDR's border in the area of Boizenburg or just slipped over it!

'Had there ever been an order to shoot down the intruder, the MiG-25 crews would have been ready! But the routine of this event never escalated to such a dramatic situation. After a short time with the aircraft flying next to each other, the MiG-25PD headed home. The normal flight path home to Finow was over Poland.

'Beside the airborne defenders, missile defence forces were also on alarm status. It would have been possible to successfully destroy the intruder, but the parameters for a successful lock-on and shoot down included a slightly lateral fly by of the SR-71 to the missile's launch ramp to reduce the extreme altitude. Troops from the missile air-defence forces remained on alert as long as SR-71 Blackbirds were inside the spectrum of the Soviet radio-listening troops.'

In 1972, the Mikoyan-Gurevich OKB began working on a new design which was destined to replace the MiG-25 interceptors. Designed around two D-30F6 afterburning turbofans, the aircraft would have both a lower top speed and ceiling than the MiG-25PD. However, this fourth-generation interceptor, equipped with a weapons control system based on the SBI-16 Zaslon (ASCC 'Flash Dance') phased-array radar, enabled its two crewmembers to intercept and destroy targets in either the front or rear hemisphere, day or night, in any weather conditions and while operating in a passive or an active jamming environment, while flying at high supersonic speeds. Designated MiG-31 (ASCC 'Foxhound'), the type's final Act of Acceptance was signed in December 1981 and deliveries to PVO units began in 1982.

Like the MiG-25PD before it, the new MiG also had a full IRST capability. Located in a retractable pod, the STP IRST enabled the aircraft to execute attacks without recourse to its radar. Typical armament consisted of four R-33 (AA-9 'Amos') long-range air-to-air missiles carried semi-recessed in the fuselage on AKU-410 ejector racks, or four R-60M missiles if the target was to be engaged at short range. Each R-33 missile weighed around 1,058 lb (480 kg), including its 103-lb (48-kg) HE/fragmentation warhead and had a range of about 75 miles (120 km). The new Zaslon radar touted a detection range of 180 km (111 miles) and a target-tracking range of 120 km (75 miles). The aircraft's avionics suite also included the BAN-75 command link, the SAU-155M automatic flight control system, the APD-518 digital secure data link system – this enabled a flight of four MiG-31s to swap data generated by their radars provided that they were within 200 km (124 miles) of one another, the RK-RLDN secure data link and the SPO-15SL radar homing and warning system (RHAWS). A highly capable navigation suite enabled the MiG-31's crew to operate confidently in the Arctic theatre of operations.

The major units to be equipped with the type were the 153rd IAP stationed at Morshansk, the 786th IAP, at Pravdinsk, the 180th IAP at Gromovo, the 174th IAP at Monchegorsk, the 72nd IAP at Amderma and the 518th IAP at Talagi.

Russian military aviation writer Valery

Romanenko has undertaken detailed research for *Beyond the Secret Missions* and has pieced together, for the first time, a unique insight into MiG-31 operations against Det 4 SR-71s. With the help of translators James F. Gebhardt, Ilya Grinberg and Dr Heinz Berger, the fruits of that effort are detailed below: 'Military 1st Class Pilot Mikhail Myagkiy, Guards Major (ret.), is one of the PVO (Protivo-vozdushnoy Ororony, or air defence force) pilots who executed intercepts of the SR-71 near the border of the USSR in the far north. Between 1984 and 1987, he was a Mikoyan MiG-31 'Foxhound' commander with the 174th GvIAP (Gvardeiskaya Istrebeitel'nyi Aviatsionnyi Polk, or Guards Fighter Aviation Regiment). During this period he conducted 14 successful SR-71 intercepts.

'Myagkiy graduated from Armavir VVAKUL PVO (Higher Military Aviation Red Banner Academy of Pilots of the PVO) in 1977. He started his front-line service on the Sukhoi Su-9 "Fishpot". He then qualified as a 1st Class Pilot on the Mikoyan-Gurevich MiG-23ML "Flogger-G", having accumulated approximately 600 hours of total flying time. At that time he held the rank of Captain.

'In 1983, only two regiments flew the MiG-31. The 786th IAP at Pravdinsk (near Gorkiy) was the first of these units, followed by the 174th GvIAP at Monchegorsk (near Murmansk). Before operating the MiG-31, the 174th GvIAP flew the Yakovlev Yak-28P "Firebar". During the transition to the MiG-31, many pilots left the unit – apparently they did not want to master the new aircraft. The majority of the remaining 174th trainees were therefore weapon systems operators (WSOs). Therefore, pilots had to be selected from other regiments, because at that time only 1st Class Pilots were being selected to fly the MiG-31.

'Consequently, the PVO's 14th Air Army was required to supply one pilot. At that time Captain Myagkiy was acting as a flight commander. Transfer onto the MiG-31 meant a reduction in position, since the air army commander did not release pilots from their permanent duty positions, but allowed transfer to temporary positions.

'Myagkiy arrived at the 174th GvIAP in October 1983. The regiment had already been flying the MiG-31 for 18 months and had frequently flown missions against the SR-71.

'After a month, Myagkiy was sent for transition training to the TsBP IA-PVO (Tsentry Boyevoy Podgotovki, IA-PVO, or centre for combat readiness, PVO fighter aviation) in Savasleyka. The MiG-31 WSOs, with two of whom Myagkiy would later fly, also underwent transition training at Savasleyka.

'Only conversion training onto type was taught at Savasleyka. Over the course of two months, the pilots studied two aircraft: the MiG-31 and the

Majs Jim Jiggens and Ted Ross begin accelerating '960 down Mildenhall's runway for another operational sortie, the slight flash from the right engine coming from TEB ignition. The left engine is already delivering maximum thrust. On 'light up', a sharp rudder deflection was often necessary to correct for the asymmetric thrust resulting from one afterburner lighting before the other. (Paul F. Crickmore)

Mikoyan-Gurevich MiG-25PU "Foxbat-C" (the students took a separate examination on each aircraft). Initially, they flew the dual-control MiG-25PU two-seat trainers. Four flights were conducted in the MiG-25PU, and the fifth, sixth, and seventh flights in the MiG-31 (with an instructor). On the eighth MiG-31 flight, the pilots went solo (with a WSO in the back seat rather than an instructor). After this, training was solely on the MiG-31.

'The flight-training programme was very short. On 21 May 1984, Captain Myagkiy received his authorisation for independent flights in the MiG-31, and on 21 June 1984, he received his authorisation for combat readiness. This meant that he could now fly and conduct a combat patrol in daytime and in bad weather. By the end of July, the Captain was carrying out combat patrols.

Mikhail Myagkiy executed his first mission against the SR-71 from a combat readiness posture on 21 August 1984. According to his recollection, the procedures for a successful intercept were crazy, and completely inadequate when considered against the threat posed by the SR-71's spy flights. The speed and altitude of the American aircraft simply hypnotised everyone. Therefore, each attempted SR-71 interception was considered a top priority, not only for fighter aviation but also for the PVO's entire 10th Army. The ground vectoring station on Rybachiy Peninsula typically made the first "sighting". Intercepting aircraft then took off from all the airfields in the north where weather permitted. A mistake at any level – by a pilot, the ground personnel, a command post, or a ground vectoring station – brought with it the threat of a military tribunal (court martial).

'Each fighter regiment executed an intercept in its own sector. For the 174th GvIAP, this was the sector of the Soviet border from Kharlovka to Cape Svyatoy Nos. For the unit's MiG-31 crews, 16 minutes elapsed from the moment the alert was sounded to the take-off command being given. Of this time, two minutes were used to put on the VKK-3 (vysotnyy kompensiruyushchiy kostyum, or altitude-compensating suit), two minutes to run 50 to 60 m [55 to 66 yards] in the VKK and get strapped into the aircraft, and the remainder of the time to check out the systems, start engines, and taxi. After 16 minutes the fighter would be parked at the end of the runway, with its engines running, fully prepared for take-off.

'When the SR-71 alert was first given, the technical personnel ran to the aircraft and initially removed its R-60 (AA-8 "Aphid") short-range missiles, because they would be disabled at velocities above Mach 1.75 (the standard MiG-31 ordnance load included four R-60s and four long-range R-33s (AA-9 "Amos")).

'Before the aircraft was launched, its INS had to be activated in minimum time. As soon as the green lights confirming that the INS was aligned came on (after approximately three minutes), the engines could be fired up.

'The two crews of the ready flight prepared immediately. Everything was accomplished in a somewhat tense environment. Since these aircraft were from the first production series, there were occasions of system failure, particularly during the turning off of ground power. If the ground power plug was pulled out too abruptly, the INS system malfunctioned. The crew that managed to reach full readiness first was the crew that launched.

'Having received permission to taxi, the aircraft took up a position at the end of the runway. Here, the crews sometimes had to "cool their jets" for several minutes. The scheme for intercepting the SR-71 was computed down to the second, and therefore the MiGs had to launch exactly 16 minutes after the initial alert. During this period of time the ground vectoring station determined what route (out route or return route) the SR-71 was following.

'Five minutes after take-off, the MiG was already at an altitude of 16000 m [52,493 ft]. The afterburners would still be lit and the crew experiencing significant g. In addition, the MiG-31 had a disconcerting idiosyncrasy. At high supersonic speeds (above Mach 2.35), the control stick moved all the way forward, pushing up against the instrument panel. The pilot had to extend his arm fully, which was very uncomfortable, and quickly caused fatigue. However, the MiG-31 was significantly more benign in its flight characteristics at supersonic speeds than the MiG-25. The great weight of the MiG-31's on board equipment and systems had an effect on its performance compared to the "Foxbat", but its instrumentation was significantly greater and a generation more modern.

'During an SR-71 intercept, many commonly accepted practices were broken. For example, take-off was executed in a northerly direction, while normal procedure called for a take off to the south. A number of limitations were also removed: for example, the altitude for transition to supersonic flight was established as 11000 m [36,089 ft], but during SR-71 intercepts Soviet aircraft were permitted to pass through the sound barrier at 8000 m [26,247 ft]. Ground vectoring was usually conducted at an altitude of 16000 m [52,493 ft], but during an attack the MiG-31s reached 18500–19500 m [60,696–63,976 ft] (aiming to establish the best missile launch

trajectory, the MiGs gained as much altitude as they could, right up to 20000 m/65,617 ft).

'Information about the Blackbird normally arrived at the command post when the spyplane was three hours out (this information coming from a radio intercept station). As the SR-71s flew out of Mildenhall conversations between their crews and those of their supporting tankers were "captured" during in-flight refuelling, so if tankers showed up, the IA-PVO waited for the SR-71.

'The standard SR-71 route was normally loop shaped. If the spyplane appeared from the direction of Norway, it tracked toward the White Sea, farther to the north toward Novaya Zemlya, then turned around on a reverse course to the west over the Arctic Ocean. This track was called a "straight loop". If it initially flew from the direction of the Arctic Ocean toward Novaya Zemlya, then south toward the White Sea, then to the west along the coast of the USSR toward Norway, its track was called the "return loop". The tactics of the intercept were geared toward the type of loop the spyplane was flying.

'The SR-71 was intercepted using only a thermal channel (infra-red, IR). The massive IR emissions of its engines permitted it to be detected at a distance of 100–120 km [62–75 miles]. The MiG-31's thermal detection system was called OMB (or optical multi-functional apparatus) and was mounted in the lower nose of the aircraft. The device was lowered and turned on by the WSO. The MiG's radar was not turned on. On combat alert the radar was set on a combat frequency, and in order not to expose this frequency to a "probable enemy", the radar was not turned on. A passive system (the thermal apparatus) was adequate for a reliable intercept.

'After capture of the target by the OMB, a target indicator showing the range to the target appeared on the SEI (sistema edinoy indikatsii, or unified display system) in the pilot's head-up display (HUD). A voice indicator, using a pleasant female voice (known as "Rita" to the crews), announced "Attack!." The range to the target was calculated by the aircraft's BTsVM (on board digital computer), using a triangulation method that employed other on-board sensors. This was very good, because, for example, on the MiG-25 the pilot did not receive range-to-target data, it was only passed from ground vectoring stations. Also the ZDR (or zone of range of missiles, basically the engagement envelope for the missiles) was projected on the HUD.

'After the "Attack!" signal, missile preparation began. Targeting instructions were handed off to the GSN (golovka samonavedeniya, or the target-seeking device of the missile, ie. its seeker head). Four green triangles appeared on the image

Majs Brian Shul and Walt Watkins are busy working through the challenge and response checklist prior to launching '973 on an operational sortie. Note the rudder deflection, which is the result of controllability tests. (Paul F. Crickmore)

of the MiG in the cockpit display after the missiles had been prepared for launch.

'The BRLS (bortovaya radiolokatsionnaya stantsiya, or on-board radar) was turned on only in the event that the vectoring station issued an order to destroy the target. In this case, the WSO would turn the radar on. Information regarding the target would then be instantly transferred from the OMB to the radar. After this the pilot had only to push the firing button and the missiles would be launched.

'If the SR-71 had violated Soviet airspace, a live missile launch would have been carried out. There was practically no chance that the aircraft could avoid an R-33. But in the early 1980s the Blackbirds did not violate the border, although they sometimes "tickled" it (came right up to it). Indeed, local counter-intelligence dreamt of finding pieces of the SR-71, if not on land then in the territorial waters of the USSR.'

Mikhail Myagkiy particularly remembers his eighth intercept, when he managed to gain visual contact with an SR-71, and not just in the form of a spot on a screen. As a keepsake he preserved the printout of the recording from the 'black box' through which all the intercept data was processed.

Here is how he describes that flight: 'I went on combat alert on 31 January 1986 as normal. I drew my personal weapon in the morning and then headed for the on-duty crew hut.

'They alerted us for an SR-71 intercept at approximately 11:00. They sounded the alarm with a shrill bell and then confirmed it with a loudspeaker. To this day I have been averse even to ordinary school bells, because a bell was the first signal for a burst of adrenaline. The appearance of an SR-71 was always accompanied by nervousness. Everyone began to talk in frenzied voices, to scurry about, and react to the situation with excessive emotion.

'I ran to put on my VKK and GSh-6 [germoshlem, or flight helmet], and over that a fur-lined flight jacket with IPS [individualnaya podvesnaya systema, or parachute harness], and ran the 60 m [55 yards] to the aircraft. I was not flying with my own WSO, but with Aleksey Parshin, our flight WSO. When I sat down and was being strapped in (it was simple and convenient to be strapped in wearing a jacket and IPS, which is why we flew in them), the readiness lamps for the INS were lit. I pressed the engine start button, reported to the command post, and immediately received the command to taxi to the runway. We sat on the runway for about five minutes; my WSO "read the prayer" [loudly went through the pre-take off checklist].

'After the take-off order from the command post we lit the afterburners and took off. Our take-off speed was approximately 360 km/h [224 mph]. Not coming off afterburners, we went for altitude with a 60° right bank and turned to a course of 100°. We attained 8000 m [26,247 ft] and reached the horizontal area (for acceleration) in which we passed through the sound barrier. Here vectoring station "Gremikha" had already assumed responsibility for vectoring us. Our indicated speed at this time was 1190 km/h [739 mph]. We went for altitude again, up to 16000 m [52,493 ft]. At 16000 m we were flying at Mach 2.3 and made a left turn to a combat course of 360°. The WSO lowered and turned on the OMB and within five seconds had captured the target. A feminine voice in the earphones announced, "Attack!", and a symbol was illuminated on the SEI. The SR-71 was proceeding on the "return loop", from east to west, so we began the intercept immediately.

'As usual, we executed an "aiming run" from 16000 m, gaining altitude to 18900 m [62,008 ft]. After closing to 60 km [37 miles] I spotted the contrail of the SR-71 on an intersecting course. I reported the heading to my WSO over the SPU [samoletnoye peregovornoye ustroystvo, or intercom], "I have visual!" A contrail at 22000–23000 m [69,000–72,000 ft] is very rare, but on this day the weather was excellent and the air was transparent, and the contrail was clearly visible. I passed under the spyplane, it was 3000-4000 m [8,843–13,123 ft] above us, and even managed to make out its black silhouette. The SR-71 was flying over the ocean ever so carefully on a track 60 km [37 miles] out from, and parallel to, the coast. I reported, "we're breaking off," to the command post and came off afterburners. We had been airborne for 15 minutes 40 seconds.

'The Blackbird was flying its normal route, over neutral waters, and it made no sense to follow it. Therefore the vectoring station gave the command to turn onto a course for our airfield. We dropped down to 15000 m [49,213 ft], transitioned to horizontal flight, and engaged a stopwatch. This was the so-called "area for canopy cooling". During flight at speeds in excess of Mach 2, the skin, including the canopy, heated up to 800°C [1,472°F]. Therefore, it was necessary to cool it. Failure to do so might result in cracking or catastrophic failure during subsequent altitude reduction. Our speed remained in the order of Mach 1.6.

'After 30 seconds we once again began to lose altitude. We went subsonic at the normal 12000 m [39,370 ft]. Dropping down to 8000 m [26,247 ft], we tracked toward our airfield. After the last vector was issued the command centre handed us off to our regiment command post, which directed me to a checkpoint at an altitude of 4100 m [13,451 ft]. At

32 km [20 miles] out from the airfield I lowered the gear and began to descend. We conducted a straight-in landing at a speed of 310 km/h [193 mph]. The entire flight had lasted 50 minutes.

'During the 15 to 20 minutes when I was on a combat course, the second alert crew was sitting on the ground with engines running. Later they shut down their engines, but the pilot and WSO sat in their aircraft in readiness until our landing.

'This was the only occasion in my 14 intercepts when I saw the SR-71 with my own eyes. It was obvious that a combination of circumstances facilitated this event: good weather that was rare in the north, clear air and unusual atmospheric conditions, when the contrail was clearly visible at an altitude of 23000 m [75,459 ft].'

Mikhail Myagkiy retired in 1992 with the rank of Guards Major at the age of 36.

The SR-71's awesome performance capabilities also provided a unique opportunity for allied fighter controllers and fighter pilots to evaluate various intercept solutions against a high-speed, high-altitude threat, as Rolf Jonsson, a retired Swedish air force fighter controller now recalls: 'The most spectacular alerts in the Swedish air force during the 1980s occurred about once a week, when the Blackbird was operating in the Baltic. These were also probably the most frustrating events of the entire Cold War, with our fighters trying to reach the same altitude and position as this high-speed, high-altitude target, efforts which, if successful, would allow the fortunate pilot to catch a brief glimpse of the fantastic SR-71 at quite close quarters.

'When the SR-71 first began operating in Europe our air force was equipped with the Saab J 35F Draken and although intercept attempts were made, the aircraft's performance wasn't up to the task, but one point was clear, the method that offered the greatest opportunity of success was a frontal attack, with both aircraft exactly on a 180° divergent heading – always assuming of course that the SR-71 didn't turn! Other very important factors to try to determine when planning an intercept were the high altitude air temperature and the SR-71's altitude.

'When the Saab 37 Viggen entered service, suddenly the mix was right; the aircraft's performance and avionics capabilities, combined with the eagerness of its pilots and a high degree of teamwork with the Air Command and Control Centres, including the radar tracker (a conscript), the intercept controller and the pilots.

'For everything to work, the pilot needed to reach the speed and altitude that corresponded with information derived from the data tracker system in the Air Operations Centre (AOC). This data determined exactly where and when the pilot needed to initiate a pull-up from cruising altitude to acquire a radar contact. If the pilot failed to lock his radar on first time, that was it; the opportunity was gone – at least for another week. On some occasions, our pilots had problems locking-on because the SR-71 crew activated their defensive countermeasure systems, but pilots soon learned how to avoid triggering such systems – also an electronic counter-countermeasures system was built into the JA 37 fighter version of the Viggen.

'Another high-performance aircraft operating from bases around the Baltic was the Mikoyan-Gurevich MiG-25 "Foxbat"; this had a speed advantage on the JA 37 Viggen, but the latter had a superior weapon system and, from 1981, was already using an information dissemination system similar to JTIDS (Joint Tactical Information Distribution System), which the US later deployed on tactical aircraft such as the F-15C Eagle.

'The most difficult phase of the intercept for pilots was during the steep climb, since they had to monitor their engine instruments to ensure they remained within the Volvo Flygmotor RM8B turbofan's EGT limits, and also scan their radar screens. During this phase the pilot tilted his radar scan angle down, to its maximum of -15°. The radar then had just a few seconds to locate and then lock-on to the target before the two aircraft passed one another with a combined closing speed of Mach 5; it was an extremely impressive spectacle to watch on radar from the ground! The intercept window was incredibly tight, and all the SR-71 pilot needed to do during the fighter's final climb phase was manoeuvre just slightly and the intercept solution changed and failed. One of the main problems facing our Viggen pilots was that one of the rules in their OSF (Orders for Safe Flight) stipulated that flight above 16000 m [52,493 ft] was prohibited without the use of a full pressure suit and these weren't available, so our pilots needed to be careful or they could be grounded by their divisional commanders.

'The SR-71 "Baltic Express" flights were usually known about an hour before the aircraft entered the area. The Habu always entered the Baltic Sea over a reporting point named "Codan", (located about 50 miles/80 km south of Copenhagen) and on a heading of about 090°. This usually triggered a scramble by a pair of JA 37s that were kept on alert at either F10 Ängelholm, F17 Ronneby or F13 Norrköping, although sometimes even temporary bases like Visby were used. The best base for an SR-71A intercept, however, was F17 Ronneby because this was best positioned for the acceleration and climb phase – about 19–31 miles [30–50 km] southeast of Gotland. The SR-71's Baltic flight path remained the same throughout the time it operated in Europe and consisted of a single anticlockwise loop that took about

30 minutes to complete. During this time, the SR-71 would have been monitoring Soviet submarine positions in their harbours at Rostock (Warnemünde), Peenemünde, Gdansk, Baltijsk, Klaipeda, Liepaja and Ventspils. It remained in international airspace and first flew off the Polish coast, then just before the Bay of Gdanska, well inside the Kalingrad enclave, the aircraft turned left, onto a heading of about 015°. With the Habu now flying at 70–80,000 ft [21336–24384 m] only the Sukhoi Su-15 "Flagons" based at Vainode, in Latvia, had a chance of making an intercept and it's doubtful that any of them were actually successful – certainly the MiG-21 "Fishbeds" and MiG-23 "Floggers" based at Pamu, Haapsalu and Tapa in Estonia had no chance; their trails on our radar screens in Sweden were so harmless it was painful!

'The Habu then proceeded to a point about 37 miles [60 km] west of the Estonian island of Saaremaa, where it began a long, programmed, left turn, taking it onto a southerly heading of about 190°, rolling out east of Stockholm. It then passed between the islands of Gotland and Oland, and this always impressed us because the corridor of international airspace between the two islands is only two miles wide: the Habu only violated our airspace once (this was the only time that it became necessary for the Swedish foreign department to protest about an airspace violation) when an SR-71 was forced to interrupt its high speed left turn, reduce speed and descend from its position in the north of its route, due to an in-flight emergency. [On that occasion, the SR-71 was forced to fly directly over Gotland. At this point AJ 37 Viggen pilots took hand-held photos of the Habu and it is clear to see from these that the aircraft was flying on one engine]. It was in this area that our JA 37 pilots carried out their practice intercepts. Once 35–46 miles (56–74 km) southeast of Gotland the "Baltic Express" turned onto a heading of about 265° and exited the area over the same point that it had entered.

'Almost every time the SR-71 was about to leave the Baltic, a lone MiG-25PD "Foxbat-E", belonging to the Soviet air force's 787th IAP, stationed at Finow-Eberswalde in the German Democratic Republic, scrambled. The 787th maintained three squadrons (around 40 aircraft) which may have flown only the MiG-25PD, but probably consisted of two MiG-23M "Flogger-B" units and one of MiG-25PDs. A detachment of the latter was also maintained at Wittstock. Another detachment might have been based at another southern airfield in East Germany. Arriving at its exit point, the "Baltic Express" was flying at about 72,000 ft [21946 m], and the lone MiG would reach about 63,000 ft [19202 m] in a left turn, before rolling out and always completing its stern attack 1.6 nm [1.8 miles; 2.9 km] behind its target. We

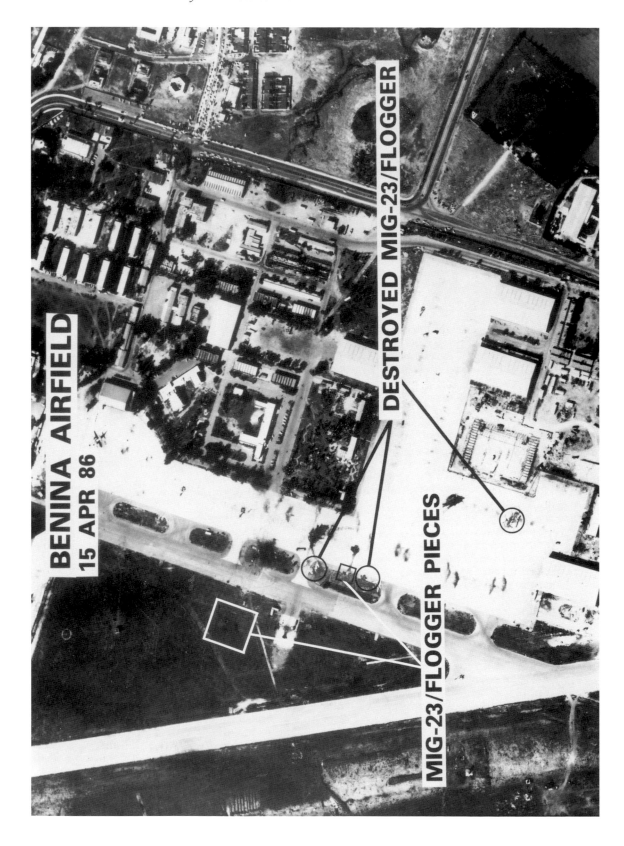

BENINA AIRFIELD
15 APR 86

DESTROYED MIG-23/FLOGGER

MIG-23/FLOGGER PIECES

were always impressed by this precision, it was always 63,000 ft and 1.6 nm behind the SR-71.

'When the SR-71 detachment at Mildenhall was deactivated, the Soviet 787th IAP re-equipped with new Mikoyan MiG-29 "Fulcrum-Cs", but even after the withdrawl, we believe that at least three "Foxbats" remained behind at Finow-Eberswalde – just in case the "Baltic Express" returned!'

It is interesting to note when reading Rolf Jonsson's account involving a lone MiG-25PD out of Finow-Eberswalde, that the simulated attack consistently terminated when the interceptor was at 63,000 ft and 1.6 nm behind its target; this would seem to suggest that these were the parameters necessary for its weapons system to effect a successful intercept if the order to fire was ever given. However, this will of course forever remain supposition.

The key to the JA 37's success was the integration of a highly sophisticated data link which, until recently, remained highly classified. The Swedish air force gained significant expertise in the data link field with a system installed in the J 35F back in 1965. However, the system installed in the JA 37 Jaktviggen (or fighter Viggen) is far more capable than that of its predecessor, and entered service in 1982. It has the ability to uplink and download data to four active aircraft on the same link, it also has the capability to downlink data from an airborne JA 37 to others still on the ground. Data link information is displayed on the Horizontal Situation Display (HSD) and a tactical display, the latter utilising link symbology that can be overlaid with an electronic map displayed on a multifunction display (MFD). As an integral part of the Stri-60 command-and-control system that was built around it, the JA 37 can take-off, attack, land, refuel and re-arm, then re-engage, with little or no voice communications, while enduring heavy jamming.

The first successful intercept of an SR-71 in the Baltic was carried out by Per-Olof Eldh, who now recalls the incident: 'In 1980, I joined 2nd Squadron "Blue Martins" of Fighter Wing 13, equipped with the JA 37 fighter Viggen and based at Bravalla, just outside the town of Norrköping, on the Baltic coast. Our task was to conduct operational tasks and evaluations that were focused on air defence and air superiority. We were already equipped with a data link from the air defence network, the next step was to establish it between fighters and we achieved this

Det 4's SR-71s provided analysts in the Pentagon with concrete proof of the damage inflicted on Benina airfield by the US Navy strikes during the operations against Libya. The quality of the images taken allowed destroyed MiG-23s on the tarmac and burnt-out hangars to be seen clearly. (USAF)

in 1981; integrating this with the PS-46 air-to-air pulse-Doppler radar and the SkyFlash missile provided the JA 37 with a significantly enhanced capability. Looking at the map display on the MFD, the pilot could see other friendlies, the enemy, SAM sites, etc, and this information was constantly updated via the data link by fighter controllers and other JA 37s giving the pilot unprecedented levels of situational awareness. In fact, the system was so good that we could employ the same tactics – line abreast, box formations or scissors manoeuvres day or night, in VFR (Visual Flight Rules) or IFR (Instrument Flight Rules) conditions. When I conducted the first Swedish air force intercept of an SR-71, the target had completed its northbound pass, off the Soviet coastline, and had turned west, south of the Finnish island of Aland and was tracking south, on a heading that would take it between Gotland and Oland. The data link from the fighter controller was on and I lined up for a head-on attack with a target angle of 180°. From my altitude of 8000 m [26,247 ft], I accelerated to Mach 1.35 then pulled up, very gently, continuing to accelerate to between Mach 1.7 and Mach 2.0, topping out at between 18500 and 20000 m [60,696 and 65,617 ft]. All the target data was on my map display, including radar detection of the target at maximum range, which then locked on, immediately afterwards. I simulated missile launches – the closing velocity was very high, between Mach 4.5 and 5.0; the SR-71 was flying at Mach 2.98 and at 21500 m [70,538 ft]. I had visual contact.

'In total I have five hot intercepts against the SR-71 to my credit. All can be described as successful. I was visual three times. On a couple of occasions the SR-71 was contrailing; this was very useful because you could do a visual check to ensure you ended up in the right spot!

'When we began conducting these SR-71 intercepts, the squadron began a special air safety programme and we all underwent an intense series of emergency procedure checks in the simulator, because we were flying at the outer edges of the envelope and at higher risk.

'On 9 January 1986, while leading a JA 37 three-ship in aircraft tail number "38", we received target data immediately after take-off from Bravalla. We flew in trail, receiving updated target information over the link from both the fighter controller and the other fighters in the formation. All three of us carried out successful intercepts, between 13:14 hours and 13:25 hours, about 31 miles (50 km) west of the town of Visby, on the island of Gotland. Major Moller was number two in tail number "60" and Captain Ulf Johansson number three in tail number "53". I remember that the SR-71 was flying at an altitude of 72,178 ft [22000 m] and a speed of Mach 2.9. Ulf had some difficulties coming back to earth, he actually reached the target's altitude and passed the SR-71 head-on, at the same altitude with some side separation, but suffered a high temperature engine stall! A cartoon drawn by SAS Captain Stefan Lofren to commemorate this event was used as a poster in our briefing room.'

UNDER THREAT?

At 10:10 hours on 3 June 1986, Majs 'Stormy' Boudreaux and Ted Ross left Mildenhall in '980, heading out across the North Sea toward their first refuelling west of Norway on another Barents/Baltic sortie. At 26,000 ft in the refuelling track, they found the sun directly ahead of them and clouds all around as they closed for contact with the KC-135s in diffuse and strangely-angled sunlight, which reflected brightly off the bottoms of the tankers.

As soon as the boomer made contact, 'Stormy' found himself flying formation in almost blinding conditions, with the SR-71's cockpit instruments obscured (in the dark shadow of the dashboard below the windscreen), forcing him to arrange his tiltable car-like sun-visor to shield against the high contrast conditions. That effort proved of little value for while the SR-71 was in the contact position on the boom, the tanker's reference lights for formation flying were flashing in such extreme contrast that they appeared to be surrounded by 'sea, or sky, or whatever'. A strong sensation of vertigo overtook 'Stormy', leaving him with a false sense of diving and climbing (and with the even more powerful sensation of flying inverted while refuelling). An interphone call to Ted assured 'Stormy' that he was not upside-down; he was then able to continue filling '980's tanks while fighting his sense of flying 'straight up, or straight down'.

After clearing the tanker, and his senses, 'Stormy' climbed through 60,000 ft (18288 m), where he noted through his periscope that '980 was still pulling contrails which should have stopped above that altitude. Another check at 70,000 ft (21336 m) revealed that he was still 'conning', a process which he hoped would surely stop before they approached their target area. Upon entering the Barents Sea zone, the aircraft began a programmed left turn to the north east and then reversed in a large sweeping right turn to roll out on a westerly heading, which would take them on the 'collection run' and back across the entry point. When established on the westerly heading north of Archangel, they noted that they were still 'conning', which was most abnormal at high altitudes. To add to their dismay, 'Stormy' spotted three other contrails ahead of them and to the left, but turning to converge in what might be an intercept. Another southerly glance revealed

more 'cons' closing from the left, but at a lower altitude.

These six Soviet fighters, each separated by approximately 15 miles (24 km), were executing what appeared to be a well-rehearsed turning intercept manoeuvre to pop up somewhere in the vicinity of the fast-moving Habu and fire off some sophisticated air-to-air missiles. The Soviet fighter pilots had executed an in-place turn, which would have placed them in a perfect position for a head-on attack had '980's track penetrated Soviet air space. As Ted monitored the fighters' electronic activities, 'Stormy' increased speed and altitude.

Suddenly a contrail shot by just beneath the nose of '980, leaving both crewmembers waiting for a missile or another aircraft to appear which might have 'spoiled their whole day'. It was with great relief that 'Stormy' realised that they were now parallelling their inbound contrail, and the contrail they had just crossed was their own that they had laid while turning northeast before heading west. For a few moments their hearts missed several beats in the thought of having unwanted high-Mach company 15 miles above the cold Arctic seas.

'Stormy' eased off some power and settled back into their routine of high-Mach cruise. The autopilot completed a long 'lazy turn' around the north shore of Norway, before 'Stormy' started his descent toward another refuelling. To complete the mission, the crew made an easy high-altitude dash into the Baltic corridor and down through West Germany, before heading home to Mildenhall.

LEBANON

By the mid-1970s, the complicated politics that had bonded the Middle East's Christian and Moslem factions together in relative peace in the Lebanon since that country had declared its independence in November 1943, had broken down. Soon after, a long and tragic civil war erupted which was further complicated by the wider implications of the region's power politics. In an effort to restore peace, President Assad of Syria dispatched more than 40,000 of his best troops in a series of fruitless battles. Assad's forces were backed by a number of Palestine Liberation Organisation (PLO) fanatics who stiffened the resolve of the various Moslem militia groups in the area. In August 1982, the grim catalogue of human carnage had reached many thousand dead on both sides of the rising conflict.

Some 15 terrorist organisations sympathetic to the Palestinian cause operated from numerous bases in Southern Lebanon, and periodically launched attacks against neighbouring Israel. These acts of terrorism became progressively more numerous and violent. After several retaliatory strikes, Israel responded on 6 June 1982 with a major land, sea and air invasion aimed at destroying the PLO leadership and its armed forces. Twenty-three days later Israeli troops were at the gates of Beirut, and were in a position to fulfil their stated objective. Prime Minister Mechachem Begin was forced to modify his fierce demands, however, when faced with threats of Soviet intervention to aid Syria, and American disapproval of the invasion. An Israeli siege of Beirut then culminated in some 7,000 PLO fighters abandoning the city and fleeing the Lebanon into sympathetic Arab sanctuaries in Algeria, Iraq, Jordan, the Sudan, Syria, North and South Yemen, and Tunisia, where their leader, Yasser Arafat, set up his headquarters.

On 28 September President Reagan announced that the US Marines were to resume their peacekeeping role in Beirut, a role which had been interrupted by the Israeli invasion of the Lebanon. Reagan said that he believed it was important that the US maintain a military presence in the area until the Lebanese government was in full control. France, Italy and the United Kingdom also dispatched contingents of troops to the region in an attempt to add world pressure to the policing of the area, for the departure of the PLO heralded the beginning of a new era of terrorism in the Lebanon.

On 18 April 1983 a suicidal member of Islamic Jihad, a pro-Iranian network of fanatical Shi'ites, drove a truck loaded with 300 lb (136 kg) of explosives up to the entrance of the US Embassy in Beirut. He detonated the explosives, killing 40 people, including eight Americans. Two more of these kamikaze-type raids followed. On 23 October, the resulting explosion killed 241 US Marines and 58 French paratroopers. Another such raid on 4 November claimed the lives of 39 Israeli troops within their guarded camp. By early 1984, the peacekeeping positions had become untenable and the troops were withdrawn, leaving behind only the Syrians and the Israelis. By February, the Lebanon was once again embroiled in an ever-worsening civil war.

The resurgence of Islamic fundamentalism was sparked off by the Ayatollah Khomeini on 1 April 1979, when he declared Iran to be an Islamic Republic. Khomeini was a zealot whose unquestioned devotion to Islam was only equalled by his all-consuming hatred for the West and, in particular, the United States. According to most Western intelligence sources, Islamic fundamentalism would represent the most destabilising influence in the Middle East throughout the 1980s.

Once again, the capabilities of the SR-71 would be called upon in this hot spot to serve the needs of the transatlantic intelligence community, and of those friendly nations who also shared in the

revelations of the Habu's high-quality photographic and electronic surveillance. Missions over the Lebanon were flown by Mildenhall Det 4 crews to keep tabs on the Syrian and Israeli armies, as well as on various contraband movements which supplied Islamic Jihad warriors and other supporting groups. The Habu flights also monitored the movements of key terrorist leaders as their small executive aircraft slipped from one tiny airstrip to another in the desert.

One such Middle Eastern SR-71 sortie took place on 27 July 1984, when, at 07:30 hours, 'Stormy' Boudreaux and Ted Ross again departed Mildenhall in '979, using the call sign BOYCE 64. This important flight (the crew's 30th together) was complicated by several factors: the usual refusal of overflight transit across France, which necessitated entering the Mediterranean area via the Straits of Gibraltar; inlet control problems during acceleration to high Mach, which forced 'Stormy' to 'go manual' on bypass door operations; and spike control problems at 2.2 Mach which caused further aggravated control.

By this time '979 was eastbound and nearing Mach 2.5, and the flight path was committed to entering the 'Med' on the pre-planned heading, or overflying West Africa or Spain during an abort. Consequently, 'Stormy' elected to 'go manual' on both inlet spike and door operations. Emergency operating procedures dictated that an aircraft in a 'double-manual' configuration should not be flown above Mach 3 and 70,000 ft (21336 m). Therefore, 'Stormy' held '979 at that degraded limit and pressed on through the Straits of Gibraltar high over the Mediterranean. Off the southern coast of Italy they decelerated and descended for a second refuelling. Standard procedures (once returning to subsonic flight) included resetting all inlet switches back to 'automatic', and to continue the next leg of the flight in 'auto' since inlet glitches often tended to clear themselves on another acceleration cycle.

'Stormy' and Ted followed this logical procedure, but '979 repeated the previous disturbances. At that point, according to the 'book', they should have aborted the flight. The mission had been planned around a single high-speed, high-altitude pass over the target area. The well-seasoned crew reasoned that they had already come so far that they could make that one pass easily and collect the needed reconnaissance data within imposed operating constraints, especially since they could easily break off over the waters of the eastern Mediterranean should they have any serious difficulties over land.

Consequently, they completed the recce run 'manually' but found that '979 (operated in the less fuel-efficient 'manual' inlet configuration) ended the run in a notably depleted fuel state. Ted urgently contacted the tankers which were orbiting near the island of Crete and asked that they head east to meet the thirsty Habu. As the SR-71 descended 'Stormy' caught sight of the tankers some 30,000 ft (9144 m) below, and executed what he described loosely as 'an extremely large variation of a barrel roll' to slide in behind the tankers 'in no time flat'. The boomer plugged in immediately and '979 began taking on the much needed JP-7. Hooking up well east of the normal ARCP, BOYCE 64 had to stay with the tankers much longer than the normal 12 to 15 minutes of on the boom time to drop off at the scheduled 'end-AR' point, before proceeding back to England.

With '979's tanks filled to a pressure disconnect, 'Stormy' and Ted climbed to high altitude on the final leg back through the Straits of Gibraltar and home to Mildenhall, where they landed after nearly seven hours, four of which had been spent at supersonic speed while carefully controlling both the inlet spikes and doors manually. The good news was that their 'take' was of exceptional quality as a result of a cold front which covered the eastern Mediterranean and produced very clear air for razor-sharp photographic imagery. Det 4's commander, Col Jay Murphy, was especially proud of his crew's very notable mission accomplishments, but the bad news was that they had flown a 'degraded' aircraft within range of a known Soviet SA-5 SAM site. Overriding that concern, however, was word from Washington that the 'take' was 'most valuable' for the analysts back at the National Photographic Interpretation Center (NPIC).

LIBYA

A group of revolutionary army officers seized power on 1 September 1969 while King Idris of Libya was on holiday in Turkey. In revolt, led by a subaltern named Moamar Ghadaffi, the officers proclaimed Libya to be a republic in the name of 'freedom, socialism and unity'. Washington recognised the new regime just five days later, allowing Ghadaffi to consolidate his position of power over the next two-and-a-half years, during which time he nationalised foreign banking and petroleum interests within Libya and was called a 'strongman' by Western news editors.

Ghadaffi made his interpretation of 'freedom, socialism and unity' clear to the world on 11 June 1972, when he announced he was giving aid to the Irish Republican Army. That support was also extended to similar terrorist organisations within Europe and the Middle East.

In the summer of 1981, Ghadaffi decided to lay claim to territorial rights over much of the Gulf of

Three dark red camels were painted on the left nose-gear door of '980 after its participation in the April raid. The apparent light colouration of the middle camel is due to photographic flash bouncing back. (Paul F. Crickmore)

Sidra on Libya's northern shore. The United Stated refused to recognise any extension beyond the traditional 3-mile limit and, to back up the 'international waters' claim to the Gulf, USS *Nimitz* (CVN-68), attached to the 6th Fleet, began an exercise within the disputed area on 18 August. Interference by Libyan Mirages, Sukhoi Su-22 'Fitters', MiG-23s and MiG-25s culminated in the shooting down of two Su-22 'Fitter-Js' by F-14 Tomcats from VF-41 'Black Aces'. Libyan/American relations plunged to an all time low as Ghadaffi's aggression continued. Northern Chad was annexed by Libyan forces, an English police woman was shot dead by a Libyan 'diplomat' in London, arms were sent to Nicaraguan Sandinistas and continued support was given to countless terrorist organisations throughout the world.

US patience was running out. In an address to the American Bar Association on 8 July 1985, President Reagan branded Libya, Iran, North Korea, Cuba and Nicaragua as members of a 'confederation of terrorist states'. Libya's political ruse finally reached its end after further actions in the Gulf of Sidra, the hijacking of a TWA Boeing 727 airliner on a flight from Rome to Athens and the bombing of the La Belle discotheque in Berlin.

THE PLANNING BEGINS

Frank Stampf recalls the planning process prior to committing the SR-71 to the skies above Libya: 'The week before Christmas, 1985, for those of us assigned to SAC HQ in Omaha, Nebraska, it was pretty much the same as many other past holiday seasons. Plenty of parties and social get togethers, and lots of opportunities for frustrated aviators now stuck in headquarters staff jobs to swap war stories about the "good old days". The pace of work activity had slowed down a bit, although not very much. Those of us at the Strategic Reconnaissance Center (SRC) within HQ SAC were still kept fairly busy planning, tasking, and coordinating "real-world" reconnaissance sorties being flown by U-2, TR-1, various models of RC-135, and SR-71 aircraft all over the globe on a 24-hour basis. These daily sorties were a critical component of the eyes and ears of the free world as our nation kept close watch, not only on our long-time adversaries of the Cold War – the Soviet Union – but pretty much all of the Third World hot spots and rogue nations that appeared determined to cause the US and our allies as much trouble as possible during their own quests for power.

'The action officers who staffed the SRC were all experienced former strategic reconnaissance crewmembers – pilots, recon systems officers, electronic warfare officers – relatively fresh out of the cockpit and sent to "do their time" at headquarters staff jobs. The official Air Force reason for us being at least temporarily "banished" from operational flying and sent to the headquarters staff was that we needed the opportunity for "career-broadening" assignments to enhance our potential for eventual promotion. We all knew the real reason was that the senior leadership didn't want us to get the idea that all the Air Force was about was flying airplanes. Silly us …

'Meanwhile, our counterparts at the Joint Reconnaissance Center in the Pentagon – also former recce crew dogs – did their best to decipher the myriad requirements they received daily from the military and civilian intelligence agencies demanding SR-71 coverage all over the world. The JRC would then pass those needs to us at SRC. The idea was for us to eventually task the SR-71 wing and operational detachments with specific missions in some reasonably clear terms that would allow the crews (our former squadron mates) to actually fly them.

BACK TO LATE 1985 …

'It was while enjoying the holiday company of a group of friends, their wives and significant others, at one of those evening cocktail parties a few days before Christmas, that my pager started to buzz. I had to fight off the urge to make believe I hadn't noticed it. I was finally beginning to relax and get into the holiday spirit, and now it appeared I was to be slapped back into reality by a call from "Mother SAC". I excused myself and called in to the SRC operations desk to see what

was up. I was hoping it was just a routine notification of a sortie delayed or cancelled for weather somewhere very, very far away. No such luck. I was told by the duty officer that I was needed at the headquarters immediately, and that I should bypass the SRC and go directly to the tanker shop downstairs in the bowels of the headquarters building. I made my apologies to the hosts, and very reluctantly left the warm glow of the party for the cold, wet, snowy December streets of Omaha.

'Driving toward the base, I was perplexed as to the reason for my "recall". Not that I hadn't been called in at all odd hours many times before in the almost three years I had been chief of the SR-71 branch at SRC, it was just that normally, the duty officer could give me a hint as to the reason. For example just the word "delay" or "cancel" or "weather" would be enough to give me the general idea of what was going on (without compromising classified information about specific missions, locations, times, etc) so I could begin to formulate possible options on my way to the base. Not this time. And being told to report to the tanker operations shop, rather than the SRC, was another surprise. Of course, we worked with the tanker guys all the time – their support was critical to the success of the SR mission. In fact, air-refuelling support for all kinds of fighter, bomber, reconnaissance, and mission-support operations worldwide was coordinated and tasked through the tanker shop at SRC. They definitely had the "big picture" as far as tanker availability and capabilities.

'As I walked into the tanker vault (pretty much all of the operations areas in the HQ SAC building were in secure "walk-in vaults" where classified information could be openly displayed and readily handled by those authorised), I recognised most of the people standing around as tanker guys, some folks from the airborne command and control division, and a bunch of intelligence types. Almost all were in civilian clothes, as I was, since they had also been called in unexpectedly from what they thought would be a quiet evening with friends or family.

'After a few more minutes, when someone decided that everyone who needed to be there had arrived, we were quieted down and the colonel who ran the tanker ops division stood up. He told us that SAC had just received orders from the Pentagon to develop plans for tanker and reconnaissance support of a bombing raid on Libya. The targets were to be terrorist training compounds and a number of various military facilities such as airfields, air defences, command and control centres, etc. The raid would take place before dawn and be immediately followed (at first light) by an SR-71 overflight of the target areas to assess bomb damage, which would be critical in determining whether follow-on strikes would be necessary. My first thought was that the timing for the SR-71 overflight would put the crew overhead just when the Libyans were fully alerted ... and very pissed off. Apparently, President Reagan finally decided he had had just about enough of Moamar Ghadaffi. The decision for the US response to Ghadaffi was an interesting proposition to begin with, and it would become even more interesting as the mission plans evolved. The operation was to be called El Dorado Canyon.

The specific date for the attack was not given, but we were to begin planning our respective roles immediately, and have enough information assembled to provide an initial briefing to the SAC Deputy Commander for Operations and Director of Intelligence – both two-star generals – by 07:00 the next morning, about ten hours from our initial notification. It was going to be the first of many long nights. We obviously wouldn't have the whole operation nailed down in great detail by then, but we were to be prepared to present the various courses of action and recommendations to the SAC General Staff. Then the rest of our resources would be called in and we would begin in earnest to put together the many pieces of what would turn out to be a pretty complex operation. The actual attacks would be carried out by Navy fighter-bombers operating from a carrier in the Med, and USAF F-111s flying out of RAF Lakenheath. They would be supported by USAF EF-111s (electronic jamming aircraft), a number of command and control aircraft, and, of course, about a "bazillion" tankers.

MORE GENERALS – MORE AIRPLANES

'Obviously, the Navy and USAF fighter-bomber community did the planning for their attack aircraft. The USAF F-111 planners passed on their fuel-load and mission-timing requirements to SAC, and the SAC tanker crowd figured out how many and what types of tankers would be needed, where they could locate the tracks to safely (both militarily and politically) conduct air refuelling operations, where the tankers would operate from, and how and when to get them where they needed to be. This was never going to be an easy task, although it started out significantly less complex than it ended up. The original concept for the Air Force strike component called for eight primary USAF F-111 aircraft actually on target, with another four air-spare aircraft launching and flying to a "Go-No-Go" point where they would be told whether they were needed or not (based upon the status of the primary aircraft). The "operators" – the folks who knew the aircraft and mission capabilities first-hand and were best qualified to make the call – seemed pretty satisfied that those numbers would do the trick.

'However, because the specific date for the attack had not yet been set (or at least it had not yet been shared with us planning the missions), there must have been sufficient time for more and more general officers to get involved in the game. The plan went through several ever-increasingly complex evolutions until the final strike package of USAF F-111s eventually reached eighteen aircraft with six air spares. This, of course, exponentially increased the number of tanker aircraft required to get the "armada" of airplanes from the UK to Libya and hopefully back again. Just to make matters worse, several weeks into the process the planners were told that the French would not allow any US aircraft, strike or support,

This Libyan air force Ilyushin Il-76 'Candid' was seen at Tripoli airport through the Pave Tack laser target designation pod of an F-111F. The Libyan transport is directly beneath the cross hairs of the bomber's laser 'sparkle'. (USAF)

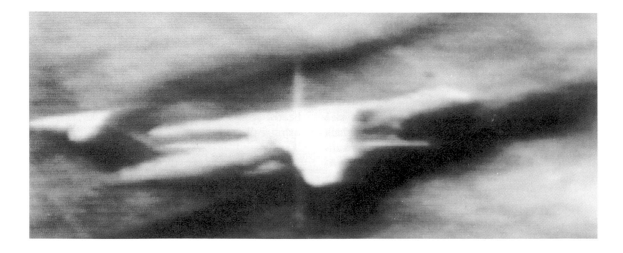

to overfly their landmass either on the way to, or returning from, the strike. All of the airplanes would have to fly south, just off the western coast of France, then turn east and thread their way through the straits of Gibraltar to get over the Mediterranean Sea. That translated into several more hours of flying time for all the aircraft, which in turn would require even more tankers than before. Eventually the plan called for more than 20 KC-135 and KC-10 tanker aircraft to support the USAF strike force, not to mention the SR-71 primary and air-spare aircraft. This was not going to be a low-profile operation. In fact, one of the most serious concerns was how to avoid mid-air collisions between the dozens of airplanes that would be traversing the extremely narrow gap of the Straits of Gibraltar, in both directions, within a short span of time, while radio-silent and without being under air traffic control.

THE HABU MISSION

'Fortunately for us recce types, that planning problem was one of many logistical and operational challenges that were left to the tanker troops to resolve. All we had to do was put together a plan to get an SR-71 over all the targets on time, with cameras and electronic sensors blazing, defeat what we expected would be very alert and active Libyan defences, and then get the jet back to RAF Mildenhall. There, the mission "take" would be processed and the intelligence immediately disseminated to all the people who would be anxiously awaiting the strike results. Among those people were numerous military and civilian high rollers, including the Chairman of the Joint Chiefs of Staff and the President of the United States, who wanted to be personally assured that the job had been done.

'Normally, non-routine SR-71 missions such as this one would be developed by the planners at the operational detachment from which the sortie was to be flown, and the plan would then be passed back to our people at the SR-71 branch of the SRC for review and approval. This made sense, since the folks at the Dets were the ones who had first-hand knowledge of the operational environment in which the missions would be flown. However, in this case there were way too many operational, logistical, and political variables that were changing on an almost daily basis (and too many senior officers continuing to get involved) for the Det 4 mission planners to keep up with by themselves. Fortunately, in addition to the very capable and experienced planners at the detachments, we had a couple of pretty solid folks working the task at SRC, including one Major "Chuck" Holte. Although "Chuck" was not a former SR-71 crewmember, he had extensive operational experience as an

Electronic Warfare Officer (EWO), having flown many real-world reconnaissance missions in the RC-135. He was assigned to the SR-71 branch because of his in-depth knowledge of the ever-changing electronic threat environment, and his expertise was most welcome in not only planning specific SR-71 missions, but in helping us develop strategic plans for future defensive systems that would be needed for the SR-71's continued viability. "Chuck's" quiet, efficient manner and subtle sense of humour made him highly respected, and, equally important, very well liked and trusted by all the SR people who knew him, both at the headquarters and at the operational sites. As a result, the Det 4 planners at RAF Mildenhall, from where this mission would be flown, welcomed his input in the planning process for this complex, highly visible tasking.

'As the weeks and months went on and the Omaha winter gave way to spring, we still hadn't received a specific date for the attack. However, it seemed that every general in the building wanted daily updates on the plan. The plan, as initially envisioned and quite well laid out, would have been ready to go months earlier, but it seemed as though every general officer to whom it was briefed wanted another change or tweak, so it became the proverbial "perpetual motion machine". Consequently, most of us involved in planning the mission had worked every day and some nights, without break, from the first night we were called out pre-Christmas. That pattern was to continue right up to the day of the attack in April, and for several weeks following, due to the same general officers wanting "after-action" reports and "lesson learned" briefings.

TIME TO GO – ALMOST

'"Chuck's" patient nature allowed him to do a remarkable job keeping up with all the changes for the SR-71 mission plan and coordinating them with the Det 4 folks as they came up. Then, one day in mid-spring, almost four months after we'd been given the order to develop the plan for the mission, the morning news headlines told of a terrorist bombing at the "La Belle" discotheque in Berlin. A number of people were killed and injured, among them American soldiers. Almost immediately, links were reported between the terrorist bombers and Libya. We had the feeling that would be the trigger for the President to give the go-ahead for the strike. We were right. The date for the attack was set for April 15, 1986, and the SR-71 plan was ready. At Det 4 – the "pointy end of the spear" – the Habu crews and all their ops-support, maintenance, intel, and tanker-support people were well prepared and waiting to go.

'About 48 hours prior to the scheduled SR launch from Mildenhall, the CINCSAC's executive officer called down to SRC and said the general wanted my boss and me to come up to his office and brief him on the SR element of the mission. I dutifully folded up the mission charts, packed them into our secure briefcase, and the colonel and I weaved our way through the lower vaults of the headquarters building where we went about our classified work every day (and many nights). We eventually came to the stairs that took us up the several flights to where the sunlight and air were, and, not surprisingly, the generals' offices. I'm not sure how many general officers were assigned to SAC headquarters at the time, but I think it would have been easier to count the stars in the Milky Way than the collective stars on their shoulders. We made our way to the CINC's office and waited outside under the watchful eye of his trusty exec until the general was ready to receive us. As one of the SAC operations briefers, I had stood in front of the CINC quite a few times before, while presenting the daily SAC operations briefing, with emphasis on the results of all the worldwide reconnaissance missions that had been flown during the previous 24 hours.

'As a frame of reference for this briefing, it was no secret that SAC did not like having the SR-71 in its operating budget. As I was also responsible for articulating and advocating the SR-71 operating budget within SAC, I was constantly locked in a state of mortal combat within the command to increase, or at times just sustain funding for the flying hours we needed to meet our growing tasking. The problem was that the majority of that tasking was coming from many sources outside SAC, and even outside the Air Force. For example, the driving reason we established a permanent SR-71 detachment in Europe was to meet the US Navy's critical need to monitor the status of the Soviet Northern Fleet, and, in particular, their nuclear submarine operations out of Murmansk on the Barents Sea. Once permanent SR-71 operations were set up and operating in Europe, the US Army realised we could provide excellent coverage of the Eastern Bloc countries around the Federal Republic of Germany, particularly during the darkness and cloud-covered weather of the European winter. The Army was also the primary driver of the regular coverage we provided to monitor hostile force status and movements in and around the Korean Peninsula in the Pacific theatre. SAC was not too happy about having to pick up the tab as the benevolent provider of all that great intelligence to other commands and services. Especially when they felt it cut into funding for their strategic bombers, intercontinental ballistic missiles, and tankers. So it was no surprise that the CINC was not a huge supporter of the SR-71 programme (other than of course, when SAC wanted to make a splash at air shows or other exhibitions, where the SR-71 was always their star performer and biggest crowd pleaser.)

'The general had us lay out the chart with the SR-71 track on his desk, and we were to brief him straight from the map. I had gotten about as far as, "Sir, this is ..." when he jabbed his finger at the two large rings representing the coverage of the Soviet-made SA-5 SAM sites, both of which were clearly bisected by the SR-71's planned track. One was located at Sirt, near the first target area at Benina airfield in eastern Libya, and the other at Tripoli, to the west. The CINC then asked (while continuing to stare at the very large circles on the map), "Will these SA-5s be taken out prior to the SR going in?" My response, I thought at the time, was pretty obvious, even for a lowly major like me ... "Sir, we'll know if the sites were destroyed when the SR returns and the intel folks analyse the 'take'." Wrong answer. The remainder of the "briefing" went something like this:

'The General: "I don't want the airplane penetrating those SAMs unless we know they've been neutralised prior to the pass."

'The Lowly Major: "Sir, there is no way for the SR to collect all of the tasked targets without going through the SA-5 coverage. The SR will be at better than Mach 3 and at or above 80,000 feet. The best intel we have on the SA-5 and the SR's ability to defeat it with the airplane's combination of on board systems and speed and altitude, puts this at an acceptable risk level for the mission."

'The General: "Like I said, Major, I don't want the SR to penetrate those rings unless we know the sites have been taken out."

'The Lowly Major: "Sir, if we could just ... "

'The General (this time in a clearly angered tone): "Major — you are not listening — I'm not going to risk one of MY SR-71s for this piddly little operation!"

'The Lowly Major: (In thought only ...): "One of 'his' SR-71s? Piddly little operation?"

'End of discussion. End of briefing. Back to the drawing boards and with less than 48 hours to come up with an alternative approach.

PLAN 'A' AND PLAN 'B'

'Although the SA-5 was the most modern, and only existing Soviet SAM system with a postulated capability against the SR-71, none had yet been fired at the Habu, and therefore its capability against a high-altitude, Mach 3+ manoeuvring target was still hypothetical. Additionally, we had more than reasonable confidence in the SR-71's on board electronic defensive systems, when coupled with the airplane's speed and altitude, to handle the threat. On top of all that, this was the very type of mission for which the SR-71 had been designed, and had proven itself so well in successfully

accomplishing for over 20 years up to that point. In fact, even when the programme was eventually terminated four years later, the SR-71 could boast a record that no other USAF aircraft could claim. That is – after 26 years of operational service and hundreds of missions over and around hostile territory, with hundreds of SA-2 SAM firings against it during the Vietnam war alone – not a single Air Force crewmember had ever been killed in an SR-71, and none had ever been lost to enemy action.

'Notwithstanding the reality of all that, we were clearly going to have to come up with another approach if we were going to meet the tasking that had been levied on us. (In hindsight, if we failed to come up with a workable plan, this would have been a perfect way for SAC to say that the SR was tasked, but couldn't support the mission. Another arrow in its quiver to get rid of the programme).

'After a lot of scurrying and many secure phone calls, we were told by our people in D.C. that there was a slight possibility the status of the SA-5 sites could be assessed (by a highly-classified intelligence source) in the short period between the time that the last bomb was dropped and the SR-71 came over the target. So we came up with another plan that none of us liked very much.

'The status of the SAM sites, if known by then, could be transmitted via satellite communications to the KC-10 tanker that would be waiting for the SR-71 over the Mediterranean Sea prior to the SR accelerating into the target area. Once the SR-71 was on the tanker's boom and taking gas, the tanker crew would simply pass the words "Option Alpha" or "Option Bravo" to the SR crew via the secure boom interphone. The SR-71 RSO would then select one of two flight paths pre-programmed into the ANS computer. From the end of the air refuelling track, "Option A" would direct the airplane along the originally planned

Tom McCleary and Stan Gudmundson arrive at the 'barn' and say their last farewells to the team of Mildonhall ground technicians. (Paul F. Crickmore)

flight path, directly through the SA-5 rings, assuming that intel confirmed the sites had been destroyed. If the sites were either confirmed as still operational, or the information simply wasn't available, then the RSO would select "Option B," which would take the SR on a peripheral flight path just skirting the operational range of the SA-5s. This flight path would obviously allow the SR-71 to avoid the potential SA-5 threat, but it would also unfortunately reduce the number of targets its sensors could collect, and therefore degrade the usefulness of the intelligence it would bring back.

'We at SRC didn't like this plan for any number of reasons. First of all, NO SR-71 crew liked to mess around with the ANS once the aircraft was airborne and operating smoothly. The system was certainly capable of doing what was planned in this case, but it just didn't feel right to the crews. But more importantly, by not allowing the SR to fly the mission as originally planned to acquire all the tasked damage assessment of the targets hit by the strike force, there was a great risk of not knowing what was and what wasn't destroyed. This would very likely result in sending more aircraft in for a second strike. As it was, we lost one F-111 crew in the first attack. Another strike, especially if launched unnecessarily – only because the SR-71 wasn't allowed to confirm the targets had already been hit – would just expose more aircrews to the danger of losing their lives for no reason.

'But, as ordered, we passed the revised "Option A" and "B" plan to the Det planners, and they prepared to execute it as the SR's launch time approached. Frustration levels were high all

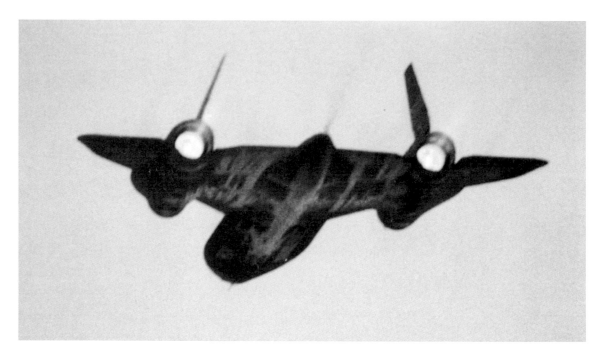

Aircraft '964 made a sharp getaway as Tom McCleary and Stan Gudmundson departed Mildenhall for the last time. Shortly after, they performed the final UK flyby for the press, before heading to California. (Paul F. Crickmore)

around. This was one of those times when the crews on the line, getting ready to fly the mission, no doubt wondered what in the world was going on in the minds of their former crewmates at the headquarters who tasked this crazy sortie ...

THE END GAME

'As somewhat of an anticlimax, the "Option A" and "B" plan was scrapped for some reason undisclosed to us, pretty much at the last hour. The SR crew wound up flying the mission as originally tasked and obviously survived the SA-5 threat to come back with the "take". No surprise to those of us who knew and understood the Habu and its incredible capabilities. It is not unreasonable to speculate that the "highly classified source" that was supposed to provide the status of the SAM sites prior to the SR going in wasn't up to the task, and the SAC general staff were beginning to feel the pressure, both from the Joint Staff and from the White House, to produce the much-needed intelligence.'

THE DET COMMANDER

Lt-Col Barry MacKean was the Det 4 Commander during this period and it was he and his team that had to implement the plan, as he now recalls: 'Planning for the raids on Libya in April 1986 began weeks before the actual flights. Lt-Col Frank Stampf from the Strategic Reconnaissance Center at HQ Strategic Air Command in Omaha, Nebraska, initially advised me of the pending operation, code named El Dorado Canyon. At that point everything was handled as Top Secret because of the implications of overflying foreign territory. There was also a great deal of uncertainty about whether the missions would ever be flown due to the necessary approvals required from several foreign countries – most notably the British government. US Air Force involvement in the plan was to be exclusively executed from England. The F-111 strike would launch from RAF Lakenheath, the EF-111 Raven electronic support aircraft from RAF Upper Heyford, KC-135 and KC-10 refuelling support from RAF Fairford and RAF Mildenhall, and the SR-71 reconnaissance support would be fielded from RAF Mildenhall. Given the enormity of the plan, world sensitivities at the time and the lack of British involvement, I had my doubts that Prime Minister Margaret Thatcher would approve air strikes flown from England. But fortunately for the free world, and in spite of mounting opposition from within her own party as well as that of Labour, she ultimately approved the missions.

'The SR-71 mission was to provide bomb damage assessment (BDA) for all the target areas struck in Libya; US Navy fighters were targeted against Banghazi in the eastern part of Libya, while the Air Force were targeted against Tripoli and the surrounding area. An additional burden was placed on all Air Force sorties to fly around France, Spain, Portugal then through the Straits of Gibraltar, because France refused overflight clearance.

'The sensor chosen by the Pentagon for the Blackbird mission was the suite of highly sensitive cameras. This choice was based on their ability to declassify the photo images for release to the world press, whereas products generated from our high-resolution radar system would reveal their capabilities and therefore could not be declassified. This decision would prove costly because, while the radar was day/night all weather capable, the cameras were definitely restricted to daytime operations and clear weather.

'Our mission-planning team, led by Maj Bruce Blakely under the supervision of the Director of Operations, Lt-Col Bob Behler, developed a very creative flight profile for the Blackbird that maximised target collection while minimising exposure to surface-to-air missiles and Libyan fighters. Since we had previously flown missions into the eastern Mediterranean area, the same air-refuelling route was selected to help disguise this mission. It consisted of a high-altitude route that unexpectedly turned back to the west covering the targets in eastern Libya and proceeded at Mach 3+ to the capital, Tripoli, before the air defence systems could respond.

'When it appeared El Dorado Canyon might be approved, the build up of tanker aircraft, both KC-10s and KC-135s, began at RAF Mildenhall. Part of the cover story for this highly visible addition of tankers parked everywhere was that a large European exercise, normally scheduled for this time of year, was taking place. There were even photos and stories in the local British newspapers to that effect, which helped minimise any potential leaks. To further add credence to the cover and disguise the real operation, at 5 am on the morning of the actual mission (the strike aircraft and tankers launched around 5 pm in England), the 48th Tactical Fighter Wing at RAF Lakenheath initiated a typical base "exercise". This included a recall of all military personnel to their duty stations, generation of aircraft for alert, including uploading conventional weapons, and general exercise activities. Many of the "exercise" participants were completely unaware of what was about to happen later that day.

'Launch of the strike force and tankers occurred in the late afternoon, on Monday, 15 April. The day prior (Sunday), I received a call from Lt-Col Stampf at SRC directing us to cancel our regularly scheduled sorties and configure both of our jets for the pending Libyan mission. One aircraft was designated as primary, the other scheduled to follow a little more than an hour later as back-up, in case the primary aircraft had to abort for aircraft or sensor problems.

'Our maintenance team, led by Mr Mel Rushing, consisted of 45 Lockheed personnel with 15 subcontractors and associates from other companies that supported systems/sensors on the aircraft. I had two blue-suit (Air Force) technical sergeants (Robby Butterfield and Jerry Gresham) that provided me quality assurance of the contractor maintenance. The intelligence branch consisted of about 100 military personnel led by Maj Rod Mitchell. This team provided the targeting data for mission planning, processed the film after the mission, analysed the imagery for weapons' effects, and managed all the electrical and conditioned air requirements for the American

The grey overcast sky at Mildenhall reflected the UK 'birdwatchers' gloom, as Don Watkins and Bob Fowlkes took off to head west in an SR-71 for the final time from the Suffolk base. (Paul F. Crickmore)

systems operating under British standards. Bottom line, the entire team was extremely anxious to participate in Operation El Dorado Canyon.

'Our scheduled launch time was 5 am on Tuesday 16 April, to allow for enough light in the target areas to effectively expose the camera film and reveal the damage. With our aircraft and team in full readiness, I departed my office around 5 pm for my on-base quarters located on RAF Lakenheath. My staff car was equipped with UHF/VHF radios that allowed me to monitor our operation, as well as that of the tower at RAF Mildenhall. The most amazing thing was happening on the taxiways and runway – tankers were taxing and taking off with no communication with the tower or departure control. The entire operation was what we call "comm out" – all movement and approvals were done with lights from the tower based on timing. It was truly an amazing sight to behold!

'As I approached my quarters, I witnessed the same "comm out" launch of the F-111s, fully loaded with their conventional stores. My wife Terri, an Air Force nurse stationed at the hospital at RAF Lakenheath, had participated in the early morning "exercise"/recall that day. When I entered the house she told me how, for the first time ever, an "exercise" was terminated early. The cover story was that the "exercise" had gone so well, the wing staff chose to terminate the remaining events. I gave her a set of binoculars and told her to look at the next F-111 that took off. She too was amazed to see the conventional weapons on the wings. I then told her about El Dorado Canyon.

'After a few hours of restless sleep I returned to our unit to find everything in perfect shape. We launched the primary aircraft flown by Lt-Col Jerry Glasser and Maj Ron Tabor uneventfully "on the hack, comm out". After our spare aircraft, flown by Maj Brian Shul and Maj Walt Watson launched successfully, several of us went for breakfast. As we got out of the car, the F-111s were returning one by one, back into RAF Lakenheath, but this time there were no weapons on the wings – definitely an eerie sight watching combat aircraft return. Unfortunately one F-111 was lost with its crew and another had to land in Spain with engine problems.

'Remember the earlier comment about cameras requiring good weather? Well, we encountered our nemesis; cloud cover over the target area. The primary aircraft flew perfectly and did everything required, our problem – clouds. Both aircraft came back "code one", meaning not one maintenance discrepancy. Before we even received word from SRC as to a return engagement, I had the maintenance teams preparing both aircraft for possible flights the next day. Everyone was so

mission oriented, there was no problem making it happen. While we awaited the go-ahead from SRC, our intelligence team was poring over the film with hopes of getting enough usable imagery to complete a full BDA report. Unfortunately, when it came to the area around Tripoli, there was none to be had.

'With SRC approval, we swapped the aircrews and jets and flew the very next day. Our mission planners cleverly altered the flight plan to preclude predictability and to minimise potential threats. However, on this occasion the lead aircraft experienced a malfunction of the optical bar camera. Although the other cameras performed flawlessly, the target areas were obscured by sand storms. Because of the high level of national interest, joining our imagery analysts to review the film was Maj-Gen Thomas McInerny, the Third Air Force commander stationed at RAF Mildenhall. He understood we had no control over Mother Nature and was very supportive of the efforts of our personnel. However, senior leadership was adamant that we provide releasable BDA.

'Without missing a beat, our team prepared both aircraft for a third consecutive flight. SRC gave approval and the two jets departed RAF Mildenhall for the third and finally successful time. This time the primary crew was Lt-Col Bernie Smith and Lt-Col Denny Whalen with the spare crew being Lt-Col Jerry Glasser and Maj Ron Tabor. As fate would have it, the target area was clear and we were able to provide good BDA as tasked. However, this was all very frustrating to us, in the recce team, because we knew that we could have provided BDA imagery after the very first sortie, had we been allowed to use our very sophisticated radar system.

'Besides finally providing the much sought after BDA, our team established a benchmark for SR-71 sorties generated and flown that was and remains unparalleled. We flew six sorties in three days with only two aircraft supported by a maintenance team that was staffed to support only two to three sorties a week. As the commander of the unit, I was extremely proud of their accomplishments and the manner in which everyone pulled together. Definitely in keeping with the Habu tradition!'

MISSION EXECUTION

Lt-Col Jerry Glasser, an SR-71 Instructor Pilot and Director of Simulator Training, with over 900 hours of Habu flight time already under his belt, together with his RSO Maj Ron Tabor an RSO Instructor and the chief back-seat simulator instructor, were the primary aircraft crew for the initial post-strike BDA surveillance after the attack. Majors Brian Shul and his RSO Walt

Watson, were nominated to fly back-up first time around. A third crew, Lt-Col Bernie Smith, the Chief of the Standards Board and instructor RSO Lt-Col Dennie Whalen, were en route to join their colleagues via KC-135; they would fly a later mission over Libya. Jerry now provides a unique insight into that first sortie: 'As the tasking came down and the F-111s geared up, we were directed to equip the aircraft with optical sensors, an OBC in the nose and TEOCs in the chine bays. The weather could always be a problem with visual sensors, but they provided the best image quality and this was very important for Washington.

'The plan was to launch the two aircraft with a time interval between them would ensure that if all went according to plan, "primary" would just be coming off the target as the back-up air spare was just about to turn into the Mediterranean refuelling track. If "primary" had sustained some kind of mechanical or sensor malfunction, back-up would continue into the area and get the take. If, however, "primary" cleared the target area and reported "Ops Normal", back-up would turn back to England prior to the Straits of Gibraltar. Three air refuelling tracks were planned to support the mission, one off Lands End, England, and two in the Mediterranean. This was due to the French refusing to grant us overflight permission (which we weren't particularly pleased about, but politically made sense for the French).

'An area of concern for us as crewmembers was the decision that the second air refuelling in the Med was to be conducted from a KC-10 at 31,000 ft [9449 m]. This was 6,000 ft [1829 m] above our usual refuelling block altitude, checking the Mach/IAS limits for the KC-10 confirmed that we'd be "well behind the subsonic power curve while behind the boom". From what I recall, even the KC-10/SR-71 compatibility checks carried out at Palmdale didn't get up to 31,000 ft. A second and common problem as we learned later at first-hand, was the brutal sun angle, which would be directly down the boom.

'Mission brief was at 3:00 am, Brian and Walt were also our mobile crew, so after seeing us off, they had to get suited and launch as airborne back-up. Our route was subsonic to Lands End, where we'd be topped-off by two KC-135s. We'd then climb and accelerate south along the Portuguese coast, then make a left turn through the Straits of Gibraltar, decel and refuel in the western Med. Our second accel was on an easterly heading and we'd then make a right, climbing turn to the south and head directly for our first target – Benghazi. We'd then perform a hard right, to slip by the SA-5 sites at Sirte and then fly on to Tripoli, our second target. The plan then called for a post target decel for our third and final AR in the western Med before our final accel exiting again

through the Straits, then on to a northerly heading that would take us back to the UK.'

The main thrust of the strike was to be conducted by 18 F-111Fs from RAF Lakenheath, split into six flights of three aircraft each using call signs PUFFY, LUJAN, REMIT, ELTON, KARMA and JEWEL. More than 20 KC-10s and KC-135s were used to provide air refuelling support for the strike force. In addition, three EF-111 Ravens provided ECM support.

Hours before the Habu launched, the first of its support tankers got airborne. Four KC-135s and three KC-10s left the base for their refuelling orbits:

FINEY 50 (KC-135 59-1520) and FINEY 51 (KC-10 83-0079) launched at 02:30 and 02:40 hours, respectively;

FINEY 52 (KC-135 58-0125) and FINEY 53 (KC-10 83-0082) launched at 04:02 and 04:05 hours, respectively;

FINEY 54 (KC-135 60-0342) and FINEY 55 (KC-135 58-0094) launched at 04:12 and 04:15 hours, respectively;

FINEY 56 (KC-10 83-0075) launched at 07:40 hours.

Lt-Col Jerry Glasser and Maj Ron Tabor took off as scheduled at 05:00 in SR-71 number '980 (call sign TROMP 30) and Jerry continues: 'For take off we carried 55,000 lb [24948 kg] of fuel, which was 10,000 lb [4536 kg] more than normal. A night launch down Mildenhall's 8,500-ft [2591-m] runway was always exciting. From a safety aspect, I always had concerns for the buildings at the end of runway 29, especially when we were heavy. We rendezvoused as planned with FINEY 54 and FINEY 55 which had entered a holding pattern off the southwest coast of England. Our first AR was fine except for a little turbulence, we then made our first accel towards the Med. The early morning accel with the sunrise and the coast of Europe to the left painted a wonderful scene and the turn through the Straits of Gibraltar was quite spectacular – we were prohibited from taking random photos of the Straits. Our second AR was planned to have a KC-135Q act as lead to a KC-10 in trail; this was due to the special comm/ranging equipment carried by our KC-135Q tankers. We thought it was overkill, but it worked out fine. The '135 flew 1 mile [1.6 km] ahead of the KC-10 and we ranged on both. The weather was clear but the sun angle was a big problem. As we hooked up at 31,000 ft, I couldn't see the tanker's director lights due to the glare. I'd talked to the KC-10 boomer prior to the mission and this proved to be an invaluable conversation. As a result, he fully understood the speed/altitude incompatibility issue and that the sun angle was likely to cause a problem. I had two boom disconnects before I settled down and to further help reduce the glare, Ron got the tanker to turn 10° right and I "hid"

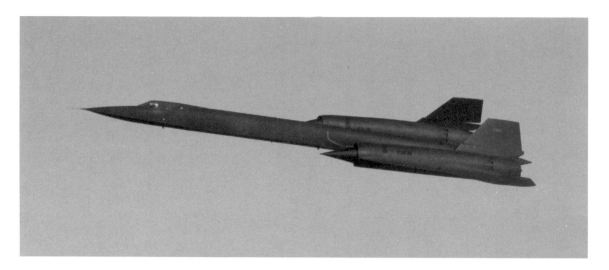

The last Det 4 SR-71 was returned to Beale by Majs Don Watkins and Bob Fowlkes soon after '964's departure from RAF Mildenhall. (Paul F. Crickmore)

under its number one engine nacelle. When we reached 53,000 lb [24041 kg] of JP-7 on-load, I put both throttles into 'min-burner' to stay on the boom – normally we'd engage the left burner at about 77,000 lb [34927 kg] (dependent on the outside air temperature), in order to get a full fuel load from a KC-135 at our usual altitude. Ron, my RSO, did a masterful job managing the on-load, he knew I was just hanging-on for the last 27,000 lb [12247 kg] to complete a full off-load. Knowing that the director lights were of no help to me, the KC-10 boomer also did a fine job keeping us plugged in. When we'd finally finished, we began our second accel. I have to say, I've completed many air refuellings in the SR, in good and bad weather, pitch black night, even in an area we called the "black hole" – off Kadena over the Pacific, at night, with no moon and rough weather – but that second AR was my most challenging.

'As we began the second accel the right AB wouldn't light, but a little manual rise in exhaust temperature, together with another shot of TEB and we were off again. We entered a solid cirrus deck at 41,000 ft [12497 m] and I began to get a little concerned, as we didn't break out until we reached 60,000 ft [18288 m]. However, as soon as we were clear, there dead ahead of us was the coast of Africa and Ron got set for the Benghazi take. As we levelled off at 75,000 ft [22860 m] and at our cruising speed of Mach 3.15, the bird was running just beautifully. I knew to leave Ron alone during this phase, as he was really busy. The DEF warning lights started to flash and Ron signaled that all was a "Go". The take seemed normal as we made our hard right turn towards Tripoli and we were tuned for the SA-5 site at Sirte. Again warning lights flashed, but nothing was visible – we truly felt invincible at Mach 3.15.

'The weather over Tripoli wasn't good. As we completed the run and turned out of the area, Ron gave an "Ops normal" call, so Brian and Walt who were fast approaching the pre-designated abort point, made a right turn short of Gibraltar and headed back to Mildenhall. As it subsequently turned out, morning fog cut out some of the optical take around Tripoli and two more missions would be required to complete the BDA picture; one due to weather, the other to sensor failure – the OBC.

'Our third and final refuelling conducted down at 26,000 ft [7925 m], was uneventful; we pressure disconnected off the boom and headed home, once again through the straits. The remainder of the mission was normal, normal, normal, as Ron and I made our final descent into the UK and called "London Mil". I still plainly recall the impeccable English that gave us both a little lift, "Good morning gentleman, it's been a long day for you." It's with some nostalgia and a great sense of pride that I've enjoyed such a professional association with British controllers. As we were handed over to the various controlling agencies as we made our way back to Mildenhall, we were eventually vectored to runway 11, for a GCA approach. The landing was uneventful and as we taxied back to the "Barn", there was Brian, Walt, Bernie and Dennie in the "mobile car" to greet us. But, as was my habit, as I stepped from the gantry ladder, the people I first made sure to shake hands with were the maintenance chiefs who, through their professionalism, had enabled Ron and I to fulfil our part of the mission.'

As planned, Majs Brian Shul and Walt Watson had launched at 06:15 hours in aircraft '960 (call sign TROMP 31) and duplicated the route flown by Glasser and Tabor to the first ARCP with FINEY

54 and FINEY 55 off Cornwall. Shul spotted the returning F-111s approaching head-on, several thousand feet below. LUJAC 21's pilot (LUJAC flight leader) rocked his wings in recognition and Shul returned the time-honoured aviation salute with a similar manoeuvre.

The final tanker (KC-10 83-0075) joined El Dorado Canyon to support the return of the two Habus.

At 09:10 a KC-135Q (call sign JAVA 90) landed at Mildenhall carrying senior members of the 9th SRW staff from Beale to witness the mission debriefing. Twenty minutes later, tankers FINEY 54 and FINEY 55 touched down, followed at 09:35 by TROMP 30, which had flown a mission lasting four hours 30 minutes. One hour and 13 minutes later, Brian landed the Habu back-up, TROMP 31. The five remaining tankers returned over the next four hours 30 minutes. FINEY 51 flew a 12 hour 30 minute sortie. When FINEY 56 landed at 15:26 hours, El Dorado Canyon was completed, with the exception of search efforts for Capts Ribas-Dominicci and Lorance, whose F-111 had been lost the previous night off the coast of Libya.

The mission's 'take' was processed in the Mobile Processing Center and it was then transported by a KC-135 (TROUT 99) to Andrews AFB, Maryland, (only 25 miles/40 km from the Pentagon and the White House), where national-level officials were eagerly awaiting post-strike briefings that showed both the good and bad effects of the strike. The world's news media had shown the bad side of the story under Libyan guidance, BBC reporter Kate Adie being used to show not only where one F-111's bomb load went astray near the French embassy, but also where Libyan SAMs had fallen back on the city to be blamed as US bombs. Fortunately, she also proved useful in post-strike reconnaissance by showing the accurately bombed terrorist camp, referred to by her as a 'cadet' school.

As mentioned earlier, the marginal weather around the Libyan capital forced another Habu sortie to be flown the following day. This time Jerry and Ron were back up again in aircraft '980, for Brian and Walt who were the primary crew in aircraft '960; Bernie and Dennie were the mobile crew, charged with overseeing both launches and the recoveries back into Mildenhall. However, during this sortie the primary aircraft suffered a sensor failure and, for whatever reason, the back-up aircraft, which was in the air and operational, wasn't contacted. This required a third mission, which was completed on 17 April by Bernie and Dennie as the primary crew in aircraft '980, backed up by Brian and Walt, yet again in '960. To preserve security, the call signs were changed, FATTY and LUTE being allocated to the tankers and SR-71s, respectively, for the 16 April mission, and MINOR and PHONY being

used the next day. Photographs taken in the vicinity of Banghazi by TROMP 30 on 15 April were released to the press, although the source was never officially admitted and image quality was purposely degraded to hide the system's true capabilities.

Bellicose rumblings from Ghadaffi continued after the raid, and 14 months later the West's intelligence services believed that Libya had received a number of MiG-29 'Fulcrums'. This outstanding fighter would considerably enhance Libya's air defence network. It was therefore decided that Det 4 should fly another series of sorties over the Libyan region to try and confirm these intelligence reports. On 27, 28 and 30 August, both SR-71s were launched from Mildenhall to photograph all the Libyan bases. Tanker support for each operation consisted of three KC-135s and two KC-10s. The tankers and the Habus used call signs of MUG, SOKEY and BAFFY. Two other KC-135s (GAMMIT 99 and MYER 99) flew courier missions to Andrews AFB, Maryland, on 29 August and 9 September to transport the 'take' to the Pentagon, where intelligence analysts failed to find the MiGs they had suspected.

Thereafter, until 22 December 1988, it appeared as though the Libyan leader and his regime may have learned a lesson about US intolerance towards international terrorism; however, on that night, high over the small Scottish town of Lockerbie, Pan American Boeing 747, Flight 102 was blown from the sky by a bomb that had been planted on the aircraft earlier. In all, 259 passengers and crew and at least 11 people on the ground were killed, making this Britain's worst air disaster.

DET 4'S NEAR LOSSES

On 29 June 1987, Majs Duane Noll and Tom Veltri launched in '964 for a Barents/Baltic mission. They had just completed their anti-clockwise run off the coasts of Lithuania, Latvia and Estonia, when there was an explosion in the aircraft's right engine. Since 'denied territory' was off to their right, they had no alternative but to turn left, decelerate and descend. They were north of Gotland and as the aircraft descended, Tom turned on the IFF and declared an emergency on guard frequency. He now takes up the story: 'That got the Swede's attention and a pair of Viggens were on our wing before we reached 18,000 ft [5486 m]. Given that the Soviets were monitoring our activity, I was glad to see a friendly escort. We later found out that the Soviets had launched numerous fighters with orders to force us to land in Soviet territory or shoot us down. The descent from 80,000 to 25,000 ft [24384 to 7620 m] where the plane began to stabilise took just a few minutes. The Viggens continued to escort us through the Baltic and along the Polish and East German borders until F-15s out of West Germany intercepted and took over escort duties, but the worst was not yet over. Since fuel constraints made it impossible to make it back to Mildenhall, we were forced to land at Nordholz AB, West Germany. The engine explosion also caused the complete loss of our auxiliary hydraulic fluids. That meant no brakes or steering on landing. The base closed off all the surrounding roads prior to our arrival in anticipation of our going off the runway. Fortunately for everyone, there was just enough residual hydraulic fluid left in the lines for one application of the brakes. The airplane stopped just short of the end of the runway and that's where we left it for the rest of the day until a maintenance crew from Mildenhall arrived and moved it.'

During the late autumn, the Det again came within a breath of losing an aircraft, as Larry Brown elucidates: 'Keith [Carter] and I were scheduled to launch at 17:30 hours local, for a Barents mission on the evening of 20 October in aircraft '980. There was weather forecasted in the refuelling area off the coast of Norway; this was our first tour to Det 4, RAF Mildenhall, so we were the new guys. Mike Smith and Doug Soifer were actually scheduled for this mission but due to a conflict with another activity, we swapped flights.

'Launch went as scheduled and the aircraft performed well throughout as we exited the sensitive area. Our descent profile into the last refuelling track was going well with our altitude profile in check. So far, a great mission. We had a good lock on with the tanker's ranging system and fuel was above planned. Just one more hook-up, ACCEL, and we'd be back on the ground in no time, or so I thought …

'Decelerating through Mach 1.3 we completed our final "Decel" checklist. Altitude was on profile and as we passed through 31,000 ft [9449 m], the triple display indicator showed us decelerating through the Mach to subsonic speed. "OK Larry, range 40 to go, ready with the refuelling checks," Keith said. "OK, go with the checks." By level-off at 26,000 ft [7925 m], we had completed our refuelling checks and now we could concentrate on the rendezvous. Our range to the tanker quickly counted down to 20 miles [32 km] as the tanker made its final turn that would put us in trail and on the same heading. There was no moon or horizon and everything outside looked pretty black. At 10 miles [16 km] range, I picked up the tanker's lights, they were in a left turn about 10° off the nose. At 5 miles [8 km], I began a slow descent to their altitude of 25,000 ft [7620 m].

'The tanker had just about rolled out on heading and I began to slowly retard the throttles back to begin slowing from 0.9 Mach. Moments later I heard something through my earphones that

An ex-B-52 driver, Don Watkins illustrates a manoeuvre that he could perform easily in the SR-71 but that was unattainable in the 'BUFF'. Bob Fowlkes looks on unimpressed! (Paul F. Crickmore)

seemed to be a high pitched buzzing sound, similar to the sound heard when switching the generators on after engine start during ground operations. Immediately, the master warning light illuminated signaling me to check the tele-light panel [Central Annunciator Panel]. I glanced down to discover an amber "R GEN OFF" light illuminated indicating that the right electrical ac engine-driven generator had disconnected from the main ac bus. In the SR we had two ac generators, each driven by its respective engine. The electrical system, as with other aircraft, was designed with an ac bus tie to allow one generator to power the ac electrical requirements in case the other dropped off line.

'My first reaction was to look back up at the tanker. I was at their altitude with closure speed and needed to first stabilise our position behind them before working our problem. As I stabilised behind the tanker I told Keith we had a right generator off light and he responded that we had also lost the ANS, which was our primary navigation system. We went ahead and hooked up with the tanker taking on 5,000 lb [2268 kg] of fuel before disconnecting. The nature of a single generator out was not a serious emergency, especially since the other generator had picked up the load. I knew we had two chances to reset it, otherwise it was mandatory for us to land as soon as possible. After going through the checks, the generator dropped off again and then again, now we had no choice but to divert to Bødo, Norway. We explained to the tanker crew the nature of our problem and directed them to proceed to Bødo. I elected to remain on their wing until we had everything ironed out before taking the lead. Since the tanker had a good platform and navigation system the choice was simple to keep them in front, especially considering the solid deck of weather, night and no moon!

'We again hooked back up with the tanker for an additional 10,000 lb [4536 kg] of fuel – one thing I didn't need was to make a poor situation even worse by running low on fuel just in case we had to go somewhere else other than Bødo. I then slid back on the tanker, flying a loose formation. We finished up our checks and prepared for the approach, setting up the ILS and TACAN. We were still too far out for a check on the ILS and our TACAN wouldn't lock on, but the INS seemed to be OK. One of our UHF radios was on the tanker's frequency and the other with ATC.

'With 70 miles [113 km] to go I could see we were too high and tried to communicate with the tanker but with no luck. I kept trying, but got no reply and we were not receiving ATC either. Fuel looked good at 28,000 but the cg was getting aft so I began to transfer fuel to the forward tanks. We then tried the VHF radios and guard, but again, no luck. As we penetrated the deck, the tanker began a left turn away from where I thought we should be heading; now I wasn't sure if Bødo was closed, or if the tanker was just circling to get down. We were getting ready to try them on the HF radio when we heard them over guard, "come on up on victor 127.0." Having finally made contact, I planned on getting a position check, but then things really took a turn for the worse.

'The cockpit lights suddenly came on, making it extremely bright in the cockpit and very difficult to see the tanker. At about the same time that familiar buzzing sound came through my head-phones. I immediately looked down at the tele-light panel to discover a host of amber caution and red warning lights. The two red warning lights that caught my attention were the "LEFT" and "RIGHT" "ENGINE FUEL LOW PRESSURE" lights indicating loss of our remaining generator and imminent engine failure. I immediately placed both generator control switches to the emergency position as called for by the bold face procedures. Keith, also aware of the failure, called out the bold face actions without hesitation. Now, I went from bright floods to very dim lighting. However, my immediate concern was the back-up ac generator system (also known as emergency generators) and the supply of ac power to the fuel-tank boost pumps ensuring fuel pressure to the engines. I quickly looked down to where my fuel-control panel was supposed to be located, but the entire panel was black with no lighting whatsoever. To further complicate matters, none of the fuel tank selection buttons illuminated, either because the pumps were tripped off or because no power was going to any of the status indicator lights.

'I then remembered a warning in the manual stating that during emergency ac operation, the normal auto fuel sequencing system is disabled and the pilot must manually select the tanks. Auto transfer and ullage systems would also be inoperative. I felt across my panel until I located the tank selection buttons, then, beginning from the top I counted down, including the cross-feed button, to the 5th button and pushed it in, which was tank 4. Tank 4 had the most fuel and feed from this tank would have less impact on the centre of gravity. I still had no tank 4 "ON" light but observed that both red "LEFT" and "RIGHT" "ENGINE FUEL LOW PRESSURE" lights went out indicating at least some of the four boost pumps in tank 4 were operating and supplying adequate fuel pressure to the engines.

'Now at last, I had a chance to assess our situation; we were still over water, north of the Arctic Circle and it was hours before sunrise, this would make for a very serious situation if it became necessary for us to bail out. In the SR-71, fuel boost pumps are required to sustain engine operation. These pumps operate under ac voltage and required high enough current that only the engine driven ac generators could deliver it. If one generator failed or dropped off line for any number of reasons, then the electrical cross-over system provided ac voltage from the remaining ac generator. However, if a failure also occurred in the other ac generator, then the boost pumps failed to supply fuel to the engines. To guard against this remote possibility, an emergency back up feature was installed, this allowed the pilot to switch over to a more direct routing to the generator, or what was termed emergency generator. If one or both generators were intact and producing some amount of current, then this emergency bypass system would allow you to tap into any ac power coming from them. This emergency mode was intended as a last resort in order to provide unregulated and reduced power for running certain critical components necessary for flight. In the case of a non-rotating or seized generator, then no power would be available to power the boost pumps.

'We were now operating on emergency generator power with sufficient ac current for fuel pump operation. We were still in the weather flying formation off the tanker but had dropped back near my visual limits with the tanker. I reviewed our status with Keith – the RSO's cockpit didn't have a tele-light panel, so I needed to keep Keith informed. I then informed the tanker that our situation had gotten worse and we needed to get over land. It was hard to believe we had two totally independent failures, I was convinced there was a single failure at the route cause of all this.

'I shifted my attention to what we had working while the tanker continued the descent through the weather. Keith said he was in a totally dark cockpit with no lights, no INS information, no navigation and no radio control! I had a faint light on my airspeed and heading indicators but the rest of my instrument panel was dark. I knew that under emergency power I was supposed to have boost pumps, cross-feed, cg and fuel indicators, together with pitch and yaw trim. I also knew that my dc essential bus and the ac emergency bus (different from the back up emergency AC system to run the boost pumps), were being powered by either the number one battery or one or both of the transformer rectifiers. With the emergency ac voltage high enough from the generators then the transformer rectifiers would power the emergency ac and essential dc buses, if not, then they would only be powered by the number one battery, which would only last for a very limited time. My VHF radio was another concern, as well as the intercom for talking with Keith. Cross checking my tele-light panel I saw that the "EMER BAT ON" status light was not illuminated indicating I had good ac voltage from my emergency generators. Both transformer rectifier lights were also out assuring me I had good DC voltage to run my essential DC bus. My instrument inverter light was "On", which was supposed to be the case for this condition. These status lights indicated the electrical system was operating as designed while under emergency power. I could now see that the tanker had increased the descent rate and was still in an orbit, but I couldn't see any coastal lights.

'We had been operating under emergency ac power for about three minutes and things at least looked stable. It would just be a matter of picking up the coastal lights and then manoeuvring to final approach and landing. I was about to ask for our position and heading when the red master warning light illuminated again. "This can't be good, I thought." Checking my tele-light panel, I discovered the left generator fail light was on, indicating we had a complete loss of the left emergency AC back up system, probably due to a seized generator. I made a call to the tanker that we were down to our last source of emergency ac power. ATC informed us that a rescue helicopter had been despatched.

'We went from a simple single generator failure to losing our nav and radios, then losing the right generator to losing the emergency left generator system. Out of four ac generator modes, we had lost three of them and were now down to our last one and all within 15 minutes! There was no reason to believe that the remaining right generator would not completely fail. I still couldn't make out the coast, or for that matter a horizon. I asked for range and bearing to Bødo and ATC replied with, "on the nose for 25 miles."

'With the left generator completely gone, I knew I had lost half my tank 4 boost pumps.

It fell to Lt-Col Tom Henichek to reluctantly officiate over the deactivation of Det 4. His obvious fatigue says much about the thoughts of the Habu community at the time. (Paul F. Crickmore)

Pumps 4-2 and 4-3 were now without power, leaving me with just pumps 4-1 and 4-4; basically one pump for each engine. I wasn't sure of the voltage or current output of that remaining ac generator. If it was too low, then the boost pumps might not have sufficient ac power to meet fuel demands under the high engine power settings required during approach or go-around. The fuel cross-feed valve had been selected open but there was no light to indicate that it was functioning. I selected tank 2, but there was no light to indicate that the pumps were operating.

'Finally, I made out the surrounding lights of Bødo air base. I still could not read most of my indicators. I lowered the gear as soon as I was sure of making it to the coast. Thankfully, all three green gear down and locked indicator lights came on. I knew I didn't have a taxi light, but at least I retained control for deploying the drag chute. At about 10 miles [16 km] from Bødo, I picked up the runway, cleared the tanker off and manoeuvred to about a 5 mile [8 km] final. I wasn't sure of my exact speed, but kept it high in case I lost an engine. Over the overrun, I brought both throttles to idle, touching down about 1,500 ft [457 m] down the runway. With a good chute we came to a stop about 5,000 ft [1524 m] down the runway, the time was about 20:50 hours, local. We radioed the tanker that we had landed safely and they in

Although it remained primarily a transport and tanking base, RAF Mildenhall will always be remembered for its association with the SR-71. The aircraft was a favourite of the enthusiasts which gathered at the base fences, as well as all those who visited the annual Air Fete. The local area proved popular with the I-abu community in return, as Det 4's dartboard motif indicates. (Paul F. Crickmore)

An aircraft of impressive performance, with a Habu-chasing Mach 2.8 top speed, the MiG-25PD 'Foxbat-E' has now passed out of Russian service, where only reconnaissance versions of the big MiG survive, although it remains in service with countries including Libya. Undoubtedly the aircraft's systems and avionics were inferior to those of contemporary Western types, but its powerful missile armament, launched under exact parameters, might have given the aircraft a chance for a successful Habu shootdown. The R-40 (AA-6 'Acrid') missile shown on this aircraft's inner underwing pylons may have been capable of reaching and killing an SR-71, especially given the Soviet practice of launching salvoes of radar- and IR-guided versions of the same weapon. The R-60 missile mounted outboard on this MiG would not be carried on a Habu intercept. (Yefim Gordon)

Right: Military 1st Class Pilot Mikhail Myagkiy flew MiG-31 intercepts against SR-71s.

Although it cannot match the MiG-25 in terms of outright speed, the MiG-31 'Foxhound' is a much more capable interceptor, especially when armed with the R-33 missile as seen under the belly of 'Blue 31'. R-33 is believed to owe much to America's AIM-54 Phoenix, ironically derived from the YF-12's GAR-9, anc when combined with the MiG-31 it must be seen as the most serious threat to the SR-71 ever conceived. Russia had in excess of 300 R-33 armed MiG-31s available at the end of 2003. (Yefim Gordon)

JA 37 pilots, including Per-Olof Eidh, managed to fly hazardous interception profiles which bought them within range of cruising Habus. Although the JA 37, if carefully managed, could provide the performance to reach within striking range of the SR-71, the performance of its SkyFlash missiles in such an engagement is open to question. This F13 aircraft is armed with SkyFlash (inboard) and Sidewinder AAMs. Artech/Aerospace

Aircraft '964 prepares to leave its 'barn' on 17 December 1987 for an 07:45 launch. Ground technicians would have begun their activities four-and-a-half hours earlier. Their first task was to warm the tar-like engine o1 prior to start up, which in UK winter temperatures cooled to a solid mass. (Paul F. Crickmore)

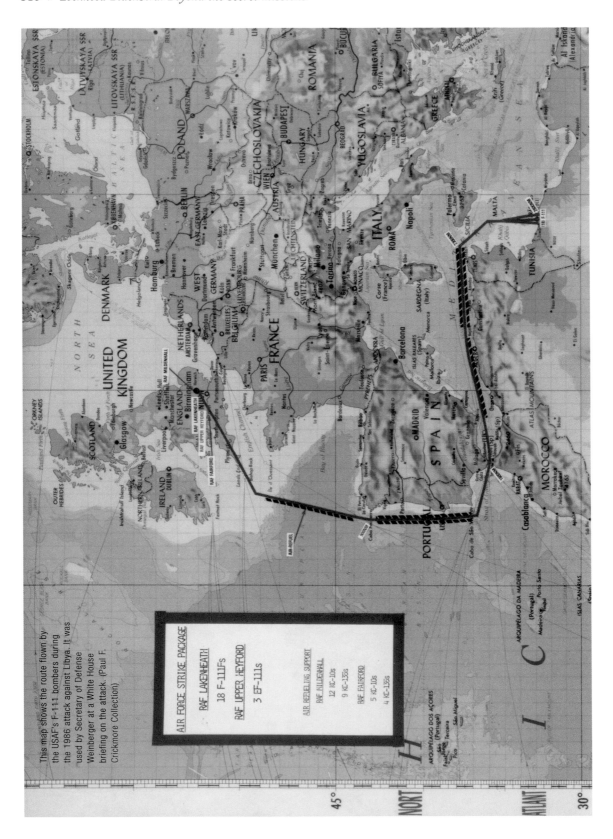

This map shows the route flown by the USAF's F-111 bombers during the 1986 attack against Libya. It was used by Secretary of Defense Weinberger at a White House briefing on the attack. (Paul F. Crickmore Collection)

AIR FORCE STRIKE PACKAGE

RAF LAKENHEATH

18 F-111Fs

RAF UPPER HEYFORD

3 EF-111s

AIR REFUELING SUPPORT

RAF FILDENHALL

12 KC-10s

9 KC-135s

RAF FAIRFORD

5 KC-10s

4 KC-135s

The Habu was always a spectacular air show performer, even though it was flying outside its optimum envelope. As the high point of Mildenhall's Air fetes, the aircraft was always flown with enthusiasm, at least one aircraft being permanently overstressed and more than one display resulting in dramatic fireballs as the afterburners ignited clouds of unburnt fuel. (E. W. F. Eden)

The radome housing the C3
Com data-link antenna, fitted
along with the ASARS
equipment, was located below
bay C, just forward of the nose-
undercarriage well. A digital
cassette recorder system
provided for the recording and
playback of both ASARS and
Elint data. Data could be
transmitted in real-time if the
aircraft was within range of a
receiving station; if not, it could
be downloaded quickly once
the aircraft was in range.
(USAF)

NASA 832 is shown on a two-mile, ILS final approach for landing on Runway 25 at Air Force Plant 42, Palmdale, California, to complete its NASA Dryden-crewed functional test flight on 26 June 1995. Palmdale Canyon Country and the San Gabriel Mountains lie in the background. (Jim Ross/NASA)

A gathering of Blackbirds large and small – Det 2's 29 March 1996 ribbon-cutting ceremony saw all its aircraft on display, including a pair of gloss-black Talons. Ironically, the programme was terminated just 17 days after this photograph was taken. (Lt-Col Blair Bozek/USAF)

With vortices streaming form its nacelle chine/wing leading-edge junctions,
NASA 831 (SR-71B 64-17956) moves in under a tanker for refuelling. NASA
made good use of this aircraft, operating it intensively from July 1991 to
August 1998. Inevitably, most of its flying related to crew proficiency and
training work in support of the NASA SR-71As and the short-term reactivation
of USAF Habu operations. (NASA)

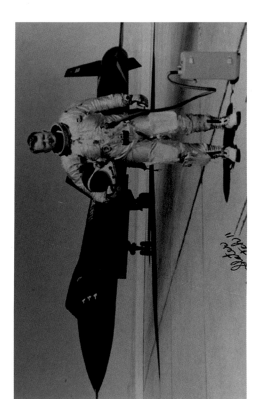

Above: Buzz Carpenter suffered a diarrhoea attack on a mission to Yemen.

Top: Ed Yielding and Curt Osterheld (at right) enjoy their final flight, end-of-tour celebration after an ASARS sortie over Cuba on 9 October 1987. The lady is Lisa Osterheld, Curt's wife and a KC-135 pilot. (via Curt Osterheld)

Above: Larry Brown and Keith Carter enjoyed the hospitality of the Norwegian air force after they were forced to divert into Bodø.

Top: Colone. Hugh C. 'Slip' Slater checked out as Ride Number 127. He was involved in the A-12 and YF-12 (as here) programmes.

Above: SR-71A 64-17962 is the only Habu on display outside the US. It is held at the Imperial War Museum Duxford, near Cambridge in the UK. The aircraft flew its fair share of missions out of Kadena, as well as raising the record for altitude in horizontal flight to 85,068.997 ft (25,929.031 m) in the period 27/28 July 1976. (Paul F. Crickmore)

Below: The same aircraft is shown during the 1976 record attempts, streaming its brake chute after a sortie. The machines used to set the records were standard, apart from the application of large white-cross calibration markings on their undersides. One arm of the cross can just be seen on '962's engine nacelle. (Lockheed)

For NASA service from 1990, the SR-71 gained a NASA tail number, which was applied to the fins in white under a red and white NASA title band. Otherwise the aircraft's colour schemes remained more or less standard. Here 831 makes a smart take-off, with its main gear already into its retraction cycle. (NASA)

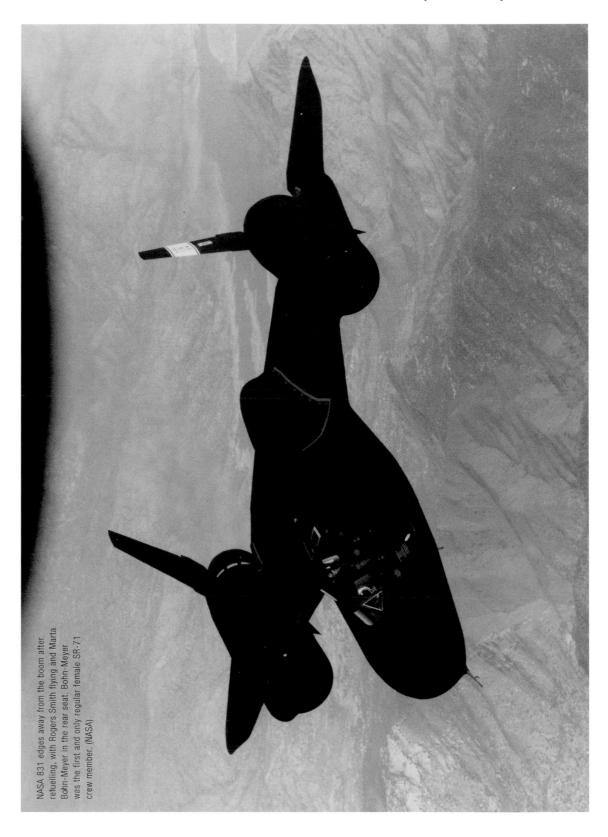

NASA 831 edges away from the boom after refuelling, with Rogers Smith flying and Marta Bohn-Meyer in the rear seat. Bohn-Meyer was the first and only regular female SR-71 crew member. (NASA)

Among the final NASA SR-71 flights were those supporting the LASRE programme. In the event, the LASRE aerospike engine was never fired in flight since insurmountable problems with fuel leaks made this too hazardous. (NASA Dryden Flight Test Center)

turn informed the tower, as they couldn't see us, since we had no exterior lights. After tuning to the tower frequency on VHF, we were able to communicate and coordinate our movement around the airfield. Keith and I were pretty glad to be on the ground, to say the least! We taxied to a remote hangar where we shut down and were greeted by an officer overseeing the operation. Now we were safely down, the security of the aircraft and the "take" was our next priority.

'Norwegian military security personnel were soon on the scene and they brought with them about a dozen very well armed guards. We instructed their officer in charge that no one other than Keith or myself were allowed past them into the secure zone. They secured the perimeter with armed guards all in view of each other. Keith and I felt confident it was safe to leave the aircraft and its valuable intelligence cargo.

'We were then transported to their command post, where we were patched through to our operations post at Mildenhall. We had a lengthy discussion with maintenance describing the extent of our problems. No doubt, they were at a loss as to what systems failed and to that extent, what they needed to bring over with them. Afterwards we were given rooms at the officers' quarters along with some "flights" to wear and an invitation to join the base commander at his table for dinner.

'The following day a KC-135Q arrived from Mildenhall carrying our maintenance and security personnel and, most importantly, our personal belongings. I always had a "grab and go bag" with all the necessary clothing in my room, just in case of a land away. I was also glad to see they'd included a generous amount of refreshments –

refreshments were very expensive in Bødo! We had an access list of all personnel allowed into the secure area which Keith and I reviewed. We then coordinated with the Norwegian officer in charge to transfer security over to our military security personnel. Keith and I were very grateful to our Norwegian friends and we were certainly impressed with their ability to respond with such little notice and with such a high degree of professionalism. Every detail was covered, and we were treated with the utmost courtesy.

'During the next four days of our stay Keith and I went out to the hanger to check on progress and help out, including conducting engine runs. It looked like the aircraft was going to be ready for the flight back to Mildenhall on 24 October. I was hoping for a daylight departure, but system checks took a bit longer than anticipated so we finally launched out of Bødo that evening, for the night subsonic return to RAF Mildenhall. Other than a little apprehension on the reliability of the electrical systems, the aircraft flew quiet well with no abnormal occurrences. The aircraft was put right back on schedule after a few more checks, once again demonstrating what a superior ground crew we had, a real test of our capability.

'During the tear down, maintenance discovered we had suffered two completely separate failures. The loss of the right generator was due to a failure of the right voltage regulator, while the loss of the left generator was due to a failure in the accessory drive unit. This failure of the left side, caused the generator to seize and would have also resulted in complete left utility hydraulic failure. I guess it was fitting that on 18 January 1989, Keith and I flew our last SR-71 flight in aircraft '980!'

SHUTDOWN
Chapter 10

With changes in technology radically modifying the state of the art in reconnaissance systems, the Senior Crown programme was increasingly living on borrowed time without an electro-optical back plate for its camera system and a data-link system that would permit both camera and radar imagery to be down linked in near real time. Eventually funds were appropriated for the development of Senior King, a secure data link via satellite, but its development would prove too late to save the SR-71.

By the late 1980s the people on the long list of those articulating an anti-SR-71 posture were as varied in position as they were powerful. Dewain Andrews and Bob Fitch, serving on the Senate's House Permanent Select Committee on Intelligence (HPSCI), appeared to make the shutdown of the Senior Crown programme a personal crusade. Within the Air Force at the time detractors included Chief of Staff Gen Larry Welch, AF/XO (Air Force/Executive Officer) Gen Dougan, CINCSAC Gen John Chain, AF/Programme Requirements Gen Ron Fogleman, Chief of SAC Intelligence (SAC/IN) Gen Doyle and SAC/IN Col Tanner, and Gen Leo Smith of the Budget Review Board. The main thrust of their argument orientated itself around cost issues versus the 'marginal benefits' of operating the SR-71 compared to satellites. In addition, the Pentagon contended that an air-breathing replacement platform was under development and during a meeting on Capitol Hill, Welch testified (incorrectly) that the SR-71 had become vulnerable to SA-5 and SA-10 'Grumble' SAMs.

By 1988 it looked as though these combined efforts would be successful. But all was not quite lost. CINCLANT, Admiral Lee Baggott, still required SR-71 coverage of the Kola peninsula as there were no other systems (including satellites) that were capable of meeting the Navy's requirements. He took the battle to retain the SR-71 in Europe right to the JCS and obtained funding for Det 4 for a further year. Meanwhile, the SR-71 Program Element Monitor (PEM) and his action officer were able to secure a commitment from a staffer on the Senate Appropriations Committee for $46 million to keep both Kadena and Palmdale open for another year. Thereafter, however, the antagonists got their way

Ed Yeilding and JT Vida established a coast-to-coast speed record in '972 on 6 March 1990, when they 'ferried' it from Palmdale to the National Air and Space Museum at Dulles Airport, Washington DC, the last USAF SR-71 flight. (Lockheed)

Above: This was the back seat of the $50-million flight simulator that was purchased just prior to the SR-71 programme's cancellation. Within NASA this crew space is known as the Research Systems Operator's position.

Right: This was the instructor's position in the same simulator. (both Paul F. Crickmore Collection)

and what was to be the Air Force's final SR-71 flight took place on 6 March 1990, when Ed Yeilding and JT Vida flew '972 on a west-to-east coast record-breaking flight of the United States, before landing at the Smithsonian National Aerospace Museum, Washington DC, where the aircraft was handed over for permanent display. With the SR-71 fleet retired from the inventory, three were placed in storage at Site 2 Palmdale, and two 'A' models and the sole surviving two-seater were loaned to NASA. The remaining 13 aircraft (including the hybrid trainer designated SR-71C), were donated to various museums in the United States and United Kingdom, this despite more than 40 members of Congress, together with many other well placed officials and senior officers voicing their concern over the decision.

Subsequently, during the course of Desert Storm – the 1991 Gulf War – two requests were made to reactivate the Senior Crown programme. However, perhaps not surprisingly, both were turned down by the same SECDEF who had presided over the aircraft's shutdown a year earlier – Dick Cheney. That Desert Storm was an overwhelming success for Coalition forces is beyond dispute, but there were lessons to be learned from the 41-day campaign, not the least of which was the inability of US forces to make timely reconnaissance material available to Gen Schwarzkopf's field commanders.

The SR-71 programme remained quiet until March/April 1994, when events in the

international arena once more took a turn. Relations between North Korea and the United States (at best always strained) reached a new low over North Korea's refusal to allow inspection of its nuclear facilities. At this point Senator Robert Byrd took centre stage. He, together with several members of the armed services and various members of Congress, contended that back in 1990 the Pentagon had consistently lied about the supposed readiness of a replacement for the SR-71. The motivation behind such comments did not appear to be the usual politicking, but one of genuine concern for the maintenance of a platform capable of survivable broad-area synoptic coverage.

The campaigning and lobbying paid off as short-term provision was made for a modest 'three-plane SR-71 aircraft contingency reconnaissance capability', at a cost of $100 million, for Fiscal Year 1995 (FY95). Of the three SR-71As that were stored at Palmdale, only '967 was called to arms. The other 'A' model to be re-commissioned was '971, which had been loaned to NASA, re-numbered 832 and regularly ground tested, but never flown by its civilian caretakers. The pilot-trainer SR-71B, together with the brand new flight simulator purchased just months before shut down, would be shared between the Air Force and NASA, and in a further move to keep operating

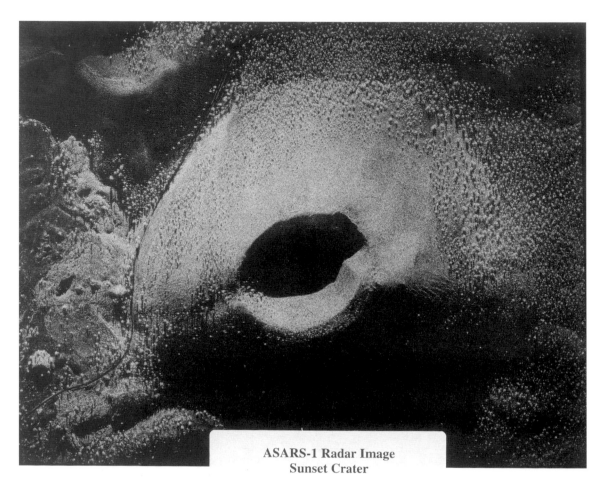

ASARS-1 Radar Image
Sunset Crater

This incredible picture was the first of the SR-71/ASARS-1 images to be released. It shows Sunset Crater, Arizona, in superb detail. (Goodyear)

costs to a minimum, the new detachment, designated Det 2, would, like the NASA operation, be based at Edwards AFB, California.

Aircraft reactivation began on 5 January 1995 with a fuel leak evaluation of '967. Seven days later, at 11:26 hours, NASA crew Steve Ishmael and Research Systems Operator Marta Bohn-Meyer got airborne from Edwards in '971 on a 26-minute ferry flight that terminated at Lockheed Martin's Skunk Works, Plant 10, Building 602, Palmdale. Over the next three months, ASARS, together with other sensors previously in storage at Luke AFB, Arizona, were installed in the aircraft. At 10:18 hours on 26 April, NASA crew Ed Schneider and Marta Bohn-Meyer completed a 34-minute FCF on '971. A month later, Ed and Marta's husband, Bob Meyer, conducted '971's second and final FCF which lasted 2 hours 30 minutes. However, it took seven further check flights to wring out all the

glitches in '967, the final one being successfully completed on 12 January 1996.

Three Air Force crews were selected to fly the aircraft, the plan being that two crews would always be Mission Ready qualified and the third crew Mission Capable. While crew proficiency training got underway in the simulator and the 'B' model, research and development funds were used to develop and install the long awaited data link, which was manufactured by C3 Com., of Salt Lake City. Its antenna was housed in a small radome, just forward of the front undercarriage wheel well. A digital cassette recorder system (DCRsi) provided recording and playback of both Elint and ASARS data, enabling the SR-71 to provide near-real-time data provided it was within 300 nm (345 mile; 555 km) line-of-sight range of a receiving station. If not, the entire recorded collection could be downloaded in ten minutes once the aircraft was within station range.

As the qualified Air Force crews began to acquaint themselves with their aircraft, the on-going battle between the various factions supporting or against the resurrected programme

A-12 60-6925, Article 122, was dismantled at Palmdale and trucked to New York, where it was lifted aboard USS *Intrepid*, a decommissioned aircraft-carrier which is used as a military museum in New York Harbour. The aircraft had been used for ground tests before its first flight and spent a good deal of time mounted on 'the Pole' at Area 51's RCS test range. Today the aircraft is displayed on the port side of the carrier's flight deck, near the port aircraft elevator, alongside exhibits including an AV-8C Harrier, an F-14 Tomcat and an F-16 Fighting Falcon. (both via Don Emmons)

came to a head. Exploiting a complex technical loophole in the legislation, the antagonists asserted that it was technically illegal to operate the SR-71. Consequently, at 23:00 (Z) on 16 April 1996, a signal was despatched from the Pentagon once again suspending all SR-71 operations with immediate effect. This was overturned when supporters serving on the Senate Appropriations Committee threatened to defeat the Intelligence Authorization Act for FY1997. This would have halted all intelligence activities, not only within the Air Force, but also at the DIA, CIA, NSA, etc! Some $39 million was therefore allocated to the programme: $30 million for operations and maintenance and $9 million for procurement. Once again, expectations in Det 2 were running high as the next phase of sensor enhancement involving the development of an electro-optical backplate for the TEOCs, by Recon Optical located at Barrington, Illinois, got underway. This development replaced the traditional film with a charged coupled device (CCD), enabling digitised, high-quality, close-look imagery from the cameras, together with that acquired by ASARS, to be transmitted by data link directly to theatre commanders.

LAST BREATH

However, the political prevarication and lobbying continued and on 10 October 1997, President Clinton line-item vetoed the SR-71 programme and everything drew to a halt. Routine maintenance work continued until 30 September 1999 (the end of the military fiscal year), after which the remaining monies ran out and Senior Crown finally succumbed. On 6 October 1999, Detachment 2 of the 9th Strategic Reconnaissance Wing was

deactivated. For 30 years the SR-71 had operated with impunity over the most heavily fortified areas of the world. By 1981, over 1,000 SA-2s had been launched against the aircraft, but due to its speed and altitude capabilities, and sophisticated DEF systems, all missed. Unfortunately, Kelly Johnson's masterpiece was not immune from attacks launched from Capitol Hill.

The projection of military power, in the form of a carrier battle group, is a useful deterrent to potential conflict and underpins political rhetoric. Similarly, the SR-71's unique ability to overfly the capital of any potential enemy with impunity, gathering as it goes reconnaissance data, while laying down a triple sonic boom, re-enforced military superiority and intent, in a manner that an enemy's state-run propaganda machine would find difficult to dismiss.

Since the A-12 and SR-71 first took to the air, the world's geopolitical systems have changed dramatically. Today, the Cold War is a phenomenon researched by students of contemporary history. But the contribution made by Oxcart, Senior Crown and all those associated with the programmes during those years is almost incalculable. Quite apart from the obvious benefits derived by Western intelligence agencies from its surveillance-gathering systems, the aircraft's very existence represented such a threat to the Soviet Union that it spent billions of roubles developing weapons systems like the SA-5 SAM and MiG-25/MiG-31 interceptors, solely in an effort to

Call sign NASA 832 vents JP-7 from its rear fuselage vent several minutes after take-off during its functional test flight from Runway 25 at Air Force Plant 42, Palmdale, California. The test pilot is Ed Schneider and the flight-test engineer is Bob Meyer. (Jim Ross/NASA)

defeat the SR-71 and similar-performing aircraft should they ever violate its sovereign airspace.

The sickening events of 11 September 2001 vividly demonstrated the vulnerability of an open society to an attack, the like of which has not been witnessed since the kamikaze attacks of World War II – attacks which also ultimately failed to achieve their military and political objectives. But the attack also demonstrated, in gut-wrenching terms, what happens when intelligence agencies rely too heavily on a limited number of collection sources. Today, the United States is extremely reliant upon satellites for the collection of strategic reconnaissance data from otherwise 'denied' areas. Shortly after 'Nine Eleven', various members of Congress wrote to Secretary of Defense Donald Rumsfeld, urging him to consider reactivating two SR-71As in a bid to bolster US reconnaissance gathering capabilities. Alas, the only sure way of tracking small, hardened terrorist cells is via an effective Humint network. Notwithstanding, the SR-71 is in a unique position to make an unrivalled contribution to countering global terrorism due to the various systems upgrades described earlier. If President George W. Bush is serious about tackling states that arm, train and support terrorists, or that prepare weapons of mass destruction for them, he might well be advised to listen to the words from some of his Senators.

COMPLETE OL-8, OLRK, OLKA AND DET 1 SR-71 MISSION RECORD
Appendix 1

During more than 20 years of its existence, the SR-71 detachment at Kadena AB, Okinawa, was scheduled to fly in excess of 2,700 Habu missions. Deducting ground and air aborts from this total reveals that the unit completed a staggering 2,410 Habu missions.

Intelligence requirements of the Vietnam war dominated the Det's early activities. Flight duration times varied from two hours 30 minutes to five hours 30 minutes, depending upon the number of targets scheduled into the mission; this in turn dictating the aircraft's air refuelling requirements, etc.

It was not until 25 July 1970 that the Det broadened its area of interest to include North Korea. Again, flight duration varied between two and four hours, the determining factor of course being the intelligence community's requirements.

PARPRO sorties were also flown from Okinawa off China and the Soviet Union. Round-robin missions from the island lasted about four hours. Often, though, these collection areas were targeted during aircraft change-arounds, as an SR-71 returned to Beale or conversely was positioned to complete a stint of TDY on the island.

Later still came the 11-hour return flights to the Arabian Gulf.

An analysis of Det 4's flight log clearly demonstrates the reach capability of this remarkable aircraft, together with the willingness of successive US administrations to deploy this high-value asset to all hot spots of the world in the pursuit of truth. It also depicts in bold relief the ability of both the flight crews and the ground support staff to successfully execute the most demanding of missions.

FOOTNOTES TO OL-8, OLRK, OLKA AND DET 1 SR-71 MISSION RECORD

1. First confirmed firing of an SA-2 against an SR-71.
2, 3, 4 and 5. First aircraft changeovers.
6. First and only aircraft recall due to enemy preparedness along the aircraft's intended route.
7. Aircraft stalled post air refuelling and crashed in Thailand, the crew ejected safely.
8. First SR-71 mission over North Korea (all prior operational sorties from Kadena were flown in support of the Vietnam War).
9. First night operational sortie flown from Kadena, the collection area was Vladivostok.
10. Co-ordinated sorties to lay down sonic booms over the Hanoi Hilton PoW camp. Take-off times were: '979, 14:16 hours (L); '980, 14:18 hours (L); and '968, 15:22 hours (L).
11. Second series of missions to boom the Hanoi Hilton. Take-off times were: '980, 14:16 hours (L); '978, 14:18 hours (L); and '968, 15:22 hours (L).
12. Close call over Hanoi following generator failure and double flame-out.
13. Aircraft was written-off during recovery back at Kadena. Crew escaped injury.
14. Missions for the remainder of the year flown in support of Linebacker II.
15. First operational mission flown over North Vietnam at night.
16. Mission flown in support of the SS Mayaguez incident.
17. Successful mission flown off the coast of Okinawa to locate a Soviet Intelligence gathering 'trawler'.
18. On 6 Septembrr 1976, Viktor Belenko successfully defected to Habodate Air Base, Japan, in a MiG-25P. SR-71 missions from Kadena to points off the coast of Petropavlovsk were typically of about four-hours duration.
19. Special flight co-ordinated with the US Navy.
20. Special mission.
21. Special flight co-ordinated with the US Navy.
22. Brave Shield mission flown in the region of Kawajelin Island and co-ordinated with missile tests from Vandenberg AFB in order to validate elements of SIOP.

23. Fight off the coast of Petropavlovsk.
24. Aircraft flown to Diego Garcia to 'exercise' facilities should they be required to support future SR-71 operations.
25. Aircraft returned from Diego Garcia.
26. Special flight conducted over North Vietnam, Cambodia and Laos in search of substantive evidence claims of MIA PoW camps.
27. Nearing completion of a third pass along the DMZ between North and South Korea, the crew were fired upon by an SA-2.
28. Flight conducted off the eastern coast of China and North Korea; the crew reported an unusual massing of shipping.
29. Flight path of the 26 August 1981 mission repeated with full support of strike and Wild Weasel aircraft in case North Korea again elected to launch an SA-2 – wisely, it refrained.
30. The aircraft was airborne at 14:I5 hours (L), the collection area being the vicinity of the Kamchatka Peninsula. Upon return to Kadena the RSO reported increased tracking and ECM activity in the collection area. Later that night an RC-135 Elint/Comint gathering aircraft of the 55th SRW undertook a mission to the same area. Shortly thereafter, Korean Airlines flight KE007, a Boeing 747-200B on a commercial flight from Anchorage, Alaska to Seoul, was shot down having strayed well into Soviet airspace and the highly sensitive area of Kamchatka. The aircraft failed to respond to various warnings and was eventually shot down by a force consisting of three Su-15s and a MiG-23. All 269 passengers and crew on board the airliner lost their lives.
31. Co-ordinated mission off the coast of Vladivostok between II '964 flying a round-robin and '973 inbound from Beale.
32. First mission flown from Kadena into the Gulf and back, during the war between Iran and Iraq.
33. Second mission to the Gulf.
34. Third mission to the Gulf.
35. Fourth mission to the Gulf.
36. Aircraft crashed into the sea off Luzon, Philippines. The crew ejected safely.

COMPLETE DET 1 MISSION RECORD

Date	Instal. No.	T.O. Time	Pilot Name	RSO Name	Mission Type	Duration	Remarks
09/03/68	978	10:00	BROWN Buddy	JENSEN Dave	Ferry to OL-8	6.6	
11/03/68	976	10:00	O'MALLEY Jerome/Jerry	PAYNE Edward/Ed.	Ferry to OL-8	6.5	
13/03/68	974	10:00	SPENCER Bob	BRANHAM Keith	Ferry to OL-8	6.3	
18/03/68	978	10:00	BROWN Buddy	JENSEN Dave	CCTM	1.5	
21/03/68	976	12:30	O'MALLEY Jerry	PAYNE Ed.	HABU	5.1	
24/03/68	976	11:00	O'MALLEY Jerry	PAYNE Ed.	RTB FERRY	1.5	
26/03/68	974	11:51	WATKINS Jim	DEMPSTER Dave	CCTM	1.7	
28/03/68	976	11:00	SPENCER Bob	BRANHAM Keith	CCTM	1.7	
01/04/68	978	12:00	BROWN Buddy	JENSEN Dave	CCTM	1.7	
04/04/68	976	12:00	O'MALLEY Jerry	PAYNE Ed.	FCF/E	1.7	
05/04/68	974	14:00	WATKINS Jim	DEMPSTER Dave	CCTM	1.7	
08/04/68	978	12:00	SPENCER Bob	BRANHAM Keith	CCTM	1.6	
10/04/68	978		BROWN Buddy	JENSEN Dave	CCTM		A
10/04/68	976	14:00	O'MALLEY Jerry	PAYNE Ed.	HABU	3.9	
12/04/68	974	12:00	BROWN Buddy	JENSEN Dave	CCTM	1.7	
15/04/68	976	13:22	WATKINS Jim	DEMPSTER Dave	CCTM	2.4	
16/04/68	976	16:00	SPENCER Bob	BRANHAM Keith	FCF/E	1.1	
18/04/68	978	11:00	BROWN Buddy	JENSEN Dave	HABU	2.4	A
19/04/68	974	12:00	WATKINS Jim	DEMPSTER Dave	HABU	5.4	
20/04/68	978	13:00	BROWN Buddy	JENSEN Dave	RTB FERRY	2.3	
22/04/68	974	11:00	SPENCER Bob	BRANHAM Keith	HABU	5.6	
24/04/68	978	10:00	O'MALLEY Jerry	PAYNE Ed.	FCF/E	1.9	A
27/04/68	976	12:20	BROWN Buddy	JENSEN Dave	HABU	3	A
28/04/68	974	14:00	WATKINS Jim	DEMPSTER Dave	HABU	3.8	
28/04/68	978	15:00	O'MALLEY Jerry	PAYNE Ed.	FCF/ELECT	1.6	
29/04/68	976	10:58	BROWN Buddy	JENSEN Dave	RTB FERRY TO OL-8	2.3	
02/05/68	976	12:00	SPENCER Bob	BRANHAM Keith	CCTM	2.6	
04/05/68	974		WATKINS Jim	DEMPSTER Dave	FCF/E	1.6	
05/05/68	978		SPENCER Bob	BRANHAM Keith	HABU	5.4	
08/05/68	976		WATKINS Jim	DEMPSTER Dave	HABU	5.7	
09/05/68	978		DEVALL Larry	SHOEMAKER Clyde	FCF/E	2.3	
11/05/68	976		STORRIE John	MALLOZZIE Cos	FCF/E	1.7	
11/05/68	974		SPENCER Bob	BRANHAM Keith	HABU	4.5	
13/05/68	974		WATKINS Jim	DEMPSTER Dave	HABU	5.6	
16/05/68	976		STORRIE John	MALLOZZIE Cos	HABU	5.2	
17/05/68	978		DEVALL Larry	SHOEMAKER Clyde	HABU	4.3	
19/05/68	976		WALBRECHT Don	LOIGNON Phil	FCF/E	1.7	
19/05/68	978		WATKINS Jim	DEMPSTER Dave	FCF/E	1.9	
22/05/68	974		STORRIE John	MALLOZZIE Cos	HABU	3.1	
24/05/68	976		DEVALL Larry	SHOEMAKER Clyde	HABU	5.5	
25/05/68	978		WALBRECHT Don	LOIGNON Phil	HABU	5.3	
27/05/68	978		WALBRECHT Don	LOIGNON Phil	FCF/E	1.8	
29/05/68	974		WATKINS Jim	DEMPSTER Dave	CCTM	2.5	
03/06/68	976		STORRIE John	MALLOZZIE Cos	HABU	1.3	A
03/06/68	978		DEVALL Larry	SHOEMAKER Clyde	HABU	4.3	
05/06/68	974		BEVACQUA Tony	CREWS Mac	CCTM	2.3	
07/06/68	978		WALBRECHT Don	LOIGNON Phil	CCTM	2.3	
11/06/68	976		STORRIE John	MALLOZZIE Cos	CCTM	2.7	
14/06/68	974		DEVALL Larry	SHOEMAKER Clyde	CCTM	1.7	
15/06/68	978		BEVACQUA Tony	MALLOZZIE Cos	CCTM	1.8	
17/06/68	976		WALBRECHT Don	LOIGNON Phil	CCTM		A
18/06/68	974		WALBRECHT Don	LOIGNON Phil	HABU	4.1	
19/06/68	976		STORRIE John	MALLOZZIE Cos	CCTM	1.9	
23/06/68	978		BEVACQUA Tony	CREWS Mac	HABU	5.4	
25/06/68	974		STORRIE John	MALLOZZIE Cos	HABU	4.3	
26/06/68	976		DEVALL Larry	SHOEMAKER Clyde	CCTM	0.8	A
29/06/68	974		COLLINS Pete	SHOEMAKER Clyde	CCTM	2.3	A
30/06/68	978		WALBRECHT Don	LOIGNON Phil	HABU	5.2	
03/07/68	974		COLLINS Pete	SEAGROVES Connie	CCTM		A
04/07/68	976		BEVACQUA Tony	CREWS Mac	HABU	6	
05/07/68	974		COLLINS Pete	SEAGROVES Connie	CCTM	1.6	A
07/07/68	978		STORRIE John	MALLOZZIE Cos	CCTM	2.7	
08/07/68	976	11:00	WALBRECHT Don	LOIGNON Phil	CCTM	1.5	
10/07/68	978	11:00	BEVACQUA Tony	CREWS Mac	CCTM	1.7	A
12/07/68	976	14:00	STORRIE John	MALLOZZIE Cos	HABU	3.9	
14/07/68	978	10:00	COLLINS Pete	SEAGROVES Connie	CCTM	2.3	
15/07/68	974	10:00	WALBRECHT Don	LOIGNON Phil	CCTM	1.6	
17/07/68	976	10:15	STORRIE John	MALLOZZIE Cos	CCTM	2.6	
18/07/68	976	14:00	COLLINS Pete	SEAGROVES Connie	HABU	5.3	
19/07/68	974	12:00	BEVACQUA Tony	CREWS Mac	CCTM	1.8	
20/07/68	978	15:00	HALLORAN Pat	JARVIS Mort	CCTM	2.1	
23/07/68	978	13:45	WALBRECHT Don	LOIGNON Phil	HABU	5.1	
24/07/68	976	14:00	COLLINS Pete	SEAGROVES Connie	FCF/PHASE	2.3	
26/07/68	974	09:01	HALLORAN Pat	JARVIS Mort	HABU	2.1	A
26/07/68	976	10:08	BEVACQUA Tony	CREWS Mac	HABU	6	1
28/07/68	974	09:10	HALLORAN Pat	JARVIS Mort	HABU	5.3	
01/08/68	978	10:15	WALBRECHT Don	LOIGNON Phil	CCTM	2.5	
02/08/68	974	10:30	COLLINS Pete	SEAGROVES Connie	CCTM	1.6	
04/08/68	974	10:00	ST MARTIN Roy	BREADEN Cecil	FCF	1.7	
05/08/68	976	13:25	BEVACQUA Tony	CREWS Mac	CCTM	2.3	
07/08/68	978	10:45	HALLORAN Pat	JARVIS Mort	CCTM	2.3	
09/08/68	974	10:45	COLLINS Pete	SEAGROVES Connie	CCTM	2.3	
11/08/68	978	10:05	ST MARTIN Roy	BREADEN Cecil	CCTM	0.5	
12/08/68	974	08:50	BEVACQUA Tony	CREWS Mac	HABU	5.5	
14/08/68	976	10:50	HALLORAN Pat	JARVIS Mort	CCTM	2.4	
16/08/68	976	10:25	COLLINS Pete	SEAGROVES Connie	FCF	2.1	
17/08/68	974	14:58	HALLORAN Pat	JARVIS Mort	HABU	0.6	A
17/08/68	978	14:00	COLLINS Pete	SEAGROVES Connie	HABU	1.9	A
18/08/68	978	13:35	COLLINS Pete	SEAGROVES Connie	HABU	4	
18/08/68	974	14:35	HALLORAN Pat	JARVIS Mort	HABU	4.1	

Date	Instal. No.	T.O. Time	Pilot Name	RSO Name	Mission Type	Duration	Remarks
19/08/68	976	11:05	BULL George	Mc NEER Red	CCTM	2.4	
21/08/68	978	08:50	ST MARTIN Roy	BREADEN Cecil	HABU	5.4	
23/08/68	978	11:55	COLLINS Pete	SEAGROVES Connie	CCTM	2.3	
29/08/68	974	10:06	COLLINS Pete	SEAGROVES Connie	HABU	1.7	A
01/09/68	976	12:55	HALLORAN Pat	JARVIS Mort	CCTM	1.3	
02/09/68	974	11:35	BULL George	Mc NEER Red	CCTM	1.3	
06/09/68	978	12:00	ST MARTIN Roy	BREADEN Cecil	CCTM	1.1	
06/09/68	974	13:00	HALLORAN Pat	JARVIS Mort	CCTM	1	
08/09/68	974	09:05	BULL George	Mc NEER Red	HABU	4.3	
09/09/68	978	12:05	COLLINS Pete	SEAGROVES Connie	CCTM	0.9	
10/09/68	976	09:50	HALLORAN Pat	JARVIS Mort	CCTM	2.3	
12/09/68	980	08:00	SHELTON Dale	BOGGESS Larry	FERRY TO OL-8	6.3	2
13/09/68	976	06:00	COLLINS Pete	SEAGROVES Connie	FERRY TO SC-5		2
14/09/68	980	11:55	SHELTON Dale	BOGGESS Larry	CCTM K3	2.5	
15/09/68	970	02:00	HICHEW Al	SCHMITTOU Tom	FERRY TO OL-8	6.3	3
16/09/68	974	06:00	HALLORAN Pat	JARVIS Mort	FERRY TO SC-5		3
17/09/68	980	10:00	ST MARTIN Roy	BREADEN Cecil	HABU	3.9	
17/09/68	970	11:16	BULL George	Mc NEER Red	CCTM K3	2.4	
18/09/68	962	02:00	CAMPBELL Bill	PENNINGTON Al	FERRY TO OL-8	5.9	4
18/09/68	980	13:00	BULL George	Mc NEER Red	HABU	4	
19/09/68	978	06:00	HICHEW Al	SCHMITTOU Tom	FERRY TO SC-5		5
19/09/68	962	13:05	CAMPBELL Bill	PENNINGTON Al	CCTM K3	2.3	
20/09/68	980	09:05	SHELTON Dale	BOGGESS Larry	CCTM K3	2.2	
25/09/68	970	09:25	SHELTON Dale	BOGGESS Larry	HABU	5.7	
26/09/68	980		ST MARTIN Roy	BREADEN Cecil	CCTM		A
30/09/68	962	12:00	CAMPBELL Bill	PENNINGTON Al	HABU	5.8	
01/10/68	970	10:55	ST MARTIN Roy	BREADEN Cecil	HABU	6.1	
02/10/68	980	10:55	BULL George	Mc NEER Red	CCTM K3	0.4	A
03/10/68	962	11:20	BULL George	Mc NEER Red	HABU	5.7	
04/10/68	970	09:15	SHELTON Dale	BOGGESS Larry	HABU	1	R,6
05/10/68	980	10:15	Mc CALLUM Brian	LOCKE Bobby	CCTM K3	0.6	A
07/10/68	980	10:40	CAMPBELL Bill	PENNINGTON Al	CCTM K3	2.4	
10/10/68	970	09:30	BULL George	Mc NEER Red	CCTM K3	2.2	
12/10/68	980	11:55	SHELTON Dale	BOGGESS Larry	CCTM K3	2.4	
13/10/68	970	11:40	SHELTON Dale	BOGGESS Larry	HABU	4.1	
16/10/68	980	10:55	CAMPBELL Bill	PENNINGTON Al	HABU	4.6	A
17/10/68	962	12:00	Mc CALLUM Brian	LOCKE Bobby	HABU	4.6	A
18/10/68	980	14:32	CAMPBELL Bill	PENNINGTON Al	RTB FERRY	2.3	
20/10/68	970	12:00	BULL George	Mc NEER Red	HABU	5.7	
23/10/68	980	11:31	SHELTON Dale	BOGGESS Larry	CCTM K3	1.1	A
25/10/68	980	09:30	CAMPBELL Bill	PENNINGTON Al	CCTM K3	2.3	A
26/10/68	962	10:30	DAUBS Larry	ROETCISOENDER Bob	CCTM K3	2.4	
26/10/68	980	11:40	Mc CALLUM Brian	LOCKE Bobby	CCTM K3	2.4	
27/10/68	970		SHELTON Dale	BOGGESS Larry	CCTM K3		A
29/10/68	980	10:30	SHELTON Dale	BOGGESS Larry	CCTM K3	2.4	
30/10/68	970	11:30	CAMPBALL Bill	PENNINGTON Al	CCTM K3	2.4	
03/11/68	970	11:45	CAMPBALL Bill	PENNINGTON Al	HABU	5.7	
04/11/68	962	10:00	CAMPBELL Bobby	KRAUS Jon	CCTM K3	2.6	
04/11/68	980	12:00	Mc CALLUM Brian	LOCKE Bobby	CCTM K4	1	
05/11/68	962	10:00	DAUBS Larry	ROETCISOENDER Bob	CCTM K3	2.7	
10/11/68	970	11:30	DAUBS Larry	ROETCISOENDER Bob	CCTM K4	1.1	
10/11/68	980	10:10	Mc CALLUM Brian	LOCKE Bobby	HABU	5.9	
11/11/68	962	10:00	CAMPBELL Bill	PENNINGTON Al	CCTM K3	2.2	
12/11/68	962	10:00	CAMPBELL Bobby	KRAUS Jon	CCTM K3	2.5	
13/11/68	980	10:00	Mc CALLUM Brian	LOCKE Bobby	CCTM K3	2.4	
15/11/68	962	10:30	DAUBS Larry	ROETCISOENDER Bob	CCTM K3	2.5	
16/11/68	970	10:30	CAMPBELL Bobby	KRAUS Jon	CCTM K3	2.5	
18/11/68	962	09:50	BOWLES Ben	FAGG Jimmy	CCTM K3	2.3	
21/11/68	980		DAUBS Larry	ROETCISOENDER Bob	HABU		A
21/11/68	970	11:10	CAMPBELL Bobby	KRAUS Jon	HABU	5.9	
22/11/68	962	09:30	DAUBS Larry	ROETCISOENDER Bob	HABU	5.9	
23/11/68	980	10:35	BOWELS Ben	FAGG Jimmy	HABU	5.8	
24/11/68	962	11:45	Mc CALLUM Brian	LOCKE Bobby	CCTM K4	1.1	
26/11/68	962	14:15	CAMPBELL Bobby	KRAUS Jon	CCTM K3	2.5	
27/11/68	970	11:55	Mc CALLUM Brian	LOCKE Bobby	CCTM K3	2.4	
29/11/68	962	09:30	DAUBS Larry	ROETCISOENDER Bob	CCTM K3	0.9	A
30/11/68	962	09:30	BOWELS Ben	FAGG Jimmy	CCTM K3	2.5	
02/12/68	980	12:45	DAUBS Larry	ROETCISOENDER Bob	HABU	4.1	
03/12/68	962	10:00	CAMPBELL Bobby	KRAUS Jon	HABU	1.5	A
03/12/68	970	11:00	BOWELS Ben	FAGG Jimmy	HABU	5.7	
04/12/68	980	10:45	SPENCER Bob	BRANHAM Keith	CCTM K4	0.9	
04/12/68	962	09:30	CAMPBELL Bobby	KRAUS Jon	HABU	5.4	
05/12/68	980	12:00	SPENCER Bob	BRANHAM Keith	HABU	1.7	A
07/12/68	980	10:00	DAUBS Larry	ROETCISOENDER Bob	CCTM K3	2.5	
08/12/68	970	09:30	BOWELS Ben	FAGG Jimmy	CCTM K3	2.5	
09/12/68	962	11:00	SPENCER Bob	BRANHAM Keith	HABU	5.3	
10/12/68	970	11:50	DAUBS Larry	ROETCISOENDER Bob	HABU	5.4	
10/12/68	980	13:06	CAMPBELL Bobby	KRAUS Jon	CCTM K3	1	
11/12/68	962	10:55	CAMPBELL Bobby	KRAUS Jon	HABU	5.5	
13/12/68	970	11:45	BOWELS Ben	FAGG Jimmy	HABU	5.7	
13/12/68	980	13:00	SPENCER Bob	BRANHAM Keith	CCTM K4	1	
17/12/68	970	10:00	LAWSON Willie	MARTINEZ Gil	CCTM K3	2.7	
19/12/68	980	12:15	CAMPBELL Bobby	KRAUS Jon	CCTM K4	1.2	
20/12/68	962	10:30	SPENCER Bob	BRANHAM Keith	HABU	5.7	
21/12/68	980	10:00	BOWELS Ben	FAGG Jimmy	CCTM K3	2.3	
24/12/68	970	10:00	LAWSON Willie	MARTINEZ Gil	HABU	6.2	
27/12/68	970	10:00	POWELL Robert (Bob)	KENDRICK Bill	CCTM K3	2.5	
29/12/68	980	11:50	POWELL Bob	KENDRICK Bill	HABU	5.8	
30/12/68	962	11:35	BOWELS Ben	FAGG Jimmy	HABU	6.1	
30/12/68	970	12:50	SPENCER Bob	BRANHAM Keith	CCTM K4	1	

Date	Instal. No.	T.O. Time	Pilot Name	RSO Name	Mission Type	Duration	Remarks
03/01/69	980	10:00	LAWSON Willie	MARTINEZ Gil	CCTM K3	2.5	
06/01/69	962	10:00	POWELL Bob	KENDRICK Bill	CCTM K3	2.3	
10/01/69	970	12:25	SPENCER Bob	BRANHAM Keith	HABU	4.2	
10/01/69	980	13:41	LAWSON Willie	MARTINEZ Gil	CCTM K4	1.3	
13/01/69	980	10:00	O'MALLEY Jerry	PAYNE Ed	CCTM K3	2.3	
14/01/69	962	10:15	POWELL Bob	KENDRICK Bill	CCTM K3	2.2	
16/01/69	980	10:30	SPENCER Bob	BRANHAM Keith	CCTM K3	2.4	
18/01/69	970		LAWSON Willie	MARTINEZ Gil	CCTM		A
20/01/69	980	12:00	POWELL Bob	KENDRICK Bill	CCTM K4	1.1	
20/01/69	962	11:55	LAWSON Willie	MARTINEZ Gil	CCTM K3	2.3	
21/01/69	970	09:55	O'MALLEY Jerry	PAYNE Ed	CCTM K3	2.3	
23/01/69	962	12:30	LAWSON Willie	MARTINEZ Gil	CCTM K3	2.5	
25/01/69	980	13:56	POWELL Bob	KENDRICK Bill	CCTM K4	1.2	
26/01/69	970	09:30	KARDONG Abe	KOGLER Jim	CCTM K3	2.5	
27/01/69	980	12:00	LAWSON Willie	MARTINEZ Gil	HABU	5.9	
28/01/69	970	12:00	POWELL Bob	KENDRICK Bill	HABU	6	
29/01/69	962	12:00	O'MALLEY Jerry	PAYNE Ed	HABU	5.3	
31/01/69	980	10:00	KARDONG Abe	KOGLER Jim	FCF/S/K3	0.7	A
02/02/69	980	10:00	KARDONG Abe	KOGLER Jim	CCTM K3	2.4	
03/02/69	980	10:15	LAWSON Willie	MARTINEZ Gil	CCTM K3	2.5	
06/02/69	962	12:10	POWELL Bob	KENDRICK Bill	CCTM K3	2.3	
07/02/69	980	10:15	O'MALLEY Jerry	PAYNE Ed	FCF/E/K3	2.6	
08/02/69	970		FRUEHAUF Dave	PAYNE Al	CCTM K3		A
11/02/69	980	10:55	FRUEHAUF Dave	PAYNE Al	FCF/E/K3	2.1	
12/02/69	970	10:15	KARDONG Abe	KENDRICK Bill	CCTM K5	2	
13/02/69	980	11:45	POWELL Bob	KOGLER Jim	FCF/E/K3	2.3	
14/02/69	962	13:00	KARDONG Abe	KOGLER Jim	HABU	4.1	
15/02/69	970	12:55	POWELL Bob	KENDRICK Bill	HABU	4.2	
17/02/69	980	09:50	O'MALLEY Jerry	PAYNE Ed	FCF/E/K3	2.5	
19/02/69	970		FRUEHAUF Dave	PAYNE Al	CCTM		
20/02/69	980	13:06	KARDONG Abe	PAYNE Al	CCTM K3	1.7	A
21/02/69	962	10:30	KARDONG Abe	KOGLER Jim	FCF/PHASE/K3	2.4	
23/02/69	980	09:50	DEVALL Larry	SHOEMAKER Clyde	CCTM K5	2.4	
25/02/69	970	10:30	O'MALLEY Jerry	PAYNE Ed	CCTM K3	0.4	A
26/02/69	962	10:30	FRUEHAUF Dave	PAYNE Al	CCTM K5	2.6	
28/02/69	970	09:30	KARDONG Abe	KOGLER Jim	CCTM K3	2.5	
03/03/69	962	09:30	DEVALL Larry	SHOEMAKER Clyde	CCTM K3	2.3	
04/03/69	980	09:30	O'MALLEY Jerry	PAYNE Ed	FCF/PHASE/K3	2.5	
06/03/69	980		FRUEHAUF Dave	PAYNE Al	CCTM K3		A
07/03/69	980	10:15	FRUEHAUF Dave	PAYNE Al	CCTM K3	2.5	
09/03/69	962	11:30	FRUEHAUF Dave	PAYNE Al	HABU	6.1	
10/03/69	980	11:55	DEVALL Larry	SHOEMAKER Clyde	HABU	5.3	
11/03/69	970	11:00	BROWN Buddy	JARVIS Mort	FCS/PHASE/K4	1.2	
12/03/69	962	11:00	KARDONG Abe	KOGLER Jim	HABU	5.2	
13/03/69	962	11:35	KARDONG Abe	KOGLER Jim	RTB FERRY	0.7	
14/03/69	980	13:00	BROWN Buddy	JARVIS Mort	CCTM K3	2.5	
18/03/69	962	13:00	DEVALL Larry	SHOEMAKER Clyde	CCTM K4	1.2	
18/03/69	970	12:20	FRUEHAUF Dave	PAYNE Al	CCTM K3	2.4	
19/03/69	980	13:10	BROWN Buddy	JARVIS Mort	HABU	4.2	
20/03/69	962	12:30	FRUEHAUF Dave	PAYNE Al	HABU	6	
21/03/69	970		DEVALL Larry	SHOEMAKER Clyde	HABU		A
21/03/69	980	13:50	KARDONG Abe	KOGLER Jim	HABU	4	
25/03/69	962	11:40	HUDSON Jim	BUDZINSKI Norb	CCTM K3	2.4	
26/03/69	970	13:00	DEVALL Larry	SHOEMAKER Clyde	HABU	5.3	
27/03/69	980	13:05	BROWN Buddy	JARVIS Mort	HABU	4.2	
27/03/69	962	14:40	HUDSON Jim	BUDZINSKI Norb	CCTM K3	2.3	
01/04/69	980	11:00	FRUEHAUF Dave	PAYNE Al	CCTM K3	2.4	
05/04/69	970	12:30	DEVALL Larry	SHOEMAKER Clyde	CCTM K3	1.3	A
06/04/69	962	11:30	HUDSON Jim	BUDZINSKI Norb	HABU	5.5	
07/04/69	980	10:00	DEVALL Larry	SHOEMAKER Clyde	HABU	4.1	
08/04/69	962	13:20	BROWN Buddy	JARVIS Mort	HABU	4.2	
08/04/69	980	14:35	ESTES Tom	VICK Dewain	CCTM K3	2.4	
09/04/69	970	11:40	ESTES Tom	VICK Dewain	HABU	0.9	A
09/04/69	962	12:40	HUDSON Jim	BUDZINSKI Norb	HABU	5.6	
11/04/69	970	11:00	DEVALL Larry	SHOEMAKER Clyde	CCTM K3	1.6	A
13/04/69	962	10:00	BROWN Buddy	JARVIS Mort	CCTM K3	2.3	
15/04/69	962	13:30	ESTES Tom	VICK Dewain	HABU	4.2	
16/04/69	970		HUDSON Jim	BUDZINSKI Norb	CCTM		A
17/04/69	970	11:00	HUDSON Jim	BUDZINSKI Norb	CCTM K4	1	
18/04/69	971	03:00	BULL George	Mc NEER Red	FERRY TO OL-8	5.6	
19/04/69	980	06:00	DEVALL Larry	SHOEMAKER Clyde	FERRY TO SC-5		
21/04/69	979	03:27	STORRIE John	MALLOZZIE Cos	FERRY TO OL-8	5.3	
22/04/69	970	06:00	BULL George	Mc NEER Red	FERRY TO SC-5		
23/04/69	971	14:00	BROWN Buddy	JARVIS Mort	HABU	4.1	
24/04/69	975	03:53	WATKINS Jim	LOIGNON Phil	FERRY TO OL-8	5.5	
25/04/69	962	06:00	BROWN Buddy	JARVIS Mort	FERRY TO SC-5		
26/04/69	979	10:00	ESTES Tom	VICK Dewain	CCTM K3	1.8	
29/04/69	975	10:30	HUDSON Jim	BUDZINSKI Norb	CCTM K3	2.3	
01/05/69	979	12:30	HUDSON Jim	BUDZINSKI Norb	HABU	0.7	A
01/05/69	971	13:30	ESTES Tom	VICK Dewain	HABU	5.2	
02/05/69	975	10:15	STORRIE John	MALLOZZIE Cos	CCTM K3	2.4	
04/05/69	979	10:30	WATKINS Jim	LOIGNON Phil	CCTM K3	2.4	
09/05/69	975	11:06	HUDSON Jim	BUDZINSKI Norb	CCTM K5	2.3	
10/05/69	979	13:35	HUDSON Jim	BUDZINSKI Norb	HABU	0.4	A
10/05/69	971	14:35	STORRIE John	MALLOZZIE Cos	HABU	0.7	A
11/05/69	975	13:00	HUDSON Jim	BUDZINSKI Norb	HABU	5.4	
12/05/69	971	13:35	STORRIE John	MALLOZZIE Cos	HABU	4.2	
14/05/69	971	13:35	WATKINS Jim	LOIGNON Phil	HABU	3.4	A
14/05/69	975	14:50	ESTES Tom	VICK Dewain	CCTM K3	2.4	
16/05/69	971	14:00	WATKINS Jim	LOIGNON Phil	RTB FERRY	2.5	
16/05/69	979	13:50	ESTES Tom	VICK Dewain	HABU	1.2	A
16/05/69	975	14:50	STORRIE John	MALLOZZIE Cos	HABU	2.2	A
18/05/69	971	13:50	ESTES Tom	VICK Dewain	HABU	4	
18/05/69	975	15:05	STORRIE John	MALLOZZIE Cos	CCTM K3	2.3	
20/05/69	979	11:15	WATKINS Jim	LOIGNON Phil	CCTM K5	0.7	A
20/05/69	975	10:00	SHELTON Jim	SCHMITTOU Tom	CCTM K3	2.5	
21/05/69	979	13:50	WATKINS Jim	LOIGNON Phil	CCTM K5	2.4	
22/05/69	975	12:40	STORRIE John	MALLOZZIE Cos	HABU	5.1	
23/05/69	971	10:15	ESTES Tom	VICK Dewain	CCTM K3	2.4	
24/05/69	979	10:00	WATKINS Jim	LOIGNON Phil	HABU	3.5	
25/05/69	975	13:00	SHELTON Jim	SCHMITTOU Tom	HABU	5.4	
26/05/69	979	10:00	STORRIE John	MALLOZZIE Cos	CCTM K3	2.3	
28/05/69	979	09:05	ESTES Tom	VICK Dewain	HABU	5.9	
29/05/69	971	09:30	STORRIE John	MALLOZZIE Cos	HABU	4.1	
31/05/69	975	10:00	ST MARTIN Roy	BREADEN Cecil	CCTM K3	2.5	
03/06/69	975	11:00	WATKINS Jim	LOIGNON Phil	CCTM K3	2.4	
04/06/69	979	10:15	SHELTON Jim	SCHMITTOU Tom	CCTM K5	2.3	
05/06/69	971		SHELTON Jim	SCHMITTOU Tom	HABU		A
05/06/69	975	13:55	WATKINS Jim	LOIGNON Phil	HABU	5.6	A
07/06/69	975	09:05	WATKINS Jim	LOIGNON Phil	RTB FERRY	1.2	
10/06/69	975	10:15	STORRIE John	MALLOZZIE Cos	CCTM K3	2.3	
11/06/69	971	10:48	ST MARTIN Roy	BREADEN Cecil	CCTM K3	2.3	
13/06/69	979	12:50	SHELTON Jim	SCHMITTOU Tom	HABU	1.3	A
13/06/69	975	13:50	ST MARTIN Roy	BREADEN Cecil	HABU	5.4	
17/06/69	975	10:01	BULL George	Mc NEER Red	CCTM K3	1.3	A
18/06/69	975	14:15	STORRIE John	MALLOZZIE Cos	CCTM K3	2.3	
22/06/69	979	09:46	ST MARTIN Roy	BREADEN Cecil	CCTM K3	2.3	
23/06/69	971	10:15	SHELTON Jim	SCHMITTOU Tom	CCTM K3	2.3	
25/06/69	975		BULL George	Mc NEER Red	CCTM K3		A
29/06/69	975		STORRIE John	MALLOZZIE Cos	HABU		A
29/06/69	971	09:45	BULL George	Mc NEER Red	CCTM K3	1.6	A
30/06/69	979	09:15	ST MARTIN Roy	BREADEN Cecil	HABU	3.5	
01/07/69	975	10:00	STORRIE John	MALLOZZIE Cos	CCTM K4	0.4	A
02/07/69	979	12:30	STORRIE John	MALLOZZIE Cos	HABU	3.8	
04/07/69	975		Mc CALLUM Brian	LOCKE Bobby	CCTM		A
04/07/69	971	10:00	SHELTON Jim	SCHMITTOU Tom	CCTM K3	2.5	
05/07/69	971	14:00	SHELTON Jim	SCHMITTOU Tom	HABU	4.1	
06/07/69	975	10:50	Mc CALLUM Brian	LOCKE Bobby	CCTM K3	2.6	
08/07/69	979	10:10	ST MARTIN Roy	BREADEN Cecil	HABU	3.5	
08/07/69	975	09:10	BULL George	Mc NEER Red	HABU	1.5	A
10/07/69	971		Mc CALLUM Brian	LOCKE Bobby	CCTM		A
11/07/69	971	10:40	Mc CALLUM Brian	LOCKE Bobby	CCTM K3	2.4	
12/07/69	975	10:15	CAMPBELL Bobby	KRAUS Jon	CCTM K3	2.5	
15/07/69	971	10:10	BULL George	Mc NEER Red	CCTM K3	2.4	
16/07/69	979	10:20	ST MARTIN Roy	BREADEN Cecil	CCTM K3	2.3	
18/07/69	975	09:30	Mc CALLUM Brian	LOCKE Bobby	CCTM K3	2.5	
21/07/69	971	10:47	CAMPBELL Bobby	KRAUS Jon	CCTM K4	1.1	
22/07/69	979	10:30	ST MARTIN Roy	BREADEN Cecil	CCTM K3	1.6	A
23/07/69	975	13:30	BULL George	Mc NEER Red	HABU	5.8	
25/07/69	979	09:45	Mc CALLUM Brian	LOCKE Bobby	CCTM K3	2.4	
26/07/69	971	09:45	DAUBS Larry	ROETCISOENDER Bob	FCF K3	2.4	A
28/07/69	979	12:45	Mc CALLUM Brian	LOCKE Bobby	HABU	5.7	
30/07/69	971	10:17	CAMPBELL Bobby	KRAUS Jon	FCF K3	2.3	A
01/08/69	975	10:00	BULL George	Mc NEER Red	FCF K4	1.2	A
03/08/69	971		CAMPBELL Bobby	KRAUS Jon	FCF K4		A
03/08/69	975	14:50	DAUBS Larry	ROETCISOENDER Bob	HABU	4.2	
04/08/69	979	09:45	CAMPBELL Bobby	KRAUS Jon	HABU	4.8	
09/08/69	971	10:00	Mc CALLUM Brian	LOCKE Bobby	FCF K3	1.9	A
11/08/69	979	10:00	DAUBS Larry	ROETCISOENDER Bob	FCF K3	2.4	
13/08/69	979		BOWLES Ben	FAGG Jimmy	FCF K3		A
14/08/69	975	10:00	BOWLES Ben	FAGG Jimmy	CCTM K3	2.6	
15/08/69	979	12:05	CAMPBELL Bobby	KRAUS Jon	FCF K4	1.2	A
16/08/69	971	12:00	Mc CALLUM Brian	LOCKE Bobby	HABU	3.6	
18/08/69	979		DAUBS Larry	ROETCISOENDER Bob	FCF		A
22/08/69	979	12:00	DAUBS Larry	ROETCISOENDER Bob	FCF K3	2.3	A
23/08/69	975	12:35	DAUBS Larry	ROETCISOENDER Bob	HABU	5.4	
24/08/69	971	13:35	BOWLES Ben	FAGG Jimmy	HABU	4	
25/08/69	975	11:00	CAMPBELL Bobby	KRAUS Jon	FCF K3	2.4	A
27/08/69	971	10:00	POWELL Bob	COLEMAN Gary	FCF K3	2.4	A
31/08/69	979		CAMPBELL Bobby	KRAUS Jon	HABU		A
31/08/69	975	14:30	POWELL Bob	COLEMAN Gary	HABU	4	
03/09/69	979		DAUBS Larry	ROETCISOENDER Bob	FCF		A
04/09/69	979	10:00	DAUBS Larry	ROETCISOENDER Bob	FCF K3	2.3	
06/09/69	975	14:35	BOWLES Ben	FAGG Jimmy	CCTM K4	1.1	
08/09/69	971	13:20	DAUBS Larry	ROETCISOENDER Bob	HABU	4.1	
09/09/69	979	13:20	BOWLES Ben	FAGG Jimmy	HABU	4.3	
10/09/69	975	13:15	LAWSON Willie	MARTINEZ Gil	HABU	2.1	A
10/09/69	971	14:20	POWELL Bob	COLEMAN Gary	HABU	4.1	
12/09/69	971		BOWLES Ben	FAGG Jimmy	FCF		A
15/09/69	979	12:30	LAWSON Willie	MARTINEZ Gil	HABU	5.4	
15/09/69	971	13:30	BOWLES Ben	FAGG Jimmy	K7	2.5	
16/09/69	975	11:20	DAUBS Larry	ROETCISOENDER Bob	HABU	5.7	
18/09/69	975	10:00	POWELL Bob	COLEMAN Gary	FCF K3	2.2	A
19/09/69	971	10:00	BOWLES Ben	FAGG Jimmy	HABU	1.4	A
19/09/69	979	11:00	POWELL Bob	COLEMAN Gary	HABU	3.7	
21/09/69	974	03:00	BEVACQUA Tony	KOGLER Jim	FERRY TO OL-8	2.9	A
24/09/69	969	09:00	SHELTON Jim	SCHMITTOU Tom	FERRY TO OL-8	5.4	
25/09/69	979	06:00	BOWELS Ben	FAGG Jimmy	FERRY OUT		
27/09/69	973	02:00	FRUEHAUF Dave	PAYNE Al	FERRY TO OL-8	5.2	
28/09/69	971	06:00	SHELTON Jim	SCHMITTOU Tom	FERRY TO SC-5	2.7	A
29/09/69	971	13:00	SHELTON Jim	SCHMITTOU Tom	FCF K3	2.2	A
29/09/69	969	11:40	LAWSON Willie	MARTINEZ Gil	HABU	5.3	
30/09/69	972	09:00	SPENCER Bob	SHEFFIELD Butch	FERRY TO OL-8	5.3	
01/10/69	971	06:00	SHELTON Jim	SCHMITTOU Tom	FERRY OUT		
03/10/69	974	02:17	BEVACQUA Tony	KOGLER Jim	FERRY TO OL-8	2.9	
03/10/69	973	12:30	POWELL Bob	COLEMAN Gary	HABU	4.5	
04/10/69	973	09:45	FRUEHAUF Dave	PAYNE Al	HABU	1.6	A
04/10/69	972	10:45	SPENCER Bob	SHEFFIELD Butch	HABU	6	
08/10/69	969	10:00	LAWSON Willie	MARTINEZ Gil	K3	2.5	
08/10/69	973	11:01	POWELL Bob	COLEMAN Gary	K7	2.4	
09/10/69	973	10:00	FRUEHAUF Dave	PAYNE Al	HABU	3.8	
10/10/69	969	10:00	SPENCER Bob	SHEFFIELD Butch	K3	1.6	A
12/10/69	972		LAWSON Willie	MARTINEZ Gil	HABU		A
12/10/69	973	11:50	POWELL Bob	COLEMAN Gary	HABU	5.6	
13/10/69	969	10:15	LAWSON Willie	MARTINEZ Gil	K7	2.4	
17/10/69	972	10:20	LAWSON Willie	MARTINEZ Gil	HABU	3.7	

Date	Instal. No.	T.O. Time	Pilot Name	RSO Name	Mission Type	Duration	Remarks
20/10/69	972		FRUEHAUF Dave	PAYNE Al	K3		A
20/10/69	969	11:00	FRUEHAUF Dave	PAYNE Al	K7	2.5	
22/10/69	975	06:00	DAUBS Larry	ROETCISOENDER Bob	FERRY OUT		
22/10/69	972	10:00	DEVALL Larry	SHOEMAKER Clyde	K3	2.5	
22/10/69	973	11:00	SPENCER Bob	SHEFFIELD Butch	K7	2.5	
24/10/69	969	10:15	LAWSON Willie	MARTINEZ Gil	K7	2.5	
27/10/69	972	10:00	FRUEHAUF Dave	PAYNE Al	K3	2.4	
29/10/69	969	09:50	LAWSON Willie	MARTINEZ Gil	K3	2.4	
31/10/69	973	09:30	DEVALL Larry	SHOEMAKER Clyde	K3	2.3	
31/10/69	972	10:30	SPENCER Bob	SHEFFIELD Butch	K3	2.3	
03/11/69	972	10:00	HUDSON Jim	BUDZINSKI Norb	K3	2.2	
06/11/69	973	12:20	SPENCER Bob	SHEFFIELD Butch	HABU	4.1	
07/11/69	974	10:05	FRUEHAUF Dave	PAYNE Al	K7	2.4	
09/11/69	973	12:00	DEVALL Larry	SHOEMAKER Clyde	HABU	4.2	
10/11/69	974	09:55	HUDSON Jim	BUDZINSKI Norb	K3	2.4	
11/11/69	969	12:00	FRUEHAUF Dave	PAYNE Al	HABU	4.2	
13/11/69	973	09:45	SPENCER Bob	SHEFFIELD Butch	K3	2.4	
16/11/69	972	10:00	ESTES Tom	VICK Dewain	K3	2.3	
22/11/69	974	11:00	SPENCER Bob	SHEFFIELD Butch	HABU	3.4	A
22/11/69	972	13:30	DEVALL Larry	SHOEMAKER Clyde	K3	2.3	
23/11/69	974	16:03	SPENCER Bob	SHEFFIELD Butch	RTB FERRY	1.5	
24/11/69	969		HUDSON Jim	BUDZINSKI Norb	K3		A
26/11/69	973	11:00	HUDSON Jim	BUDZINSKI Norb	HABU	4	A
27/11/69	969	11:15	ESTES Tom	VICK Dewain	K3	2.3	
27/11/69	972	10:00	DEVALL Larry	SHOEMAKER Clyde	HABU	5.2	
28/11/69	969	11:00	ESTES Tom	VICK Dewain	HABU	6	
01/12/69	974	10:50	BROWN Buddy	JARVIS Mort	K7	2.4	
03/12/69	972	10:00	HUDSON Jim	BUDZINSKI Norb	K3	2.3	
03/12/69	974	11:00	DEVALL Larry	SHOEMAKER Clyde	K3	2.5	
05/12/69	969	10:30	HUDSON Jim	BUDZINSKI Norb	HABU	5.6	
06/12/69	974	10:19	ESTES Tom	VICK Dewain	K7	2.4	
08/12/69	974	10:15	BROWN Buddy	JARVIS Mort	K3	2.2	
09/12/69	972	10:15	DEVALL Larry	SHOEMAKER Clyde	K3	2.1	
11/12/69	973	10.10	HUDSON Jim	BUDZINSKI Norb	K3	2.3	
12/12/69	974	10:20	BROWN Buddy	JARVIS Mort	HABU	5.2	
15/12/69	969	10:15	ESTES Tom	VICK Dewain	K3	2.4	
16/12/69	973	10:00	SHELTON Jim	SCHMITTOU Tom	K3	1.4	A
17/12/69	974	10:15	HUDSON Jim	BUDZINSKI Norb	K3	2.3	
19/12/69	973	10:00	SHELTON Jim	SCHMITTOU Tom	K3	2.4	
20/12/69	972	10:15	BROWN Buddy	JARVIS Mort	K3	2.3	
22/12/69	972	10:15	HUDSON Jim	BUDZINSKI Norb	K7	2.3	
23/12/69	974	12:10	ESTES Tom	VICK Dewain	HABU	2.1	A
23/12/69	973	13:16	SHELTON Jim	SCHMITTOU Tom	HABU	4.1	
26/12/69	972	10:43	ST MARTIN Roy	BREADEN Cecil	K7	2.3	
29/12/69	972	10:30	ESTES Tom	VICK Dewain	HABU	5.8	
30/12/69	969	09:55	BROWN Buddy	JARVIS Mort	K8	2	
01/01/70	972	12:20	BROWN Buddy	JARVIS Mort	HABU	4	
02/01/70	973	12:05	SHELTON Jim	SCHMITTOU Tom	K3	2.2	
06/01/70	972	10:15	ESTES Tom	VICK Dewain	K3	2.4	
06/01/70	969	11:15	ST MARTIN Roy	BREADEN Cecil	K3	2.3	
07/01/70	972	10:15	BROWN Buddy	JARVIS Mort	K3	2.3	
09/01/70	972	11:10	SHELTON Jim	SCHMITTOU Tom	HABU	5.3	
12/01/70	974	10:15	BULL George	KRAUS Jon	K3	2.3	
13/01/70	969	10:15	ST MARTIN Roy	BREADEN Cecil	K7	2.3	
15/01/70	972	11:53	ST MARTIN Roy	BREADEN Cecil	HABU	3.9	
16/01/70	974	14:20	SHELTON Jim	SCHMITTOU Tom	K3	2.3	
19/01/70	972	10:15	BROWN Buddy	JARVIS Mort	K11	2.1	
20/01/70	969	10:15	BULL George	KRAUS Jon	K11	2.2	
21/01/70	974	10:15	ST MARTIN Roy	BREADEN Cecil	K3	2.3	
24/01/70	974	12:58	STORRIE John	MALLOZZIE Cos	K3	2.3	
28/01/70	972	10:15	SHELTON Jim	SCHMITTOU Tom	K3	2.4	
28/01/70	969	11:15	BULL George	KRAUS Jon	K7	2.3	
29/01/70	973	12:55	ST MARTIN Roy	BREADEN Cecil	K3	1.3	A
29/01/70	974	11:35	BULL George	KRAUS Jon	HABU	5.5	
01/02/70	973	12:45	STORRIE John	MALLOZZIE Cos	K3	2.3	
03/02/70	969	11:30	SHELTON Jim	SCHMITTOU Tom	HABU	1.4	A
03/02/70	974	12:30	ST MARTIN Roy	BREADEN Cecil	HABU	5.5	
04/02/70	973	10:15	BULL George	KRAUS Jon	K7	2.4	
07/02/70	969	10:15	POWELL Bob	COLEMAN Gary	K3	2.4	
08/02/70	969	11:50	STORRIE John	MALLOZZIE Cos	HABU	5.6	
09/02/70	974	10:15	ST MARTIN Roy	BREADEN Cecil	K10	2.2	
11/02/70	972	10:15	BULL George	KRAUS Jon	K11	2.4	
13/02/70	972	10:15	POWELL Bob	COLEMAN Gary	K11	2.3	
14/02/70	973	11:02	STORRIE John	MALLOZZIE Cos	K11	2.3	
16/02/70	973	10:00	ST MARTIN Roy	BREADEN Cecil	HABU	2.6	A
18/02/70	974	11:55	BULL George	KRAUS Jon	K3	2.3	
19/02/70	972	10:14	POWELL Bob	COLEMAN Gary	K7	2.4	
20/02/70	973	12:00	STORRIE John	MALLOZZIE Cos	K3	2.2	
21/02/70	972	12:00	BEVACQUA Tony	KOGLER Jim	K3	2.3	
23/02/70	974	09:45	BULL George	KRAUS Jon	K7	2.4	
25/02/70	974	12:00	BULL George	KRAUS Jon	HABU	5.6	
28/02/70	972	10:10	POWELL Bob	COLEMAN Gary	K11	2.2	
02/03/70	973	10:15	STORRIE John	MALLOZZIE Cos	K11	2.5	
04/03/70	973	11:50	BEVACQUA Tony	KOGLER Jim	K7	2.4	
06/03/70	973	10:24	POWELL Bob	COLEMAN Gary	K7	2.3	
08/03/70	974	10:15	Mc CALLUM Brian	LOCKE Bobby	K11	2.4	
09/03/70	969	10:15	STORRIE John	MALLOZZIE Cos	K11	2.4	
11/03/70	973	11:00	BEVACQUA Tony	KOGLER Jim	K3	1.4	A
12/03/70	969	10:14	POWELL Bob	COLEMAN Gary	K7	2.5	
14/03/70	972	11:00	BEVACQUA Tony	KOGLER Jim	K11	2.4	
14/03/70	973	10:00	Mc CALLUM Brian	LOCKE Bobby	K3	2.3	
19/03/70	969	09:26	POWELL Bob	COLEMAN Gary	HABU	5.3	
20/03/70	972	13:25	BEVACQUA Tony	KOGLER Jim	K11	2.6	
22/03/70	973	10:15	BOWELS Ben	FAGG Jimmy	K3	2.5	
22/03/70	969	11:15	Mc CALLUM Brian	LOCKE Bobby	K11	2.5	
24/03/70	972	10:15	POWELL Bob	COLEMAN Gary	K11	2.3	
25/03/70	973	10:15	BEVACQUA Tony	KOGLER Jim	K11	1.5	A
30/03/70	973	11:50	Mc CALLUM Brian	LOCKE Bobby	K7	2.5	
31/03/70	972	10:15	BOWELS Ben	FAGG Jimmy	K3	2.4	
03/04/70	972	11:20	BEVACQUA Tony	KOGLER Jim	HABU	5.7	
04/04/70	969	10:15	LAWSON Willie	MARTINEZ Gil	K11	2.4	
06/04/70	972	10:15	Mc CALLUM Brian	LOCKE Bobby	K11	2.4	
09/04/70	969	12:00	Mc CALLUM Brian	LOCKE Bobby	HABU	5.5	
10/04/70	973	12:00	BOWELS Ben	FAGG Jimmy	HABU	5.3	
12/04/70	972		BEVACQUA Tony	KOGLER Jim	K7		A
12/04/70	973	11:30	LAWSON Willie	MARTINEZ Gil	K11	2.2	
13/04/70	972	10:15	BEVACQUA Tony	KOGLER Jim	K7	2.4	
17/04/70	972	10:00	Mc CALLUM Brian	LOCKE Bobby	K7	2.4	
19/04/70	972	10:15	FRUEHAUF Dave	PAYNE Al	K3	2.2	
19/04/70	973	11:15	BOWLES Ben	FAGG Jimmy	K11	2.4	
21/04/70	974	12:15	LAWSON Willie	MARTINEZ Gil	K11	2.5	
22/04/70	969		Mc CALLUM Brian	LOCKE Bobby	K7		A
23/04/70	974	12:45	BOWLES Ben	FAGG Jimmy	K3	2.4	
23/04/70	969	11:15	FRUEHAUF Dave	PAYNE Al	K7	2.3	
25/04/70	969	10:15	DEVALL Larry	SHOEMAKER Clyde	K11	2.4	
26/04/70	974	10:22	BOWLES Ben	FAGG Jimmy	HABU	1.8	A
26/04/70	973	11:43	LAWSON Willie	MARTINEZ Gil	HABU	5.4	A
28/04/70	974		FRUEHAUF Dave	PAYNE Al	K3		A
29/04/70	974	10:15	FRUEHAUF Dave	PAYNE Al	K3	2.5	
30/04/70	973	13:10	DEVALL Larry	SHOEMAKER Clyde	K7	2.4	
01/05/70	969	12:10	LAWSON Willie	MARTINEZ Gil	HABU	5.5	
02/05/70	973	12:05	BOWLES Ben	FAGG Jimmy	HABU	5.5	
04/05/70	969	10:15	FRUEHAUF Dave	PAYNE Al	K3	2.4	
05/05/70	973	10:15	DEVALL Larry	SHOEMAKER Clyde	K3	2.3	
06/05/70	974	08:30	FRUEHAUF Dave	PAYNE Al	HABU	4.2	
07/05/70	969	10:56	BOWLES Ben	FAGG Jimmy	HABU	3.6	
08/05/70	972	10:15	LAWSON Willie	MARTINEZ Gil	K3	2.3	
09/05/70	973	12:10	DEVALL Larry	SHOEMAKER Clyde	HABU	5.4	
10/05/70	969	10:30	LAWSON Willie	MARTINEZ Gil	HABU		
CRASH,7							
17/05/70	974	10:15	SPENCER Bob	SHEFFIELD Butch	K7	2.5	
18/05/70	973	10:45	FRUEHAUF Dave	PAYNE Al	K3	2.3	
19/05/70	972	10:15	BOWLES Ben	FAGG Jimmy	K3	2.3	
21/05/70	973	10:15	DEVALL Larry	SHOEMAKER Clyde	K3	2.3	
23/05/70	974	10:15	HUDSON Jim	BUDZINSKI Norb	K3	2.3	
25/05/70	972		SPENCER Bob	SHEFFIELD Butch	K7		A
29/05/70	972	10:15	SPENCER Bob	SHEFFIELD Butch	K7	2.2	
02/06/70	972	12:11	HUDSON Jim	BUDZINSKI Norb	K7	1.1	A
02/06/70	974	13:30	FRUEHAUF Dave	PAYNE Al	HABU	4.1	
03/06/70	972	12:10	DEVALL Larry	SHOEMAKER Clyde	K3	2.3	
05/06/70	974	10:50	FRUEHAUF Dave	PAYNE Al	HABU	3.6	
06/06/70	973	14:50	SPENCER Bob	SHEFFIELD Butch	K3	2.3	
06/06/70	972	13:30	DEVALL Larry	SHOEMAKER Clyde	HABU	4	
09/06/70	974	10:35	HUDSON Jim	BUDZINSKI Norb	K7	2.4	
10/06/70	972		FRUEHAUF Dave	PAYNE Al	K7		A
11/06/70	972	10:00	FRUEHAUF Dave	PAYNE Al	K4	1.1	
15/06/70	973	12:00	SPENCER Bob	SHEFFIELD Butch	HABU	4.1	
17/06/70	973	12:15	HUDSON Jim	BUDZINSKI Norb	HABU	5.8	
17/06/70	972	13:35	ESTES Tom	VICK Dewain	K7	2.4	
26/06/70	974	11:00	SPENCER Bob	SHEFFIELD Butch	HABU	5	
12/07/70	972	11:04	ESTES Tom	VICK Dewain	K4	0.9	A
12/07/70	973	11:15	HUDSON Jim	BUDZINSKI Norb	K4	1.3	
14/07/70	973		SPENCER Bob	SHEFFIELD Butch	K4		A
14/07/70	974	10:10	STORRIE John	MALLOZZIE Cos	K4	1.2	
14/07/70	973	13:30	SPENCER Bob	SHEFFIELD Butch	K4	1.2	
15/07/70	972	11:24	ESTES Tom	VICK Dewain	K4	1.3	
15/07/70	973	12:21	HUDSON Jim	BUDZINSKI Norb	K4	1.3	
17/07/70	973	10:30	STORRIE John	MALLOZZIE Cos	K4	1.2	
18/07/70	972	10:05	SHELTON Jim	SCHMITTOU Tom	K4	1.3	
20/07/70	972	16:01	HUDSON Jim	BUDZINSKI Norb	K4	1.1	
21/07/70	974	10:00	STORRIE John	MALLOZZIE Cos	K4	1	
22/07/70	973	10:00	ESTES Tom	VICK Dewain	HABU	2	A
22/07/70	972	11:39	SHELTON Jim	SCHMITTOU Tom	K4	1.1	
22/07/70	974	11:00	HUDSON Jim	BUDZINSKI Norb	HABU	1.6	A
25/07/70	974		STORRIE John	MALLOZZIE Cos	HABU		A
25/07/70	972	10:00	STORRIE John	MALLOZZIE Cos	HABU	2.1	8
26/07/70	973	10:04	COBB Darryl	GANTT Myron	K4	1.2	
27/07/70	972	10:15	SHELTON Jim	SCHMITTOU Tom	K7	2.4	
28/07/70	974	09:10	ESTES Tom	VICK Dewain	HABU	0.7	A
28/07/70	972	10:10	STORRIE John	MALLOZZIE Cos	HABU	1.8	A
31/07/70	973	13:15	COBB Darryl	GANTT Myron	K3	2.3	
31/07/70	974	11:50	ESTES Tom	VICK Dewain	HABU	5.8	
05/08/70	972	09:45	STORRIE John	MALLOZZIE Cos	K4	0.9	
05/08/70	974	10:00	SHELTON Jim	SCHMITTOU Tom	K4	1.1	
06/08/70	973	09:50	COBB Darryl	GANTT Myron	K4	1.1	
08/08/70	974	10:15	BULL George	KRAUS Jon	K3	2.3	
10/08/70	972	10:30	STORRIE John	MALLOZZIE Cos	K7	1.5	A
11/08/70	974		SHELTON Jim	SCHMITTOU Tom	K3		A
15/08/70	972	11:15	SHELTON Jim	SCHMITTOU Tom	K3	2.3	
16/08/70	974	09:45	COBB Darryl	GANTT Myron	K3	2.3	
17/08/70	973	12:00	BULL George	KRAUS Jon	K7	2.3	
19/08/70	972	09:45	STORRIE John	MALLOZZIE Cos	K3	2.4	
21/08/70	973	09:45	COBB Darryl	GANTT Myron	K9	2.4	
21/08/70	974	11:15	BULL George	KRAUS Jon	K7	2.3	
22/08/70	972	10:00	ST MARTIN Roy	BREADEN CECIL	K7	2.6	
24/08/70	974	09:45	COBB Darryl	GANTT Myron	K9	2.4	
25/08/70	974		BULL George	KRAUS Jon	K3		A
25/08/70	973	10:00	STORRIE John	MALLOZZIE Cos	K3	2.2	
26/08/70	974	09:45	BULL George	KRAUS Jon	K3	2.1	
30/08/70	973	13:10	STORRIE John	MALLOZZIE Cos	HABU	4.1	
01/09/70	974	09:45	ST MARTIN Roy	BREADEN Cecil	K9	2.3	
01/09/70	972	11:42	COBB Darryl	GANTT Myron	K9	2.3	
02/09/70	973	12:50	COBB Darryl	GANTT Myron	HABU	4.1	
08/09/70	972	11:00	BROWN Buddy	JARVIS Mort	HABU	3.7	
09/09/70	972	11:45	BULL George	KRAUS Jon	HABU	2.9	A
11/09/70	974	10:00	ST MARTIN Roy	BREADEN Cecil	K9	2.2	A

Date	Instal. No.	T.O. Time	Pilot Name	RSO Name	Mission	Duration	Remarks
11/09/70	972	10:32	BULL George	KRAUS Jon	RTB FERRY	0.3	A
13/09/70	972	15:35	BULL George	KRAUS Jon	RTB FERRY	2.6	
14/09/70	974	13:05	COBB Darryl	GANTT Myron	K9	2.4	
17/09/70	973	11:30	ST MARTIN Roy	BREADEN Cecil	HABU	5.5	
18/09/70	974	10:00	BULL George	KRAUS Jon	HABU	3.5	
19/09/70	973	09:10	BULL George	KRAUS Jon	HABU	5	
20/09/70	972	10:00	BROWN Buddy	JARVIS Mort	K7	2.3	
21/09/70	972	09:30	POWELL Bob	COLEMAN Gary	HABU	3.5	
23/09/70	973	11:30	BROWN Buddy	JARVIS Mort	HABU	4.2	
24/09/70	974	10:15	ST MARTIN Roy	BREADEN Cecil	K9	2.4	
26/09/70	972	12:00	ST MARTIN Roy	BREADEN Cecil	HABU	3.5	
28/09/70	972	10:23	BULL George	KRAUS Jon	K7	2.4	
30/09/70	974	10:15	POWELL Bob	COLEMAN Gary	K9	2.2	
01/10/70	972	10:00	BROWN Buddy	JARVIS Mort	K9	2.3	
03/10/70	974	10:00	ST MARTIN Roy	BREADEN Cecil	HABU	5.5	
06/10/70	974	13:00	BEVACQUA Tony	KOGLER Jim	HABU	3.6	
07/10/70	973	11:00	BROWN Buddy	JARVIS Mort	HABU	5.4	
08/10/70	972	09:45	POWELL Bob	COLEMAN Gary	K9	2.2	
10/10/70	972	10:00	ST MARTIN Roy	BREADEN Cecil	K9	2.4	
12/10/70	972		BEVACQUA Tony	KOGLER Jim	K9		A
13/10/70	972	09:45	BEVACQUA Tony	KOGLER Jim	K9	2.4	
13/10/70	974	11:00	BROWN Buddy	JARVIS Mort	K9	2.3	
15/10/70	974	07:00	POWELL Bob	COLEMAN Gary	HABU	3.7	
19/10/70	973	10:15	FRUEHAUF Dave	PAYNE Al	K3	2.5	
22/10/70	972		BEVACQUA Tony	KOGLER Jim	K9		A
23/10/70	973	12:15	POWELL Bob	COLEMAN Gary	HABU	4.1	
24/10/70	972		FRUEHAUF Dave	PAYNE Al	HABU B/U		A
24/10/70	974	11:15	BEVACQUA Tony	KOGLER Jim	HABU	5.5	
26/10/70	972	10:00	BROWN Buddy	JARVIS Mort	K7	2.4	
27/10/70	973	10:45	FRUEHAUF Dave	PAYNE Al	HABU	3.6	
28/10/70	974	10:15	POWELL Bob	COLEMAN Gary	K7	2.3	
31/10/70	974	11:30	BOWLES Ben	FAGG Jimmy	HABU	2	A
31/10/70	973	12:30	BEVACQUA Tony	KOGLER Jim	HABU	3.6	
02/11/70	972	11:15	POWELL Bob	COLEMAN Gary	HABU	5.1	
02/11/70	974	12:30	BEVACQUA Tony	KOGLER Jim	K9	2.3	
04/11/70	974	10:50	BEVACQUA Tony	KOGLER Jim	HABU	5.6	
05/11/70	974	11:00	FRUEHAUF Dave	PAYNE Al	HABU	3.7	
06/11/70	973	12:10	BOWLES Ben	FAGG Jimmy	K9	2.3	
06/11/70	974	10:50	FRUEHAUF Dave	PAYNE Al	HABU	5.6	
09/11/70	972	10:00	POWELL Bob	COLEMAN Gary	K7	2.4	
11/11/70	973	09:45	BEVACQUA Tony	KOGLER Jim	HABU	3.5	
11/11/70	974	12:30	FRUEHAUF Dave	PAYNE Al	K7	2.5	
13/11/70	972	10:50	BOWLES Ben	FAGG Jimmy	HABU	5.4	
16/11/70	973	10:15	PUGH Tom	RICE Ron	K3	2.5	
18/11/70	974	11:30	PUGH Tom	RICE Ron	HABU	4.2	A
20/11/70	972	08:25	BEVACQUA Tony	KOGLER Jim	HABU	5.5	
20/11/70	974	13:35	PUGH Tom	RICE Ron	RTB FERRY	2.4	
21/11/70	973	09:20	FRUEHAUF Dave	PAYNE Al	HABU	5.5	
24/11/70	974	10:15	BOWLES Ben	FAGG Jimmy	K7	2.4	
25/11/70	972	08:17	BOWLES Ben	FAGG Jimmy	HABU	3.6	
27/11/70	972	11:45	PUGH Tom	RICE Ron	K3	2.5	
28/11/70	973	10:00	FRUEHAUF Dave	PAYNE Al	K7	2.4	
29/11/70	974	12:29	PUGH Tom	RICE Ron	HABU	3.5	A
30/11/70	972	10:15	BUSH Denny	LOIGNON Phil	K7	2.4	
03/12/70	974	10:00	BOWLES Ben	FAGG Jimmy	K3	0.7	A
04/12/70	974	13:15	BUSH Denny	FAGG Jimmy	K4	0.9	
04/12/70	972	12:59	PUGH Tom	RICE Ron	HABU	1.7	A
04/12/70	973	11:53	FRUEHAUF Dave	PAYNE Al	HABU	1.8	A
07/12/70	973	10:30	BOWLES Ben	FAGG Jimmy	HABU	3.5	
11/12/70	972	10:00	PUGH Tom	RICE Ron	K7	2.4	
13/12/70	974	10:10	HUDSON Jim	BUDZINSKI Norb	K3	2.4	
14/12/70	972	10:00	BUSH Denny	LOIGNON Phil	K3	2.3	
16/12/70	973	10:00	BOWLES Ben	FAGG Jimmy	K3	2.5	
18/12/70	975	10:00	SPENCER Bob	SHEFFIELD Butch	FERRY TO OL-8	5.7	
18/12/70	972	12:00	PUGH Tom	RICE Ron	HABU	6.1	
19/12/70	974	12:05	BUSH Denny	LOIGNON Phil	HABU	6	A
21/12/70	973	11:00	HUDSON Jim	BUDZINSKI Norb	HABU	3.6	
23/12/70	974	10:00	SPENCER Bob	SHEFFIELD Butch	K3	2.3	
24/12/70	973	10:00	PUGH Tom	RICE Ron	HABU	3.6	
25/12/70	972	08:35	PUGH Tom	RICE Ron	HABU	1.5	A
25/12/70	974	10:18	PUGH Tom	RICE Ron	HABU	2.2	A
29/12/70	973	11:00	HUDSON Jim	BUDZINSKI Norb	HABU	1.8	A
29/12/70	972	12:00	SPENCER Bob	SHEFFIELD Butch	HABU	2.1	A
02/01/71	974	10:00	SPENCER Bob	SHEFFIELD Butch	K3	2.2	
02/01/71	972	11:15	BUSH Denny	LOIGNON Phil	K9	2.3	
03/01/71	973	12:20	HUDSON Jim	BUDZINSKI Norb	K3	2.3	
03/01/71	972	11:00	PUGH Tom	RICE Ron	HABU	5.8	
04/01/71	975	09:00	BUSH Denny	LOIGNON Phil	K7	2.4	
04/01/71	974	08:09	SPENCER Bob	SHEFFIELD Butch	HABU	3.9	
07/01/71	974	17:30	HUDSON Jim	BUDZINSKI Norb	K12	0.7	
08/01/71	975	12:15	BUSH Denny	LOIGNON Phil	HABU	5.3	
09/01/71	973	08:55	HUDSON Jim	BUDZINSKI Norb	HABU	3.9	A
09/01/71	975	14:14	SPENCER Bob	SHEFFIELD Butch	HABU	1.5	A
10/01/71	972	13:30	ESTES Tom	VICK Dewain	K3	2.6	
11/01/71	975	13:00	BUSH Denny	LOIGNON Phil	K3	1.8	A
13/01/71	975	10:30	HUDSON Jim	BUDZINSKI Norb	HABU	3.7	
13/01/71	973	13:40	ESTES Tom	VICK Dewain	K9	1	A
15/01/71	975	11:30	SPENCER Bob	SHEFFIELD Butch	HABU	3.7	
15/01/71	973	14:30	ESTES Tom	VICK Dewain	K9	2.2	
16/01/71	972	11:00	HUDSON Jim	BUDZINSKI Norb	HABU	3	A
18/01/71	972	12:00	HUDSON Jim	BUDZINSKI Norb	RTB FERRY	2.5	
19/01/71	973	16:30	SPENCER Bob	SHEFFIELD Butch	K3	2.3	
22/01/71	975	11:40	ESTES Tom	VICK Dewain	HABU	3.8	
24/01/71	972	11:00	SHELTON Jim	SCHMITTOU Tom	K3	2.4	
25/01/71	973	10:00	HUDSON Jim	BUDZINSKI Norb	K3	2.4	
28/01/71	973	11:50	SPENCER Bob	SHEFFIELD Butch	HABU	3.8	
31/01/71	975	16:15	ESTES Tom	VICK Dewain	NK3	2.3	
01/02/71	974	10:00	SHELTON Jim	SCHMITTOU Tom	K9	2.3	
02/02/71	975	10:00	HUDSON Jim	BUDZINSKI Norb	HABU	3.7	
06/02/71	973	12:30	SPENCER Bob	SHEFFIELD Butch	HABU	1.5	A
06/02/71	972	13:30	ESTES Tom	VICK Dewain	HABU	1.8	A
07/02/71	973	11:15	SHELTON Jim	SCHMITTOU Tom	K7	0.8	A
07/02/71	974	10:00	COBB Darryl	GANTT Myron	K3	2.3	
08/02/71	972	13:00	ESTES Tom	VICK Dewain	RTB FERRY OL-RK	1.5	
10/02/71	974	11:00	SPENCER Bob	SHEFFIELD Butch	HABU	1.6	A
10/02/71	973	12:15	COBB Darryl	GANTT Myron	HABU	3.7	
10/02/71	972	14:30	SHELTON Jim	SCHMITTOU Tom	K7	2.4	
12/02/71	973	11:01	COBB Darryl	GANTT Myron	K7	2.3	
13/02/71	972	10:00	ESTES Tom	VICK Dewain	K9	2.5	
13/02/71	974	11:04	SPENCER Bob	SHEFFIELD Butch	RTB FERRY (OL-RK)	1.6	
15/02/71	973	12:50	SHELTON Jim	SCHMITTOU Tom	HABU	4	
15/02/71	974	14:30	COBB Darryl	GANTT Myron	K9	2.4	
18/02/71	973	17:45	SHELTON Jim	SCHMITTOU Tom	NK4	1.2	
19/02/71	974	10:00	ESTES Tom	VICK Dewain	K7	2.4	
20/02/71	973	12:20	ESTES Tom	VICK Dewain	HABU	5.4	
21/02/71	975	10:15	STORRIE John	MALLOZZIE Cos	FCF K9	2.4	
23/02/71	974	12:30	SHELTON Jim	SCHMITTOU Tom	HABU	5.3	
23/02/71	972	14:35	COBB Darryl	GANTT Myron	K7	1.4	A
25/02/71	973	10:45	COBB Darryl	GANTT Myron	HABU	3.8	
25/02/71	972	12:45	ESTES Tom	VICK Dewain	K7	2.4	
26/02/71	974	13:37	STORRIE John	MALLOZZIE Cos	HABU	1.8	A
26/02/71	973	14:40	SHELTON Jim	SCHMITTOU Tom	HABU	3.7	
27/02/71	975	11:00	COBB Darryl	GANTT Myron	K9	2.3	
01/03/71	974	12:00	ESTES Tom	VICK Dewain	HABU	5.2	
01/03/71	972	18:00	STORRIE John	MALLOZZIE Cos	NK12	0.8	
02/03/71	975	10:00	SHELTON Jim	SCHMITTOU Tom	K7	2.4	
04/03/71	972	11:51	STORRIE John	MALLOZZIE Cos	HABU	3.7	
05/03/71	975	12:15	COBB Darryl	GANTT Myron	K9	2.5	
07/03/71	974	11:30	SHELTON Jim	SCHMITTOU Tom	HABU	3.9	
07/03/71	975	14:00	BULL George	KRAUS Jon	K3	2.4	
09/03/71	972		COBB Darryl	GANTT Myron	K9		A
10/03/71	972	12:00	COBB Darryl	GANTT Myron	K9	1.7	A
12/03/71	974	11:35	BULL George	KRAUS Jon	HABU	4	
12/03/71	973	13:30	STORRIE John	GANTT Myron	K9	2.3	
14/03/71	975	09:30	SHELTON Jim	SCHMITTOU Tom	HABU	5.1	
15/03/71	973	10:00	COBB Darryl	GANTT Myron	K7	2.4	
16/03/71	974	10:15	BULL George	KRAUS Jon	K9	2.4	
16/03/71	975	11:15	STORRIE John	SCHMITTOU Tom	K9	2.3	
17/03/71	972	11:50	COBB Darryl	GANTT Myron	HABU	7.6	
20/03/71	973	10:00	ST MARTIN Roy	BREADEN Cecil	K9	0.7	A
21/03/71	973	13:20	ST MARTIN Roy	BREADEN Cecil	K9	2.1	
21/03/71	974	12:00	STORRIE John	MALLOZZIE Cos	HABU	3.9	
24/03/71	975	12:30	BULL George	KRAUS Jon	HABU	4.2	
25/03/71	974	10:00	COBB Darryl	GANTT Myron	HABU	3.5	
27/03/71	975	12:00	ST MARTIN Roy	BREADEN Cecil	HABU	1.7	A
27/03/71	974	13:00	COBB Darryl	GANTT Myron	HABU	3.9	A
28/03/71	975	12:20	ST MARTIN Roy	BREADEN Cecil	HABU	5.1	
29/03/71	973	12:10	STORRIE John	MALLOZZIE Cos	HABU	5.4	
30/03/71	974	10:00	BULL George	KRAUS Jon	HABU	3.5	
04/04/71	975	11:30	ST MARTIN Roy	BREADEN Cecil	HABU	1.7	A
04/04/71	974	12:30	STORRIE John	MALLOZZIE Cos	HABU	2.1	A
05/04/71	973	10:00	HERTZOG Randy	CARNOCHAN John	K7	1.6	A
06/04/71	975	13:30	STORRIE John	MALLOZZIE Cos	HABU	3.9	
07/04/71	973	10:15	HERTZOG Randy	CARNOCHAN John	K7	2.1	
09/04/71	972		STORRIE John	MALLOZZIE Cos	K9		A
10/04/71	972	14:40	STORRIE John	MALLOZZIE Cos	K9	2.4	
12/04/71	975	12:00	BULL George	KRAUS Jon	HABU	1.8	A
12/04/71	974	13:03	ST MARTIN Roy	BREADEN Cecil	HABU	2.5	
12/04/71	972	13:49	HERTZOG Randy	CARNOCHAN John	K9	1.8	
13/04/71	975	09:45	STORRIE John	MALLOZZIE Cos	K7	2.4	
15/04/71	975	12:50	BULL George	KRAUS Jon	HABU	3.8	
19/04/71	974	10:15	BROWN Buddy	JARVIS Mort	K9	2.4	
20/04/71	972	10:15	HERTZOG Randy	CARNOCHAN John	K9	2.2	
21/04/71	974	12:00	HERTZOG Randy	CARNOCHAN John	HABU	5.5	
23/04/71	975	11:45	BULL George	KRAUS Jon	HABU	3.5	
24/04/71	974		BROWN Buddy	JARVIS Mort	K3		A
25/04/71	974	10:00	BROWN Buddy	JARVIS Mort	K3	2.2	
28/04/71	972	11:30	ST MARTIN Roy	BREADEN Cecil	K3	2.2	
29/04/71	974	11:30	HERTZOG Randy	CARNOCHAN John	HABU	3.4	
30/04/71	975	09:30	BROWN Buddy	JARVIS Mort	HABU	1.7	A
30/04/71	972	11:36	ST MARTIN Roy	BREADEN Cecil	HABU	3.7	
02/05/71	975	09:30	FRUEHAUF Dave	PAYNE Al	K7	2.5	
03/05/71	973	10:00	BROWN Buddy	JARVIS Mort	K9	2.1	
07/05/71	975	10:00	HERTZOG Randy	CARNOCHAN John	K9	2.4	
08/05/71	972	12:00	ST MARTIN Roy	BREADEN Cecil	HABU	1.6	A
08/05/71	973	13:00	FRUEHAUF Dave	PAYNE Al	HABU	3.5	
09/05/71	973	10:00	ST MARTIN Roy	BREADEN Cecil	HABU	5.8	A
09/05/71	972	11:15	HERTZOG Randy	CARNOCHAN John	K9	2.2	
10/05/71	975	10:00	BROWN Buddy	JARVIS Mort	K9	2.2	
11/05/71	972	13:45	HERTZOG Randy	CARNOCHAN John	HABU	3.9	
12/05/71	975	09:45	ST MARTIN Roy	BREADEN Cecil	K9	1.5	A
14/05/71	973	11:00	FRUEHAUF Dave	PAYNE Al	HABU	2.3	
15/05/71	974	10:00	POWELL Bob	COLEMAN Gary	K9	2.3	
16/05/71	975	10:00	BROWN Buddy	JARVIS Mort	K9	2.1	
17/05/71	972	11:30	HERTZOG Randy	CARNOCHAN John	HABU	3.3	
18/05/71	974	10:00	FRUEHAUF Dave	PAYNE Al	K9	2.4	
20/05/71	973	10:10	POWELL Bob	COLEMAN Gary	HABU	3.5	
23/05/71	974	10:00	BROWN Buddy	JARVIS Mort	K9	2.2	
24/05/71	973	10:00	HERTZOG Randy	CARNOCHAN John	K9	2.3	
25/05/71	974	10:00	FRUEHAUF Dave	PAYNE Al	K9	2.3	
25/05/71	973	10:00	POWELL Bob	COLEMAN Gary	K9	2.2	
27/05/71	972	12:50	BROWN Buddy	JARVIS Mort	HABU	1.6	A
27/05/71	973	13:50	FRUEHAUF Dave	PAYNE Al	HABU	5.6	
28/05/71	975	13:45	POWELL Bob	COLEMAN Gary	K9	2.3	
28/05/71	974	12:30	BROWN Buddy	JARVIS Mort	HABU	5.5	
29/05/71	972	13:00	HERTZOG Randy	CARNOCHAN John	HABU	3.4	

Date	Instal. No.	T.O. Time	Pilot Name	RSO Name	Mission	Duration	Remarks
01/06/71	973	09:45	FRUEHAUF Dave	PAYNE Al	K9	1	A
03/06/71	973	09:45	POWELL Bob	COLEMAN Gary	K9	2.4	
04/06/71	972	09:45	BROWN Buddy	JARVIS Mort	K9	2.3	
06/06/71	975	09:30	FRUEHAUF Dave	PAYNE Al	HABU	3.2	
08/06/71	973	06:00	BROWN Buddy	JARVIS Mort	FERRY OUT		
10/06/71	968	03:00	BEVACQUA Tony	KOGLER Jim	FERRY TO OL-RK	5.3	
11/06/71	972	06:00	HERTZOG Randy	CARNOCHAN John	FERRY OUT		
13/06/71	979	03:00	ESTES Tom	VICK Dewain	FERRY TO OL-RK	5.4	
14/06/71	974	06:00	FRUEHAUF Dave	PAYNE Al	FERRY OUT		
14/06/71	968	07:30	POWELL Bob	COLEMAN Gary	K7	2.4	
16/06/71	978	03:00	BOWLES Ben	FAGG Jimmy	FERRY TO OL-RK	5.3	
16/06/71	968	10:30	POWELL Bob	COLEMAN Gary	HABU	3.9	
17/06/71	975	06:00	ESTES Tom	VICK Dewain	FERRY OUT		
17/06/71	979	10:20	BEVACQUA Tony	KOGLER Jim	HABU	2.3	
18/06/71	978	10:30	BEVACQUA Tony	KOGLER Jim	HABU	4	
19/06/71	980	03:09	PUGH Tom	RICE Ron	FERRY TO OL-RK	5.2	
19/06/71	979	11:00	POWELL Bob	COLEMAN Gary	K9	2.3	
21/06/71	978	10:00	BOWLES Ben	RICE Ron	K2	2.4	
22/06/71	980		PUGH Tom	RICE Ron	K2		A
23/06/71	978		BEVACQUA Tony	KOGLER Jim	HABU-BACKUP		
23/06/71	979	13:51	PUGH Tom	RICE Ron	HABU	3.5	
24/06/71	980	10:00	BEVACQUA Tony	KOGLER Jim	K2	2.2	
26/06/71	979	13:30	BOWLES Ben	FAGG Jimmy	HABU	5.7	
27/06/71	978	13:00	PUGH Tom	RICE Ron	HABU	3.9	
30/06/71	980	13:00	POWELL Bob	COLEMAN Gary	HABU	3.4	
01/07/71	968	10:15	PUGH Tom	RICE Ron	K9	2.3	
03/07/71	968	10:00	BEVACQUA Tony	KOGLER Jim	K9	2.3	
04/07/71	980	11:00	POWELL Bob	COLEMAN Gary	HABU	3.7	A
05/07/71	978	13:00	BEVACQUA Tony	KOGLER Jim	HABU	5.3	
08/07/71	968	10:00	BOWLES Ben	FAGG Jimmy	K9	2.4	
10/07/71	979	10:19	BUSH Denny	LOIGNON Phil	K9	2.3	
11/07/71	978	13:00	BOWLES Ben	FAGG Jimmy	HABU	5.5	
13/07/71	978	12:00	PUGH Tom	RICE Ron	HABU	3.5	
15/07/71	979	10:00	BEVACQUA Tony	KOGLER Jim	K7	2.3	
17/07/71	979	11:30	BUSH Denny	LOIGNON Phil	HABU	1.5	A
17/07/71	978	12:30	BOWLES Ben	FAGG Jimmy	HABU	3.5	
19/07/71	980	10:00	PUGH Tom	RICE Ron	K9	2.3	
21/07/71	968		PUGH Tom	RICE Ron	HABU		A
21/07/71	979	14:30	BUSH Denny	LOIGNON Phil	HABU	5.8	
23/07/71	968	12:00	BOWLES Ben	FAGG Jimmy	HABU	3.4	
24/07/71	979	10:00	SHELTON Jim	SCHMITTOU Tom	K9	1.8	A
27/07/71	979		PUGH Tom	RICE Ron	K9		A
28/07/71	980		BUSH Denny	MARTINEZ Gil	K9		A
28/07/71	979		PUGH Tom	RICE Ron	K9		A
28/07/71	979	13:00	PUGH Tom	RICE Ron	K9	2.3	
29/07/71	978	10:00	BUSH Denny	LOIGNON Phil	K9	1.5	A
30/07/71	979	11:30	BOWLES Ben	FAGG Jimmy	HABU	3.5	
31/07/71	968	13:30	SHELTON Jim	SCHMITTOU Tom	K9	2.3	
01/08/71	980	12:00	PUGH Tom	RICE Ron	K9	2.2	
06/08/71	978		BUSH Denny	LOIGNON Phil	K7		A
07/08/71	979	13:30	BUSH Denny	LOIGNON Phil	HABU	1.5	A
07/08/71	968	14:35	SHELTON Jim	SCHMITTOU Tom	HABU	3.6	
08/08/71	978	10:10	SPENCER Bob	SHEFFIELD Butch	K9	2.2	
08/08/71	979	13:55	BUSH Denny	LOIGNON Phil	RTB FERRY TO OL-KA	1.4	
11/08/71	978	11:16	PUGH Tom	RICE Ron	K9	2.3	
12/08/71	979	10:00	SHELTON Jim	SCHMITTOU Tom	K9	1.5	A
13/08/71	968	13:00	SPENCER Bob	SHEFFIELD Butch	HABU	1.4	A
13/08/71	978	14:00	BUSH Denny	LOIGNON Phil	HABU	3.5	
14/08/71	979	10:00	SPENCER Bob	SHEFFIELD Butch	K9	2.3	
15/08/71	968	12:15	SHELTON Jim	SCHMITTOU Tom	K9	2.2	
18/08/71	978	09:07	PUGH Tom	RICE Ron	K9	1.4	A
19/08/71	968	09:00	BUSH Denny	LOIGNON Phil	K7	2.4	
20/08/71	980	13:15	SPENCER Bob	SHEFFIELD Butch	K7	2.4	
21/08/71	979	09:30	SHELTON Jim	SCHMITTOU Tom	HABU	3.5	
23/08/71	980	10:15	CUNNINGHAM Bob	MORGAN George	K9	2.4	
24/08/71	968	09:00	BUSH Denny	LOIGNON Phil	K7	1.6	A
26/08/71	978	09:45	SPENCER Bob	SHEFFIELD Butch	K9	1.6	A
27/08/71	978	10:00	SHELTON Jim	SCHMITTOU Tom	K7	2.3	
30/08/71	978	12:30	SHELTON Jim	SCHMITTOU Tom	HABU	3.3	A
31/08/71	980	08:50	CUNNINGHAM Bob	MORGAN George	HABU	3.7	
31/08/71	978	14:18	SHELTON Jim	SCHMITTOU Tom	RTB FERRY TO OL-RK	3.9	
01/09/71	979	09:00	SPENCER Bob	SHEFFIELD Butch	K4	1.1	
01/09/71	980	08:30	BUSH Denny	LOIGNON Phil	HABU	1.9	
02/09/71	968	09:45	CUNNINGHAM Bob	MORGAN George	K9	2.5	
03/09/71	979	11:30	SHELTON Jim	SCHMITTOU Tom	HABU	4.1	
04/09/71	978	10:00	HERTZOG Randy	CARNOCHAN John	K7	1.5	A
09/09/71	968	08:24	SPENCER Bob	SHEFFIELD Butch	HABU	2.3	
10/09/71	978	10:15	CUNNINGHAM Bob	MORGAN George	K7	0.5	A
11/09/71	968	11:30	SPENCER Bob	SHEFFIELD Butch	HABU	5.3	
12/09/71	968	11:00	HERTZOG Randy	CARNOCHAN John	HABU	3.5	
13/09/71	978	10:30	HERTZOG Randy	CARNOCHAN John	K9	2.3	
15/09/71	979	10:00	CUNNINGHAM Bob	MORGAN George	HABU	4	
16/09/71	978	10:00	SHELTON Jim	SCHMITTOU Tom	K9	2.1	
17/09/71	968	11:30	HERTZOG Randy	CARNOCHAN John	HABU	5.8	
18/09/71	980	10:38	COBB Darryl	BLACKWELL Reggie	K4	1.1	A
19/09/71	968	13:00	CUNNINGHAM Bob	MORGAN George	HABU	1.7	
20/09/71	980	12:55	COBB Darryl	BLACKWELL Reggie	K9	2.3	
20/09/71	979	11:30	SPENCER Bob	SHEFFIELD Butch	HABU	4.9	
25/09/71	979	12:30	COBB Darryl	BLACKWELL Reggie	HABU	1.5	A
25/09/71	980	13:30	CUNNINGHAM Bob	MORGAN George	HABU	0.8	A
26/09/71	978	13:30	HERTZOG Randy	CARNOCHAN John	K9	1.6	A
27/09/71	979	11:32	COBB Darryl	BLACKWELL Reggie	K9	2.2	
27/09/71	980	18:15	SPENCER Bob	SHEFFIELD Butch	N/HABU	2.6	A,9
28/09/71	978		CUNNINGHAM Bob	MORGAN George	K9		A
28/09/71	980	19:43	SPENCER Bob	SHEFFIELD Butch	N/RTB FERRY	1.4	
28/09/71	979	12:30	HERTZOG Randy	CARNOCHAN John	HABU	1.9	
29/09/71	979	13:30	COBB Darryl	BLACKWELL Reggie	HABU	1.9	A
29/09/71	980	14:35	CUNNINGHAM Bob	MORGAN George	HABU	5.2	
30/09/71	980		COBB Darryl	BLACKWELL Reggie	HABU		A
30/09/71	978	10:05	HERTZOG Randy	CARNOCHAN John	K9	2.5	
03/10/71	978	09:00	ESTES Tom	MORGAN George	K2	3.5	
03/10/71	968	10:00	COBB Darryl	BLACKWELL Reggie	K9	2.3	
04/10/71	980	11:00	HERTZOG Randy	CARNOCHAN John	K7	2.3	
05/10/71	978	12:00	CUNNINGHAM Bob	MORGAN George	HABU	3.4	
07/10/71	980	12:30	CUNNINGHAM Bob	MORGAN George	HABU	5.4	
07/10/71	968	13:55	ESTES Tom	VICK Dewain	K9	2.3	
10/10/71	978	10:00	COBB Darryl	BLACKWELL Reggie	K9	2.4	
12/10/71	968	10:40	CUNNINGHAM Bob	MORGAN George	HABU	3.6	
14/10/71	980	09:55	ESTES Tom	VICK Dewain	HABU	2.2	
14/10/71	978	14:00	HERTZOG Randy	CARNOCHAN John	HABU	3.8	
16/10/71	978	10:00	FRUEHAUF Dave	MARTINEZ Gil	K9	2.3	
16/10/71	979	11:00	COBB Darryl	BLACKWELL Reggie	K9	2.2	
17/10/71	968	11:15	ESTES Tom	VICK Dewain	HABU	1.5	A
17/10/71	980	12:15	HERTZOG Randy	CARNOCHAN John	HABU	1.6	A
18/10/71	979	11:30	COBB Darryl	BLACKWELL Reggie	HABU	1.6	A
18/10/71	980	12:30	ESTES Tom	VICK Dewain	HABU	5.1	
19/10/71	968	12:15	FRUEHAUF Dave	MARTINEZ Gil	HABU	3.6	
20/10/71	979	09:00	HERTZOG Randy	CARNOCHAN John	K9	2.3	
22/10/71	979	12:00	COBB Darryl	BLACKWELL Reggie	HABU	5.1	
24/10/71	978	10:00	ESTES Tom	VICK Dewain	K9	1.8	A
25/10/71	978	12:00	FRUEHAUF Dave	MARTINEZ Gil	K9	1.7	A
27/10/71	980	08:50	HERTZOG Randy	CARNOCHAN John	HABU	2.3	
31/10/71	979	12:00	POWELL Bob	COLEMAN Gary	HABU	1.8	
01/11/71	980	10:00	ESTES Tom	VICK Dewain	K5	0.8	A
01/11/71	978	09:45	COBB Darryl	BLACKWELL Reggie	K9	2.3	
02/11/71	978	11:00	COBB Darryl	BLACKWELL Reggie	HABU	7.2	A
03/11/71	979	11:00	FRUEHAUF Dave	MARTINEZ Gil	HABU	2.2	A
04/11/71	980	09:00	POWELL Bob	COLEMAN Gary	K5	1.6	A
06/11/71	980	10:00	ESTES Tom	VICK Dewain	K5	2.3	
07/11/71	978	13:30	ESTES Tom	VICK Dewain	HABU	3.8	
09/11/71	980	10:10	COBB Darryl	BLACKWELL Reggie	K5	2.4	
10/11/71	979	12:00	FRUEHAUF Dave	MARTINEZ Gil	HABU	1.8	
11/11/71	980	08:10	POWELL Bob	COLEMAN Gary	HABU	2.3	
16/11/71	980	12:31	PUGH Tom	RICE Ron	K7	2.5	
17/11/71	978	11:15	FRUEHAUF Dave	MARTINEZ Gil	HABU	5.6	
18/11/71	980	11:30	ESTES Tom	VICK Dewain	HABU	3.4	
18/11/71	968	12:45	POWELL Bob	COLEMAN Gary	K5	2.4	
21/11/71	979	09:30	PUGH Tom	RICE Ron	K7	2.3	
23/11/71	979	06:24	ESTES Tom	VICK Dewain	HABU	2.3	
27/11/71	980	12:30	FRUEHAUF Dave	MARTINEZ Gil	HABU	1.9	
27/11/71	968	13:45	POWELL Bob	COLEMAN Gary	K5	2.2	
30/11/71	968	10:30	PUGH Tom	RICE Ron	K9	2.3	
02/12/71	968	10:57	BULL George	KRAUS Jon	K5	2.3	
05/12/71	979	11:15	FRUEHAUF Dave	MARTINEZ Gil	HABU	1.9	
05/12/71	980	13:00	PUGH Tom	RICE Ron	K7	2.4	
07/12/71	979	11:15	FRUEHAUF Dave	MARTINEZ Gil	HABU	3.3	
09/12/71	980	11:30	POWELL Bob	COLEMAN Gary	K7	2.4	
10/12/71	979	12:30	PUGH Tom	RICE Ron	HABU	3.8	
10/12/71	968	13:45	BUSH Denny	KOGLER Jim	K5	2.4	
12/12/71	979	11:45	POWELL Bob	COLEMAN Gary	HABU	5.4	
13/12/71	978	10:00	PUGH Tom	RICE Ron	K7	2	
13/12/71	968	13:52	BULL George	KRAUS Jon	HABU	2.4	
15/12/71	968		BUSH Denny	KOGLER Jim	K7		A
16/12/71	968	09:45	BUSH Denny	KOGLER Jim	K7	2.4	
17/12/71	978	11:30	POWELL Bob	COLEMAN Gary	HABU	3.3	A
19/12/71	980	11:00	PUGH Tom	RICE Ron	HABU	5.5	
20/12/71	978	10:00	BUSH Denny	KOGLER Jim	K9	2.3	
20/12/71	968	13:15	BULL George	KRAUS Jon	HABU	2.4	
21/12/71	968	12:15	BULL George	KRAUS Jon	HABU	5.3	
21/12/71	980	13:30	BUSH Denny	KOGLER Jim	K9	2.3	
23/12/71	980	09:45	PUGH Tom	RICE Ron	K9	1.8	A
28/12/71	978		BUSH Denny	KOGLER Jim	HABU		A
28/12/71	980	13:00	BULL George	KRAUS Jon	HABU	1.9	
28/12/71	979	09:00	SHELTON JIm	SCHMITTOU Tom	K3	2.5	
31/12/71	979	10:00	BUSH Denny	KOGLER Jim	K3	2.3	
02/01/72	978	11:00	BUSH Denny	KOGLER Jim	HABU	3.5	
04/01/72	978	10:00	PUGH Tom	RICE Ron	K9	2.3	
06/01/72	980	10:15	SHELTON Jim	SCHMITTOU Tom	K9	2.4	
07/01/72	979	09:45	JUDKINS Ty	SHOEMAKER Clyde	K9	2.6	
08/01/72	980	10:15	BULL George	KRAUS Jon	K3	2.3	
12/01/72	980		JUDKINS Ty	SHOEMAKER Clyde	K5		A
13/01/72	980	12:00	BUSH Denny	KOGLER Jim	HABU	4.2	
14/01/72	978	10:00	SHELTON Jim	SCHMITTOU Tom	K9	2.4	
16/01/72	980	12:30	SHELTON Jim	SCHMITTOU Tom	HABU	1.9	
16/01/72	979	13:45	JUDKINS Ty	SHOEMAKER Clyde	K5	2.3	
17/01/72	968	10:17	BULL George	KRAUS Jon	K9	2.3	
18/01/72	978	10:15	BUSH Denny	KOGLER Jim	K7	2.5	
20/01/72	978	12:47	BUSH Denny	KOGLER Jim	HABU	5.5	
21/01/72	979	12:00	SHELTON Jim	SCHMITTOU Tom	HABU	5.1	
22/01/72	968	12:30	JUDKINS Ty	SHOEMAKER Clyde	HABU	3.6	
22/01/72	978	13:45	BOWLES Ben	FAGG Jimmy	K7	2.6	
24/01/72	968	12:45	SHELTON Jim	SCHMITTOU Tom	K9	2.4	
24/01/72	979	11:40	JUDKINS Ty	SHOEMAKER Clyde	HABU	5.4	
27/01/72	968		SHELTON Jim	SCHMITTOU Tom	K9		A
27/01/72	979	13:45	BOWLES Ben	FAGG Jimmy	HABU	2.3	
28/01/72	968		BUSH Denny	KOGLER Jim	K5		A
28/01/72	978	11:30	SHELTON Jim	SCHMITTOU Tom	HABU	1.9	
30/01/72	968	10:00	BUSH Denny	KOGLER Jim	K9	2.3	
01/02/72	978	13:00	BUSH Denny	KOGLER Jim	HABU	5.5	
02/02/72	968	11:15	SHELTON Jim	SCHMITTOU Tom	K7	2.3	
02/02/72	979	10:00	JUDKINS Ty	SHOEMAKER Clyde	HABU	3.6	
04/02/72	968	12:00	SHELTON Jim	SCHMITTOU Tom	K5	2.4	
05/02/72	979	12:15	BOWLES Ben	FAGG Jimmy	HABU	3.6	
08/02/72	978	10:15	CUNNINGHAM Bob	MORGAN George	K4	1	
10/02/72	979	10:35	JUDKINS Ty	SHOEMAKER Clyde	HABU	3.4	A
11/02/72	968	13:15	CUNNINGHAM Bob	MORGAN George	HABU	1.5	A

Date	Instal. No.	T.O. Time	Pilot Name	RSO Name	Mission	Duration	Remarks
11/02/72	978	14:15	SHELTON Jim	SCHMITTOU Tom	HABU	3.8	
14/02/72	979	11:15	BOWLES Ben	FAGG Jimmy	HABU	1.8	
15/02/72	980	10:15	CUNNINGHAM Bob	MORGAN George	K9	1.7	A
16/02/72	968	11:15	JUDKINS Ty	SHOEMAKER Clyde	K9	2.3	
17/02/72	980	10:00	BOWLES Ben	FAGG Jimmy	K9	2.2	
18/02/72	968	09:45	HERTZOG Randy	FAGG Jimmy	K9	2.2	
19/02/72	979	13:00	BOWLES Ben	FAGG Jimmy	HABU	5.5	
24/02/72	979	10:30	JUDKINS Ty	SHOEMAKER Clyde	K9	2.3	
25/02/72	980	13:00	JUDKINS Ty	SHOEMAKER Clyde	HABU	5.4	
29/02/72	968	13:00	CUNNINGHAM Bob	MORGAN George	K9	2.3	
02/03/72	979	10:15	HERTZOG Randy	CARNOCHAN John	K9	2.3	
03/03/72	980	10:00	SULLIVAN Jim	WIDDIFIELD Noel	K9	2.3	
03/03/72	968	11:15	BOWLES Ben	FAGG Jimmy	K9	2.3	
04/03/72	979	13:00	BOWLES Ben	FAGG Jimmy	HABU	4.1	A
05/03/72	968	10:30	CUNNINGHAM Bob	MORGAN George	HABU	3.5	
05/03/72	979	17:10	BOWLES Ben	FAGG Jimmy	RTB FERRY	3.7	
06/03/72	980	13:15	CUNNINGHAM Bob	MORGAN George	HABU	5.3	
08/03/72	979	10:30	HERTZOG Randy	CARNOCHAN John	K9	2.3	
09/03/72	980	08:00	SULLIVAN Jim	WIDDIFIELD Noel	HABU	2.3	
11/03/72	968	10:00	BOWLES Ben	FAGG Jimmy	K9	2.3	
12/03/72	980	10:30	HERTZOG Randy	CARNOCHAN John	K9	2.2	
15/03/72	979	13:45	HERTZOG Randy	CARNOCHAN John	HABU	4	
16/03/72	980	10:15	CUNNINGHAM Bob	MORGAN George	K9	2.3	
17/03/72	978	11:15	SPENCER Bob	SHEFFIELD Butch	K9	2.4	
17/03/72	968	12:30	SULLIVAN Jim	WIDDIFIELD Noel	HABU	1.5	A
18/03/72	968	09:45	SULLIVAN Jim	WIDDIFIELD Noel	RTB FERRY	1.3	
20/03/72	980	12:30	SULLIVAN Jim	WIDDIFIELD Noel	HABU	4.1	
22/03/72	968	09:15	HERTZOG Randy	CARNOCHAN John	K9	2.2	
22/03/72	979	10:30	CUNNINGHAM Bob	MORGAN George	K9	1.5	A
23/03/72	978	14:00	SPENCER Bob	SHEFFIELD Butch	HABU	4.1	
26/03/72	980	10:00	HERTZOG Randy	CARNOCHAN John	K9	2.3	
26/03/72	978	14:00	CUNNINGHAM Bob	MORGAN George	HABU	1.8	
28/03/72	979	10:25	SULLIVAN Jim	WIDDIFIELD Noel	K9	2.3	
29/03/72	978	07:14	SPENCER Bob	SHEFFIELD Butch	HABU	2.3	
30/03/72	980	10:00	SULLIVAN Jim	WIDDIFIELD Noel	K9	1.5	A
31/03/72	980	15:16	COBB Darryl	BLACKWELL Reggie	K4	1.2	
01/04/72	979	08:30	HERTZOG Randy	CARNOCHAN John	HABU	1.9	
02/04/72	968	10:15	SPENCER Bob	SHEFFIELD Butch	K9	2.4	
03/04/72	979		SULLIVAN Jim	WIDDIFIELD Noel	HABU		A
04/04/72	980	09:15	COBB Darryl	BLACKWELL Reggie	K7	2.4	
04/04/72	968	13:30	SULLIVAN Jim	WIDDIFIELD Noel	HABU	3.6	
05/04/72	980	14:00	HERTZOG Randy	CARNOCHAN John	HABU	3.8	
07/04/72	979	11:05	SULLIVAN Jim	WIDDIFIELD Noel	HABU	4	
08/04/72	980	10:00	COBB Darryl	BLACKWELL Reggie	K4	1.1	
09/04/72	968	11:30	HERTZOG Randy	CARNOCHAN John	HABU	1.9	
11/04/72	968	13:30	SPENCER Bob	SHEFFIELD Butch	HABU	3.7	A
12/04/72	968	12:15	COBB Darryl	BLACKWELL Reggie	HABU	3.9	
13/04/72	978	14:00	SULLIVAN Jim	WIDDIFIELD Noel	HABU	3.9	
14/04/72	978	14:00	FRUEHAUF Dave	MARTINEZ Gil	HABU	4.1	
16/04/72	980	14:55	SPENCER Bob	SHEFFIELD Butch	HABU	3.8	A
17/04/72	978	13:00	COBB Darryl	BLACKWELL Reggie	HABU	4.1	
17/04/72	968	14:00	SULLIVAN Jim	WIDDIFIELD Noel	HABU	4.1	A
18/04/72	980	09:00	SPENCER Bob	SHEFFIELD Butch	K9	2.3	
18/04/72	979	10:00	SULLIVAN Jim	WIDDIFIELD Noel	K9	2	A
19/04/72	968	09:00	FRUEHAUF Dave	MARTINEZ Gil	K9	2.3	
19/04/72	980	10:00	COBB Darryl	BLACKWELL Reggie	K9	2.3	
20/04/72	978		FRUEHAUF Dave	MARTINEZ Gil	HABU		A
20/04/72	980	13:00	SPENCER Bob	SHEFFIELD Butch	HABU	4.2	
23/04/72	979	14:30	FRUEHAUF Dave	MARTINEZ Gil	HABU	4.1	
25/04/72	979	10:00	SULLIVAN Jim	WIDDIFIELD Noel	K9	2.3	
26/04/72	978	10:00	COBB Darryl	BLACKWELL Reggie	HABU	3.9	
27/04/72	980	14:30	SPENCER Bob	SHEFFIELD Butch	HABU	4.1	
29/04/72	979	12:09	PUGH Tom	RICE Ron	HABU	2.4	A
30/04/72	980	11:00	COBB Darryl	BLACKWELL Reggie	K9	2.3	
30/04/72	968	14:54	FRUEHAUF Dave	MARTINEZ Gil	K9	2.3	
01/05/72	979	10:30	PUGH Tom	RICE Ron	RTB FERRY	2.1	
02/05/72	980	14:18	COBB Darryl	BLACKWELL Reggie	HABU	3.8	10
02/05/72	979	14:16	SPENCER Bob	SHEFFIELD Butch	HABU	4.8	A,10
02/05/72	968	15:22	FRUEHAUF Dave	MARTINEZ Gil	HABU	4.1	10
03/05/72	978	13:00	PUGH Tom	RICE Ron	K9	2.3	
04/05/72	980	14:16	SPENCER Bob	SHEFFIELD Butch	HABU	3.9	11
04/05/72	978	14:18	COBB Darryl	BLACKWELL Reggie	HABU	4.1	11
04/05/72	968	15:22	PUGH Tom	RICE Ron	HABU	4.2	11
08/05/72	979		FRUEHAUF Dave	MARTINEZ Gil	HABU		A
08/05/72	978	15:05	COBB Darryl	BLACKWELL Reggie	HABU	4.1	
09/05/72	980	12:00	SPENCER Bob	SHEFFIELD Butch	HABU	4.2	
10/05/72	980	14:03	FRUEHAUF Dave	MARTINEZ Gil	HABU	4.2	
10/05/72	979	15:50	PUGH Tom	RICE Ron	K9	1.8	
11/05/72	978	12:00	PUGH Tom	RICE Ron	HABU	4.4	
12/05/72	979	13:00	ESTES Tom	VICK Dewain	HABU	4.2	
13/05/72	968		ESTES Tom	VICK Dewain	K9		A
13/05/72	978	13:00	COBB Darryl	BLACKWELL Reggie	HABU	4.2	
14/05/72	968	09:30	ESTES Tom	VICK Dewain	K9	1.7	
14/05/72	979	12:50	FRUEHAUF Dave	MARTINEZ Gil	HABU	4	A
15/05/72	978	11:45	PUGH Tom	RICE Ron	HABU	1.6	A,12
16/05/72	979	14:15	COBB Darryl	BLACKWELL Reggie	K9	1.6	
16/05/72	968	13:00	ESTES Tom	VICK Dewain	HABU	4.1	
17/05/72	979	13:00	COBB Darryl	BLACKWELL Reggie	HABU	2.3	A
17/05/72	978	14:00	PUGH Tom	RICE Ron	RTB FERRY	3.6	
17/05/72	968	14:14	FRUEHAUF Dave	MARTINEZ Gil	HABU	2.5	A
18/05/72	968	11:52	FRUEHAUF Dave	MARTINEZ Gil	RTB FERRY	2.6	
18/05/72	978	12:42	PUGH Tom	RICE Ron	K9	2.3	
18/05/72	979	11:40	COBB Darryl	BLACKWELL Reggie	HABU	4	
19/05/72	978	11:50	PUGH Tom	RICE Ron	HABU	4.1	
20/05/72	979	12:15	ESTES Tom	VICK Dewain	HABU	4.1	
21/05/72	978	12:00	FRUEHAUF Dave	MARTINEZ Gil	HABU	4.1	
22/05/72	968	11:50	COBB Darryl	BLACKWELL Reggie	HABU	4.2	
23/05/72	980		COBB Darryl	BLACKWELL Reggie	K9		A

Date	Instal. No.	T.O. Time	Pilot Name	RSO Name	Mission	Duration	Remarks
23/05/72	979	12:20	PUGH Tom	RICE Ron	HABU	4.1	
24/05/72	980	09:30	COBB Darryl	BLACKWELL Reggie	K9	2.3	
24/05/72	978	12:50	ESTES Tom	VICK Dewain	HABU	3.8	A
25/05/72	968	14:30	FRUEFAUF Dave	MARTINEZ Gil	HABU	4	
26/05/72	980	16:05	PUGH Tom	RICE Ron	K9	2.3	
26/05/72	979	14:50	POWELL Bob	COLEMAN Gary	HABU	4.1	
27/05/72	968	12:30	PUGH Tom	RICE Ron	HABU	4.1	
28/05/72	980	14:45	FRUEHAUF Dave	MARTINEZ Gil	HABU	1.9	
28/05/72	978	13:00	ESTES Tom	VICK Dewain	HABU	4.2	
29/05/72	968	14:00	FRUEHAUF Dave	MARTINEZ Gil	HABU	4.1	
30/05/72	978	13:30	POWELL Bob	COLEMAN Gary	HABU	4.2	
31/05/72	980	14:15	PUGH Tom	RICE Ron	HABU	4.2	
01/06/72	968	12:00	FRUEHAUF Dave	MARTINEZ Gil	HABU	4.2	A
02/06/72	978	13:00	ESTES Tom	VICK Dewain	HABU	3.8	A
03/06/72	979	12:00	POWELL Bob	COLEMAN Gary	HABU	4.3	A
04/06/72	968	11:30	PUGH Tom	RICE Ron	HABU	2.3	A
05/06/72	979	13:30	FRUEHAUF Dave	MARTINEZ Gil	HABU	4.3	A
06/06/72	980	13:05	ESTES Tom	VICK Dewain	HABU	4.2	
07/06/72	978	13:30	POWELL Bob	COLEMAN Gary	HABU	4.4	
08/06/72	979	13:40	PUGH Tom	RICE Ron	HABU	2	A
08/06/72	980	15:20	ESTES Tom	VICK Dewain	HABU	4	A
09/06/72	968	09:00	GUNTHER Bud	ALLOCCA Tom	K7	2.4	
09/06/72	978	10:45	POWELL Bob	COLEMAN Gary	HABU	6.3	A
10/06/72	979	12:00	PUGH Tom	RICE Ron	HABU	4.2	A
11/06/72	980	14:00	GUNTHER Bud	ALLOCCA Tom	HABU	4.2	
12/06/72	979	13:00	ESTES Tom	VICK Dewain	HABU	4.1	
13/06/72	978	13:30	POWELL Bob	COLEMAN Gary	HABU	4.5	
14/06/72	980	12:00	PUGH Tom	RICE Ron	HABU	4.2	
15/06/72	968	10:30	GUNTHER Bud	ALLOCCA Tom	HABU	4.1	
16/06/72	978	10:00	ESTES Tom	VICK Dewain	HABU	4.2	
17/06/72	980	11:00	POWELL Bob	COLEMAN Gary	HABU	4.1	
18/06/72	978		PUGH Tom	RICE Ron	HABU		A
19/06/72	968	13:30	PUGH Tom	RICE Ron	HABU	4.1	A
20/06/72	978		GUNTHER Bud	ALLOCCA Tom	HABU		A
20/06/72	980	13:30	ESTES Tom	VICK Dewain	HABU	3.9	A
21/06/72	978	14:15	GUNTHER Bud	ALLOCCA Tom	HABU	4.1	
22/06/72	979	13:00	POWELL Bob	COLEMAN Gary	HABU	4	
23/06/72	979	13:30	ESTES Tom	VICK Dewain	HABU	4.1	A
24/06/72	980	13:00	BUSH Denny	FAGG Jimmy	HABU	4	
25/06/72	968	12:30	GUNTHER Bud	ALLOCCA Tom	HABU	4.2	
26/06/72	978	13:30	POWELL Bob	COLEMAN Gary	HABU	4	
27/06/72	979	13:00	ESTES Tom	VICK Dewain	HABU	3.8	A
29/06/72	968	12:00	BUSH Denny	FAGG Jimmy	HABU	4.1	
30/06/72	980	11:00	GUNTHER Bud	ALLOCCA Tom	HABU	4.3	A
01/07/72	978	12:30	POWELL Bob	COLEMAN Gary	HABU	1.9	A
01/07/72	979	14:10	ESTES Tom	VICK Dewain	HABU	3.8	A
02/07/72	978	12:25	POWELL Bob	COLEMAN Gary	RTB FERRY	2.2	A
02/07/72	968	13:30	BUSH Denny	FAGG Jimmy	HABU	4.2	A
03/07/72	980	12:15	GUNTHER Bud	ALLOCCA Tom	HABU	6.3	A
04/07/72	978	13:40	ESTES Tom	VICK Dewain	HABU	4	A
05/07/72	979	13:00	POWELL Bob	COLEMAN Gary	HABU	2.1	A
05/07/72	968	14:30	BUSH Denny	FAGG Jimmy	HABU	4	A
06/07/72	968	12:30	GUNTHER Bud	ALLOCCA Tom	HABU	4.1	
07/07/72	979	13:00	POWELL Bob	COLEMAN Gary	HABU	1.9	A
07/07/72	980	14:30	BUSH Denny	FAGG Jimmy	HABU	4.1	A
08/07/72	968	13:00	JUDKINS Ty	KRAUS Jon	HABU	4.3	A
09/07/72	980	09:15	GUNTHER Bud	ALLOCCA Tom	HABU	4.1	
10/07/72	968	11:30	POWELL Bob	COLEMAN Gary	HABU	4.3	
11/07/72	979		GUNTHER Bud	ALLOCCA Tom	K9		A
11/07/72	968	11:00	BUSH Denny	FAGG Jimmy	HABU	4	A
13/07/72	979		GUNTHER Bud	ALLOCCA Tom	K9		A
13/07/72	978	09:30	JUDKINS Ty	KRAUS Jon	K7	2.4	A
13/07/72	979	12:38	GUNTHER Bud	ALLOCCA Tom	K9	1.9	
14/07/72	968	12:00	JUDKINS Ty	KRAUS Jon	HABU	4.2	A
14/07/72	979	14:00	POWELL Bob	COLEMAN Gary	K9	2.1	
15/07/72	978	11:30	GUNTHER Bud	ALLOCCA Tom	HABU	4.2	A
16/07/72	978	08:34	GUNTHER Bud	ALLOCCA Tom	RTB FERRY TO OL-KA	1.2	A
16/07/72	980	09:10	POWELL Bob	COLEMAN Gary	HABU	1.9	A
16/07/72	979	10:40	JUDKINS Ty	KRAUS Jon	HABU	1.5	A
17/07/72	979	10:00	POWELL Bob	COLEMAN Gary	HABU	4.1	A
18/07/72	978	11:00	GUNTHER Bud	ALLOCCA Tom	HABU	4.1	A
18/07/72	980	13:00	POWELL Bob	COLEMAN Gary	K9	2.2	
19/07/72	979	13:00	JUDKINS Ty	KRAUS Jon	HABU	4.1	A
20/07/72	978	12:20	BUSH Denny	FAGG Jimmy	HABU	4	,13 CRASH
27/07/72	980	11:15	CUNNINGHAM Bob	MORGAN George	HABU	1.7	A
27/07/72	979	12:45	GUNTHER Bud	ALLOCCA Tom	HABU	1.2	A
28/07/72	968		JUDKINS Ty	KRAUS Jon	K9		A
28/07/72	979	10:30	CUNNINGHAM Bob	MORGAN George	HABU	4	A
29/07/72	968		CUNNINGHAM Bob	MORGAN George	K9		A
29/07/72	979	13:00	GUNTHER Bud	ALLOCCA Tom	HABU	4	A
30/07/72	979	13:15	CUNNINGHAM Bob	MORGAN George	HABU	3.9	
30/07/72	968	16:00	GUNTHER Bud	ALLOCCA Tom	K9	2.2	A
31/07/72	968		JUDKINS Ty	KRAUS Jon	HABU		A
31/07/72	979	13:45	GUNTHER Bud	ALLOCCA Tom	HABU	4.5	A
01/08/72	979		CUNNINGHAM Bob	MORGAN George	HABU		A
01/08/72	968	12:30	JUDKINS Ty	KRAUS Jon	HABU	0.6	A
02/08/72	968	13:20	CUNNINGHAM Bob	MORGAN George	K9	2.2	A
02/08/72	979	11:30	JUDKINS Ty	KRAUS Jon	HABU	4.2	
03/08/72	968	11:00	CUNNINGHAM Bob	MORGAN George	HABU	4.2	
03/08/72	980	12:50	GUNTHER Bud	ALLOCCA Tom	K9	2.4	
04/08/72	968	12:34	GUNTHER Bud	ALLOCCA Tom	HABU	4.5	
05/08/72	980	11:30	JUDKINS Ty	KRAUS Jon	HABU	4	A
06/08/72	968	12:30	CUNNINGHAM Bob	MORGAN George	HABU	4.1	
06/08/72	979	14:20	GUNTHER Bud	ALLOCCA Tom	K7	2.3	
07/08/72	979	12:00	GUNTHER Bud	ALLOCCA Tom	HABU	4.4	
08/08/72	968		JUDKINS Ty	KRAUS Jon	HABU		A
08/08/72	979	14:00	JUDKINS Ty	KRAUS Jon	HABU	4	A

Date	Instal. No.	T.O. Time	Pilot Name	RSO Name	Mission	Duration	Remarks
09/08/72	979	11:00	CUNNINGHAM Bob	MORGAN George	HABU	4.1	
10/08/72	968	?	JUDKINS Ty	KRAUS Jon	HABU	4	
11/08/72	975	11:00	POWELL Bob	COLEMAN Gary	FERRY TO OL-KA	5.4	
11/08/72	979	?	CUNNINGHAM Bob	MORGAN George	HABU	3.3	
12/08/72	980		GUNTHER Bud	ALLOCCA Tom	FERRY OUT BACKUP		
12/08/72	979	06:30	JUDKINS Ty	KRAUS Jon	FERRY OUT		
12/08/72	968	15:30	POWELL Bob	COLEMAN Gary	HABU	0.7	A
12/08/72	975	15:45	CUNNINGHAM Bob	MORGAN George	HABU	4.1	A
13/08/72	975	12:30	GUNTHER Bud	ALLOCCA Tom	HABU	4.1	
14/08/72	968	11:30	POWELL Bob	COLEMAN Gary	HABU	4.1	A
14/08/72	971	03:00	SULLIVAN Jim	WIDDIFIELD Noel	FERRY TO OL-KA	5.3	
15/08/72	980	06:00	GUNTHER Bud	ALLOCCA Tom	FERRY OUT		
15/08/72	971	13:00	SULLIVAN Jim	WIDDIFIELD Noel	HABU	3.1	A
18/08/72	961	03:00	SHELTON Jim	SCHMITTOU Tom	FERRY TO OL-KA	5.3	A
18/08/72	975	12:00	SULLIVAN Jim	WIDDIFIELD Noel	HABU	4.2	
19/08/72	968	06:00	POWELL Bob	COLEMAN Gary	FERRY OUT		
19/08/72	961	12:30	CUNNINGHAM Bob	MORGAN George	HABU	4.2	A
20/08/72	975	12:15	SHELTON Jim	SCHMITTOU Tom	HABU	4.3	
21/08/72	963	03:00	COBB Darryl	BLACKWELL Reggie	FERRY TO OL-KA	5.1	A
21/08/72	961	11:00	SULLIVAN Jim	WIDDIFIELD Noel	HABU	4	
22/08/72	971	13:00	COBB Darryl	BLACKWELL Reggie	HABU	4.1	
23/08/72	963	12:00	CUNNINGHAM Bob	MORGAN George	HABU	4.3	
23/08/72	961	14:45	SHELTON Jim	SCHMITTOU Tom	K5	2.3	
24/08/72	975	10:30	SULLIVAN Jim	WIDDIFIELD Noel	HABU	1.6	A
24/08/72	971	12:00	SHELTON Jim	SCHMITTOU Tom	HABU	4.3	A
25/08/72	961		SHELTON Jim	SCHMITTOU Tom	K5		A
25/08/72	963	12:15	SULLIVAN Jim	WIDDIFIELD Noel	HABU	4.3	A
26/08/72	975	11:00	COBB Darryl	BLACKWELL Reggie	HABU	3.5	A
27/08/72	975	13:15	COBB Darryl	BLACKWELL Reggie	RTB FERRY	2.4	A
27/08/72	971	12:00	CUNNINGHAM Bob	MORGAN George	HABU	4.1	
28/08/72	963	11:30	SHELTON Jim	SCHMITTOU Tom	HABU	4.3	
29/08/72	961	11:20	CUNNINGHAM Bob	MORGAN George	K4	0.7	A
29/08/72	971	09:30	SULLIVAN Jim	WIDDIFIELD Noel	HABU	3.9	
29/08/72	963	12:30	COBB Darryl	BLACKWELL Reggie	HABU	2.3	
31/08/72	971		CUNNINGHAM Bob	MORGAN George	HABU		A
31/08/72	963	12:44	CUNNINGHAM Bob	MORGAN George	HABU	3.9	A
01/09/72	971	14:15	SHELTON Jim	SCHMITTOU Tom	HABU	4	
02/09/72	975		SHELTON Jim	SCHMITTOU Tom	K4		A
02/09/72	961		SULLIVAN Jim	WIDDIFIELD Noel	HABU		A
02/09/72	963	11:30	COBB Darryl	BLACKWELL Reggie	HABU	4.1	A
03/09/72	961	08:30	SULLIVAN Jim	WIDDIFIELD Noel	HABU	2.5	A
04/09/72	961	16:15	SULLIVAN Jim	WIDDIFIELD Noel	RTB FERRY	2	A
04/09/72	971	09:30	CUNNINGHAM Bob	MORGAN George	HABU	4.1	A
05/09/72	971	11:30	SHELTON Jim	SCHMITTOU Tom	HABU	4.1	
06/09/72	961	13:00	COBB Darryl	BLACKWELL Reggie	HABU	1.6	A
06/09/72	975	14:30	SULLIVAN Jim	WIDDIFIELD Noel	HABU	4.2	A
07/09/72	961	12:00	COBB Darryl	BLACKWELL Reggie	HABU	4.3	
08/09/72	975	13:45	SHELTON Jim	SCHMITTOU Tom	HABU	4.3	A
09/09/72	975		SULLIVAN Jim	WIDDIFIELD Noel	HABU		A
09/09/72	971	15:15	COBB Darryl	BLACKWELL Reggie	HABU	4.1	A
10/09/72	975	11:45	SULLIVAN Jim	WIDDIFIELD Noel	HABU	4	
11/09/72	975	13:30	SHELTON Jim	SCHMITTOU Tom	HABU	4.1	
12/09/72	961	12:00	COBB Darryl	BLACKWELL Reggie	HABU	4.1	
12/09/72	963	14:37	HALLER Carl	FULLER John	K9	2.2	
13/09/72	961	08:30	SULLIVAN Jim	WIDDIFIELD Noel	HABU	1.7	A
13/09/72	971	10:00	HALLER Carl	FULLER John	HABU	4.4	A
14/09/72	963	09:30	SULLIVAN Jim	WIDDIFIELD Noel	HABU	4	A
15/09/72	961	08:30	COBB Darryl	BLACKWELL Reggie	HABU	1.7	A
15/09/72	963	10:00	SHELTON Jim	SCHMITTOU Tom	HABU	4	A
15/09/72	971	11:00	HALLER Carl	FULLER John	HABU	3.6	A
17/09/72	963	11:30	COBB Darryl	BLACKWELL Reggie	HABU	4.1	
18/09/72	963	12:00	SULLIVAN Jim	WIDDIFIELD Noel	HABU	4.2	
18/09/72	975	14:03	COBB Darryl	BLACKWELL Reggie	HABU	3.4	
19/09/72	975	13:00	HALLER Carl	FULLER John	HABU	4	
20/09/72	975	08:00	SHELTON Jim	SCHMITTOU Tom	HABU	4.2	A
21/09/72	971	09:30	COBB Darryl	BLACKWELL Reggie	HABU	3.8	
22/09/72	975	11:00	SULLIVAN Jim	WIDDIFIELD Noel	HABU	4.1	
22/09/72	961	12:50	COBB Darryl	BLACKWELL Reggie	K9	2.3	A
23/09/72	963	12:00	HALLER Carl	FULLER John	HABU	4.3	A
23/09/72	971	12:45	SULLIVAN Jim	WIDDIFIELD Noel	HABU	3.6	
24/09/72	961	13:00	SHELTON Jim	SCHMITTOU Tom	HABU	4.1	
25/09/72	963	13:15	COBB Darryl	BLACKWELL Reggie	HABU	1.8	A
25/09/72	971	14:45	SULLIVAN Jim	WIDDIFIELD Noel	HABU	2.3	A
26/09/72	961	10:30	COBB Darryl	BLACKWELL Reggie	HABU	4.1	A
27/09/72	961	12:00	HALLER Carl	FULLER John	HABU	2.2	A
27/09/72	963	13:30	SHELTON Jim	SCHMITTOU Tom	HABU	4	A
28/09/72	963	10:00	HALLER Carl	FULLER John	HABU	4.3	
28/09/72	971	11:50	COBB Darryl	BLACKWELL Reggie	K4	1.1	A
29/09/72	971	12:00	POWELL Bob	COLEMAN Gary	HABU	3.9	A
30/09/72	971	11:30	COBB Darryl	BLACKWELL Reggie	HABU	4.1	
30/09/72	961	14:00	POWELL Bob	COLEMAN Gary	HABU	3.4	A
01/10/72	961	12:10	SHELTON Jim	SCHMITTOU Tom	HABU	4.1	
02/10/72	961	09:45	HALLER Carl	FULLER John	HABU	4	A
03/10/72	963	09:15	POWELL Bob	COLEMAN Gary	HABU	3.9	
04/10/72	975		POWELL Bob	COLEMAN Gary	K9		A
04/10/72	961	10:00	COBB Darryl	BLACKWELL Reggie	HABU	4	A
05/10/72	975	10:00	COBB Darryl	BLACKWELL Reggie	K9	1.8	
05/10/72	971	13:00	SHELTON Jim	SCHMITTOU Tom	HABU	4.1	A
06/10/72	963	12:15	HALLER Carl	FULLER John	HABU	4.1	A
07/10/72	971	09:30	POWELL Bob	COLEMAN Gary	HABU	4.1	
07/10/72	975	11:20	HALLER Carl	FULLER John	K9	2.2	
08/10/72	975	12:00	COBB Darryl	BLACKWELL Reggie	HABU	4.1	
09/10/72	971	12:30	SHELTON Jim	SCHMITTOU Tom	HABU	4.2	
10/10/72	963	12:15	HALLER Carl	FULLER John	HABU	6.9	
10/10/72	975	13:50	POWELL Bob	COLEMAN Gary	K4	0.9	
11/10/72	971	10:00	POWELL Bob	COLEMAN Gary	HABU	3.4	A
12/10/72	963	11:30	COBB Darryl	BLACKWELL Reggie	HABU	1	A
12/10/72	971	13:00	HALLER Carl	FULLER John	HABU	4	A
13/10/72	963	12:30	COBB Darryl	BLACKWELL Reggie	HABU	2.2	A
13/10/72	975	14:20	HERTZOG Randy	RICE Ron	K4	1	A
14/10/72	971	13:00	COBB Darryl	BLACKWELL Reggie	HABU	4.1	
14/10/72	961	14:58	POWELL Bob	COLEMAN Gary	K9	2.2	
15/10/72	975	08:45	HERTZOG Randy	RICE Ron	HABU	3.9	
16/10/72	975	11:00	POWELL Bob	COLEMAN Gary	HABU	3.9	A
16/10/72	961	14:15	HERTZOG Randy	RICE Ron	HABU	1.7	A
17/10/72	963	12:30	HALLER Carl	FULLER John	HABU	4.2	A
18/10/72	961	12:04	COBB Darryl	BLACKWELL Reggie	HABU	4.2	
20/10/72	975	12:20	HERTZOG Randy	RICE Ron	HABU	4	
21/10/72	961	10:00	POWELL Bob	COLEMAN Gary	HABU	3.5	
24/10/72	963	11:45	HALLER Carl	FULLER John	HABU	4.2	
25/10/72	975	10:00	COBB Darryl	BLACKWELL Reggie	K5	2.3	
26/10/72	961	14:13	HERTZOG Randy	RICE Ron	HABU	1.7	
28/10/72	975	12:00	POWELL Bob	COLEMAN Gary	HABU	3.8	
29/10/72	971	10:00	BLEDSOE Pat	CARNOCHAN John	K9	2.3	A
30/10/72	961	12:45	BLEDSOE Pat	CARNOCHAN John	HABU	4	
31/10/72	963	12:15	HALLER Carl	FULLER John	HABU	3.5	
02/11/72	975		HALLER Carl	FULLER John	HABU		A
02/11/72	963	11:33	HERTZOG Randy	RICE Ron	HABU	4.1	A
02/11/72	975	13:18	POWELL Bob	COLEMAN Gary	HABU	0.3	A
03/11/72	971	12:44	HALLER Carl	FULLER John	HABU	4.3	A
04/11/72	971	13:30	POWELL Bob	COLEMAN Gary	HABU	4.9	
07/11/72	975	10:00	BLEDSOE Pat	CARNOCHAN John	HABU	3.4	A
09/11/72	961	10:00	HERTZOG Randy	RICE Ron	K9	2.3	
10/11/72	971	11:00	BLEDSOE Pat	CARNOCHAN John	HABU	4.1	
11/11/72	971	13:45	POWELL Bob	COLEMAN Gary	HABU	1.8	
12/11/72	975	12:00	JUDKINS Ty	MORGAN George	HABU	4.1	A
14/11/72	963	13:00	HERTZOG Randy	RICE Ron	HABU	4.2	
15/11/72	963	11:00	BLEDSOE Pat	CARNOCHAN John	HABU	4	A
18/11/72	961		JUDKINS Ty	MORGAN George	HABU		A
18/11/72	961	13:15	JUDKINS Ty	MORGAN George	HABU	3.5	A
19/11/72	975	12:30	HERTZOG Randy	RICE Ron	HABU	1.6	A
19/11/72	961	14:00	JUDKINS Ty	MORGAN George	HABU	4.2	A
21/11/72	975	10:00	BLEDSOE Pat	CARNOCHAN John	K9	2.4	
21/11/72	961	11:00	GUNTHER Bud	ALLOCCA Tom	HABU	3.6	A
25/11/72	971	13:30	SULLIVAN Jim	WIDDDIFIELD Noel	HABU	1.9	
28/11/72	961	10:20	BLEDSOE Pat	CARNOCHAN John	K9	2.4	A
01/12/72	975	08:30	BLEDSOE Pat	CARNOCHAN John	HABU	2.2	A
02/12/72	971	12:00	GUNTHER Bud	ALLOCCA Tom	HABU	4.1	A
02/12/72	975	12:50	BLEDSOE Pat	CARNOCHAN John	RTB FERRY	3.8	
04/12/72	963		RANSOM Lee	GERSTEN Mark	K9		A
04/12/72	961	11:00	SULLIVAN Jim	WIDDIFIELD Noel	HABU	4.1	A
05/12/72	971	10:30	JUDKINS Ty	MORGAN George	HABU	4	A
05/12/72	963	12:12	RANSOM Lee	GERSTEN Mark	K9	2.4	A
06/12/72	971	12:00	RANSOM Lee	GERSTEN Mark	HABU	4	
08/12/72	963	12:30	GUNTHER Bud	ALLOCCA Tom	HABU	4	
11/12/72	975	10:00	RANSOM Lee	GERSTEN Mark	K9	2.2	
11/12/72	961	11:30	SULLIVAN Jim	WIDDIFIELD Noel	HABU	4	
12/12/72	975	13:30	RANSOM Lee	GERSTEN Mark	HABU	3.7	
15/12/72	975	10:00	COBB Darryl	BLACKWELL Reggie	HABU	4.2	
15/12/72	963	13:00	RANSOM Lee	GERSTEN Mark	HABU	3.5	
19/12/72	975		SULLIVAN Jim	WIDDIFIELD Noel	HABU		A
19/12/72	961	14:00	SULLIVAN Jim	WIDDIFIELD Noel	HABU	4.1	A,14
20/12/72	961	12:00	COBB Darryl	BLACKWELL Reggie	HABU	4.2	
21/12/72	975	11:45	RANSOM Lee	GERSTEN Mark	HABU	4.1	
22/12/72	963	12:10	COBB Darryl	BLACKWELL Reggie	HABU	4	
23/12/72	975	12:30	CUNNINGHAM Bob	FAGG Jimmy	HABU	4.9	A
23/12/72	961	14:12	RANSOM Lee	GERSTEN Mark	HABU	4.3	A
24/12/72	971	13:00	COBB Darryl	BLACKWELL Reggie	HABU	4.1	A
25/12/72	975	13:00	CUNNINGHAM Bob	FAGG Jimmy	HABU	4	
27/12/72	963		RANSOM Lee	GERSTEN Mark	HABU		A
27/12/72	963	14:20	RANSOM Lee	GERSTEN Mark	HABU	3.8	A
28/12/72	975	22:43	COBB Darryl	BLACKWELL Reggie	N-HABU	3.9	A,15
29/12/72	971	13:00	CUNNINGHAM Bob	FAGG Jimmy	HABU	4.1	
01/01/73	975		RANSOM Lee	GERSTEN Mark	HABU		A
01/01/73	963		COBB Darryl	BLACKWELL Reggie	HABU		A
02/01/73	975	10:00	RANSOM Lee	GERSTEN Mark	HABU	5.9	A
03/01/73	963	12:39	COBB Darryl	BLACKWELL Reggie	HABU	4.3	A
04/01/73	961	12:40	CUNNINGHAM Bob	FAGG Jimmy	HABU	3.4	
07/01/73	971	11:46	BLEDSOE Pat	CARNOCHAN John	HABU	4.4	A
08/01/73	963	10:00	COBB Darryl	BLACKWELL Reggie	HABU	4.3	A
10/01/73	961	12:30	BLEDSOE Pat	CARNOCHAN John	HABU	3.5	A
13/01/73	963	12:00	CUNNINGHAM Bob	FAGG Jimmy	HABU	4	A
14/01/73	971	14:00	SHELTON Jim	SCHMITTOU Tom	HABU	4.2	
15/01/73	961	12:00	BLEDSOE Pat	CARNOCHAN John	HABU	3.9	
16/01/73	963	12:05	SHELTON Jim	SCHMITTOU Tom	HABU	2.3	
19/01/73	963	12:00	CUNNINGHAM Bob	FAGG Jimmy	K9	2.3	A
20/01/73	961	12:45	CUNNINGHAM Bob	FAGG Jimmy	HABU	4	
20/01/73	975	15:15	SHELTON Jim	SCHMITTOU Tom	K9	2	
21/01/73	961	12:00	SHELTON Jim	SCHMITTOU Tom	HABU	4.1	A
22/01/73	971	12:00	BLEDSOE Pat	CARNOCHAN John	HABU	4.1	
23/01/73	975	12:00	CUNNINGHAM Bob	FAGG Jimmy	HABU	4.3	
24/01/73	971	12:50	SHELTON Jim	SCHMITTOU Tom	HABU	4.3	
25/01/73	963	12:30	BLEDSOE Pat	CARNOCHAN John	HABU	3.9	
26/01/73	975	11:45	SHELTON Jim	SCHMITTOU Tom	K9	2.2	A
30/01/73	971	10:00	JUDKINS Ty	MORGAN George	K10	2.2	
31/01/73	963	12:45	JUDKINS Ty	MORGAN George	HABU	3.5	
01/02/73	971	11:00	SHELTON Jim	SCHMITTOU Tom	HABU	4	
06/02/73	975	12:00	JUDKINS Ty	MORGAN George	HABU	3.9	
07/02/73	961	09:35	SHELTON Jim	SCHMITTOU Tom	K10	2.2	A
07/02/73	963	11:00	GUNTHER Bud	ALLOCCA Tom	HABU	3.5	
10/02/73	971	12:00	GUNTHER Bud	ALLOCCA Tom	HABU	4.1	
11/02/73	963	13:00	POWELL Bob	COLEMAN Gary	HABU	3.9	
13/02/73	971	12:30	JUDKINS Ty	MORGAN George	HABU	4	A
14/02/73	975	12:00	GUNTHER Bud	ALLOCCA Tom	HABU	4.2	A
15/02/73	961	10:00	POWELL Bob	COLEMAN Gary	HABU	5.2	
16/02/73	971	12:00	JUDKINS Ty	MORGAN George	HABU	4.1	

Date	Instal. No.	T.O. Time	Pilot Name	RSO Name	Mission	Duration	Remarks
17/02/73	975	13:00	GUNTHER Bud	ALLOCCA Tom	HABU	4	
18/02/73	963	10:00	POWELL Bob	COLEMAN Gary	HABU	3.7	
19/02/73	975	11:00	JUDKINS Ty	MORGAN George	HABU	4	
20/02/73	961	10:00	GUNTHER Bud	ALLOCCA Tom	HABU	4	A
22/02/73	975	10:40	POWELL Bob	COLEMAN Gary	HABU	3.8	
23/02/73	975	12:30	JUDKINS Ty	MORGAN George	HABU	3.5	A
24/02/73	961	11:00	GUNTHER Bud	ALLOCCA Tom	HABU	4	A
25/02/73	963	10:40	POWELL Bob	COLEMAN Gary	HABU	2.2	
27/02/73	975		JUDKINS Ty	MORGAN George	HABU		A
27/02/73	961		JUDKINS Ty	MORGAN George	HABU		A
27/02/73	975	11:14	GUNTHER Bud	ALLOCCA Tom	HABU	4.1	A
28/02/73	963	09:45	POWELL Bob	COLEMAN Gary	HABU	3.5	
01/03/73	975	10:00	JUDKINS Ty	MORGAN George	HABU	2	A
01/03/73	963	11:30	GUNTHER Bud	ALLOCCA Tom	HABU	3.7	A
03/03/73	975	11:00	JUDKINS Ty	MORGAN George	HABU	4	
06/03/73	961	12:30	POWELL Bob	COLEMAN Gary	HABU	3.9	
07/03/73	971	10:00	JUDKINS Ty	MORGAN George	K3	2.4	
08/03/73	963	12:30	GUNTHER Bud	ALLOCCA Tom	HABU	3.6	
10/03/73	961	10:00	SULLIVAN Jim	WIDDIFIELD Noel	HABU	3.6	A
11/03/73	971	12:00	POWELL Bob	COLEMAN Gary	HABU	2.6	A
13/03/73	975	09:15	GUNTHER Bud	ALLOCCA Tom	HABU	4.3	A
14/03/73	971	10:00	SULLIVAN Jim	WIDDIFIELD Noel	HABU	3.6	A
18/03/73	961	14:00	RANSOM Lee	GERSTEN Mark	HABU	3.6	
19/03/73	975	11:50	RANSOM Lee	GERSTEN Mark	HABU	4.2	
23/03/73	971	10:00	SULLIVAN Jim	WIDDIFIELD Noel	HABU	3.9	
26/03/73	961	08:20	RANSOM Lee	GERSTEN Mark	HABU	2.3	
26/03/73	971	10:00	ADAMS Buck	MACHOREK Bill	K9	2.4	A
27/03/73	961	11:00	ADAMS Buck	MACHOREK Bill	HABU	4	
30/03/73	971	12:00	SULLIVAN Jim	WIDDIFIELD Noel	HABU	3	
31/03/73	975	09:45	RANSOM Lee	GERSTEN Mark	HABU	3.7	
03/04/73	971	10:30	SULLIVAN Jim	WIDDIFIELD Noel	HABU	3.9	
04/04/73	963	12:00	SULLIVAN Jim	WIDDIFIELD Noel	K4	0.8	A
04/04/73	961	10:00	ADAMS Buck	MACHOREK Bill	HABU	3.7	A
06/04/73	961	09:10	ADAMS Buck	MACHOREK Bill	HABU	4.5	A
08/04/73	961	12:30	BLEDSOE Pat	BLACKWELL Reggie	HABU	3.2	
09/04/73	975	10:30	SULLIVAN Jim	WIDDIFIELD Noel	HABU	0.6	A
09/04/73	971	10:35	ADAMS Buck	MACHOREK Bill	HABU	4.4	A
11/04/73	963	12:50	BLEDSOE Pat	BLACKWELL Reggie	HABU	3.5	
12/04/73	975	08:30	SULLIVAN Jim	WIDDIFIELD Noel	HABU	3.8	A
14/04/73	963	10:45	ADAMS Buck	MACHOREK Bill	HABU	2.2	A
14/04/73	961	12:15	BLEDSOE Pat	BLACKWELL Reggie	HABU	0.4	A
16/04/73	971	12:15	SULLIVAN Jim	WIDDIFIELD Noel	HABU	3.9	A
18/04/73	961	07:05	BLEDSOE Pat	BLACKWELL Reggie	HABU	2.3	A
19/04/73	971	12:00	ADAMS Buck	MACHOREK Bill	HABU	4.1	
22/04/73	963	11:44	CUNNINGHAM Bob	FAGG Jimmy	HABU	5.3	
24/04/73	963	11:45	BLEDSOE Pat	BLACKWELL Reggie	HABU	5.5	A
26/04/73	961	14:00	ADAMS Buck	MACHOREK Bill	HABU	3.5	A
28/04/73	971	09:15	CUNNINGHAM Bob	FAGG Jimmy	HABU	3.5	A
30/04/73	963	10:00	BLEDSOE Pat	BLACKWELL Reggie	HABU	3.5	
01/05/73	975	10:00	ADAMS Buck	MACHOREK Bill	K5	2.2	
05/05/73	975	12:25	CUNNINGHAM Bob	FAGG Jimmy	K5	2	
06/05/73	961	09:46	RANSOM Lee	GERSTEN Mark	K4	1	A
07/05/73	975	12:00	ADAMS Buck	MACHOREK Bill	HABU	3	A
08/05/73	975	18:30	ADAMS Buck	MACHOREK Bill	N-RTB FERRY	2.3	A
11/05/73	971	10:00	CUNNINGHAM Bob	FAGG Jimmy	K4	1.1	
12/05/73	971	10:00	CUNNINGHAM Bob	FAGG Jimmy	HABU	4.3	
13/05/73	963	10:25	RANSOM Lee	GERSTEN Mark	HABU	4	
16/05/73	963	09:40	CUNNINGHAM Bob	FAGG Jimmy	HABU	3.8	A
17/05/73	975	13:30	RANSOM Lee	GERSTEN Mark	HABU	2.6	A
19/05/73	971	10:30	HERTZOG Randy	CARNOCHAN John	HABU	4.3	A
19/05/73	963	13:30	CUNNINGHAM Bob	FAGG Jimmy	HABU	1.8	
20/05/73	961	11:30	RANSOM Lee	GERSTEN Mark	HABU	3.1	A
21/05/73	975	11:00	HERTZOG Randy	CARNOCHAN John	K3	2.2	A
24/05/73	961	10:00	RANSOM Lee	GERSTEN Mark	HABU	2	A
27/05/73	963	12:15	CUNNINGHAM Bob	FAGG Jimmy	HABU	4.3	A
28/05/73	971	10:00	HERTZOG Randy	CARNOCHAN John	K4	1	
30/05/73	961	10:45	HERTZOG Randy	CARNOCHAN John	HABU	2.3	
30/05/73	975	11:45	RANSOM Lee	GERSTEN Mark	K5	2.2	A
31/05/73	971	12:30	JUDKINS Ty	MORGAN George	K4	1	
01/06/73	961		CUNNINGHAM Bob	FAGG Jimmy	HABU		A
01/06/73	975	13:58	RANSOM Lee	GERSTEN Mark	HABU	3.1	A
03/06/73	971	10:00	HERTZOG Randy	CARNOCHAN John	HABU	3.9	
04/06/73	975	06:00	CUNNINGHAM Bob	FAGG Jimmy	FERRY OUT		A
06/06/73	962	03:00	BLEDSOE Pat	BLACKWELL Reggie	FERRY IN (OL-KA)	5.3	
07/06/73	961	06:00	BLEDSOE Pat	BLACKWELL Reggie	FERRY OUT		
08/06/73	963	09:30	BLEDSOE Pat	BLACKWELL Reggie	HABU	4	
08/06/73	962	10:00	JUDKINS Ty	MORGAN George	K5	2.1	
09/06/73	972	03:00	ADAMS Buck	MACHOREK Bill	FERRY TO OL-KA	5.3	
10/06/73	971	06:00	RANSOM Lee	GERSTEN Mark	FERRY OUT		
11/06/73	972	11:00	HERTZOG Randy	CARNOCHAN John	HABU	3.6	
12/06/73	968	03:08	HELT Bob	ELLIOTT Larry	FERRY TO OL-KA	5.5	
13/06/73	963	06:00	ADAMS Buck	MACHOREK Bill	FERRY OUT		
14/06/73	972	10:00	JUDKINS Ty	MORGAN George	HABU	0.6	A
14/06/73	968	10:19	HELT Bob	ELLIOTT Larry	K9	2.3	A
15/06/73	968	07:00	JUDKINS Ty	MORGAN George	HABU	3.5	A
16/06/73	972	10:00	HERTZOG Randy	CARNOCHAN John	K9	2.5	
19/06/73	962	10:00	HELT Bob	ELLIOTT Larry	K9	3.9	
20/06/73	968	11:15	JUDKINS Ty	MORGAN George	HABU	4.3	A
21/06/73	972	10:00	HERTZOG Randy	CARNOCHAN John	K5	1.8	
22/06/73	968	16:00	HERTZOG Randy	CARNOCHAN John	HABU	2.2	
23/06/73	962	12:20	HELT Bob	ELLIOTT Larry	HABU	3.3	
24/06/73	968		JUDKINS Ty	MORGAN George	K4		A
24/06/73	972	11:30	HERTZOG Randy	CARNOCHAN John	HABU	3.9	A
26/06/73	972	10:00	JUDKINS Ty	MORGAN George	K9	2.1	
28/06/73	962	10:10	JUDKINS Ty	MORGAN George	HABU	3.9	
29/06/73	968	13:25	HELT Bob	ELLIOTT Larry	HABU	3.5	
02/07/73	972	10:00	GUNTHER Bud	ALLOCCA Tom	K9	2.1	
05/07/73	962	11:30	JUNKINS Ty	MORGAN George	HABU	2.2	A
05/07/73	968	13:08	HELT Bob	ELLIOTT Larry	HABU	3.6	A
06/07/73	962		JUDKINS Ty	MORGAN George	RTB FERRY		A
07/07/73	972	12:00	GUNTHER Bud	ALLOCCA Tom	HABU	2	A
07/07/73	962	18:06	JUDKINS Ty	MORGAN George	N-RTB FERRY	2.4	A
10/07/73	972	10:10	HELT Bob	ELLIOTT Larry	K9/5	2.1	A
11/07/73	962	12:00	GUNTHER Bud	ALLOCCA Tom	HABU	3.6	A
13/07/73	972	09:30	JOERSZ Al	FULLER John	K3	2.3	
13/07/73	962	14:15	HELT Bob	ELLIOTT Larry	HABU	3.6	
21/07/73	968	13:30	JOERSZ Al	FULLER John	HABU	3.3	
22/07/73	962	11:10	HELT Bob	ELLIOTT Larry	HABU	3.6	
24/07/73	972	11:00	GUNTHER Bud	ALLOCCA Tom	K4	1	
25/07/73	962	14:30	JOERSZ Al	FULLER John	HABU	3.5	
27/07/73	972	09:30	SHELTON Jim	COLEMAN Gary	HABU	3.8	
29/07/73	968	11:00	GUNTHER Bud	ALLOCCA Tom	HABU	3.5	A
31/07/73	962	09:30	JOERSZ Al	FULLER John	HABU	3.9	
02/08/73	968	14:30	SHELTON Jim	COLEMAN Gary	HABU	3.6	
03/08/73	962	10:30	GUNTHER Bud	ALLOCCA Tom	HABU	3.1	
04/08/73	972		WILSON Jim	DOUGLASS Bruce	K10		A
05/08/73	968	10:08	WILSON Jim	DOUGLASS Bruce	K10	2.4	A
07/08/73	972	11:00	JOERSZ Al	FULLER John	HABU	1.9	A
07/08/73	968	12:41	SHELTON Jim	COLEMAN Gary	HABU	3.9	A
10/08/73	962	13:30	JOERSZ Al	FULLER John	HABU	3.5	A
17/08/73	968	13:00	JOERSZ Al	FULLER John	HABU	3.9	
17/08/73	962	14:50	WILSON Jim	DOUGLASS Bruce	K9	2.3	
19/08/73	972		ADAMS Buck	MACHOREK Bill	K11		A
19/08/73	972	14:40	ADAMS Buck	MACHOREK Bill	K4	1.1	A
20/08/73	962	14:00	SHELTON Jim	COLEMAN Gary	HABU	3.6	A
24/08/73	972	13:00	WILSON Jim	DOUGLASS Bruce	HABU	4.2	A
26/08/73	968		ADAMS Buck	MACHOREK Bill	K11B		A
28/08/73	962	10:00	ADAMS Buck	MACHOREK Bill	K11B	2.3	A
28/08/73	968	11:00	SHELTON Jim	COLEMAN Gary	K11A	2.1	
30/08/73	962		WILSON Jim	DOUGLASS Bruce	HABU		A
30/08/73	972	14:07	WILSON Jim	DOUGLASS Bruce	HABU	3.5	A
31/08/73	968	10:00	ADAMS Buck	MACHOREK Bill	K6	2.7	
03/09/73	962	10:00	WILSON Jim	DOUGLASS Bruce	K11B	2.2	
04/09/73	972	10:00	ADAMS Buck	MACHOREK Bill	K11C	2.2	
06/09/73	962	11:00	WILSON Jim	DOUGLASS Bruce	HABU	4.5	A
07/09/73	972	12:00	ADAMS Buck	MACHOREK Bill	HABU	3.5	
09/09/73	972	09:30	ADAMS Buck	MACHOREK Bill	HABU	3.7	A
10/09/73	962	10:00	SULLIVAN Jim	WIDDIFIELD Noel	K11	2.3	A
11/09/73	968	12:30	SULLIVAN Jim	WIDDIFIELD Noel	HABU	3.5	
13/09/73	972	10:00	SULLIVAN Jim	WIDDIFIELD Noel	HABU	3.9	A
15/09/73	962	10:00	WILSON Jim	DOUGLASS Bruce	K11A	2.4	A
18/09/73	972	07:00	WILSON Jim	DOUGLASS Bruce	K13	2.1	
20/09/73	962	13:15	ADAMS Buck	MACHOREK Bill	HABU	3.4	
23/09/73	962	11:55	SULLIVAN Jim	WIDDIFIELD Noel	K4	0.9	
23/09/73	972	10:10	BLEDSOE Pat	BLACKWELL Reggie	HABU	4.4	
26/09/73	968	10:00	ADAMS Buck	MACHOREK Bill	K12	3.8	A
27/09/73	962	13:30	BLEDSOE Pat	BLACKWELL Reggie	HABU	3.5	
30/09/73	968	10:00	SULLIVAN Jim	WIDDIFIELD Noel	K12	3.4	A
02/10/73	968		SULLIVAN Jim	WIDDIFIELD Noel	HABU		A
02/10/73	962	11:00	ADAMS Buck	MACHOREK Bill	HABU	0.8	A
04/10/73	972	09:30	SULLIVAN Jim	WIDDIFIELD Noel	HABU	3.9	A
05/10/73	962	13:30	BLEDSOE Pat	BLACKWELL Reggie	HABU	3.6	A
07/10/73	972	13:03	RANSOM Lee	ALLOCCA Tom	K12	2	A
08/10/73	968	13:12	SULLIVAN Jim	WIDDIFIELD Noel	HABU	1.9	A
10/10/73	968	10:00	BLEDSOE Pat	BLACKWELL Reggie	K11B	3.3	A
12/10/73	972		RANSOM Lee	ALLOCCA Tom	K12		A
13/10/73	962		SULLIVAN Jim	WIDDIFIELD Noel	K4		A
13/10/73	972	13:07	RANSOM Lee	ALLOCCA Tom	K11B	1	A
13/10/73	962	13:28	SULLIVAN Jim	WIDDIFIELD Noel	K4	1	A
15/10/73	968	13:17	RANSOM Lee	ALLOCCA Tom	HABU	2.5	A
17/10/73	972	10:06	BLEDSOE Pat	BLACKWELL Reggie	K9	2.2	A
18/10/73	968	13:30	BLEDSOE Pat	BLACKWELL Reggie	HABU	3.6	
19/10/73	962	10:00	HERTZOG Randy	CARNOCHAN John	K9	2.4	
21/10/73	968	09:30	BLEDSOE Pat	BLACKWELL Reggie	HABU	4.1	
23/10/73	972	10:09	RANSOM Lee	ALLOCCA Tom	K9	2.2	A
25/10/73	962	10:00	HERTZOG Randy	CARNOCHAN John	K9	1.8	A
28/10/73	972	10:00	BLEDSOE Pat	BLACKWELL Reggie	K9	2.3	A
29/10/73	962		RANSOM Lee	ALLOCCA Tom	K9		A
30/10/73	968	11.00	RANSOM Lee	ALLOCCA Tom	HABU	4	A
31/10/73	972	14:00	RANSOM Lee	ALLOCCA Tom	K9	2.2	
01/11/73	962	10:00	HERTZOG Randy	ALLOCCA Tom	K9	1.8	A
03/11/73	972	12:30	JUDKINS Ty	MORGAN George	HABU	3.5	A
06/11/73	962	10:00	HERTZOG Randy	CARNOCHAN John	K9	2.3	
08/11/73	968	12:00	RANSOM Lee	ALLOCCA Tom	HABU	4.1	A
08/11/73	972	15:45	JUDKINS Ty	MORGAN George	K4	0.9	A
12/11/73	962	10:00	HERTZOG Randy	CARNOCHAN John	K9	2.2	
14/11/73	972	10:00	RANSOM Lee	ALLOCCA Tom	K9	2.1	
14/11/73	968	11:00	JUDKINS Ty	MORGAN George	K9	2.1	A
17/11/73	962	10:00	HELT Bob	ELLIOTT Larry	K12	3.4	
18/11/73	968	12:30	HELT Bob	ELLIOTT Larry	HABU	3.6	
19/11/73	972	11:30	HERTZOG Randy	CARNOCHAN John	HABU	4.2	
21/11/73	968	10:00	JUDKINS Ty	MORGAN George	HABU	4.4	
22/11/73	972	12:30	HERTZOG Randy	CARNOCHAN John	HABU	3.6	
26/11/73	968	10:00	HELT Bob	ELLIOTT Larry	K4	1.4	
28/11/73	962	11:15	HELT Bob	ELLIOTT Larry	HABU	3.9	
29/11/73	968	12:20	JUDKINS Ty	MORGAN George	HABU	3.6	
02/12/73	972	10:10	HELT Bob	ELLIOTT Larry	K9	2.5	
03/12/73	962	11:00	JUDKINS Ty	MORGAN George	HABU	4.1	
04/12/73	962	11:15	SHELTON Jim	COLEMAN Gary	HABU	4.8	
05/12/73	968	09:30	HELT Bob	ELLIOTT Larry	K9	2.3	
07/12/73	968	10:15	HELT Bob	ELLIOTT Larry	K10	2.5	
08/12/73	962	09:30	HELT Bob	ELLIOTT Larry	HABU	4.1	
10/12/73	962	11:30	JUDKINS Ty	MORGAN George	HABU	4.8	A
11/12/73	972	10:00	SHELTON Jim	COLEMAN Gary	K4	1	
16/12/73	972	13:23	SHELTON Jim	COLEMAN Gary	HABU	0.5	A
17/12/73	972	12:15	SHELTON Jim	COLEMAN Gary	HABU	4.2	A

Date	Instal. No.	T.O. Time	Pilot Name	RSO Name	Mission	Duration	Remarks
18/12/73	968	10:00	JOERSZ Al	FULLER John	K9	0.8	
19/12/73	972	12:15	JOERSZ Al	FULLER John	HABU	4.9	
21/12/73	968	10:00	HELT Bob	ELLIOTT Larry	K9	1.5	
26/12/73	962	10:00	JOERSZ Al	FULLER John	K9	2.1	A
27/12/73	962	10:06	SHELTON Jim	COLEMAN Gary	K9	2.6	A
28/12/73	972	12:15	JOERSZ Al	FULLER John	HABU	3.5	
29/12/73	968	10:00	WILSON Jim	DOUGLASS Bruce	K9	2.5	A
31/12/73	972	11:15	JOERSZ Al	FULLER John	HABU	4.2	
03/01/74	962	10:00	WILSOM Jim	DOUGLASS Bruce	K9	1.8	A
04/01/74	972	11:45	SHELTON Jim	COLEMAN Gary	HABU	4.9	A
06/01/74	968	10:00	JOERSZ Al	FULLER John	K9	2.6	
08/01/74	972	10:30	WILSON Jim	DOUGLASS Bruce	HABU	4.1	
09/01/74	962	10:00	JOERSZ Al	FULLER John	K9	2.6	
12/01/74	968	11:00	WILSON Jim	DOUGLASS Bruce	HABU	3.6	
14/01/74	972	11:20	SULLIVAN Jim	WIDDIFIELD Noel	K9	2.5	
15/01/74	962	11:00	ROSENBERG Maury	BULLUCH Don	K9	2.5	
17/01/74	968	10:11	ROSENBERG Maury	BULLUCH Don	K1	3.7	
18/01/74	972	10:00	WILSON Jim	DOUGLASS Bruce	K9	2.6	
19/01/74	972	12:00	SULLIVAN Jim	WIDDIFIELD Noel	HABU	4.8	
22/01/74	972	12:00	WILSON Jim	DOUGLASS Bruce	K9	2.4	
23/01/74	968	10:31	ROSENBERG Maury	BULLUCH Don	K9	2.6	A
24/01/74	962	11:30	WILSON Jim	DOUGLASS Bruce	HABU	4.1	A
25/01/74	968	10:00	ROSENBERG Maury	BULLUCH Don	K9	1.4	A
28/01/74	968	13:10	ROSENBERG Maury	BULLUCH Don	K9	2.4	A
30/01/74	972	12:00	SULLIVAN Jim	WIDDIFIELD Noel	HABU	3.5	A
31/01/74	968	10:00	WILSON Jim	DOUGLASS Bruce	K9	2.3	
02/02/74	962	11:30	WILSON Jim	DOUGLASS Bruce	HABU	4.1	
04/02/74	968	09:45	ROSENBERG Maury	BULLUCH Don	K9	2.5	
05/02/74	968	10:00	ROSENBERG Maury	BULLUCH Don	K1	1.4	A
06/02/74	962	10:00	SULLIVAN Jim	WIDDIFIELD Noel	HABU	3.8	A
07/02/74	968	10:00	ROSENBERG Maury	BULLUCH Don	K1	3.7	
10/02/74	962	12:15	ADAMS Buck	MACHOREK Bill	HABU	3.6	
11/02/74	972	10:05	ROSENBERG Maury	BULLUCH Don	K1	4.1	
13/02/74	962	12:30	SULLIVAN Jim	WIDDIFIELD Noel	HABU	1.9	A
15/02/74	962	11:55	SULLIVAN Jim	WIDDIFIELD Noel	HABU	3.9	A
18/02/74	968	12:30	ADAMS Buck	MACHOREK Bill	HABU	3.5	
19/02/74	972	10:00	RANSOM Lee	ALLOCCA Tom	K9	2.3	
22/02/74	968		RANSOM Lee	ALLOCCA Tom	HABU		A
23/02/74	962		RANSOM Lee	ALLOCCA Tom	HABU		A
25/02/74	968	11:30	RANSOM Lee	ALLOCCA Tom	HABU	3.7	A
26/02/74	972	10:15	BLEDSOE Pat	BLACKWELL Reggie	K9	2.4	
27/02/74	968	09:05	ADAMS Buck	MACHOREK Bill	HABU	3.6	A
02/03/74	962	12:00	BLEDSOE Pat	BLACKWELL Reggie	HABU	4.4	
04/03/74	962		RANSOM Lee	ALLOCCA Tom	K9		A
05/03/74	962	10:17	RANSOM Lee	ALLOCCA Tom	K9	2.2	A
06/03/74	972	10:20	ADAMS Buck	MACHOREK Bill	K9	1.1	A
07/03/74	962	12:00	RANSOM Lee	ALLOCCA Tom	HABU	1.1	A
08/03/74	968	09:30	RANSOM Lee	ALLOCCA Tom	HABU	3.7	A
11/03/74	972	11:00	ADAMS Buck	MACHOREK Bill	HABU	4.4	
12/03/74	962	13:15	RANSOM Lee	ALLOCCA Tom	K4	0.9	
12/03/74	972	12:15	BLEDSOE Pat	BLACKWELL Reggie	HABU	4.3	A
16/03/74	968	10:00	JUDKINS Ty	MORGAN George	K9	2.4	A
18/03/74	962	12:00	RANSOM Lee	ALLOCCA Tom	HABU	3.5	
19/03/74	972		BLEDSOE Pat	BLACKWELL Reggie	K9		A
20/03/74	972	09:45	BLEDSOE Pat	BLACKWELL Reggie	K9	2.3	A
25/03/74	962	10:00	HELT Bob	ELLIOTT Larry	K9	2.4	A
26/03/74	968	13:00	JUDKINS Ty	MORGAN George	K9	2.1	
27/03/74	972	10:00	JUDKINS Ty	MORGAN George	HABU	3.7	
28/03/74	972	13:00	BLEDSOE Pat	BLACKWELL Reggie	HABU	4.3	
31/03/74	972	12:15	HELT Bob	ELLIOTT Larry	HABU	3.8	
04/04/74	962	13:00	BLEDSOE Pat	BLACKWELL Reggie	K4	1.1	
05/04/74	972	11:30	JUDKINS Ty	MORGAN George	HABU	4.8	
07/04/74	962	10:30	BLEDSOE Pat	BLACKWELL Reggie	HABU	4.1	
10/04/74	972	09:45	HELT Bob	ELLIOTT Larry	K9	2.8	
11/04/74	962	11:00	HELT Bob	ELLIOTT Larry	HABU	5	
13/04/74	972	10:00	HERTZOG Randy	CARNOCHAN John	K9	2.4	
16/04/74	962	09:46	JUDKINS Ty	MORGAN George	K9	2.4	A
20/04/74	972	11:30	HERTZOG Randy	CARNOCHAN John	HABU	3.7	A
22/04/74	968	10:00	JOERSZ Al	FULLER John	D1	1.3	
23/04/74	962	10:00	HELT Bob	ELLIOTT Larry	D1	1.2	A
27/04/74	968	12:20	JOERSZ Al	FULLER John	D3	2	
29/04/74	972	14:30	HELT Bob	ELLIOTT Larry	HABU	3.9	
30/04/74	968	10:00	HERTZOG Randy	CARNOCHAN John	D3	2.5	
01/05/74	962	12:35	JOERSZ Al	FULLER John	HABU	5	
06/05/74	962	11:10	HERTZOG Randy	CARNOCHAN John	HABU	5.1	
07/05/74	972	10:00	WILSON Jim	DOUGLASS Bruce	D4	2.7	
10/05/74	972	10:00	JOERSZ Al	FULLER John	HABU	3.9	
13/05/74	962	10:00	HERTZOG Randy	CARNOCHAN John	D6	2.4	
14/05/74	962	13:35	WILSON Jim	DOUGLASS Bruce	D4	2.8	
17/05/74	968	11:03	WILSON Jim	DOUGLASS Bruce	HABU	3.7	
18/05/74	962	10:05	JOERSZ Al	FULLER John	D4	2.4	
19/05/74	968	09:30	JOERSZ Al	FULLER John	HABU	3.7	
20/05/74	962	18:50	WILSON Jim	DOUGLASS Bruce	D1	1	
22/05/74	968	10:00	ROSENBERG Maury	BULLUCH Don	D4	2.4	
27/05/74	968	10:45	ROSENBERG Maury	BULLUCH Don	HABU	5.1	
28/05/74	962	10:00	JOERSZ Al	FULLER John	D3	2.5	
03/06/74	972	10:15	WILSON Jim	DOUGLASS Bruce	D5	2.1	
04/06/74	962	09:45	SULLIVAN Jim	WIDDIFIELD Noel	D4	2.5	
05/06/74	968	10:05	WILSON Jim	DOUGLASS Bruce	HABU	2.3	A
06/06/74	972	10:20	ROSENBERG Maury	BULLUCH Don	D8	4.2	
07/06/74	972	10:15	SULLIVAN Jim	WIDDIFIELD Noel	D8	4	
10/06/74	968	10:03	WILSON Jim	DOUGLASS Bruce	D8	4.3	
11/06/74	968	10:45	ROSENBERG MAURY	BULLUCH Don	D8	4.2	
12/06/74	962	10:45	WILSON Jim	DOUGLASS Bruce	D8	4.2	
14/06/74	972	13:00	ROSENBERG Maury	BULLUCH Don	HABU	2	A
15/06/74	972	14:00	ROSENBERG Maury	BULLUCH Don	HABU	4.7	
17/06/74	962	09:00	ADAMS Buck	MACHOREK BIll	D8	3.9	
18/06/74	972	09:02	SULLIVAN Jim	WIDDIFIELD Noel	D7	2	
21/06/74	962		ROSENBERG Maury	BULLUCH Don	D8		A
22/06/74	972	11:00	SULLIVAN Jim	WIDDIFIELD Noel	HABU	3.6	
24/06/74	962	10:00	ROSENBERG Maury	BULLUCH Don	D8	2.3	A
25/06/74	972	10:04	ADAMS Buck	MACHOREK Bill	D8	4	
26/06/74	972		SULLIVAN Jim	WIDDIFIELD Noel	D8		A
27/06/74	962	13:44	ADAMS Buck	MACHOREK Bill	HABU	1.8	A
28/06/74	972	13:30	ADAMS Buck	MACHOREK Bill	HABU	1.3	A
29/06/74	972	11:30	SULLIVAN Jim	WIDDIFIELD Noel	HABU	3.6	
02/07/74	968	10:06	HELT Bob	ELLIOTT Larry	D8	2	A
03/07/74	962	10:20	ADAMS Buck	MACHOREK Bill	D8	2.1	
08/07/74	972	11:00	HELT Bob	ELLIOTT Larry	HABU	3	A
09/07/74	962	10:00	SULLIVAN Jim	WIDDIFIELD Noel	D3	2.2	
10/07/74	962	11:30	SULLIVAN Jim	WIDDIFIELD Noel	HABU	4.1	
11/07/74	968	10:05	ADAMS Buck	MACHOREK Bill	D8	3.9	
12/07/74	972		HELT Bob	ELLIOTT Larry	D8		A
15/07/74	968	12:30	ADAMS Buck	MACHOREK Bill	HABU	3.6	
16/07/74	972	10:30	HELT Bob	ELLIOTT Larry	D8	4.1	
18/07/74	968		BLEDSOE Pat	BLACKWELL Reggie	D7		A
19/07/74	968	10:30	BLEDSOE Pat	BLACKWELL Reggie	D1	1.1	
23/07/74	968	11:03	HELT Bob	ELLIOTT Larry	HABU	4	
24/07/74	972	10:30	ADAMS Buck	MACHOREK Bill	D4	2.3	
26/07/74	968	09:10	BLEDSOE Pat	BLACKWELL Reggie	HABU	4.2	
29/07/74	972	10:00	HELT Bob	ELLIOTT Larry	HABU	2.1	A
30/07/74	962	11:23	RANSOM Lee	PAYNE Al	D8	4.1	
31/07/74	968	11:00	BLEDSOE Pat	BLACKWELL Reggie	D7	2.3	
02/08/74	968	10:15	HELT Bob	ELLIOTT Larry	D8	4.1	
06/08/74	972	12:30	RANSOM Lee	PAYNE Al	HABU	1.5	A
07/08/74	962	10:15	BLEDSOE Pat	BLACKWELL Reggie	D8	4	
08/08/74	968	10:30	RANSOM Lee	PAYNE Al	HABU	4	
09/08/74	962	12:00	HELT Bob	ELLIOTT Larry	HABU	2.3	A
09/08/74	968	13:23	BLEDSOE Pat	BLACKWELL Reggie	HABU	4.2	
11/08/74	968		RANSOM Lee	PAYNE Al	D4		A
12/08/74	968	10:00	HELT Bob	ELLIOTT Larry	D1	1.1	
13/08/74	963	03:00	JOERSZ Al	FULLER John	FERRY IN	5.3	
13/08/74	972	10:00	RANSOM Lee	PAYNE Al	D3	2.4	
14/08/74	968	06:00	HELT Bob	ELLIOTT Larry	FERRY OUT		
15/08/74	962	11:00	BLEDSOE Pat	BLACKWELL Reggie	HABU	3.7	
15/08/74	963	10:00	JOERSZ Al	FULLER John	D3	2.4	
16/08/74	961	03:00	WILSON Jim	DOUGLASS Bruce	FERRY IN	5.3	
17/08/74	972	06:00	BLEDSOE Pat	BLACKWELL Reggie	FERRY OUT		
18/08/74	963	12:34	RANSOM Lee	PAYNE Al	HABU	3.4	A
19/08/74	976	03:00	HERTZOG Randy	MORGAN George	FERRY IN	5.3	
20/08/74	962	06:00	WILSON Jim	DOUGLASS Bruce	FERRY OUT		
20/08/74	961	09:30	JOERSZ Al	FULLER John	D3	0.8	A
22/08/74	963	09:45	RANSOM Lee	PAYNE Al	HABU	1.5	A
22/08/74	976	11:00	JOERSZ Al	FULLER John	HABU	1.7	A
23/08/74	963	09:45	RANSOM Lee	PAYNE Al	HABU	4.3	
26/08/74	976	10:00	HERTZOG Randy	MORGAN George	D4	2.3	
26/08/74	961	10:35	JOERSZ Al	FULLER John	HABU	4.8	
27/08/74	963	10:00	RANSOM Lee	PAYNE Al	D1	1.1	
28/08/74	976	10:15	HERTZOG Randy	MORGAN George	D4	1.5	A
03/09/74	976	10:15	JOERSZ Al	FULLER John	D8	4.1	
04/09/74	961	10:17	RANSOM Lee	PAYNE AL	D1	1	
04/09/74	963	10:30	HERTZOG Randy	MORGAN George	D3	2.4	
05/09/74	963	10:30	HERTZOG Randy	MORGAN George	HABU	4.9	
09/09/74	976	10:52	ROSENBERG Maury	BULLUCH Don	D8	4	
10/09/74	963	10:30	JOERSZ Al	FULLER John	HABU	4.9	
11/09/74	961	11:55	JOERSZ Al	FULLER John	HABU	4	
13/09/74	963	10:45	HERTZOG Randy	MORGAN George	D3	2.4	
17/09/74	961	10:32	JOERSZ Al	FULLER John	D3	2.5	
19/09/74	976	10:00	ROSENBERG Maury	BULLUCH Don	HABU	4.9	
20/09/74	963	10:15	HERTZOG Randy	MORGAN George	D3	2.3	
23/09/74	961	10:40	WILSON Jim	DOUGLASS Bruce	D8	4.1	
24/09/74	976	10:15	ROSENBERG Maury	BULLUCH Don	D4	1.8	A
25/09/74	963	10:45	HERTZOG Randy	MORGAN George	HABU	5	
27/09/74	961	12:00	HERTZOG Randy	MORGAN George	HABU	2.1	A
27/09/74	963	13:24	ROSENBERG Maury	BOLLUCH Don	HABU	4.3	
02/10/74	963	10:14	WILSON Jim	DOUGLASS Bruce	D2	2.5	
04/10/74	961	10:13	ROSENBERG Maury	BULLUCH Don	D1	1.2	
09/10/74	961	11:45	ROSENBERG Maury	BULLUCH Don	HABU	3.7	
10/10/74	963	10:34	WILSON Jim	DOUGLASS Bruce	D8	3.6	
12/10/74	963	12:30	WILSON Jim	DOUGLASS Bruce	HABU	4.2	
15/10/74	963		ADAMS Buck	MACHOREK Bill	D4		A
16/10/74	961	11:44	WILSON Jim	DOUGLASS Bruce	HABU	5.1	
17/10/74	963		ADAMS Buck	MACHOREK Bill	D4		A
18/10/74	961	12:27	ROSENBERG Maury	BULLUCH Don	D7	1.8	
18/10/74	963	10:34	ADAMS Buck	MACHOREK Bill	HABU	4.1	
22/10/74	961	10:15	WILSON Jim	DOUGLASS Bruce	D3	2.5	
26/10/74	963	12:50	ADAMS Buck	MACHOREK Bill	HABU	3.7	
28/10/74	963	12:50	WILSON Jim	DOUGLASS Bruce	HABU	3.8	
29/10/74	961	10:15	SULLIVAN Jim	WIDDIFIELD Noel	D3	2.4	
01/11/74	963		SULLIVAN Jim	WIDDIFIELD Noel	HABU		A
02/11/74	963	10:30	SULLIVAN Jim	WIDDIFIELD Noel	HABU	3.6	
11/11/74	961	13:15	HELT Bob	ELLIOTT Larry	D3	2.5	
12/11/74	963	10:35	SULLIVAN Jim	WIDDIFIELD Noel	D3	2.3	
13/11/74	961	11:00	HELT Bob	ELLIOTT Larry	HABU	5.1	
15/11/74	963	13:30	SULLIVAN Jim	WIDDIFIELD Noel	D3	2.4	
17/11/74	961	10:00	RANSOM Lee	PAYNE Al	D8	2.6	A
23/11/74	963	11:30	HELT Bob	ELLIOTT Larry	HABU	4.2	
25/11/74	963	13:00	RANSOM Lee	PAYNE Al	D8	3.9	
26/11/74	971	03:31	BLEDSOE Pat	BLACKWELL Reggie	FERRY IN (DET 1)	5.5	
28/11/74	963	11:30	HELT Bob	ELLIOTT Larry	HABU	4.2	
29/11/74	961	10:50	RANSOM Lee	PAYNE Al	D3	2.5	
02/12/74	971	10:31	BLEDSOE Pat	BLACKWELL Reggie	D8	1.5	A
03/12/74	961	11:30	BLEDSOE Pat	BLACKWELL Reggie	HABU	4.4	
04/12/74	971	10:15	HELT Bob	ELLIOTT Larry	D8	1.4	A
06/12/74	961	10:45	RANSOM Lee	PAYNE Al	HABU	5	
09/12/74	971	12:00	HELT Bob	ELLIOTT Larry	D8	2	A

Date	Instal. No.	T.O. Time	Pilot Name	RSO Name	Mission	Duration	Remarks
10/12/74	971		BLEDSOE Pat	BLACKWELL Reggie	D9		A
11/12/74	971	11:15	BLEDSOE Pat	BLACKWELL Reggie	D1	1.1	
11/12/74	963	10:15	HELT Bob	ELLIOTT Larry	HABU	3.7	
13/12/74	971	10:15	RANSOM Lee	PAYNE Al	D9	2.7	
17/12/74	971	12:00	KINEGO Joe	JACKS Roger	D3	2.5	
19/12/74	963		BLEDSOE Pat	BLACKWELL Reggie	HABU		A
20/12/74	961	10:30	BLEDSOE Pat	BLACKWELL Reggie	D8	3.8	
21/12/74	963		BLEDSOE Pat	BLACKWELL Reggie	HABU		A
23/12/74	961	10:50	RANSOM Lee	PAYNE Al	D1	1	
23/12/74	963	09:30	BLEDSOE Pat	BLACKWELL Reggie	HABU	3.7	
27/12/74	971	11:30	KINEGO Joe	JACKS Roger	D5	3.9	
28/12/74	963	11:15	KINEGO Joe	JACKS Roger	HABU	3.7	
30/12/74	961	11:30	BLEDSOE Pat	BLACKWELL Reggie	HABU	2.1	A
30/12/74	971	12:45	KINEGO Joe	JACKS Roger	HABU	1.4	A
31/12/74	961	11:30	BLEDSOE Pat	BLACKWELL Reggie	HABU	6.2	A
02/01/75	963	10:30	ROSENBERG Maury	BULLUCH Don	HABU	4.3	
03/01/75	961	09:30	ROSENBERG Maury	BULLUCH Don	D4	2.4	
04/01/75	961		KINEGO Joe	JACKS Roger	HABU		A
04/01/75	963	12:15	ROSENBERG Maury	BULLUCH Don	HABU	4.1	
06/01/75	971	10:00	BLEDSOE Pat	BLACKWELL Reggie	D8	4.2	
07/01/75	961	10:30	KINEGO Joe	JACKS Roger	HABU	3.3	
09/01/75	961	10:30	ROSENBERG Maury	BULLUCH Don	HABU	4.3	
10/01/75	976	10:00	SMITH Tom	CARNOCHAN John	FCF	0.7	A
10/01/75	971	11:30	KINEGO Joe	JACKS Roger	HABU	5	
11/01/75	961	11:31	KINEGO Joe	JACKS Roger	HABU	4.3	
13/01/75	976		PUGH Tom	CARNOCHAN John	FCF		A
13/01/75	976	13:15	PUGH Tom	CARNOCHAN John	FCF	1.4	A
14/01/75	976	13:30	SMITH Tom	CARNOCHAN John	FCF	2.4	
15/01/75	963	11:00	JOERSZ Al	MACHOREK Bill	D9	2.5	
16/01/75	971	10:50	ROSENBERG Maury	BULLUCH Don	HABU	5.2	
17/01/75	976	13:00	PUGH Tom	CARNOCHAN John	D1	1	
17/01/75	961	11:00	JOERSZ Al	MACHOREK Bill	HABU	3.9	
23/01/75	963	10:00	KINEGO Joe	MACHOREK Bill	D1	1	
24/01/75	961	11:30	JOERSZ Al	MACHOREK Bill	HABU	4.1	
25/01/75	963	10:45	ROSENBERG Maury	BULLUCH Don	HABU	4	
27/01/75	961	11:00	ROSENBERG Maury	BULLUCH Don	HABU	1.7	A
28/01/75	961	11:00	HERTZOG Randy	MORGAN George	HABU	3.6	A
29/01/75	976	13:00	PUGH Tom	CARNOCHAN John	D1	1	
29/01/75	963	11:45	JOERSZ Al	MACHOREK Bill	HABU	3.1	A
30/01/75	976	06:50	PUGH Tom	CARNOCHAN John	FERRY OUT		
31/01/75	971		ROSENBERG Maury	BULLUCH Don	HABU		A
31/01/75	961	12:30	HERTZOG Randy	MORGAN George	HABU	4.2	
01/02/75	971	10:28	ROSENBERG Maury	BULLUCH Don	D8	4	
04/02/75	971	10:32	JOERSZ Al	MACHOREK Bill	D8	4	
07/02/75	961	10:15	HERTZOG Randy	MORGAN George	HABU	4.2	
08/02/75	963		JOERSZ Al	MACHOREK Bill	HABU		A
10/02/75	971		JOERSZ Al	MACHOREK Bill	HABU		A
10/02/75	971	12:33	JOERSZ Al	MACHOREK Bill	HABU	4.9	
11/02/75	963	10:15	WILSON Jim	DOUGLASS Bruce	D3	2.1	
13/02/75	971	10:45	HERTZOG Randy	MORGAN George	HABU	4.9	
18/02/75	971	11:20	WILSON Jim	DOUGLASS Bruce	HABU	4.3	
18/02/75	961	12:50	JOERSZ Al	MACHOREK Bill	D3	2.3	
19/02/75	963	10:15	HERTZOG Randy	MORGAN George	D1	1.1	
24/02/75	961	12:00	HERTZOG Randy	MORGAN George	HABU	4.3	
25/02/75	971	11:30	WILSON Jim	DOUGLASS Bruce	HABU	3.8	
28/02/75	971	11:05	ADAMS Buck	GERSTEN Mark	HABU	4.8	
04/03/75	961	12:15	HERTZOG Randy	MORGAN George	D3	2.4	
06/03/75	971	12:00	WILSON Jim	DOUGLASS Bruce	HABU	4.2	
07/03/75	961	12:00	WILSON Jim	DOUGLASS Bruce	HABU	5	
09/03/75	963	09:00	SULLIVAN Jim	WIDDIFIELD Noel	D1	1.1	
10/03/75	963	12:38	ADAMS Buck	GERSTEN Mark	D8 MODIFIED	2.5	
12/03/75	961	11:00	ADAMS Buck	GERSTEN Mark	HABU	0.6	A
13/03/75	971		ADAMS Buck	GERSTEN Mark	HABU		A
14/03/75	971		ADAMS Buck	GERSTEN Mark	HABU		A
14/03/75	971	13:10	ADAMS Buck	GERSTEN Mark	HABU	4.1	
15/03/75	971	12:00	SULLIVAN Jim	WIDDIFIELD Noel	HABU	4.9	
17/03/75	963	11:00	WILSON Jim	DOUGLASS Bruce	D8	4.1	
19/03/75	961	11:00	ADAMS Buck	GERSTEN Mark	D8	2.2	
20/03/75	963	11:00	SULLIVAN Jim	WIDDIFIELD Noel	D1	1.1	
21/03/75	971	11:15	ADAMS Buck	GERSTEN Mark	HABU	5	
22/03/75	963	10:16	SULLIVAN Jim	WIDDIFIELD Noel	D1	0.9	
24/03/75	961	10:15	RANSOM Lee	PAYNE Al	D3	1.3	A
25/03/75	963	10:45	SULLIVAN Jim	WIDDIFIELD Noel	HABU	4.8	
26/03/75	963	13:10	SULLIVAN Jim	WIDDIFIELD Noel	HABU	3.3	
27/03/75	963	12:00	RANSOM Lee	PAYNE Al	HABU	4	
28/03/75	963	11:30	ADAMS Buck	GERSTEN Mark	HABU	3.5	
28/03/75	971	13:00	SULLIVAN Jim	WIDDIFIELD Noel	D1	0.8	A
01/04/75	971	11:30	ADAMS Buck	GERSTEN Mark	HABU	4	
02/04/75	961	11:37	RANSOM Lee	PAYNE Al	D1	1	
03/04/75	963		RANSOM Lee	PAYNE Al	HABU		A
03/04/75	963	12:32	RANSOM Lee	PAYNE Al	HABU	4.9	
04/04/75	961	10:30	SULLIVAN Jim	WIDDIFIELD Noel	D3	2.2	
05/04/75	971	12:00	SULLIVAN Jim	WIDDIFIELD Noel	HABU	4.2	
07/04/75	961		HELT Bob	ELLIOTT Larry	D1		A
09/04/75	971	11:00	HELT Bob	ELLIOTT Larry	D8	3.9	
10/04/75	963	11:20	RANSOM Lee	PAYNE Al	HABU	4.9	A
11/04/75	961	10:15	SULLIVAN Jim	WIDDIFIELD Noel	D1	0.9	
12/04/75	961	10:00	HELT Bob	ELLIOTT Larry	HABU	0.9	A
13/04/75	961	11:01	HELT Bob	ELLIOTT Larry	HABU	3.6	
15/04/75	971	09:30	SULLIVAN Jim	WIDDIFIELD Noel	HABU	4.4	
16/04/75	963	11:30	SULLIVAN Jim	WIDDIFIELD Noel	HABU	3.5	
17/04/75	971	10:15	RANSOM Lee	PAYNE Al	HABU	1	A
17/04/75	963	11:35	HELT Bob	ELLIOTT Larry	HABU	3.5	
19/04/75	963		RANSOM Lee	PAYNE Al	HABU		A
19/04/75	971	11:20	RANSOM Lee	PAYNE Al	HABU	0.9	A
21/04/75	963	10:00	RANSOM Lee	PAYNE Al	HABU	4.4	
22/04/75	961	10:33	CIRINO AL	LIEBMAN Bruce	D3	2.5	
23/04/75	963	09:30	CIRINO AL	LIEBMAN Bruce	HABU	0.6	A
24/04/75	961		CIRINO AL	LIEBMAN Bruce	HABU		A
24/04/75	961	10:50	CIRINO AL	LIEBMAN Bruce	HABU	4.4	
25/04/75	963	10:00	HELT Bob	ELLIOTT Larry	HABU	3.3	A
26/04/75	971	09:05	RANSOM Lee	PAYNE Al	HABU	4.5	
27/04/75	971	10:30	CIRINO Al	LIEBMAN Bruce	HABU	3.5	
27/04/75	963	22:40	HELT Bob	ELLIOTT Larry	RTB FERRY NITE	2	
28/04/75	971	09:50	RANSOM Lee	PAYNE Al	HABU	3.4	
29/04/75	961	10:09	HELT Bob	ELLIOTT Larry	HABU	3.4	
30/04/75	971	09:30	CIRINO Al	LIEBMAN Bruce	HABU	3.5	
06/05/75	963	10:20	BLEDSOE Pat	BLACKWELL Reggie	D3	2.2	
07/05/75	961	11:40	HELT Bob	ELLIOTT Larry	D4	2.3	
09/05/75	963	11:30	HELT Bob	ELLIOTT Larry	HABU	1.6	A
10/05/75	961	11:30	CIRINO Al	LIEBAMN Bruce	HABU	3.8	
11/05/75	971	10:30	CIRINO Al	LIEBAMN Bruce	D1	0.9	
11/05/75	971	08:30	HELT Bob	ELLIOTT Larry	HABU	4.2	
15/05/75	963	11:20	BLEDSOE Pat	BLACKWELL Reggie	D1	1.1	
17/05/75	963	09:30	KINEGO Joe	JACKS Roger	D1	1	
19/05/75	961	08:30	CIRINO Al	LIEBMAN Bruce	HABU	7.4	A,16
20/05/75	963	12:20	BLEDSOE Pat	BLACKWELL Reggie	HABU	5.1	
22/05/75	961	09:50	BLEDSOE Pat	BLACKWELL Reggie	HABU	4.1	
24/05/75	961	12:00	CIRINO Al	LIEBMAN Bruce	HABU	0.5	A
26/05/75	963	10:30	CIRINO Al	LIEBMAN Bruce	HABU	2.2	A
27/05/75	971	10:35	KINEGO Joe	JACKS Roger	D9	1.2	
28/05/75	961	10:30	CIRINO Al	LIEBMAN Bruce	HABU	2.4	A
30/05/75	963	11:01	KINEGO Joe	JACKS Roger	HABU	3.9	
02/06/75	971		RANSOM Lee	PAYNE Al	D9		A
03/06/75	963	11:00	BLEDSOE Pat	BLACKWELL Reggie	HABU	3.7	
03/06/75	971	11:40	RANSOM Lee	PAYNE Al	D4	2.4	
06/06/75	971		KINEGO Joe	JACKS Roger	D8		A
06/06/75	971	15:02	KINEGO Joe	JACKS Roger	D4	1.9	A
10/06/75	971	11:32	BLEDSOE Pat	BLACKWELL Reggie	D4	1.9	A
13/06/75	961	09:16	RANSOM Lee	PAYNE Al	D4	1.9	A
13/06/75	963	10:10	KINEGO Joe	JACKS Roger	HABU	5	
16/06/75	971	10:15	WILSON Jim	DOUGLASS Bruce	D3	2.6	
17/06/75	963	10:15	JOERSZ AL	MORGAN George	D4	2.4	
18/06/75	961		KINEGO Joe	JACKS Roger	D4		A
19/06/75	963	10:15	WILSON Jim	DOUGLASS Bruce	D6	2.4	
20/06/75	971	11:15	KINEGO Joe	JACKS Roger	HABU	2.4	
23/06/75	961	09:30	JOERSZ Al	MORGAN George	D8	1.7	A
24/06/75	963	09:30	KINEGO Joe	JACKS Roger	HABU	3.2	
24/06/75	961	13:30	WILSON Jim	DOUGLASS Bruce	D9	2.5	
25/06/75	971	10:15	JOERSZ Al	MORGAN George	D9	1.3	
27/06/75	961	12:27	JOERSZ Al	MORGAN George	D9	2.2	
30/06/75	971		MURPHY Jay	BILLINGSLEY John	D4		A
01/07/75	963	10:15	MURPHY Jay	BILLINGSLEY John	D3	2.3	
02/07/75	963	09:00	WILSON Jim	DOUGLASS Bruce	D4	2.3	
02/07/75	971	13:03	JOERSZ Al	MORGAN George	HABU	3.6	
03/07/75	971	11:53	WILSON Jim	DOUGLASS Bruce	HABU	3.5	
07/07/75	963		MURPHY Jay	BILLINGSLEY John	D9		A
07/07/75	963	11:30	MURPHY Jay	BILLINGSLEY John	D9	1.3	
09/07/75	961	10:15	MURPHY Jay	BILLINGSLEY John	D9	2.9	
11/07/75	971	10:00	WILSON Jim	DOUGLASS Bruce	HABU	3.7	
11/07/75	963	12:33	JOERSZ Al	MORGAN George	K9	2.7	
14/07/75	961	12:49	MURPHY Jay	BILLINGSLEY John	D8	1.7	A
16/07/75	963	11:59	WILSON Jim	DOUGLASS Bruce	D9	2.7	
17/07/75	971	13:00	MURPHY Jay	BILLINGSLEY John	HABU	2.2	
18/07/75	961	13:37	JOERSZ Al	MORGAN George	D9	2.4	
19/07/75	971	09:15	JOERSZ Al	MORGAN George	HABU	3.5	
21/07/75	971	09:26	MURPHY Jay	BILLINGSLEY John	D8	3.8	
22/07/75	961	10:18	WILSON Jim	DOUGLASS Bruce	D8	2.5	A
23/07/75	961	10:00	JOERSZ Al	MORGAN George	D8	4.1	
24/07/75	963		MURPHY Jay	BILLINGSLEY John	HABU		A
25/07/75	963		MURPHY Jay	BILLINGSLEY John	D1		A
25/07/75	963	13:00	MURPHY Jay	BILLINGSLEY John	D3	1	
28/07/75	961	10:10	MURPHY Jay	BILLINGSLEY John	HABU	4.2	A
30/07/75	961	11:20	HELT Bob	ELLIOTT Larry	HABU	3.6	
31/07/75	963	08:35	HELT Bob	ELLIOTT Larry	HABU	4.3	
01/08/75	961	11:15	SULLIVAN Jim	GERSTEN Mark	D4	2.4	
04/08/75	963	09:30	SULLIVAN Jim	GERSTEN Mark	HABU	1.4	A
08/08/75	961	11:14	SULLIVAN Jim	GERSTEN Mark	HABU	3.5	
13/08/75	971	12:51	ROSENBERG Maury	BULLUCH Don	D10	2.2	
14/08/75	963	12:00	HELT Bob	ELLIOTT Larry	D10	2.4	
15/08/75	963	09:30	HELT Bob	ELLIOTT Larry	HABU	3.8	
15/08/75	971	12:09	SULLIVAN Jim	GERSTEN Mark	D10	2.3	
22/08/75	961		ROSENBERG Maury	BULLUCH Don	D10		A
22/08/75	963	14:20	SULLIVAN Jim	GERSTEN Mark	D4	2.4	
24/08/75	971		SULLIVAN Jim	GERSTEN Mark	HABU		A
25/08/75	963	10:30	SULLIVAN Jim	GERSTEN Mark	HABU	2.1	A
26/08/75	963	10:30	SULLIVAN Jim	GERSTEN Mark	HABU	3.6	
26/08/75	961	13:15	ROSENBERG Maury	BULLUCH Don	D10	2.2	
27/08/75	971	11:18	CIRINO Al	LIEBMAN Bruce	HABU	3.8	
28/08/75	961	10:30	SULLIVAN Jim	GERSTEN Mark	D10	2.2	
29/08/75	971		SULLIVAN Jim	GERSTEN Mark	HABU		A
29/08/75	961	14:13	CIRINO Al	LIEBMAN Bruce	HABU	3.6	
02/09/75	961	10:00	ROSENBERG Maury	BULLUCH Don	D8	2.6	
03/09/75	961	10:35	SULLIVAN Jim	GERSTEN Mark	D4	2.5	
04/09/75	971	09:45	CIRINO Al	LIEBMAN Bruce	D8	4.2	
05/09/75	963		ROSENBERG Maury	BULLUCH Don	D10		A
05/09/75	963	16:01	ROSENBERG Maury	BULLUCH Don	D10	2.3	
08/09/75	963		BLEDSOE Pat	BLACKWELL Reggie	D10		A
08/09/75	961	09:50	ROSENBERG Maury	BULLUCH Don	HABU	3.5	
09/09/75	963	10:00	BLEDSOE Pat	BLACKWELL Reggie	D8	4	
09/09/75	971	10:45	CIRINO Al	LIEBMAN Bruce	D3	2.6	A
10/09/75	963	10:28	ROSENBERG Maury	BULLUCH Don	D8	3.8	
11/09/75	971	10:00	BLEDSOE Pat	BLACKWELL Reggie	D8	1.4	A
15/09/75	961	10:15	ROSENBERG Maury	BULLUCH Don	D8	4.2	
16/09/75	971	14:42	CIRINO Al	LIEBMAN Bruce	HABU	3.5	
17/09/75	961	10:30	BLEDSOE Pat	BLACKWELL Reggie	D8	4.1	

Date	Instal. No.	T.O. Time	Pilot Name	RSO Name	Mission	Duration	Remarks
19/09/75	961		CIRINO Al	LIEBMAN Bruce	D8		A
22/09/75	971	10:15	BLEDSOE Pat	BLACKWELL Reggie	HABU	4.9	
22/09/75	961	12:30	GRAHAM Rich	EMMONS Don	D5	3.6	
24/09/75	961	11:15	CIRINO Al	LIEBMAN Bruce	D8	2.5	A
26/09/75	961		GRAHAM Rich	EMMONS Don	D8		A
29/09/75	961		CIRINO Al	LIEBMAN Bruce	D5		A
29/09/75	961	14:47	CIRINO Al	LIEBMAN Bruce	D8	2.6	
30/09/75	971	11:00	GRAHAM Rich	EMMONS Don	HABU	3.6	
03/10/75	961	11:00	BLEDSOE Pat	BLACKWELL Reggie	D8	2.8	
06/10/75	971		BLEDSOE Pat	BLACKWELL Reggie	HABU		A
07/10/75	971	09:00	KINIGO Joe	JACKS Roger	D11	5.6	
09/10/75	961	10:10	BLEDSOE Pat	BLACKWELL Reggie	HABU	4.9	
10/10/75	971	09:38	GRAHAM Rich	EMMONS Don	D11	5.7	
13/10/75	971	10:07	GRAHAM Rich	EMMONS Don	HABU	3.5	
17/10/75	961	11:15	KINEGO Joe	JACKS Roger	HABU	1.9	
22/10/75	963		RANSOM Lee	PAYNE Al	D8		A
23/10/75	963	10:15	RANSOM Lee	PAYNE Al	D8	4.1	
28/10/75	971	10:15	GRAHAM Rich	EMMONS Don	D11	2.1	
29/10/75	963	12:30	RANSOM Lee	PAYNE Al	HABU	3.6	
30/10/75	961	11:00	KINEGO Joe	JACKS Roger	HABU	2.6	A
31/10/75	963	11:00	KINEGO Joe	JACKS Roger	HABU	1	A
31/10/75	961	12:15	RANSOM Lee	PAYNE Al	HABU	3.5	
03/11/75	971	10:14	WILSON Jim	DOUGLASS Bruce	D8	4.1	
05/11/75	961	11:10	WILSON Jim	DOUGLASS Bruce	HABU	3.8	
06/11/75	963	10:15	KINEGO Joe	JACKS Roger	D8	4.2	
07/11/75	961		RANSOM Lee	PAYNE Al	D8		A
12/11/75	971	11:00	KINEGO Joe	JACKS Roger	HABU	3.7	
14/11/75	963	10:15	RANSOM Lee	PAYNE Al	D4	2.5	
17/11/75	971	12:55	WILSON Jim	DOUGLASS Bruce	HABU	3.7	
18/11/75	963	12:00	MURPHY Jay	BILLINGSLEY John	HABU	3.8	
19/11/75	971		RANSOM Lee	PAYNE Al	D8		A
21/11/75	971	10:17	RANSOM Lee	PAYNE Al	D8	3.8	
24/11/75	963	10:15	WILSON Jim	DOUGLASS Bruce	D4	2.6	
26/11/75	971	10:15	RANSOM Lee	PAYNE Al	D8	3.9	
27/11/75	963	12:15	MURPHY Jim	BILLINGSLEY John	HABU	1.9	
01/12/75	963	09:31	JOERSZ Al	MORGAN George	D4	2.5	
04/12/75	963	10:00	WILSON Jim	DOUGLASS Bruce	HABU	2.6	
05/12/75	963	10:15	MURPHY Jay	BILLINGSLEY John	D8	4.1	
08/12/75	971	10:16	JOERSZ Al	MORGAN George	D8	4.3	
09/12/75	963	11:00	JOERSZ Al	MORGAN George	HABU	3.6	
10/12/75	971	10:15	WILSON Jim	DOUGLASS Bruce	D4	2.7	
12/12/75	963	11:00	MURPHY Jay	BILLINGSLEY John	HABU	5	
15/12/75	971	09:10	JOERSZ Al	MORGAN George	HABU	0.7	A
16/12/75	963	10:30	JOERSZ Al	MORGAN George	HABU	3.6	
16/12/75	971	12:05	ALISON Tom	VIDA Joe (J.T.)	D4	2.7	
18/12/75	963	10:00	ALISON Tom	VIDA Joe	HABU	3.6	A
20/12/75	963	07:00	MURPHY Jay	BILLINGSLEY John	HABU	3.8	
22/12/75	971	10:50	ALISON Tom	VIDA Joe	HABU	4.9	
29/12/75	963	10:04	JOERSZ Al	MORGAN George	D4	2.6	
30/12/75	971	09:30	ROSENBERG Maury	BULLUCH Don	HABU	3.6	
31/12/75	963	10:05	ALISON Tom	VIDA Joe	D4	2.5	
05/01/76	963	10:50	JOERSZ Al	MORGAN George	HABU	4.9	
08/01/76	971	09:30	ALISON Tom	VIDA Joe	HABU	3.7	
10/01/76	963	10:14	ROSENBERG Maury	BULLUCH Don	D4	2.5	
12/01/76	963	10:15	ROSENBERG Maury	BULLUCH Don	HABU	3.6	
14/01/76	961	14:04	ALISON Tom	VIDA Joe	D4	2.6	
17/01/76	963	12:15	HELT Bob	ELLIOTT Larry	HABU	1.1	A
20/01/76	971	11:42	ALISON Tom	VIDA Joe	HABU	3.5	A
21/01/76	971	10:03	ROSENBERG Maury	BULLUCH Don	D8	4.1	
23/01/76	961	11:30	HELT Bob	ELLIOTT Larry	HABU	3.7	
23/01/76	963	13:05	ROSENBERG Maury	BULLUCH Don	D7	1.7	
24/01/76	971	10:30	ROSENBERG Maury	BULLUCH Don	HABU	3.7	
27/01/76	961	11:00	BLEDSOE Pat	FULLER John	HABU	3.6	
29/01/76	963	12:40	HELT Bob	ELLIOTT Larry	HABU	4.3	
02/02/76	961	10:15	ROSENBERG Maury	BULLUCH Don	D4	2.7	
06/02/76	963	10:02	BLEDSOE Pat	FULLER John	HABU	4.8	
07/02/76	961	10:31	HELT Bob	ELLIOTT Larry	HABU	3.8	
10/02/76	963	11:30	CIRINO Al	LIEBMAN Bruce	HABU	2.4	
11/02/76	961	10:15	HELT Bob	ELLIOTT Larry	D4	2.6	
12/02/76	963		BLEDSOE Pat	FULLER John	HABU		A
13/02/76	963	11:22	BLEDSOE Pat	FULLER John	HABU	3.9	
16/02/76	971	10:56	CIRINO Al	LIEBMAN Bruce	D8	4.5	
18/02/76	961	11:50	HELT Bob	ELLIOTT Larry	HABU	3.7	
19/02/76	963	10:20	BLEDSOE Pat	FULLER John	D4	2.4	
20/02/76	971	09:10	CIRINO Al	LIEBMAN Bruce	HABU	1.3	A
20/02/76	961	10:10	BLEDSOE Pat	FULLER John	HABU	2	
23/02/76	961	10:17	GRAHAM Rich	EMMONS Don	D8	4.1	
24/02/76	971		CIRINO Al	LIEBMAN Bruce	HABU		A
24/02/76	961	11:30	GRAHAM Rich	EMMONS Don	HABU	3.6	
26/02/76	971	10:18	CIRINO Al	LIEBMAN Bruce	D4	2.6	
27/02/76	963	11:05	BLEDSOE Pat	EMMONS Don	D4	2.7	
27/02/76	961	12:30	CIRINO Al	LIEBMAN Bruce	HABU	3.7	
01/03/76	971		GRAHAM Rich	EMMONS Don	D4		A
02/03/76	961	10:30	BLEDSOE Pat	FULLER John	HABU	2.7	A
03/03/76	971	10:15	GRAHAM Rich	EMMONS Don	D4	2.6	
04/03/76	971	10:30	GRAHAM Rich	EMMONS Don	HABU	3.5	
08/03/76	971	10:15	CIRINO Al	LIEBMAN Bruce	D8	4	
09/03/76	971	10:00	CIRINO Al	LIEBMAN Bruce	HABU	2.4	
10/03/76	961	10:15	RANSOM Lee	PAYNE Al	D4	2.6	
12/03/76	961	11:00	GRAHAM Rich	EMMONS Don	SPECIAL-CAPSTAN DRAGON SNAPPER	1.9	17
15/03/76	971	10:18	CIRINO Al	LIEBMAN Bruce	D4	2.6	
17/03/76	961	10:50	GRAHAM Rich	EMMONS Don	HABU	3.6	
19/03/76	971		RANSOM Lee	PAYNE Al	D4		A
20/03/76	961	09:30	RANSOM Lee	PAYNE Al	HABU	4.8	
22/03/76	971	10:30	MURPHY Jay	BILLINGSLEY John	D4	2	A
23/03/76	963		GRAHAM Rich	EMMONS Don	D8		A
24/03/76	961	09:45	GRAHAM Rich	EMMONS Don	HABU	3.7	
25/03/76	963		RANSOM Lee	PAYNE Al	D8		A
25/03/76	963		RANSOM Lee	PAYNE Al	D8		A
26/03/76	963	11:47	RANSOM Lee	PAYNE Al	D4	2.4	
26/03/76	971	10:17	MURPHY Jay	BILLINGSLEY John	D4	2.3	
29/03/76	961	10:58	MURPHY Jay	BILLINGSLEY John	HABU	3.6	
30/03/76	963	10:19	GRAHAM Rich	EMMONS Don	D4	2.5	
02/04/76	971	14:05	RANSOM Lee	PAYNE Al	D4	1.7	A
05/04/76	961	10:22	KINEGO Joe	JACKS Roger	D4	2.4	
06/04/76	961	12:08	RANSOM Lee	PAYNE Al	HABU	2.1	A
07/04/76	963	10:15	WILSON Jim	DOUGLASS Bruce	D8	4.3	
08/04/76	971	13:05	WILSON Jim	DOUGLASS Bruce	HABU	2	A
10/04/76	971	11:30	KINEGO Joe	JACKS Roger	HABU	2.3	
12/04/76	961	11:46	RANSOM Lee	PAYNE Al	D8	2.3	A
13/04/76	963	10:16	WILSON Jim	DOUGLASS Bruce	D4	2.6	
14/04/76	971	10:48	KINEGO Joe	JACKS Roger	D8	4.2	
19/04/76	963	10:20	JOERSZ Al	MORGAN George	D4	2.5	
20/04/76	971	10:22	WILSON Jim	DOUGLASS Bruce	HABU	3.7	
22/04/76	963	10:25	KINEGO Joe	JACKS Roger	D4	2.5	
23/04/76	971	09:30	KINEGO Joe	JACKS Roger	HABU	3.5	
26/04/76	971	10:00	JOERSZ Al	MORGAN George	HABU	3.5	
27/04/76	961	10:42	WILSON Jim	DOUGLASS Bruce	D8	4.2	
28/04/76	963		KINEGO Joe	JACKS Roger	D4		A
28/04/76	963	11:20	KINEGO Joe	JACKS Roger	D4	2.5	
30/04/76	961	11:15	JOERSZ Al	MORGAN George	D4	2.5	
03/05/76	971	10:31	WILSON Jim	DOUGLASS Bruce	D4	2.5	
04/05/76	961	12:30	WILSON Jim	DOUGLASS Bruce	HABU	4	A
06/05/76	963	09:30	KINEGO Joe	JACKS Roger	HABU	0.8	A
06/05/76	971	10:37	JOERSZ Al	MORGAN George	HABU	4.6	
08/05/76	961	09:40	KINEGO Joe	JACKS Roger	HABU	4.9	
10/05/76	971	10:30	WILSON Jim	DOUGLASS Bruce	D4	2.6	
11/05/76	961	10:00	JOERSZ Al	MORGAN George	D4	2.3	
12/05/76	963	10:15	KINEGO Joe	JACKS Roger	D4	2.4	
17/05/76	971	10:15	MURPHY Jay	BILLINGSLEY John	D4	1.5	A
18/05/76	963	13:47	WILSON Jim	DOUGLASS Bruce	HABU	3.6	
21/05/76	963	10:15	JOERSZ Al	MORGAN George	HABU	1	A
24/05/76	963	10:15	JOERSZ Al	MORGAN George	HABU	3.1	A
25/05/76	961	10:01	WILSON Jim	DOUGLASS Bruce	D2	2.4	
26/05/76	971	09:45	MURPHY Jay	BILLINGSLEY John	HABU	3.9	
28/05/76	971		MURPHY Jay	BILLINGSLEY John	HABU		A
28/05/76	971	14:55	MURPHY Jay	BILLINGSLEY John	HABU	2.2	
01/06/76	963	10:17	ALISON Tom	VIDA Joe	D4	2.3	
02/06/76	961	11:15	ROSENBERG Maury	BULLUCH Don	D4	2.2	
03/06/76	971	10:15	ALISON Tom	VIDA Joe	HABU	3.8	
07/06/76	963	10:27	MURPHY Jay	BILLINGSLEY John	D4	2.3	
08/06/76	961	11:05	ROSENBERG Maury	BULLUCH Don	HABU	2.1	
09/06/76	971	10:17	ALISON Tom	VIDA Joe	D2	2.3	
10/06/76	961	13:00	ALISON Tom	VIDA Joe	HABU	2.2	
14/06/76	963	10:15	BLEDSOE Pat	FULLER John	D2	2.2	
15/06/76	971	11:30	ROSENBERG Maury	BULLUCH Don	HABU	3.7	
18/06/76	963	10:39	ALISON Tom	VIDA Joe	D4	2.3	
21/06/76	963	12:00	BLEDSOE Pat	FULLER John	D4	2.5	
22/06/76	971	09:30	ALISON Tom	VIDA Joe	HABU	3.6	
23/06/76	963	10:15	ROSENBERG Maury	BULLUCH Don	D4	2.6	
26/06/76	971		BLEDSOE Pat	FULLER John	HABU		A
26/06/76	963	12:57	ROSENBERG Maury	BULLUCH Don	HABU	3.6	
27/06/76	971	13:00	BLEDSOE Pat	FULLER John	HABU	2.4	
28/06/76	963		ALISON Tom	VIDA Joe	D11		A
29/06/76	963	12:15	ALISON Tom	VIDA Joe	HABU	3.9	
03/07/76	961	11:17	ROSENBERG Maury	BULLUCH Don	D4	2.4	
06/07/76	963	11:48	BLEDSOE Pat	FULLER John	D4	2.4	
07/07/76	971	10:15	ROSENBERG Maury	BULLUCH Don	HABU	3.6	
07/07/76	961	15:43	ALISON Tom	VIDA Joe	D4	2.2	
08/07/76	963	12:00	BLEDSOE Pat	FULLER John	HABU	2.2	
12/07/76	961	13:10	ALISON Tom	VIDA Joe	HABU	2.7	A
13/07/76	979	04:00	GRAHAM Rich	EMMONS Don	FERRY IN	5.3	
13/07/76	963	10:23	BLEDSOE Pat	FULLER John	D4	2.2	
14/07/76	971	06:00	ROSENBERG Maury	BULLUCH Don	FERRY OUT		
14/07/76	979	13:38	BLEDSOE Pat	FULLER John	HABU	2.3	
15/07/76	972	04:00	MURPHY Jay	BILLINGSLEY John	FERRY IN	5.1	
16/07/76	963	06:00	ALISON Tom	VIDA Joe	FERRY OUT		
16/07/76	961	06:42	MURPHY Jay	BILLINGSLEY John	D1	1.2	
20/07/76	976	04:00	CIRINO Al	LIEBMAN Bruce	FERRY IN	5.2	
20/07/76	979	13:30	GRAHAM Rich	EMMONS Don	HABU	3.7	
21/07/76	961	06:42	MURPHY Jay	BILLINGSLEY John	FERRY OUT		
21/07/76	972	10:15	BLEDSOE Pat	FULLER John	D4	2.3	
23/07/76	976	14:05	CIRINO Al	LIEBMAN Bruce	HABU	3.6	
26/07/76	976	13:15	GRAHAM Rich	EMMONS Don	HABU	3.8	
27/07/76	979	10:17	KINEGO Joe	JACKS Roger	D4	2.5	
29/07/76	972	10:45	CIRINO Al	LIEBMAN Bruce	D4	2.5	
30/07/76	976		KINEGO Joe	JACKS Roger	HABU	3	A
02/08/76	976	10:21	GRAHAM Rich	EMMONS Don	D4	2.5	
03/08/76	972	10:15	CIRINO Al	LIEBMAN Bruce	D4	1.9	A
05/08/76	976	11:50	KINEGO Joe	JACKS Roger	D4	2.4	
06/08/76	979	13:45	CIRINO Al	LIEBMAN Bruce	HABU	3.9	
11/08/76	979	11:03	GRAHAM Rich	EMMONS Don	HABU	3.6	
12/08/76	972	10:19	KINEGO Joe	JACKS Roger	D4	2.5	
13/08/76	976	10:15	CIRINO Al	LIEBMAN Bruce	D8	3.4	A
14/08/76	972	09:50	KINEGO Joe	JACKS Roger	HABU	3.7	
16/08/76	979	10:18	CIRINO Al	LIEBMAN Bruce	D4	2.3	
18/08/76	976	11:00	GRAHAM Rich	EMMONS Don	D1	0.9	
19/08/76	972	14:15	KINEGO Joe	JACKS Roger	HABU	2.4	
21/08/76	976	09:01	MURPHY Jay	BILLINGSLEY John	HABU	3.9	
23/08/76	979	08:00	GILMORE Bill	PAYNE Al	HABU	4	
26/08/76	976	13:00	KINEGO Joe	JACKS Roger	HABU	2.1	
28/08/76	979	10:00	MURPHY Jay	BILLINGSLEY John	HABU	3.3	
31/08/76	976	10:00	MURPHY Jay	BILLINGSLEY John	HABU	2.2	
03/09/76	976	10:30	GILMORE Bill	PAYNE Al	HABU	3.9	
04/09/76	979	09:30	JOERSZ AL	MORGAN George	HABU	3.5	

Date	Instal. No.	T.O. Time	Pilot Name	RSO Name	Mission	Duration	Remarks
07/09/76	972		GILMORE Bill	PAYNE Al	D8		A
07/09/76	976	10:00	MURPHY Jay	BILLINGSLEY John	HABU	4.2	18
11/09/76	979	10:31	GILMORE Bill	PAYNE Al	D4	2.3	
13/09/76	976	10:30	GILMORE Bill	PAYNE Al	HABU	2.4	
15/09/76	979	10:46	JOERSZ Al	MORGAN George	D3	2.3	
16/09/76	972	11:01	GILMORE Bill	PAYNE Al	D8	4.1	
17/09/76	979	13:30	JOERSZ Al	MORGAN George	HABU	3.5	
20/09/76	976	10:30	ALISON Tom	VIDA Joe	D8	4	
21/09/76	976	11:02	GILMORE Bill	PAYNE Al	D4	2.4	
22/09/76	972	11:00	GILMORE Bill	PAYNE Al	HABU	5.3	
23/09/76	976	09:30	ALISON Tom	VIDA Joe	HABU	2.2	
24/09/76	972	10:13	JORESZ Al	MORGAN George	D8	4.1	
27/09/76	979	10:25	GILMORE Bill	PAYNE Al	D5	3.7	
28/09/76	972	11:16	ALISON Tom	VIDA Joe	D5	3.6	
29/09/76	979	11:15	JOERSZ Al	MORGAN George	HABU	2.4	A
01/10/76	972	11:01	ALISON Tom	VIDA Joe	D8	4	
04/10/76	972	10:14	ROSENBERG Maury	BULLUCH Don	D8	4	
06/10/76	976	09:30	ALISON Tom	VIDA Joe	HABU	3.6	
07/10/76	972	11:10	JOERSZ Al	MORGAN George	D8	3.7	
12/10/76	976	10:00	JOERSZ Al	MORGAN George	HABU	3.5	
13/10/76	972	10:01	ROSENBERG Maury	BULLUCH Don	D8	4.1	
14/10/76	976	10:30	ROSENBERG Maury	BULLUCH Don	HABU	5.2	
15/10/76	972	11:00	ALISON Tom	VIDA Joe	HABU	3.7	
18/10/76	972	14:25	BLEDSOE Pat	FULLER John	D12	2.4	
19/10/76	976	10:00	ALISON Tom	VIDA Joe	D3	2.2	
21/10/76	972	10:30	ROSENBERG Maury	BULLUCH Don	D8	1.6	A
22/10/76	976	11:31	BLEDSOE Pat	FULLER John	HABU	2.5	A
25/10/76	979	10:00	ALISON Tom	VIDA Joe	D8	4.1	
26/10/76	972	14:00	ROSENBERG Maury	BULLUCH Don	HABU	4	A
27/10/76	979		BLEDSOE Pat	FULLER John	D8		A
28/10/76	979	10:34	BLEDSOE Pat	FULLER John	D3	1.6	A
29/10/76	972	14:30	ALISON Tom	VIDA Joe	HABU	3.8	
30/10/76	976	12:00	ROSENBERG Maury	BULLUCH Don	SAROO1	4.1	
02/11/76	972	11:10	BLEDSOE Pat	FULLER John	D3	2.6	
04/11/76	972	08:20	BLEDSOE Pat	FULLER John	HABU	4	
05/11/76	976	10:55	ALISON Tom	VIDA Joe	D12	1.8	A
08/11/76	979		ROSENBERG Maury	BULLUCH Don	D8		A
12/11/76	979	11:15	BLEDSOE Pat	FULLER John	D7	2.3	
13/11/76	972	09:45	GRAHAM Rich	EMMONS Don	D3	2.3	
15/11/76	972	11:00	BLEDSOE Pat	FULLER John	HABU	5.3	
16/11/76	979	09:25	CIRINO Al	LIEBMAN Bruce	D7	2.5	
18/11/76	979	10:46	CIRINO Al	LIEBMAN Bruce	HABU	3.9	
19/11/76	976	10:07	GRAHAM Rich	EMMONS Don	D12	2.4	
20/11/76	979		GRAHAM Rich	EMMONS Don	HABU		A
22/11/76	976	13:00	GRAHAM Rich	EMMONS Don	HABU	3.6	
23/11/76	979	11:30	BLEDSOE Pat	FULLER John	HABU	5.5	
27/11/76	976	09:30	CIRINO Al	LIEBMAN Bruce	HABU	3.6	
29/11/76	979	10:50	GRAHAM Rich	EMMONS Don	HABU	3.9	
30/11/76	972	11:10	KINEGO Joe	JACKS Roger	HABU	2.1	
03/12/76	972	12:00	CIRINO Al	LIEBMAN Bruce	HABU	3.6	
07/12/76	979	13:15	GRAHAM Rich	EMMONS Don	HABU	3.7	
11/12/76	972	10:30	KINEGO Joe	JACKS Roger	HABU	2.3	
13/12/76	979	10:20	CROWDER Bob	MORGAN John	D3	2.5	
15/12/76	972	11:15	GRAHAM Rich	EMMONS Don	HABU	3.5	
17/12/76	976		KINEGO Joe	JACKS Roger	D8		A
20/12/76	979	13:45	GRAHAM Rich	EMMONS Don	HABU	3.6	
21/12/76	976		CROWDER Bob	MORGAN John	D8		A
23/12/76	976	10:08	KINEGO Joe	JACKS Roger	D8	4.2	
24/12/76	972	10:12	CROWDER Bob	MORGAN John	HABU	3.9	
28/12/76	976	10:34	CROWDER Bob	MORGAN John	D8	4.3	
29/12/76	979	12:08	KINEGO Joe	JACKS Roger	HABU	2.8	A
30/12/76	972	10:10	CROWDER Bob	MORGAN John	D5	3.7	
03/01/77	976	11:00	KINEGO Joe	JACKS Roger	D4	2.7	
05/01/77	979	06:55	CROWDER Bob	MORGAN John	HABU	3.5	
07/01/77	972	11:08	MURPHY Jay	BILLINGSLEY John	D12	2.6	
10/01/77	979	09:58	JOERSZ Al	PAYNE Al	D8	2.2	A
11/01/77	976	11:00	CROWDER Bob	MORGAN John	HABU	3.6	
12/01/77	972	10:41	MURPHY Jay	BILLINGSLEY John	D3	2.4	
13/01/77	976	10:40	JOERSZ Al	PAYNE Al	HABU	3.5	
14/01/77	979	10:00	CROWDER Bob	MORGAN John	D11	6.1	
15/01/77	972	09:55	MURPHY Jay	BILLINGSLEY John	HABU	3.7	
17/01/77	972	12:30	CROWDER Bob	MORGAN John	HABU	4	
20/01/77	976	11:00	MURPHY Jay	BILLINGSLEY John	D8	2.3	A
21/01/77	979	13:15	JOERSZ Al	PAYNE Al	HABU	4	
24/01/77	972	10:59	ROSENBERG Maury	BULLUCH Don	D3	2.3	
26/01/77	979	09:30	ROSENBERG Maury	BULLUCH Don	HABU	3.1	A
27/01/77	976	13:50	JOERSZ Al	PAYNE Al	HABU	3.8	
31/01/77	979	10:03	MURPHY Jay	BILLINGSLEY John	D8	4.2	
04/02/77	972	09:30	ROSENBERG Maury	BULLUCH Don	D2	2.4	
05/02/77	976	10:00	MURPHY Jay	BILLINGSLEY John	HABU	1.5	A
07/02/77	979	09:30	JOERSZ Al	PAYNE Al	D4	2.6	
08/02/77	976	11:02	MURPHY Jay	BILLINGSLEY John	HABU	4.1	
10/02/77	972		ROSENBERG Maury	BULLUCH Don	HABU		A
14/02/77	976	14:17	ROSENBERG Maury	BULLUCH Don	HABU	1.5	A
16/02/77	976	11:00	JOERSZ Al	PAYNE Al	HABU	2.3	
17/02/77	976	09:30	ROSENBERG Maury	BULLUCH Don	HABU	2.4	
18/02/77	979	10:00	CIRINO Al	LIEBMAN Bruce	P2	2.5	
19/02/77	976	09:10	ROSENBERG Maury	BULLUCH Don	HABU	4.2	
21/02/77	979	10:15	ALISON Tom	VIDA Joe	HABU	4	
22/02/77	976	13:15	CIRINO Al	LIEBMAN Bruce	HABU	2.3	A
24/02/77	979	10:00	ROSENBERG Maury	BULLUCH Don	HABU	3.7	
26/02/77	976	10:30	ALISON Tom	VIDA Joe	HABU	4	
28/02/77	979	10:00	ROSENBERG Maury	BULLUCH Don	P2	2.5	
01/03/77	976	09:10	ALISON Tom	VIDA Joe	P2	2.4	
03/03/77	979	12:00	ALISON Tom	VIDA Joe	HABU	3.6	
07/03/77	976	11:00	CIRINO Al	LIEBMAN Bruce	HABU	2.2	
08/03/77	972	10:37	BLEDSOE Pat	FULLER John	P8	3.6	A
09/03/77	979	09:52	BLEDSOE Pat	FULLER John	HABU	4.1	
10/03/77	972	09:45	CIRINO Al	LIEBMAN Bruce	P8	4.1	
11/03/77	976	11:03	ALISON Tom	VIDA Joe	P4	3.8	
15/03/77	979	12:22	CIRINO Al	LIEBMAN Bruce	HABU	2.7	A
17/03/77	976	10:30	BLEDSOE Pat	FULLER John	P2	2.3	
18/03/77	979	09:30	ALISON Tom	VIDA Joe	HABU	4.1	
21/03/77	972	10:20	CARPENTER Buzz	MURPHY John	P8	4.2	
22/03/77	976	10:15	BLEDSOE Pat	FULLER John	D8	1.8	A
23/03/77	979	11:30	BLEDSOE Pat	FULLER John	HABU	4.1	
24/03/77	972	13:02	ALISON Tom	VIDA Joe	P8	4.2	
25/03/77	976	10:30	CARPENTER Buzz	MURPHY John	D8	4.1	
28/03/77	979	11:36	CARPENTER Buzz	MURPHY John	HABU	4	
01/04/77	976	10:30	BLEDSOE Pat	FULLER John	P8	3.8	
04/04/77	972	11:00	GRAHAM Rich	EMMONS Don	P8	4.1	
05/04/77	979	09:30	BLEDSOE Pat	FULLER John	HABU	4.2	
06/04/77	972	10:30	CARPENTER Buzz	MURPHY John	P8	3.8	
08/04/77	979	13:00	CARPENTER Buzz	MURPHY John	HABU	4.2	
11/04/77	976	10:33	BLEDSOE Pat	FULLER John	P8	4.3	
12/04/77	972	11:00	GRAHAM Rich	EMMONS Don	P8	3.6	
14/04/77	976	10:16	CARPENTER Buzz	MURPHY John	D8	3.8	
16/04/77	972	09:05	GRAHAM Rich	EMMONS Don	HABU	4	
19/04/77	972	13:00	CARPENTER Buzz	MURPHY John	HABU	2.4	
19/04/77	976	09:30	KINEGO Joe	JACKS Roger	HABU	1.4	A
22/04/77	972	10:06	GRAHAM Rich	EMMONS Don	HABU	2.6	
22/04/77	976		KINEGO Joe	JACKS Roger	HABU		A
22/04/77	972		GRAHAM Rich	EMMONS Don	HABU		A
25/04/77	976	11:00	KINEGO Joe	JACKS Roger	HABU	2.5	A
26/04/77	972	12:00	GRAHAM Rich	EMMONS Don	HABU	2.5	A
29/04/77	976	09:20	KINEGO Joe	JACKS Roger	HABU	3.8	
02/05/77	979	10:12	CROWDER Bob	MORGAN John	D8	4	
03/05/77	972	10:13	GRAHAM Rich	EMMONS Don	P8	3.9	
04/05/77	976		GRAHAM Rich	EMMONS Don	HABU		A
06/05/77	979	09:20	GRAHAM Rich	EMMONS Don	HABU	4.1	
07/05/77	972	11:00	CROWDER Bob	MORGAN John	HABU	3.5	
10/05/77	976	09:45	KINEGO Joe	JACKS Roger	HABU	3.6	
12/05/77	976	14:15	CROWDER Bob	MORGAN John	HABU	4.3	
13/05/77	972	10:09	KINEGO Joe	JACKS Roger	FERRY TO GUAM	2.5	
					STATIC DISPLAY		
15/05/77	972	11:00	CROWDER Bob	MORGAN John	RTB FERRY	3	
17/05/77	979	10:30	MURPHY Jay	BILLINGSLEY John	P8	1.2	A
18/05/77	976	10:15	CROWDER Bob	MORGAN John	D8	4.1	
19/05/77	972	13:07	KINEGO Joe	JACKS Roger	P2	2.5	
21/05/77	976	14:00	KINEGO Joe	JACKS Roger	HABU	3.9	
23/05/77	972		MURPHY Jay	BILLINGSLEY John	D8		A
23/05/77	972	11:45	MURPHY Jay	BILLINGSLEY John	P8	4.1	
24/05/77	979	10:15	CROWDER Bob	MORGAN John	P8	4	
26/05/77	976	12:11	MURPHY Jay	BILLINGSLEY John	P2	2.3	
27/05/77	979	15:00	MURPHY Jay	BILLINGSLEY John	HABU	2.2	A
31/05/77	979	14:00	JOERSZ Al	BULLUCH Don	HABU	3.5	
01/06/77	976	10:45	CROWDER Bob	MORGAN John	D8	3.9	
03/06/77	972	10:30	MURPHY Jay	BILLINGSLEY John	D8	3.7	
04/06/77	979		CROWDER Bob	MORGAN John	HABU		A
04/06/77	979	11:05	CROWDER Bob	MORGAN John	HABU	1.8	A
06/06/77	972	11:00	MURPHY Jay	BILLINGSLEY John	HABU	2.4	
07/06/77	979		CROWDER Bob	MORGAN John	HABU		A
07/06/77	979	12:49	CROWDER Bob	MORGAN John	HABU	4	A
10/06/77	972	11:04	JOERSZ Al	BULLUCH Don	P7	2.1	
14/06/77	979	09:20	JOERSZ Al	BULLUCH Don	HABU	3.8	
15/06/77	972	10:15	ROSENBERG Maury	PAYNE Al	P7	2.3	
17/06/77	979	10:05	MURPHY Jay	BILLINGSLEY John	HABU	2.6	A
23/06/77	972	11:00	ROSENBERG Maury	PAYNE Al	P13	2.5	
24/06/77	979	13:33	ROSENBERG Maury	PAYNE Al	HABU	4.1	
25/06/77	972	09:30	CIRINO Al	LIEBMAN Bruce	HABU	4.1	
27/06/77	979	13:39	ALISON Tom	VIDA Joe	HABU	2.5	A
27/06/77	976	12:44	CIRINO Al	LIEBMAN Bruce	P7	2.5	
27/06/77	979		ALISON Tom	VIDA Joe	HABU		A
30/06/77	976		ROSENBERG Maury	PAYNE Al	HABU		A
30/06/77	976	12:18	ROSENBERG Maury	PAYNE Al	HABU	3.9	
01/07/77	976	10:51	ALISON Tom	VIDA Joe	D13	2.5	
05/07/77	976	10:00	CIRINO Al	LIEBMAN Bruce	P8	4	
07/07/77	979	11:44	ROSENBERG Maury	PAYNE Al	D8	3.8	
07/07/77	979		ROSENBERG Maury	PAYNE Al	D8		A
08/07/77	976	07:00	CIRINO Al	LIEBMAN Bruce	HABU	2.3	A
11/07/77	976	14:00	ALISON Tom	VIDA Joe	HABU	3.8	
12/07/77	979	09:53	ROSENBERG Maury	PAYNE Al	D8	3.3	A
14/07/77	976	08:00	ALISON Tom	VIDA Joe	HABU	4.1	
15/07/77	979	10:00	CIRINO Al	LIEBMAN Bruce	P5	3.7	
18/07/77	972		ALISON Tom	VIDA Joe	D7		A
19/07/77	979	09:29	ROSENBERG Maury	PAYNE Al	HABU	4.1	
19/07/77	972	09:00	ALISON Tom	VIDA Joe	P1	1.1	
19/07/77	979		ROSENBERG Maury	PAYNE Al	HABU		A
21/07/77	976	10:07	CIRINO Al	LIEBMAN Bruce	P5	2.5	
23/07/77	976	09:15	CIRINO Al	LIEBMAN Bruce	HABU	4.3	
25/07/77	972	21:20	BLEDSOE Pat	FULLER John	N-D7	2.4	
27/07/77	972	13:00	CARPENTER Buzz	MURPHY John	HABU	4.2	A
28/07/77	976	10:09	CIRINO Al	LIEBMAN Bruce	D7	3.1	A
31/07/77	976	14:00	BLEDSOE Pat	FULLER John	HABU	2.3	
01/08/77	979	10:00	CARPENTER Buzz	MURPHY John	D4	2.5	A
02/08/77	976	09:33	CIRINO Al	LIEBMAN Bruce	HABU	1	A
04/08/77	976	14:58	BLEDSOE Pat	FULLER John	HABU	4.2	
05/08/77	972	13:07	CARPENTER Buzz	MURPHY John	HABU	2.5	
08/08/77	979	08:50	CIRINO Al	FULLER John	P4	3.5	
09/08/77	976	06:00	CIRINO Al	LIEBMAN Bruce	H/FERRY OUT		
10/08/77	960	04:00	ROSENBERG Maury	PAYNE Al	FERRY IN / HABU	5.5	
11/08/77	972	06:00	BLEDSOE Pat	FULLER John	FERRY OUT		
12/08/77	960	08:45	ROSENBERG Maury	PAYNE Al	D4	2.6	
12/08/77	975	04:00	GRAHAM Rich	EMMONS Don	FERRY IN	5	
13/08/77	979	06:20	ROSENBERG Maury	PAYNE Al	FERRY OUT		
14/08/77	967	04:00	KINEGO Joe	ELLIOTT Larry	FERRY IN	5.3	

Date	Instal. No.	T.O. Time	Pilot Name	RSO Name	Mission	Duration	Remarks
15/08/77	967	09:52	CARPENTER Buzz	MURPHY John	HABU	5.4	
18/08/77	967	10:18	GRAHAM Rich	EMMONS Don	HABU	4	
19/08/77	960	10:09	CARPENTER Buzz	MURPHY John	D4	4.1	
23/08/77	960	15:12	CARPENTER Buzz	MURPHY John	HABU	2.1	A
23/08/77	967		GRAHAM Rich	EMMONS Don	D4		A
24/08/77	975	10:00	GRAHAM Rich	EMMONS Don	D4	2.4	
25/08/77	975	09:26	KINEGO Joe	ELLIOTT Larry	HABU	2.2	A
27/08/77	975	12:32	CARPENTER Buzz	MURPHY John	HABU	4.2	
29/08/77	967	12:00	KINEGO Joe	ELLIOTT Larry	D4	4.4	
30/08/77	975	09:15	GRAHAM Rich	EMMONS Don	HABU	3.8	
02/09/77	967	10:48	KINEGO Joe	ELLIOTT Larry	HABU	3.8	
02/09/77	960	10:48	VETH Jack	KELLER Bill	D7	2.5	
07/09/77	960	09:30	GRAHAM Rich	EMMONS Don	HABU	2.4	
07/09/77	975	10:31	VETH Jack	KELLER Bill	D7	2.4	
12/09/77	967	10:23	KINEGO Joe	ELLIOTT Larry	D4	3.4	A
13/09/77	975	09:10	VETH Jack	KELLER Bill	HABU	3.8	
15/09/77	967	11:55	VETH Jack	KELLER Bill	D7	4.1	A
16/09/77	960	13:00	KINEGO Joe	ELLIOTT Larry	HABU	3.9	
19/09/77	960	21:05	VETH Jack	KELLER Bill	N-HABU	4.1	
21/09/77	960		CROWDER Bob	MORGAN John	D11		A
22/09/77	975	10:20	CROWDER Bob	MORGAN John	HABU	4.1	
23/09/77	960	10:03	KINEGO Joe	ELLIOTT Larry	D4	2.5	
23/09/77	967	09:53	VETH Jack	KELLER Bill	P13	2.1	
26/09/77	960	09:36	CROWDER Bob	MORGAN John	P11	6.3	
27/09/77	967	21:30	KINEGO Joe	ELLIOTT Larry	N-HABU	4.3	
29/09/77	960	12:18	VETH Jack	KELLER Bill	P11	5.9	
03/10/77	975	10:45	VETH Jack	KELLER Bill	HABU	4.3	
04/10/77	960	09:30	MURPHY Jay	BILLINGSLEY John	D4	2.5	
07/10/77	975	09:12	CROWDER Bob	MORGAN John	HABU	3.9	
11/10/77	967	09:15	VETH Jack	KELLER Bill	HABU	3.8	
12/10/77	960	06:50	MURPHY Jay	BILLINGSLEY John	D4	2.4	
14/10/77	967	09:05	MURPHY Jay	BILLINGSLEY John	HABU	4.2	
19/10/77	975	11:15	CROWDER Bob	MORGAN John	HABU	2.3	A
20/10/77	967	10:00	ROSENBERG Maury	PAYNE Al	D8	4.4	
21/10/77	975	10:15	MURPHY Jay	BILLINGSLEY John	D8	4.1	
22/10/77	967	10:40	ROSENBERG Maury	PAYNE Al	HABU	4.3	
25/10/77	975	18:30	CROWDER Bob	MORGAN John	N-D4	2.5	
27/10/77	967	14:00	ROSENBERG Maury	PAYNE Al	HABU	4.2	A
28/10/77	975	10:00	ALISON Tom	VIDA Joe	D8	3.3	A
01/11/77	967	10:15	MURPHY Jay	BILLINGSLEY John	HABU	2	A
03/11/77	967	14:00	MURPHY Jay	BILLINGSLEY John	RTB FERRY	1.8	
05/11/77	975	14:33	ALISON Tom	VIDA Joe	HABU	4.3	
07/11/77	967	09:58	ROSENBERG Maury	PAYNE Al	D4	2.3	
08/11/77	975	10:00	MURPHY Jay	BILLINGSLEY John	D8	2.4	A
10/11/77	975	09:53	ROSENBERG Maury	PAYNE Al	D4	2.5	
11/11/77	967	09:30	ROSENBERG Maury	PAYNE Al	HABU	3.4	
14/11/77	960	10:18	CARPENTER Buzz	MURPHY John	D8	3.4	
15/11/77	975	11:00	ALISON Tom	VIDA Joe	D8	4.6	
16/11/77	967	20:15	ALISON Tom	VIDA Joe	N-HABU	2.5	A
18/11/77	960		CARPENTER Buzz	MURPHY John	HABU		A
21/11/77	967	10:02	ROSENBERG Maury	PAYNE Al	D8	3.9	
22/11/77	960		CARPENTER Buzz	MURPHY John	P4		A
23/11/77	967	09:15	CARPENTER Buzz	MURPHY John	HABU	3.6	
23/11/77	960	14:45	ALISON Tom	VIDA Joe	P2	2.4	
25/11/77	960	20:00	ALISON Tom	VIDA Joe	N-HABU	2.3	
28/11/77	967	12:48	CARPENTER Buzz	MURPHY John	HABU	4.4	
29/11/77	960	10:00	GRAHAM Rich	EMMONS Don	P13	3.2	A
02/12/77	960	10:40	GRAHAM Rich	EMMONS Don	HABU	3.8	
05/12/77	967	12:19	ALISON Tom	VIDA Joe	D8	2.5	A
06/12/77	960	10:00	ALISON Tom	VIDA Joe	HABU	5.3	
08/12/77	967	10:24	CARPENTER Buzz	MURPHY John	D8	3.8	
10/12/77	960	11:02	GRAHAM Rich	EMMONS Don	GIANT BARNACLE	3.9	19
12/12/77	967	11:00	GRONINGER Bill	SOBER Chuck	GIANT BARNACLE	4.1	19
13/12/77	960	21:00	CARPENTER Buzz	MURPHY John	N-HABU	2.4	
15/12/77	975	10:06	GRONINGER Bill	SOBER Chuck	D8	3.2	
16/12/77	960	13:15	GRAHAM Rich	EMMONS Don	HABU	4	
19/12/77	960	11:15	GRONINGER Bill	SOBER Chuck	HABU	2.3	
20/12/77	975	10:14	CARPENTER Buzz	MURPHY John	P4	2.4	
22/12/77	960	19:00	GRAHAM Rich	EMMONS Don	N-HABU	2.4	
23/12/77	975	13:00	VETH Jack	KELLER Bill	P2	2.3	
28/12/77	975	14:45	GRAHAM Rich	EMMONS Don	D8	3.2	
28/12/77	960	12:03	GRONINGER Bill	SOBER Chuck	HABU	4	
03/01/78	975	13:16	VETH Jack	KELLER Bill	HABU	4.3	
06/01/78	967	08:56	VETH Jack	KELLER Bill	D4	1.4	
06/01/78	975	08:04	GRONINGER Bill	SOBER Chuck	SPECIAL MISSION	4.4	20
09/01/78	975	10:06	KINEGO Joe	ELLIOTT Larry	D8	4.3	
10/01/78	967	10:10	GRONINGER Bill	SOBER Chuck	HABU	2.5	
11/01/78	960	08:05	VETH Jack	KELLER Bill	D8	4.7	
13/01/78	960	10:00	KINEGO Joe	ELLIOTT Larry	D8	5.1	A
16/01/78	967	13:15	VETH Jack	KELLER Bill	D8	2	A
17/01/78	960	09:36	GRONINGER Bill	SOBER Chuck	D11	2.7	A
19/01/78	975	10:00	VETH Jack	KELLER Bill	P2	2.4	
20/01/78	967		KINEGO Joe	ELLIOTT Larry	HABU		A
20/01/78	967		KINEGO Joe	ELLIOTT Larry	HABU		A
20/01/78	960	14:30	CROWDER Bob	MORGAN John	P2	2.6	
23/01/78	960	09:40	KINEGO Joe	ELLIOTT Larry	HABU	4.1	
24/01/78	975	13:30	CROWDER Bob	MORGAN John	P2	2.6	
25/01/78	967	08:15	VETH Jack	KELLER Bill	HABU	4.1	
27/01/78	960		CROWDER Bob	MORGAN John	HABU		A
27/01/78	960		CROWDER Bob	MORGAN John	HABU		A
28/01/78	975	10:05	CROWDER Bob	MORGAN John	HABU	4.3	
30/01/78	967	09:15	KINEGO Joe	ELLIOTT Larry	HABU	3.7	
30/01/78	960		VETH Jack	KELLER Bill	D4		A
01/02/78	960	10:15	VETH Jack	ELLIOTT Larry	P2	2.8	A
03/02/78	967	10:15	CROWDER Bob	MORGAN John	HABU	2.4	
03/02/78	960	13:15	MURPHY Jay	BILLINGSLEY John	P2	2.8	A
04/02/78	975	10:30	KINEGO Joe	ELLIOTT Larry	D1	1.1	
06/02/78	975	20:33	KINEGO Joe	ELLIOTT Larry	N-HABU	2.3	
07/02/78	960	14:30	CROWDER Bob	MORGAN John	D4	2.6	
08/02/78	967		MURPHY Jay	BILLINGSLEY John	D3		A
09/02/78	967	10:15	MURPHY Jay	BILLINGSLEY John	D4	2.2	
10/02/78	960	09:30	KINEGO Joe	ELLIOTT Larry	HABU	4	
13/02/78	960	13:15	CROWDER Bob	MORGAN John	HABU	3.9	
14/02/78	960	10:33	KINEGO Joe	ELLIOTT Larry	D4	2.2	
18/02/78	975	18:00	CROWDER Bob	MORGAN John	N-HABU	2.4	
18/02/78	960		CROWDER Bob	MORGAN John	HABU		A
20/02/78	960	09:43	MURPHY Jay	BILLINGSLEY John	HABU	3.7	
23/02/78	975	16:15	ALISON Tom	VIDA Joe	HABU	2.3	
25/02/78	960	14:48	CROWDER Bob	MORGAN John	HABU	2.2	
02/03/78	960	16:30	MURPHY Jay	BILLINGSLEY John	N-HABU	2.3	
06/03/78	960	13:40	ALISON Tom	VIDA Joe	HABU	2.2	
11/03/78	960	19:00	MURPHY Jay	BILLINGSLEY John	N-HABU	0.9	A
12/03/78	975	19:00	ROSENBERG Maury	PAYNE Al	N-HABU	2.3	
14/03/78	960	21:30	ALISON Tom	VIDA Joe	N-HABU	2.4	
17/03/78	975	10:00	ROSENBERG Maury	PAYNE Al	HABU	3.8	
20/03/78	960	15:16	CARPENTER Buzz	MURPHY John	D4	0.9	A
22/03/78	975	11:25	ALISON Tom	VIDA Joe	HABU	4.1	
22/03/78	960	13:35	ROSENBERG Maury	PAYNE Al	D4	2.5	
24/03/78	975	11:30	CARPENTER Buzz	MURPHY John	D8	2.9	A
29/03/78	975	15:30	ROSENBERG Maury	PAYNE Al	HABU	4.1	
30/03/78	975	17:30	CARPENTER Buzz	MURPHY John	N-HABU	2.2	
03/04/78	975	18:30	CARPENTER Buzz	MURPHY John	N-HABU	1.9	A
05/04/78	967	12:15	THOMAS B.C.	REID Jay	D8	4.2	
06/04/78	975	13:15	ROSENBERG Maury	PAYNE Al	HABU	4.1	
07/04/78	967		CARPENTER Buzz	MURPHY John	D4		A
08/04/78	967	11:00	CARPENTER Buzz	MURPHY John	D4	1.2	A
11/04/78	975	10:10	CARPENTER Buzz	MURPHY John	HABU	3.7	
15/04/78	975	10:30	THOMAS B.C.	REID Jay	HABU	4.1	
18/04/78	967	10:35	GRAHAM Rich	EMMONS Don	P4	3.9	
20/04/78	975	13:16	CARPENTER Buzz	MURPHY John	HABU	2.4	A
21/04/78	967	11:00	GRAHAM Rich	EMMONS Don	HABU	3.9	
21/04/78	975	10:38	CARPENTER Buzz	MURPHY John	RTB FERRY	1.6	
24/04/78	967	12:55	THOMAS B.C.	REID Jay	D8	4.1	
24/04/78	960	15:30	CARPENTER Buzz	MURPHY John	D9	2.6	A
25/04/78	975	20:05	CARPENTER Buzz	MURPHY John	N-HABU	2.3	
27/04/78	967	13:35	GRAHAM Rich	EMMONS Don	D8	4.2	
28/04/78	960	07:30	THOMAS B.C.	REID Jay	HABU	3.9	
01/05/78	960	10:00	GRONINGER Bill	SOBER Chuck	D8	3.9	
02/05/78	967		GRAHAM Rich	EMMONS Don	HABU		A
03/05/78	960	10:27	THOMAS B.C.	REID Jay	D9	3.9	
04/05/78	967	09:05	GRAHAM Rich	EMMONS Don	HABU	4.1	A
08/05/78	960	14:00	GRONINGER Bill	SOBER Chuck	HABU	4.1	
09/05/78	967	14:00	THOMAS B.C.	REID Jay	D4	2.5	
11/05/78	960	10:00	GRAHAM Rich	SOBER Chuck	D8	3.9	
12/05/78	967		GRONINGER Bill	SOBER Chuck	HABU		A
13/05/78	967	08:30	GRONINGER Bill	SOBER Chuck	HABU	2.3	
15/05/78	975		VETH Jack	ELLIOTT Larry	D9		A
17/05/78	967	12:45	GRAHAM Rich	EMMONS Don	HABU	1.8	A
19/05/78	967	06:38	VETH Jack	KELLER Bill	HHQ GIANT BARNACLE	3.3	21
20/05/78	975	06:30	GRAHAM Rich	EMMONS Don	HABU	2.3	
21/05/78	967	11:08	VETH Jack	KELLER Bill	RTB FERRY	2.9	
22/05/78	967	11:20	GRONINGER Bill	SOBER Chuck	HABU	4.4	
25/05/78	967	21:13	VETH Jack	KELLER Bill	N-HABU	2.4	
30/05/78	967	11:25	GRONINGER Bill	SOBER Chuck	HABU	2	A
31/05/78	967	13:25	GRONINGER Bill	SOBER Chuck	HABU	3.6	
01/06/78	975	10:30	KINEGO Joe	KELLER Bill	D8	3.8	
02/06/78	967	09:30	KINEGO Joe	LIEBMAN Bruce	HABU	4.2	
06/06/78	967	13:45	VETH Jack	KELLER Bill	HABU	4.2	
08/06/78	975	13:05	KINEGO Joe	LIEBMAN Bruce	P4	2.6	
08/06/78	975		KINEGO Joe	LIEBMAN Bruce	P4		A
09/06/78	960	13:38	VETH Jack	ELLIOTT Larry	P4 / FCF COMPLETED	2.5	
12/06/78	975	10:00	CROWDER Bob	MORGAN John	D8	4	
13/06/78	967		KINEGO Joe	LIEBMAN Bruce	D5		A
15/06/78	960	10:30	KINEGO Joe	LIEBMAN Bruce	HABU	3.9	
16/06/78	975	10:30	VETH Jack	LIEBMAN Bruce	D8	4.3	
20/06/78	975	21:00	VETH Jack	KELLER Bill	N-HABU	2.4	
22/06/78	975	09:27	CROWDER Bob	MORGAN John	HABU	2.3	
23/06/78	975	11:40	KINEGO Joe	LIEBMAN Bruce	HABU	3.9	
26/06/78	960	11:54	KECK Tom	SHAW Tim	D8	3.9	
26/06/78	960		KECK Tom	SHAW Tim	D8		A
27/06/78	967	10:28	CROWDER Bob	MORGAN John	P4	5.7	
28/06/78	960	09:30	KECK Tom	SHAW Tim	HABU	0.7	A
29/06/78	960	09:51	KECK Tom	SHAW Tim	HABU	4.3	
30/06/78	975	10:00	KINEGO Joe	LIEBMAN Bruce	D3	2.5	
05/07/78	960	09:15	KECK Tom	SHAW Tim	D3	2.5	
06/07/78	967	21:25	CROWDER Bob	MORGAN John	N-HABU	2.3	
10/07/78	967	10:00	ALISON Tom	VIDA Joe	D8	3.8	
12/07/78	960	06:00	KECK Tom	SHAW Tim	HABU	4.3	
14/07/78	967	10:10	CROWDER Bob	MORGAN John	HABU	2.9	A
17/07/78	967	13:15	ALISON Tom	VIDA Joe	HABU	2.2	A
18/07/78	960	10:00	KECK Tom	SHAW Tim	D8	4	
21/07/78	967	14:44	KECK Tom	SHAW Tim	HABU	4.2	
24/07/78	960	18:31	ALISON Tom	VIDA Joe	HABU	1.1	A
26/07/78	967	07:15	ALISON Tom	VIDA Joe	HABU	3.9	
30/07/78	967	12:15	CARPENTER Buzz	MURPHY John	HABU	0.5	A
31/07/78	967	12:15	CARPENTER Buzz	MURPHY John	HABU	2.3	
01/08/78	960	09:27	KECK Tom	SHAW Tim	D8	3.2	A
03/08/78	960	14:55	ALISON Tom	VIDA Joe	HABU	3.7	
05/08/78	967	09:33	CARPENTER Buzz	MURPHY John	HABU	2.3	
07/08/78	960	09:15	THOMAS B.C.	REID Jay	HABU	3.8	
09/08/78	975		ALISON Tom	VIDA Joe	P4		A
10/08/78	975	14:20	ALISON Tom	VIDA Joe	D8	3.8	
11/08/78	967	13:16	CARPENTER Buzz	MURPHY John	D7	2.4	
14/08/78	975	10:35	THOMAS B.C.	REID Jay	FCF2	3.9	
18/08/78	975	04:02	CARPENTER Buzz	MURPHY John	HABU	4.1	

Date	Instal. No.	T.O. Time	Pilot Name	RSO Name	Mission	Duration	Remarks
21/08/78	975	09:16	THOMAS B.C.	REID Jay	HABU	2.8	A
23/08/78	975	11:24	GRAHAM Rich	EMMONS Don	HABU	3.6	
24/08/78	960	12:14	CARPENTER Buzz	MURPHY John	FCF2	2.7	A
24/08/78	960		CARPENTER Buzz	MURPHY John	FCF2		A
25/08/78	967	09:15	CARPENTER Buzz	MURPHY John	HABU	3.8	
28/08/78	967	10:34	GRAHAM Rich	EMMONS Don	D8	2.2	
28/08/78	960	12:35	THOMAS B.C.	REID Jay	D7	2.5	A
29/08/78	975	21:24	THOMAS B.C.	REID Jay	N-HABU	1.7	A
30/08/78	975	21:43	THOMAS B.C.	REID Jay	N-HABU	2.3	
01/09/78	967		GRAHAM Rich	EMMONS Don	HABU		A
05/09/78	975	21:04	GRAHAM Rich	EMMONS Don	N-HABU	2.2	
06/09/78	960	14:41	CROWDER Bob	MORGAN John	D8	2.5	A
08/09/78	960	11:30	CROWDER Bob	MORGAN John	HABU	4.2	
08/09/78	975	12:45	THOMAS B.C.	REID Jay	D1	1.2	
11/09/78	960	10:35	THOMAS B.C.	REID Jay	HABU	3.9	
12/09/78	975	10:35	GRAHAM Rich	EMMONS Don	HABU	2.3	
14/09/78	960	09:58	CROWDER Bob	MORGAN John	D4	2.5	
15/09/78	975	13:00	CROWDER Bob	MORGAN John	HABU	4.1	
18/09/78	960	12:53	GRONINGER Bill	SOBER Chuck	D8	4.2	
19/09/78	975	21:30	GRAHAM Rich	EMMONS Don	N-HABU	2.4	
20/09/78	960	13:00	CROWDER Bob	MORGAN John	FCF2	2.5	
22/09/78	975	04:30	GRONINGER Bill	SOBER Chuck	HABU	4.3	
25/09/78	960	09:40	CROWDER Bob	MORGAN John	HABU	3.7	
25/09/78	975	10:48	GRAHAM Rich	EMMONS Don	D1	1.2	
26/09/78	967	10:20	GRONINGER Bill	SOBER Chuck	FCF2	4.1	
28/09/78	975	14:45	GRONINGER Bill	SOBER Chuck	HABU	2.2	A
29/09/78	967	10:15	CROWDER Bob	MORGAN John	D8	4	
02/10/78	967	13:04	CROWDER Bob	MORGAN John	HABU	2.3	
04/10/78	967	09:01	VETH Jack	KELLER Bill	HABU	4.3	
05/10/78	975	10:15	VETH Jack	KELLER Bill	D8	4.2	
06/10/78	967	10:00	CROWDER Bob	MORGAN John	HABU	2.4	
10/10/78	975	13:48	VETH Jack	KELLER Bill	HABU	1.1	A
10/10/78	967	14:19	CROWDER Bob	MORGAN John	HABU	4.4	
12/10/78	960		VETH Jack	KELLER Bill	D7		A
16/10/78	960	13:29	KECK Tom	SHAW Tim	D1	1	
16/10/78	967	11:15	GRONINGER Bill	SOBER Chuck	HABU	2.4	
17/10/78	967	19:45	VETH Jack	KELLER Bill	N-HABU	2.3	
19/10/78	967	07:10	KECK Tom	SHAW Tim	HABU	1.4	A
20/10/78	967	15:00	KECK Tom	SHAW Tim	HABU	3.9	
22/10/78	960	12:10	GRONINGER Bill	SOBER Chuck	HABU	1.4	A
24/10/78	960	21:00	VETH Jack	KELLER Bill	N-HABU	2	A
25/10/78	967	21:15	VETH Jack	KELLER Bill	N-HABU	2.3	
26/10/78	960	12:00	GRONINGER Bill	SOBER Chuck	HABU	1.4	
28/10/78	960	10:15	KECK Tom	SHAW Tim	HABU	1.3	A
30/10/78	967	07:10	KECK Tom	SHAW Tim	HABU	4.3	
31/10/78	960	12:15	VETH Jack	KELLER Bill	HABU	0.9	A
01/11/78	967	21:45	VETH Jack	KELLER Bill	N-HABU	2.3	
03/11/78	967	10:10	KINEGO Joe	LIEBMAN Bruce	HABU	4.1	
03/11/78	975	13:19	KECK Tom	SHAW Tim	D4	2.6	
06/11/78	960	14:21	KECK Tom	SHAW Tim	HABU	4.4	
08/11/78	967	06:00	VETH Jack	KELLER Bill	HABU	2.5	
09/11/78	960	13:00	KINEGO Joe	LIEBMAN Bruce	FCF2	4.2	
11/11/78	960	07:00	KINEGO Joe	LIEBMAN Bruce	HABU	4.4	
13/11/78	960	09:31	KECK Tom	SHAW Tim	HABU	1.4	
14/11/78	975	10:04	PETERS Dave	BETHART Ed	D4	1.4	A
15/11/78	960	09:05	PETERS Dave	BETHART Ed	HABU	4.1	
16/11/78	960	20:20	KINEGO Joe	LIEBMAN Bruce	N-HABU	3.2	A
17/11/78	975	13:00	KECK Tom	SHAW Tim	D8	3.4	A
20/11/78	967	13:00	KECK Tom	SHAW Tim	HABU	4.2	
21/11/78	975	21:30	KINEGO Joe	LIEBMAN Bruce	N-HABU	2.3	
27/11/78	967	11:15	PETERS Dave	BETHART Ed	HABU	4.1	A
28/11/78	975	10:02	CARPENTER Buzz	MURPHY John	D2	2.2	
29/11/78	967	10:43	PETERS Dave	BETHART Ed	RTB FERRY	1.9	
30/11/78	967	10:30	KINEGO Joe	LIEBMAN Bruce	HABU	2.4	A
01/12/78	975	10:05	CARPENTER Buzz	MURPHY John	D8	4.1	
04/12/78	975	11:45	CARPENTER Buzz	MURPHY John	HABU	4.3	A
05/12/78	967		PETERS Dave	BETHART Ed	HABU		A
06/12/78	975		CARPENTER Buzz	MURPHY John	RTB FERRY		A
07/12/78	975	11:22	CARPENTER Buzz	MURPHY John	RTB FERRY	1.8	
09/12/78	975	11:10	CARPENTER Buzz	MURPHY John	HABU	2.2	A
11/12/78	967	12:40	ALISON Tom	VIDA Joe	HABU	2.9	A
11/12/78	960	14:44	CARPENTER Buzz	BETHART Ed	P2	2.2	A
13/12/78	960	09:58	CARPENTER Buzz	MURPHY John	FCF2	2.4	
13/12/78	967	14:47	ALISON Tom	VIDA Joe	RTB FERRY	1.6	
14/12/78	960	11:01	CARPENTER Buzz	MURPHY John	HABU	2.3	
15/12/78	967	12:00	ALISON Tom	VIDA Joe	HABU	1.2	A
16/12/78	967	11:15	ALISON Tom	VIDA Joe	HABU	4.2	
19/12/78	967	19:45	CARPENTER Buzz	MURPHY John	N-HABU	2.4	
20/12/78	960	15:08	PETERS Dave	BETHART Ed	FCF2	2.3	
20/12/78	960		PETERS Dave	BETHART Ed	FCF2		A
21/12/78	967	10:30	ALISON Tom	VIDA Joe	HABU	3.7	
27/12/78	960	13:19	CARPENTER Buzz	MURPHY John	HABU	1.4	A
28/12/78	960	10:04	CARPENTER Buzz	MURPHY John	HABU	4.3	
29/12/78	967	11:00	THOMAS B.C.	REID Jay	HABU	2.3	
02/01/79	975	10:31	CARPENTER Buzz	MURPHY John	FCF	2.6	
02/01/79	960	10:30	ALISON Tom	VIDA Joe	HABU	3.8	
04/01/79	960	14:10	THOMAS B.C.	REID Jay	HABU	2.4	
05/01/79	975	10:00	ALISON Tom	VIDA Joe	FCF	4	
06/01/79	960	09:11	ALISON Tom	VIDA Joe	HABU	1.4	
08/01/79	975	09:43	GRONINGER Bill	SOBER Chuck	FCF	4.1	
09/01/79	967	10:15	GRONINGER Bill	SOBER Chuck	HABU	2.3	A
11/01/79	960	19:10	THOMAS B.C.	REID Jay	N-HABU	2.4	
15/01/79	975	08:30	ALISON Tom	VIDA Joe	HABU	3.9	
17/01/79	967	13:45	THOMAS B.C.	REID Jay	HABU	3.1	A
17/01/79	960	12:55	GRONINGER Bill	SOBER Chuck	HABU	1.5	A
19/01/79	975	20:05	GRONINGER Bill	SOBER Chuck	N-HABU	2.3	
23/01/79	975	10:09	THOMAS B.C.	REID Jay	HABU	1.3	A
24/01/79	960	10:00	THOMAS B.C.	REID Jay	HABU	2.4	

Date	Instal. No.	T.O. Time	Pilot Name	RSO Name	Mission	Duration	Remarks
26/01/79	960	18:30	GRAHAM Rich	EMMONS Don	N-HABU	1.3	
30/01/79	960	09:16	GRONINGER BIll	SOBER Chuck	HABU	2.4	
31/01/79	967	11:10	THOMAS B.C.	REID Jay	HABU	2.4	
03/02/79	960	10:30	GRAHAM Rich	EMMONS Don	HABU	1.5	
05/02/79	960	19:00	GRONINGER BIll	SOBER Chuck	N-HABU	2.3	
07/02/79	960	13:15	GRAHAM Rich	EMMONS Don	HABU	3.6	
08/02/79	967	09:30	SHELTON Lee	MACKEAN Barry	FCF2	2.5	
09/02/79	967	08:33	SHELTON Lee	MACKEAN Barry	HABU	2.5	
12/02/79	960	20:16	GRONINGER Bill	SOBER Chuck	N-HABU	2.3	
15/02/79	967	10:30	GRAHAM Rich	EMMONS Don	HABU	2.4	
16/02/79	960	11:50	SHELTON Lee	MACKEAN Barry	HABU	4.1	
19/02/79	960	08:00	GRAHAM Rich	EMMONS Don	HABU	4	
22/02/79	967	09:28	VETH Jack	KELLER Bill	HABU	2.3	
23/02/79	967	13:42	SHELTON Lee	MACKEAN Barry	HABU	3.9	
23/02/79	960		SHELTON Lee	MACKEAN Barry	HABU		A
26/02/79	967	21:30	GRAHAM Rich	EMMONS Don	N-HABU	2.3	
27/02/79	967		VETH Jack	KELLER Bill	HABU		A
27/02/79	975	11:47	VETH Jack	KELLER Bill	FCF2	4.2	
02/03/79	967	13:10	SHELTON Lee	MACKEAN Barry	HABU	4.5	
05/03/79	975	10:11	KINEGO Joe	LIEBMAN Bruce	FCF2	4.3	
06/03/79	967	10:35	VETH Jack	KELLER Bill	HABU	4.2	
08/03/79	975	22:00	KINEGO Joe	LIEBMAN Bruce	N-HABU	2.1	A
10/03/79	960	12:00	SHELTON Lee	MACKEAN Barry	HABU	2.1	A
12/03/79	975	10:00	VETH Jack	KELLER Bill	FCF2	2.2	
13/03/79	960	09:10	VETH Jack	KELLER Bill	HABU	4.1	
16/03/79	960	23:30	KINEGO Joe	LIEBMAN Bruce	N-HABU	2.4	
20/03/79	960	10:15	VETH Jack	KELLER Bill	HABU	2.4	
22/03/79	960	19:45	CROWDER Bob	MORGAN John	N-HABU	2.4	
24/03/79	975	11:30	KINEGO Joe	LIEBMAN Bruce	HABU	3.9	
25/03/79	960	10:00	VETH Jack	KELLER Bill	HABU	0.5	A
25/03/79	960	12:14	VETH Jack	KELLER Bill	HABU	1.6	A
27/03/79	975	10:15	CROWDER BOb	MORGAN John	HABU	2.3	
30/03/79	960	09:10	KINEGO Joe	LIEBMAN Bruce	HABU	4.2	
02/04/79	975	18:05	CROWDER Bob	MORGAN John	N-HABU	2.3	
04/04/79	967		KECK Tom	SHAW Tim	HABU		A
05/04/79	960	09:10	KECK Tom	SHAW Tim	HABU	1.4	
06/04/79	967	16:00	KINEGO Joe	LIEBMAN Bruce	HABU	2.2	A
10/04/79	975	12:45	CROWDER Bob	MORGAN John	HABU	4.1	
11/04/79	967		KECK Tom	SHAW Tim	FCF2		A
11/04/79	967	10:05	KECK Tom	SHAW Tim	FCF2	4	
12/04/79	960	19:30	KECK Tom	SHAW Tim	N-HABU	2.5	
14/04/79	967	09:30	CROWDER Bob	MORGAN John	HABU	4.4	
16/04/79	975	21:45	PETERS Dave	BETHART Ed	N-HABU	2.2	A
18/04/79	960	10:55	KECK Tom	SHAW Tim	HABU	4.1	
20/04/79	975	10:21	CROWDER Bob	MORGAN John	HABU	2.3	
20/04/79	975		CROWDER Bob	MORGAN John	HABU		A
23/04/79	975	23:30	PETERS Dave	BETHART Ed	N-HABU	2.2	
27/04/79	967	13:47	KECK Tom	SHAW Tim	HABU	4.1	
28/04/79	960	10:35	PETERS Dave	BETHART Ed	HABU	1.4	A
30/04/79	967	12:09	ALISON Tom	VIDA Joe	FCF2	3.8	
02/05/79	975	09:40	KECK Tom	SHAW Tim	HABU	2.4	A
03/05/79	960		PETERS Dave	BETHART Ed	D4		A
04/05/79	960	16:31	PETERS Dave	BETHART Ed	FCF1	2.3	A
04/05/79	967	16:30	ALISON Tom	VIDA Joe	HABU	2.3	A
07/05/79	967	09:05	KECK Tom	SHAW Tim	HABU	4.1	
10/05/79	975	10:30	ALISON Tom	VIDA Joe	D1	1.2	
11/05/79	967	08:00	PETERS Dave	BETHART Ed	HABU	1.2	A
12/05/79	960	10:00	ALISON Tom	VIDA Joe	HABU	2.3	
14/05/79	967		PETERS Dave	BETHART Ed	HABU		A
15/05/79	975	13:00	ALISON Tom	VIDA Joe	D8	4.1	
16/05/79	960	19:30	PETERS Dave	BETHART Ed	N-HABU	2.3	
18/05/79	975	11:43	CARPENTER Buzz	MURPHY John	HABU	3.8	
19/05/79	967	09:50	ALISON Tom	VIDA Joe	HABU	4.1	A
21/05/79	975	13:15	PETERS Dave	BETHART Ed	HABU	0.5	A
25/05/79	960	14:10	ALISON Tom	VIDA Joe	HABU	4.1	
29/05/79	967	20:10	CARPENTER Buzz	MURPHY John	N-HABU	2.3	
01/06/79	975	10:00	PETERS Dave	MURPHY John	FCF	2.3	
02/06/79	967	11:25	ALISON Tom	VIDA Joe	HABU	4.2	
04/06/79	960	17:15	CARPENTER Buzz	MURPHY John	N-HABU	4.1	
05/06/79	975		ALISON Tom	VIDA Joe	?		A
07/06/79	967	13:32	CARPENTER Buzz	MURPHY John	HABU	4	
09/06/79	975	09:05	CARPENTER Buzz	MURPHY John	HABU	4.1	
13/06/79	967	15:05	GRAHAM Rich	EMMONS Don	HABU	2.3	
15/06/79	975	09:05	GRONINGER Bill	SOBER Chuck	HABU	2.5	
18/06/79	967	14:11	CARPENTER Buzz	MURPHY John	HABU	4.4	
19/06/79	960	13:00	GRAHAM Rich	EMMONS Don	FCF	2.3	
20/06/79	975	11:10	GRONINGER Bill	SOBER Chuck	HABU	2.4	
22/06/79	962	02:00	SHELTON Lee	MacKEAN Barry	FERRY IN - H	6.7	
23/06/79	960	06:00	CARPENTER Buzz	MURPHY John	H-FERRY OUT		
25/06/79	975	09:30	GRAHAM Rich	EMMONS Don	HABU	4.1	
26/06/79	967	19:25	GRONINGER Bill	SOBER Chuck	N-HABU	2.3	
28/06/79	975	10:43	SHELTON Lee	MACKEAN Barry	HABU	4.1	
02/07/79	975	10:02	GRAHAM Rich	EMMONS Don	HABU	5.2	
05/07/79	962	20:20	SHELTON Lee	MacKEAN Barry	N-HABU	2.5	
09/07/79	967	14:09	GRAHAM Rich	EMMONS Don	HABU	4.2	
11/07/79	975		THOMAS B.C.	REID Jay	HABU		A
11/07/79	975	06:23	SHELTON Lee	MACKEAN Barry	HABU	1.4	
11/07/79	962	03:58	THOMAS B.C.	REID Jay	HHQ SPECIAL - NIGHT GLOBAL SHIELD	4.5	22
13/07/79	975	10:45	GRAHAM Rich	EMMONS Don	HABU	4	
16/07/79	975	18:45	SHELTON Lee	MACKEAN Barry	N-HABU	2.3	
19/07/79	972	02:00	KINEGO Joe	KELLER Bill	FERRY IN / HABU	6.4	
20/07/79	967	08:15	SHELTON Lee	MACKEAN Barry	HABU	2.3	
20/07/79	975	06:00	GRAHAM Rich	EMMONS Don	H-FERRY OUT		
24/07/79	962	00:13	THOMAS B.C.	REID Jay	N-HABU	2.3	
25/07/79	962	09:35	KINEGO Joe	KELLER Bill	HABU	2.2	
27/07/79	962	09:45	SHELTON Lee	MacKEAN Barry	HABU	3.8	
30/07/79	972	09:45	THOMAS B.C.	REID Jay	HABU	4.1	

Date	Instal. No.	T.O. Time	Pilot Name	RSO Name	Mission	Duration	Remarks
31/07/79	967	10:00	KINEGO Joe	KELLER Bill	FCF	2.3	
02/08/79	979	02:03	VETH Jack	MACHOREK Bill	FERRY IN / HABU	6.1	A
03/08/79	967	06:00	SHELTON Lee	MACKEAN Barry	FERRY OUT		
06/08/79	962		THOMAS B.C.	REID Jay	HABU		A
06/08/79	962	13:26	THOMAS B.C.	REID Jay	HABU	4.2	
07/08/79	972	19:50	KINEGO Joe	KELLER Bill	N-HABU	2.3	
10/08/79	962	10:45	VETH Jack	MACHOREK Bill	HABU	3.8	
11/08/79	979	08:30	THOMAS B.C.	REID Jay	HABU	2.4	
20/08/79	979	13:43	VETH Jack	KELLER Bill	FCF	2.2	
25/08/79	972	11:30	YOUNG Rich	SZCZEPANIK Russ	FCF	2.5	A
27/08/79	962	15:22	VETH Jack	MACHOREK Bill	HABU	4.1	
30/08/79	979	08:05	YOUNG Rich	SZCZEPANIK Russ	HABU	3.9	
31/08/79	962	20:05	VETH Jack	MACHOREK Bill	N-HABU	2.3	
03/09/79	972	10:05	YOUNG Rich	SZCZEPANIK Russ	HABU	2.6	A
05/09/79	962	10:25	ALISON Tom	VIDA Joe	HABU	2.3	
07/09/79	962	18:00	VETH Jack	MACHOREK Bill	N-HABU	2.2	
10/09/79	979	21:20	ALISON Tom	VIDA Joe	N-HABU	2.3	
11/09/79	972	13:30	VETH Jack	MACHOREK Bill	FCF	2.4	
12/09/79	962	12:15	YOUNG Rick	SZCZEPANIK Russ	HABU	3.2	A
14/09/79	979	09:10	ALISON Tom	VIDA Joe	HABU	4.1	
17/09/79	979	10:35	YOUNG Rick	SZCZEPANIK Russ	HABU	4	
18/09/79	979	22:30	KECK Tom	SHAW Tim	N-HABU	2.4	
19/09/79	972		ALISON Tom	VIDA Joe	FCF		A
20/09/79	962	11:10	ALISON Tom	VIDA Joe	HABU	3.7	
21/09/79	972	14:47	KECK Tom	SHAW Tim	FCF	2.5	
21/09/79	962	14:46	YOUNG Rick	SZCZEPANIK Russ	HABU	4.1	
24/09/79	972	10:15	ALISON Tom	VIDA Joe	HABU	3.5	A
01/10/79	979	11:30	KECK Tom	SHAW Tim	HABU	4.2	
03/10/79	972	19:40	ALISON Tom	VIDA Joe	N-HABU	2.3	
05/10/79	979	12:30	KECK Tom	SHAW Tim	HABU	2.3	
10/10/79	972	09:05	PETERS Dave	BETHART Ed	HABU	2.3	
11/10/79	972	13:45	ALISON Tom	VIDA Joe	HABU	3.8	
13/10/79	979	10:40	KECK Tom	SHAW Tim	HABU	2.2	
20/10/79	972	15:05	PETERS Dave	BETHART Ed	HABU	2.3	
22/10/79	962	13:59	KECK Tom	SHAW Tim	FCF	4.3	
22/10/79	979	20:02	GRAHAM Rich	EMMONS Don	N-HABU	2.3	
24/10/79	972	11:15	PETERS Dave	BETHART Ed	HABU	2.4	A
25/10/79	979	22:35	KECK Tom	SHAW Tim	N-HABU	2.4	
29/10/79	962	09:17	GRAHAM Rich	EMMONS Don	HABU	3.9	23
30/10/79	979	20:20	CARPENTER Buzz	SOBER Chuck	N-HABU	2.3	
05/11/79	972	19:25	PETERS Dave	BETHART Ed	N-HABU	2.4	
07/11/79	962	11:45	GRAHAM Rich	EMMONS Don	HABU	3.7	
08/11/79	979	10:45	CARPENTER Buzz	SOBER Chuck	HABU	2.4	
09/11/79	972	18:40	GRAHAM Rich	EMMONS Don	N-HABU	2.3	
13/11/79	962	07:40	CARPENTER Buzz	SOBER Chuck	HABU	2.4	A
14/11/79	972	19:05	GRAHAM Rich	EMMONS Don	N-HABU	2.3	
16/11/79	962	12:15	THOMAS B.C.	REID Jay	HABU	4.2	
21/11/79	979	15:10	CARPENTER Buzz	SOBER Chuck	N-HABU	4.8	
24/11/79	972	10:30	SHELTON Lee	MacKEAN Barry	HABU	2.2	
26/11/79	962	11:45	CARPENTER Buzz	SOBER Chuck	HABU	3.9	
27/11/79	972	20:10	SHELTON Lee	MacKEAN Barry	N-HABU	2.3	
29/11/79	979	14:50	CARPENTER Buzz	SOBER Chuck	HABU	2.4	
03/12/79	962	18:55	SHELTON Lee	MacKEAN Barry	N-HABU	2.3	
05/12/79	972	09:05	CARPENTER Buzz	SOBER Chuck	HABU	4.2	
10/12/79	979	11:00	SHELTON Lee	MacKEAN Barry	HABU	2.3	
12/12/79	962	07:55	THOMAS B.C.	REID Jay	HABU	4	
13/12/79	979	17:45	SHELTON Lee	MacKEAN Barry	N-HABU	2.3	
14/12/79	962	12:30	THOMAS B.C.	REID Jay	HABU	4	A
17/12/79	962	09:25	SHELTON Lee	MacKEAN Barry	HABU	4.3	
18/12/79	979	21:45	THOMAS B.C.	REID Jay	N-HABU	2.3	
20/12/79	962	12:30	THOMAS B.C.	REID Jay	HABU	2.3	
21/12/79	979	11:15	SHELTON Lee	MacKEAN Barry	HABU	2.3	
27/12/79	962	13:15	YOUNG Rick	SZCZEPANIK Russ	HABU	4.3	
29/12/79	979	08:21	SHELTON Lee	MacKEAN Barry	HABU	3.9	
03/01/80	962		YOUNG Rick	SZCZEPANIK Russ	N-HABU		A
03/01/80	962	21:30	YOUNG Rick	SZCZEPANIK Russ	N-HABU	2.5	A
04/01/80	972	15:30	SHELTON Lee	MacKEAN Barry	FCF-2	2	A
05/01/80	979		YOUNG Rick	SZCZEPANIK Russ	HABU		A
07/01/80	962	09:05	YOUNG Rick	SZCZEPANIK Russ	HABU	4.2	
09/01/80	979	11:10	ALISON Tom	VIDA Joe	HABU	4.2	
10/01/80	962	10:55	SHELTON Lee	MacKEAN Barry	HABU	2.3	
15/01/80	972		YOUNG Rick	SZCZEPANIK Russ	HABU		A
16/01/80	972	10:00	YOUNG Rick	SZCZEPANIK Russ	HABU	2.3	A
17/01/80	979	20:20	ALISON Tom	VIDA Joe	N-HABU	2.3	
19/01/80	962	10:20	YOUNG Rick	SZCZEPANIK Russ	HABU	2.7	A
21/01/80	962	10:00	ALISON Tom	VIDA Joe	HABU	2.3	A
22/01/80	962	19:05	KECK Tom	SHAW Tim	HABU	2.4	
24/01/80	962	10:46	YOUNG Rick	SZCZEPANIK Russ	HABU	2.3	A
25/01/80	962	14:30	ALISON Tom	VIDA Joe	HABU	3.8	
28/01/80	979	07:30	KECK Tom	SHAW Tim	HABU	3.9	
29/01/80	972	09:20	YOUNG Rick	SZCZEPANIK Russ	HABU	2.4	A
30/01/80	979	20:15	ALISON Tom	VIDA Joe	N-HABU	2.4	
01/02/80	979	10:50	KECK Tom	SHAW Tim	HABU	2.3	
01/02/80	972	10:51	YOUNG Rick	SZCZEPANIK Russ	FCF	1.2	A
04/02/80	962	19:00	KECK Tom	SHAW Tim	HABU	2.6	
05/02/80	972	15:00	ALISON Tom	VIDA Joe	FCF	2.3	
07/02/80	979	07:15	ALISON Tom	VIDA Joe	HABU	4.1	
09/02/80	972	07:35	PETERS Dave	BETHART Ed	HABU	2.5	A
11/02/80	979	09:55	KECK Tom	SHAW Tim	HABU	4.3	
12/02/80	962	22:45	ALISON Tom	VIDA Joe	N-HABU	2.3	
15/02/80	972	10:30	PETERS Dave	BETHART Ed	HABU	1.8	A
17/02/80	979	09:15	KECK Tom	SHAW Tim	HABU	5.9	
20/02/80	962	18:45	CROWDER Bob	EMMONS Don	N-HABU	2.3	
22/02/80	972	13:12	KECK Tom	SHAW Tim	HABU	4.1	
25/02/80	979	09:05	PETERS Dave	BETHART Ed	HABU	2.3	
25/02/80	972	09:06	CROWDER Bob	EMMONS Don	FCF	4.1	
27/02/80	972	12:10	KECK Tom	SHAW Tim	HABU	3.9	
28/02/80	962	11:36	PETERS Dave	BETHART Ed	HABU	2.1	A

Date	Instal. No.	T.O. Time	Pilot Name	RSO Name	Mission	Duration	Remarks
03/03/80	962	20:05	CROWDER Bob	EMMONS Don	N-HABU	2.3	
05/03/80	972	10:10	CARPENTER Buzz	SOBER Chuck	HABU	4.2	
06/03/80	962	15:50	CROWDER Bob	EMMONS Don	HABU	2.3	
10/03/80	972	07:50	CARPENTER Buzz	SOBER Chuck	HABU	4.2	
11/03/80	962	22:05	CROWDER Bob	EMMONS Don	N-HABU	2.4	
15/03/80	972	10:38	CARPENTER Buzz	SOBER Chuck	HABU	2.4	
17/03/80	962	18:50	CROWDER Bob	EMMONS Don	N-HABU	2.2	
18/03/80	979	13:00	THOMAS B.C.	REID Jay	FCF	4.3	
19/03/80	972	11:33	CARPENTER Buzz	SOBER Chuck	HABU	3.9	
21/03/80	979	08:40	CROWDER Bob	EMMONS Don	HABU	3.8	
24/03/80	972	11:30	THOMAS B.C.	REID Jay	HABU	4	
25/03/80	962	21:20	CARPENTER Buzz	SOBER Chuck	N-HABU	2.3	
27/03/80	979	11:00	CROWDER Bob	EMMONS Don	HABU	2.4	
28/03/80	962	22:00	THOMAS B.C.	REID Jay	N-HABU	2.4	
29/03/80	972	19:10	CARPENTER Buzz	SOBER Chuck	N-HABU	2.3	
31/03/80	979		KINEGO Joe	KELLER Bill	HABU		A
31/03/80	979	19:53	KINEGO Joe	KELLER Bill	N-HABU	2.3	
02/04/80	962	19:05	THOMAS B.C.	REID Jay	N-HABU	2.4	
04/04/80	972	10:35	CARPENTER Buzz	SOBER Chuck	HABU	1.4	A
07/04/80	979		CARPENTER Buzz	SOBER Chuck	HABU		A
07/04/80	979	13:44	CARPENTER Buzz	SOBER Chuck	HABU	0.5	A
08/04/80	979	19:49	CARPENTER Buzz	SOBER Chuck	N-HABU	2.4	
12/04/80	962	09:15	KINEGO Joe	KELLER Bill	HABU	4.1	A
14/04/80	972	10:46	THOMAS B.C.	REID Jay	HABU	4.4	
15/04/80	962	20:30	SHELTON Lee	MacKEAN Barry	N-HABU	2.4	
17/04/80	979	12:20	KINEGO Joe	KELLER Bill	HABU	1.9	A
19/04/80	972	09:51	THOMAS B.C.	REID Jay	HABU	2.5	
21/04/80	962	10:30	SHELTON Lee	MacKEAN Barry	HABU	2.4	
23/04/80	979	09:25	THOMAS B.C.	REID Jay	HABU	2.5	A
24/04/80	972	21:40	KINEGO Joe	KELLER Bill	N-HABU	2.2	
29/04/80	972	11:15	SHELTON Lee	MacKEAN Barry	HABU	4.4	
01/05/80	979	10:30	KINEGO Joe	KELLER Bill	HABU	2.3	
03/05/80	979	09:15	YOUNG Rick	SZCZEPANIK Russ	HABU	6	
05/05/80	962	10:00	SHELTON Lee	MacKEAN Barry	FCF	2.5	
06/05/80	972	18:30	KINEGO Joe	KELLER Bill	N-HABU	2.3	
07/05/80	979	19:15	YOUNG Rick	SZCZEPANIK Russ	N-HABU	2.3	
09/05/80	962	09:05	SHELTON Lee	MacKEAN Barry	HABU	2.6	
12/05/80	962	13:08	YOUNG Rick	SZCZEPANIK Russ	HABU	2.5	
13/05/80	972	21:05	ALISON Tom	VIDA Joe	N-HABU	2.3	
15/05/80	979	12.30	SHELTON Lee	MacKEAN Barry	HABU	2.4	A
19/05/80	962	11:15	YOUNG Rick	SZCZEPANIK Russ	HABU	4.4	
23/05/80	972	20:45	ALISON Tom	VIDA Joe	N-HABU	2.5	
28/05/80	979	09:30	YOUNG Rick	SZCZEPANIK Russ	HABU	2.4	
30/05/80	962	06:00	KECK Tom	SHAW Tim	HABU	4.3	
02/06/80	979	11:30	ALISON Tom	VIDA Joe	HABU	2.4	
04/06/80	962	11:09	YOUNG Rick	SZCZEPANIK Russ	HABU	2.3	
05/06/80	972	20:40	KECK Tom	SHAW Tim	N-HABU	2.4	
09/06/80	979	21:05	ALISON Tom	VIDA Joe	N-HABU	2.3	
11/06/80	962	19:55	PETERS Dave	BETHART Ed	N-HABU	2.3	
13/06/80	972	14:50	KECK Tom	SHAW Tim	HABU	4.1	
16/06/80	962	09:10	ALISON Tom	VIDA Joe	HABU	2.3	A
18/06/80	979	07:20	KECK Tom	SHAW Tim	HABU	3.8	A
19/06/80	962	20:50	ALISON Tom	VIDA Joe	N-HABU	2.3	
23/06/80	979	07.02	PETERS Dave	BETHART Ed	FCF	2.3	
24/06/80	972	09:23	ALISON Tom	VIDA Joe	H-FERRY OUT		
24/06/80	962	09:42	KECK Tom	SHAW Tim	H-FERRY OUT	1.3	
					AIR SPARE		
24/06/80	976	03:08	CROWDER Bob	EMMONS Don	FERRY IN-H	5.7	
26/06/80	979	12:10	PETERS Dave	BETHART Ed	HABU	1.1	A
28/06/80	976	12:00	KECK Tom	SHAW Tim	HABU	2.9	A
01/07/80	962	10:05	CROWDER Bob	EMMONS Don	SPECIAL	4.4	24
03/07/80	979		PETERS Dave	BETHART Ed	HABU		A
04/07/80	962	10:55	CROWDER Bob	EMMONS Don	SPECIAL RTB FERRY	4.9	25
05/07/80	979	12:00	PETERS Dave	BETHART Ed	HABU	2.3	
08/07/80	979	09:05	CROWDER Bob	EMMONS Don	HABU	4.1	
09/07/80	962	20:40	PETERS Dave	BETHART Ed	N-HABU	2.1	
10/07/80	976	12:00	BERTELSON Gil	STAMPF Frank	FCF	4.1	
11/07/80	979	11:10	BERTELSON Gil	STAMPF Frank	HABU	4	
14/07/80	976	08:10	CROWDER Bob	EMMONS Don	HABU	3.9	
15/07/80	962	21:50	PETERS Dave	BETHART Ed	N-HABU	2.2	
17/07/80	958	08:30	THOMAS B.C.	REID Jay	FERRY IN-H	6.5	
19/07/80	962	09:15	PETERS Dave	BETHART Ed	H-FERRY OUT		
21/07/80	979		BERTELSON Gil	STAMPF Frank	HABU		A
21/07/80	979	12:40	BERTELSON Gil	STAMPF Frank	HABU	2.3	A
23/07/80	958	10:10	CROWDER Bob	EMMONS Don	HABU	4.1	
24/07/80	976	20:00	THOMAS B.C.	REID Jay	N-HABU	2.2	
29/07/80	976	06:00	BERTELSON Gil	STAMPF Frank	HABU	4.2	
30/07/80	979	13:10	CROWDER Bob	EMMONS Don	HABU	2.4	
01/08/80	976	09:15	THOMAS B.C.	REID Jay	HABU	1.9	A
03/08/80	979	08:15	BERTELSON Gil	STAMPF Frank	HABU	6.2	
05/08/80	976	10:10	CARPENTER Buzz	KELLER Bill	HABU	3.8	
07/08/80	958	14:05	BERTELSON Gil	STAMPF Frank	HABU	4.1	
11/08/80	976	07:55	CARPENTER Buzz	KELLER Bill	HABU	3.9	
12/08/80	979	20:03	THOMAS B.C.	REID Jay	N-HABU	2.3	
14/08/80	976	10:42	BERTELSON Gil	STAMPF Frank	HABU	2.4	
19/08/80	958	11:19	CARPENTER Buzz	KELLER Bill	HABU	4.1	
20/08/80	979	21:10	THOMAS B.C.	REID Jay	N-HABU	2.2	
23/08/80	958	12:50	SHELTON Lee	MacKEAN Barry	HABU	2.3	
25/08/80	979	20:50	CARPENTER Buzz	KELLER Bill	N-HABU	2.1	
26/08/80	976	10:03	THOMAS B.C.	REID Jay	FCF	2.2	
29/08/80	979	12:13	SHELTON Lee	MacKEAN Barry	HABU	2.5	A
02/09/80	979	19:59	CARPENTER Buzz	KELLER Bill	N-HABU	2.3	
04/09/80	976	09:44	SHELTON Lee	MacKEAN Barry	HABU	2.4	
04/09/80	960	05:57	ALISON Tom	VIDA Joe	H-FERRY IN	6.2	
05/09/80	979	10:30	CARPENTER Buzz	KELLER Bill	H/FERRY OUT		
08/09/80	958	10:15	YOUNG Rick	SZCZEPANIK Russ	HABU	2.2	
12/09/80	976	14:00	SHELTON Lee	MacKEAN Barry	HABU	2.3	
16/09/80	960	08:00	ALISON Tom	VIDA Joe	HABU	4.2	

Date	Instal. No.	T.O. Time	Pilot Name	RSO Name	Mission	Duration	Remarks
17/09/80	958		YOUNG Rick	SZCZEPANIK Russ	HABU		A
18/09/80	958	21:10	YOUNG Rick	SZCZEPANIK Russ	N-HABU	2.4	
20/09/80	960	09:30	SHELTON Lee	MacKEAN Barry	HABU	2.3	
22/09/80	958	12:05	ALISON Tom	VIDA Joe	HABU	4.1	
24/09/80	976	08:20	YOUNG Rick	SZCZEPANIK Russ	HABU	0.4	A
25/09/80	960	19:10	YOUNG Rick	SZCZEPANIK Russ	N-HABU	2.3	
26/09/80	960	13:00	ALISON Tom	VIDA Joe	HABU	2.3	
29/09/80	958	10:10	YOUNG Rick	SZCZEPANIK Russ	HABU	2.3	
01/10/80	960	10:05	PETERS Dave	BETHART Ed	HABU	4	
02/10/80	976	22:35	ALISON Tom	VIDA Joe	N-HABU	2.4	
06/10/80	960	15:05	YOUNG Rick	SZCZEPANIK Russ	N-HABU	4.2	
10/10/80	976	12:05	PETERS Dave	BETHART Ed	HABU	2.3	
14/10/80	960	20:00	ALISON Tom	VIDA Joe	N-HABU	2.4	
16/10/80	976	14:02	PETERS Dave	BETHART Ed	HABU	2.3	
18/10/80	960	10:40	ALISON Tom	VIDA Joe	HABU	2.3	
20/10/80	960	10:15	PETERS Dave	BETHART Ed	HABU	2.4	
21/10/80	976	14:50	ALISON Tom	VIDA Joe	HABU	4.3	
23/10/80	976		PETERS Dave	BETHART Ed	N-HABU		A
25/10/80	976	11:00	PETERS Dave	BETHART Ed	HABU	2.3	
28/10/80	960	10:30	CROWDER Bob	MORGAN John	HABU	2.4	
29/10/80	976	12:43	JUDSON Rich	KELLY Frank	FCF	4.2	
30/10/80	960	20:15	CROWDER Bob	MORGAN John	N-HABU	2.3	
31/10/80	958	14:00	JUDSON Rich	KELLY Frank	FCF	3.9	
03/11/80	976	13:00	JUDSON Rich	KELLY Frank	HABU	4.2	
04/11/80	960	19:50	PETERS Dave	BETHART Ed	N-HABU	2.3	
06/11/80	976	11:05	CROWDER Bob	MORGAN John	HABU	4.1	
08/11/80	960	12:10	JUDSON Rich	KELLY Frank	HABU	2.3	
10/11/80	960	11:15	CROWDER Bob	MORGAN John	HABU	4.3	
13/11/80	960	11:15	THOMAS B.C.	REID Jay	HABU	2.5	
14/11/80	960	11:15	JUDSON Rich	KELLY Frank	HABU	2.4	
17/11/80	976	07:50	CROWDER Bob	MORGAN John	HABU	4.2	
18/11/80	960	21:05	THOMAS B.C.	REID Jay	N-HABU	2.3	
20/11/80	958	20:30	THOMAS B.C.	REID Jay	N-HABU	2.2	A
21/11/80	976	12:00	JUDSON Rich	KELLY Frank	FCF	2.5	
22/11/80	960	10:25	CROWDER Bob	MORGAN John	HABU	5.7	
24/11/80	976	10:30	THOMAS B.C.	REID Jay	HABU-S	5.8	26
25/11/80	976	21:20	BERTELSON Gil	STAMPF Frank	N-HABU	2.3	
26/11/80	958	12:00	CROWDER Bob	MORGAN John	FCF	1.7	A
28/11/80	958	13:10	THOMAS B.C.	REID Jay	HABU	4.2	
01/12/80	958	12:55	BERTELSON Gil	STAMPF Frank	HABU	1.2	A
02/12/80	958	11:43	CROWDER Bob	MORGAN John	HABU	4.2	
03/12/80	976	18:40	THOMAS B.C.	REID Jay	N-HABU	2.3	
05/12/80	960	10:35	BERTELSON Gil	STAMPF Frank	HABU	3.8	
09/12/80	958	07:51	THOMAS B.C.	REID Jay	HABU	2.3	A
10/12/80	976	15:10	PETERS Dave	BETHART Ed	HABU	1.9	A
11/12/80	976	15:10	BERTELSON Gil	STAMPF Frank	HABU	2.3	
12/12/80	958	12:08	THOMAS B.C.	REID Jay	HABU	2.3	
15/12/80	960	19:30	PETERS Dave	BETHART Ed	N-HABU	2.3	
17/12/80	958		BERTELSON Gil	STAMPF Frank	HABU		A
18/12/80	958	09:30	BERTELSON Gil	STAMPF Frank	HABU	4.2	
19/12/80	960	10:30	BERTELSON Gil	STAMPF Frank	HABU	4.1	
23/12/80	976	08:02	BERTELSON Gil	STAMPF Frank	HABU	3.8	
23/12/80	960	08:41	CUNNINGHAM Nevin	QUIST Gene	FCF	3.3	
27/12/80	976	12:00	CUNNINGHAM Nevin	QUIST Gene	HABU	4.2	
29/12/80	958	18:30	CARPENTER Buzz	SHAW Tim	N-HABU	2.4	
03/01/81	958	10:40	CUNNINGHAM Nevin	QUIST Gene	HABU	4.1	
05/01/81	976	15:17	CARPENTER Buzz	SHAW Tim	HABU	4.2	A
06/01/81	960	20:15	SHELTON Lee	MacKEAN Barry	N-HABU	2.4	
08/01/81	976	10:00	CUNNINGHAM Nevin	QUIST Gene	HABU	4.3	
10/01/81	958	12:00	SHELTON Lee	MacKEAN Barry	HABU	2.2	
14/01/81	960	10:00	CARPENTER Buzz	SHAW Tim	HABU	4.1	
15/01/81	960	08:05	CARPENTER Buzz	SHAW Tim	RTB FERRY	4.8	
15/01/81	976	14:05	CUNNINGHAM Nevin	QUIST Gene	HABU	2.3	
19/01/81	976	12:30	SHELTON Lee	MacKEAN Barry	HABU	4.2	
20/01/81	958	10:11	CUNNINGHAM Nevin	QUIST Gene	HABU	1.6	A
21/01/81	960	12:00	CUNNINGHAM Nevin	QUIST Gene	HABU	4.2	
22/01/81	960	21:00	ALISON Tom	REID Jay	N-HABU	2.5	
26/01/81	958	07:55	SHELTON Lee	MacKEAN Barry	HABU	2.3	A
28/01/81	960	10:40	CUNNINGHAM Nevin	QUIST Gene	HABU	3.9	
29/01/81	976	18:30	ALISON Tom	REID Jay	N-HABU	2.5	A
30/01/81	958	18:30	ALISON Tom	REID Jay	N HABU	2.2	
02/02/81	958	12:30	SHELTON Lee	MacKEAN Barry	HABU	3.9	
04/02/81	976	14:00	YOUNG Rick	SZCZEPANIK Russ	HABU	2.4	
06/02/81	958	09:10	ALISON Tom	REID Jay	HABU	4.2	
09/02/81	976	10:35	SHELTON Lee	MacKEAN Barry	HABU	3.9	
11/02/81	958	14:55	YOUNG Rick	SZCZEPANIK Russ	HABU	2.3	
13/02/81	958	19:55	ALISON Tom	REID Jay	N-HABU	2.4	
17/02/81	976	20:15	YOUNG Rick	SZCZEPANIK Russ	N-HABU	2.3	
19/02/81	958	13:19	ALISON Tom	REID Jay	HABU	3.9	
21/02/81	976	10:25	YOUNG Rick	SZCZEPANIK Russ	HABU	4	
23/02/81	976	19:30	ALISON Tom	REID Jay	N-HABU	2.3	
25/02/81	958	13:45	ALISON Tom	REID Jay	HABU	2.4	
27/02/81	958	07:45	YOUNG Rick	SZCZEPANIK Russ	HABU	4.2	
02/03/81	976	20:05	PETERS Dave	BETHART Ed	N-HABU	2	A
04/03/81	958	12:05	YOUNG Rick	SZCZEPANIK Russ	HABU	4.3	
05/03/81	960	09:30	PETERS Dave	BETHART Ed	FCF	2.2	
06/03/81	958	10:30	YOUNG Rick	SZCZEPANIK Russ	HABU	3.9	
09/03/81	958	21:00	PETERS Dave	BETHART Ed	N-HABU	2.4	
11/03/81	960	09:30	YOUNG Rick	SZCZEPANIK Russ	FCF	2.5	
12/03/81	976	06:45	JUDSON Rich	KELLY Frank	HABU	4.3	
14/03/81	976	12:05	JUDSON Rich	KELLY Frank	HABU	4.3	
16/03/81	960	13:00	JUDSON Rich	KELLY Frank	HABU	2.4	
17/03/81	958	22:00	JUDSON Rich	KELLY Frank	N-HABU	2.3	
20/03/81	960	08:30	PETERS Dave	BETHART Ed	HABU	1.5	A
21/03/81	960	08:30	JUDSON Rich	KELLY Frank	HABU	3.2	A
24/03/81	958	10:00	PETERS Dave	BETHART Ed	HABU	4.1	
26/03/81	960	11:55	JUDSON Rich	KELLY Frank	HABU	4.2	
27/03/81	958	10:30	JUDSON Rich	KELLY Frank	HABU	3.7	
01/04/81	958	09:05	CROWDER Bob	MORGAN John	HABU	4	
02/04/81	958	20:05	JUDSON Rich	KELLY Frank	N-HABU	2.3	
06/04/81	960	07:32	CROWDER Bob	MORGAN John	HABU	4.4	
07/04/81	958	10:10	JUDSON Rich	KELLY Frank	HABU	4.1	
09/04/81	960	13:45	CROWDER Bob	MORGAN John	HABU	3.7	
13/04/81	958	21:02	BERTELSON Gil	STAMPF Frank	N-HABU	2.3	
15/04/81	958	12:55	CARPENTER Buzz	SHAW Tim	HABU	4.2	
16/04/81	976	09:30	CROWDER Bob	MORGAN John	FCF	2.5	A
17/04/81	958	08:30	BERTELSON Gil	STAMPF Frank	HABU	4	
20/04/81	976	19:45	CARPENTER Buzz	SHAW Tim	N-HABU	2.3	
22/04/81	960	14:20	CROWDER Bob	MORGAN John	HABU	4.3	
25/04/81	976	09:55	BERTELSON Gil	STAMPF Frank	HABU	2.4	
28/04/81	960	12:50	CUNNINGHAM Nevin	QUIST Gene	HABU	2.2	A
29/04/81	960	12:50	CUNNINGHAM Nevin	QUIST Gene	HABU	4.1	
01/05/81	976	10:31	BERTELSON Gil	STAMPF Frank	HABU	2.4	
04/05/81	960	20:17	CUNNINGHAM Nevin	QUIST Gene	N-HABU	2.2	
06/05/81	976	09:05	CARPENTER Buzz	SHAW Tim	HABU	4	
07/05/81	960	13:40	BERTELSON Gil	STAMPF Frank	HABU	4.1	
11/05/81	960	19:45	CUNNINGHAM Nevin	QUIST Gene	N-HABU	2.3	
13/05/81	960	10:30	CARPENTER Buzz	SHAW Tim	HABU	4	
14/05/81	958	09:19	SHELTON Lee	MacKEAN Barry	FCF	3.8	
15/05/81	958	10:00	CUNNINGHAM Nevin	QUIST Gene	HABU	4.2	
18/05/81	976	11:45	CARPENTER Buzz	SHAW Tim	HABU	4.1	
19/05/81	958	20:15	SHELTON Lee	MacKEAN Barry	N-HABU	2.3	
22/05/81	960	09:55	CUNNINGHAM Nevin	QUIST Gene	HABU	3.9	
26/05/81	976	14:00	SHELTON Lee	MacKEAN Barry	HABU	1.1	A
27/05/81	976	14:30	SHELTON Lee	MacKEAN Barry	HABU	4.1	
29/05/81	958	09:30	ALISON Tom	REID Jay	HABU	5.8	
30/05/81	976	16:00	CUNNINGHAM Nevin	QUIST Gene	N-HABU	5.2	
02/06/81	958	10:30	SHELTON Lee	MacKEAN Barry	HABU	3.9	
04/06/81	960	09:15	ALISON Tom	REID Jay	HABU	2	
08/06/81	960	10:00	ALISON Tom	REID Jay	HABU	3.9	
09/06/81	976	14:00	SHELTON Lee	MacKEAN Barry	HABU	4.1	
11/06/81	958	20:15	YOUNG Rich	SZCZEPANIK Russ	N-HABU	2.3	
13/06/81	976	07:50	ALISON Tom	REID Jay	HABU	4.2	
15/06/81	958	19:45	SHELTON Lee	MacKEAN Barry	N-HABU	2.2	
17/06/81	960	09:15	YOUNG Rich	SZCZEPANIK Russ	HABU	4.1	
19/06/81	958	10:35	ALISON Tom	REID Jay	HABU	2.3	
22/06/81	958	21:10	ALISON Tom	REID Jay	N-HABU	2.3	
25/06/81	958	09:50	BERTELSON Gil	STAMPF Frank	HABU	4.1	
25/06/81	960	10:05	GLASSER Jerry	HORNBAKER Mac	FCF	4.2	
26/06/81	976	13:00	ALISON Tom	REID Jay	HABU	4.1	
29/06/81	976	14:00	GLASSER Jerry	HORNBAKER Mac	HABU	4.1	
02/07/81	960	08:00	BERTELSON Gil	STAMPF Frank	HABU	4.1	
06/07/81	958	12:05	GLASSER Jerry	HORNBAKER Mac	HABU	4	
07/07/81	960	20:30	BERTELSON Gil	STAMPF Frank	N-HABU	2.2	
09/07/81	958	10:00	PETERS Dave	BETHART Ed	HABU	4	
10/07/81	976	14:20	GLASSER Jerry	HORNBAKER Mac	HABU	4.1	
14/07/81	975	03:40	ROSENBERG Maury	McKIM E.D.	FERRY IN-H	6.3	
15/07/81	960	05:00	BERTELSON Gil	STAMPF Frank	H-FERRY OUT		
16/07/81	958	05:52	YOUNG Rich	SZCZEPANIK Russ	H-FERRY OUT		
16/07/81	976	05:58	GLASSER Jerry	HORNBAKER Mac	FERRY OUT AIR SPARE	1.2	
16/07/81	967	04:19	JUDSON Rich	KELLY Frank	FERRY IN-H	6.7	
20/07/81	975	21:00	PETERS Dave	BETHART Ed	N-HABU	2	A
23/07/81	976	10:00	GLASSER Jerry	HORNBAKER Mac	HABU	1.7	A
24/07/81	975	10:00	GLASSER Jerry	HORNBAKER Mac	HABU	3.6	A
24/07/81	976	12:00	ROSENBERG Maury	McKIM E.D.	FCF	3.9	
27/07/81	975	15:25	GLASSER Jerry	HORNBAKER Mac	RTB FERRY	1.5	
27/07/81	976	20:38	PETERS Dave	BETHART Ed	N-HABU	2.3	
29/07/81	976	10:15	ROSENBERG Maury	McKIM E.D.	HABU	3.9	
31/07/81	976	09:30	PETERS Dave	BETHART Ed	HABU	2.4	
03/08/81	975	20:45	JUDSON Rich	KELLY Frank	N-HABU	1	A
04/08/81	967	11:00	PETERS Dave	BETHART Ed	FCF	2.2	
05/08/81	975	09:18	ROSENBERG Maury	McKIM E.D.	HABU	2.1	A
06/08/81	975	17:00	JUDSON Rich	KELLY Frank	N-HABU	4.1	
11/08/81	967	07:40	PETERS Dave	BETHART Ed	HABU	4.2	
12/08/81	975	20:48	JUDSON Rich	KELLY Frank	N-HABU	2.3	
14/08/81	975	10:15	ROSENBERG Maury	McKIM E.D.	HABU	2.3	
15/08/81	967	20:00	JUDSON Rich	KELLY Frank	N-HABU	2.3	
17/08/81	975	09:30	CUNNINGHAM Nevin	QUIST Gene	HABU	4.2	
19/08/81	976	10:00	ROSENBERG Maury	McKIM E.D.	HABU	4	
20/08/81	967	14:00	JUDSON Rich	KELLY Frank	HABU	2.3	
24/08/81	975	12:00	CUNNINGHAM Nevin	QUIST Gene	HABU	1	A
25/08/81	967	10:00	CUNNINGHAM Nevin	QUIST Gene	HABU	4.2	
26/08/81	976	13:15	ROSENBERG Maury	McKIM E.D.	HABU	4.1	27
02/09/81	976		JUDSON Rich	KELLY Frank	HABU		A
02/09/81	967	11:00	CROWDER Bob	MORGAN John	HABU	2.4	
03/09/81	967	11:45	BERTELSON Gil	STAMPF Frank	HABU	0.9	
03/09/81	975	11:00	JUDSON Rich	KELLY Frank	HABU	4	
04/09/81	967	09:15	BERTELSON Gil	STAMPF Frank	HABU	3.5	A
08/09/81	967	12:00	CROWDER Bob	MORGAN John	HABU	2.9	
10/09/81	975	04:15	JUDSON Rich	KELLY Frank	N-HABU	2.3	
12/09/81	976	09:15	BERTELSON Gil	STAMPF Frank	HABU	2.3	
14/09/81	976	18:50	CROWDER Bob	MORGAN John	N-HABU	2.4	
16/09/81	976	11:10	CUNNINGHAM Nevin	QUIST Gene	HABU	3.9	
18/09/81	976		BERTELSON Gil	STAMPF Frank	HABU		A
18/09/81	967		CROWDER Bob	MORGAN John	HABU		A
21/09/81	976	19:25	BERTELSON Gil	STAMPF Frank	N-HABU	2.3	
24/09/81	967	08:55	CUNNINGHAM Nevin	QUIST Gene	HABU	1.4	
24/09/81	976	08:45	CROWDER Bob	MORGAN John	HABU	4.8	
28/09/81	975	10:00	BERTELSON Gil	STAMPF Frank	HABU	4.2	
29/09/81	976	16:05	CUNNINGHAM Nevin	QUIST Gene	HABU	2.4	
02/10/81	967	14:00	THOMAS B.C.	REID Jay	HABU	2.4	28
03/10/81	975	09:30	CUNNINGHAM Nevin	QUIST Gene	HABU	4	
05/10/81	967	13:00	BERTELSON Gil	STAMPF Frank	HABU	3.1	
08/10/81	975		THOMAS B.C.	REID Jay	HABU		A
09/10/81	967	10:15	THOMAS B.C.	REID Jay	HABU	2.2	
14/10/81	975	19:03	CUNNINGHAM Nevin	QUIST Gene	N-HABU	2.3	

Date	Instal. No.	T.O. Time	Pilot Name	RSO Name	Mission	Duration	Remarks
15/10/81	975	12:20	THOMAS B.C.	REID Jay	HABU	2.3	
19/10/81	975	13:05	CUNNINGHAM Nevin	QUIST Gene	HABU	2.3	
20/10/81	975	10:00	CUNNINGHAM Nevin	QUIST Gene	HABU	3.9	
23/10/81	975	11:00	THOMAS B.C.	REID Jay	HABU	2.5	
24/10/81	967	18:30	CUNNINGHAM Nevin	QUIST Gene	N-HABU	3.2	
26/10/81	975	08:12	THOMAS B.C.	REID Jay	HABU	4.2	29
27/10/81	975	08:30	YOUNG Rick	BETHART Ed	HABU	4.2	
02/11/81	975	08:00	THOMAS B.C.	REID Jay	HABU	3	
03/11/81	975		YOUNG Rick	BETHART Ed	HABU		A
03/11/81	967	08:00	THOMAS B.C.	REID Jay	HABU	4.3	
04/11/81	976	10:00	McCRARY Rick	LAWRENCE Dave	FCF	4.2	
05/11/81	967	08:30	YOUNG Rick	BETHART Ed	HABU	4	
09/11/81	976	18:45	YOUNG Rick	BETHART Ed	N-HABU	2.3	
12/11/81	967	09:30	McCRARY Rick	LAWRENCE Dave	HABU	4.2	
13/11/81	976	10:30	PETERS Dave	SZCZEPANIK Russ	HABU	1.7	A
15/11/81	976	10:25	PETERS Dave	SZCZEPANIK Russ	RTB FERRY	1.6	
16/11/81	967	07:12	YOUNG Rick	BETHART Ed	HABU	4.1	
17/11/81	976	07:05	McCRARY Rick	LAWRENCE Dave	HABU	1.8	A
17/11/81	967	08:01	PETERS Dave	SZCZEPANIK Russ	HABU	4.1	
20/11/81	976		McCRARY Rick	LAWRENCE Dave	HABU		A
20/11/81	967		PETERS Dave	SZCZEPANIK Russ	HABU		A
23/11/81	976	11:45	McCRARY Rick	LAWRENCE Dave	HABU	2.3	
24/11/81	967	09:56	PETERS Dave	SZCZEPANIK Russ	HABU	2.5	A
28/11/81	976	12:30	GLASSER Jerry	HORNBAKER Mac	HABU	2.4	
30/11/81	967	08:31	McCRARY Rick	LAWRENCE Dave	HABU	4.2	
01/12/81	976	18:15	PETERS Dave	SZCZEPANIK Russ	N-HABU	2.3	
03/12/81	967	23:00	GLASSER Jerry	HORNBAKER Mac	N-HABU	2.4	
07/12/81	976	10:30	PETERS Dave	SZCZEPANIK Russ	HABU	3.8	
08/12/81	967	13:00	ROSENBERG Maury	McKIM E.D.	HABU	4.1	
09/12/81	975	09:15	GLASSER Jerry	HORNBAKER Mac	FCF	3.8	
10/12/81	976	08:57	PETERS Dave	SZCZEPANIK Russ	HABU	4	
14/12/81	967	08:30	ROSENBERG Maury	McKIM E.D.	HABU	2.4	
15/12/81	976	12:00	GLASSER Jerry	HORNBAKER Mac	HABU	4.2	
17/12/81	975	09:01	ROSENBERG Maury	McKIM E.D.	HABU	3.9	
21/12/81	967	09:02	GLASSER Jerry	HORNBAKER Mac	HABU	3.9	
23/12/81	975	09:27	CROWDER Bob	MORGAN John	HABU	4	
29/12/81	967	10:02	GLASSER Jerry	HORNBAKER Mac	HABU	4	
30/12/81	975	18:30	ROSENBERG Maury	McKIM E.D.	N-HABU	2.3	
04/01/82	976	07:10	CROWDER Bob	MORGAN John	HABU	3.9	
06/01/82	967	10:47	SMITH Bernie	WHALEN Denny	FCF	4.2	
07/01/82	975	09:30	ROSENBERG Maury	McKIM E.D.	HABU	4.4	
08/01/82	976	12:05	SMITH Bernie	WHALEN Denny	HABU	4.4	
12/01/82	975	17:30	ROSENBERG Maury	McKIM E.D.	N-HABU	2.3	
14/01/82	967	07:20	CROWDER Bob	MORGAN John	HABU	4	
15/01/82	976	09:30	SMITH Bernie	WHALEN Denny	HABU	2.3	
16/01/82	967	10:30	CROWDER Bob	MORGAN John	HABU	3.8	
18/01/82	975	18:00	JUDSON Rich	KELLY Frank	N-HABU	2.3	
20/01/82	976	10:00	SMITH Bernie	WHALEN Denny	HABU	3.9	
25/01/82	975	08:15	CROWDER Bob	MORGAN John	HABU	2.4	
26/01/82	967	18:25	JUDSON Rich	KELLY Frank	N-HABU	2.3	
28/01/82	976	11:00	SMITH Bernie	WHALEN Denny	HABU	1.6	A
29/01/82	975	09:30	SMITH Bernie	WHALEN Denny	HABU	3.9	
01/02/82	967	10:02	JUDSON Rich	KELLY Frank	HABU	4	
02/02/82	975	18:45	THOMAS B.C.	REID Jay	N-HABU	2.3	
05/02/82	976	10:00	SMITH Bernie	WHALEN Denny	HABU	3.9	
08/02/82	975	20:00	JUDSON Rich	KELLY Frank	N-HABU	2.3	
10/02/82	967	07:45	THOMAS B.C.	REID Jay	HABU	2.3	
12/02/82	976	10:38	JUDSON Rich	KELLY Frank	HABU	3.7	
16/02/82	975	19:05	THOMAS B.C.	REID Jay	N-HABU	2.3	
19/02/82	975	10:18	JUDSON Rich	KELLY Frank	HABU	4.4	
20/02/82	967	10:10	BERTELSON Gil	STAMPF Frank	HABU	2.3	
22/02/82	976	08:30	THOMAS B.C.	REID Jay	HABU	4.2	
24/02/82	975	09:30	JUDSON Rich	KELLY Frank	HABU	4.3	
25/02/82	967	10:15	BERTELSON Gil	STAMPF Frank	HABU	2.4	
01/03/82	975	09:05	BERTELSON Gil	STAMPF Frank	HABU	1.7	A
02/03/82	976	10:01	CUNNINGHAM Nevin	QUIST Gene	HABU	4	
04/03/82	975	10:00	SHELTON Lee	KELLER Bill	HABU	4.1	
05/03/82	976	12:30	BERTELSON Gil	STAMPF Frank	HABU	4.3	
08/03/82	976	18:45	CUNNINGHAM Nevin	QUIST Gene	N-HABU	2.3	
10/03/82	976	15:00	SHELTON Lee	KELLER Bill	HABU	2.4	
12/03/82	976	11:45	BERTELSON Gil	STAMPF Frank	HABU	2.4	
16/03/82	976	14:40	CUNNINGHAM Nevin	QUIST Gene	HABU	4	
17/03/82	967	14:46	SHELTON Lee	KELLER Bill	FCF	3	A
18/03/82	976		BERTELSON Gil	STAMPF Frank	HABU		A
20/03/82	975		BERTELSON Gil	STAMPF Frank	HABU		A
20/03/82	975	13:15	BERTELSON Gil	STAMPF Frank	HABU	0.4	A
22/03/82	967	19:00	SHELTON Lee	KELLER Bill	HABU	2.3	
24/03/82	976	09:05	BERTELSON Gil	STAMPF Frank	HABU	4	
25/03/82	967	10:15	CUNNINGHAM Nevin	QUIST Gene	HABU	4.2	
29/03/82	976	06:50	CUNNINGHAM Nevin	QUIST Gene	HABU	2.3	
30/03/82	967	20:50	McCRARY Rick	LAWRENCE Dave	N-HABU	2.4	
01/04/82	976	09:15	YOUNG Rick	BETHART Ed	HABU	2.8	A
02/04/82	967	13:00	CUNNINGHAM Nevin	QUIST Gene	HABU	2.4	
05/04/82	967	09:20	McCRARY Rick	LAWRENCE Dave	HABU	4.1	
06/04/82	976	21:07	CUNNINGHAM Nevin	QUIST Gene	N-HABU	2.2	
09/04/82	976	12:40	McCRARY Rick	LAWRENCE Dave	HABU	2.2	A
12/04/82	967	19:05	YOUNG Rick	BETHART Ed	N-HABU	2.3	
14/04/82	976	12:30	McCRARY Rick	LAWRENCE Dave	HABU	4.1	
16/04/82	967	10:00	YOUNG Rick	BETHART Ed	HABU	4	
19/04/82	976	19:45	YOUNG Rick	BETHART Ed	N-HABU	2.3	
22/04/82	967	08:30	McCRARY Rick	LAWRENCE Dave	HABU	4.2	
27/04/82	967	11:00	McCRARY Rick	LAWRENCE Dave	HABU	4.3	
29/04/82	976	10:30	CROWDER Bob	MORGAN John	HABU	4.1	
03/05/82	976	11:15	CROWDER Bob	MORGAN John	HABU	4.2	
04/05/82	967	19:30	McCRARY Rick	LAWRENCE Dave	N-HABU	2.3	
05/05/82	975	?	CROWDER Bob	MORGAN John	FCF	4.2	
07/05/82	976	10:30	McCRARY Rick	LAWRENCE Dave	HABU	2.3	
08/05/82	967	10:00	CROWDER Bob	LAWRENCE Dave	FCF	2.7	
10/05/82	976	09:35	GLASSER Jerry	HORNBAKER Mac	HABU	4	
12/05/82	976	20:03	GLASSER Jerry	HORNBAKER Mac	N-HABU	2.4	
13/05/82	975	14:00	CROWDER Bob	HORNBAKER Mac	FCF	2.4	
17/05/82	976	20:05	CROWDER Bob	MORGAN John	N-HABU	2.2	
19/05/82	967	09:20	GLASSER Jerry	HORNBAKER Mac	HABU	4.3	
20/05/82	967	11:00	CROWDER Bob	MORGAN John	HABU	1.7	A
22/05/82	967		CROWDER Bob	MORGAN John	RTB FERRY		A
24/05/82	976	09:30	GLASSER Jerry	HORNBAKER Mac	HABU	3.6	
26/05/82	975	08:00	ROSENBERG Maury	McKIM E.D.	HABU	2.4	
27/05/82	976	10:15	GLASSER Jerry	HORNBAKER Mac	HABU	4.1	
28/05/82	975	12:10	ROSENBERG Maury	McKIM E.D.	HABU	1.6	A
29/05/82	975	14:00	ROSENBERG Maury	McKIM E.D.	HABU	2.2	
31/05/82	975	11:00	GLASSER Jerry	HORNBAKER Mac	HABU	2.3	
01/06/82	976	20:15	ROSENBERG Maury	McKIM E.D.	N-HABU	2.2	
03/06/82	975	15:00	GLASSER Jerry	HORNBAKER Mac	HABU	2.2	
06/06/82	980	04:25	SHELTON Lee	SZCZEPANIK Russ	FERRY IN	5.9	
07/06/82	976	6:00	CROWDER Bob	MORGAN John	FERRY OUT		
09/06/82	975	09:05	GLASSER Jerry	HORNBAKER Mac	HABU	3.8	
11/06/82	980	08:40	SHELTON Lee	SZCZEPANIK Russ	HABU	2.4	
15/06/82	980	08:22	GLASSER Jerry	HORNBAKER Mac	HABU	4	
16/06/82	967	09:50	SHELTON Lee	SZCZEPANIK Russ	RTB FERRY	1.9	
17/06/82	980	12:00	LULOFF Gil	COATS Bob	FCF	4.1	
17/06/82	975	16:45	SHELTON Lee	SZCZEPANIK Russ	FCF	2	A
18/06/82	975	12:51	LULOFF Gil	COATS Bob	HABU	2.3	A
19/06/82	975	10:00	LULOFF Gil	COATS Bob	HABU	2.4	
22/06/82	975	09:31	SHELTON Lee	SZCZEPANIK Russ	HABU	2.6	
23/06/82	980	21:00	SMITH Bernie	WHALEN Denny	N-HABU	2.2	
24/06/82	967		SHELTON Lee	SZCZEPANIK Russ	FCF		A
24/06/82	967	14:01	SHELTON Lee	SZCZEPANIK Russ	FCF	1.7	A
25/06/82	975		LULOFF Gil	COATS Bob	HABU		A
25/06/82	975	12:00	LULOFF Gil	COATS Bob	HABU	4	
26/06/82	980	11:00	SMITH Bernie	WHALEN Denny	HABU	2.3	
26/06/82	967	15:00	SHELTON Lee	SZCZEPANIK Russ	FCF	2.2	
28/06/82	980	19:30	SHELTON Lee	SZCZEPANIK Russ	N-HABU	2.3	
30/06/82	967	06:00	SMITH Bernie	WHALEN Denny	FERRY OUT		
02/07/82	980	11:00	LULOFF Gil	COATS Bob	HABU	2.3	
06/07/82	975	10:15	SHELTON Lee	SZCZEPANIK Russ	HABU	4.1	
07/07/82	980	19:45	SHELTON Lee	SZCZEPANIK Russ	N-HABU	2.4	
09/07/82	980	09:45	LULOFF Gil	COATS Bob	HABU	4.2	
13/07/82	975	10:35	SHELTON Lee	SZCZEPANIK Russ	HABU	2.6	
13/07/82	980	09:40	LULOFF Gil	COATS Bob	HABU	3.8	
15/07/82	975	10:00	JUDSON Rich	HORNBAKER Mac	HABU	4	
19/07/82	975	20:09	LULOFF Gil	COATS Bob	N-HABU	2.2	
21/07/82	980	13:15	JUDSON Rich	HORNBAKER Mac	HABU	4.1	
23/07/82	975	09:30	LULOFF Gil	COATS Bob	HABU	2.3	
27/07/82	980	20:45	LULOFF Gil	COATS Bob	N-HABU	2.3	
29/07/82	975	10:15	JUDSON Rich	HORNBAKER Mac	HABU	2.3	
02/08/82	980	10:06	JUDSON Rich	HORNBAKER Mac	HABU	4.2	
03/08/82	975	20:05	SMITH Bernie	WHALEN Denny	N-HABU	2.3	
05/08/82	980	10:22	JUDSON Rich	HORNBAKER Mac	HABU	4.1	
12/08/82	975	11:09	SMITH Bernie	WHALEN Denny	HABU	2.4	
13/08/82	980	11:00	JUSDON Rich	HORNBAKER Mac	HABU	4	
19/08/82	975	08:00	SMITH Bernie	WHALEN Denny	HABU	2.3	
21/08/82	975	10:00	JUDSON Rich	HORNBAKER Mac	HABU	1.8	A
23/08/82	975	12:00	SMITH Bernie	WHALEN Denny	HABU	3.7	
27/08/82	975	11:30	SMITH Bernie	WHALEN Denny	HABU	2.4	
28/08/82	975	13:00	SMITH Bernie	WHALEN Denny	HABU	2.3	
30/08/82	975		SMITH Bernie	WHALEN Denny	HABU		A
31/08/82	975	18:45	SMITH Bernie	WHALEN Denny	N-HABU	2.3	
01/09/82	975	12:00	BERTELSON Gil	STAMPF Frank	HABU	3.9	
02/09/82	980	19:15	SMITH Bernie	WHALEN Denny	N-HABU	2.3	
06/09/82	975	11:00	BERTELSON Gil	STAMPF Frank	HABU	3.8	
08/09/82	980	20:30	SMITH Bernie	WHALEN Denny	N-HABU	2.5	
10/09/82	980	09:45	BERTELSON Gil	STAMPF Frank	HABU	2.3	
14/09/82	980	08:30	BERTELSON Gil	STAMPF Frank	HABU	4	
15/09/82	980	11:30	DYER Les	GREENWOOD Dan	FCF	4.1	
17/09/82	980	10:00	DYER Les	GREENWOOD Dan	HABU	4.1	
20/09/82	980	10:30	BERTELSON Gil	STAMPF Frank	HABU	3.9	
22/09/82	980	10:45	DYER Les	GREENWOOD Dan	HABU	3.8	
23/09/82	975	07:57	BERTELSON Gil	STAMPF Frank	FCF	1.1	
24/09/82	980	14:02	DYER Les	GREENWOOD Dan	HABU	2.3	
27/09/82	975	20:07	BERTELSON Gil	STAMPF Frank	N-HABU	2.3	
29/09/82	980	11:30	DYER Les	GREENWOOD Dan	HABU	4	
02/10/82	975	10:30	BERTELSON Gil	STAMPF Frank	HABU	3.8	
04/10/82	975	12:25	BERTELSON Gil	STAMPF Frank	HABU	3.8	
08/10/82	980	08:00	CUNNINGHAM Nevin	QUIST Gene	HABU	4.6	
08/10/82	975	08:46	DYER Les	GREENWOOD Dan	HABU	5.5	
12/10/82	975	10:04	CUNNINGHAM Nevin	QUIST Gene	HABU	2.3	
13/10/82	980	19:30	DYER Les	GREENWOOD Dan	N-HABU	2.2	
15/10/82	975	09:30	CUNNINGHAM Nevin	QUIST Gene	HABU	0.5	A
15/10/82	975	14:00	CUNNINGHAM Nevin	QUIST Gene	HABU	2.3	
18/10/82	980	12:30	DYER Les	GREENWOOD Dan	HABU	4.1	
19/10/82	975	20:15	CUNNINGHAM Nevin	QUIST Gene	N-HABU	2.2	
22/10/82	980	11:00	DYER Les	GREENWOOD Dan	HABU	4	
26/10/82	980	10:45	DYER Les	GREENWOOD Dan	HABU	2.2	
28/10/82	975	10:00	CUNNINGHAM Nevin	QUIST Gene	HABU	2.6	
30/10/82	980	08:45	CUNNINGHAM Nevin	QUIST Gene	HABU	5.4	
02/11/82	980	21:30	McCRARY Rick	WHALEN Denny	N-HABU	2.3	
04/11/82	975	10:36	CUNNINGHAM Nevin	QUIST Gene	HABU	3.7	
06/11/82	980		McCRARY Rick	WHALEN Denny	HABU		A
06/11/82	980	11:04	McCRARY Rick	WHALEN Denny	HABU	2.2	
08/11/82	975	09:30	McCRARY Rick	WHALEN Denny	HABU	2.2	
12/11/82	960	04:15	ROSENBERG Maury	BETHART Ed	FERRY IN-H	6.2	
13/11/82	980	08:12	CUNNINGHAM Nevin	QUIST Gene	H-FERRY OUT		
15/11/82	975	14:58	McCRARY Rick	WHALEN Denny	HABU	2.2	
17/11/82	960	09:15	McCRARY Rick	WHALEN Denny	HABU	2.3	
18/11/82	960	09:45	ROSENBERG Maury	BETHART Ed	HABU	2.3	
24/11/82	975	10:30	ROSENBERG Maury	BETHART Ed	HABU	3.8	

Date	Instal. No.	T.O. Time	Pilot Name	RSO Name	Mission	Duration	Remarks
26/11/82	960	11:00	BURK Bill	HENICHEK Tom	FCF	2.5	
27/11/82	975	09:45	BURK Bill	HENICHEK Tom	HABU	2.8	A
30/11/82	960	12:15	ROSENBERG Maury	BETHART Ed	HABU	2.3	
01/12/82	960	10:00	BURK Bill	HENICHEK Tom	HABU	3.9	
03/12/82	960	10:00	ROSENBERG Maury	BETHART Ed	HABU	2.3	
06/12/82	975	10:03	BURK Bill	HENICHEK Tom	HABU	2.5	
08/12/82	960	10:00	BURK Bill	HENICHEK Tom	HABU	3.6	
09/12/82	975	09:05	BURK Bill	HENICHEK Tom	HABU	2.3	
14/12/82	975	13:00	ROSENBERG Maury	BETHART Ed	HABU	2.3	
16/12/82	960	10:30	BURK Bill	HENICHEK Tom	HABU	3.2	A
18/12/82	975	11:00	ROSENBERG Maury	BETHART Ed	HABU	3.6	
20/12/82	960	18:00	BURK Bill	HENICHEK Tom	N-HABU	2.3	
22/12/82	975	14:09	ROSENBERG Maury	BETHART Ed	HABU	2.3	
27/12/82	960	18:30	ROSENBERG Maury	BETHART Ed	N-HABU	2.3	
29/12/82	975	10:00	BURK Bill	HENICHEK Tom	HABU	2.3	
05/01/83	960		SHELTON Lee	MORGAN John	HABU		A
06/01/83	975	19:00	SHELTON Lee	MORGAN John	N-HABU	2.5	
08/01/83	960	10:43	GLASSER Jerry	LAWRENCE Dave	HABU	2.3	
10/01/83	975	10:30	SHELTON Lee	MORGAN John	HABU	3.7	
12/01/83	960	11:30	GLASSER Jerry	LAWRENCE Dave	HABU	2.4	
14/01/83	975	08:00	SHELTON Lee	MORGAN John	HABU	2.4	
17/01/83	960	11:00	GLASSER Jerry	LAWRENCE Dave	HABU	2.8	A
18/01/83	975	14:00	SHELTON Lee	MORGAN John	HABU	2.4	
20/01/83	975	09:30	GLASSER Jerry	MORGAN John	HABU	2.3	
21/01/83	960	10:30	SHELTON Lee	MORGAN John	HABU	2.4	A
25/01/83	960	09:05	GLASSER Jerry	LAWRENCE Dave	HABU	2.8	
26/01/83	975	18:45	GLASSER Jerry	LAWRENCE Dave	N-HABU	1.7	A
27/01/83	960	18:45	GLASSER Jerry	LAWRENCE Dave	N-HABU	2.3	
28/01/83	960	13:00	LULOFF Gil	COATS Bob	HABU	2.4	
01/02/83	975	09:45	GLASSER Jerry	LAWRENCE Dave	HABU	4.1	
02/02/83	975	21:00	LULOFF Gil	COATS Bob	N-HABU	2.3	
04/02/83	960	12:13	GLASSER Jerry	LAWRENCE Dave	HABU	2.3	
07/02/83	975	11:30	LULOFF Gil	COATS Bob	HABU	2.3	
12/02/83	960		LULOFF Gil	COATS Bob	HABU		A
13/02/83	975	11:00	GLASSER Jerry	LAWRENCE Dave	HABU	2.3	
14/02/83	975	10:00	LULOFF Gil	COATS Bob	HABU	2.4	
15/02/83	964	04:00	JUDSON Rich	HORNBAKER Mac	FERRY IN-H	6.2	A
17/02/83	975	08:00	GLASSER Jerry	LAWRENCE Dave	H-FERRY OUT		
18/02/83	960	10:00	JUDSON Rich	HORNBAKER Mac	HABU	4	
22/02/83	960	18:45	LULOFF Gil	COATS Bob	N-HABU	2.4	
24/02/83	964	09:30	JUDSON Rich	HORNBAKER Mac	HABU	2.3	
25/02/83	960	10:00	LULOFF Gil	COATS Bob	HABU	4.1	
01/03/83	964	20:30	LULOFF Gil	COATS Bob	N-HABU	2.3	
03/03/83	960	08:30	JUDSON Rich	HORNBAKER Mac	HABU	2.2	
07/03/83	960	09:30	JUDSON Rich	HORNBAKER Mac	HABU	3.5	
09/03/83	960	09:30	SMITH Bernie	McKIM E.D.	HABU	2.3	
11/03/83	964	11:30	JUDSON Rich	HORNBAKER Mac	HABU	3.8	
15/03/83	964	06:00	SMITH Bernie	McKIM E.D.	HABU	2.3	
16/03/83	960	13:00	JUDSON Rich	HORNBAKER Mac	HABU	2.5	
18/03/83	964	10:00	SMITH Bernie	McKIM E.D.	HABU	4	
21/03/83	960	20:00	JUDSON Rich	HORNBAKER Mac	N-HABU	2.3	
23/03/83	960	08:20	JUDSON Rich	HORNBAKER Mac	HABU	4.2	
24/03/83	960	09:05	SMITH Bernie	McKIM E.D.	HABU	2.8	
28/03/83	964	19:30	SMITH Bernie	McKIM E.D.	N-HABU	2.3	
30/03/83	960	10:30	JIGGENS Jim	McCUE Joe	FCF	4.2	
01/04/83	960	09:15	JIGGENS Jim	McCUE Joe	HABU	2.4	
04/04/83	964	18:45	SMITH Bernie	McKIM E.D.	N-HABU	2.3	
06/04/83	960	10:15	JIGGENS Jim	McCUE Joe	HABU	4.2	
08/04/83	964	09:30	SMITH Bernie	McKIM E.D.	HABU	2.7	
11/04/83	960	10:00	JIGGENS Jim	McCUE Joe	HABU	2.3	
12/04/83	960	13:15	SMITH Bernie	McKIM E.D.	HABU	4	
14/04/83	960	09:05	JIGGENS Jim	McCUE Joe	HABU	2.4	
18/04/83	964	19:15	PETERS Dave	KELLER Bill	N-HABU	1.3	A
19/04/83	964	19:15	PETERS Dave	KELLER Bill	N-HABU	2.5	
21/04/83	964	10:30	JIGGENS Jim	McCUE Joe	HABU	3	A
22/04/83	960	12:14	PETERS Dave'	KELLER Bill	HABU	2.2	
26/04/83	964	21:00	JIGGENS Jim	McCUE Joe	N-HABU	2.3	
28/04/83	964	11:30	PETERS Dave	KELLER Bill	HABU	4	
02/05/83	964	10:17	PETERS Dave	KELLER Bill	HABU	4.1	
03/05/83	960	19:00	JIGGENS Jim	McCUE Joe	N-HABU	1.9	A
05/05/83	964	09:05	PETERS Dave	KELLER Bill	HABU	2.4	
09/05/83	960	08:15	PETERS Dave	KELLER Bill	HABU	2.2	
11/05/83	964	08:30	BEHLER Bob	TABOR Ron	FCF	4.1	
12/05/83	964	13:00	BEHLER Bob	TABOR Ron	HABU	4.1	
13/05/83	960	13:30	PETERS Dave	KELLER Bill	HABU	2.5	
16/05/83	964	11:30	BEHLER Bob	TABOR Ron	HABU	3.8	
18/05/83	960	20:58	PETERS Dave	KELLER Bill	N-HABU	2.3	
20/05/83	964	10:08	BEHLER Bob	TABOR Ron	HABU	3.9	
24/05/83	964	19:35	PETERS Dave	KELLER Bill	N-HABU	2.3	
25/05/83	960	12:30	BEHLER Bob	TABOR Ron	HABU	2.3	
27/05/83	964	10:00	BEHLER Bob	TABOR Ron	HABU	1.8	A
01/06/83	964	09:15	McCRARY Rick	LAWRENCE Dave	HABU	4.1	
02/06/83	960	20:55	BEHLER Bob	TABOR Ron	N-HABU	2.2	
06/06/83	964	08:30	McCRARY Rick	LAWRENCE Dave	HABU	3.8	
07/06/83	960	14:00	BEHLER Bob	TABOR Ron	HABU	2.2	
10/06/83	964	11:00	McCRARY Rick	LAWRENCE Dave	HABU	3.9	
13/06/83	960	12:30	BEHLER Bob	TABOR Ron	HABU	2.2	
14/06/83	964	19:30	BEHLER Bob	TABOR Ron	N-HABU	2.3	
16/06/83	964	09:05	McCRARY Rick	LAWRENCE Dave	HABU	2.4	
20/06/83	964	20:00	McCRARY Rick	LAWRENCE Dave	N-HABU	2.2	
22/06/83	960	10:00	BURK Bill	HENICHEK Tom	HABU	2.2	
27/06/83	964	05:00	BURK Bill	HENICHEK Tom	HABU	4.9	
27/06/83	960	05:30	McCRARY Rick	LAWRENCE Dave	HABU	3.9	
01/07/83	960	09:15	McCRARY Rick	LAWRENCE Dave	HABU	4.1	
05/07/83	964	19:50	BURK Bill	HENICHEK Tom	N-HABU	2.5	
07/07/83	964	09:30	McCRARY Rick	LAWRENCE Dave	HABU	2.3	
11/07/83	964	12:00	BURK Bill	HENICHEK Tom	HABU	3.9	
14/07/83	964	08:30	CUNNINGHAM Nevin	QUIST Gene	HABU	2.3	
15/07/83	964	12:00	BURK Bill	HENICHEK Tom	HABU	3.7	
18/07/83	964	11:30	CUNNINGHAM Nevin	QUIST Gene	HABU	2.3	
20/07/83	964	10:04	BURK Bill	HENICHEK Tom	HABU	4.2	
21/07/83	964	20:00	CUNNINGHAM Nevin	QUIST Gene	N-HABU	2.3	
22/07/83	960	14:00	BURK Bill	HENICHEK Tom	FCF	4.1	
25/07/83	960	10:30	CUNNINGHAM Nevin	QUIST Gene	HABU	3.9	
26/07/83	960	19:45	BURK Bill	HENICHEK Tom	N-HABU	1.4	A
27/07/83	960	24:00	BURK Bill	HENICHEK Tom	N-HABU	2.2	
28/07/83	960	09:45	CUNNINGHAM Nevin	QUIST Gene	HABU	2.2	
01/08/83	964	12:15	CUNNINGHAM Nevin	QUIST Gene	HABU	4.1	
03/08/83	960	11:48	BOUDREAUX Stormy	NEWGREEN Terry	FCF	4.2	
04/08/83	960	19:15	CUNNINGHAM Nevin	QUIST Gene	N-HABU	2.3	
06/08/83	960	12:00	BOUDREAUX Stormy	NEWGREEN Terry	HABU	3.7	
10/08/83	964	08:30	CUNNINGHAM Nevin	QUIST Gene	HABU	2.2	
16/08/83	960	19:30	CUNNINGHAM Nevin	QUIST Gene	N-HABU	2.4	
18/08/83	964	09:15	BOUDREAUX Stormy	NEWGREEN Terry	HABU	2.3	
20/08/83	964	12:13	BOUDREAUX Stormy	NEWGREEN Terry	HABU	2.3	
23/08/83	964	10:30	BOUDREAUX Stormy	NEWGREEN Terry	HABU	2.3	
24/08/83	960	20:00	DYER Les	WHALEN Denny	N-HABU	2.4	
27/08/83	960	13:15	BOUDREAUX Stormy	NEWGREEN Terry	HABU	4.3	
29/08/83	960	09:45	DYER Les	WHALEN Denny	HABU	3.9	
30/08/83	964	10:15	BOUDREAUX Stormy	NEWGREEN Terry	HABU	2.4	
01/09/83	964	09:05	DYER Les	WHALEN Denny	HABU	2.2	A,30
02/09/83	960	12:00	BOUDREAUX Stormy	NEWGREEN Terry	HABU	2.3	
06/09/83	960	11:00	DYER Les	WHALEN Denny	HABU	0.9	
06/09/83	960	14:15	DYER Les	WHALEN Denny	HABU	3.9	
08/09/83	960	09:30	DYER Les	WHALEN Denny	HABU	2.2	
12/09/83	960	18:45	ROSENBERG Maury	McKIM E.D.	HABU	1.2	A
14/09/83	960	08:30	ROSENBERG Maury	McKIM E.D.	HABU	4	
16/09/83	960	10:15	DYER Les	GREENWOOD Dan	HABU	1.7	A
19/09/83	960	13:00	DYER Les	GREENWOOD Dan	HABU	3.8	
20/09/83	960	19:15	ROSENBERG Maury	McKIM E.D.	N-HABU	2.2	
22/09/83	960	13:00	DYER Les	GREENWOOD Dan	HABU	4.4	
23/09/83	964	13:00	ROSENBERG Maury	McKIM E.D.	FCF	2.3	
24/09/83	960	09:45	DYER Les	GREENWOOD Dan	HABU	4.1	
29/09/83	964	10:00	ROSENBERG Maury	McKIM E.D.	HABU	2.3	
01/10/83	964	10:04	ROSENBERG Maury	McKIM E.D.	HABU	2.2	
03/10/83	964	18:45	LULOFF Gil	COATS Bob	N-HABU	2.3	
05/10/83	964	12:00	ROSENBERG Maury	McKIM E.D.	HABU	4.1	
06/10/83	960		LULOFF Gil	COATS Bob	HABU		A
06/10/83	960	14:16	LULOFF Gil	COATS Bob	HABU	3.6	
11/10/83	964	18:30	ROSENBERG Maury	McKIM E.D.	N-HABU	2.3	
14/10/83	960	09:45	LULOFF Gil	COATS Bob	HABU	2.4	
17/10/83	960	10:04	ROSENBERG Maury	McKIM E.D.	HABU	4.1	
18/10/83	960	09:30	LULOFF Gil	COATS Bob	HABU	2.4	
20/10/83	964	09:05	LULOFF Gil	COATS Bob	HABU	2.3	
24/10/83	960	10:30	LULOFF Gil	COATS Bob	HABU	1.3	A
25/10/83	964	10:30	LULOFF Gil	COATS Bob	HABU	3.7	
26/10/83	960	20:00	THOMAS B.C.	MORGAN John	N-HABU	2'3	
28/10/83	960	11:03	LULOFF Gil	COATS Bob	HABU	3.8	
01/11/83	964	18:00	THOMAS B.C.	MORGAN John	N-HABU	2.5	
03/11/83	960	11:20	LULOFF Gil	COATS Bob	HABU	4.1	
04/11/83	960	09:45	THOMAS B.C.	MORGAN John	HABU	2.4	
07/11/83	964	10:30	LULOFF Gil	COATS Bob	HABU	3.9	
08/11/83	960	11:00	THOMAS B.C.	MORGAN John	HABU	4.1	
10/11/83	964	09:05	THOMAS B.C.	MORGAN John	HABU	2.4	
14/11/83	960	18:15	LULOFF Gil	COATS Bob	N-HABU	2.4	
16/11/83	964	09:30	THOMAS B.C.	MORGAN John	HABU	2.4	
19/11/83	976	05:00	GLASSER Jerry	ROSS Ted	FERRY IN-H	6.6	
20/11/83	960	08:00	LULOFF Gil	COATS Bob	FERRY OUT		
23/11/83	964	07:15	THOMAS B.C.	MORGAN John	HABU	4	
28/11/83	964	21:08	GLASSER Jerry	ROSS Ted	N-HABU	2.4	
01/12/83	976		GLASSER Jerry	ROSS Ted	HABU		A
01/12/83	976	11:20	GLASSER Jerry	ROSS Ted	HABU	2.4	
05/12/83	964	18:00	GLASSER Jerry	ROSS Ted	N-HABU	2.3	
07/12/83	976	14:00	BEHLER Bob	TABOR Ron	HABU	2.3	
09/12/83	964	09:45	GLASSER Jerry	ROSS Ted	HABU	3.8	
12/12/83	964	12:00	BEHLER Bob	TABOR Ron	HABU	3.8	
14/12/83	976	09:05	GLASSER Jerry	ROSS Ted	HABU	3.9	
15/12/83	976		BEHLER Bob	TABOR Ron	HABU		A
15/12/83	964	21:46	BEHLER Bob	TABOR Ron	N-HABU	2.2	
19/12/83	964	17:45	GLASSER Jerry	ROSS Ted	N-HABU	2.4	
20/12/83	976	13:00	BEHLER Bob	TABOR Ron	HABU	2.3	
22/12/83	976	09:15	BEHLER Bob	TABOR Ron	HABU	2.3	
27/12/83	964	10:00	SMITH Bernie	WHALEN Denny	HABU	4	
29/12/83	976	12:00	BEHLER Bob	TABOR Ron	HABU	3	A
03/01/84	964	11:15	SMITH Bernie	WHALEN Denny	HABU	1.5	A
03/01/84	964	16:15	SMITH Bernie	WHALEN Denny	HABU	2.3	
05/01/84	964	09:45	BEHLER Bob	TABOR Ron	HABU	2.3	
06/01/84	964	10:00	SMITH Bernie	WHALEN Dennis	HABU	3.8	
09/01/84	964	18:00	BEHLER Bob	TABOR Ron	N-HABU	2.3	
11/01/84	976	09:30	SMITH Bernie	WHALEN Dennis	HABU	2.3	
12/01/84	976	09:30	SMITH Bernie	WHALEN Dennis	HABU	2.3	
17/01/84	964	11:00	MATTHEWS Joe	OSTERHELD Curt	FCF	2.7	
17/01/84	976	18:30	SMITH Bernie	WHALEN Dennis	N-HABU	2.2	
19/01/84	964	11:00	MATTHEWS Joe	OSTERHELD Curt	HABU	0.8	A
20/01/84	964	10:00	MATTHEWS Joe	OSTERHELD Curt	HABU	4.3	
23/01/84	976	13:00	MATTHEWS Joe	OSTERHELD Curt	HABU	1.5	A
25/01/84	964	18:15	SMITH Bernie	WHALEN DENNIS	N-HABU	2.2	
25/01/84	976	12:14	MATTHEWS Joe	OSTERHELD Curt	RTB FERRY	1.5	
27/01/84	964	10:00	MATTHEWS Joe	OSTERHELD Curt	HABU	3.9	
30/01/84	976	10:15	SMITH Bernie	WHALEN Dennis	HABU	2.3	
01/02/84	964	10:00	MATTHEWS Joe	OSTERHALD Curt	HABU	2.3	A
02/02/84	976	10:55	MATTHEWS Joe	OSTERHALD Curt	HABU	2.3	
06/02/84	976	18:38	MATTHEWS Joe	OSTERHALD Curt	HABU	2.3	
08/02/84	976	10:30	PETERS Dave	BETHART Ed	HABU	2	A
10/02/84	964	12:02	MATTHEWS Joe	OSTERHELD Curt	HABU	2.5	
14/02/84	976	12:15	PETERS Dave	BETHART Ed	HABU	2.3	

Date	Instal. No.	T.O. Time	Pilot Name	RSO Name	Mission	Duration	Remarks
15/02/84	964	18:45	MATTHEWS Joe	OSTERHELD Curt	N-HABU	2.3	
17/02/84	976	10:02	PETERS Dave	BETHART Ed	HABU	3.7	
21/02/84	964	18:35	MATTHEWS Joe	OSTERHELD Curt	N-HABU	2.3	
23/02/84	976	09:30	PETERS Dave	BETHART Ed	HABU	2.3	
27/02/84	964	10:00	PETERS Dave	BETHART Ed	HABU	3.8	
28/02/84	964	13:00	JIGGENS Jim	McCUE Joe	HABU	2.9	A
03/03/84	976	10:00	PETERS Dave	BETHART Ed	HABU	3.8	
05/03/84	964	18:45	JIGGENS Jim	McCUE JOE	N-HABU	2.3	
07/03/84	964	11:00	PETERS Dave	BETHART Ed	HABU	2.3	A
09/03/84	964	10:00	JIGGENS Jim	McCUE Joe	HABU	2.2	
12/03/84	964	19:00	PETERS Dave	BETHART Ed	N-HABU	2.4	
13/03/84	976	14:00	JIGGENS Jim	McCUE Joe	HABU	2.4	
15/03/84	976	09:30	JIGGENS Jim	McCUE Joe	HABU	2.3	
20/03/84	964	19:15	BOUDREAUX Stormy	NEWGREEN Terry	N-HABU	2.3	
23/03/84	964	11:00	JIGGENS Jim	McCUE Joe	HABU	2.3	
27/03/84	964	09:02	BOUDREAUX Stormy	NEWGREEN Terry	HABU	2.3	31
27/03/84	973	04:45	DYER Les	GREENWOOD Dan	FERRY IN-H	6.7	31
29/03/84	964		JIGGENS Jim	McCUE Joe	HABU		A
30/03/84	964	08:10	JIGGENS Jim	McCUE Joe	H-FERRY OUT		
02/04/84	976	09:45	BOUDREAUX Stormy	NEWGREEN Terry	HABU	2.5	
03/04/84	976	14:00	DYER Les	GREENWOOD Dan	HABU	2.1	
05/04/84	973	09:15	BOUDREAUX Stormy	NEWGREEN Terry	HABU	2.4	
09/04/84	976	10:15	DYER Les	GREENWOOD Dan	HABU	2.2	
11/04/84	973	19:05	BOUDREAUX Stormy	NEWGREEN Terry	N-HABU	2.3	
13/04/84	973	09:05	DYER Les	GREENWOOD Dan	HABU	2.2	
16/04/84	973	19:00	BOUDREAUX Stormy	NEWGREEN Terry	N-HABU	2.3	
18/04/84	973	14:30	DYER Les	GREENWOOD Dan	HABU	2.2	
20/04/84	976	09:30	BOUDREAUX Stormy	NEWGREEN Terry	HABU	2.2	
23/04/84	973	13:00	DYER Les	GREENWOOD Dan	HABU	2.3	
24/04/84	976	19:15	BOUDREAUX Stormy	NEWGREEN Terry	N-HABU	2.3	
29/04/84	973	10:00	DYER Les	GREENWOOD Dan	HABU	2.3	
01/05/84	976	16:00	CUNNINGHAM Nevin	QUIST Gene	HABU	1.4	A
02/05/84	976	12:00	CUNNINGHAM Nevin	QUIST Gene	HABU	2.3	
03/05/84	976	09:30	DYER Les	GREENWOOD Dan	HABU	2.2	
08/05/84	976		CUNNINGHAM Nevin	QUIST Gene	HABU		A
08/05/84	976	10:35	CUNNINGHAM Nevin	QUIST Gene	HABU	3.7	
09/05/84	973	21:00	DYER Les	GREENWOOD Dan	N-HABU	2.2	
11/05/84	976	06:00	CUNNINGHAM Nenin	QUIST Gene	HABU	2.3	
14/05/84	976	21:21	DYER Les	GREENWOOD Dan	N-HABU	2.1	
16/05/84	973	09:47	DYER Les	GREENWOOD Dan	HABU	2.3	
17/05/84	976	09:30	CUNNINGHAM Nevin	QUIST Gene	HABU	2.4	
21/05/84	976	17:30	CUNNINGHAM Nevin	QUIST Gene	N-HABU	2.1	A
23/05/84	973	22:00	BURK Bill	HENICHEK Tom	N-HABU	2.3	
25/05/84	976		CUNNINGHAM Nevin	QUIST Gene	HABU		A
25/05/84	976	11:15	CUNNINGHAM Nevin	QUIST Gene	HABU	2.4	
29/05/84	976	18:00	BURK Bill	HENICHEK Tom	HABU	2.2	
30/05/84	976	12:30	CUNNINGHAM Nevin	QUIST Gene	HABU	2.2	
01/06/84	976	13:00	BURK Bill	HENICHEK Tom	HABU	2.4	
04/06/84	976	20:00	CUNNINGHAM Nevin	QUIST Gene	N-HABU	2.5	
06/06/84	973	07:30	BURK Bill	HENICHEK Tom	HABU	2.4	
07/06/84	976	09:15	BURK Bill	HENICHEK Tom	HABU	2.2	
11/06/84	973	16:30	PETERS Dave	BETHART Ed	HABU	2.2	
13/06/84	973	20:10	BURK Bill	HENICHEK Tom	N-HABU	2.2	
15/06/84	973	08:15	PETERS Dave	BETHART Ed	HABU	1.6	A
18/06/84	973	16:50	BURK Bill	HENICHEK Tom	HABU	2.1	
21/06/84	976	14:22	PETERS Dave	BETHART Ed	FCF	0.9	A
22/06/84	973	19:30	BURK Bill	HENICHEK Tom	N-HABU	2.3	
25/06/84	976	11:25	BURK Bill	HENICHEK Tom	FCF	2.6	
27/06/84	976	07:50	PETERS Dave	BETHART Ed	HABU	3.8	
28/06/84	973	09:30	BURK Bill	HENICHEK Tom	HABU	1.7	A
29/06/84	973	11:00	PETERS Dave	BETHART Ed	HABU	2.3	
02/07/84	973	19:45	PETERS Dave	BETHART Ed	N-HABU	2.2	
05/07/84	973	13:15	MADISON Jack	ORCUTT Bill	FCF	2.5	
06/07/84	973	09:15	MADISON Jack	ORCUTT Bill	HABU	2.4	
09/07/84	973		PETERS Dave	BETHART Ed	N-HABU		A
10/07/84	976	19:30	PETERS Dave	BETHART Ed	N-HABU	2.3	
12/07/84	976	09:58	MADISON Jack	ORCUTT Bill	HABU	2.2	
13/07/84	976	09:45	PETERS Dave	BETHART Ed	HABU	2.4	
16/07/84	976	16:41	MADISON Jack	ORCUTT Bill	HABU	2.2	
18/07/84	976	14:00	PETERS Dave	BETHART Ed	HABU	2.2	
20/07/84	976	12:32	MADISON Jack	ORCUTT Bill	HABU	3.8	
23/07/84	976		MADISON Jack	ORCUTT Bill	HABU		A
24/07/84	976	20:00	LULOFF Gil	COATS Bob	N-HABU	2.3	
26/07/84	976	09:30	MADISON Jack	ORCUTT Bill	HABU	2.4	
27/07/84	976	10:00	LULOFF Gil	COATS Bob	HABU	2.3	
31/07/84	973	11:00	MADISON Jack	ORCUTT Bill	HABU	2.3	
01/08/84	976	19:45	MADISON Jack	ORCUTT Bill	N-HABU	2.2	
03/08/84	976	13:00	LULOFF Gil	COATS Bob	HABU	0.6	A
06/08/84	973	13:00	LULOFF Gil	COATS Bob	HABU	2.3	
07/08/84	973	10:15	MADISON Jack	ORCUTT Bill	HABU	2.3	
09/08/84	973	09:15	LULOFF Gil	COATS Bob	HABU	1.5	A
10/08/84	976	10:30	LULOFF Gil	COATS Bob	HABU	2.2	
13/08/84	976	19:15	GLASSER Jerry	TABOR Ron	N-HABU	2.4	
15/08/84	973	11:00	LULOFF Gil	COATS Bob	HABU	2.4	
17/08/84	973	08:00	GLASSER Jerry	TABOR Ron	HABU	2.3	
22/08/84	976	19:10	LULOFF Gil	COATS Bob	N-HABU	2.2	
24/08/84	976	09:45	GLASSER Jerry	TABOR Ron	HABU	2.4	
27/08/84	976		LULOFF Gil	COATS Bob	HABU		
28/08/84	973	10:00	LULOFF Gil	COATS Bob	HABU	2.2	
29/08/84	973	09:45	GLASSER Jerry	TABOR Ron	HABU	2.2	
30/08/84	976	09:30	GLASSER Jerry	TABOR Ron	HABU	2.3	
04/09/84	976	19:00	GLASSER Jerry	TABOR Ron	N-HABU	2.3	
05/09/84	973	13:00	YEILDING Edward	LEE Steve	FCF	2.5	
07/09/84	976	10:05	GLASSER Jerry	TABOR Ron	HABU	2.4	
08/09/84	973	10:00	YEILDING Edward	LEE Steve	HABU	2.2	
10/09/84	973	18:55	GLASSER Jerry	TABOR Ron	N-HABU	2.4	
12/09/84	973	13:00	YEILDING Edward	LEE Steve	HABU	2.2	
14/09/84	973	10:00	YEILDING Edward	LEE Steve	HABU	3.6	

Date	Instal. No.	T.O. Time	Pilot Name	RSO Name	Mission	Duration	Remarks
17/09/84	976	11:30	GLASSER Jerry	TABOR Ron	HABU	2.6	
19/09/84	976	18:35	GLASSER Jerry	TABOR Ron	N-HABU	2.6	
21/09/84	973	10:00	YEILDING Edward	LEE Steve	HABU	1.4	A
23/09/84	973	11:26	YEILDING Edward	LEE Steve	RTB FERRY	1.5	
24/09/84	976	13:30	SMITH Bernie	WHALEN Denny	HABU	2.3	
26/09/84	976	10:00	YEILDING Edward	LEE Steve	HABU	3.8	
27/09/84	973	15:15	SMITH Bernie	WHALEN Denny	HABU	2.2	
01/10/84	976	14:00	YEILDING Edward	LEE Steve	HABU	2.2	
03/10/84	973	10:00	SMITH Bernie	WHALEN Denny	HABU	2.3	
05/10/84	973	10:30	YEILDING Edward	LEE Steve	HABU	3.7	
09/10/84	976	18:15	YEILDING Edward	LEE Steve	N-HABU	2.2	
11/10/84	973	09:15	SMITH Bernie	WHALEN Denny	HABU	2.3	
15/10/84	973	21:00	JIGGENS Jim	McCUE Joe	N-HABU	2.4	
17/10/84	976	10:30	SMITH Bernie	WHALEN Denny	HABU	3.7	
19/10/84	976	10:00	JIGGENS Jim	McCUE Joe	HABU	3.8	
23/10/84	973	12:00	SMITH Bernie	WHALEN Denny	HABU	2.2	
24/10/84	973	18:31	JIGGENS Jim	McCUE Joe	N-HABU	2.3	
26/10/84	973		SMITH Bernie	WHALEN Denny	HABU		
30/10/84	976	12:42	SMITH Bernie	WHALEN Denny	HABU	2.3	
31/10/84	976	11:30	JIGGENS Jim	McCUE Joe	HABU	3.8	
01/11/84	976	09:30	CUNNINGHAM Nevin	MORGAN John	HABU	2.3	
05/11/84	976	18:30	BOUDREAUX Stormy	ROSS Ted	N-HABU	2.5	
07/11/84	976	11:30	CUNNINGHAM Nevin	MORGAN John	HABU	2.4	
08/11/84	973	10:00	BOUDREAUX Stormy	ROSS Ted	FCF	2.4	
09/11/84	976	11:00	CUNNINGHAM Nevin	MORGAN John	HABU	2.3	
13/11/84	976	17:45	BOUDREAUX Stormy	ROSS Ted	N-HABU	2.3	
14/11/84	973	16:00	CUNNINGHAM Nevin	MORGAN John	N-HABU	0.4	A
14/11/84	973	18:25	CUNNINGHAM Nevin	MORGAN John	N-HABU	2.4	
16/11/84	976		BOUDREAUX Stormy	ROSS Ted	HABU		
17/11/84	976	11:00	BOUDREAUX Stormy	ROSS Ted	HABU	3.7	
19/11/84	973	18:15	CUNNINGHAM Nevin	MORGAN John	N-HABU	2.3	
21/11/84	976	09:15	BOUDREAUX Stormy	ROSS Ted	HABU	2.3	
23/11/84	973	09:45	BOUDREAUX Stormy	ROSS Ted	HABU	2.3	
27/11/84	973	15:00	BEHLER Bob	TABOR Ron	HABU	2.3	
29/11/84	976	10:30	BOUDREAUX Stormy	ROSS Ted	HABU	4.1	
03/12/84	973	11:15	BEHLER Bob	TABOR Ron	HABU	0.6	A
04/12/84	973	19:30	BEHLER Bob	TABOR Ron	N-HABU	2.3	
06/12/84	976	10:15	BOUDREAUX Stormy	ROSS Ted	HABU	3.9	
07/12/84	973	10:00	BEHLER Bob	TABOR Ron	HABU	2.3	
11/12/84	964	06:04	BURK Bill	HENICHEK Tom	FERRY IN-H	6.6	
13/12/84	976	08:00	BOUDREAUX Stormy	ROSS Ted	H-FERRY OUT		
15/12/84	973	09:15	BEHLER Bob	TABOR Ron	HABU	2.3	
17/12/84	973	09:30	BEHLER Bob	TABOR Ron	HABU	5.6	
19/12/84	964	17:45	BURK Bill	HENICHEK Tom	N-HABU	2.2	
21/12/84	973	07:00	BURK Bill	HENICHEK Tom	HABU	6.2	A
26/12/84	964	18:15	BEHLER Bob	TABOR Ron	N-HABU	2.3	
27/12/84	973	11:00	BURK Bill	HENICHEK Tom	HABU	2.5	
28/12/84	964	09:05	BEHLER Bob	TABOR Ron	HABU	2.4	
30/12/84	973	10:00	BURK Bill	HENICHEK Tom	HABU	3.6	
02/01/85	964	10:00	BEHLER Bob	TABOR Ron	HABU	2.4	
03/01/85	973	09:15	BURK Bill	HENICHEK Tom	HABU	1.9	
07/01/85	964	10:30	MATTHEWS Joe	OSTERHELD Curt	HABU	3.8	
09/01/85	973	23:30	BURK Bill	HENICHEK Tom	N-HABU	2.2	
11/01/85	964	10:45	MATTHEWS Joe	OSTERHELD Curt	HABU	2.3	
14/01/85	964	11:00	BURK Bill	HENICHEK Tom	HABU	3.7	
17/01/85	964	07:30	MATTHEWS Joe	OSTERHELD Curt	HABU	4	
21/01/85	964	09:30	BURK Bill	HENICHEK Tom	HABU	3.8	
22/01/85	973	18:58	BURK Bill	HENICHEK Tom	HABU	0.5	A
23/01/85	973	18:30	BURK Bill	HENICHEK Tom	HABU	0.5	A
24/01/85	964	18:30	MATTHEWS Joe	OSTERHELD Curt	N-HABU	2.2	
26/01/85	964	08:00	MATTHEWS Joe	OSTERHELD Curt	HABU	2.3	
28/01/85	964	21:00	MATTHEWS Joe	OSTERHELD Curt	N-HABU	2.3	
29/01/85	973	14:00	SHUL Brian	WATSON Walter	FCF	2.8	
31/01/85	964	14:00	SHUL Brian	WATSON Walter	HABU	2.4	
01/02/85	973	11:00	MATTHEWS Joe	OSTERHALD Curt	HABU	2.3	
05/02/85	964	13:51	SHUL Brian	WATSON Walter	HABU	2.3	
06/02/85	973	19:50	MATTHEWS Joe	OSTERHELD Curt	N-HABU	2.3	
08/02/85	964	09:30	SHUL Brian	WATSON Walter	HABU	2.6	
12/02/85	973	12:00	MATTHEWS Joe	OSTERHELD Curt	HABU	2.3	
14/02/85	964	11:30	SHUL Brian	WATSON Walter	HABU	4.2	
19/02/85	964	21:04	DYER Les	TABOR Ron	N-HABU	2.3	
22/02/85	973	11:00	SHUL Brian	WATSON Walter	HABU	2.5	A
25/02/85	964	10:15	DYER Les	TABOR Ron	HABU	2.3	
27/02/85	964	12:00	SHUL Brian	WATSON Walter	HABU	2.4	
01/03/85	964	10:00	DYER Les	TABOR Ron	HABU	2.2	
04/03/85	964	19:00	SHUL Brian	WATSON Walter	N-HABU	2.2	
07/03/85	964	09:30	DYER Les	TABOR Ron	HABU	2.2	
11/03/85	973	13:00	YEILDING Edward	LEE Steve	HABU	2.3	
13/03/85	964	08:45	DYER Les	TABOR Ron	HABU	2.2	
15/03/85	973	09:10	YEILDING Edward	LEE Steve	HABU	2.3	
19/03/85	973	19:30	DYER Les	TABOR Ron	HABU	2.2	
22/03/85	964	10:00	YEILDING Edward	LEE Steve	HABU	2.3	
26/03/85	973	12:00	DYER Les	TABOR Ron	HABU	2.3	
28/03/85	964		YEILDING Edward	LEE Steve	HABU		A
28/03/85	973	14:00	YEILDING Edward	LEE Steve	HABU	2.3	
01/04/85	973	11:00	SMITH Bernie	WHALEN Denny	HABU	2.3	
03/04/85	964	11:00	YEILDING Edward	LEE Steve	HABU	2.3	
05/04/85	973	11:30	SMITH Bernie	WHALEN Denny	HABU	3.9	
09/04/85	973	09:10	YEILDING Edward	LEE Steve	HABU	2.2	
10/04/85	964	19:30	SMITH Bernie	WHALEN Denny	N-HABU	1.9	A
12/04/85	973	11:38	YEILDING Edward	LEE Steve	HABU	2.3	
15/04/85	964	11:00	SMITH Bernie	WHALEN Denny	HABU	2.4	
16/04/85	973	12:00	YEILDING Edward	LEE Steve	HABU	2.6	
18/04/85	964	15:00	SMITH Bernie	WHALEN Denny	HABU	2.3	
22/04/85	964	10:45	SMITH Bernie	WHALEN Denny	HABU	2.3	
23/04/85	964	09:50	DEAL Duane	VELTRI Tom	FCF	2.4	
24/04/85	973	10:15	SMITH Bernie	WHALEN Denny	HABU	0.4	A
26/04/85	973	09:30	DEAL Duane	VELTRI Tom	HABU	2.4	

Date	Instal. No.	T.O. Time	Pilot Name	RSO Name	Mission	Duration	Remarks
29/04/85	964	12:01	DEAL Duane	VELTRI Tom	HABU	4	
01/05/85	973	18:55	SMITH Bernie	WHALEN Denny	N-HABU	2.3	
03/05/85	964	11:00	SMITH Bernie	WHALEN Denny	HABU	2.3	
06/05/85	964	12:00	DEAL Duane	VELTRI Tom	HABU	2.4	
07/05/85	973	10:15	SMITH Bernie	WHALEN Denny	HABU	2.3	
09/05/85	964	10:00	DEAL Duane	VELTRI Tom	HABU	3.7	
13/05/85	964	23:00	JIGGENS Jim	McCUE Joe	N-HABU	1.4	A
15/05/85	973	11:34	JIGGENS Jim	McCUE Joe	HABU	2.2	A
16/05/85	964	09:45	DEAL Duane	VELTRI Tom	HABU	2.2	
21/05/85	973	19:30	DEAL Duane	VELTRI Tom	N-HABU	2.3	
27/05/85	973	08:00	JIGGENS Jim	McCUE Joe	FCF	2.1	
29/05/85	973	13:40	JIGGENS Jim	McCUE Joe	HABU	2.4	
31/05/85	973	09:30	JIGGENS Jim	McCUE Joe	HABU	2.3	
03/06/85	973	15:00	JIGGENS Jim	McCUE Joe	HABU	2.2	
04/06/85	964	10:22	NOLL Duane	MORGAN Charlie	FCF	2.5	
05/06/85	973	20:15	JIGGENS Jim	McCUE Joe	N-HABU	2.3	
07/06/85	973	10:00	NOLL Duane	MORGAN Charlie	HABU	2.3	A
10/06/85	964	09:45	NOLL Duane	MORGAN Charlie	HABU	2.2	
11/06/85	958	04:01	MADISON Jack	ORCUTT Bill	FERRY IN-H	6.6	
12/06/85	964	19:20	JIGGENS Jim	McCUE Joe	N-HABU	2.3	
13/06/85	958	11:00	TILDEN Tom	VIDA Joe	FCF DAFICS	3.6	
14/06/85	973	10:00	MADISON Jack	ORCUTT Bill	HABU	4.5	
17/06/85	958	13:10	TILDEN Tom	VIDA Joe	FCF DAFICS	3.7	
18/06/85	964	20:18	JIGGENS Jim	McCUE Joe	N-HABU	2.5	
19/06/85	958	11:53	TILDEN Tom	VIDA Joe	FCF DAFICS	2.6	
21/06/85	973	11:20	NOLL Duane	MORGAN Charlie	HABU	2.2	
24/06/85	958	10:15	NOLL Duane	MORGAN Charlie	HABU	2.3	
25/06/85	973		JIGGENS Jim	McCUE Joe	H-FERRY OUT		A
26/06/85	973	08:00	JIGGENS Jim	McCUE Joe	H-FERRY OUT		
28/06/85	964	12:00	MADISON Jack	ORCUTT Bill	HABU	2.4	
01/07/85	964	19:30	NOLL Duane	MORGAN Charlie	N-HABU	2.2	
03/07/85	958	09:30	MADISON Jack	ORCUTT Bill	HABU	2.2	
09/07/85	958	12:00	NOLL Duane	MORGAN Charlie	HABU	2.3	
11/07/85	958	09:15	MADISON Jack	ORCUTT Bill	HABU	2.3	
16/07/85	964	09:45	BOUDREAUX Stormy	ROSS Ted	HABU	2.3	
17/07/85	958	13:00	MADISON Jack	ORCUTT Bill	HABU	2.3	
18/07/85	958	10:35	BOUDREAUX Stormy	ROSS Ted	HABU	2.4	
21/07/85	958	10:00	BOUDREAUX Stormy	ROSS Ted	HABU	4.5	
22/07/85	964	20:00	MADISON Jack	ORCUTT Bill	N-HABU	2.3	
25/07/85	964	13:45	BOUDREAUX Stormy	ROSS Ted	HABU	2.3	
31/07/85	968	04:30	SMITH Bernie	WHALEN Denny	FERRY IN-H	6	
01/08/85	964	08:00	MADISON Jack	ORCUTT Bill	H-FERRY OUT		
02/08/85	968	09:20	BOUDREAUX Stormy	ROSS Ted	HABU	2.3	
05/08/85	958	19:30	SMITH Bernie	WHALEN Denny	N-HABU	2.3	
07/08/85	968	11:15	BOUDREAUX Stormy	ROSS Ted	HABU	2.3	
09/08/85	968	10:15	SMITH Bernie	WHALEN Denny	HABU	2.2	
14/08/85	958		BOUDREAUX Stormy	ROSS Ted	HABU		A
19/08/85	968	11:03	SMITH Bernie	WHALEN Denny	HABU	3.9	
23/08/85	968	11:30	BOUDREAUX Stormy	ROSS Ted	HABU	2.3	
25/08/85	968	10:00	SMITH Bernie	WHALEN Denny	HABU	4.5	
26/08/85	958	09:30	DYCKMAN Rod	BERGAM Tom	FCF	2.4	
27/08/85	968	11:00	DYCKMAN Rod	BERGAM Tom	HABU	2.3	
28/08/85	968	19:15	SMITH Bernie	WHALEN Denny	N-HABU	2.3	
03/09/85	968	20:04	SMITH Bernie	WHALEN Denny	N-HABU	2.2	
05/09/85	968	12:00	DYCKMAN Rod	BERGAM Tom	HABU	2.3	
07/09/85	958	10:00	SMITH Bernie	WHALEN Denny	HABU	2.3	
10/09/85	968	10:00	DYCKMAN Rod	BERGAM Tom	HABU	2.4	
11/09/85	968	09:15	SMITH Bernie	WHALEN Denny	HABU	2.3	
12/09/85	958		DYCKMAN Rod	BERGAM Tom	HABU		A
13/09/85	968	10:00	DYCKMAN Rod	BERGAM Tom	HABU	0.5	A
14/09/85	968	10:00	DYCKMAN Rod	BERGAM Tom	HABU	1.5	A
17/09/85	958	11:00	MATTHEWS Joe	OSTERHELD Curt	HABU	2.2	
18/09/85	968	18:35	MATTHEWS Joe	OSTERHELD Curt	N-HABU	2.3	
21/09/85	958	09:34	DYCKMAN Rod	BERGAM Tom	HABU	2.1	
23/09/85	968	18:45	DYCKMAN Rod	BERGAM Tom	N-HABU	2.3	
26/09/85	958	08:15	MATTHEWS Joe	OSTERHELD Curt	HABU	2.3	
27/09/85	968	10:30	DYCKMAN Rod	BERGAM Tom	HABU	2.3	
01/10/85	958	11:09	DYCKMAN Rod	BERGAM Tom	HABU	2.2	
02/10/85	968	11:00	MATTHEWS Joe	OSTERHELD Curt	HABU	2.5	A
07/10/85	958	18:33	MATTHEWS Joe	OSTERHELD Curt	N-HABU	2.3	
09/10/85	968	12:10	MATTHEWS Joe	OSTERHELD Curt	HABU	2.3	
11/10/85	958	09:45	GLASSER Jerry	TABOR Ron	HABU	2.4	
15/10/85	968	18:15	MATTHEWS Joe	OSTERHELD Curt	HABU	0.3	A
17/10/85	958	12:02	MATTHEWS Joe	OSTERHELD Curt	HABU	2.3	
18/10/85	958	10:45	GLASSER Jerry	TABOR Ron	HABU	3.7	
21/10/85	968	10:30	MATTHEWS Joe	OSTERHELD Curt	FCF	2.1	
22/10/85	958	13:05	GLASSER Jerry	TABOR Ron	HABU	2.3	
23/10/85	968	10:15	MATTHEWS Joe	OSTERHELD Curt	FCF	2.3	
24/10/85	958	09:12	GLASSER Jerry	TABOR Ron	HABU	2.4	
28/10/85	968	10:30	DEAL Duane	VELTRI Tom	HABU	2.4	
30/10/85	968	18:15	CUNNINGHAM Nevin	TABOR Ron	N-HABU	2.3	
01/11/85	968	10:00	DEAL Duane	VELTRI Tom	HABU	2.3	
05/11/85	958	09:30	CUNNINGHAM Nevin	TABOR Ron	HABU	2.3	
06/11/85	968	09:32	DEAL Duane	VELTRI Tom	HABU	5.8	
07/11/85	958	10:15	CUNNINGHAM Nevin	TABOR Ron	HABU	2.5	
12/11/85	958	19:00	CUNNINGHAM Nevin	TABOR Ron	N-HABU	2.3	
14/11/85	958	10:30	DEAL Duane	VELTRI Tom	HABU	3.8	
19/11/85	968	11:00	SHUL Brian	WATSON Walter	HABU	1	A
21/11/85	958	10:30	DEAL Duane	VELTRI Tom	HABU	2.3	
23/11/85	968	12:15	SHUL Brian	WATSON Walter	HABU	2.3	
26/11/85	958	13:30	DEAL Duane	VELTRI Tom	HABU	2.2	
27/11/85	958	11:30	SHUL Brian	WATSON Walter	HABU	2.4	
29/11/85	958	09:10	DEAL Duane	VELTRI Tom	HABU	2.3	
02/12/85	958	17:00	SHUL Brian	WATSON Walter	N-HABU	2.4	
04/12/85	968	09:30	DEAL Duane	VELTRI Tom	HABU	2.3	
07/12/85	968	11:30	SHUL Brian	WATSON Walter	HABU	2.2	
09/12/85	958	09:32	SHUL Brian	WATSON Walter	HABU	5.9	
11/12/85	968	18:15	SMITH Bernie	WHALEN Denny	N-HABU	2.3	

Date	Instal. No.	T.O. Time	Pilot Name	RSO Name	Mission	Duration	Remarks
13/12/85	968	09:03	SHUL Brian	WATSON Walter	HABU	2.3	
17/12/85	958		SMITH Bernie	WHALEN Denny	N-HABU		A
17/12/85	958	21:35	SMITH Bernie	WHALEN Denny	N-HABU	2.3	
19/12/85	968	12:00	SHUL Brian	WATSON Walter	HABU	2.3	
20/12/85	958	09:45	SMITH Bernie	WHALEN Denny	HABU	3.7	
23/12/85	958	09:35	SHUL Brian	WATSON Walter	HABU	0.8	A
23/12/85	958	13:20	SHUL Brian	WATSON Walter	HABU	2.3	
27/12/85	958	13:10	SMITH Bernie	WHALEN Denny	HABU	2.3	
30/12/85	958	12:30	SMITH Bernie	WHALEN Denny	HABU	2.3	
02/01/86	968	18:55	BOUDREAUX Stormy	ROSS Ted	N-HABU	2.3	
07/01/86	958	12:00	SMITH Bernie	WHALEN Denny	HABU	2.3	
09/01/86	968	09:00	BOUDREAUX Stormy	ROSS Ted	HABU	2.4	
10/01/86	968	11:00	SMITH Bernie	WHALEN Denny	HABU	3.8	
13/01/86	958	11:15	BOUDREAUX Stormy	ROSS Ted	HABU	2.3	
15/01/86	958	09:45	SMITH Bernie	WHALEN Denny	HABU	2.3	
16/01/86	968	09:11	BOUDREAUX Stormy	ROSS Ted	HABU	2.3	
21/01/86	958	17:35	BOUDREAUX Stormy	ROSS Ted	N-HABU	2.4	
22/01/86	968	10:58	SMITH Mike	SOIFER Douglas	ACFAM	2.5	
23/01/86	958	10:00	BOUDREAUX Stormy	ROSS Ted	HABU	4	
25/01/86	968	10:20	SMITH Mike	SOIFER Douglas	HABU	3.2	
27/01/86	958	19:00	BOUDREAUX Stormy	ROSS Ted	N-HABU	2.4	
29/01/86	958	13:30	SMITH Mike	SOIFER Douglas	HABU	2.4	
03/02/86	958	17:55	BOUDREAUX Stormy	ROSS Ted	N-HABU	2.3	
05/02/86	968		SMITH Mike	SOIFER Douglas	HABU		A
06/02/86	968	09:15	SMITH Mike	SOIFER Douglas	HABU	2.3	
07/02/86	958	10:45	SMITH Mike	SOIFER Douglas	HABU	2.3	
11/02/86	958	10:00	MADISON Jack	ORCUTT Bill	HABU	2.4	
12/02/86	958	10:50	SMITH Mike	SOIFER Douglas	HABU	3.9	
14/02/86	968	10:30	MADISON Jack	ORCUTT Bill	HABU	2.3	
17/02/86	958	09:10	SMITH Mike	SOIFER Douglas	HABU	2.3	
20/02/86	968	13:00	MADISON Jack	ORCUTT Bill	HABU	2.3	
21/02/86	958	10:30	SMITH Mike	SOIFER Douglas	HABU	3.9	
24/02/86	958	10:10	MADISON Jack	ORCUTT Bill	HABU	2.5	
26/02/86	968	11:00	SMITH Mike	SOIFER Douglas	HABU	4	
27/02/86	968	13:00	MADISON Jack	ORCUTT Bill	HABU	2.3	
03/03/86	968	10:16	NOLL Duane	VELTRI Tom	HABU	2.3	
04/03/86	958	10:00	MADISON Jack	ORCUTT Bill	HABU	3.9	
06/03/86	968	18:30	NOLL Duane	VELTRI Tom	N-HABU	2.4	
10/03/86	958	19:00	NOLL Duane	VELTRI Tom	N-HABU	2.3	
12/03/86	968	11:30	MADISON Jack	ORCUTT Bill	HABU	2.4	
17/03/86	958	11:00	MADISON Jack	ORCUTT Bill	HABU	3.9	
18/03/86	968	10:30	NOLL Duane	VELTRI Tom	HABU	2.3	
21/03/86	958	10:30	MADISON Jack	ORCUTT Bill	HABU	1.8	A
22/03/86	958	09:30	MADISON Jack	ORCUTT Bill	HABU	2.2	
24/03/86	968	19:15	YEILDING Ed	LEE Steve	N-HABU	2.3	
26/03/86	968	10:00	NOLL Duane	VELTRI Tom	HABU	2.3	
27/03/86	968	09:35	YEILDING Ed	LEE Steve	HABU	2.3	
28/03/86	958	09:15	NOLL Duane	VELTRI Tom	HABU	2.3	
01/04/86	968	11:30	YEILDING Ed	LEE Steve	HABU	2.3	
02/04/86	968		NOLL Duane	VELTRI Tom	HABU		A
04/04/86	967	06:15	DYCKMAN Rod	BERGAM Tom	FERRY IN-H	6.6	
05/04/86	958		NOLL Duane	VELTRI Tom	H-FERRY OUT		A
06/04/86	958	10:00	NOLL Duane	VELTRI Tom	H-FERRY OUT		
08/04/86	968	10:00	YEILDING Ed	LEE Steve	HABU	3.7	
11/04/86	968	10:00	DYCKMAN Rod	BERGAM Tom	HABU	4.7	
15/04/86	967	09:45	YEILDING Ed	LEE Steve	HABU	2.2	
16/04/86	967	19:35	DYCKMAN Rod	BERGAM Tom	N-HABU	2.3	
18/04/86	968	11:45	YEILDING Ed	LEE Steve	HABU	2.3	
21/04/86	967	19:30	DYCKMAN Rod	BERGAM Tom	N-HABU	2.3	
23/04/86	968	12:00	YEILDING Ed	LEE Steve	HABU	2.2	
25/04/86	968	11:15	DYCKMAN Rod	BERGAM Tom	HABU	2.3	
29/04/86	967	13:05	YEILDING Ed	LEE Steve	HABU	2.3	
01/05/86	968	09:30	DYCKMAN Rod	BERGAM Tom	HABU	2.4	
07/05/86	968	10:06	MATTHEWS Joe	OSTERHELD Curt	HABU	3.7	
08/05/86	967	15:00	DYCKMAN Rod	BERGAM Tom	HABU	2.2	
09/05/86	968	11:00	MATTHEWS Joe	OSTERHELD Curt	HABU	2.3	
12/05/86	968	19:15	MATTHEWS Joe	OSTERHELD Curt	N-HABU	2.3	
14/05/86	968	09:45	MATTHEWS Joe	OSTERHELD Curt	HABU	2.3	
16/05/86	968	11:30	DYCKMAN Rod	TABOR Ron	HABU	3.6	
19/05/86	967		MATTHEWS Joe	OSTERHELD Curt	HABU		A
20/05/86	968	09:15	MATTHEWS Joe	OSTERHELD Curt	HABU	2.4	
21/05/86	967	10:15	DYCKMAN Rod	TABOR Ron	HABU	2.3	
22/05/86	967	09:15	MATTHEWS Joe	OSTERHELD Curt	HABU	2.3	
27/05/86	968	19:44	MATTHEWS Joe	OSTERHELD Curt	N-HABU	0.4	A
27/05/86	968	22:21	MATTHEWS Joe	OSTERHELD Curt	N-HABU	2.3	
28/05/86	967	13:00	HOUSE Dan	BOZEK Blair	CRFAM	2.4	
30/05/86	967	11:00	HOUSE Dan	BOZEK Blair	HABU	4	
02/06/86	967	09:58	MATTHEWS Joe	OSTERHELD Curt	HABU	2.3	
03/06/86	968	11:28	HOUSE Dan	BOZEK Blair	HABU	2.4	
05/06/86	967	19:25	MATTHEWS Joe	OSTERHELD Curt	N-HABU	2.3	
09/06/86	968	11:00	HOUSE Dan	BOZEK Blair	HABU	3.9	
12/06/86	967	09:30	MATTHEWS Joe	OSTERHELD Curt	HABU	2.3	
13/06/86	968	11:00	HOUSE Dan	BOZEK Blair	HABU	1.9	A
16/06/86	967	10:00	HOUSE Dan	BOZEK Blair	HABU	2.2	
17/06/86	968	09:15	JIGGENS Jim	ROSS Ted	HABU	2.4	
18/06/86	968	12:00	HOUSE Dan	BOZEK Blair	HABU	2.1	
20/06/86	968	09:45	JIGGENS Jim	ROSS Ted	HABU	2.4	
23/06/86	967	11:57	HOUSE Dan	BOZEK Blair	HABU	2.2	
25/06/86	967	19:30	JIGGENS Jim	ROSS Ted	N-HABU	2.2	
27/06/86	968	12:00	HOUSE Dan	BOZEK Blair	FCF	2.6	
02/07/86	968	09:35	HOUSE Dan	BOZEK Blair	HABU	1.9	A
03/07/86	967	10:57	JIGGENS Jim	ROSS Ted	HABU	0.7	A
03/07/86	967	15:42	JIGGENS Jim	ROSS Ted	HABU	2.2	
07/07/86	967	20:15	SHUL Brian	WATSON Walter	N-HABU	2.3	
09/07/86	968	10:17	JIGGENS Jim	ROSS Ted	HABU	2.3	
11/07/86	968	09:43	SHUL Brian	WATSON Walter	HABU	2.3	
15/07/86	967	09:43	JIGGENS Jim	ROSS Ted	HABU	2.4	
17/07/86	968	11:59	SHUL Brian	WATSON Walter	HABU	2.3	

Date	Instal. No.	T.O. Time	Pilot Name	RSO Name	Mission	Duration	Remarks
18/07/86	967	09:59	JIGGENS Jim	ROSS Ted	HABU	2.3	
21/07/86	968	19:27	JIGGENS Jim	ROSS Ted	N-HABU	2.4	
24/07/86	967	10:07	SHUL Brian	WATSON Walter	HABU	2.3	
28/07/86	968	10:42	SMITH Mike	SOIFER Douglas	HABU	2.3	
30/07/86	967	11:25	SHUL Brain	WATSON Walter	HABU	2.4	
01/08/86	968	09:26	SMITH Mike	SOIFER Douglas	HABU	2.3	
04/08/86	968	11:23	SHUL Brian	WATSON Walter	HABU	2.3	
05/08/86	968	19:20	SMITH Mike	SOIFER Douglas	N-HABU	2.3	
08/08/86	968	09:40	SHUL Brian	WATSON Walter	HABU	2.2	
11/08/86	968	19:15	SMITH Mike	SOIFER Douglas	N-HABU	2.4	
13/08/86	967	11:09	SHUL Brian	WATSON Walter	HABU	2.3	
14/08/86	968	10:00	SMITH Mike	SOIFER Douglas	HABU	2.3	
18/08/86	967	10:53	NOLL Duane	VELTRI Tom	HABU	2.4	
20/08/86	968	19:25	NOLL Duane	VELTRI Tom	N-HABU	2.2	
22/08/86	967	10:25	SMITH Mike	SOIFER Douglas	HABU	2.3	
28/08/86	967	09:26	NOLL Duane	VELTRI Tom	HABU	2.3	
29/08/86	967	10:40	SMITH Mike	SOIFER Douglas	HABU	2.3	
01/09/86	968	11:00	SMITH Mike	SOIFER Douglas	HABU	2.3	
04/09/86	967	19:30	NOLL Duane	VELTRI Tom	N-HABU	2.3	
06/09/86	967	09:30	NOLL Duane	VELTRI Tom	HABU	2.2	
08/09/86	968	11:25	MADISON Jack	LEE Steve	HABU	2.3	
10/09/86	968	10:00	NOLL Duane	VELTRI Tom	HABU	2.2	
11/09/86	967	19:30	MADISON Jack	LEE Steve	N-HABU	0.5	A
11/09/86	968	21:45	MADISON Jack	LEE Steve	N-HABU	2.2	
13/09/86	967	09:45	NOLL Duane	VELTRI Tom	HABU	2.2	
15/09/86	968	20:04	NOLL Duane	VELTRI Tom	N-HABU	2.3	
17/09/86	967	07:00	NOLL Duane	VELTRI Tom	HABU	2.4	
18/09/86	967	05:55	MADISON Jack	LEE Steve	HABU	2.7	
24/09/86	967	10:00	NOLL Duane	VELTRI Tom	HABU	3.2	
27/09/86	967	10:00	MADISON Jack	LEE Steve	HABU	4.5	
01/10/86	968	10:18	DANIELSON Tom	GUDMUNDSON Stan	ACFAM	2.3	
02/10/86	967	12:30	MADISON Jack	LEE Steve	HABU	3.5	
06/10/86	968	10:30	DANIELSON Tom	GUDMUNDSON Stan	HABU	2.3	
08/10/86	967	18:30	DANIELSON Tom	GUDMUNDSON Stan	N-HABU	2.3	
10/10/86	968	09:45	MADISON Jack	LEE Steve	HABU	2.3	
14/10/86	967	18:20	MADISON Jack	LEE Steve	N-HABU	2.5	
16/10/86	968	09:58	DANIELSON Tom	GUDMUNDSON Stan	HABU	2.2	
20/10/86	968	18:40	DANIELSON Tom	GUDMUNDSON Stan	N-HABU	2.3	
22/10/86	967	11:30	SMITH Bernie	ORCUTT Bill	HABU	3.2	
24/10/86	968	10:50	DANIELSON Tom	GUDMUNDSON Stan	HABU	2.3	
27/10/86	968	09:15	SMITH Bernie	ORCUTT Bill	HABU	2.2	
28/10/86	967	11:10	SMITH Bernie	ORCUTT Bill	HABU	2.2	
30/10/86	968	09:10	SMITH Bernie	ORCUTT Bill	HABU	3.7	
03/11/86	968	10:58	SMITH Bernie	ORCUTT Bill	HABU	2.2	
07/11/86	967	12:10	DANIELSON Tom	GUDMUNDSON Stan	HABU	4.5	
12/11/86	968	17:50	MATTHEWS Joe	MORGAN John	N-HABU	2.3	
14/11/86	968	10:15	NOLL Duane	VELTRI Tom	HABU	3.9	
17/11/86	967	12:10	MATTHEWS Joe	MORGAN John	HABU	2.2	
18/11/86	968	19:40	NOLL Duane	VELTRI Tom	N-HABU	2.3	
20/11/86	968	09:50	MATTHEWS Joe	MORGAN John	HABU	2.2	
21/11/86	967	10:30	NOLL Duane	VELTRI Tom	HABU	3.9	
24/11/86	968	10:05	MATTHEWS Joe	MORGAN John	HABU	3.5	
25/11/86	967	12:10	NOLL Duane	VELTRI Tom	HABU	2.2	
01/12/86	968	09:10	DYCKMAN Rod	BERGAM Tom	HABU	2.3	
02/12/86	967	10:01	PAPPAS Terry	MANZI John	CRFAM	2.5	
03/12/86	968	18:00	DYCKMAN Tod	BERGAM Tom	N-HABU	2.3	
05/12/86	968	09:36	PAPPAS Terry	MANZI John	HABU	2.4	
08/12/86	968	09:50	DYCKMAN Rod	BERGAM Tom	HABU	2.4	
10/12/86	967	09:10	DYCKMAN Rod	BERGAM Tom	HABU	5.7	
11/12/86	968	17:45	PAPPAS Terry	MANZI John	N-HABU	2.4	
15/12/86	967	10:35	PAPPAS Terry	MANZI John	HABU	2.4	
16/12/86	968	09:20	DYCKMAN Rod	BERGAM Tom	HABU	2.4	
18/12/86	967		PAPPAS Terry	MANZI John	HABU		A
18/12/86	967	12:50	PAPPAS Terry	MANZI John	HABU	2.4	
22/12/86	967	17:40	YEILDING Ed	OSTERHELD Curt	N-HABU	2.2	
23/12/86	968	13:00	PAPPAS Terry	MANZI John	HABU	2.3	
29/12/86	967	10:45	YEILDING Ed	OSTERHELD Curt	HABU	3.9	
02/01/87	967	09:35	PAPPAS Terry	MANZI John	HABU	2.8	
05/01/87	968	09:59	YEILDING Ed	OSTERHELD Curt	HABU	2.2	
06/01/87	967	18:00	PAPPAS Terry	MANZI John	N-HABU	2.3	
08/01/87	968	10:21	YEILDING Ed	OSTERHELD Curt	HABU	3.3	
12/01/87	967		HOUSE Dan	BOZEK Blair	N-HABU		
13/01/87	967		HOUSE Dan	BOZEK Blair	N-HABU		
14/01/87	967	10:45	HOUSE Dan	BOZEK Blair	HABU	2.4	
15/01/87	968	11:00	YEILDING Ed	OSTERHELD Curt	HABU	1.9	A
16/01/87	967	11:00	HOUSE Dan	BOZEK Blair	HABU	2.3	
20/01/87	968	18:40	YEILDING Ed	OSTERHELD Curt	N-HABU	2.3	
21/01/87	967	14:50	HOUSE Dan	BOZEK Blair	HABU	2.4	
23/01/87	967	10:20	YEILDING Ed	OSTERHELD Curt	HABU	2.3	
26/01/87	968	11:35	HOUSE Dan	BOZEK Blair	HABU	2.3	
27/01/87	967	18:05	YEILDING Ed	OSTERHELD Curt	N-HABU	2.3	
29/01/87	967	13:07	HOUSE Dan	BOZEK Blair	HABU	2.4	
02/02/87	968		HOUSE Dan	BOZEK Blair	HABU		A
02/02/87	968	09:51	HOUSE Dan	BOZEK Blair	HABU	2.3	
03/02/87	967		SHUL Brian	WATSON Walter	HABU		
04/02/87	967		SHUL Brian	WATSON Walter	HABU		
05/02/87	967	10:20	SHUL Brian	WATSON Walter	HABU	3.8	
06/02/87	968	09:54	HOUSE Dan	BOZEK Blair	HABU	2.3	
07/02/87	968	10:05	SHUL Brian	WATSON Walter	HABU	2.2	
09/02/87	967	19:07	HOUSE Dan	BOZEK Blair	N-HABU	2.4	
11/02/87	967	12:11	SHUL Brian	WATSON Walter	HABU	2.3	
13/02/87	968	09:50	HOUSE Dan	BOZEK Blair	HABU	2.4	
17/02/87	967	09:10	SHUL Brian	WATSON Walter	HABU	2.3	
18/02/87	968	10:35	HOUSE Dan	BOZEK Blair	HABU	2.3	
19/02/87	967	11:55	SHUL Brian	WATSON Walter	HABU	3.2	
24/02/87	968	19:25	SMITH Mike	SOIFER Douglas	N-HABU	2.4	
26/02/87	968	09:35	SHUL Brian	WATSON Walter	HABU	2.3	
02/03/87	968	09:05	SMITH Mike	SOIFER Douglas	HABU	2.3	
04/03/87	968	10:20	SHUL Brian	WATSON Walter	HABU	2.3	
05/03/87	967	10:28	SMITH Mike	SOIFER Douglas	FCF	1.1	
07/03/87	967	09:25	SHUL Brian	WATSON Walter	HABU	2.6	
10/03/87	967	19:15	SMITH Mike	SOIFER Douglas	N-HABU	2.4	
12/03/87	967	11:40	SHUL Brian	WATSON Walter	HABU	2.8	
17/03/87	967	18:50	NOLL Duane	VELTRI Tom	N-HABU	2.2	
20/03/87	968	10:45	SMITH Mike	SOIFER Douglas	HABU	1.8	A
20/03/87	968	15:56	SMITH Mike	SOIFER Douglas	HABU	0.5	A
21/03/87	967	10:00	NOLL Duane	VELTRI Tom	HABU	2.2	
23/03/87	967	18:50	SMITH Mike	SOIFER Douglas	N-HABU	2.3	
25/03/87	968		SMITH Mike	SOIFER Douglas	HABU		A
26/03/87	967	10:37	SMITH Mike	SOIFER Douglas	HABU	3.3	
27/03/87	968	09:50	NOLL Duane	VELTRI Tom	HABU	2.3	
01/04/87	967	09:45	SMITH Mike	SOIFER Douglas	HABU	2.3	
02/04/87	968	10:35	NOLL Duane	VELTRI Tom	HABU	2.3	
04/04/87	967	12:36	NOLL Duane	VELTRI Tom	HABU	4.2	
06/04/87	967	12:00	McKENDREE Mac	SHELHORSE Randy	CRFAM	2.5	
07/04/87	968	10:00	McKENDREE Mac	SHELHORSE Randy	HABU	2.3	
09/04/87	967	18:50	NOLL Duane	VELTRI Tom	N-HABU	2.3	
14/04/87	967		McKENDREE Mac	SHELHORSE Randy	HABU		
16/04/87	967	11:00	McKENDREE Mac	SHELHORSE Randy	HABU	4	
17/04/87	968	12:00	NOLL Duane	VELTRI Tom	HABU	2.2	
20/04/87	967	19:00	McKENDREE Mac	SHELHORSE Randy	N-HABU	2.3	
23/04/87	968	09:50	NOLL Duane	VELTRI Tom	HABU	2.3	
27/04/87	967	19:00	McKENDREE Mac	SHELHORSE Randy	N-HABU	2.4	
29/04/87	968	10:00	DANIELSON Tom	GUDMUNDSON Stan	HABU	2.3	
02/05/87	967	11:09	McKENDREE Mac	SHELHORSE Randy	HABU	2.1	
05/05/87	967		DANIELSON Tom	GUDMUNDSON Stan	HABU		A
05/05/87	967	12:11	DANIELSON Tom	GUDMUNDSON Stan	HABU	2.2	
07/05/87	968	10:45	McKENDREE Mac	SHELHORSE Randy	HABU	3.7	
11/05/87	968	09:30	DANIELSON Tom	GUDMUNDSON Stan	HABU	3.3	
13/05/87	975	11:30	YEILDING Ed	OSTERHELD Curt	FERRY IN-H	6.9	
14/05/87	968	08:00	McKENDREE Mac	SHELHORSE Randy	H-FERRY OUT		
18/05/87	967	10:45	DANIELSON Tom	GUDMUNDSON Stan	HABU	2	
20/05/87	967	12:00	YEILDING Ed	OSTERHELD Curt	HABU	3.5	
22/05/87	967	09:45	DANIELSON Tom	GUDMUNDSON Stan	HABU	2.1	
26/05/87	975	19:43	YEILDING Ed	OSTERHELD Curt	N-HABU	2.1	
28/05/87	967	09:15	DANIELSON Tom	GUDMUNDSON Stan	HABU	2.2	
01/06/87	975	11:00	YEILDING Ed	OSTERHELD Curt	HABU	2.1	
02/06/87	967	19:36	DANIELSON Tom	GUDMUNDSON Stan	N-HABU	2.1	
04/06/87	975	11:05	YEILDING Ed	OSTERHELD Curt	HABU	3.6	
08/06/87	975	19:20	SMITH Mike	SOIFER Doug	N-HABU	2.1	
12/06/87	967	10:30	YEILDING Ed	OSTERHELD Curt	HABU	2.2	
16/06/87	975	12:20	SMITH Mike	SOIFER Doug	HABU	1.6	A
17/06/87	967		YEILDING Ed	OSTERHELD Curt	HABU		A
17/06/87	967	11:54	YEILDING Ed	OSTERHELD Curt	HABU	4.2	
22/06/87	967		SMITH Mike	SOIFER Doug	N-HABU		A
22/06/87	967	21:18	SMITH Mike	SOIFER Doug	N-HABU	2.2	
24/06/87	975	11:55	YEILDING Ed	OSTERHELD Curt	HABU	3.2	
25/06/87	967	11:15	SMITH Mike	SOIFER Doug	HABU	2.2	
29/06/87	967	09:57	SMITH Mike	SOIFER Doug	HABU	2.2	
30/06/87	975		BROWN Larry	CARTER Keith	CRFAM		A
30/06/87	975	16:24	BROWN Larry	CARTER Keith	CRFAM	2.4	
01/07/87	967	13:00	BROWN Larry	CARTER Keith	HABU	2.1	
06/07/87	975	19:10	SMITH Mike	SOIFER Doug	N-HABU	2.1	
08/07/87	967	10:36	BROWN Larry	CARTER Keith	HABU	2.2	
10/07/87	975	09:32	SMITH Mike	SOIFER Doug	HABU	2.2	
13/07/87	975	09:20	BROWN Larry	CARTER Keith	HABU	2.2	
16/07/87	967	10:35	SMITH Mike	SOIFER Doug	HABU	2.5	
17/07/87	967	10:34	BROWN Larry	CARTER Keith	HABU	2.2	
20/07/87	975	09:30	PAPPAS Terry	MANZI John	HABU	2.4	
22/07/87	975	11:00	YEILDING Ed	OSTERHELD Curt	HABU	4.3	
22/07/87	967	10:16	SMITH Mike	SOIFER Doug	HABU	11.2	32
28/07/87	975	13:35	BROWN Larry	CARTER Keith	HABU	2.1	
30/07/87	967	18:52	PAPPAS Terry	MANZI John	N-HABU	2.3	
03/08/87	967	10:05	BROWN Larry	CARTER Keith	HABU	2.2	
04/08/87	975	18:50	PAPPAS Terry	MANZI John	N-HABU	1.5	A
06/08/87	975	10:45	BROWN Larry	CARTER Keith	HABU	2.1	
09/08/87	975	11:30	PAPPAS Terry	MANZI John	HABU	11.1	33
09/08/87	967	12:19	BROWN Larry	CARTER Keith	HABU	4.4	
14/08/87	967	13:41	SMITH Bernie	BERGAM Tom	HABU	2.2	
18/08/87	967	11:52	PAPPAS Terry	MANZI John	HABU	0.4	A
18/08/87	967	16:01	PAPPAS Terry	MANZI John	HABU	2.2	
24/08/87	975	12:20	SMITH Bernie	BERGAM Tom	HABU	2.1	
27/08/87	967	09:22	PAPPAS Terry	MANZI John	HABU	2.1	
01/09/87	967	13:00	SMITH Barnie	BERGAM Tom	HABU	2.1	
03/09/87	967	10:06	HOUSE Dan	BOZEK Blair	HABU	2.1	
08/09/87	967	18:25	SMITH Barnie	BERGAM Tom	N-HABU	0.4	A
08/09/87	967	21:09	SMITH Barnie	BERGAM Tom	N-HABU	2.1	
09/09/87	975	15:19	HOUSE Dan	BOZEK Blair	HABU	2.2	
11/09/87	967	13:00	SMITH Barnie	BERGAM Tom	HABU-100	2.3	
15/09/87	975	10:00	HOUSE Dan	BOZEK Blair	HABU	2.2	
17/09/87	967	12:11	SMITH Barnie	BERGAM Tom	HABU	2.5	
21/09/87	967	10:45	HOUSE Dan	BOZEK Blair	HABU	3.3	
22/09/87	975	17:50	HOUSE Dan	BOZEK Blair	N-HABU	2.1	
22/09/87	967	12:00	GRZEBINIAK Steve	GREENWOOD Jim	CRWFAM	2.5	
24/09/87	975	10:34	GRZEBINIAK Steve	GREENWOOD Jim	HABU	3.8	
26/09/87	967	09:45	HOUSE Dan	BOZEK Blair	HABU	2.1	
29/09/87	975	10:15	GRZEBINIAK Steve	GREENWOOD Jim	HABU	2.1	
02/10/87	967	10:00	HOUSE Dan	BOZEK Blair	HABU	3.7	
05/10/87	967	17:20	GRZEBINIAK Steve	GREENWOOD Jim	N-HABU	2.1	
13/10/87	975	11:47	McKENDREE Mac	SHELHORSE Randy	HABU	1.8	A
15/10/87	967	11:19	GRZEBINIAK Steve	GREENWOOD Jim	HABU	3.2	
17/10/87	975	08:45	McKENDREE Mac	SHELHORSE Randy	HABU	2.1	
19/10/87	975		GRZEBINIAK Steve	GREENWOOD Jim	HABU		A
20/10/87	967	09:35	GRZEBINIAK Steve	GREENWOOD Jim	HABU	2.1	
23/10/87	975	13:00	McKENDREE Mac	SHELHORSE Randy	HABU	2.1	
26/10/87	975	12:05	HOUSE Dan	BOZEK Blair	HABU	2.5	

Date	Instal. No.	T.O. Time	Pilot Name	RSO Name	Mission	Duration	Remarks
26/10/87	967	11:00	McKENDREE Mac	SHELHORSE Randy	HABU	10.8	34
28/10/87	975	10:30	McKENDREE Mac	SHELHORSE Randy	HABU	3.6	
02/11/87	975	10:05	NOLL Duane	VELTRI Tom	HABU	3.7	
06/11/87	967	10:15	McKENDREE Mac	SHELHORSE Randy	HABU	1.9	A
11/11/87	967	11:20	NOLL Duane	VELTRI Tom	HABU	3.2	
14/11/87	975	09:05	McKENDREE Mac	SHELHORSE Randy	HABU	2.1	
16/11/87	967	09:30	NOLL Duane	VELTRI Tom	FCF	2	
19/11/87	974		MADISON Jack	BERGAM Tom	FERRY IN/HABU	6.4	
20/11/87	967	07:00	McKENDREE Mac	SHELHORSE Randy	HABU/FERRY OUT		
23/11/87	975	09:25	NOLL Duane	VELTRI Tom	HABU	2.1	
24/11/87	975	11:00	MADISON Jack	BERGAM Tom	HABU	3.7	
02/12/87	974	11:20	NOLL Duane	VELTRI Tom	HABU	2.1	
04/12/87	975	10:05	MADISON Jack	BERGAM Tom	HABU	4	
08/12/87	974	17:55	NOLL Duane	VELTRI Tom	N-HABU	1	A
09/12/87	975	12:00	NOLL Duane	VELTRI Tom	HABU	2.2	
10/12/87	975	11:39	MADISON Jack	BERGAM Tom	HABU	3.4	
15/12/87	974	13:26	DANIELSON Tom	GUDMUNDSON Stan	HABU	2.2	
16/12/87	975	12:30	MADISON Jack	BERGAM Tom	HABU	2.2	
21/12/87	974		DANIELSON Tom	GUDMUNDSON Stan	HABU		A
21/12/87	974		DANIELSON Tom	GUDMUNDSON Stan	HABU		A
22/12/87	975	11:30	DANIELSON Tom	GUDMUNDSON Stan	HABU	2.1	
29/12/87	974	09:55	MADISON Jack	BERGAM Tom	HABU	2.1	
04/01/88	975	17:40	DANIELSON Tom	GUDMUNDSON Stan	N-HABU	2.3	
06/01/88	974	10:55	BROWN Larry	CARTER Keith	HABU	2.1	
12/01/88	974	12:15	DANIELSON Tom	GUDMUNDSON Stan	HABU	2.1	
16/01/88	974	13:20	BROWN Larry	CARTER Keith	HABU	2.1	
21/01/88	974	09:35	DANIELSON Tom	GUDMUNDSON Stan	HABU	5.5	
22/01/88	975	11:10	SMITH Bernie	CARTER Keith	FCF	2.1	
25/01/88	975	11:25	SMITH Mike	SOIFER Doug	HABU	2	
28/01/88	975		SMITH Bernie	CARTER Keith	HABU		A
28/01/88	975		SMITH Bernie	CARTER Keith	HABU		A
29/01/88	974		SMITH Bernie	CARTER Keith	HABU		
30/01/88	974	15:00	SMITH Bernie	CARTER Keith	HABU	0.7	A
31/01/88	974	15:00	SMITH Bernie	CARTER Keith	HABU	3.2	
01/02/88	974	11:15	SMITH Mike	SOIFER Doug	HABU	2.1	
04/02/88	974	13:25	SMITH Bernie	CARTER Keith	HABU	2.2	
09/02/88	975	10:40	SMITH Mike	SOIFER Doug	HABU	2.1	
12/02/88	974	08:05	SMITH Bernie	CARTER Keith	HABU	5.2	
16/02/88	975	09:40	SMITH Mike	SOIFER Doug	HABU	2.1	
17/02/88	974	10:45	McCLEARY Tom	VARDAMAN Blue	CRFAM	2.2	
18/02/88	974	15:00	McCLEARY Tom	VARDAMAN Blue	HABU	3.3	
22/02/88	975	18:05	SMITH Mike	SOIFER Doug	N-HABU	2.2	
29/02/88	974	08:35	McCLEARY Tom	VARDAMAN Blue	HABU	5.3	
03/03/88	975	10:17	DYCKMAN Rod	WATSON Walt	HABU	2	
04/03/88	975	10:45	McCLEARY Tom	VARDAMAN Blue	HABU	3.8	
09/03/88	975	09:55	DYCKMAN Rod	WATSON Walt	HABU	2.1	
14/03/88	975	08:49	McCLEARY Tom	VARDAMAN Blue	HABU	3.7	
16/03/88	975	10:20	DYCKMAN Rod	WATSON Walt	HABU	2.2	
22/03/88	974	18:27	PAPPAS Terry	MANZI John	N-HABU	2.1	
29/03/88	974	12:04	HOUSE Dan	BOZEK Blair	HABU	2.1	
05/04/88	975	13:36	PAPPAS Terry	MANZI John	HABU	2.2	
07/04/88	974	08:53	HOUSE Dan	BOZEK Blair	HABU	3.4	
14/04/88	975	10:15	PAPPAS Terry	MANZI John	HABU	2.2	
15/04/88	974		HOUSE Dan	BOZEK Blair	HABU		A
15/04/88	975	09:51	HOUSE Dan	BOZEK Blair	HABU	5.2	
20/04/88	974	18:35	GRZEBINIAK Steve	GREENWOOD Jim	N-HABU	2.1	
21/04/88	975	11:45	HOUSE Dan	BOZEK Blair	FCF	2.2	
28/04/88	974	14:00	GRZEBINIAK Steve	GREENWOOD Jim	HABU	2.4	
30/04/88	974	09:17	HOUSE Dan	BOZEK Blair	HABU	10.9	35
30/04/88	975		GRZEBINIAK Steve	GREENWOOD Jim	HABU-G/A		A
04/05/88	974	19:05	McKENDREE Mac	SHELHORSE Randy	N-HABU	2.2	
10/05/88	975	09:05	GRZEBINIAK Steve	GREENWOOD Jim	HABU	3.5	
14/05/88	974	09:50	McKENDREE Mac	SHELHORSE Randy	FCF	2	
18/05/88	975	10:30	GRZEBINIAK Steve	GREENWOOD Jim	FCF	2.3	
20/05/88	974	15:00	McKENDREE Mac	SHELHORSE Randy	HABU	1.5	A
21/05/88	974	10:00	GRZEBINIAK Steve	GREENWOOD Jim	HABU	2.2	
23/05/88	975	14:10	McKENDREE Mac	SHELHORSE Randy	HABU	2.2	
26/05/88	974	10:20	GRZEBINIAK Steve	GREENWOOD Jim	HABU	4.8	
27/05/88	975	12:25	McKENDREE Mac	SHELHORSE Randy	HABU	1.9	
02/06/88	974	13:10	PAPPAS Terry	MANZI John	FCF	2.1	
06/06/88	975	11:30	McKENDREE Mac	SHELHORSE Randy	HABU	2.3	
09/06/88	974	11:18	PAPPAS Terry	MANZI John	FCF	2.2	
14/06/88	975	09:50	McKENDREE Mac	SHELHORSE Randy	HABU	2.1	
16/06/88	974	11:00	PAPPAS Terry	MANZI John	FCF	2.1	
17/06/88	975	12:10	McCLEARY Tom	BERGAM Tom	HABU	1.9	
21/06/88	974	12:30	PAPPAS Terry	MANZI John	HABU	2.1	
22/06/88	975	09:09	McCLEARY Tom	BERGAM Tom	HABU	3.5	
28/06/88	974	10:00	McCLEARY Tom	BERGAM Tom	FCF	2.1	
30/06/88	975	07:06	PAPPAS Terry	MANZI John	HABU/FERRY OUT		
03/07/88	979	05:00	BROWN Larry	CARTER Keith	FERRY IN/HABU	6.3	
07/07/88	979	09:06	BROWN Larry	CARTER Keith	HABU	3.2	
08/07/88	974	12:00	CRITTENDEN Greg	FINAN Mike	FCF	2.1	
12/07/88	974	10:00	CRITTENDEN Greg	FINAN Mike	FCF	4.3	
15/07/88	979	10:00	CRITTENDEN Greg	FINAN Mike	FCF	2.3	
16/07/88	974		BROWN Larry	CARTER Keith	HABU		A
18/07/88	974	12:10	BROWN Larry	CARTER Keith	HABU	2.3	
20/07/88	974	10:13	CRITTENDEN Greg	FINAN Mike	FCF	1.5	A
21/07/88	979	10:55	BROWN Larry	CARTER Keith	HABU	4.2	LTO
28/07/88	974	09:35	CRITTENDEN Greg	FINAN Mike	HABU	2.2	
31/07/88	979	13:00	DYCKMAN Rod	MANZI John	HABU	2.1	
02/08/88	974	09:44	CRITTENDEN Greg	FINAN Mike	HABU	2.2	
04/08/88	979	11:00	CRITTENDEN Greg	FINAN Mike	HABU	1.9	
06/08/88	979	09:30	DYCKMAN Rod	MANZI John	HABU	4.2	
12/08/88	979	09:12	DYCKMAN Rod	MANZI John	HABU/FERRY OUT		
17/08/88	974	14:50	CRITTENDEN Greg	FINAN Mike	HABU	1.1	A
23/08/88	974	11:45	SMITH Mike	SOIFER Doug	HABU	2.2	
25/08/88	974	10:40	NOLL Duane	VELTRI Tom	HABU	2	
29/08/88	974	09:30	SMITH Mike	SOIFER Doug	HABU	2.3	
31/08/88	974	13:35	NOLL Duane	VELTRI Tom	HABU	2.1	
02/09/88	974	09:20	SMITH Mike	SOIFER Doug	HABU	3.3	
07/09/88	974	09:01	NOLL Duane	VELTRI Tom	FCF	1.9	
08/09/88	974	10:01	SMITH Mike	SOIFER Doug	FCF	2.2	
12/09/88	974	09:05	NOLL Duane	VELTRI Tom	HABU	4.7	
14/09/88	974	10:36	WATKINS Don	FOWLKES Bob	CRFAM	2.2	
16/09/88	974	09:07	WATKINS Don	FOWLKES Bob	HABU	3.3	
19/09/88	974	09:30	HOUSE Dan	BOZEK Blair	FCF	4	
20/09/88	974	09:30	WATKINS Don	VELTRI Tom	FCF	2.2	
27/09/88	974	11:45	WATKINS Don	FOWLKES Bob	FCF	1.9	A
29/09/88	974	10:31	HOUSE Dan	BOZEK Blair	FCF	2.2	
04/10/88	974	10:45	WATKINS Don	FOWLKES Bob	FCF	2.1	
12/10/88	974	09:05	HOUSE Dan	BOZEK Blair	FCF	2.1	
20/10/88	974	14:00	HOUSE Dan	BOZEK Blair	FCF	2.1	
27/10/88	974	18:15	HOUSE Dan	BOZEK Blair	N-FCF	2.2	
02/11/88	974	10:02	HOUSE Dan	BOZEK Blair	FCF	2.2	
08/11/88	974	09:32	McCLEARY Tom	BERGAM Tom	FCF	2.2	
15/11/88	974	17:50	McCLEARY Tom	BERGAM Tom	N-FCF	2.3	
21/11/88	974	11:00	McCLEARY Tom	BERGAM Tom	FCF	2.2	
29/11/88	974	17:45	McCLEARY Tom	BERGAM Tom	N-FCF	2.3	
07/12/88	974	10:06	BROWN Larry	CARTER Keith	FCF	0.6	A
08/12/88	974		BROWN Larry	CARTER Keith	FCF		A
15/12/88	974	10:00	BROWN Larry	CARTER Keith	FCF	2.1	
19/12/88	974	11:00	BROWN Larry	BERGAM Tom	FCF	4	
21/12/88	974	11:01	BROWN Larry	BERGAM Tom	FCF	2.7	
04/01/89	974	11:00	NOLL Duane	MANZI John	FCF	2.1	
19/01/89	974	08:01	NOLL Duane	MANZI John	FCF	2.7	
24/01/89	974		NOLL Duane	MANZI John	FCF		A
25/01/89	974	15:02	NOLL Duane	MANZI John	FCF	2.2	
30/01/89	974	18:30	NOLL Duane	MANZI John	N-FCF	2.5	
07/02/89	974	11:00	GRZEBINIAK Steve	GREENWOOD Jim	FCF	2.1	
17/02/89	974	12:49	GRZEBINIAK Steve	GREENWOOD Jim	FCF	2.6	
22/02/89	974	12:49	GRZEBINIAK Steve	GREENWOOD Jim	N-FCF	2.2	
28/02/89	974	11:30	GRZEBINIAK Steve	GREENWOOD Jim	FCF	2.2	
10/03/89	974	11:29	CRITTENDEN Greg	BERGAM Tom	FCF	1.2	
14/03/89	974	18:50	CRITTENDEN Greg	FINAN Mike	N-FCF	2	
16/03/89	974	09:30	CRITTENDEN Greg	FINAN Mike	FCF	2	
27/03/89	974	10:30	CRITTENDEN Greg	FINAN Mike	FCF	3.9	
31/03/89	974	10:00	HOUSE Dan	BOZEK Blair	HABU	3.3	
03/04/89	974	12:21	HOUSE Dan	BERGAM Tom	FCF	1.6	
10/04/89	974	08:46	HOUSE Dan	BOZEK Blair	HABU	3.2	
12/04/89	974	14:25	HOUSE Dan	BERGAM Tom	FCF	2.2	
14/04/89	974	09:46	HOUSE Dan	BOZEK Blair	HABU	3.5	
21/04/89	974	09:30	HOUSE Dan	BOZEK Blair	HABU		C,36
09/06/89	962	07:04	McKENDREE Mac	SHELHORSE Randy	FERRY IN/HABU	6.2	
15/06/89	962	08:45	McKENDREE Mac	SHELHORSE Randy	HABU	3	A
20/06/89	962	19:51	McKENDREE Mac	SHELHORSE Randy	N-HABU	5.4	A
22/06/89	962	10:00	McKENDREE Mac	SHELHORSE Randy	FCF	2.1	
23/06/89	962	14:00	McKENDREE Mac	SHELHORSE Randy	HABU	3.2	
27/06/89	962	08:00	McKENDREE Mac	SHELHORSE Randy	HABU	4.8	
29/06/89	962	09:30	McKENDREE Mac	SHELHORSE Randy	HABU	3.4	
06/07/89	962	08:45	McKENDREE Mac	SHELHORSE Randy	HABU	3.6	
11/07/89	962	09:15	McKENDREE Mac	SHELHORSE Randy	HABU	3.7	
13/07/89	962	09:30	McKENDREE Mac	SHELHORSE Randy	HABU	3.6	
17/07/89	962	07:00	McKENDREE Mac	SHELHORSE Randy	HABU	5.4	
24/07/89	962	10:11	McKENDREE Mac	SHELHORSE Randy	HABU	3.5	
28/07/89	962	08:07	McCLEARY Thomas	GUDMUNDSON Stan	FCF	4.2	
03/08/89	962	12:00	McCLEARY Thomas	GUDMUNDSON Stan	FCF	2.2	
04/08/89	962		McCLEARY Thomas	GUDMUNDSON Stan	HABU		
09/08/89	962	09:15	McCLEARY Thomas	GUDMUNDSON Stan	HABU	3.8	
11/08/89	962	10:00	McCLEARY Thomas	GUDMUNDSON Stan	HABU	3.8	
15/08/89	962	09:05	McCLEARY Thomas	GUDMUNDSON Stan	HABU	3.7	
21/08/89	962	09:48	CRITTENDEN Greg	FINAN Mike	HABU	3.7	
23/08/89	962	15:00	CRITTENDEN Greg	FINAN Mike	N-HABU	5.3	
28/08/89	962	11:02	CRITTENDEN Greg	GUDMUNDSON Stan	FCF	3.9	
01/09/89	962	08:59	CRITTENDEN Greg	FINAN Mike	HABU	3.6	
06/09/89	962		CRITTENDEN Greg	FINAN Mike	HABU		A
18/09/89	962		WATKINS Don	FOWLKES Bob	HABU		
19/09/89	962	09:05	WATKINS Don	FOWLKES Bob	HABU	3.3	A
22/09/89	962	11:00	SMITH Mike	FOWLKES Bob	RTB FERRY	2.3	
25/09/89	962	09:10	WATKINS Don	FOWLKES Bob	HABU	3.4	
05/10/89	962	12:30	SMITH Mike	FOWLKES Bob	FCF	1.6	
06/10/89	962	12:00	WATKINS Don	FOWLKES Bob	FCF	1.5	A
23/10/89	962	10:08	HOUSE Dan	BOZEK Blair	FCF	2.3	
26/10/89	962	18:09	HOUSE Dan	BOZEK Blair	Nite-FCF	2.3	
31/10/89	962	11:30	HOUSE Dan	BOZEK Blair	FCF	2.1	
02/11/89	962	09:00	HOUSE Dan	BOZEK Blair	FCF	0.6	A
03/11/89	962	10:30	HOUSE Dan	BOZEK Blair	FCF	1.9	
06/11/89	962	09:30	HOUSE Dan	BOZEK Blair	FCF	2.2	
07/11/89	962	10:00	HOUSE Dan	SHELHORSE Randy	FCF	1.1	
14/11/89	962	11:50	GRZEBINIAK Steve	GREENWOOD Jim	FCF	2.3	
17/11/89	962	09:15	GRZEBINIAK Steve	GREENWOOD Jim	FCF	1.9	
21/11/89	962	11:30	GRZEBINIAK Steve	GREENWOOD Jim	FCF	2.2	
28/11/89	962	11:30	GRZEBINIAK Steve	WALTON Charles	HIGH SPEED TAXI		
05/12/89	962		GRZEBINIAK Steve	GREENWOOD Jim	FCF		A
06/12/89	962	10:00	GRZEBINIAK Steve	GREENWOOD Jim	FCF/CREW PROFICIENCY	0.9	
14/12/89	962	11:00	GRZEBINIAK Steve	ADRIAN David	HIGH SPEED TAXI		
18/12/89	962	08:10	GRZEBINIAK Steve	GREENWOOD Jim	FCF	2.5	
18/01/90	962	10:28	GRZEBINIAK Steve	GREENWOOD Jim	FCF	3.7	
21/01/90	962	05:00	GRZEBINIAK Steve	GREENWOOD Jim	FERRY OUT		

THE HABU'S DEAD, LONG LIVE THE HABU

A-12, YF-12 AND SR-71 CHECK FLIGHTS

Appendix 2

Check Ride No.	Category	Position/Rank	Name	Check Ride No.	Category	Position/Rank	Name
001	Plt	ADP	Lou Schalk	027	Eng	ADP	Glen Fulkerson
000	VIP	ADP	Kelly Johnson	028	Plt	CIA	Jack J. Layton
002	Plt	ADP	Bill Park	029	Plt	CIA	Mele Vojvodich
003	Plt	ADP	Jim Eastham	030	Plt	CIA	Jack C. Weeks
004	Plt	ADP	Bob Gilliland	031	RSO	ADP	Kenneth E. Moeller
005	Plt	CIA	William L. Skliar	032	VIP	ADP	Rus Daniell
006	Plt	CIA	Kenneth S. Collins	033	Plt	CIA	Francis J. Murray
007	Plt	CIA	Walter L. Ray	034	Plt	CIA	Russell J. Scott
008	Plt	CIA	Dennis B. Sullivan	101	Plt	Col	Robert I. Stephens
009	Plt	CIA	Alonzo J. Walter	102	FCO	Lt-Col	Daniel Andre
010	Eng	ADP	Larry Edgar	103	FCO	Maj	Noel T. Warner
011	Eng	ADP	Hank Stockham	104	FCO	Capt	James P. Cooney
012	Eng	ADP	Torrey Larsen	105	Plt	Maj	Walter F. Daniel
013	Plt	ADP	Darrell Greenamyer	106	FCO	Capt	Sammel M. Ursini
014	FCO	Hughes	Tony Byland	107	RSO	Maj	Kenneth D. Hurley
015	FCO	Hughes	Ray Scalise	108	Plt	Maj	Charles C. Bock
016	Eng	ADP	R. L. Dick Miller	109	Plt	Col	Vern Henderson
017	Plt	ADP	Art Peterson	110	Plt	Lt-Col	Jacqres G. Beezley
018	FCO	Hughes	George Parsons	111	Plt	Col	H. A. Templeton
019	Plt	ADP	Bill Weaver	112	Plt	Maj	Mervin L. Evenson
020	RSO	ADP	Jim Zwayer	113	Plt	Maj	Allen L. Hichew
021	FCO	Hughes	John Archer	114	RSO	Capt	Tom W. Schmittou
022	Eng	ADP	Keith Beswick	115	Plt	Maj	Robert G. Sowers
023	RSO	ADP	George Andre	116	RSO	Capt	Richard E. Sheffield
024	RSO	ADP	Steven A. Belgeau	117	RSO	Capt	Cosimo B. Mallozzi
025	RSO	ADP	Ray Torick	118	Plt	Lt-Col	Ray Haupt
026	Eng	ADP	Larry Bohanan	119	RSO	Lt-Col	Cecil H. Braeden
				120	RSO	Capt	James W. Fagg
				121	RSO	Maj	William R. Payne
				122	Plt	Col	Frenchy D. Bennett
				123	VIP	Brig-Gen	H. B. Manson
				124	Plt	Lt-Col	Joe Rogers
				125		Lt-Col	Ralph Richardson
				126	Plt	Col	Robert J. Holbury
				127	Plt	Col	Hugh C. Slater
				128	Plt	Maj	Harold E. Burgeson
				129	Plt	Lt-Col	B. S. Barrett
				130	Plt	Lt-Col	Roland L. Perkim
				131	RSO	Lt-Col	Norman S. Drake
				132	Plt	Maj	Ben Bowles
				133	RSO	Lt-Col	Harold C. Peterson
				134	Plt	Maj	William J. Campbell
				135	RSO	Capt	Albert N. Pennington
				136	Plt	Col	Douglas T. Nelson
				137	RSO	Lt-Col	Russel L. Lewis
				138	Plt	Maj	Patrick J. Halloran
				139	RSO	Capt	Mortimer J. Jarvis
				140	RSO	Capt	David P. Dempster

This group of A-12 personnel includes, from left to right, Jack Layton, Dennis Sullivan, Mele Vojvodich, Lt-Col Burt Barrett, Jack Weeks, Ken Collins, Walt Ray, Gen Ledford, Bill Skliar, Lt-Col Cy Perins, Col Holbury, Col Kelly and Col Slater.

Check Ride No.	Category	Position/ Rank	Name	Check Ride No.	Category	Position/ Rank	Name
141	Plt	Maj	Buddy L. Brown	192	RSO	Maj	Jon P. Kraus
142	RSO	Capt	David J. Jensen	193	Plt	Maj	Lothar J. Maier
143	Plt	Capt	Charles W. Collins	194	Plt	Maj	William E. Lawson III
144	RSO	Capt	Jean C. Seagroves				
145	Plt	Maj	John H. Storrie	195	RSO	Maj	James A. Kogler
146	Plt	Maj	Jack Kennon	196	RSO	Maj	Gary L. Coleman
147	Plt	Capt	Franklin D. Shelton	197	RSO	Maj	Gilbert Martinez
148	RSO	Capt	Lawrence L. Boggess	198	RSO	Lt-Col	Harold E. Chapman
				199	Plt	Capt	David E. Fruehauf
149	Plt	Lt-Col	William L. Skliar	200	VIP	Col	Benjamin N. Bellis
150	Plt	Maj	Jerome F. O'Malley	201	RSO	Capt	Allen R. Payne
151	RSO	Capt	Edward D. Payne	202	Plt	Maj	James W. Hudson
152	Plt	Maj	Donald A. Walbrecht	203	RSO	Capt	Norbet L. Budzinske
153	RSO	Capt	Phillip G. Loignon	204	RSO	Maj	Donn A. Byrnes
154	Plt	Capt	Earle M. Boone	205	RSO	Maj	Bruce Hartman
155	RSO	Capt	Dewain C. Vick	206	RSO	Maj	R. W. Weaver Jr
156	Staf	Col	Russell K. Weller	207	Plt	Lt-Col	Harlon A. Hain
157	Plt	Maj	James L. Watkins	208	RSO	Maj	Don Rhude
158	Plt	Maj	Anthony P. Bevacqua	209	Plt	Maj	Richard C. Gerard
				210	Plt	Maj	Thomas B. Estes
159	Staf	Col	William P. Hayes	211	RSO	Maj	Charles G McLean
160	RSO	Capt	Robert J. Rotcisoender	212	RSO	Maj	Ken G. Moeller
				213	Plt	Lt-Col	Kenneth S. Collins
161	RSO	Maj	William C. Keller	214	Plt	Maj	James H. Shelton Jr
162	RSO	Maj	Donald E. Mathers	215	Plt	Capt	Reverdy J. Allender
163	Plt	Capt	Robert C. Spencer	216		Lt-Col	Fred Trost
164	Plt	Col	Harold E. Confer	217	Plt	Lt-Col	Dennis B. Sullivan
165	RSO	Capt	Clyde L. Shoemaker	218	Plt	Lt-Col	Mel Vojvodich
166	Plt	Maj	Brian K. McCallom	219	Plt	Capt	Bruce E. Wilcox
167		Lt-Col	James C. Schever	220	Plt	Maj	E. L. Payne (EAFB)
168	RSO	Maj	Jerald L. Crew	221	VIP	Senator	Barry Goldwater
169	Plt	Maj	Larry S. Devall	222	Staf	Lt-Col	Ronald J. Layton
170	RSO	Capt	Ruel K. Branham	223	Staf	Col	James E. Anderson
171	RSO	Maj	Thomas A. Casey	224	VIP	Brig-Gen	Alton Slay
172	Plt	Maj	Roy L. St Martin	225	VIP	Col	William R. Payne
173	RSO	Capt	Robert M. Locke	226	Plt	Maj	Darrel W. Cobb
174	Plt	Maj	George M. Bull	227	RSO	Capt	Myron L. Gantt
175	RSO	Capt	John F. Carnochan	228	Plt	NASA	Fitzhugh L. Fulton Jr
176	Staf	Col	John B. Boynton	229	Plt	Maj	Thomas S. Pugh
177	Plt	Maj	Robert M. Powell	230	Plt	NASA	Donald L. Mallick
178	RSO	Maj	Charles J. McNeer	231	RSO	Maj	Ronnie C. Rice
179	Plt	Maj	Charles E. Daubs	232	Plt	Capt	Dennis K. Bush
180	Eng	Maj	William A. Lusby	233	Plt	Capt	Randolph B. Hertzog
181	Eng	Civ	Robert W. Sudderth				
182	RSO	Capt	William I. Kendrick	234	Plt	Col	D. B. Sullivan
183	Staf	Col	Charles F. Minter Sr	235	RSO	Maj	Ronald L. Selberg
184	Eng	Civ	Richard Abrams	236	Staf	Lt-Col	Roy W. Owen Jr
185	Plt	Capt	Bobby L. Campbell	237	RSO	Maj	Billy A. Curtis
186	VIP	Gen	Bruce Holloway (CINC)	238	Plt	Maj	George H. Sewell Jr
				239	RSO	Capt	Reginald T. Blackwell
187	VIP	Lt Gen	Arthur C. Agan	240	VIP	Lt Gen	P. K. Carlton 15th AF/CC
188	VIP	Lt Gen	William K. Martin				
189	Plt	Maj	Gabriel A. Kardong				
190	VIP	Lt Gen	Jack J. Catton (15th AF/CC)	241	RSO	Capt	George T. Morgan
				242	Plt	Capt	Robert J. Cunningham
191	RSO	Capt	Gary Heidlebauch				

Check Ride No.	Category	Position/Rank	Name
251	VIP	Congress-man	Robert Price
252	Plt	Capt	Carl A. Haller
253	VIP	Maj-Gen	Salvador E. Felices
254			cancelled
255	Plt	Maj	A. H. Bledsoe
256	RSO	Maj	Cletius C. Rogers
257	Plt	Maj	James V. Sullivan
258	RSO	Capt	Noel F. Widdifield
259	RSO	Capt	John T. Fuller
260	Plt	Capt	Leland B. Ransom III
261	RSO	Maj	Mark H. Gersten
262	Plt	Capt	Harold B. Adams
263	RSO	Capt	William C. Machorek
264	Plt	Capt	Robert C. Helt
265	RSO	Capt	Larry A. Elliott
266	Plt	Capt	Eldon W. Joersz
267	Plt	Capt	James F. Wilson
268	VIP	Maj-Gen	George W. McLaughlin
269	RSO	Capt	Bruce S. Douglass
270	VIP	Sec of AF	John L. McLucas
271	VIP	Lt Gen	William F. Pitts (15th AF/CC)
272	VIP	Brig-Gen	Don D. Pittman (14th AD/CC)
273	Plt	Capt	Maury Rosenberg

Below: Bill Park joined Schalk on the A-12 test team as the type's second pilot, with Check Ride number 002.

Above: With Check Ride number 001, Lou Schalk was the first person ever to fly an aircraft in the 'Blackbird' family.

Check Ride No.	Category	Position/Rank	Name
243	RSO	NASA	Victor W. Horton
244	VIP	Col	Ross Spinkle
245	Plt	Capt	Monty T. Judkin
246	VIP	Brig-Gen	Lukeman
247	Plt	Maj	Caroll D. Gunther
248	RSO	NASA	William R. Young
249	RSO	Capt	Thomas R. Allocca
250	Staf	Brig-Gen	Edgar S. Harris Jr

Check Ride No.	Category	Position/Rank	Name
274	RSO	Capt	Donald C. Bulloch
275	VIP	Lt-Col	Hal Rupard
276	VIP	Lt-Col	Jackie G. Reed
277	Plt	Lt-Col/AFLC	Tom Smith
278	Staf	Lt-Col	Raphael S. Samay
279	Plt	Capt	Joseph C. Kinego
280	RSO	Capt	Roger L. Jacks
281	VIP	Maj-Gen	Ray B. Sitton
282	VIP	Hon	Malcom R. Currie
283	VIP	Hon	Walter B. Laberge
284	Plt	Capt	Alan B. Cirino
285	RSO	Capt	Bruce L. Liebman
286	Plt	Capt	Justin J. Murphy
287	VIP	Gen	Albert L. Melton
288	RSO	Maj	John A. Billingsley
289	VIP	Lt Gen	James M. Keck (Vice CINC)
290	VIP	Maj-Gen	Billy J. Ellis
291	Plt	Capt	Richard H. Graham
292	RSO	Capt	Donald R. Emmons
293	VIP	Maj-Gen	Herbert J. Gavin
294	Plt	Capt	Thomas M. Alison
295	Plt	Maj./AFLC	Robert L. Riedenauer AFLC
296	RSO	Maj./AFLC	William J. Frazier AFIC
297	RSO	Maj	Joseph T. Vida
298	VIP	Col	Merlyn H. Dethlefsen
299	VIP	Lt Gen	Bryan M. Shotts (15th AF/CC)
300	VIP	Lt Gen	Andrew B. Anderson Jr
301	VIP	Maj-Gen	John W. Burkhart
302	Staf	Col	Robert D. Beckel
303	VIP	Maj-Gen	Otis Moore

Lt-Col B. S. Barrett gained his SR-71 'wings' on Check Ride number 129.

From left to right, Doug Nelson and Ray Haupt were both among the first cadre of SR-71 pilots. The second pressure-suited crewmember is likely RSO Lt-Col Cecil H. Braeden, while Bill Hayes was a staff officer.

Check Ride No.	Category	Position/Rank	Name
304	Staf	Col	Richard J. Bower
305	Plt	Capt	William G. Gilmore
306	Plt	Maj	Robert W. Crowder
307	RSO	Capt	John G. Morgan
308	VIP	Gen	Russ E. Dougherty (CINC)
309	Plt	Capt	Adelbert W. Carpenter
310	VIP	Lt Gen	John W. Roberts
311	RSO	Capt	John E. Murphy
312	VIP	Brig-Gen	Gerald E. Cooke
313	VIP	Mr	James W. Plummer
314	RSO	Capt	William C. Keller
315	VIP	Lt Gen	Robert E. Hails
316	Staf	Col	Lyman M. Kidder
317	VIP	Hon	James B. Connor
318	Plt	Maj	John J. Veth
319	Plt	Maj	William G. Groninger
320	RSO	Capt	Charles T. Sober Jr
321	Plt	Maj	Bredette Thomas
322	VIP	Brig-Gen	Bill V. Brown (14th AD/CC)
323	RSO	Capt	Jay Reid
324	VIP	Maj-Gen	Earl G. Peck
325	Staf	Col	John W. Fenimore
326	Plt	Capt	Thomas J. Keck
327	RSO	Capt	Timothy J. Shaw
328	Plt	NASA	John Manke
329	Plt	NASA	Bill Dana
330	Plt	NASA	Gary E. Krier
331	Plt	NASA	Einar K. Enevoldson
332	Plt	NASA	Thomas C. McMurtry
333	Plt	Maj	David M. Peters
334	RSO	Capt	Michael L. Stockton
335	VIP	Col	Ted H. Shadburn

Check Ride number 139 saw Captain Mortimer J. Jarvis qualify as an SR-71 RSO.

Check Ride No.	Category	Position/ Rank	Name
336	RSO	Capt	Edgar J. Bethart Jr
337	Plt	Maj	Lee M. Shelton III
338	Staf	Col	Andrew G. Terry
339	Staf	Col	David G. Young
340	VIP	Lt Gen	Robert C. Mathis
341	RSO	Maj	Barry C. MacKean
342	Plt	Lt-Col/AFLC	Calvin F. Jewett AFIC
343	Plt	Capt	Richard A. Young
344			cancelled
345	RSO	Capt	Russell L. Szczepanik
346	VIP	Reverend	Theodore M. Hesburgh
347	VIP	Lt Gen	James P. Mullins (15th AF/CC)
348	Plt	NASA	Stephen D. Ishmael
349	Plt	NASA	Michael R. Swann
350	VIP	Brig-Gen	John A. Brashear (14th AD/CC)
351	Plt	Capt	Calvin J. Augustin
352	RSO	Maj	Frank K. Kelly
353	VIP	Col	Joseph S. Stanton

Below: Phil Loignon (left) is greeted by a samurai sword-wielding 'Chief-Master Necktie Cutter' CMSgt Bill Gornik on his debut outing, while his pilot, Don Walbrecht, looks on. (USAF via Don Walbrecht)

Check Ride No.	Category	Position/ Rank	Name	Check Ride No.	Category	Position/ Rank	Name
354	VIP	Senator	Howard W. Cannon	376	RSO	Maj	Dennis W. Whalen
355	Plt	Capt	Gilbert M. Bertelson	377	VIP	Brig-Gen	Monroe W. Hatch
356	RSO	Capt	Frank W. Stampf				(14th AD/CC)
357	VIP	Civ	Frank A. Fishburne	378	Plt	Capt	Gary I. Luloff
358	Plt	Capt	Richard W. Judson	379	VIP	Gen	Bennie L. Davis
359			cancelled				(CINC)
360	VIP	Lt Gen	Lloyd R. Leavitt Jr	380	RSO	Capt	Robert L. Coats
361	Plt	Maj	Nevin N.	381	VIP	Lt Gen	John J. Murphy
			Cunningham	382	VIP	Congress-	Robert K. Dornan
362	RSO	Capt	Gene R. Quist			man	
363			cancelled	383	Plt	Maj	Leslie R. Dyer
364	Plt	Capt	Dennis R. Berg	384	RSO	Capt	Daniel Greenwood
365	RSO	Maj./AFLC	Bill Flanagan	385	VIP	Lt Gen	George D. Miller
366	VIP	Civ	Jim Hartz				(Vice CINC)
367	RSO	Capt	ED McKim	386	VIP	Maj-Gen	Louis C. Buckman
368	Plt	Maj	Gerald T. Glasser				(SAC/DO)
369			cancelled	387	Staf	Col	Lonnie L. Liss
370	RSO	Capt	David M.	388	Plt	Capt	William Burk
			Hornbaker	389	Plt	Maj./AFLC	Thomas V. Tilden
371	VIP	Civ	Robert R.	390	VIP	Gen	Lew Allen (CS/Air
			Ropelewske				Force)
372	Plt	Capt	Richard S. McCrary	391	RSO	Capt	Thomas J. Henichek
373	RSO	Capt	David A. Lawrence	392	VIP	Brig-Gen	Jesse S. Hocker
374	Plt	Maj	Bernard J. Smith				(14th AD/CC)
375	VIP	Maj-Gen	John T. Chain Jr	393	Plt	Capt	James M. Jiggins
				394	RSO	Capt	Joseph J. McCue
				395	VIP	Sec of AF	Edward 'Pete' Aldridge

Tom Allison (pilot) and JT Vida teamed up as a crew for the period 1976–1977. (Paul F. Crickmore Collection)

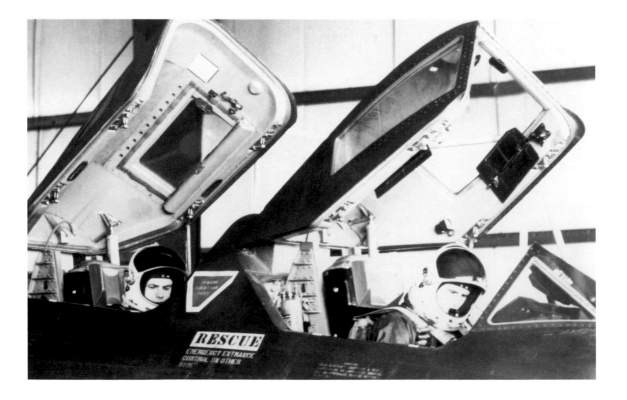

On 6 March 1990, Ed Yeilding and JT Vida set a new US coast-to-coast speed record of 1 hour 8 minutes, flying 64-17972. (USAF)

Check Ride No.	Category	Position/ Rank	Name
396	VIP	Lt Gen	Andrew P. Iosue
397	Plt	Maj	Robert F. Behler
398	RSO	Capt	Ronald D. Tabor
399	VIP	Congress-man	'Bill' C. W. Young
400	Plt	Maj	Lionel P. Boudreax
401	RSO	Capt	Walter F. Newgreen
402	VIP	Lt Gen	Lawrence A. Skantze
403	Plt	Maj	Joseph E. Matthews
404	RSO	Capt	Edward W. Ross
405	VIP	Brig-Gen	Charles Yeager
406	RSO	Capt	Douglas C. Osterheld
407	Staf	Col	George V. Freese
408	Staf	Col	David H. Pinsky
409	Plt	Capt	Jack E. Madison
410	VIP	Lt Gen	James E. Light (15th AF/CC)
411	RSO	Maj	William D. Orcutt
412	Plt	Capt	Ed Yeilding
413	RSO	Capt	Stephen M. Lee
414	Plt	Maj	Brian Shul
415	RSO	Maj	Waiter I. Watson
416	Plt	Capt	Duane W. Deal
417	RSO	Capt	Thomas F. Veltri

Shown here with Col Pat Bledsoe, RSO Capt Reggie Blackwell went on to fly mission GS663 with Col Darrell Cobb, beginning on 27 December 1972 and the only night sortie flown during the Vietnam War. They used aircraft 64-17975 for the operation. (USAF)

Check Ride No.	Category	Position/ Rank	Name
418	Plt	Maj	Duane M. Noll
419	RSO	Capt	Charles A. Morgan
420	VIP	Congress-man	Bob Stump
421	Plt	Maj	William R. Dyckman
422	RSO	Maj	Thomas E. Bergam
423	Staf	Brig-Gen	John Farrington (14th AD/CC)
424	Plt	Maj	Michael L. Smith
425	RSO	Capt	Douglas B. Soifer
426	Staf	Col	Robert B. McConnell
427	Staf	Maj-Gen	Alexander Davidson (AF/XO)
428	RSO	Maj	Phillip I. Soucy
429	VIP	Congress-man	Beverly Byron
430	Plt	Maj	Dan E. House
431	RSO	Capt	Blair L. Bozek
432	VIP	Gen	Larry D. Welch (CINC)
433	Plt	Maj	Thomas J. Danielson
434	VIP	Congress-man	Robert E. Badham
435	RSO	Maj	Stanley J. Gudmundson
436	Plt	Maj	Terry D. Pappas
437	RSO	Capt	John D. Manzi
438	Staf	Col	James Sarvada
439	VIP	Maj-Gen	Hansford T. Johnson SAC/DO
440	Plt	Maj	Warren C. Mckendree
441	RSO	Maj	Randy F. Shelhorse
442	VIP	Congress-man	Larry J. Hopkins
443	Plt	Maj	Larry Brown
444	RSO	Maj	Keith E. Carter
445	Plt	Capt	Steven Grzebiniak
446	RSO	Capt	James F. Greenwood
447	Plt	Maj	Thomas R. McCleary
448	RSO	Capt	Hunter W. Vardaman
449	VIP	Lt Gen	Kenneth L. Peek (Vice CINC)
450	Staf	Brig-Gen	Howell M. Estes (14th AD/C)
451	Staf	Col	Donald R. Schreiber
452	Plt	Capt	Gregory N. Crittenden
453	RSO	Maj./AFLC	Tom Fuhrman AFIC
454	RSO	Maj	Michael J. Finan
455	Plt	Maj	Donald T. Watkins
456	RSO	Capt	Robert E. Fowlkes
457	Plt	Capt	Ben Snyder

Check Ride No.	Category	Position/ Rank	Name
458	RSO	Capt	Briggs Shade
459	Staf	Brig-Gen	Kenneth F. Keller (14th AD/CC)
460	VIP	Lt Gen	Ellie G. Shuler Jr (8AF/CC)
461			cancelled
462	Plt	Maj./AFLC	Jim Halsell
463	Staf	Maj-Gen	John L. Borling
464	Plt	NASA	Roger Smith
465	FE	NASA	Marta Bohn-Meyer
466	FE	NASA	Robert E. Meyer

Note the jump in check ride numbers from 034 to 101. This is due to the allocation of numbers 000 to 100 to the Oxcart programme, some of which were not taken up prior to its termination. The Senior Crown programme was allocated the numbers 101 onward.

Here 'Buzz' Carpenter and his RSO John Murphy pose in celebration of their first operational sortie. (USAF)

DISPOSITION OF A-12, YF-12A AND SR-71 AIRFRAMES

Appendix 3

A-12

Tail No: LAC No:	First Flt Date: Last Flt Date:	No. of Flts Total Hrs:	Remarks:
60-6924 121	26 April 1962 ?	322 Flts 418.2 hrs	Prototype. Towed from Plant 42, Palmdale storage area to display area and now displayed at Palmdale Air Musem, NV.
60-6925 122	? ?	161 Flts 177.9 hrs	Used for ground tests prior to first flight. Transported from Plant 42, Palmdale to USS *Intrepid,* NY, for display.
60-6926 123	? 24 May 1963	79 Flts 135.3 hrs	Second A-12 to fly. Lost during training/test flight after aircraft stalled due to inaccurate data being displayed to pilot. Pilot Ken Collins ejected safely.
60-6927 124	? ?	614 Flts 1076.4 hrs	Only two-seat pilot trainer. Displayed at California Museum of Science, Los Angeles.
60-6928 125	? 5 Jan 1967	202 Flts 334.9 hrs	Lost during training/test flight. Pilot Walter L. Ray successfully ejected but was killed after he failed to separate from his ejection seat.
60-6929 126	? 28 Dec 1967	105 Flts 169.2 hrs	Lost seconds after take-off from Groom Lake following incorrect installation of SAS. Pilot Mel Vojvodich ejected safely.
60-2930 127	? ?	258 Flts 499.2 hrs	Deployed to Kadena from 24 May 1967 until June 1968 in support of operation Black Shield. Was stored at Plant 42, Palmdale. Trucked to Space and Rocket Center Museum, Huntsville, AL, for display.
60-2931 128	? ?	232 Flts 453 hrs	Was stored at Plant 42, Palmdale. Transported by C-5 on 27 October 1991 to Minneapolis Air National Guard for display at Minnesota ANG Museum, St Paul, Minneapolis.
60-6932 129	? 5 June 1968	268 Flts 409.9 hrs	Deployed to Kadena from 26 May 1967, in support of operation Black Shield. Lost off the Philippine islands during an FCF prior to its scheduled return to USA. Pilot Jack Weeks was killed.
60-6933 130	27 Nov 1963 August 1965	217 Flts 406.3 hrs	Was stored at Plant 42, Palmdale. Trucked to San Diego Aerospace Museum, CA, for display. Now displayed at Kennedy Space Center, FL.
60-6937 131	? ?	177 Flts 345.8 hrs	Deployed to Kadena from 22 May 1967 until June 1968, in support of operation Black Shield. Stored at Plant 42, Palmdale.
60-6938 132	? ?	197 Flts 369.9 hrs	Was stored at Plant 42, Palmdale. Trucked to USS *Alabama,* located at Mobile, AL, for display.
60-6939 133	? 9 July 1964	10 Flts 8.3 hrs	Lost while on approach into Groom Lake during test flight due to complete hydraulic failure. Lockheed Test Pilot Bill Park ejected safely.

Tail No: LAC No:	First Flt Date: Last Flt Date:	No. of Flts Total Hrs:	Remarks:
60-6940 134	? ?	80 Flts 123.9 hrs	One of two A-12s converted for project Tagboard – the carriage of D-21 drones. Trucked to the Museum of Flight, Seattle, WA, for display, where it is the sole surviving example of its type.
60-6941 135	? 30 July 1966	95 Flts 152.7 hrs	One of two A-12s converted for project Tagboard – the carriage of D-21 drones. Lost during tests off the coast of California. Pilot Bill Park and Launch Control Engineer Ray Torick, both Lockheed employees, ejected safely, however, Ray Torick tragically drowned in the subsequent feet-wet landing.

Tail No: LAC No: **YF-12**	First Flt Date: Last Flt Date:	First Flt Crew Total Hrs:	Remarks:
60-6934 1001	8 Aug 1963 14 Aug 1966	Jim Eastham 180.9 hrs	First YF-12 was used by Col Robert L. Stephens and his FCO Lt-Col Daniel Andre to establish a new speed (as YF-12) and altitude record; however, due to technical problems, these records were obtained in '936. Aircraft was transformed into SR-71C serial 64-17981, now displayed at Hill AFB, UT.
60-6935 1002	26 Nov 1963 7 Nov 1979	Lou Schalk 534.7 hrs	After initial YF-12 test programme the aircraft was placed in storage at Edwards. It was later made available to NASA and flew again on 11 December 1969. On completion of this programme it was delivered to Wright-Patterson Air Force museum, where it remains as the sole YF-12.
60-6936 1003	13 March 1964 24 July 1971	Bob Gilliland 439.8 hrs	This aircraft was used to obtain all world absolute speed and altitude records of 1 May 1965. After a brief period of retirement the aircraft was made available to a joint Air Force, NASA and ADP test programme but was lost on 24 June 1971. Lt-Col Jack Layton and Maj Billy Curtis ejected safely.

SR-71

64-17950 2001	23 Dec 1964 10 Jan 1967	Bob Gilliland ?	Lost during anti-skid brake system evaluation at Edwards AFB. Pilot Art Peterson survived.
64-17951 2002	5 March 1965 22 Dec 1978	Gilliland/Zwayer 796.7 hrs	Operated by NASA from 16 July 1971 and known as YF-12C, serialled 60-6937. Removed from Palmdale storage and trucked to Pima Museum, Tucson, AZ, for display.
64-17952 2003	24 March 1965 25 Jan 1966	? ?	Lost during test flight from Edwards AFB. Pilot Bill Weaver survived, RSO Jim Zwayer killed, incident occurred near Tucumcari, NM.
64-17953 2004	4 June 1965 18 Dec 1969	Weaver/Andre ?	Lost during test flight from Edwards AFB. Pilot Lt-Col Joe Rogers, RSO Lt-Col Gary Heidelbaugh ejected safely, incident occurred near Shoshone, CA.
64-17954 2005	20 July 1965 11 April 1969	Weaver/Andre ?	Lost on runway at Edwards AFB during take-off. Pilot Lt-Col Bill Skliar, RSO Maj Noel Warner escaped without injury.
64-17955 2006	17 Aug 1965 24 Jan 1985		Operated extensively by AFLC from Palmdale Plant as the dedicated SR-71 test aircraft. This aircraft is on display at Edwards AFB, CA.
64-17956 2007		Gilliland/Belgau 3,760 hrs	One of two SR-71B two-seat pilot trainers. It is currently on loan to NASA at the Ames Research Center Hugh L. Dryden Flight Research Facility, Edwards AFB, CA. Renumbered NASA 831. Likely to go on display at Kennedy Space Center, FL.

Tail No: LAC No:	First Flt Date: Last Flt Date:	First Flt Crew Total Hrs:	Remarks:
64-17957 2008	18 Dec 1965 11 Jan 1968	Gilliland/Eastham ?	One of two SR-71B two-seat pilot trainers. It was lost following fuel cavitation while on approach to Beale AFB. IP Lt-Col Robert G. Sowers, student Capt David E. Fruehauf ejected safely.
64-17958 2009	15 Dec 1965 23 Feb 1990	Weaver/Andre 2,288.9 hrs	Used on 27/28 July 1979 by Capt Eldon W. Joersz and RSO Maj George T. Morgan Jr to establish speed run over 15/25 kilometre course of 2,193.67 mph (3529.464 km/h). Flown to Robbins AFB, GA, for display.
64-17959 2010	19 Jan 1966 29 Oct 1976	Weaver/Andre 866.1 hrs	Underwent 'Big Tail' modification to increase and enhance sensor capacity/capability. Trucked to Air Force Armament, Eglin AFB, FL, for display.
64-17960 2011	9 Feb 1966 27 Feb 1990	Weaver/Andre 2,669.6 hrs	This aircraft flew 342 combat missions, more than any other SR-71. Flown to Castle AFB for display.
64-17961 2012	13 April 1966 2 Feb 1977	Weaver/Andre 1,601 hrs	Displayed at the Kansas Cosmophere & Space Center, Hutchinson, KS.
64-17962 2013	29 April 1966 14 Feb 1990	Weaver/Belgau 2,835.9 hrs	Displayed at the Imperial War Museum, Duxford, UK.
64-17963 2014	9 June 1966 28 Oct 1976	Weaver/Belgau 1,604.4 hrs	Towed to current display area at Beale AFB.
64-17964 2015	11 May 1966 20 March 1990	Weaver/Belgau 3,373.1 hrs	Displayed at the Strategic Air Command Museum, Omaha, NE.
64-17965 2016	10 June 1966 25 Oct 1976	Weaver/Moeller ?	Lost during night training sortie, following INS platform failure. Pilot St Martin, RSO Carnochan ejected safely. Incident occurred near Lovelock, NV.
64-17966 2017	1 July 1966 13 April 1967	Gilliland/Belgau ?	Lost after night refuelling, subsonic high-speed stall. Pilot Boone and RSO Sheffield both ejected safely. Incident occurred near Las Vegas, NM
64-17967 2018	3 Aug 1966 14 Feb 1990	Weaver/Andre 236.8 hrs	Displayed at Barksdale AFB Museum, LA.
64-17968 2019	3 Aug 1966 12 Feb 1990	Weaver/Andre 2,279.0 hrs	Displayed at Richmond Air Museum, VA.
64-17969 2020	18 Oct 1966 10 May 1970	Weaver/Belgau ?	Lost after refuelling, subsonic high-speed stall. Pilot Lawson, RSO Martinez ejected safely. Incident occurred near Korat RTAFB.
64-17970 2021	21 Oct 1966 17 June 1970	Weaver/Belgau ?	Lost following mid-air collision between KC-135Q tanker. Tanker able to limp back to Beale AFB. Pilot Buddy Brown, RSO Mort Jarvis both ejected safely. Incident 20 miles (32 km) east of El Paso, NM.
64-17971 2022	17 Nov 1966 Still Flying	Weaver/Moeller 3,512.5 hrs	One of two SR-71As loaned to NASA and the Ames Research Center Hugh L. Dryden Research Facility, Edwards AFB. Renumbered NASA 832. Now displayed at Edwards AFB, CA.
64-17972 2023	12 Dec 1966 6 March 1990	Weaver/Belgau 2801.1hrs	Flown on 1 September 1974 by Majs James Sullivan, Noel Widdifield, from New York to London in record time of 1 hour 54 minutes 56.4 seconds. Flown on 6 March 1990 by Lt-Col Ed Yeilding RSO Lt-Col Joseph T Vida from Los Angeles to Washington DC in 1 hour 4 minutes 20 seconds, West to East coast in 1 hour 7 minutes 54 seconds. It is now on display at the Smithsonian Institution, Dulles Airport, Washington DC.

Tail No: LAC No:	First Flt Date: Last Flt Date:	First Flt Crew Total Hrs:	Remarks:
64-17973 2024	8 Feb 1967 21 July 1987	Weaver/Greenamyer 1,729.9 hrs	Damaged while being demonstrated at the RAF Mildenhall Air Fete May 1987 by Maj Jim Jiggens. Displayed at the Blackbird Airpark, Palmdale, CA
64-17974 2025	16 Feb 1967 21 April 1989	Weaver/Belgau ?	One of three aircraft used on the first operational deployment to Kadena AB, Okinawa. Lost in 1989 while out-bound from Kadena on an ops sortie following engine explosion and complete hydraulic failure. Pilot Maj Dan F. House, RSO Capt Bozek both ejected safely.
64-17975 2026	13 April 1967 28 Feb 1990	Greenamyer/Belgau 2,854 hrs	Flown from Beale AFB to March AFB, where it is now on display.
64-17976 2027	? May 1967 27 March 1990	Gilliland/Belgau 2,985.7 hrs	One of three aircraft used on the first operational deployment to Kadena AB, Okinawa. '976 was flown by Maj Jerome F. O'Malley and RSO, Capt Edward D. Payne on 9 March 1968, on the first-ever SR-71 operational sortie. Flown to the Air Force Museum at Wright-Patterson AFB.
64-17977 2028		Gilliland/ Greenamyer	Lost at the end of the runway at Beale AFB, following a wheel explosion and runway abort. Pilot Maj Gabriel A. Kardong rode the aircraft to a standstill, RSO Capt James A. Kogler ejected – both survived.
64-17978 2029		Weaver/Belgau	One of three aircraft used on the first operational deployment to Kadena AB, Okinawa. Lost four years later after a landing incident at Kadena AB, Okinawa. Pilot Capt Dennis K. Bush, RSO Jimmy Fagg, both escaped unhurt.
64-17979 2030	10 Aug 1967 6 March 1990	Greenamyer/Belgau 3,321.7 hrs	This aircraft flew the first three of nine sorties from the eastern seaboard of the USA to the Middle East and back, during the 1973 Yom Kippur War. The aircraft was flown to Lackland AFB, TX, for display at the History and Traditions Museum.
64-17980 2031	25 Sep 1967 5 Feb 1990	Gilliland/Belgau 2,255.6 hrs	One of two SR-7lAs loaned to NASA and flown from the Ames Research Center, Hugh L. Dryden Flight Research Facility, Edwards AFB, CA. Renumbered NASA 844. To be displayed at NASA Dryden Test Center, Edwards AFB, CA.
64-17981 2000	14 March 1969 11 April 1976	Gilliland/Belgau 556.4 hrs*	Designated SR-71C, this hybrid consists of the forward fuselage from a static test specimen mated to the wing and rear section of YF-12A, 60-6934. It was trucked to Hill AFB, UT, for display.

* This figure does not include 180.9 hrs accumulated on the aircraft as YF-12A serial 60-6934.

COMMANDERS AND AWARDS
Appendix 4

9TH STRATEGIC RECONNAISSANCE WING COMMANDERS

Name	From	To
Col Douglas T. Nelson	Jan 1966	Dec 1966
Col William R. Hayes	Jan 1967	Jun 1969
Col Charles E. Minter	Jun 1969	Jun 1970
Col Harold E. Confer	Jul 1970	May 1972
Col Jerome F. O'Malley	May 1972	May 1973
Col Patrick J. Halloran	May 1973	Jun 1975
Col John H. Storrie	Jul 1975	Sep 1977
Col Lyman M. Kidder	Sep 1977	Jan 1979
Col Dale Shelton	Feb 1979	Jul 1980
Col David Young	Jul 1980	Jul 1982
Col Thomas S. Pugh	Jul 1982	Jul 1983
Col Hector Freese	Aug 1983	Jan 1985
Col David H. Pinsky	Jan 1985	Jul 1987
Col Richard H. Graham	Jul 1987	Nov 1988
Col James Savarda	Dec 1988	Jun 1990
Col Thomas J. Keck	Jun 1990	Nov 1991
Col Richard Young	Nov 1991	*1

9TH SRW VICE WING COMMANDERS

Name	From	To
Col Marvin L. Speer	Jan 1966	Dec 1966
Col Charles F. Minter	Dec 1966	Jun 1969
Col Harold E. Confer	Jun 1969	Jun 1970
Col James E. Anderson	Jul 1970	Dec 1971
Col Dennis B. Sullivan	Dec 1971	Jul 1972
Col Patrick J. Halloran	Jul 1972	Jun 1973
Col Donald A. Walbrecht	Jun 1973	May 1974
Col John H. Storrie	Jun 1974	Jun 1975
Col Robert D. Beckel	Jun 1975	Sep 1976
Col Lyman M. Kidder	Oct 1976	Sep 1977
Col William E. Lawson III	Sep 1977	Jan 1979
Col David G. Young	Feb 1979	Jul 1980
Col Thomas S. Pugh	Jul 1980	Jul 1982
Col Lonnie S. Liss	Jul 1982	Jan 1983
Col David H. Pinsky	Jan 1983	Jan 1985
Col Robert B. McConnell	Jan 1985	Aug 1987

Col Donald R. Schreiber	Aug 1987	Aug 1989
Col Tom Atkinson	Aug 1989	Jun 1990
Col Rich Salsbury	Jun 1990	Jul 1991
Col Rich Young	Jul 1991	Nov 1991
Col Tieman	Nov 1991	*2

1ST STRATEGIC RECONNAISSANCE SQUADRON COMMANDERS

Name	From	To
Lt-Col William R. Griner	Jan 1966	Mar 1966
Lt-Col Harold E. Confer	Apr 1966	Oct 1966
Lt-Col Raymond Haupt	Nov 1966	Jul 1967
Lt-Col Alan L. Hichew	Jul 1967	Sep 1968
Lt-Col Patrick J. Halloran	Sep 1968	Nov 1969
Lt-Col James L. Watkins	Dec 1969	Mar 1971
Lt-Col Harlon A. Hain	Apr 1971	Jul 1971
Lt-Col Larry S. DeVall	Jul 1971	Jan 1972
Lt-Col Kenneth S. Collins	Jan 1972	Jun 1972
Lt-Col George M. Bull	Jun 1972	Jul 1973
Lt-Col Brian K. McCallum	Jul 1973	Jan 1974
Lt-Col James H. Shelton Jr	Jan 1974	Aug 1975
Lt-Col Raphael S. Samay	Aug 1975	Jun 1977
Lt-Col Adolphus H. Bledsoe	Jul 1977	Dec 1978
Lt-Col Randolph B. Hertzog	Dec 1978	Dec 1979
Lt-Col Richard H. Graham	Jan 1980	Jul 1981
Lt-Col Eldon W. Joersz	Aug 1981	Jul 1983
Lt-Col Alan B. Cirino	Jul 1983	Aug 1985
Lt-Col Joseph Kinego	Aug 1985	
Lt-Col William D. Orcutt	*3	
Lt-Col William R. Dyckman		

99TH STRATEGIC RECONNAISSANCE SQUADRON COMMANDERS

Name	From	To
Lt-Col John B. Boynton	Jun 1966	Dec 1967
Lt-Col Robert G. Sowers	Jan 1967	Mar 1968
Lt-Col John C. Kennon	Apr 1968	Nov 1969
Lt-Col Harlon A. Hain	Nov 1969	Mar 1971

9TH STRATEGIC RECONNAISSANCE WING AWARDS DURING SR-71 OPERATIONS

PRESIDENTIAL UNIT CITATION	31 Mar 1968	31 Dec 1968
AIR FORCE OUTSTANDING UNIT AWARD	1 Jul 1970	30 Jun 1971
AIR FORCE OUTSTANDING UNIT AWARD, WITH 'VALOR'	1 Jul 1972	30 Jun 1973
AIR FORCE OUTSTANDING UNIT AWARD	1 Jul 1974	30 Jun 1975
AIR FORCE OUTSTANDING UNIT AWARD	1 Jul 1975	30 Jun 1977
AIR FORCE OUTSTANDING UNIT AWARD	1 Jul 1981	30 Jun 1982
AIR FORCE OUTSTANDING UNIT AWARD	1 Jul 1983	30 Jun 1984
AIR FORCE OUTSTANDING UNIT AWARD	1 Jul 1985	30 Jun 1986
AIR FORCE OUTSTANDING UNIT AWARD	1 Jul 1986	30 Jun 1987

OL-8 was also awarded the:
REPUBLIC OF VIETNAM GALLANTRY CROSS & PALM
31 Dec 1970

*1 Col Young Nov 1991–Jun 1993; Col Larry Tieman to Jul 1994; Gen John Rutledge to Sep 1995; Gen Bob Behler, final
*2 Col Tieman Nov 1991–Jun 1993; Col Carpenter to Jan 1995; Col George Lafferty to Aug 1995; Col Dale Smith, final
*3 Lt-Col Kinego Aug 1985–Aug 1987; Lt-Col Orcutt Aug 1987–Nov 1988; Lt-Col Dyckman Nov 1988–Jun1990

AIR FORCE LOGISTICS COMMAND SR-71 CREW HISTORY
Appendix 5

Pilots	From	To
Merv Evenson	Jan 1970	Jul 1974
Dick Gerard	Jan 1971	Jul 1973
Tom Pugh	Jul 1973	Jul 1978
T. Smith	Oct 1973	Jul 1975
B. Riedenauer	Nov 1973	Nov 1978
Jim Sullivan	Jul 1978	Aug 1980
Cal Jewett	Jul 1978	Jul 1982
Bob Helt	Jul 1980	Jul 1984
Tom Tilden	Feb 1982	Jul 1989
BC Thomas	Jul 1984	Dec 1987
Ed Yeilding	Jan 1988	Jan 1990
J. Halsell	Feb 1989	Jan 1990

RSO	From	To
Col Red McNeer	Jan 1970	Jul 1971
Ron Selberg	Jan 1971	Aug 1974
Coz Mallozzi	Jul 1971	Jul 1974
B. Frazier	Jul 1974	Jul 1980
John Carnochan	Aug 1974	Feb 1978
George Morgan	Jan 1978	Jul 1985
Bob Flanagan	Jan 1980	Aug 1985
Joe Vida	Jan 1981	Jan 1990
P. Soucy	Jul 1985	Dec 1987
Tom Fuhrman	Dec 1987	Jan 1990

CHRONOLOGY OF SIGNIFICANT EVENTS

Appendix 6

Year	Date	Event
1957	24 Dec	Christmas Eve, first J58 engine run
1959	29 Aug	US accepts A-12 Design
	30 Jan	CIA approves Oxcart Project
1962	26 Apr	First flight of A-12, pilot Lou Schalk
	4 Jun	SR-71 mock-up reviewed by Air Force
	30 Jul	J58 completes pre-flight rating test
	28 Dec	Lockheed contracted to build six production SR-71 aircraft
1963	31 Jan	First J58 air tested
	24 May	First A-12 lost in accident
	7 Aug	First flight of YF-12, pilot J. Eastham
1964	29 Feb	Existence of Oxcart (A-12) announced
	25 Jul	President Johnson makes first public announcement of Mach-3 aircraft, twists letters RS-71 and says SR-71. Designation sticks.
	29 Oct	SR-71 prototype to Palmdale
	7 Dec	SR-71s to be based at Beale AFB, announced
	18 Dec	First engine run of SR-71 prototype
	21 Dec	SR-71 taxi tests
	22 Dec	First flight of SR-71, Palmdale, pilot Bob Gilliland
	22 Dec	First flight M-12/D-21, Groom Dry Lake, Nevada
1965	3 Mar	First flight of YF-12C
	1 May	YF-12 sets nine speed and altitude records
	1 Jun	SR-71/YF-12 Test Force formed, Edwards AFB
	7 Jul	First two T-38 companion trainers delivered to Beale AFB

Year	Date	Event
1965	2 Nov	SR-71B maiden flight from Palmdale, pilot B. Gilliland, with Bill Weaver
1966	6 Jan	First SR-71 delivered to USAF. Crew Ray Haupt and Charlie Bock
	7 Jan	SR-71B arrives at Beale AFB. Crew, Ray Haupt and Doug Nelson
	25 Jan	First SR-71A lost in accident
	10 May	First SR-71A delivered to Beale AFB
	25 Jun	Ninth Strategic Reconnaissance Wing formed at Beale AFB
	3 Jul	First launch attempt of D-21 drone from M-12
	30 Jul	M-12/D-21 programme ends
1967	17 Apr	SR-71 flies 14,000 miles (22,530 km), much at Mach 3, wins FAI Gold Medal, ('Silverfox') Stephens
	31 May	First A-12 operational sortie
1968	11 Jan	SR-71B lost, Beale AFB
	26 Jan	First overflight of North Korea by an A-12
	21 Mar	First SR-71 operational sortie over Southeast Asia
	26 Jul	First confirmed firings of two SA-2s at an SR-71
	1 Nov	9th SRW receives Air Force Outstanding Unit Award
1969	14 Mar	First flight of SR-71C
	13 Apr	9th SRW loses its first SR-71A
	11 Dec	YF-12 NASA/USAF test programme begins
1970	16 Jan	SR-71/YF-12 Test Force redesignated 4786th Test Squadron

Year	Date	Event	Year	Date	Event
1971	1 Apr	99th SRS deactivated as an SR-71unit	1984	7 Nov	First SR-71 sortie over Nicaragua
	26 Apr	SR-71A completes 15,000 miles (24,140 km) non-stop around US, time 10 hours 30 minutes	1986	13 Apr	Two SR-71s conduct post-strike reconnaissance over Libya after Operation El Dorado Canyon
1973	12 Oct	First SR-71A reconnaissance flights over Middle East, Yom Kippur War	1987	22 Jul	First operational mission into the Gulf by an SR-71
1974	1 Sep	New York to London record 1 hour 56 minutes. Pilot J. Sullivan, RSO N. Widdefield	1989	1 Oct	USAF operations suspended (except for minimum proficiency sorties) while awaiting budget outcome
	13 Sep	SR-71 London to Los Angeles record 3 hours 47 minutes. Pilot Buck Adams, RSO Bill Machorek		22 Nov	All USAF operations terminated
1976	27 Jul	Speed record, 2,092 mph (3367 km/h), pilot P. Bledsoe and RSO J. Fuller	1990	26 Jan	SR-71 is decommissioned in ceremony at Beale AFB
	28 Jul	Speed record, 2,193 mph (3529 km/h), pilot F. Joersz and G. Morgan		6 Mar	Ed Yeilding and J T Vida flew '972 on the Air Force's final SR-71 flight, a West–East coast record-breaking flight of the United States, time 1 hour 7 minutes
	28 Jul	Altitude record, 85,068 ft (25929 m), pilot R. Helt and RSO L. Elliot	1995	5 Jan	SR-71 reactivation began with '967
1978	16 Nov	First SR-71 overflight of Cuba	1996	16 Apr	The Pentagon once again suspended all SR-71 operations
1979	31 Mar	Det 4, 9th SRW, formed at RAF Mildenhall	1997	10 Oct	President Clinton line-item vetoed the SR-71 programme
	31 Oct	NASA flight test programme ended	1999	6 Oct	Detachment 2 of the 9th Strategic Reconnaissance Wing deactivated
	7 Nov	YF-12 lands at Wright-Patterson AFB for Air Force Museum			
1981	1 Aug	4029th SRTS formed to train SR-71 crews			
	26 Aug	North Korea launches two SA-2s at SR-71 flight conducted over DMZ			

RECORD BREAKING

Appendix 7

While reading the records established below that were verified at the time by the Federation Aéronautique Internationale (FAI), it should be remembered that, impressive as these figures are, they are not demonstrations of the aircraft's absolute capabilities. For example, on 20 November 1965, an A-12 attained speeds in excess of Mach 3.2 and a sustained altitude capability above 90,000 ft (27432 m). During the first operational deployment of a CIA A-12 from Area 51 to Kadena Air Base, on the island of Okinawa, the pilot, Mele Vojvodich, covered the distance in aircraft Article Number 131, in just six hours six minutes. Had it not been for security considerations, this could easily have been recognised as a new transpacific speed record. With the passage of time, several earlier SR-71 records were broken by a highly-modified, stripped-down Soviet MiG-25. However, the inability of that country to subsequently build an operational aircraft with truly similar performance capabilities to the SR-71, provides a useful perspective on the research-only status of that particular MiG.

Col Robert L. 'Fox' Stephens and his FCO, Lt-Col Daniel Andre, set new Absolute Altitude and Absolute Speed records in YF-12A 60-6936, on 1 May 1965. (USAF)

YF-12A RECORDS

It is probably not a coincidence that the date chosen to demonstrate some of the YF-12A's awesome capabilities was 1 May 1965 – exactly five years to the day after Francis Gary Powers was shot down in his U-2 by a Soviet SA-2.

Date: 1 May 1965
Record: Absolute Altitude,
80,257.86 ft (24,390 m)
Crew: Pilot, Col Robert L 'Fox' Stephens.
FCO, Lt-Col Daniel Andre
Aircraft: YF-12A 60-6936

Date: 1 May 1965
Record: Absolute Speed over a straight course.
2,070.101 mph (3331.141 km/h)
Crew: Pilot, Col Robert L. 'Fox' Stephens.
FCO, Lt-Col Daniel Andre
Aircraft: YF-12A 60-6936

Date: 1 May 1965
Record: Absolute Speed over a 500-km closed course 1688.889 mph (2717.929 km/h)
Crew: Pilot, Lt-Col Walter F. Daniel.
FCO, Maj James P. Cooney
Aircraft: YF-12A 60-6936

Date: 1 May 1965
Record: Absolute Speed over a 1000-km closed course 1643.041 mph (2644.146 km/h)
Crew: Pilot, Lt-Col Walter F. Daniel.
FCO, Maj Noel T. Warner
Aircraft: YF-12A 60-6936

SR-71 RECORDS

The first big, attention-grabbing SR-71 headlines were undoubtedly those which heralded the transatlantic speed records. Both still stand unbroken, more than 35 years later.

Date: 1 September 1974
Record: Speed Over a Recognised Course –
New York to London
Crew: Pilot Maj James V. Sullivan.
RSO Maj Noel F. Widdifield
Distance: 3,490 miles (5616 km), time 1 hour 54 minutes 56.4 seconds
Aircraft: SR-71A 64-17972

Date: 13 September 1974
Record: Speed Over a Recognised Course –
London to Los Angeles
Crew: Pilot Capt Harold B. Adams.
RSO Capt William C. Machorek
Distance: 5,645 miles (9084 km), time 3 hours 47 minutes 35.8 seconds.
Aircraft: SR-71A 64-17972

Next came celebrations commemorating the United States' bicenntenial year.

Date: 27/28 July 1976
Record: Altitude in Horizontal Flight,
85,068.997 ft (25,929.031 m)
Crew: Pilot Capt Robert C. Helt.
RSO Maj Larry A. Elliott
Aircraft: SR-71A, 61-7962

Date: 27/28 July 1976
Record: Speed Over Straight Course (15/25 km), 2193.167 mph (3529.56 km/h)
Crew: Pilot Capt Eldon W. Joersz.
RSO MajGeorge T. Morgan
Aircraft: SR-71A, 61-7958

Date: 27/28 July 1976
Record: Speed Over a Closed Course (1000 km), 2092.294 mph (3367.221 km/h)
Crew: Pilot Maj Adolphus H. Bledsoe Jr.
RSO Maj John T. Fuller
Aircraft: SR-7 IA, 61-7958

STRATEGIC AIR COMMAND

Finally, despite all that some Strategic Air Command officials could do to prevent more headline attentionafter the programme was prematurely closed down, the following records were set.

Date: 6 March 1990
Record: Speed Over A Recognised Course – Los Angeles to East Coast
Crew: Pilot Lt-Col Ed Yeilding. RSO Lt-Col Joseph T. Vida
Coast to Coast (2,086 miles/3357 km), time 1 hour 7 minutes 53.69 seconds, average speed 2,124.5 mph (3419 km/h); Los Angeles to Washington DC (1,998 miles/3215 km), time 1 hour 4 minutes 19.89 seconds, average speed 2,144.83 mph (3451.67 km/h); St Louis to Cincinnati (311.44 miles/501.20 km), time 8 minutes 31.97 seconds, average speed 2,189.94 mph (3524.27 km/h); Kansas City to Washington DC (942.08 miles/ 1516.09 km), time 25 minutes 58.53 seconds, average speed 2,176.08 mph (3501.97 km/h)
Aircraft: SR-71A 64-17972

Gen Al Joersz, a captain at the time of setting his 1976 speed record recalls the event: 'The record-breaking flight was flown out of Beale AFB, unrefuelled, down to and over the Edwards AFB ranges and back. The criteria for breaking the

Above: The Habus gather at Beale to celebrate the 1976 series of records. From left to right, those pictured are Maj George T. Morgan Jr, Kelly Johnson, Capt Eldon W. Joersz, Maj John T. Fuller, Maj Adolphus H. Bledsoe Jr, Maj Larry A. Elliot and Capt Robert C. Helt. The officer at the microphone is Lt-Gen Bryan M. Shotts. (USAF)

record included the requirement to fly through a 25-km [15½-mile[course in level flight (we had to exit the course within 150 ft [46 m] of the entry altitude). After entering, we completed a 90°/270° turn (which had us fly through three states, Arizona, Nevada and California). We then re-entered the course, flying through in the opposite direction. In this instance the rules required that you again enter the course within 300 ft [91 m] of the first exit altitude and then leave within 150 ft of the second entry altitude. While this may not seem like a big deal, flying at 80,600 ft [24567 m] it was more difficult than is readily apparent. The SR-71 is a cruise-climb airplane, so the desired altitude for each pass was considerably different. For the first pass we had to be higher than desired and during the second we had to be lower than desired (we actually had to throttle back to keep from exceeding the max design limit of the airplane on the second pass).

'We actually flew for the record on the 27th, but since weather precluded accurate altitude measurement of our flight, we were required to fly it again on the 28th. That flight was tracked

More celebrations for the 1976 record-breaking teams. The Lockheed/USAF placard lists their accomplishments, while each has received a model Habu in recognition. From left to right the crews are John Fuller, Pat Bledsoe, 'G T' Morgan, Al Joersz, Larry Elliot and Bob Helt. (USAF)

satisfactorily, so was the counter. Actually, during the flight on the first day (the 27th) we had an inlet unstart mid-way through the course at 3.3 Mach, which made our ability to stay within the 150 ft altitude requirement problematic. No one ever said we exceeded the limit, but it was close at least, an unstart at any speed and condition is always interesting, but the one that day was even more unwelcome than normal. The airplane is pretty delicate to fly while at max speed and altitude, and that day was no exception.

'We were selected to fly the mission pretty much at random. We were one of the more senior crews available and since there were only nine qualified crews flying the airplane at that time and four of them were unavailable due to operational deployments, the chance of getting to do the record was pretty high. In any case, we were honoured and enjoyed the chance to put some new numbers in the books. We decided we would shoot for about 2,200 mph [3540 km/h], but our translation from knots to mph was a little off, so we ended up at 2,193 mph [3529 km/h]. Actually we flew the course at the maximum compressor inlet temperature limit for the airplane, so we didn't have much wiggle room to do more. The airplane we flew (tail number '958), was just one of the planes in the hanger. The only mod made was to paint a big white 'X' on the bottom so that they could track us better with the cameras as we flew through the range at Edwards. (The Nun Baker cameras they used are the ones used to track the space shuttle when it comes in to land at Edwards and to photograph other test flights out of that facility.)'

A-12, YF-12 AND SR-71 LOSSES
Appendix 8

1963	24 May	A-12, 60-6926, Article 123, pilot Ken Collins survived.
1964	9 July	A-12, 60-6939, Article 133, pilot Bill Park survived.
1966	25 Jan	SR-71A, 64-17952, Article 2003, pilot Bill Weaver survived, RSO Jim Zwayer killed.
	30 July	M-12, 60-6941, Article 135, pilot Bill Park survived, LCO Ray Torick killed.
1967	5 Jan	A-12, 60-6928, Article 125, pilot Walt Ray killed.
	10 Jan	SR-71A, 64-17950, Article 2001, pilot Art Peterson survived, back seat was unoccupied.
	13 April	SR-71A, 64-17966, Article 2017, pilot Earle Boone and RSO 'Butch' Sheffield both survived.
	25 Oct	SR-71A, 64-17965, Article 2016, pilot Roy St Martin and RSO John Carnochan both survived.
	28 Dec	A-12, 60-6929, Article 126, pilot Mel Vojvodich survived.
1968	11 Jan	SR-71B, 64-17957, Article 2008, Instructor Pilot 'Gray' Sowers and student John Freuhauf both survived.
	5 June	A-12, 60-6932, Article 129, pilot Jack Weeks killed.
1968	10 Oct	SR-71A, 64-17977, Article 2028, pilot 'Abe' Kardong and RSO Kim Kogler both survived.
1969	11 April	SR-71A, 64-17954, Article 2005, pilot Bill Skliar and RSO Noel Warner both survived.
	18 Dec	SR-71A, 64-17953, Article 2004, pilot Joe Rogers and RSO Garry Heidlebaugh both survived.
1970	10 May	SR-71A, 64-17969, Article 2020, pilot Willie Lawson and RSO 'Gil' Martinez both survived.
	17 Jun	SR-71A, 64-17970, Article 2021, pilot Buddy Brown and RSO 'Mort' Jarvis both survived.
1971	24 June	YF-12A, 60-6936, Article 1003, pilot Jack Layton and FCO Billy Curtis both survived.
1972	20 July	SR-71A 64-17978, Article 2029, pilot Denny Bush and RSO Jimmy Fagg both survived.
1989	21 April	SR-71A, 64-17974, Article 2025, pilot Dan House and RSO Blair Bozek both survived.

NASA FLIGHT ACTIVITY
Appendix 9

In 1967, the Ames Flight Research Center of the National Aeronautics and Space Administration (NASA) negotiated with the US Air Force for access to early A-12 wind tunnel data. These wind tunnel tests had been conducted at Ames sometime earlier in conditions of utmost secrecy. The Air Force decided to release the information and in return NASA provided a small team of highly skilled engineers to work on the SR-71 flight-test programme. In the summer of 1967 a team from the Flight Research Center (FRC), under the leadership of Gene Matranga, was engaged on various stability and control aspects of the SR-71 flight-research effort at Edwards. This work helped to speed the SR-71 into the inventory and led to the establishment of a close working relationship between the Air Force and NASA's 'Blackbird' team.

Later, the Office of Advanced Research Technology viewed the F-12 not only as a superb technical achievement but also as a potential source of flight data applicable to future commercial supersonic transports (SSTs). NASA therefore requested an instrumented SR-71 to conduct research, or to have its instrumentation packages installed on other USAF Lockheed research and development aircraft. Unable to accommodate either request, the Air Force offered NASA the two remaining YF-12s, which were then in storage at Edwards. With funds available from

the cancelled North American X-15 and XB-70 programmes, NASA accepted the offer and agreed to pay for the operational expenses. Aerospace Defense Command (ADC) supplied maintenance and logistic support and on 5 June 1969, a memorandum of understanding (MoU) was signed between the two parties and announced on 18 July.

Utilisation of these high-speed research platforms would be high, since NASA engineers at Langley were interested in using them for aerodynamic experiments and for testing advanced structures. In addition, Lewis Research Establishment wanted to study propulsion, while Ames wanted to concentrate on inlet aerodynamics and the correlation of wind tunnel and flight data. Finally, the aircraft could be used to support various specialised experimentation packages. It was thus hoped that many problems worked around during earlier test programmes could be designed out of any future commercial venture, so avoiding expensive mistakes.

Three months' work was needed to ready the two YF-12s (60-6935 and 60-6936) for flight.

Three classic designs from Kelly Johnson are featured in this formation – F-104, YF-12 and SR-71. The Starfighter was being flown by John Manke, while Fitz Fulton and Vic Horton crewed the YF-12 and Don Mallick and Ray Young were flying SR-71A '951, which was then referred to as a YF-12C. (NASA)

During this time, readily-available instrumentation for the study of aerodynamic loads and structural effects was installed aboard 60-6935 by FRC technicians. Strain gauges were installed within the wing and fuselage and thermocouples were mounted on the left side of the aircraft to measure high-Mach temperature readings.

On 11 December 1969, the joint NASA/US Air Force flight-test programme was launched when, for the first time in three years, a YF-12 climbed away from Edwards. In the front seat was Col Joseph Rogers and Maj Heidelbaugh occupied the FCO position. Phase one of the programme was controlled by the Air Force and consisted of developing procedures and establishing limitations for command and control, and for working out possible bomber-penetration tactics against an interceptor with the YF-12's capabilities.

This phase of the programme was terminated rather early during the closing stages of the 63rd flight on 24 June 1971. 60-6936 had been used throughout the tests by the Air Force and as Lt-Col Ronald J. Layton and systems operator Maj William A. Curtis were approaching the traffic pattern before recovery at Edwards on 24 June, a fire broke out as a result of a fuel line fatigue failure. The flames quickly enveloped the entire aircraft and while on the base leg both crew members ejected. '936 crashed into the middle of the dry lakebed and was totally destroyed.

In contrast, the NASA programme was a long-running success. While the YF-12s were being prepared to fly again Donald L. Mallick and Fitzhugh L. Fulton Jr, the two NASA pilots that flew the majority of phase two of the programme, were quickly checked out in the type. Fitz Fulton flew his first mission in the front seat of an SR-71B with Lt-Col William Campbell as the instructor pilot. Fulton flew his first YF-12A, '936, the next day, on 5 March 1970, followed by further familiarisation sorties on 9 and 11 March.

On 26 March Lt-Col 'Bill' Campbell flew Victor Horton in '935, marking the first flight of a NASA engineer in the YF-12. Ray Young flew in the back seat a few days later and together these two engineers flew most of the NASA back-seat sorties.

YF-12 60-6935 became a real workhorse for NASA. A 'flight loads' research programme pursued by FRC and Langley engineers studied the data gathered. In-flight measurements were correlated against the effects of thermal heating and stress, which together change the aircraft's shape and load distribution pattern. A Hasselblad camera was installed within the fuselage to photograph the structure during moderate-*g* manoeuvres. It revealed that under certain conditions the aft end of the fuselage deflected some 6 in (15 cm) from the centreline.

A major objective of the flight-test programme was to compare actual flight data against that predicted by computers in an effort to assess the accuracy of predictive techniques. In order to predict loads and structural response, NASA had developed two computer modelling programmes using a technique known as finite element analysis. Both these Flexstab and Nastran programmes were applied to the YF-12.

After the 22nd flight of '935 on 16 June 1970, the aircraft was grounded for nine months for instrumentation changes. Once these were completed, Don Mallick and Victor Horton flew a check flight on 22 March 1971. The folding ventral fin was then removed for four flights to assess directional stability up to Mach 2.8.

TEST SR-71

NASA needed more aircraft, and the Air Force supplied an SR-71A (Article 2002, serial 64-17951) on 16 July 1971. This aircraft had been involved in the contractor flight-test programme from the beginning, and the Air Force stipulated that it should only be used for propulsion testing. The first NASA flight of this aircraft was undertaken by Fitz Fulton and Victor Horton on 24 May 1972.

Studies carried out on various aspects of the aircraft's handling qualities revealed that inlet spike movement and bypass door operations were almost as effective as the elevons and rudders in influencing the aircraft's flight path at high speed. Propulsion system and flight control integration were an aspect of control testing tackled by the NASA programme in an effort to improve future mixed-compression inlet design. Airflow disturbance often culminated in an unstart and the accompanying aerodynamic hiccups could hardly be tolerated in a supersonic passenger aircraft. This work led Lewis Research Center to develop a throat-bypass stability system, which was successfully tested on the YF-12. It used relief-type poppet valves in the inlet which could react to internal airflow transients much faster than the bypass doors. This valve-stabilised airflow mechanism complemented the inlet control system by providing sufficient time for the inlet shockwave geometry to reconfigure itself to maintain a 'started' inlet.

Another Lockheed system funded, installed, and tested by NASA technicians and prepared by a Honeywell engineer, proved so successful that it was later fitted to operational SR-71s – the Central Airborne Performance Analyser (CAPA). This integrated, automatic support system isolated faults and recorded the performance of 170 subsystems (relating primarily to the inlet controls) on $\frac{1}{2}$-in magnetic tape. Pre- and post-flight analysis of this on-board monitoring and diagnostic system proved highly cost effective

The final NASA team, from top to bottom, was
Rogers Smith, Ed Schneider, Bob Meyer and
Marta Bohn-Meyer. (NASA)

and reduced maintenance man-hours significantly.

Between 1974 and 1976, a research programme was undertaken by NASA's Langley Research Center to investigate and evaluate titanium and composite materials. This metallurgic database would be useful to support decisions affecting future civil and military supersonic-cruise aircraft. Lockheed's Skunk Works was the prime contractor for the three wing panel samples evaluated. These lightweight structures consisted of a weld-brazed titanium skin/stringer panel, a Rohr-bond titanium honeycomb core panel and a boron/aluminium/titanium core panel. All three components exceeded strength requirements.

For maximum range at high Mach number and high altitude, both flight path and speed parameters must be precisely controlled. During extended periods in autopilot, NASA identified deficiencies in the original system and introduced a two-phase improvement programme. Shortfalls in both the altitude-hold and Mach-hold modes were attributed to decreased aircraft stability, low static pressure, and temperature variations. The altitude-hold mode received data via the air data computer through the pitot/static system and low atmospheric static pressure made precise control difficult because of poor instrument resolution. Therefore, during the first phase of the improvement programme, the altitude-hold mode was improved by compensating for angle-of-attack static pressure sensitivity and pitot/static tube bending.

Cruising on Mach-hold at Mach 3.2 and above 80,000 ft (24390 m), the aircraft would often be subjected to altitude variations of as much as 3,000 ft (914 m). This unacceptable situation was caused by a combination of high altitude and high speed, which sometimes leads to an imbalance between kinetic and potential energy. In turn, large altitude changes are often necessary to correct for small Mach-number changes. The second major objective of the autopilot improvement programme was to develop an auto-throttle control system which could control Mach or KEAS. The programme was so successful that the Air Force incorporated the modifications to both modes.

HEAT-TRANSFER EXPERIMENTS

One of the more unusual heat-transfer experiments supported by NASA was Coldwall. All of the Coldwall tests were flown by Fitz Fulton, with Vic Horton as test engineer. For these flights a hollow stainless steel cylinder was mounted under the fuselage of YF-12 '935, equipped with thermocouples and pressure-sensing equipment. It was then encased in a ceramic shell closed off at each end. Before flight

the cylinder was filled with liquid nitrogen to supercool it to about -60°F (-51°C). At Mach 3.0 the ceramic shell was ballistically removed, resulting in a classic heat transfer experiment as the cylinder went from very cold to very hot almost instantaneously. Using the same cylinder, this experiment was then repeated in a wind tunnel, thereby validating ground research methods for future heat-transfer experiments. It was a relatively difficult test to fly, since it was important to be at the proper speed and altitude over the test range and to minimise the flight time at high speed and high temperature. Unfortunately, on 21 October 1976 the instruments fired the ceramic coating off prematurely when the sensors got too hot. These sorties were also interesting as Don Mallick had the added difficulty of flying close formation in '937 as a Mach-3 chase aircraft.

Aircraft 60-6937 was retired from the programme after its 88th flight with NASA on 28 September 1978. YF-12 60-6935 continued operating until the flight programme ceased after its 145th NASA flight, which was flown by Fitz Fulton and Victor Horton on 31 October 1979. A week later, Col J. Sullivan and Col R. Uppstrom ferried the aircraft to the Air Force Museum at Wright-Patterson AFB, Ohio, where the sole surviving example of the YF-12 is on permanent display.

TESTING IN THE 1990S

In early 1990 NASA once again became involved with Kelly Johnson's trisonic masterpiece when it was decided to conduct a number of advanced aeronautical experiments that required the use of the SR-71 as a supersonic test platform. The Department of Defense bailed NASA two SR-71As, numbers 64-17971, 64-17980 and SR-71B 64-17956. However, before the SR-71B could join its new civilian operators, the Air Force flew three training sorties in order to check-out a NASA instructor pilot:

Date:	Pilot:	Mach:
Time:	IP:	Altitude:
1 Jul 91	Steve Ishmael	3:10
1:00	Rod Dyckman	76,000 ft/23165 m
10 Jul 91	Rod Dyckman	3:23
1:25	Steve Ishmael	80,800 ft/24628 m
25 Jul 91	Rod Dyckman	3:09
1:35	Steve Ishmael	74,000 ft/22555 m

On 25 July 1991, SR-71B 64-17956 was officially delivered to NASA Dryden, Edwards AFB, California, and Steve Ishmael, the newly qualified instructor pilot (IP) began checking out a fellow NASA pilot, Rogers Smith:

| 14 Aug 91 | Rogers Smith | 3.13 |
| 1:18 | Steve Ishmael | 75,000 ft/22860 m |

| 26 Aug 91 | Rogers Smith | 3.10 |
| 2:31 | Steve Ishmael | 76,000 ft/23165 m |

Next to be checked out were the two NASA engineers who would conduct the high altitude experiments: husband and wife, Robert Meyer and Marta Bohn-Meyer, on 9 and 4 October 1991, respectively.

| 23 Sep 91 | Rogers Smith | 3.18 |
| 3:00 | Steve Ishmael | 78,700 ft/23988 m |

| 4 Oct 91 | Steve Ishmael | 3.23 |
| 1:27 | Marta Meyer | 81,450 ft/24826 m |

| 9 Oct 91 | Rogers Smith | 3.23 |
| 1:26 | Robert F Meyer | 81,450 ft/24826 m |

A change to accompany the SR-71's period of duty with NASA was a change in the aircraft's serial numbers in order to comply with FAA regulations, hence 64-17956 became NASA 831, 64-17971 became 832 and 64-17980 became 844.

USAF Serial Number	NASA Number
64-17956	831
64-17971	832
64-17980	844

Far and away the most ambitious experiment got under way on 31 October 1997 and involved hauling the largest external payload since Project Tagboard. The first flight, lasting one hour and 50 minutes, marked the beginning of the Linear Aerospike SR-71 Experiment (LASRE), during which NASA 844 reached a maximum speed of Mach 1.2 and an altitude of 33,000 ft (10058 m). On 4 March 1998, the first of three cold-flow flights was made, during which gaseous helium and liquid nitrogen were cycled through the Boeing-Rocketdyne J2-S linear aerospike engine. However, numerous cryogenic leaks were discovered and despite the engine being 'hot fired' on the ground on two occasions, for a total of three seconds, it was deemed to be too dangerous to fire it up with itsliquid-hydrogen fuel while aloft. Further investigation into the leaks determined that these would be too difficult and expensive to rectify and therefore the programme was cancelled in November 1998.

Since participating in the Edwards AFB open house weekend of 9/10 October 1999, the NASA SR-71s have been placed in 'flyable storage' while awaiting requests and funding for future 'access to space' projects.

On the following page is a complete record of NASA's SR-71 flight activity to date, and the 1995 return of the SR-71 to the USAF.

NASA FLIGHTS & 1995/96 USAF

LOG OF SR-71A, 64-17971

Date	Location	Pilot Name	Rso Name	Flight Duration	Max Mach	Max Altitude/ft	Remarks
12/01/95	E	I	BM	0.2	0.39	3,200	Ferry to Palmdale
26/04/95	E	SC	BM	1.4	0.96	29,000	FCF
23/05/95	PMD	SC	M	2.5	3.23	81,000	
02/06/95	PMD	SC	BM				
26/06/95	PMD	SC	M	1.3	3.21	77,800	
06/07/95	PMD	SC	BM	4.3	3.20	79,100	
12/07/95	PMD	SC	M	4.1	3.06	77,500	
17/10/95	PMD	SC	BM	1.2	3.05	76,000	
01/02/96	PMD			2.7	3.05	77,200	Participated in Red Flag
08/02/96				0.6	0.90	20,000	
27/02/96				2.6	3.00	75,000	
01/03/96				2.3	3.19	78,400	
10/04/96				2.5	3.02	77,000	
14/06/96		SC	BOZEK	4.0	3.05	78,600	ASARS/Data Link Test

LOG OF SR-71A, 64-17967

Date	Location	Pilot Name	Rso Name	Flight Duration	Max Mach	Max Altitude/ft	Remarks
28/08/95	PMD	SC	M	1.4	0.95	26,000	FCF
06/09/95	PMD	S	BM	1.5	0.92	24,000	
13/09/95	PMD	S	BM	1.4	0.93	23,500	
06/10/05	PMD	S	M	1.6	3.01	70,200	
25/10/95	PMD	SC	M	2.5	3.23	79,000	FCF diverts into Nellis
15/12/95	PMD	S	BM	2.3	3.15	74,100	FCF
09/01/96	PMD	S	M	2.3	3.15	74,100	FCF
12/01/96	PMD	S	BM	1.9	3.22	78,300	Final FCF
30/01/96	PMD			2.6	3.02	76,500	USAF flight & position to E
09/02/96	E			2.9	3.15	79,700	First Flight of data link randome
15/02/96	E			3.1	3.01	72,700	
16/04/96	E	LULOFF	FINAN	2.5	3.02	76,600	
09/05/96	E	LULOFF	GREENWOOD	2.3	???	???	ASARS/Data Link Test

LOG OF SR-71B, 64-17956 (NASA 831)

Date	Location	Pilot Name	Rso Name	Flight Duration	Max Mach	Max Altitude/ft	Remarks
01/07/91	PMD	I	DYCKMAN	1.0	3.10	71,400	FCF
10/07/91	PMD	I	DYCKMAN	1.4	3.23	80,800	FCF
25/07/91	PMD	I	DYCKMAN	1.6	3.09	74,500	DELIVERY TO NASA
14/08/91	E	S	I	1.3	3.06	75,500	FIRST NASA FLIGHT
29/10/91	E	I	BM	1.7	3.20	79,500	
01/11/91	E	S	M	2.1	3.25	81,500	
07/11/91	E	I	BM	3.3	3.21	81,500	

Date	Location	Pilot Name	Rso Name	Flight Duration	Max Mach	Max Altitude/ft	Remarks
14/11/91	E	I	M	3.8	3.21	81,800	
28/01/92	E	I	M	1.8	3.26	77,400	
26/02/92	E	S	BM	1.5	3.26	81,100	
10/03/92	E	I	M	1.4	3.12	78,000	
22/04/92	E	S	I	1.7	3.22	81,800	OPERATION
20/05/92	E	S	I	1.6	3.21	83,500	CREW PROFICIENCY
04/06/92	E	I	McMURTRY	1.5	3.23	83,000	OPERATIONAL
26/06/92	E	I	BARTHELEMY	1.4	3.23	82,160	
24/10/92	E	I	BM	1.3	3.20	78,600	FCF
24/11/92	E	S	M	1.8	3.26	80,500	CREW PROFICIENCY & TANKER
08/12/92	E	I	BM (I)	5.2	3.09	76,500	WITH KC10
20/01/93	E	S	M	3.0	3.22	80,000	INLET TEST & CREW PROFICIENCY
14/04/93	E	S	BM	1.4	3.23	81,500	FCF/CREW PROFICIENCY
09/11/93	E	I	BM	1.9	3.07	75,850	FCF/CREW PROFICIENCY
18/02/94	E	I	M	1.7	3.20	81,200	FCF/CREW PROFICIENCY
25/02/94	E	I	GEN DAILY	1.6	3.17	82,100	
04/03/94	E	S	BM	1.5	3.23	80,800	FCF
24/08/94	E	S	M	1.3	3.23	79,300	FCF
06/10/94	E	I	M	1.7	3.22	83,600	CREW PROFICIENCY
18/10/94	E	SC	I	1.6	3.22	84,700	FIRST FLIGHT FOR ED
17/11/94	E	I	FULLERTON	2.8	3.23	82,300	CREW PROFICIENCY
08/12/94	E	I	S	2.5	3.23	82,500	CREW PROFICIENCY
20/01/95	E	SC	I	1.9	3.05	75,400	CREW PROFICIENCY

From left to right, NASA's early test team, which flew the YF-12, was Ray Young, Fitz Fulton, Don Mallick and Vic Horton. Note their early-style pressure suits. (NASA)

Date	Location	Pilot Name	Rso Name	Flight Duration	Max Mach	Max Altitude/ft	Remarks
22/02/95	E	SC	S	2.3	3.11	77,000	CREW PROFICIENCY
18/05/95	E	SC	M	1.7	3.22	80,800	CREW PROFICIENCY
31/05/95	E	SC	BM	1.3	3.22	81,290	CREW PROFICIENCY
27/06/95	E	LULOFF	S	3.1	3.23	78,245	CREW PROFICIENCY
15/07/95	E	LULOFF	S	3.1	3.03	75,100	CREW PROFICIENCY
20/07/95	E	S	SC	3.1	3.04	76,200	
28/07/95	E	McCLEARY	S	2.8	3.15	76,650	AF-FIRST FLIGHT FOR TOM
02/08/95	E	McCLEARY	S	4.0	3.05	77,450	
11/08/95	E	McCLEARY	SC	2.8	3.15	78,000	
17/08/95	E	SC	BM	1.5	3.20	80,500	CREW PROFICIENCY
24/08/95	E	LULOFF	S	3.0	3.04	75,850	AF-NIGHT QUAL FOR LULOFF
29/08/95	E	McCLEARY	BOZEK	2.8	3.15	76,500	AF CREW RE QUALIFICATION
31/08/95	E	S	M	2.2	3.24	79,800	CREW PROFICIENCY
27/09/95	E	S	SC	1.4	3.21	80,300	FCF
30/10/95	E	McCLEARY	SC	1.5	3.05	74,500	AF RE ACTIVATION
09/11/95	E	LULOFF	S	2.2	3.18	80,000	AFA RE ACTIVATION
16/11/95	E	McCLEARY	SC	220	3.02	77,050	NIGHT QUAL McCLEARY
22/11/95	F	WATKINS	SC	2.9	3.22	78,950	FIRST FLIGHT FOR DON
11/12/95	E	WATKINS	SC	2.9	3.21	80,250	
18/01/96	E	McCLEARY	SC	2.4	3.02	77,700	
01/02/96	E	SC	M	1.5	3.21	80,150	CREW PROFICIENCY
06/02/96	E	LULOFF	S	2.4	3.17	75,300	
16/02/96	E	SC	BM	1.5	1.50	48,000	CREW PROFICIENCY
20/03/96	E	SC	BM	1.4	3.09	79,000	FCF
29/03/96	E	S	M	2.3	3.22	80,000	CREW PROFICIENCY
04/04/96	E	SC	BM	2.1	3.04	76,400	CREW PROFICIENCY
10/04/96	E	S	M	2.5	3.22	80,100	CREW PROFICIENCY
25/04/96	E	SC	M	2.7	3.26	82,200	CREW PROFICIENCY
16/05/96	E	S	BM	2.9	3.01	74,000	CREW PROFICIENCY
05/06/96	E	SC	M	1.3	3.04	78,600	CREW PROFICIENCY
22/08/96	E	SC	BM	1.4	3.23	80,800	CREW PROFICIENCY

LOG OF SR-71A, 64-17980 (NASA 844)

Date	Location	Pilot Name	Rso Name	Flight Duration	Max Mach	Max Altitude/ft	Remarks
24/09/92	E	I	BM	1.7	3.25	76,680	OSC EXPERIMENT
06/10/92	E	S	M	1.5	3.26	80,000	OSC EXPERIMENT
09/03/93	E	I	BM (2)	1.5	3.17	82,350	UV CCD
16/03/93	E	S	M (3)	1.7	3.24	84,050	UV CCD
15/07/93	E	I	M (4)	3.0	3.23	81,800	NUVS (NEAR ULTRA-VIOLET SPECTROMETER)
28/07/93	E	S	BM (5)	1.5	1.85	48,500	NUVS & SONIC BOOM TESTS
03/08/93	E	I	M (6)	1.7	3.23	83,950	UV SPECTROMETER & HANDLING QUALITIES
17/09/93	E	S	I (7)	1.7	3.00	76,070	HANDLING QUALITIES
01/10/93	E	I	BM (8)	1.7	3.17	76,500	NUVS
06/10/93	E	S	M (9)	1.7	3.03	73,025	NUVS
13/10/93	E	I	BM	1.8	3.23	83,700	NUVS
20/10/93	E	S	M	1.5	3.05	75,635	NUVS
08/12/93	E	I	M	1.5	3.21	77,375	NUVS
22/12/93	E	I	BM (10)	1.4	3.11	76,000	NUVS & LEOEX (LOW EARTH ORBIT EXPERIMENT)
22/12/93	E	I	BM (10)	1.5	3.11	76,150	NUVS & LEOEX

Date	Location	Pilot Name	Rso Name	Flight Duration	Max Mach	Max Altitude/ft	Remarks
25/01/94	E	S	M	1.5	3.04	77,600	NUVS & LEOEX
25/01/94	E	S	M	1.4	3.04	77,600	DAVE (DYNAMIC AURORAL EXPERIMENT)
07/07/94	E	I	M	1.3	3.16	77,750	DAVE
13/07/94	E	S	M	1.4	3.18	77,700	NUVS & DAVE
21/07/94	E	S	BM	1.5	3.19	80,300	NUVS & DAVE
31/08/94	E	S	BM	1.4	3.05	75,700	NUVS & DAVE
25/10/94	E	S	BM	1.4	3.21	80,000	NUVS & DAVE
15/02/95	E	S	M	1.5	1.27	31,500	SONIC BOOM WITH F-16XL CHASE
16/03/95	E	SC	BM	1.4	1.26	34,100	SONIC BOOM WITH F-16XL & AMES Y03A
22/03/95	E	I	M	1.5	1.28	33,000	SONIC BOOM WITH F-16XL & AMES Y03A
24/03/95	E	SC	BM	1.6	1.63	48,000	SONIC BOOM WITH F-16XL & AMES Y03A
29/03/95	E	SC	M	2.2	1.56	48,200	SONIC BOOM WITH F-16XL & AMES Y03A & F-18
05/04/95	E	S	BM	2.2	1.54	47,600	SONIC BOOM WITH F-16XL & AMES Y03A
12/04/95	E	I	BM	2.0	1.28	44,300	SONIC BOOM WITH F-16XL & AMES Y03A & F-18
20/04/95	E	SC	M	2.0	1.35	44,300	SONIC BOOM WITH F-16XL & AMES Y03A & F-18
25/05/95	E	S	BM	1.7	1.92	49,000	SONIC BOOM WITH Y-01A LANDED PMD & F-18
14/03/95	PMD	SC	BM	0.8	0.98	26,650	LOW FCF RETURN TO DFRC
22/03/96	E	SC	BM	2.4	3.22	80,400	HIGH HOT FCF
12/07/96	E	SC	M	3.1	2.15	60,000	FIRST LASER POD OFF FLIGHT

Key
E = Edwards
I = Ishmael
S = Smith
BM = Bohn-Meyer
M =Meyer
SC =Schnieder
PMD = Palmdale

1 Experiment using the SR-71 as a target to check radars that were modified for use on Aegis ships. This flight was the first time the SR-71B trainer had flown east of the Mississippi. The collection track was over the Atlantic Ocean east of the Virginia coast.

2. Evaluation of two ultraviolet spectrometers for multi-spectral (IR-UV) imagery. This was the initial experiment (using a Winkler Nose) to check UV (looking up).

3. JPL experiment in nose with UV sensor (looking up).

4. First time the SR-71 flew with JP-8 fuel. Initial 'boom' experiment for 'Glove'.

5. Boom experiment (SR-71, F-16XL, F/A-18, F-15). F-16XL flew close formation with the SR-71 at Mach 1.8, flying in and out of the SR-71's shock wave. F-16XL flew to within 50 ft (15 m) of the SR.

6. Initial OADS (Optical Air Data System) flight (nose mounted). Initial flight with TM telemetry package on board.

7. OADS flight No. 2. OADS had to be shut down during descent due to

overheating. Overheating was caused from radiated heat from the TEOC window into the OADS system. The organic cooling system within the OADS could not cool the lasers enough to continue operation.

8. This flight terminated early due to compressor stalls and engine inlet un-starts. The return leg was subsonic.

9. LEO (Low Earth Orbit) experiment flown for Motorola. The LEO component used the 'L' and 'S' band frequency range. Collection track was south of Chandler, Arizona. The SR-71 collected a total of 16 minutes of data for both missions. The SR-71 was 'hot refuelled'; the right engine and all electronic equipment were shut down during the ground refuelling.

10. NASA flight No. 44 was an orientation/familiarisation flight for General Jack Daily, Deputy Director of NASA (Gen Daily received a Mach 3+ pen).

MIG-31 INTERCEPTS OF SR-71A BY MAJ M. MYAGKIY

Appendix 10

All take-offs, except the first, were from DS (which may be a reference to 'alert status') to intercept and escort the SR-71:

Date	Duration
21 August 1984	50 minutes
14 March 1985	1 hour 5 minutes
18 March 1985	1 hour 10 minutes
15 April 1985	54 minutes
17 July 1985	1 hour 8 minutes
19 December 1985	1 hour
20 January 1986	1 hour 28 minutes
31 January 1986	50 minutes
21 February 1986	52 minutes
28 February 1986	48 minutes
1 April 1986	1 hour 2 minutes
6 October 1986	34 minutes
23 December 1986	53 minutes
8 January 1987	40 minutes

TECHNICAL AND CUTAWAY DRAWINGS

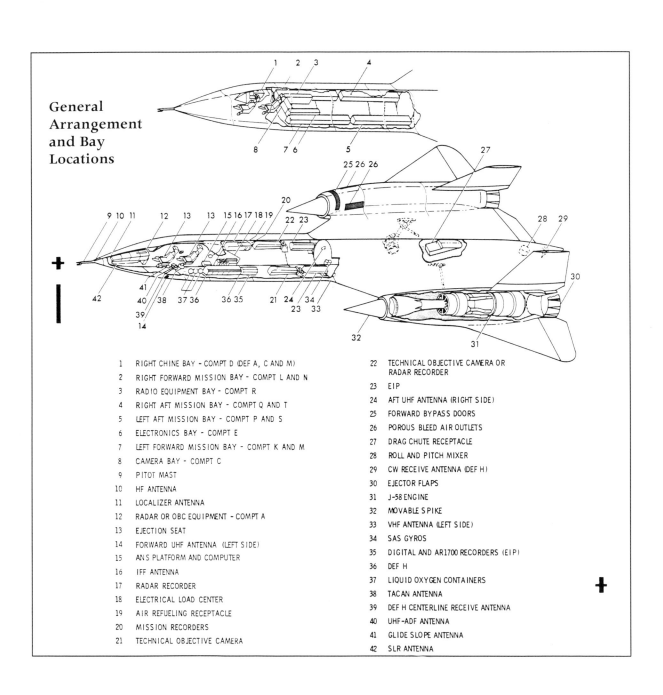

General
Arrangement
and Bay
Locations

1	RIGHT CHINE BAY - COMPT D (DEF A, C AND M)	22	TECHNICAL OBJECTIVE CAMERA OR RADAR RECORDER
2	RIGHT FORWARD MISSION BAY - COMPT L AND N	23	EIP
3	RADIO EQUIPMENT BAY - COMPT R	24	AFT UHF ANTENNA (RIGHT SIDE)
4	RIGHT AFT MISSION BAY - COMPT Q AND T	25	FORWARD BYPASS DOORS
5	LEFT AFT MISSION BAY - COMPT P AND S	26	POROUS BLEED AIR OUTLETS
6	ELECTRONICS BAY - COMPT E	27	DRAG CHUTE RECEPTACLE
7	LEFT FORWARD MISSION BAY - COMPT K AND M	28	ROLL AND PITCH MIXER
8	CAMERA BAY - COMPT C	29	CW RECEIVE ANTENNA (DEF H)
9	PITOT MAST	30	EJECTOR FLAPS
10	HF ANTENNA	31	J-58 ENGINE
11	LOCALIZER ANTENNA	32	MOVABLE SPIKE
12	RADAR OR OBC EQUIPMENT - COMPT A	33	VHF ANTENNA (LEFT SIDE)
13	EJECTION SEAT	34	SAS GYROS
14	FORWARD UHF ANTENNA (LEFT SIDE)	35	DIGITAL AND AR1700 RECORDERS (EIP)
15	ANS PLATFORM AND COMPUTER	36	DEF H
16	IFF ANTENNA	37	LIQUID OXYGEN CONTAINERS
17	RADAR RECORDER	38	TACAN ANTENNA
18	ELECTRICAL LOAD CENTER	39	DEF H CENTERLINE RECEIVE ANTENNA
19	AIR REFUELING RECEPTACLE	40	UHF-ADF ANTENNA
20	MISSION RECORDERS	41	GLIDE SLOPE ANTENNA
21	TECHNICAL OBJECTIVE CAMERA	42	SLR ANTENNA

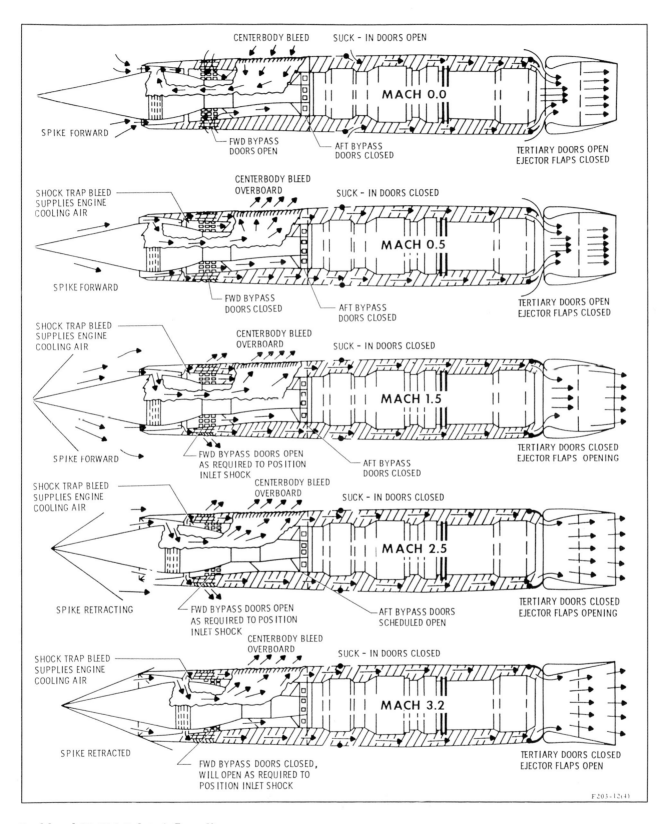

Lockheed SR-71A Inlet airflow diagram

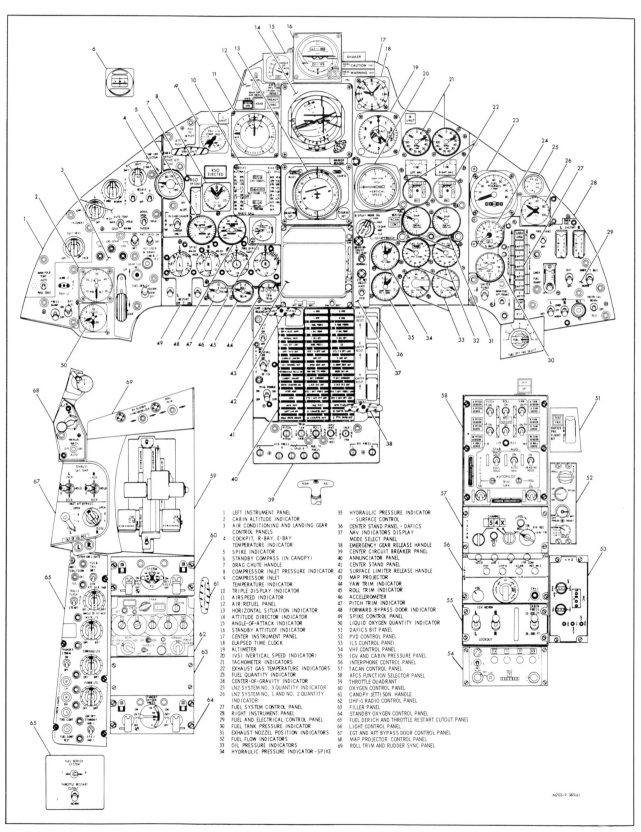

1	LEFT INSTRUMENT PANEL	35	HYDRAULIC PRESSURE INDICATOR
2	CABIN ALTITUDE INDICATOR		- SURFACE CONTROL
3	AIR CONDITIONING AND LANDING GEAR	36	CENTER STAND PANEL - DAFICS
	CONTROL PANELS	37	NAV INDICATORS DISPLAY
4	COCKPIT, R-BAY, E-BAY		MODE SELECT PANEL
	TEMPERATURE INDICATOR	38	EMERGENCY GEAR RELEASE HANDLE
5	SPIKE INDICATOR	39	CENTER CIRCUIT BREAKER PANEL
6	STANDBY COMPASS (IN CANOPY)	40	ANNUNCIATOR PANEL
7	DRAG CHUTE HANDLE	41	CENTER STAND PANEL
8	COMPRESSOR INLET PRESSURE INDICATOR	42	SURFACE LIMITER RELEASE HANDLE
9	COMPRESSOR INLET	43	MAP PROJECTOR
	TEMPERATURE INDICATOR	44	YAW TRIM INDICATOR
10	TRIPLE DISPLAY INDICATOR	45	ROLL TRIM INDICATOR
11	AIRSPEED INDICATOR	46	ACCELEROMETER
12	AIR REFUEL PANEL	47	PITCH TRIM INDICATOR
13	HORIZONTAL SITUATION INDICATOR	48	FORWARD BYPASS DOOR INDICATOR
14	ATTITUDE DIRECTOR INDICATOR	49	SPIKE CONTROL PANEL
15	ANGLE-OF-ATTACK INDICATOR	50	LIQUID OXYGEN QUANTITY INDICATOR
16	STANDBY ATTITUDE INDICATOR	51	DAFICS BIT PANEL
17	CENTER INSTRUMENT PANEL	52	PVD CONTROL PANEL
18	ELAPSED TIME CLOCK	53	ILS CONTROL PANEL
19	ALTIMETER	54	VHF CONTROL PANEL
20	IVSI (VERTICAL SPEED INDICATOR)	55	IGV AND CABIN PRESSURE PANEL
21	TACHOMETER INDICATORS	56	INTERPHONE CONTROL PANEL
22	EXHAUST GAS TEMPERATURE INDICATORS	57	TACAN CONTROL PANEL
23	FUEL QUANTITY INDICATOR	58	AFCS FUNCTION SELECTOR PANEL
24	CENTER-OF-GRAVITY INDICATOR	59	THROTTLE QUADRANT
25	LN2 SYSTEM NO. 3 QUANTITY INDICATOR	60	OXYGEN CONTROL PANEL
26	LN2 SYSTEM NO. 1 AND NO. 2 QUANTITY	61	CANOPY JETTISON HANDLE
	INDICATOR	62	UHF-1 RADIO CONTROL PANEL
27	FUEL SYSTEM CONTROL PANEL	63	FILLER PANEL
28	RIGHT INSTRUMENT PANEL	64	STANDBY OXYGEN CONTROL PANEL
29	FUEL AND ELECTRICAL CONTROL PANEL	65	FUEL DERICH AND THROTTLE RESTART CUTOUT PANEL
30	FUEL TANK PRESSURE INDICATOR	66	LIGHT CONTROL PANEL
31	EXHAUST NOZZLE POSITION INDICATORS	67	EGT AND AFT BYPASS DOOR CONTROL PANEL
32	FUEL FLOW INDICATORS	68	MAP PROJECTOR CONTROL PANEL
33	OIL PRESSURE INDICATORS	69	ROLL TRIM AND RUDDER SYNC PANEL
34	HYDRAULIC PRESSURE INDICATOR -SPIKE		

M203-9-385(d)

**SR-71A Forward cockpit instrument panel and
side consoles**

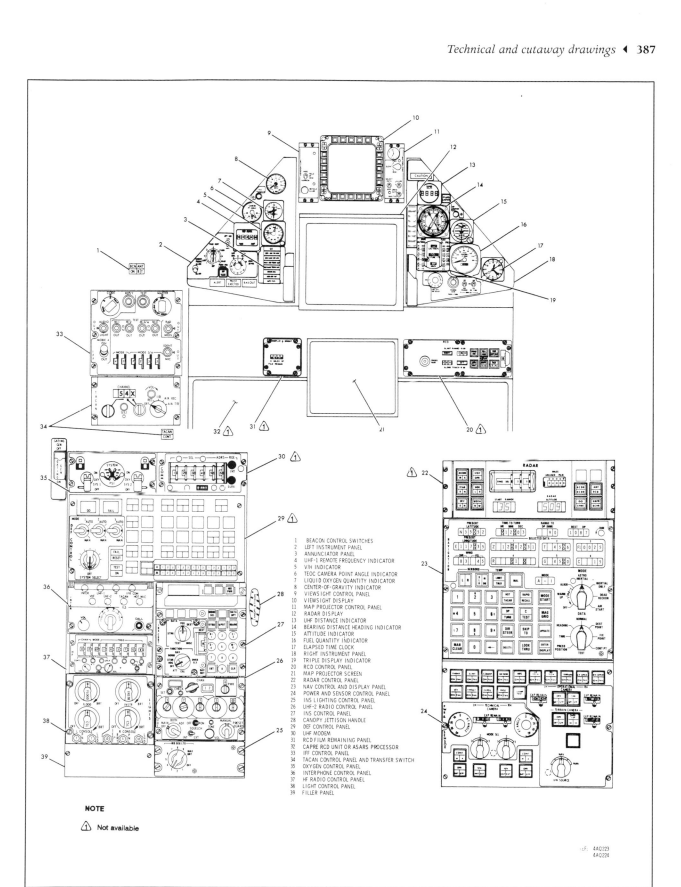

1. BEACON CONTROL SWITCHES
2. LEFT INSTRUMENT PANEL
3. ANNUNCIATOR PANEL
4. UHF-1 REMOTE FREQUENCY INDICATOR
5. V/H INDICATOR
6. TEOC CAMERA POINT ANGLE INDICATOR
7. LIQUID OXYGEN QUANTITY INDICATOR
8. CENTER-OF-GRAVITY INDICATOR
9. VIEWSIGHT CONTROL PANEL
10. VIEWSIGHT DISPLAY
11. MAP PROJECTOR CONTROL PANEL
12. RADAR DISPLAY
13. UHF DISTANCE INDICATOR
14. BEARING DISTANCE HEADING INDICATOR
15. ATTITUDE INDICATOR
16. FUEL QUANTITY INDICATOR
17. ELAPSED TIME CLOCK
18. RIGHT INSTRUMENT PANEL
19. TRIPLE DISPLAY INDICATOR
20. RCD CONTROL PANEL
21. MAP PROJECTOR SCREEN
22. RADAR CONTROL PANEL
23. NAV CONTROL AND DISPLAY PANEL
24. POWER AND SENSOR CONTROL PANEL
25. INS LIGHTING CONTROL PANEL
26. UHF-2 RADIO CONTROL PANEL
27. INS CONTROL PANEL
28. CANOPY JETTISON HANDLE
29. DEF CONTROL PANEL
30. UHF MODEM
31. RCD FILM REMAINING PANEL
32. CAPRE RCD UNIT OR ASARS PROCESSOR
33. IFF CONTROL PANEL
34. TACAN CONTROL PANEL AND TRANSFER SWITCH
35. OXYGEN CONTROL PANEL
36. INTERPHONE CONTROL PANEL
37. HF RADIO CONTROL PANEL
38. LIGHT CONTROL PANEL
39. FILLER PANEL

NOTE

⚠ Not available

REF: 4AQ223
    4AQ224

SR-71A Aft cockpit instrument panel and side consoles

Lockheed SR-71A Blackbird

Cutaway key
1. Pitot head
2. Alpha/beta probe, incidence and yaw measurement
3. RF isolation segment
4. RWR Antennae
5. VOR Antenna
6. Interchangeable nose mission equipment bay
7. Loral CAPRE side-looking ground mapping radar antenna
8. Antenna mounting and drive mechanism
9. Detachable nose bay mounting bulkhead
10. Cockpit front pressure bulkhead
11. Fuselage chine section framing
12. Rudder pedals and control column, Digital Automatic Flight and Inlet Control System (DAFICS)
13. Pilot's instrument panel
14. Windscreen panels, port only with electrical de-icing
15. Heat dispersion fairing
16. Upward hingeing cockpit canopy
17. Ejection seat headrest
18. Canopy actuator and hinge point
19. Pilot's 'zero-zero' ejection seat
20. Side console panel with engine throttle levers
21. Canopy external release
22. Retractable ventral UHF antenna
23. Liquid oxygen bottles (3)
24. Rear cockpit side console with ECM equipment controls
25. Reconnaisance Systems Officer's (RSO) instrument console and viewsight display

26. SR-71B dual control variant, nose section profile
27. Conversion Pilot's cockpit
28. Elevated Instructor's cockpit enclosure
29. RSO's upward hingeing cockpit canopy
30. RSO's ejection seat
31. Cockpit's sloping rear pressure bulkhead
32. Canopy hinge point
33. Honeycomb composite chine skin panelling
34. Astro-navigation star tracker aperture
35. Platform computer
36. Air conditioning equipment bay, port and starboard
37. Avionics equipment, port and starboard, access via nose undercarriage wheel bay
38. ELINT equipment package, port and starboard
39. Twin-wheel nose undercarriage, forward retracting
40. Hydraulic retraction jack
41. Infra-red unit
42. IFF transceiver
43. Flight refuelling receptacle, open
44. Recording equipment bay
45. Starboard sensor equipment bays
46. Fuselage upper main longeron

47. Close-pitched fuselage frame structure
48. Forward fuselage fuel tankage, total internal capacity 12,219 US gal of JP-7 (80,280 lb)

49. Tactical Objective Camera (TEOC), port and starboard
50. Operational Objective Camera (OOC), port and starboard
51. Camera mounting pallets/access hatches
52. Quartz glass viewing apertures
53. Stability Augmentation System (SAS) gyros
54. Forward/centre fuselage joint ring frame
55. Centre fuselage integral fuel tankage
56. Beta B.120 titanium skin panelling
57. Corrugated wing skin panelling
58. Starboard main undercarriage, stowed position
59. Intake centre-body bleed air spill louvres
60. By-pass suction relief louvres
61. Starboard engine air intake
62. Movable conical intake centrebody (spike)
63. Spike retracted (high speed) position
64. Boundary layer bleed air perforations
65. DAFICS air data probe
66. Diffuser chamber
67. Spike hydraulic actuator

68. Engine inlet guide vanes
69. Pratt & Whitney J58 afterburning turbojet engine
70. Nacelle by-pass duct
71. By-pass duct suction relief doors
72. Split nacelle and integral outer wing panel hinged to vertical for engine access/removal
73. Starboard outer wing panel
74. Starboard outboard elevon

75. All-moving s
76. Fixed fin roc
77. Afterburner
78. Afterburner
79. Tertiary air c
80. Exhaust noz
81. Variable are
82. Starboard ir
83. Inboard elev actuators (6
84. Inboard elev
85. Starboard w fuel tank ba

86. Corrugated
87. Brake para
88. Parachute
89. Parachute, linkage
90. Skin double
91. Centre fuse
92. Aft fuselage

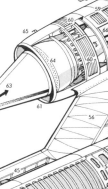

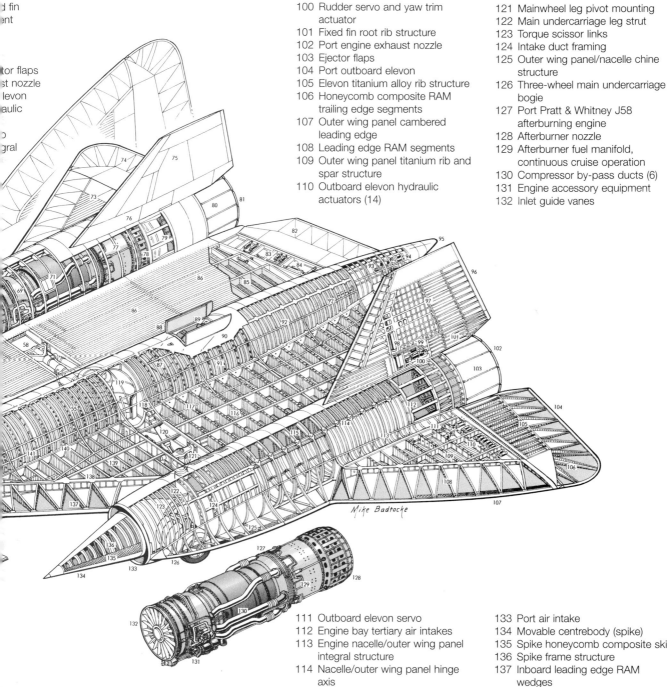

100 Rudder servo and yaw trim actuator
101 Fixed fin root rib structure
102 Port engine exhaust nozzle
103 Ejector flaps
104 Port outboard elevon
105 Elevon titanium alloy rib structure
106 Honeycomb composite RAM trailing edge segments
107 Outer wing panel cambered leading edge
108 Leading edge RAM segments
109 Outer wing panel titanium rib and spar structure
110 Outboard elevon hydraulic actuators (14)

121 Mainwheel leg pivot mounting
122 Main undercarriage leg strut
123 Torque scissor links
124 Intake duct framing
125 Outer wing panel/nacelle chine structure
126 Three-wheel main undercarriage bogie
127 Port Pratt & Whitney J58 afterburning engine
128 Afterburner nozzle
129 Afterburner fuel manifold, continuous cruise operation
130 Compressor by-pass ducts (6)
131 Engine accessory equipment
132 Inlet guide vanes

111 Outboard elevon servo
112 Engine bay tertiary air intakes
113 Engine nacelle/outer wing panel integral structure
114 Nacelle/outer wing panel hinge axis
115 Port nacelle ring frame structure
116 Inboard wing panel integral fuel tank bays
117 Multi-spar titanium alloy wing panel structure
118 Main undercarriage wheel bay
119 Wheel bay thermal lining
120 Hydraulic retraction jack

133 Port air intake
134 Movable centrebody (spike)
135 Spike honeycomb composite skin
136 Spike frame structure
137 Inboard leading edge RAM wedges
138 Leading edge spar
139 Inner wing panel leading edge integral fuel tankage
140 Wing/root fuselage attachment root rib
141 Close pitched fuselage frames
142 Wing/fuselage chine blended fairing panels

93 Inboard elevon servo input linkage and mixer
94 Roll and pitch trim actuators
95 Fuel jettison
96 Port all-moving fin
97 Fin rib structure
98 Torque shaft hinge mounting
99 Rudder hydraulic actuator

Mike Badtocke

BIBLIOGRAPHY

Burrows, William E., *By Any Means Necessary*, Farrar, Straus & Giroux, 2001

Burrows, William E., *Deep Black*, Random House, 1986

Byrnes, Donn A. & Hurley, Kenneth D., *Blackbird Rising*, Sage Mesa Publications, 1999

Goodall, James C. & Goodall, Norah D., *Senior Bowl, From The Shadow of Black, International Air Power Review*, AIRtime Publishing, 2001

Goodall, James & Miller, Jay, *Lockheed's SR-71 'Blackbird' Family*, Aerofax, 2002

Gordon, Yefim, *MiG-25 'Foxbat' and MiG-31 'Foxhound'*, Aerofax, 1997

Graham, Col Richard H., *SR-71 Revealed*, Motorbooks International, 1996

Johnson, Clarence L. 'Kelly' with Maggie Smith, *Kelly*, Smithsonian Institution, 1985

Miller, Jay, *Lockheed's Skunk Works*, Aerofax, 1995

Pocock, Chris, *The U-2 Spyplane Toward the Unknown*, Schiffer Military History, 2000

Price, Dr Alfred, *The History of US Electronic Warfare, Volume III*, The Association of Old Crows, 2000

Remak, Jeannette & Ventolo, Joseph, *A-12 Blackbird Declassified*, MBI Publishing Company, 2001

Rich, Ben R. & Janos, Leo, *Skunk Works*, Little, Brown & Co, 1994

Richelson, Jeffrey T., *The US Intelligence Community*, Westview Press, 1999

Richelson, Jeffrey T., *The Wizards of Langley*, Westview Press, 2001

Samuel, Wolfgang W. E., *I always wanted to fly*, University Press of Mississippi, 2001

Sontag, Sherry & Drew, Christopher with Drew, Annette L., *Blind Man's Bluff*, Arrow Books, 1998

Tart, Larry & Keefe, Robert., *The Price of Vigilance*, Ballantine Books, 2001

Truscott, Peter., *Kursk*, Simon & Schuster, 2002

INDEX